# UNDERSTANDING CHILDREN'S DEVELOPMENT

## BASIC PSYCHOLOGY

# UNDERSTANDING CHILDREN'S DEVELOPMENT

## Second Edition

Peter K. Smith and Helen Cowie

Basil Blackwell

First published 1988
Reprinted 1988, 1989
Second Edition 1991

Basil Blackwell Ltd
108 Cowley Road, Oxford OX4 1JF, UK

Basil Blackwell, Inc.
3 Cambridge Center
Cambridge, Massachusetts 02142, USA

*British Library Cataloguing in Publication Data*

A CIP catalogue record for this book is available from the British Library.

*Library of Congress Cataloging in Publication Data*

Smith, Peter K.
    Understanding children's development/Peter K. Smith and Helen
Cowie.—2nd ed.
        p. cm.—(Basic psychology)
    Includes bibliographical references and index.
    ISBN 0–631–17792–2
    1. Child psychology.   2. Child development.   I. Cowie, Helen.
II. Title.   III. Series: Basic psychology (Oxford, England)
BF721.S57325   1991
155.4—dc20                                         90–19343
                                                        CIP

Typeset in 11 on 11½pt Palatino
by APS Salisbury, Wilts
Printed in Great Britain by Cambridge University Press

# Contents

# Series Preface

Psychology is a relatively new science which has already made notable achievements; yet its methods are constantly being questioned and redefined. This book is one of a series of introductory psychology texts, designed to convey the fast-moving and relevant nature of contemporary research while at the same time encouraging the reader to develop a critical perspective on the methodology and data presented. The format of the book is intended to aid such independent inquiry, as is shown in particular by the boxes at the end of each chapter that concentrate on individual studies as 'worked examples'.

The books in the Basic Psychology series should be accessible to those who have no previous knowledge of the discipline. *Understanding Children's Development* can profitably be used by students on their own without a teacher, but resources aimed at group work, for example as part of social work or teacher training courses, are also included: a further reading section, discussion points and practical exercises follow each chapter.

Peter K. Smith

# Preface

We are bombarded by opinions on child development. Everyone has a view of how children should be brought up, and explanations for why people have turned out the way they have.

Even if you have not studied psychology before, you no doubt already have views on how children develop. You may agree or disagree with the following statements, but you will probably have heard them or opinions very much like them:

1 'Animal behaviour is instinctive; human behaviour is learned. That's the difference.'

2 'She gave me a lovely smile. I'm sure she recognized me even though she's only two months old.'

3 'I wouldn't leave my child at a nursery. If you have a baby you should look after it yourself.'

4 'A good smack never did a child any harm. That's how they learn what is right and what is wrong.'

5 'If things go wrong in the early years of a child's life there's not much you can do about it.'

6 'Parents shouldn't try to teach their children to read. That's best left to the school.'

7 'They don't do any work at Paul's school. They just play all day.'

8 'You can't understand how a child's mind works. They just think differently from us, and that's all there is to it.'

9 'Children see far too much violence on television these days.'

10 'Just wait until they are teenagers. That's when the trouble starts.'

11 'IQ tests don't tell us anything about real intelligence. They're a means of social control.'

12 'Psychologists can't teach us much. What they say is just common sense.'

In this book we don't aim to provide absolute answers to the many questions which arise in the course of rearing children. But we do aim to provide up-to-date accounts of research in this area. We hope to present controversies and to outline the various ways in which child psychologists' research findings enhance our understanding of the developmental process.

The material is arranged in three major sections. In Part One an introductory chapter describes to the reader the ways in which psychologists study developmental processes. It also raises issues about the specific status of psychology, its methods of inquiry and ethical questions in research. This chapter, or parts of it, could profitably be re-read after the rest of the book or taught course has been completed. Chapter 2 surveys the biological and evolutionary background of behavioural development, as well as being a self-contained unit on animal behaviour. It introduces conceptual terms such as 'instinct', 'learning' and 'canalization', which are used later in the book. Students interested in child development only could omit this chapter, but a reading of pp. 34–46 would be advisable.

Part Two deals with social and moral development in childhood, up to and including adolescence. Topics include parent–child attachment, sex differences, peer relationships, the influence of television on social behaviour, play and prosocial behaviour. Part Three covers perceptual, linguistic and cognitive development in children. The contribution of Jean Piaget is given particular attention, as are psychometric and other more recent approaches to assessing intelligence and attainment. Part Three concludes with a consideration of how disadvantage and deprivation affect children from different social classes and ethnic minority groups. Appendices give details of ethical guidelines in carrying out research, resources for teachers and careers in psychology.

We have tried to emphasize the variety, strengths and weaknesses of different kinds of psychological investigation. To bring this out more vividly, each chapter (after the first) concludes with two 'boxes'. Each box consists of a detailed description of one particular study, discussing its aims, design, results, analysis and strengths and limitations. Study of these boxes should be useful not only in terms of the content of the studies themselves, but also in helping the reader get a feel for how psychological research is carried out. More advanced students may wish to pursue the references to original work given throughout the text, while beginners should read the book without being distracted by them. The references are provided primarily for use by teachers, and also because we feel that acknowledgement should be made to those psychologists who have put forward certain theories or carried out particular studies.

Each chapter offers suggestions for further reading, giving indications of level and content. There are also ideas for discussion points which might be taken up as essay titles or topics for debate in class; and examples are given of practical exercises that might be carried out by students on the basis of the material in the foregoing chapter.

Peter K. Smith and Helen Cowie

The authors and publishers are grateful to the following for permission to reproduce photographs and figures: David Bygott for figure 2.11, from 'The Thinking Primate's Guide to Deception' by Richard Byrne and Andrew Whiten, *New Scientist*, 116, 1987; Axel Scheffler for figure 5.1.1, from *Autism* by Uta Frith, Basil Blackwell, © 1989; G. L. Vygodskaya and R. van der Veer for plate 12.1; David Wood for figure 12.1.1, from *How Children Think and Learn*, Basil Blackwell, © 1988; Sidney Harris for figure 13.5, © 1989.

*On Aggression*, and figure 2.3, from Eibl-Eibesfeldt, *Love and Hate*, 1971; The National Council on Family Relations for figure 8.9, from Floyd and South, 'Dilemma of youth', in the *Journal of Marriage and Family*, 34, 1972, Oxford University Press for figures 2.7, 2.8 and 2.9, from Tinbergen, *Study of Instinct*; Pan Books Ltd for figures 14.8, 14.9 and 14.10 from Wedge and Essen, *Children in Adversity*; Penguin Books Ltd for figure 6.1, from Foss (ed.), *New Perspectives in Child Development*, © Penguin Books, 1974; Pergamon Journals Ltd for figure 4.2, from Clark, Wyon and Richards, *Journal of Child Psychiatry and Psychology*, 10. 1969, and Pergamon Books Ltd for figure 5.4, from Lefkowitz et al., *Growing Up To Be Violent*: Plenum Publishing Cooporation for figures 9.7 and 9.9, from Mitchell, 'Effects of early visual experience on the development of certain perceptual abilities in animals and man', in Walk and Pick (ed.), *Perception and Experience*; *Science* for figure 9.10 and plate 9.4, from Annis et al., 'Human visual ecology and orientation anisotropies in acuity', 182, pp. 729–31, 16 November 1973, and Timney et al., 'Orientation anisotropaly: Incidence and magnitude in Caucasian and Chinese subjects', 193, pp. 699–701, 20 August 1976, copyright © American Association for the Advancement of Science; The Society for the Psychological Study of Social Issues for figure 8.8, from Hopkins, 'Sexual behavior in adolescence', in the *Journal of Social Issues*, 33, 2, pp. 67–85; The Society for Research in Child Development for figures 7.1, from *Monographs of the Society for Research in Child Development*, 48, and for figures 2.11, 9.4 and 11.7 from Hess, *Child Development*, 36, pp. 869–86, and Maurer and Barrera, *Child Development* 52, pp. 196–202, and Danner and Day, 48, pp. 1600–6; Scott, Foresman and Co. for figure 2.6, from Fishbein, *Evolution, Development and Children's Language*, copyright © Scott, Foresman and Co. 1976; W. H. Freeman and Company for box figure 9.1.1, from Bower, *Development in Infancy*, and for figure 8.1, from Herant Katchadourian, *The Biology of Adolescence*, copyright © 1977, W. H. Freeman and Company; W. H. Freeman and Scientific American for figures 9.1, 9.4, 9.6 and plates 2.1, 8.1, 9.1, 9.4, from Fantz, 'The origin of form perception', May 1961; Boss, 'The perception of speech in early infancy', January 1985; Held, 'Plasticity in sensory-motor systems', November 1965; Clutton-Brock, 'Reproductive success in Red Deer', February 1985; Tanner, 'Growing-up', September 1973; Gibson and Walk, 'The visual cliff', April 1960, and Vandivert, May 1961; John Wiley and Sons, Inc. Publishers, for figure 4.1, from Young et al., *The Beginning of Friendship*, in Lewis and Rosenblum (eds), *Friendship and Peer Relations*; The Zoological Society of London for box plate 6.1.2, from Hutt, 'Play, exploration and territory in mammals', in *Symposia of the Zoological Society of London*, 18, 1966.

## Acknowledgements for Second Edition

For the new material and revisions in this edition, we have had helpful comments from a number of colleagues. We would like to thank Simon Baron-Cohen, Mark Blades, Valerie Binney, Jill Boucher, Michael Boulton, Kevin Browne, Richard Byrne, Charlie Lewis, Ted Melhuish, Lorraine Pinnington, Andrew Whiten and David Wood.

Jerome Bruner, Philip Hwang, Charlie Lewis, Fernando Vidal and Jacques Voneche helpfully provided photographs which have been used in this edition.

# Acknowledgements

The book is a cooperative venture by the two authors, each of whom, however, has had primary responsibility for different sections. Peter Smith undertook the overall editing of the book, as well as preparing Parts One and Two; Helen Cowie was responsible for Part Three. We have had helpful comments and advice from many colleagues and students, and would particularly like to thank John Archer, Michael Banks, Martyn Barrett, Patrick Bateson, Julie Croll, Kevin Durkin, Chris Henney, Paul Martin, David Messer, Helen Weinreich-Haste, Cecile Wright, and students at Granville College, Sheffield, and Rowlinson School, Sheffield. Help in typing the script came from Anne Clifton, Ruth Farrance, Brenda Finney, Carole Gillespie, Gay Rich and Christine Wood. The original photographs were taken by Geoff Watson, with the cooperation of Leatrice Black and the University of Sheffield Nursery (plates 3.1, 4.1, 6.1, 6.2, 6.3, 6.4, 10.1, 10.2, 11.2, 13.1).

The authors and publishers are grateful to the following for permission to reproduce photographs and figures: Academic Press, Inc. (London) Ltd for box figure 6.1.1; The American Psychological Association and T. J. Berndt for figures 4.3 and 8.6; Annual Review of Psychology, vol. 31, © 1980 by Annual Reviews Inc., for figure 1.1; Ballière Tindall and *Animal Behaviour* for box plates 2.1.1 and 2.1.2; The British Psychological Society, and the *British Journal of Educational Psychology*, 48, 1978, for figure 11.6; Brooks/Cole Publishing Company Pacific Grove, California 93950, for figure 14.3, © 1985, by Wadsworth, Inc.; Jonathan Cape Ltd and Julian Huxley for figure 2.1; Cambridge University Press for figures 2.3, 6.1, and 10.1; Delachaux and Niestlé, Editeurs, for figures 11.2, and 11.5, from Piaget and Inhelder, *The Growth of Logical Thinking from Childhood to Adolescence*; Grafton Books, a division of The Collins Publishing Group, for figure 2.2, from Ewer, *The Ethology of Mammals*; Harcourt Brace Jovanovich, Inc. and Allen and Beatrice Gardener for plate 2.2; Michael Horniman for figure 13.1; Jossey-Bass, Inc. Publishers for figure 6.2, from Krasnor and Pepler, 'The study of children's play', in Rubin (ed.) *Children's Play*; Longman Ltd and the National Children's Bureau, for figure 8.7, from Schofield, *The Sexual Behaviour of Young People*, and 14.1, 14.2, and 14.3, from Davie et al., *From Birth to Seven*; Macmillan Journals Ltd for box figure 9.2, from *Nature*, 228, 1970; Merrill-Palmer Quarterly, 18/4, 1972, for box figure 3.1.2, from Watson, 'Smiling, cooing and "the game" '; Methuen and Co. Publishers for figure 2.13, from Lorenz,

# Part One

# Theories and Methods

# 1

# Studying Development

The study of how behaviour develops forms part of the science of psychology. But what do we mean by terms such as 'science', 'psychology' and 'development'? This chapter aims to supply the answer, but although it comes first in the book, it may not necessarily be best to read it thoroughly at the outset. Especially if you have not studied psychology before, it might be useful to read it through quickly at this stage, and return to it later, even after finishing the rest of the book, for a more thorough understanding. The issues raised in this chapter are important, but understanding them fully will be easier if you already know something of psychological theories and methods of investigation.

In an important sense, we are all psychologists. We are all interested in understanding behaviour, both our own and that of our parents, children, family and friends. We try to understand why we feel the way we do about other people, why we find certain tasks easy or difficult, or how certain situations affect us; and we try to understand and predict how other people behave, or how their present behaviour and situation may affect their future development. Will a child settle well with a childminder, or do well at school? Will watching violent films on television be harmful? What level of moral reasoning can we expect a child to understand? And so on.

In an interesting and perceptive book, Nicholas Humphrey (1984) has described us as 'nature's psychologists', or *homo psychologicus*. By this he means that, as intelligent social beings, we use our knowledge of our own thought and feelings – 'introspection' – as a guide for understanding how others are likely to think, feel and therefore behave. Indeed, Humphrey goes further and argues that we are conscious, that is, we have self-awareness, precisely because this is so useful to us in this process of understanding others and thus having a successful social existence. He argues that consciousness is a biological adaptation to enable us to perform this introspective psychology. Whether this is right or not (and you might like to think about this again after you have read chapter 2), we do know that the process of understanding others' thoughts, feelings and behaviour is something that develops through childhood and probably throughout our lives. According to one of the greatest child psychologists, Jean Piaget, a crucial phase of this process occurs in middle childhood (see chapter 11); though more recent research has revealed how much has developed before this (see chapter 5).

If we are already nature's psychologists, then why do we need an organized study of science of psychology? A professional psychologist would probably answer that by systematically gathering knowledge and by carrying out controlled experiments we can develop a greater understanding and awareness of ourselves than would otherwise be possible. There is still much progress to be made in psychology and in the psychological study of development. We are still struggling to understand areas such as the role of play in development, the causes of delinquency, the nature of stages in cognitive development. Most psychologists would argue, however, that the discipline of child development has made some progress and even in the most difficult areas knowledge has now become more systematic, with theories being put forward. Our understanding has clearly advanced in some areas. We now know more, for example, about the importance of social attachments in infancy (chapter 3), or the process by which a child learns its native language (chapter 10), than previous generations ever did or could have done without organized study.

## Development Observed

The biologist Charles Darwin, famous for his theory of evolution, made one of the earliest contributions to child psychology in his article 'A biographical sketch of an infant' (1877), which was based on observations of his own son's development. By the early twentieth century, however, most of our understanding of psychological development could still not have been described as 'scientific' knowledge; much was still at the level of anecdote and opinion. Nevertheless, knowledge was soon being organized through both observation and experiment and during the 1920s and 1930s the study of child development got seriously under way in the USA with the founding of institutes of child study or child welfare in university centres such as Iowa and Minnesota. Careful observations were made of development in young children and of normal and abnormal behaviour and adjustment. In the 1930s Jean Piaget started out on his long career as a child psychologist, blending observation and experiment in his studies of children's thinking (see chapter 11).

Observation of behaviour in natural settings fell out of favour with psychologists in the 1940s and 1950s (though it continued in the study of animal behaviour by zoologists, chapter 2). Perhaps as a reaction against the absence of experimental rigour in philosophy and early psychology, and the reliance on introspection (that is, trying to understand behaviour by thinking about one's own mental processes), many psychologists moved to doing experiments under laboratory conditions. As we will discuss later, such experiments do have advantages, but they also have drawbacks. Much of the laboratory work carried out in child development in the 1950s and 1960s has been described by Urie Bronfenbrenner (1979) as 'the science of the behavior of children in strange situations with strange adults'. In more recent decades child psychologists have generally come back to recognizing the complementary virtues of various different methods of investigation.

## What Is 'Development'?

The term 'development' refers to the process by which a child, or more generally an organism (human or animal), grows and changes through its life-span. In humans the most dramatic developmental changes occur in infancy and childhood, as the newborn develops into a young adult capable of becoming a parent himself or herself. From its origins much of developmental psychology has thus been concerned with child psychology, and with the changes from infancy through to adolescence. These are the primary areas covered in this book.

Generally, developmental processes have been related to age. A typical 3-year-old has, for example, a particular mastery of spoken language (see chapter 10), and a 4-year-old has typically progressed further. A developmental psychologist may then wish to find out, and theorize about, the processes involved in this progression. What experiences, rewards, interactions, feedback, have helped the child develop in this way?

Two important but different research strategies have commonly been used in this endeavour. These are 'cross-sectional' and 'longitudinal' designs. In a cross-sectional design an investigator might look at several age groups simultaneously. For example, she might record language ability in 3-year-olds and 4-year-olds, at the same point in time. In a longitudinal design, the investigator follows certain subjects over a given time period, measuring change. For example, our investigator might have recorded the language ability for a sample of 3-year-olds and a year later visited the same children to get a sample of what 4-year-olds can do.

Each method has advantages and disadvantages. The cross-sectional design is quick to do, and is appropriate if the main interest is in what abilities or behaviours are typical at certain ages. Because of the convenience of the method, the majority of developmental studies have been cross-sectional. Longitudinal designs are generally preferable if the focus of interest is the process of change, and the relationship between earlier and later behaviour. In our example above, it is longitudinal data which give us the most ready access to information on what kinds of experience foster language development, and whether individual differences at 3 years of age predict anything about individual differences a year later, at age 4.

Although longitudinal studies are more powerful in this way they have a number of drawbacks. One is simply the possibility of subject attrition – some participants may move away, lose contact, or refuse or be unable to participate by the next time of testing. This could influence the generality of conclusions, especially if the reason for participant loss may be related to the dependent variables of the study (for an example, see box 8:1).

Another problem with longitudinal designs is that they are time-consuming! In our example a wait of one year may not be too off-putting. But, if you wanted to see whether friendships in childhood related to happiness as an adult (see chapter 4), you might find yourself having to wait 20 years! Some longitudinal studies have now in fact proceeded for this length of time and longer. A few major studies which originated in the USA in the 1930s, as well as some nation-wide surveys in Britain during the years after the Second World War, have provided or are providing longitudinal data spanning 20, 30 or 40 years.

Such long-term studies give us some of our most powerful evidence on the nature of development, so far available. However, when a study goes on for so long, another problem may arise. When the study was initially designed decades ago, it may not have asked the sort of questions that we now find most interesting. Any long-term longitudinal study will be dated in its conception. It will also be dated in its conclusions, which will refer to developmental outcomes for people born decades ago. Such conclusions may not always be applicable to today's children. For example, the effects of parental divorce on a child's later adjustment may be different now, when divorce is more frequent and socially acceptable, than 20 or 30 years ago when the social stigma attached to divorce in Western societies was much greater (see pp. 23–4).

### Baltes's conceptualization of life-span development

Paul Baltes, a German psychologist, has been influential in emphasizing the life-span nature of development and the importance of historical influences (see Baltes et al., 1980). Baltes points out that age-related trends, the traditional staple of developmental psychology, constitute only one of three important influences on development throughout the life-span (figure 1.1). Each of these influences is determined by an interaction of biological and environmental factors (cf. chapter 2), though one or the other may predominate in particular cases.

Of the three kinds of influence, 'normative age-graded' are those which have a fairly strong relationship with chronological age. The advent of puberty at adolescence (see chapter 8) would be an example of a normative age-graded influence with a strong biological component, while entering school at 5 years (in Britain) would be a normative age-graded influence with little biological determination.

'Normative history-graded' influences are those associated with historical time for most members of a given generation (or 'cohort', see below). A famine, for example the Ethopian famine of the 1980s, would be an example of strong biological determinants on development. The advent of television (see box 5:2), or historical

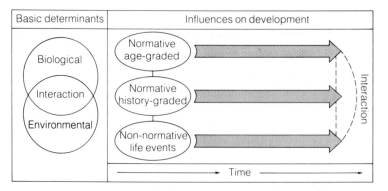

FIGURE 1.1   *Three major influence systems on life-span development: normative age-graded, normative history-graded and non-normative life events. These influence systems interact and differ in their combinational profile for different individuals and for different behaviours (adapted from Baltes et al., 1980)*

changes in family size (for example the 'one-child' policy in China in the early 1980s) are examples with little biological determination.

Finally, 'non-normative life events' are those which do not occur in any normative age-graded or history-graded manner for most individuals. The effects of brain damage in an accident would be an example with strong biological determinants; the effects of job loss, or moving house, or divorce, examples with less strong biological determinants. All are significant events that can occur in the life-span of an individual at many age points and at many historical times.

This sort of conceptualization leads to further consideration of designs for studying development, apart from the cross-sectional and longitudinal ones already mentioned. One of these is cohort design, in which different cohorts (i.e. samples of children born in different years) are compared at the same ages. The characteristics of the three designs mentioned so far are thus:

*Cross-sectional design*
Different subjects          Different ages          Same historical time

*Longitudinal design*
Same subjects          Different ages          Different historical times

*Cohort design*
Different subjects          Same ages          Different historical times

Yet another design is a combination called cohort-sequential design. As an example of this, we might look at the effects of compensatory preschool programmes (see chapter 14) on children born in 1970, 1975 and 1980, following each cohort longitudinally through from age 3 years to, say, age 18 years. As well as several sets of cross-sectional and longitudinal data, this hypothetical design (figure 1.2) would let us see whether historical change over the last decade or so (for example in educational policy, or the relative position of minority groups in society) had an impact on whatever long-term effects of the programmes might be detected. Obviously, this would be immensely time-consuming, and indeed such a study has not been carried out! Even one set of actual longitudinal studies originating in the 1970s has proved a major research undertaking (see chapter 14). So far, cohort-

FIGURE 1.2   *A hypothetical study design, combining cross-sectional, longitudinal and cohort comparisons, to examine the effects of compensatory preschool programmes at different ages and different historical periods. If started in 1973, the study would continue until 1998. The ages of each sample of children from each cohort and at each year of study are shown in years*

sequential designs have been rarely used, and only on a smaller scale. An example is given in box 4.2.

A different approach is to examine the effects of a particular kind of non-normative life event when it happens, perhaps irrespective of age, or with age as another factor. The effects of divorce on children, mentioned earlier, is one example. Investigators of this topic typically record the adjustment of children, often of a range of ages, over a period of time from when the parental separation occurred. Other examples would be the study of bereavement, or the effects of sudden unemployment.

### Bronfenbrenner's ecological model of human development

The American psychologist Urie Bronfenbrenner has proposed another influential conceptualization of development (1979). He emphasizes the importance of studying 'development-in-context', or the ecology of development. 'Ecology' refers here to the environmental settings which the person or organism is experiencing, or is linked to directly or indirectly. Bronfenbrenner conceives of this ecological environment as a set of four nested systems (see figure 1.3). Most familiar to the psychologist is the 'microsystem' – what an individual experiences in a given setting. For a young child, one microsystem may comprise the home environment,

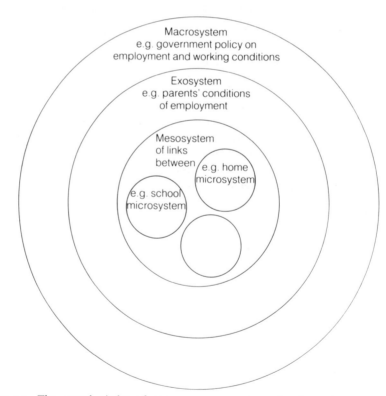

FIGURE 1.3 *The nested circles of macro-, exo-, meso- and microsystems proposed by Bronfenbrenner (1979), with examples relevant to a school-age child*

with parents and siblings. Another microsystem may be the school environment, with teachers and peers. Most psychological research is carried out at the level of one microsystem, for example looking at mother's talk and child's speech in the home (chapter 10), or peer popularity and aggression at school (chapter 4).

At the next level is the 'mesosystem'. This refers to links amongst settings which the individual directly participates in. For example, the quality of the child's home environment might affect his or her school performance or confidence with peers.

The third level is the 'exosystem'. This refers to links to settings which the individual does not participate in directly, but which do affect the individual. For example, the mother's or father's work environment may affect their behaviour at home, and hence the quality of parental care. The child does not directly experience the parent's work environment, but he or she experiences the effects indirectly.

The fourth and final level is the 'macrosystem'. This refers to the general pattern of ideology and organization of social institutions in the society or subculture the individual is in. Thus, the effects of parental stress at work, or unemployment, will be affected by such factors as working hours in that society, rates of pay, holiday and leave entitlement, occupational status, or the degree of social stigma attached to unemployment.

Bronfenbrenner's model illustrates how a decision or change in the macrosystem (e.g. change in employment conditions) may affect the exosystem (parent's work experience) and hence a child's mesosystem and microsystem. This is not controversial in itself. However, recognizing these links does suggest the importance of trying to conceptualize and design psychological investigations extending beyond just the microsystem level.

Bronfenbrenner proposes that we view human development as the process of understanding and restructuring our ecological environment at successively greater levels of complexity. The child first comes to understand its primary caregivers (chapter 3), then its home and nursery or school environment, then wider aspects of society. Changes in the ecological environment (or 'ecological transitions') are especially important in development. Examples might be: having a new sibling; entering school; getting a job; being promoted; getting married; taking a holiday. (Note the similarity to Baltes's ideas of life events.) At such times the person is faced with a challenge, has to adapt, and thus development takes place. Indeed, Bronfenbrenner feels that seeing how a person copes with change is essential to understanding that person: 'If you want to understand something, try to change it.'

## Obtaining Information about Behaviour and Development

As you read through this book, you will see that psychologists have used a wide variety of means to obtain useful information, whatever their theoretical or conceptual orientation has been. Some form of experimental study is perhaps the most common form of investigation reported in psychological books and journals. Nevertheless, non-experimental methods, such as naturalistic observation or field surveys, are also respectable procedures provided there is a clear aim to the research. The crucial variable is the *degree of control* the investigator has over what is happening. We shall discuss this variable in some detail, together with two other aspects of project design – the way behaviour is recorded and the selection of participants. All these aspects are also highlighted in the boxes that follow all the subsequent chapters.

### What degree of control?

A great deal can be learnt from recording behaviour in natural situations or settings. Suppose we were interested in what kinds of help are shown by preschool children to others in distress (chapter 7). Perhaps the most suitable approach here is for the investigator simply to observe children in natural settings such as the home, or ask parents or adults to keep diary records of events. Or, we might try to save time simply by interviewing parents, or giving a questionnaire. The investigator interferes as little as possible, only to the extent of making sure he or she gets reliable data. This kind of approach is most suitable when we do not yet have much systematic knowledge about the phenomenon, and need to gather this descriptive data.

From this kind of study we can learn what kinds of behaviour occur, and how frequently. But do we advance our understanding of the processes involved? To some extent, the answer is yes. For instance, we can carry out 'correlational analyses' of various kinds. In a correlation we examine whether a certain behaviour occurs systematically or more frequently together with some other particular behaviour or in some particular situation. For example, we may find that helpful behaviour by children is correlated with clear communications by the mother (p. 211).

Such findings certainly suggest explanations as to the processes involved. Parents who communicate clearly may have children who are more helpful because the communications bring this about. However, can we be confident that this explanation is better than some other, different explanation? Not really. The relation between cause and effect might be reversed: for example, children who are for other reasons helpful may have better relations with parents, who are thus more willing to take time to explain things to them. Or, some other factor may account for both aspects separately. Perhaps parents who are less stressed and more happy have both more time to communicate to children and have less stressed children who are therefore more helpful. In that case, stress would be the crucial factor and not parental communication.

This weakness of correlational evidence is a most important concept to grasp. If you find it difficult, think of this example. Suppose you correlated, from day to day, the number of people wearing shorts and the number of people eating ice-creams. You would probably get a positive association or correlation. This does not mean that wearing shorts causes people to eat ice-creams, or vice versa; we know that in this case the daily variation in temperature, a third variable, is the likely cause of both.

At several points in this book we will draw out these limitations of correlational methods. The way psychologists have tried to proceed further is to use some form of experiment. In an experiment we focus on one or a small number of variables of interest which we think are important: then we try to exclude other variables from our possible explanations. Three kinds of experiment will be described.

The weakest form of experiment is the 'quasi-experiment' (see Cook and

Campbell, 1979, for extended discussion). In a quasi-experiment the variable which the investigator thinks is important is changed naturally, and the investigator watches what happens. For example, in box 5.2 we refer to a before-and-after study in 1955 of the effects of introducing a new television transmitter in Norwich on children's behaviour. The investigators felt that the introduction of the opportunity to watch TV was an important variable and took the opportunity to measure its effects.

Unfortunately quasi-experiments are not much more powerful than correlational studies at excluding alternative explanations. Usually, we know too little about (i.e. have too little control over) the characteristics of our participants and the circumstances of the variable which is changing. For example, in the situation just described which parents first acquired television sets when they were available? They would almost certainly be different in many ways from those who did not acquire television sets (and indeed the study identified some such differences). Also, children might differentially view programmes of certain types, depending on personality and interest. How can we tell whether changes in behaviour are due to watching the programmes, or whether the programme-watching is just a by-product of these changes?

The most powerful way to answer such cause-effect questions is to carry out a 'true' or 'controlled' experiment. We can distinguish field experiments and laboratory experiments, but both share two important features. The first is that there are two or more well-specified 'conditions' which participants can experience. The second is that participants are assigned to conditions in a systematic fashion. In these ways the experimenter seeks to ascribe an outcome definitely to differences between certain conditions. Alternative explanations in terms of other uncontrolled differences between conditions, or between participants in different conditions, can be excluded.

Let us take further the idea that television viewing may affect children's social behaviour. Suppose we invite children in small groups to a laboratory, where we randomly assign them to one of three conditions. In one condition they see several violent cartoon programmes; in another they see several non-violent cartoons; in the third (called a control condition) they do not watch television at all but do something else, like drawing. Afterwards they go to a playroom and are filmed by the experimenter, who records their social behaviour.

Suppose the experimenter finds a significant difference. Children who watched the violent cartoons are more aggressive to each other in the playroom than those who watched non-violent cartoons, or did drawing. This difference in aggressiveness can confidently be ascribed to watching the violent cartoons. It cannot be explained by systematic differences in the participants (we assigned them randomly) and it cannot be explained by unknown variations in the children's experiences (we chose the cartoons, and made the children sit through all of them).

Sometimes the investigator compares the effects of two or more conditions he or she is interested in (for example, violent and non-violent cartoon films). Sometimes it is appropriate to include a 'control group', which is a condition including all the same experiences except that which the investigator is particularly interested in. The children who experience drawing, above, were a control group for the general experience of coming to the laboratory and meeting the experimenters. Any differences between the control group and the two experimental groups showed the effects of watching cartoons. Any difference between the two experimental groups further showed the effects of whether the cartoons are violent, or non-violent.

In all experiments we can identify 'independent variables' and 'dependent variables'. Independent variables are those controlled or manipulated by the experimenter: in our example, the experience of watching cartoons, and whether the cartoons were violent or not. The dependent variables are those we choose to examine for possible effects: in our example, social behaviour in the playroom.

The laboratory experiment allows tight control of assignment of participants and of the independent variables; but is it rather artificial? What do the participants feel about coming to the laboratory? Would they normally choose to watch such cartoons? Can we expect a reasonable range of normal behaviour in this environment? Perhaps not. To some extent we can try to overcome these objections in a 'field experiment'. For example, we might try showing different kinds of television cartoons to different groups of children at a school, or at a summer camp. The children would normally be at the school, or camp, and watching some television might be part of their expected programme.

In general in a field experiment the investigator attempts to combine the rigorous control of experimental design with the advantages of a naturalistic setting. This can, at its best, be a very powerful method. However, it is difficult to maintain both experimental control and naturalness, and the field experiment may slip either into becoming a quasi-experiment, or into becoming more constrained and unnatural, like the laboratory experiment.

Thus, in all investigations the naturalness of the setting needs to be balanced against the degree of knowledge and control we have over the setting. Where the balance is best struck depends very much on the kind of behaviour or skill we are interested in. We do want to be reasonably sure that the conclusions we draw from our study apply to the 'real world'. This concern has been labelled as the need for 'ecological validity'. Bronfenbrenner (1979) has defined ecological validity as 'the extent to which the environment experienced by the participants in a scientific investigation has the properties it is supposed or assumed to have by the investigator'. In other words, is it reasonably representative as regards the conclusions we wish to draw from the study? If we felt that the results of a laboratory experiment on cartoon watching were not representative of the effects of real-life television watching, then we would say this experiment lacked ecological validity.

*Recording data*

Whatever design of investigation we are using, we also have to decide how to record the data. A variety of methods is available and whether the choice is obvious or requires some deliberation depends on the topic of investigation. Sometimes several types of data may be gathered in one study.

One method is to make observational records of behaviour (e.g. box 2.2), whereby the investigator watches the participant(s) and makes systematic records of whether certain behaviours occur. Usually the investigator defines certain 'behaviour categories' in advance, and then scores when they occur. Some method of 'time sampling' is often employed to assist in quantifying the scoring (see Martin and Bateson, 1986, for extended discussion). Sometimes the investigator asks the participant(s) to keep their own records, perhaps a diary of occurrences (e.g. box 7.1). Again, the participants will probably need some training in what and what not to record in this way.

Another set of methods involves interviews and questionnaires. In an interview, the investigator asks participants about a topic and explores their thoughts, feelings or attitudes with them. Often some degree of structure is imposed on the kinds of questions asked in the interview (e.g. box 8.2). A more structured approach still is to give participants a questionnaire in which they fill in replies to preset questions (e.g., box 5.2). A questionnaire is often given individually, but can be given in groups. A questionnaire sent to large numbers of people is called a 'survey' (e.g. pp. 232–4).

Tests can also be given individually or (in some cases) in groups. In a test the participant may be asked certain questions and also perhaps be asked to carry out certain actions, e.g. solve certain puzzles. The test differs from the interview in that it is designed to measure a particular ability or trait, and it is scored in a strictly defined way that can be compared with normative values obtained earlier in the process of test design (see chapter 13).

*Reliability and validity*

Whatever measuring instrument or method we use, we need to be sure of its 'reliability'. Basically, a reliable method is one that will give the same answer if you, or another investigator, were to repeat the measurement in the same conditions. A straight, firm ruler is reliable, a crooked or floppy one is not. Similarly, if we recorded 'aggressive behaviour' in children, but did not define our behaviour categories or method of time sampling, this would be unreliable; someone else might have a different idea of what is aggressive, and get different results even if watching the same behaviour. Methods need to be carefully specified and tried out if they are to be reliable.

The term 'reliability' is often confused with 'validity': both are very important in any investigation. We have just seen that reliability refers to the recording of data. Validity, in contrast, refers to whether the data we obtain are actually meaningful. Remember the concept of 'ecological validity' we discussed above. Our measurements in a laboratory experiment might be very reliable (well specified and repeatable) but this does not guarantee that they are valid in the sense of meaningful in the 'real world'.

Problems of validity actually arise in all kinds of investigation. If we are making records in a natural setting, we have to beware that the presence of an observer does not change the behaviour being observed. If you stand in a playground recording aggressive behaviour, will less aggression occur than usual because you are there? This is a problem of 'observer effects'. Similarly, in experiments there are 'experimenter effects'. The experimenter may unwittingly help some participants more than others, or score some participants more leniently. One type of experimenter effect is known as the 'Clever Hans' effect. Clever Hans was a horse which apparently could count. If his trainer asked 'what is three and four' Hans would tap with his front foot seven times. However the German psychologist Oskar Pfungst (1911) discovered that Hans actually relied on subtle non-verbal (and unintentional) cues from his trainer, who inclined his head slightly forward after Hans had tapped the correct number of times. Hans was clever, but not in the way originally thought.

The demonstration was a reliable one, but the conclusions drawn initially were not valid.


## Participant characteristics

One aspect of validity concerns the representativeness of the participants investigated. If we do a survey of young men's attitude to sexual relationships, they may not be representative of the views of young women (chapter 8). Or, we may not even have enough participants to give us a reliable source of data.

Data obtained from one person is called a 'case study'. Normally a case study tells us little about the general population but, if we can obtain very extensive records (for example, the records Piaget obtained of his own children described in chapter 11) or if the person is especially interesting (for example, the case studies of extreme deprivation described in chapter 14) then this method may be very valuable. A case study may often serve as a source of ideas or hypotheses for later study (e.g. p. 293).

Many psychological investigations are done on small samples of some 10–50 individuals, who can be brought to a laboratory or observed in a single setting. Usually statistical tests are then carried out to see whether the results are sufficiently stable or characteristic that it is likely they would be true of larger samples. The means of carrying out simple statistical tests (such as correlation, $t$ test, and chi-square, $\chi^2$) are described in introductory texts such as Heyes et al. (1986) or Robson (1983), together with the meaning of probability or $p$ values. Examples of the results of such tests are given in many of the boxes in this book.

Sometimes a survey or other investigation is carried out on a large sample of hundreds of participants. Such a sample may be regarded as normative, or representative, of some section of the population. For example, one longitudinal study in Britian included all the children born in one week of March 1946 (p. 222). These could reasonably be taken as representative of children born in Britain in the later 1940s. Again, statistical tests are usually employed to look at correlations, or at differences between subgroups in the sample.


## Ethical issues

Whenever an investigation is made with human or animal participants, investigators should have due respect for their rights and welfare. Investigations with animals kept for experimental purposes are in fact controlled by strict Home Office guidelines. In addition, societies such as the British Psychological Society have issued ethical guidelines for the planning of investigations. Many investigations involve some disturbance of privacy or inconvenience to participants. Some may involve temporary deception, or even some distress or pain in the case of animal experiments. Even when legally permissible, any such outcomes should be balanced very carefully against the likely benefits from carrying out the investigations. Needless to say, any negative outcomes to participants must be carefully justified and only accepted under the most unusual circumstances; they should never be a feature of student experiments or investigations. The ethical principles approved by the British Psychological Society, and revised in 1990, are reprinted in appendix A and should be consulted in case of any uncertainty on this issue.

Another ethical issue relates to the accurate reporting of results. It is clearly the duty of investigators to report their resuls in as accurate and unbiased a way as possible, but there have been occasions when this principle is known to have been violated. The British psychologist Sir Cyril Burt reported data on twins which he claimed to have gathered for many years, in order to prove that intelligence was largely inherited. His results were published in numerous articles as his sample of twins accumulated. However, it has now been shown beyond reasonable doubt that in the latter part of his life Burt did not gather more data, but invented it (Hearnshaw, 1979). Thus a great deal of his twin data set is fraudulent, and the conclusions drawn from it unwarranted. Much attention has been drawn to this deception, partly because of the social implications of the theory of hereditary intelligence, and partly because fraud on this scale is believed to be rare. Drawing attention to such misdemeanours hopefully serves to make future occurrences less probable.

## Objectivity and bias

Scientific investigation is supposed to be objective, not biased by the personal beliefs or values of the individual investigator or the wider society. In practice, this is not entirely the case. The kinds of problems chosen for study, and the way they are tackled, are inevitably affected by personal or societal ideas of what is important. This may be especially so in certain areas of psychology. Stephen Gould (1981), in a compelling book entitled *The Mismeasure of Man*, demonstrates this in the instance of the study of intelligence testing and the view held by some psychologists that there were innate racial differences in intelligence. The kinds of study carried out earlier in the century, and the way those studies were interpreted, clearly reflected bias (for example, racial prejudices) in some investigators. At times this involved misconceived inferences from results, or observer bias in scoring or testing. At extremes it bordered on fraudulence similar to the Burt example. Gould takes an optimistic view, in the sense that biases can be recognized and exposed, at least after the event. Indeed much more sophisticated studies of the issues involved in race and intelligence have now been carried out (e.g. Scarr, 1984).

## The Scientific Status of Psychology

This chapter began by briefly considering the nature of psychology as a scientific discipline. We shall conclude by discussing briefly what is meant by the term 'science', and whether this is what psychologists practice. The nature of scientific inquiry has been written about by philosophers of science: we shall summarize the views of two – Popper and Kuhn.

For a long time it was generally held that science proceeded by gathering factual data, by observation and experiment, and by deriving general laws from these facts. This has been called the 'traditional' or 'inductivist' view. However, throughout the twentieth century, scientists and philosophers of science have put more emphasis on the role of hypotheses or theories in science. A hypothesis, or theory, is a proposition that some relationship holds amongst certain phenomena. For example, some psychological hypotheses discussed in this book include:

that bird song serves to defend a territory (p. 24);

that the first hours of birth are critically important for mother–infant bonding (p. 62);

that viewing violent television programmes makes children behave more aggressively (p. 156);

that children are attracted to a level of moral reasoning just above their current level (p. 212);

that infants aged 6 weeks can perceive the depth (distance) of an object (p. 276);

that children cannot understand another's point of view until about 7 years of age (p. 327);

that preschool 'Headstart' programmes can benefit a child educationally throughout the school years (p. 430).

The 'traditional' view would be that hypotheses such as these are derived from facts we have gathered, and that if we get enough factual support then the theory will have been 'proved' correct. However, this view is not now generally held. Instead, most scientists and philososphers believe that the role of theory is a primary one, and that theories cannot be proved, only disproved. A most articulate proponent of this viewpoint is Sir Karl Popper (b. 1902), who argues that our ideas about the world, or 'common-sense beliefs', serve as the starting point for organizing knowledge from which scientific investigation proceeds. Thus, theory serves a primary role and indeed structures what and how we observe or categorize 'facts', or observations about the world. Psychologists are in a good position to appreciate this argument, as part of their discipline (and part of this book, e.g. chapters 9 and 10) is concerned with how children construct hypotheses about perceptual data and how they gain greater knowledge about the world through forming hypotheses to test against experience. Indeed, we started this chapter by considering how people are 'nature's psychologists' in this sense (see also chapter 5).

Popper considers that science and knowledge progress by advancing hypotheses, making deductions from them, and continuing to do so until some deductions are proved wrong or 'falsified'. The hypothesis is then changed to cope with this. A hypothesis can thus never be finally proved correct, as there is always the possibility that some further observation or experiment might discredit it. An hypothesis can, however, be falsified and it is through this process that science progresses.

You can think about this by examining the hypotheses we just listed. Have any been falsified (some have)? Did the falsifying lead to better hypotheses (sometimes)? Could any be 'proved' beyond question?

Popper's notion of falsification has been a powerful one, and he uses it to distinguish 'science' from 'non-science'. If propositions, hypotheses or theories cannot actually be falsified, then according to Popper, this is not science. It may be interesting and enlightening, like a novel, but it is not science.

Not all philosophers of science agree with Popper's approach. At least, not many believe that scientists spend most of their time trying to *disprove* their theories. A different view was put by Thomas Kuhn (b. 1922), who saw a mature branch of any science as having an accepted 'paradigm'. A paradigm is a basic set of assumptions, or way of trying to solve problems. Atomic theory provided a paradigm in the natural sciences, for example.

In psychology, 'psychoanalysis', 'behaviourism', 'sociobiology' (see chapter 2) and the 'information processing' approach (viewing the brain as a computer), could be taken as paradigms in this sense. However the most influential paradigm informing the present book is the 'cognitive–developmental' paradigm. This links behaviour to the kind of cognitive development or thinking ability expected at the age or level of development the individual is at. Piaget's theory of cognitive development is often taken as a reference point here (chapter 11), though the approach is not necessarily tied to Piaget's ideas.

Kuhn described how a branch of science might develop thus. It starts in a 'pre-paradigmatic stage' where it would be characterized by rather random fact-gathering, and many schools of thought which quarrel about fundamental issues. With maturity, one paradigm is accepted and directs the way observations and experiments are made. Kuhn called this phase 'normal science'. Scientists work within the paradigm, extending and defending it. The paradigm is not rejected unless many difficulties or falsifications accumulate, and in addition a superior paradigm appears. A period of 'revolutionary science' with competing paradigms then emerges, with eventually one proving superior, when 'normal science' resumes.

Kuhn characterizes science as having a fruitful paradigm which can unify the efforts and direction of study of many scientists. Falsification has a relatively minor role to play, he argues, since all theories have some anomalies (phenomena which cannot yet be well explained). Only the appearance of another paradigm can really upset things, according to Kuhn.

Kuhn's ideas have been criticized, and modified, but his idea of a paradigm, while rather vague in practice, has had considerable impact. Psychologists in particular often seem to be claiming that a particular approach or theory is setting up a 'new paradigm'! Kuhn himself seems to think that psychology and other social sciences may well still be at a pre-paradigmatic stage. It is indeed true that no single paradigm as yet unites the whole of psychology. Still, certain paradigms (e.g. the cognitive-developmental approach) do seem to be fruitful and capable of bringing together several areas of psychology. Perhaps, after working through this book, the reader may decide for himself or herself what kind of scientific status the study of psychological development has, what it has achieved, and what it may reasonably hope to achieve in the foreseeable future.

**Further reading**

A very readable introductory text on methods of studying behaviour is P. Martin and P. Bateson 1986: *Measuring Behaviour: an Introductory Guide*. Cambridge: Cambridge University Press; it has most detail on observational methods, and on studying animals. A more advanced sourcebook for research methodology and experimental design in psychology is provided by J. M. Neale and R. M. Liebert 1986: *Science and Behavior: an Introduction to Methods of Research*, 3rd ed. Englewood Cliffs, N. J.: Prentice-Hall.

There are many good statistics texts available for psychology and the social/behavioural sciences. Amongst the most suitable for introductory psychology courses are C. Robson 1983: *Experiment, Design and Statistics in Psychology*, 2nd ed. Harmondsworth: Penguin: and S. Heyes, M. Hardy, P. Humphreys and P. Rookes 1986: *Starting Statistics in Psychology and Education*. London: Weidenfeld and Nicolson. An excellent, thorough and broader text is H. Coolican 1990: *Research Methods and Statistics in Psychology*. London: Hodder & Stoughton.

The way in which psychologists can be affected by the social climate of the time, and the ethical issues involved in doing research with social policy implications, are well exemplified in S. J. Gould 1981: *The Mismeasure of Man*. Harmondsworth: Penguin.

An introduction to Popper's ideas on scientific method can be found in B. Magee 1973: *Popper*. Glasgow: Fontana. Kuhn's ideas are best expressed in T. Kuhn 1962: *The Structure of Scientific Revolutions*. London: University of Chicago Press (2nd edn, 1970). A comprehensive sourcebook is J. Losee 1980: *A Historical Introduction to the Philosophy of Science*. Oxford: Oxford University Press.

## Discussion points

1   Has our knowledge of psychological development advanced beyond 'common sense'?

2   What is meant by 'development' and how can we study it?

3   What are the advantages and disadvantages of carrying out experiments in psychology?

4   What ethical issues are involved in psychological investigation?

5   In what ways can psychology be considered to be, or not to be, a science?

# 2

# An Evolutionary Perspective

In this chapter we look at the main forms of social behaviour and development in birds and mammals – including our closest relatives, the monkeys and apes. The chapter aims to provide an evolutionary perspective on human social behaviour, and a cross-species account of how behaviour develops. First the kinds of social behaviour seen in mammals and birds are described. The second section then gives an overview of sociobiology and behavioural ecology, which many biologists believe provides the most successful approach to explaining why animals behave as they do, and which some researchers have tried to apply to human behaviour. A third section considers the process of development, constrasting instinctive and acquired aspects of social behaviour.

## Social Organization in Mammals and Birds

The basic imperatives of life for non-human species are to survive and to rear offspring. To survive, it is important to find food and to avoid being eaten oneself. To rear offspring, it is important to find a mate and, if appropriate, help the offspring through their infancy period. For many, though not all, animal species some form of social living is the best way to achieve these goals. The main types of social organization in mammals and birds are shown in table 2.1, with examples from different mammalian species, including primates (monkeys and apes).

In solitary species a female moves around with her young, and now and then encounters a male with whom she may mate (e.g. leopards). This is the bare minimum of social existence necessary for reproduction and raising offspring. In other species, however, a male may form a stable relationship with one or more females, for at least one breeding season and perhaps for many. These may be 'monogamous' families – a male–female pair with offspring (e.g. foxes) – or 'harem' families, where a male associates with several females and excess males roam in bachelor herds (e.g. wild horses).

Yet other species form cohesive social groups of many adults; perhaps some 5 to 30 in number. These are either bands of females with their young, who now and then encounter males (e.g. elephants), or bands of adult males and females together. Many of the ground-living monkeys have this latter form of social organization.

TABLE 2.1  *Types of social organization, with examples from mammals, including primates*

| Social organization | | | Non-primate mammals | Primates |
|---|---|---|---|---|
| Solitary: | female + young<br>roving males | | leopard<br>small deer | orang-utan |
| Family: | (a) | monogamous:<br>male + female<br>+ young | fox<br>jackal | gibbon<br>marmoset |
| | (b) | harem<br>male + females<br>+ young | zebra<br>wild horse | patas monkey<br>gorilla |
| Social group: | (a) | females + young;<br>roving males | elephant | — |
| | (b) | males + females<br>+ young | lion | many baboons and macaques, chimpanzee |
| Colonial or semi-social: | large aggregations of<br>males, females + young | | many bats<br>seals | gelada baboons |

Finally, some species form very large 'colonies' or aggregations; these may number hundreds or even thousands, such as seal colonies and bat roosts. Here, the aggregations are not cohesive in the way that the smaller social groups are, and (apart from mothers and infants) there is little evidence that individuals recognize each other.

Looking at table 2.1, you may notice that there are two main kinds of variation between the different forms of social organization. One is the size of the social group – ranging from single animals to thousands of individuals; the other is the kind of association between males and females – living separately or together in monogamous, polygynous or promiscuous relationships. Why should there be these various ways of living socially? We will first examine the size of social groups, and then discuss male–female associations (mating systems).

### The size of social groups

Two main factors are thought to be responsible for determining the size of social groups: the ease of getting food and the advantages in avoiding predation. An individual animal usually lives in a group of about optimum size from these points of view. For each factor we can think of the costs and benefits to the individual of being in a smaller or larger group. The main costs and benefits of a large social group are listed below. The costs and benefits of a smaller social group would be the inverse of these.

#### Getting food

Costs of living in larger group: less easy to hunt by surprise or ambush; you have to share food with others in the group.

Benefits of living in larger group: easier to find food if you can follow others, or listen for food calls; more effective predation by cooperative hunting and chasing; defend food better against other groups or species.

### Avoiding predation

Costs of living in a larger social group; less easy to hide from predators and avoid detection.

Benefits of living in a larger group: greater chance of detecting predator at a distance, if first animal to see it gives an alarm call; greater chance to confuse predator by large number of animals grouping together or running in various directions; less chance of you as an individual animal being captured, once predator has found your group; more possibility of group defence against predator.

The importance of each of these factors depends on the kind of animal. Let us consider two kinds of antelope living in Africa. One, the dik-dik, is solitary. It is a small animal, living in forests where it quietly merges with its surroundings; also, its food – tender buds and shoots on bushes – grows in small clumps which could not be readily shared with others. Solitary living both suits its feeding strategy and enables it to hide from predators more easily. By contrast, the wildebeest or gnu is a large antelope, living in vast herds in the Serengeti plains. It crops tough grass, of which there is sufficient that company does not mean competition. But company does mean that if a predator finds the herd, an individual is less likely to be caught.

Other factors may also be involved in determining the size of social groups, such as available nesting or sleeping sites, and communal care of young. However food and predation do seem to be the most important (Bertram, 1978).

### Mating systems

The other way in which social groups of animals obviously differ is in their composition, which is greatly affected by the form of mating system. Mating systems are commonly classified as:

*Monogamy*    A male–female pair mate only with each other, for at least one breeding season.

*Polygyny*    Several females mate with only one male.

*Polyandry*    Several males mate with only one female.

*Promiscuity*    Individual males or females may mate with a number of partners.

The majority of mammals are polygynous and among them a very common form of social organization is the 'harem', in which a male monopolizes mating opportunities with several females by holding a territory and excluding other adult males from it (e.g., red deer), or by herding his females with him (e.g., zebra). Another common form among mammals is that of large social groups with a promiscuous mating system, but in which dominant males have greater mating opportunities than subordinates. This is characteristic of the ground-living monkey species, such as baboons and macaques, and also of chimpanzees. The dominance hierarchy strongly influences who mates with whom. This has been called 'patterned promiscuity', since mating is not random but no long-term male–female bonds are present.

Some – rather few – mammals are monogamous. Examples are the fox, jackal, badger, mongoose, hooded seal, gibbon and marmoset. In this there is a great contrast with bird species, more than 90 per cent of which are monogamous. No mammal has been found to be polyandrous (excepting a few human societies), but a few species of birds are polyandrous (Jenni, 1979).

Why are there these differences in mating systems between mammals and birds, and an asymmetry between the frequency of polygyny and polyandry? The answer seems to be related to ways of looking after the young. In both mammals and birds the female has to spend a lot of time and energy on rearing offspring. A mother bird has to grow and lay eggs – and each egg is often 10–15 per cent of the mother's body weight. A mother mammal has to grow the fetus, give birth and then nurse the infant for some time if it is to have any chance of surviving. A father bird, or mammal, on the other hand, might help with rearing offspring, but this is not vitally necessary for the infant's development. Put simply, a female mammal or bird has two main strategies she can adopt in choosing a partner to mate with:

1    She can mate with a 'successful' male, one who is strong, or defends a good territory for feeding on, or who is high in a dominance hierarchy. This leads to polygyny (in a 'harem' type social group) or to patterned promiscuity (in a multi-male social group). The complementary male strategy is to mate with a large number of females, but not spend much time or effort helping to look after offspring.

2    She can mate with a 'good parenting' male, one who will give a lot of help in rearing offspring. This generally leads to monogamy, as it is difficult for a male to give much help to two broods or litters in the same breeding season. The complementary male strategy is then to invest time and energy in raising offspring of the one partner, rather than seeking further mates and leaving the female to cope on her own.

Be careful to note that when we talk about 'strategies' in animals, it does not mean that we think of them as making *conscious* decisions in the way humans do. The issue of instinct and learning in animals is discussed below in a later section of this chapter.

We can now understand why most birds are monogamous. Birds make nests and lay eggs which need to be kept warm (incubated) almost continuously. Most birds also have hatchlings which are helpless for some time and need a great deal of feeding. It would be difficult and sometimes impossible for one parent bird alone to incubate the eggs and feed the hatchlings without them dying from cold, predation, or lack of food, or the parent dying from exhaustion. If the father left to mate with another female, all his first brood would probably die. Hence, fathers usually stay and help with raising the young, and monogamy is very common.

The case is quite different in mammals. Only the mother can feed the infants, giving the milk when they suckle. Also in many mammals the young mature rapidly and are able to follow the mother around (e.g. deer, cattle). There is very little role for a father here, and such species are almost always polygynous or promiscuous. Even when the young are more helpless and huddle in a nest or den for some period (e.g. mice, kittens, rabbits), the litter help keep each other warm, and the possible role of a father is small. In a few species, however, the father does play an important role by regurgitating food to the mother or older pups (e.g. jackal, wild dog), or by defending the nest or den (e.g. mongoose), or by carrying the young (e.g. marmoset). These generally comprise the monogamous mammals.

We can also see why polyandry is so rare. In polyandry, a female has a brood or litter, and several males helping her; yet, only one male is the father. Other males would do better to seek another mate and help raise their own offspring. In a few cases of bird polyandry the female usually lays two or more clutches of eggs, leaving a male to tend to each. A rare kind of social structure is found in the Tasmanian native hen, where a female hen often has two males consorting with her. In this species, where there is a shortage of females in the population, it has been found that the two males are normally brothers (so even the non-father male is raising related offspring). Also, having two males helps rear more offspring successfully, perhaps because of predator defence.

The type of mating system is related to the characteristic mode of courtship of the species, and to sexual signalling. In monogamous species, there is often a long courtship period in which the male and female get to know each other and perhaps make sure that the partner is not going to desert. In an early ethological study, Julian Huxley (1914) described courtship in the great crested grebe; this involves complex routines of head shaking, diving and bringing up water weeds (see figure 2.1). In

FIGURE 2.1  *Courtship in the great crested grebe involves elaborate mutual ceremonials, some of which are illustrated here: (a) the head shaking ceremony in which the pair face each other displaying their head feathers and shaking their heads from side to side; (b) the male dive, in which the male approaches the female with head submerged and suddenly shoots high out of the water just in front of her; (c) the mutual presentation of water weeds to each other (from Huxley, 1914/1968)*

monogamous species, the male and female are usually similar in size and appearance,. In polygynous species, however, courtship is short or non-existent, and the male is often larger and more ornate or impressive in appearance than the female, so as to attract females and perhaps deter other males. This difference between the sexes is known as 'sexual dimorphism'. Sexual signalling is discussed further below in the section on communication.

### Home range and territory

An animal, or group of animals, usually obtains food within a known, limited area, only rarely venturing beyond. This area of main usage is known as the 'home range'. Home ranges may overlap but are not strongly defended. In species such as lions, grizzly bears or gorillas, for example, there are large, overlapping home ranges, which it would be impossible to patrol effectively to keep out intruders. If one animal or group encounters another, they may avoid each other, or call or display, or there may be some aggression, but the range is not systematically defended.

A small area, however, can be defended, and if an animal or group defends a discrete area from intruders, and there is a clear boundary between this area and that of neighbours, this is known as a 'territory'. Many birds have territories, and bird song (besides attracting mates in the breeding season) is a means of telling other birds that a territory is occupied and will be defended. Krebs, Ashcroft and Webber (1978) looked at the use of song in great tits. Male great tits may have repertoires of from two to eight different songs, changing perch for a different song. On a number of occasions the researchers replaced a great tit with a loudspeaker which either played a control sound (a note on a tin whistle), a single great tit song, or a repertoire. The researchers found that the great tit's empty territory would be occupied by another great tit after a period of time; however, the control sound did not deter other tits at all, and most such territories were reoccupied within six hours. If the loudspeaker played one great tit song, it was 18 hours before most territories were reoccupied; whereas if it played a repertoire of songs, most territories remained empty for about 30 hours. The song repertoire does seem to function to keep other birds out, perhaps because they think that several birds are producing the repertoire (the hypothesis Krebs favoured), or perhaps because an extensive song repertoire is a sign of a bird's strength and vigour.

Some mammals defend territories too, using calls and also scent marking. It is usually the male who defends a territory, especially during the breeding season, as it gives him mating rights over females in his territory. For example, red deer and wildebeest defend small territories against other males in this way.

### Cooperation, dominance and aggression

Animals living in a social group may cooperate, and compete, with each other in various ways. Social life in animals is not completely harmonious, but neither is it entirely a case of 'nature red in tooth and claw'. Let us consider some examples of cooperation first.

We have already seen how in some species a male and female will cooperate together to raise offspring, sharing the burden of feeding and defence. In some mammals several females will share the feeding of the litters, which are kept in a communal den. This 'communal suckling' is characteristic of lionesses, for example, who live in groups of several females with young; the lion cubs are left in a shallow den while the lionesses go out hunting, and a lionesses will nurse any of the cubs on return. Elephants are another example; they move around in herds of females and young, and females will allow offspring besides their own to suckle. With both lionesses and elephants, females in a group are likely to be related (e.g. sisters, or cousins).

In some species a monogamous pair may get help from another adult, usually a grown-up offspring, in raising young. This is true of some bird species such as the superb blue wren of Australia, or the scrub jay of Florida, and in a few mammals such as jackals and mongooses. These are referred to as 'helpers at the nest' or 'helpers at the den'. The older offspring help rear younger brothers and sisters by giving extra defence against predators and/or getting food. This is instead of going off to find a mate and have offspring of their own. Helping at the nest or den may be the best strategy if mates are few, or if the helper hopes to inherit its parents' territory on their death.

Many species have alarm calls or signals which alert others to the presence of a predator. Communal defence against enemies also occurs in some species, when several animals will group together to attack the predator; for example, elephants in a herd will cooperate in defending the young.

It is worth noting, however, that these kinds of cooperation are not characteristic of all species. For example, wildebeest live in large herds and young wildebeest are predated very heavily by lions and hyenas. In theory, fully grown adult widebeest could cooperate effectively in driving away a lion, or a group of hyenas – but they do not do so. Only the mother wildebeest will defend her young; she can do so effectively against a single hyena, but against a second hyena the young wildebeest has no chance. Other wildebeest around will ignore what is happening. Similarly, mother wildebeest will nurse their own young, but not anyone else's. The reason for this lack of cooperation is probably that wildebeest live in such large herds that another wildebeest is unlikely to be closely related (see discussion of kin selection below, p. 33).

Whether animals in a group cooperate to a great extent or not (and it seems to be more common in smaller herds or flocks, where individuals are related), there will also be conflicts of interest within the group. These conflicts may be over mating rights, or food, or use of nesting or denning sites, for example. Similarly, there are potential conflicts between individuals or groups over territories. In such cases a conflict could be resolved by fighting. Sometimes animals do fight with each other, quite viciously. Often, however, a fight is avoided, after some signalling or posturing by both parties. It is as if one animal recognizes another's greater strength, or higher dominance position or territorial rights.

Some earlier writers, such as Konrad Lorenz (1966), thought that serious fights were always avoided 'for the good of the species', but we now know that this is not so. For example a long-term study has been made of red deer on the island of Mull, in Scotland, by Clutton-Brock and his colleagues (1982). Red deer are a harem-living polygynous species where males defend individual territories in the breeding season. The large antlers of the males are used in conflicts with other males. Frequently one male may challenge another by approaching and roaring; the two males walk along in parallel, raising their heads and roaring for some time, and often one male will retire at this point, thus avoiding injury. However, sometimes a real fight will ensue, and this can cause serious damage. Clutton-Brock found that every year about a quarter of the male red deer stags under study incurred some injury from fighting, and for about 6 per cent of stags this was a serious injury such as laming, antler breakage, or blinding. The challenges and fights are important, however, as they decide which stags will hold a territory, attract females and sire offspring in that breeding season.

Within multi-male and multi-female groups potential conflicts are usually sorted out within the constraints of a dominance hierarchy. This phenomenon was first described in hens, and this is why it is sometimes called a 'pecking order'. The birds can be arranged in a vertical line or hierarchy, with an individual submitting to those above, but dominating those below. Dominance hierarchies have been observed in many species, including the ground-living monkeys and chimpanzees, for example. They usually have a simple, linear form, though in monkeys and apes it can be more complicated if two or more lower ranking animals gang up or form a 'clique' against an animal who would dominate them individually. As with territory rights, domiance tends to be enforced by signals, and it is usually in a subordinate animal's interests to comply rather than risk injury. Sometimes dominance is challenged, resulting in serious fighting (see box 2.1 for an example).

*Parent-offspring relations, peers and play*

We have already discussed how the mother mammal or bird must look after offspring if they are to survive, and how the father may also help in some species. The main ways in which the mother, sometimes the father, and sometimes older siblings, may help offspring is in providing warmth and shelter, food, transport, and protection from predators. This kind of help is often called *parental investment*. The young are usually distinguished as being of one of two types.

*Altricial young*   The young are helpless at birth, often blind and unable to move. Examples are mice, pups, kittens, and many bird fledglings. Brood or litter size is often large. The young are fed periodically when mother returns to the nest or den. The young take some time to learn the characteristics of the mother, and vice versa. Rapid bonding is not necessary, as the mother will find the young in the den or nest when she returns. As a result, experimental fostering is often relatively easy.

*Precocial young*   The young are relatively independent at or soon after birth, and able to move around often within a few hours. Examples are deer, cattle, sheep and some birds such as hens and ducks. In precocial mammals the mother often has just one young in a litter, and it is fed when it wishes, or 'on demand'. The young very rapidly learn to follow the mother around, and a bond of recognition and attachment is formed between mother and young, so that the latter will not get separated or lost. As a consequence, experimental fostering is very difficult in these species.

The primates (monkeys and apes) do not fit too well into this scheme, as they carry their young around (as distinct from putting them in a den, or having them follow).

The young are usually quite quite helpless or altricial, and, being carried around, do not need to bond as rapidly with the mother as do precocial young. However, there is usually only one young in a litter (it would be too much for a mother monkey to carry two offspring), and suckling is 'on demand'.

Young mammals and birds, after a period of high initial dependence on the mother or parents, go through a period during which they become less dependent but do not leave the mother completely. In mammals the young may range further away before returning, and may get more interested in same-age peers (e.g. littermates) than in parents. Much social interaction between littermates involves play, or grooming. Social play usually consists of wrestling or chasing, the non-serious intent being signalled by a playful face or approach (see also chapter 6). It is believed that this kind of play is useful, perhaps for exercise, developing later fighting or hunting skills, or forming social bonds, though the extent to which it is necessary or essential for this is controversial (see Smith, 1982; Martin and Caro, 1985).

Littermates may cooperate in later life, especially if they stay in the same social group. This is true of lions and elephants for example, and also of baboons and macaques, and of chimpanzees (box 2.1). They may learn to recognize each other and behave in a more cooperative way than with strangers (see discussion of kin selection, below). Experience together as young animals is probably important for this (see box 2.2 on spiny mice, for example).

*Communication systems in mammals and birds*

Animals often communicate with one another. In communication some sort of signal is sent from one individual to another, which may influence the latter's behaviour. In addition, ethologists believe that many of these signals have evolved for the purpose of communication. For example, the raised head and loud roar of the red deer (plate 2.1) signals to a nearby adult male deer that the first animal may challenge it if it approaches. The second deer may then move away, or take up the challenge by roaring itself.

Signals are important in many social interactions, and we have mentioned several already. These include:

readiness to initiate or continue courtship (e.g., great crested grebe).
readiness to mate.
readiness to defend territory (e.g., red deer roaring; bird song).
readiness to attack or dominate another animal, or to submit (see figure 2.2).
the playful nature of an approach or grapple (see figure 6.1).
alarm calls at a predator's approach.

These signals can be given in many different ways in different species. Some are visual, e.g. facial or body posture; some are auditory, e.g. deer roaring, bird song, alarm calls; some are tactile; and some rely on the sense of smell, e.g. scent-marking. Sometimes signals are graded in intensity. An interesting example from the studies of Lorenz on dogs is illustrated in figure 2.3. This shows the characteristic facial expression according to the degree to which the dog is ready to attack (aggressive

PLATE 2.1   *A male red deer, with does on left, raises his head and roars as a challenge to a younger stag (from Clutton-Brock, 1985)*

motivation) and simultaneously ready to submit (fear motivation). Aggression is signalled by bared teeth, erect ears and drawn-up nose. Fear is signalled by laid-back ears and narrowed eyes. The expression bottom right in figure 2.3 thus implies a dog which would like to attack, but is prevented by strong fear.

So far our discussion has implied that a signal gives an accurate impression of the intention of the animal sending it. This was the prevailing view but it has recently been challenged by theories and findings that suggest some communications may be

FIGURE 2.2   *A young Grant's gazelle (on left) lowers its head as a sign of submission to the adult male on the right, which holds its head high in a threat signal (from Ewer, 1968)*

Increasing aggression

Increasing fear

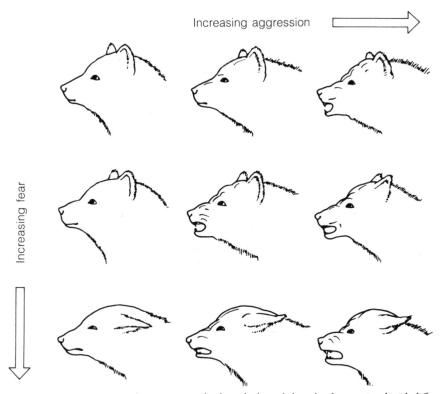

FIGURE 2.3    *Changes in facial expression in the dog which are believed to be associated with different motivational states (from Eibl-Eibesfeldt, 1971)*

deceitful. It could be in an animal's interests to send a misleading message. In fact, we have already encountered a possible example of this, in the song repertoire of the great tit. If the song repertoire is taken by other birds to imply the presence of several tits, then its message is deceitful. In apes, we even have some evidence of intentional deceit. Jane Goodall (box 2.1) has described how once, when a group of chimpanzees were crowded around bananas at the feeding area, one low-ranking chimpanzee on the periphery gave an alarm call. The other chimpanzees scattered but the chimpanzee who gave the call very quickly went to the bananas! Such examples are discussed further on pp. 43–5.

Recent research on mammalian calls is suggesting that they are more complex and sophisticated than ethologists originally thought. For example, a study of ground squirrels in Canada (Davis, 1984) has found that these animals give at least two kinds of alarm call. A short chirp is given in the presence of hawks, and squirrels hearing this immediately run to their burrow. A long whistle is given to weasels, and squirrels then stand erect, watch and flee (they do not go direct to the burrow, as the weasel might follow them in).

Signals seem especially complex in the monkeys and apes (see Seyfarth and Cheney, 1984). For example, vervet monkeys (a ground-living, social species) have three kinds of alarm call, with corresponding responses. 'Leopard alarms' cause other monkeys to run to trees; 'eagle alarms' cause them to look up in the air or run into

PLATE 2.2  Washoe, a young female chimpanzee taught to use sign language, signs 'sweet' for lollipop (left) and 'hat' for woollen cap (on right) (from Atkinson, Atkinson and Hilgard, 1981)

bushes; while 'snake alarms' cause monkeys to rise on their hind legs and look into the grass around them. These conclusions, based first on observation, have been confirmed by controlled experiments involving playback of tape-recorded calls. Vervet monkeys also 'grunt' at other monkeys, and the same methods have shown that grunts which sound the same to a human observer, differ in spectrographic analysis according to whether the grunt is directed to a dominant animal, a subordinate animal, or a monkey from another group.

The most dramatic studies of animal communication have been made with captive apes, usually chimpanzees. A husband and wife team, Gardner and Gardner (1969), taught American Sign Language (ASL) to Washoe, a young female chimpanzee who lived with them. Washoe acquired a large number of signs, and could convey messages such as 'please tickle' and 'give drink' (plate 2.2). The Gardners claimed that Washoe could use several signs strung together meaningfully, that she used signs in new situations (e.g. 'water bird' when she first saw a swan), and that altogether Washoe had language competence not dissimilar to that of a 2-year-old human child. Similar methods have been used successfully with other chimpanzees, with a female gorilla called Koko (Patterson, 1978), and with an orang-utan, Princess (Shapiro, 1982).

Other methods have also been used. Premack (1971) taught a female chimpanzee, Sarah, to communicate using plastic shapes, and Savage-Rumbaugh and Rumbaugh (1978) used a computer keyboard to similar effect, teaching Lana (another female chimpanzee) to communicate with the experimenter in verb-object phrases.

Criticisms have been made of these studies, for example that only rote-learning is taking place, or that the experimenter, as with 'Clever Hans' (see chapter 1), is giving unintentional cues to the animal as to the right response. Terrace et al. (1979), working with a chimpanzee called Nim, strongly criticized some of the Gardner's more ambitious claims, and the selective way in which they reported their data. The Gardners have defended their position, pointing out that their claims and methods of data reporting are no worse, and often better, than the methods used by those studying child language (van Cantford and Rimpau, 1982; Drumm et al., 1986; see also chapter 10).

## Sociobiology: Why Do animals Behave as They Do?

Most readers will probably have some idea of evolutionary theory, stemming from the work of Charles Darwin in the nineteenth century. A detailed knowledge of this theory is not necessary for our purposes, but a very brief summary will be useful for some understanding of recent developments in what has been called 'sociobiology' and the way in which it explains animal social behaviour.

Darwin's evolutionary theory was concerned with the ways the characteristics of an animal were selected, over generations, to be especially suited to or 'adapted' for the kind of environment in which it lived. The giraffe's long neck was adapted for feeding on the kinds of leaves and buds found high up on trees and bushes, for example. Although Darwin wrote before modern genetic theory was developed, the idea of the gene provides a crucial link in modern evolutionary theory. The gene codes information about development, and it is passed on from parent to offspring.

Giraffes, for example, have genes for long neck growth: in the past, as giraffes were evolving, those individuals which had genes for especially long necks fed better, and thus had more offspring, who themselves were more likely than average to have genes for long necks. Thus, genes for long necks, and actual long necks, came to typify the modern giraffe species.

Behaviour can be selected for during evolution, just as body characteristics can. For example, bird song, signals such as the red deer's roaring, courtship displays as in the great crested grebe, all are characteristic of a species and seem to have adaptive value. In considering social behaviour, however, a long-standing controversy has existed about whether we should think of the behaviour as being adaptive for the individual animal, or for the social group it is in, or even for the entire species.

Darwin's approach implied that behaviour should be adaptive for the individual, as the genes which are selected are only passed from parent to offspring. However, it was difficult to explain examples of cooperation and altruism on this basis. A consideration of figure 2.4 may help explain this. Consider a behaviour by animal A, which affects animal B. The behaviour might have a benefit or a cost to A, and a benefit or cost to B. We measure benefits and costs in terms of how the behaviour increases the chances of surviving and rearing offspring. Animal A's behaviour could be mutualistic, selfish, altruistic or spiteful, according to this framework. Now, if we argue that behaviour is selected for individual benefits, then we should only expect behaviour in the top two cells in figure 2.4. We would not expect altruistic behaviour, and yet we have seen that this does occur (e.g. communal suckling; communal defence of young).

The predominant response to this, until about 20 years ago, was to argue that behaviour was selected for the good of the whole social group, or species. You will still find this argument in some older textbooks. The difficulty with this approach, appealing as it may seem, is that it predicts only behaviour in the left hand cells of figure 2.4. No selfish behaviour is expected. Yet, we have seen that selfish behaviour

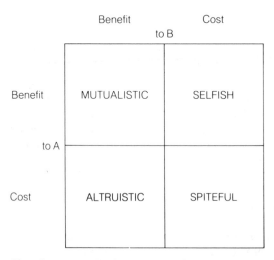

FIGURE 2.4   *Cost and benefit to two animals, A and B, of a social interaction between A and B*

is also common (e.g. failure to defend others, or nurse others' young; deceit in bird song repertoire; aggression over territory and mating rights).

Sociobiological theory provides a way out of this impasse. It predicts the mixture of mutualistic, altruistic and selfish behaviour that we actually observe in animal societies. The key idea, put forward by Hamilton (1964), and a central idea in modern sociobiology, is that of 'kin selection'. This is the hypothesis that an animal will behave altruistically toward its kin, especially those closely related. This was always taken for granted for an individual's offspring, as it was only through offspring that genes were directly passed on. Hamilton's insight was that an animal would share a greater than average proportion of genes with relatives too, especially close relatives such as siblings and cousins. Helping relatives is another way in which particular genes get passed on to the next generation, admittedly only an indirect way compared with having offspring oneself.

Kin selection theory then predicts that helpful or altruistic behaviour may be directed towards relatives, provided that it is not too harmful to the animal giving the help, and provided that the other animal is closely enough related to make it worthwhile. Close relatives will be helped more. Much evidence supports this theory. We have already seen examples, such as communal suckling in lions and elephants, and communal defence. Other examples are given in box 2.1 and box 2.2. In box 2.2 there is also some discussion of how animals might recognize kin.

In an interesting extension of kin selection theory, S. Trivers (1974) postulated that we should expect to see *parent–offspring* conflict. This is because the genetic interests of parent and offspring are not identical. The mother is related to all her offspring equally, and would be selected (other things being equal) to provide each with the same amount of parental investment or help. However, an individual offspring would be selected to favour itself over its siblings, with whom it only shares half its genes; thus, according to Trivers, it should seek more than its fair share of parental investment. This should lead to conflict with the mother, over the amount and duration of parental investment, and also to conflict with siblings, or *sibling rivalry*.

Since Trivers wrote his article, there have been many observations of parent–offspring and sibling conflict in animals. In mammals, suckling is a very important form of parental investment by the mother. In many species, the infant seems to try to continue suckling for longer than the mother wishes; the mother may reject the attempts of older infants to suckle, quite forcefully. Siblings may also compete with each other for access to the mother, in feeding situations.

There is more to sociobiology than just kin selection, however. Another way of explaining altruistic behaviour is through what is called 'reciprocal altruism' (Trivers, 1971). The hypothesis is that one individual will help another, at some smaller cost to itself, if it can expect similar help back from the other animal in the future. This is the old adage 'if you scratch my back, I'll scratch yours'. There is some evidence of reciprocal altruism, the most convincing being in monkeys and apes where it is clear that individuals do recognize each other and could thus stop helping individuals who failed to reciprocate ('cheats'). In a study of baboons, Packer (1977) found that pairs of unrelated males would help each other in challenging a dominant male. Individuals that gave such help to a particular male often received help back from the same male. As the males were unrelated, kin selection could not explain this.

Sociobiology has become the prevailing theorectical paradigm for explaining why animals behave towards others in the way they do, in terms of the evolutionary advantages of such behaviour. (A related theoretical area is that of 'behavioural ecology', which puts more emphasis on the animal in the non-social environment, for example on how animals should most efficiently forage for food). These theories have encountered problems and have severe critics. Nevertheless, they have changed the study of animal social behaviour away from being primarily an observational and descriptive science. Now, if a new species of monkey were discovered, for example, and we knew its food and its predators, we could attempt to predict such features as the size and composition of its social groups, its mating system, territorial behaviour and system of infant care. Sociobiology makes specific predictions, and field observations are now guided towards the testing of these.

## How Behaviour Develops

We have mentioned briefly the importance of genetic theory and the idea of the gene for sociobiology and for evolutionary theory. Each individual has a large number of genes, strung along the chromosomes. The whole collection of genes is called the 'genotype'. The genes are passed on from parent to offspring via the egg cells (ova) of the mother and the sperm cells of the father. The offspring receives a mixture of the genes of each parent, approximately half from each, reassembled into new combinations.

The genes regulate the production of amino acids and thus determine the first stages in cell growth and differentiation in the body and in the brain and nervous system. They thus are often thought of as providing a blueprint for the animal's growth and also for its behaviour. The actual course of growth and of behavioural development, however, depends upon, and is influenced by, the external environment. The environment not only provides the 'building materials' such as food and water; the particular environmental experiences of the animal also interact with the genetic instructions to determine in detail which exact course of development is followed.

Figure 2.5 depicts in very simple form the interaction of information from the genotype and information from the environment in determining behaviour. Both genotype and environment are obviously essential for *any* behaviour. Thus, we

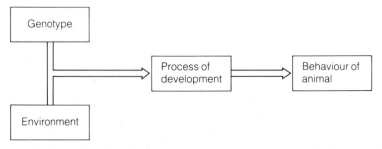

FIGURE 2.5    *Simple model of how both information from the genotype and information from the environment combine and interact to determine the course of behaviour development*

cannot say that a particular behaviour is genetic and another behaviour environmental; nor can we sensibly say that a behaviour comprises some percentage of each.

The diagram in figure 2.5 is a simple one – some psychologists and ethologists might say too simple. (For example, the information in the genotype may influence the animal's choice of environment, so the two influences are not as independent as they seem.) However, it may help in conceptualizing terms such as 'instinct', 'maturation' and 'learning', and the issue of the rigidity or flexibility of behaviour development.

Although we cannot say that a *behaviour* is mostly genetic or environmental, we can say that the *difference in behaviour* between two individuals is mostly genetic or environmental. In humans, for example, differences in eye colour can usually be ascribed to genetic differences (although both genotype and environment are necessary for the development of eye colour); whereas differences in spoken language can usually be ascribed to environmental differences (although both genotype and environment are necesary for the development of language).

Many writers have used the terms 'instinct', 'maturation' and 'learning' in discussing the development of behaviour. There are problems with the definition of these terms, and some ethologists prefer not to use the term 'instinct' at all. However, in order to understand discussion on these matters we need to know what writers who use such terms intend. Representative definitions are given below.

*Instinct*    Instinctive behaviour is observed in all normal healthy members of a species. Thus, it is little influenced by the environment. The genetic instructions provide detailed information for the development of instinctive behaviour, and only quite general environmental input (such as is necessary for healthy growth) is needed for its expression.

*Maturation*    Maturation refers to the emergence of instinctive behaviour patterns at a particular point in development. The genetic instructions facilitate the expression of certain behaviour patterns when a certain growth point is reached or a certain time period has elapsed.

*Learning*    Learning refers to the influence of specific environmental information on behaviour. Within a wide range of variation, the way an animal behaves depends on what it learns from the environment. Thus, individuals of a species may differ considerably in their learnt behaviour patterns.

### Bird song: an example of behavioural development

There are many species of song bird, each of which has a characteristic song, or song repertoire, though individuals may differ in the details of their song. We can use the development of bird song in different species to illustrate our discussion of behavioural development. Many ingenious experiments have been performed on this topic (see Thorpe, 1972, for a review).

For some species of bird the song might be described as 'instinctive'. Some birds have been reared experimentally in isolation, or deafened, or fostered by another species, so that they cannot hear the songs of birds of their own kind. In some species, such as doves, hens and song sparrows, the song develops quite normally in such circumstances. This is also true of cuckoos, which are of course regularly reared by foster parents. In such cases there is little environmentally caused variation between healthy individuals, and all members of the species sing much the same song.

Even if 'instinctive', however, the song may not appear fully formed. For example, in whitethroat, the male develops its song first as a continuous reiteration of one note, with other notes being added gradually. This occurs whether the bird is isolated, or not. Thus, this is an example of maturation.

The situation is different in chaffinches, whose song has been studied intensively by Thorpe (1972). Chaffinches sing a song consisting of three main phrases, followed by a terminal flourish. If a chaffinch is reared in isolation, it will not produce a proper chaffinch song. It will produce a much simpler song, of the right length and frequency but not divided into phrases, and without the terminal flourish. The full song is therefore not instinctive and some more specific environmental input is needed for its development. The song is more complex if chaffinches are reared in groups, but in isolation from adult chaffinches. Presumably, the experience of countersinging with other chaffinches is a helpful environmental input. Even so, the song is not perfect, and only the experience of hearing the adult chaffinch song produces a fully formed song in the young chaffinch. Clearly, learning is important in this species.

However, let us note two constraints on this learning of chaffinch song. One is that the young chaffinch will only learn its song from adult chaffinches. If fostered by another species, it will not learn that species' song. In other words, the type of learning is limited to songs that are within a narrow range characteristic of adult chaffinches. The second point to bear in mind is that this learning can only occur within a certain period. Learning capacity is at its maximum in the first spring, when the bird is 8 months old, and ceases after about 14 months, when the bird's singing behaviour becomes fixed or unalterable.

Chaffinch song provides an excellent example of how genotype and environment interact in constraining development. Some learning occurs in chaffinch song, but it is highly constrained in time and duration. As a result, chaffinch song is stable. Chaffinches introduced into New Zealand in 1862, and South Africa in 1900, still sing very much the same song as European chaffinches.

The situation is different again in other species, where learning of the adult song it much more flexible. In bullfinches, for example, the song is learned and there are few constraints on the type of song; if fostered by canaries, a young bullfinch will adopt canary song and ignore the songs of other bullfinches.

*Rigidity and flexibility*

As you can see from the bird song example, it can often be rather simplistic to say that a behaviour is either 'instinctive' or 'learned'. Many psychologists now prefer to talk in terms of the 'ridigity' or 'flexibility' of behaviour, or of how 'modifiable' or 'canalized' behavioural development is. Rigid behaviour is less susceptible to environmental modification, flexible behaviour is more so. In the examples above we can see successive increases in flexibility in the adult song of doves, chaffinches and bullfinches, respectively.

A helpful way of conceptualizing this issue is shown in figure 2.6. This type of

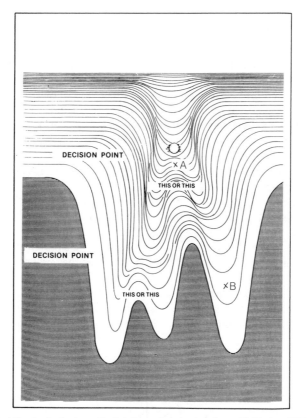

FIGURE 2.6   *Waddington's 'epigenetic landscape' (adapted from Fishbein, 1976)*

figure, produced by Waddington (1957), is called an 'epigenetic landscape'. The ball represents the organism while the landscape represents the possibilities for development constrained by the genotype. The movement of the ball down the slope represents development. The direction of travel (development) is influenced by the shape of the landscape, as it is easier for the ball to roll down the troughs, or canals. However, environmental influences can also influence the direction of travel, pushing the ball in certain directions.

At certain times there are choice or decision points in development, and environmental influences may easily affect the direction of development at such points (for example, the point marked A in figure 2.6). At other times, environmental influence, unless extreme, will have little effect (the point marked B, for instance). The development of chaffinch song could easily be interpreted within this framework.

Waddington, and others since, talk of the 'canalization' of behaviour. This is another way of referring to the rigidity as against flexibility of behaviour. We talk of canalized behaviour when the troughs or canals in the epigenetic landscape are deep and environmental variations have little effect. If the canals are shallow, the environment produces much greater variation.

*'Instinctive' behaviour: early studies*

The study of species-typical or 'instinctive' behaviour was first put on a scientific footing by Konrad Lorenz and Niko Tinbergen in the 1940s and 1950s. For this work they shared the Nobel Prize for Physiology or Medicine in 1973 (together with Karl Von Frisch for his work on dance language in honey bees). In his book *The Study of Instinct*, Tinbergen (1951) put forward a set of influential ideas about the organization of behaviour. He postulated that many sequences of behaviour were largely uninfluenced by environmental variation. He called such sequences 'fixed action patterns' or FAPs. The FAP was set off by a particular stimulus called a 'sign stimulus'. The sign stimulus was detected by an 'innate releasing mechanism' or IRM, which then activated the FAP.

Let us consider two examples. The first is illustrated in figure 2.7, which shows young blackbirds in a nest. When the mother arrives, the hatchlings stretch their necks and gape for food. This is a fixed action pattern. The sign stimulus which releases this does not need to be an actual blackbird; it is simpler. Any close moving object which is larger than 3 cm in diameter and above the level of the nestlings will do.

Another example is the alarm response of birds such as ducks and geese to aerial predators. The fixed action pattern is the alarm call and escape response. The sign stimulus need not be an actual hawk. The sufficient stimulus is an object moving

FIGURE 2.7   *Young blackbirds gaping at a model 'parent' (from Evans, 1978)*

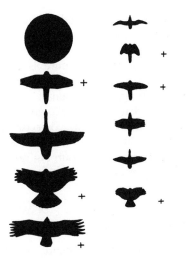

FIGURE 2.8   *Bird models used by Lorenz and Tinbergen for testing reactions of various birds of prey. Those marked + released escape responses (from Tinbergen, 1951)*

overhead, with a short neck and long tail. Figure 2.8 shows some cardboard models which did, and did not, elicit alarm behaviour in this way.

Sometimes an artificial or unusual stimulus can release a fixed action pattern even more strongly or effectively than the natural stimulus. This is called a 'supernormal stimulus'. Figure 2.9 shows an example where an oystercatcher has chosen to try to incubate an oversized egg. The FAP is incubation, and the oversized egg is a supernormal stimulus. Another example is the FAP of feeding by parent birds in response to the gape of the hatchlings. A young cuckoo in the nest will give a large, bright orange gape which often provides a supernormal stimulus and means that the young cuckoo gets most of the food brought to the nest.

FIGURE 2.9   *An oyster catcher reacting to a giant egg in preference to a normal egg (foreground) and a herring gull egg (left) (from Tinbergen, 1951)*

In the foregoing discussion we have looked at birds, but many of the examples from Tinbergen's and Lorenz's work were from fishes, amphibia and insects. 'Instinctive' behaviour, or as we might now prefer to say, 'species-typical' behaviour of a strongly canalized or rigid nature, is in fact most characteristic of these simpler species. So far as birds are concerned, and mammals especially, some of the early ideas now seem too simple. For example, Lorenz supposed that specific energy built up for each FAP, so that eventually it would find an outlet even without being released by a sign stimulus; or, he conjectured, the energy would be 'displaced' into another activity. In his book *On Aggression* (1966) he applied such ideas to mammalian and even human behaviour, but no clear evidence for a 'build-up' of aggressive energy has been found, and these ideas are not now given much credence.

### Imprinting and the concept of sensitive periods

One of Lorenz's ideas which has remained influential, is that of 'imprinting'. We saw earlier how the young in precocial species (such as ducks, hens, deer) may learn to follow their mother around very soon after birth. But how do they learn whom to follow? Lorenz discovered that while the following mechanism is highly canalized ('instinctive'), there is some flexibility in learning what (or whom) is to be followed. Generally, the young bird or mammal learns the characteristics of a conspicuous moving object nearby during a period soon after birth or hatching; it then follows this object around. It is this process of learning which object to follow that is known as imprinting. Usually imprinting occurs to the mother, since she is the main figure the offspring encounters during the critical, or sensitive, period after birth. But imprinting to other objects can occur. Lorenz imprinted some ducklings on himself, so that they then followed him everywhere (plate 2.3). This is easy to do with sheep as well (as in the nursery song, where 'everywhere that Mary went, the lamb was sure to go').

Lorenz introduced the term 'critical period' to describe the restricted period of time in which he believed imprinting took place. In ducklings this period is from about 9 hours to 17 hours after birth (see figure 2.10). Lorenz also believed that imprinting was irreversible after this period. Subsequent research has suggested that the learning which takes place in imprinting is not quite as rigid as this, but that nevertheless it is the case that such learning occurs most readily within a restricted period. Usually researchers now refer to this as a 'sensitive period'. We have seen another example of a sensitive period already, in the instance of chaffinch song. Yet another example might be the development of kin recognition in littermates (box 2.2).

Imprinting in which the young learn the characteristics of the parent is known as 'filial imprinting'. It is important in precocial species in order to ensure that the young follow the correct animal (unless an experimenter such as Lorenz intervenes!). Lorenz also believed that at the same time the young learned the characteristics of their species, so that they would ultimately choose a member of their own species to mate with. This is called 'sexual imprinting' and the evidence for it is less well established. However, Bateson (1982) has shown that early experience is important for mating preference in Japanese quail. Bateson found that Japanese quail prefer as mating partners other quail that differ in appearance slightly, but not a lot, from

PLATE 2.3    *Young ducklings 'imprinted' on Konrad Lorenz follow him wherever he goes (from Atkinson, Atkinson and Hilgard, 1981)*

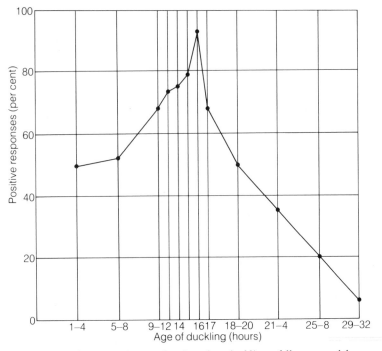

FIGURE 2.10    *Results of an experiment showing that ducklings follow a model more readily 9–17 hours after hatching than at other times (from Evans, 1978)*

quail they were reared with. If quail are reared normally with siblings, then as adults they prefer to mate with cousins, rather than with either siblings or unrelated birds. However, such choices can be altered if they are reared with non-sibling quail of different appearance. In this species imprinting seems normally to involve learning the appearance of kin, and then later selecting as a mate an individual who would be related, but not too closely, thus achieving a balance between the costs of inbreeding and outbreeding.

*Learning processes*

Imprinting is often presented as a special form of learning, highly constrained in what is learned and when it is learned. Many forms of learning are more flexible, especially in the mammals, though the idea that there are some constraints on learning (some degree of canalization in development, see figure 2.6) seems to apply widely (Hinde and Stevenson-Hinde 1973).

Learning may occur through observation and imitation of others, for example in much bird song acquisition and in the learning of food preferences and tool use in chimpanzees (box 2.1). Some learning occurs through 'trial-and-error'. The degree to which the individual is rewarded or 'reinforced', in its behaviour is also important in learning. For example, rats will learn not to eat food that produces nausea, even if the nausea occurs an hour later (Garcia et al., 1966).

In the more advanced mammals, especially the monkeys and apes, it seems as though we are encountering the beginnings of mental activity ('thinking') as we are familiar with it. This involves a kind of internal, symbolic representation of the world in the brain. Thinking consists of the internal manipulation of these symbols.

Some examples of behaviour seen in monkeys certainly suggest this kind of cognitive thinking. In species such as macaques and baboons, individuals will sometimes form cliques against a rival (for example, Packer's observations on p. 33); or will give different vocalizations to animals of different social status or relatedness (p. 31; Seyfarth and Cheney, 1984). It appears as though monkeys are thinking in quite complex ways about their social relationships. This goes along with a relatively larger cerebral cortex in these species. With this sort of brain, behaviour becomes much more flexible, and learning during development much more important.

## Thinking in primates

Researchers who have studied primates (monkeys and apes) have often been impressed by their thinking abilities; and this is especially true of the great apes – the chimpanzees, the gorilla, and the orang-utan. Studies have been made both in the wild, and in laboratories; an example of a naturalistic study of chimpanzees is provided in box 2.1.

Let's look at some examples of advanced intelligence in the great apes:

*Tool use and making*    Tool use has been observed in a number of species, but tool making – deliberately altering a natural object to a specific end – was long thought to be uniquely characteristic of humans. However it has been observed in chimpanzees in natural conditions (see p. 53) and in other great apes in experimental situations. Related to this is an ability to use objects in *insightful* ways – for example stacking boxes on top of each other to reach an out-of-reach clump of bananas; or using poles as ladders to get over fences.

*Pretence*   There are some observations of chimpanzees using objects in 'pretend' ways (for a discussion of pretend play in children see chapter 6). A classic example is of a chimpanzee called Viki, home-reared by two psychologists. Viki was observed at times to be acting as if she had an imaginary pull-toy:

> Very slowly and deliberately she was marching around the toilet, trailing the fingertips of one hand on the floor. Now and then she paused, glanced back at the hand, and then resumed her progress ... she interrupted the sport one day to make a series of tugging motions ... She moved her hands over and around the plumbing knob in a very mysterious fashion; then placing both fists one above the other in line with the knob, she strained backwards as in tug of war. Eventually there was a little jerk and off she went again, trailing what to my mind could only be an imaginary pulltoy. (Hayes, 1952).

*Self-recognition*   Chimpanzees and orang-utans can recognize themselves in a mirror. This has been shown by so-called 'mirror image stimulation' or MIS studies (Gallup, 1982). An animal is first accustomed to a mirror. Then, while anesthetized, it is marked conspicuously (for example with red dye) on an ear, nose or eyebrow in a way which it cannot see directly. Its reaction on seeing its mirror reflection is noted. Monkeys will reach for the mirror image as if it was another animal. However (after a few days of prior mirror exposure) a chimpanzee or orang-utan will reach for its *own* body part, strongly suggesting it recognizes itself in the image. Surprisingly, gorillas have not yet been found to have this ability.

*Learnt symbolic communication*   All three species of great ape have been trained to communicate using non-verbal signals (see p. 31); this is at least a rudimentary kind of learnt language. These are based on laboratory studies, but there is an example of learnt communication in natural surroundings too. Nishida (1980) has described a 'leaf-clipping display' amongst wild chimpanzees in Tanzania. A chimpanzee picks several stiff leaves and repeatedly pulls them from side to side between its teeth; this makes a distinctive and conspicuous ripping sound. It is used as possessive behaviour or courtship display by a male to a female, or a female in oestrus to a male. This display has not been seen to be used in this way in other chimpanzee populations, and may be a social custom of this particular group.

*Deception*   Deception is involved when an individual sends a signal to another individual, who then acts appropriately towards the signal according to its obvious meaning, which is however untrue. Deception is well known in many animal species, but is particularly complex in primates.

As an example, consider an observation made on chimpanzees by Plooij (in Byrne and Whiten, 1987).

> An adult male (A) was about to eat some bananas that only he knew about, when a second male (T) came into view at the edge of the feeding area. The

FIGURE 2.11   *Tactical deception in chimpanzees (after Byrne and Whiten, 1987)*

first quickly walked several metres away from the food, sat down and looked around as though nothing had happened (see figure 2.11a).

Here A is deceiving T by giving signals that 'there is nothing of interest around here' (untrue!). If A looked at the bananas, then T (being more dominant) would have taken them instead.

However, the observation continues:

The newcomer (T) left the feeding area (see figure 2.11b) but as soon as he was out of sight he hid behind a tree and peered at the male who remained (A). As soon as A approached the food and took it, T returned, displaced the other and ate the bananas.

This is actually counter-deception by the second chimpanzee, who seems to have realized that the first was hiding something!

*The evolution of high intelligence*

Why has such high intelligence evolved in the primates and especially the great apes? There is a cost to high intelligence – large brains use up more energy for maintenance, and a longer developmental period entails greater risks. So there must be benefits to counterbalance these.

The traditional view has been that high intelligence helps animals cope with the physical environment. Parker and Gibson (1979) suggested that high intelligence evolved as a means of better obtaining food. For example, tool use, tool making, and imitative learning are all involved in food gathering in chimpanzees (see box 2.1).

An alternative argument is that high intelligence has been selected for because of its advantages in social interaction (Byrne and Whiten, 1988). As we have seen, primates are clever in social contexts – recognizing and deceiving others, forming alliances, achieving dominant status. Being socially clever could have considerable advantages for an animal's reproductive success. Byrne and Whiten (1988) call this 'Machiavellian intelligence', or *tactical deception*. The example of the two chimpanzees described above illustrates this high degree of social intelligence (Whiten and Byrne, 1988).

## Deceiving others

Deception itself is not a sign of high intelligence; it depends on what level the deception is at. Mitchell (1986) has described levels of deception.

*Level one deception*    This describes situations where an animal is programmed to give a deceptive signal, irrespective of circumstances. For example, an insect which is palatable but which mimics in appearance a brightly coloured and inedible wasp.

*Level two deception*    The animal's signal is still programmed or 'instinctive', but is given only in response to certain stimuli. For example, some birds will 'pretend' to be injured when certain predators approach their nest. By feigning a broken wing, for instance, they may distract the predator and lure it away from the eggs or chicks. The display is fairly stereotyped, but only elicited if a predator appears.

*Level three deception*    Here the animal's signal can be modified by learning. The song repertoire of great tits (see p. 24) may be an example of this. Another might be a dog which, by limping (even though not injured) gets more petting and attention; this differs from the bird's feigned injury in that it has been learnt in ontogeny as a successful strategy. However it may be no more than stimulus–response learning of the type 'lifting my paw in a certain way results in my being petted'. Many cases of tactical deception (Whiten and Byrne, 1988) are likely to be of this kind.

*Level four deception*    Here the animal deliberately corrects or changes its signals so as to encourage the receiver to act in certain ways. It is as if the animal doing the deceiving knows, and calculates, the effects on the recipient. The chimpanzee example described in the last section would come at this level. Here it appears there is an *understanding of deceptive intent*, and a flexibility of response, which Whiten and Byrne (1988) highlight in their analysis of tactical deception as evidence that the animal understands the tactic it uses.

## The evolution of 'mindreading' and of metarepresentations

At these higher levels of intelligence and intentional action, it would seem as though an animal has some idea of what is going on in another animal's mind – it is, as it were, 'mindreading'. Other researchers talk of a 'theory of mind' – implying that an individual can hypothesize what is going on in another's mind (it might be thinking 'that animal is hungry' or 'that animal is hiding food', for example). Level four tactical deception is a good indicator of this. Somewhat similar skills can be seen developing in children (see chapter 5; and Whiten, 1991).

More generally, mindreading skills and also the other aspects of high intelligence mentioned previously, can be taken as examples of 'second order representation', or 'metarepresentation'. A first-order representation is symbolizing something in your mind – for example an object such as a table, or a banana; or a state such as being hungry. In a second-order or meta-representation, one or more first-order representations are themselves represented.

For example, in tool-making the first-order representation of the actual action is manipulated relative to the representation of the desired object; this process involves second-order representation. In pretence, the representation of the actual object co-exists with the representation of it as having pretend characteristics (Leslie, 1987). In self-recognition, the representation of the mirror image is related to the representation of ones own self, or body. In symbolic communication, symbols (non-verbal or verbal) stand for or represent other objects or actions. And in level four deception, the intentionality of deceit implies that the sender can represent both the true and the falsely signalled state of affairs (somewhat analogous to pretence).

Some researchers argue that these abilities all represent a metarepresentational capacity which is found in the great apes, and which is also an important aspect of children's development (Whiten and Byrne, 1991). We shall look more at the related work on children in chapter 5.

## An Evolutionary Perspective on Human Behaviour

As humans, we are primates – members of the same order of animals as the monkeys and apes. Our closest animal relatives are the great apes, the chimpanzee, gorilla and orang-utan. We know that early humans, or 'hominids', had become different from the early apes by 5 million years ago. In East Africa scientists such as Richard Leakey and Donald Johanson have unearthed fossil remains of hominids which are 3–4 millions years old (Leakey and Lewin, 1977; Johanson and Edey, 1981). These very early hominids, called australopithecines, were smaller than us (about 4 foot tall) and had smaller brains (about 500–600 cubic centimetres), but had already walked erect and had moved from the ape habitat of forest to the hominid habitat of open grassland. Over the next few million years fossil remains document the increasing body size and especially brain size of the hominids and their increasing technological and cultural sophistication as evidenced by stone tool manufacture and later by shelter construction, use of fire and cave art. By some 50,000 years ago early humans were physically much like us today: *Homo sapiens* had arrived. Changes over the past 50,000 years have been largely cultural, not biological, as people learned to domesticate animals, cultivate plants, build cities, pursue the systematic advance of knowledge and acquire modern technology.

Does our primate ancestry tell us anything useful about ourselves now? This has been a very controversial issue. Some scientists studying animal behaviour have tried to make links to human behaviour. This is true of some of the ethologists, such as Konrad Lorenz and Irenaus Eibl-Eibesfeldt; and of some recent sociobiologists, such as E. O. Wilson at Harvard University in the USA. Let us look first at some of their suggestions, and then at some of the limitations of 'human ethology' or 'human sociobiololgy'.

Lorenz (1996) and Eibl-Eibesfeldt (1971) have made use of the concepts of fixed action pattern (FAP) and sign stimulus to explain some kinds of human behaviour.

An example of a human FAP is claimed to be the facial expression involved in greeting – a smile, widening of the eyes and flash (rapid raising and lowering) of the eyebrows (figure 2.12). This has been found to be very similar in a wide variety of human societies. An example of a sign stimulus is claimed to be the 'cute' facial and bodily appearance of babies, which elicits caring and parental behaviour. In an experimental study Sternglanz et al. (1977) presented the stimuli show in figure 2.13 to a number of young adults. They rated the one shown at (b) as being most attractive. It has quite large eyes and a moderately large forehead. Dolls and 'cute' animals in film cartoons have similar facial proportions (c).

Sociobiologists such as E. O. Wilson (1978) are less interested in instinctive mechanisms of behaviour; rather, they wonder whether human behaviour, like animal behaviour, seems to maximize the survival and reproductive success of individuals. For example, do the predictions of kin selection apply to humans? It does seem to be the case that people are most generous or altruistic to close kin, even when it is not socially sanctioned. In agricultural and tribal societies (i.e. people not yet living in large cities) kinship is a very important organizing framework, affecting expectations about whom you shall marry as well as expectations for help and alliance in warfare.

There are other parallels to be drawn. For example, almost all human societies are either monogamous or polygynous (though a few tribes are polyandrous, notably in Sri Lanka and Tibet). Sociobiology can explain this, especially when it is also noted that monogamous societies tend to be those where fathers can help directly in child-rearing, whereas in polygynous societies men compete for status, for example by acquiring wealth or cattle, and do little to help their wives directly. As another example, what seem to be characteristic sex differences in men and women, for

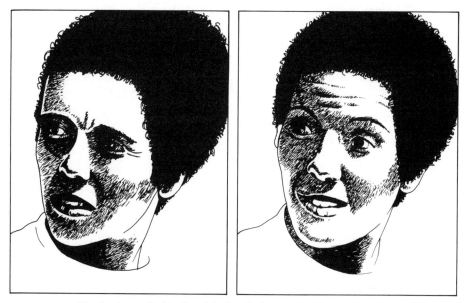

FIGURE 2.12   *The 'eyebrow flash': the right-hand photograph shows the raising of eyebrows during greeting in a Frenchman (after Eibl-Eibesfeldt, 1972)*

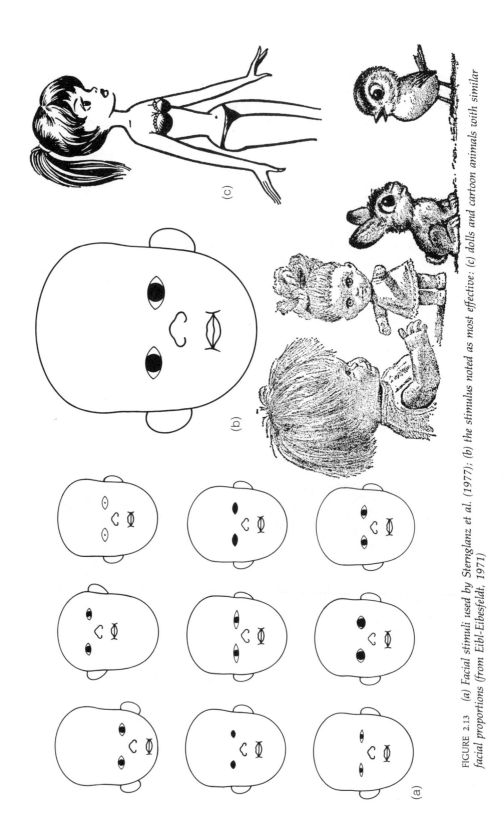

FIGURE 2.13  (a) Facial stimuli used by Sternglanz et al. (1977); (b) the stimulus noted as most effective: (c) dolls and cartoon animals with similar facial proportions (from Eibl-Eibesfeldt, 1971)

example in abilities, in aggression and in attitudes to sexual behaviour, have been given a sociobiological explanation (Wilson, 1978; Symons, 1979).

There has been some very strong reaction against these views. Some scientists believe that even to attempt such explanations is misplaced, because of the dangers of, for example, making sex differences seem natural and inevitable. These scientists believe that the flexibility of human learning is so great that nothing useful is learnt from evolutionary theorizing (e.g. Sahlins, 1977; Rose et al., 1984). At times the debate has become more personal than scientific.

## Human Behaviour Is Modifiable

A real problem for such extrapolations from sociobiology is that human behaviour seems to be of an order of magnitude more flexible even than that of other advanced mammals. There are enormous cultural variations in the behaviour of people in different societies: for example in the language spoken, technology used, moral or religious beliefs held, and methods of child-rearing used. These are learned variations. A Chinese baby brought up in China learns Chinese, and Chinese manners; brought up in the USA, it learns American English and American manners. In addition to this flexibility of learning, humans can cumulatively pass on and build up knowledge and beliefs through cultural traditions (e.g. the development of the idea of democracy; the development of electronic and computer technology). While there are some examples of traditions among animals (e.g. dialects in bird song; patterns of tool use in chimpanzees), no animal species has been found cumulatively to build up traditions of technology or behaviour in this way.

If human behaviour is so flexible, is there any scope for theorizing based on our evolutionary past? There may be, but perhaps only in limited ways. Human cultural variation is enormous, but there are still some apparent cultural universals. Examples are:

The pattern of sensori-motor development in the first 12–18 months of life.

The attachment relationship which develops between infant and caregiver.

Forms of play in children, especially rough-and-tumble play.

The structure of human language, and the way it is acquired.

Human non-verbal signals and emotional expressions.

Some sex differences in behaviour, and patterns of marriage.

Situations in which aggressive behaviour is elicited.

Of course, these could be similar simply for cultural reasons – societies just happen to have passed on the same learned tradition. However, this does seem implausible in some cases. There is little that parental treatment can do to alter the pattern of sensori-motor development in infancy; and facial expressions of emotion, such as smiling and crying, appear in blind children who cannot see such expressions in other humans.

It would certainly be misleading to call these types of behaviour 'instinctive'. To do so leads to a quagmire of misunderstanding whereby it is inferred that some behaviours are inevitable and unalterable. It may, however, be justified to think of some human behaviour development as reasonably canalized. Thus, the development of human language, from babbling to one-word utterances to syntax, may be fairly strongly canalized (see chapter 10), whereas the actual language learned is weakly canalized, if at all. Possibly some sex differences are somewhat canalized, such that they will develop unless positive steps are taken to prevent them, whereas other sex differences may not be canalized at all and could easily be changed. Whether substantiated or not, this at least is a language of reasoned debate. The metaphor of canalization, or of the modifiability of behaviour, enables us to get away from the instinctive/learned dichotomy. We can consider the possibility of there being some limited links to our evolutionary past, without having to defend the innateness, desirability or complete inevitability of certain human characteristics.

### Further reading

Accessible introductions to the subject of animal behaviour are J.M. Deag 1980: *Social Behaviour of Animals*. London: Edward Arnold; and N. Chalmers 1979: *Social Behaviour in Primates*. London: Edward Arnold.

J. Alcock 1984: *Animal Behaviour: An Evolutionary Approach*. Sunderland, Mass: Sinauer, 3rd edn is an excellent text at a more advanced level; it includes discussion of the sociobiological approach to human behaviour. Other useful resource books are J. R. Krebs and N. B. Davies 1987: *An Introduction to Behavioural Ecology* (2nd Edition). Oxford: Blackwell Scientific; and D. McFarland 1985: *Animal Behaviour*. London: Pitman.

A popular account of the earlier ethological work is N. Tinbergen's *Curious Naturalists*. Harmondsworth: Penguin, revised edn 1974. The work on chimpanzees described in box 6.1 can also be studied in J. van Lawick-Goodall 1971: *In the Shadow of Man*. Glasgow: Collins. A fascinating observational study of chimpanzees in a semi-natural habitat (an island at Arnhem zoo) is F. de Waal 1982: *Chimpanzee Politics*. London: Unwin.

### Discussion points

1  Consider the social organization of some mammal or bird species, and how that organization might be related to the costs and benefits of different group sizes and mating systems.

2  When are animals aggressive?

3  How has the study of animal behaviour changed between the 1950s and the 1990s?

4  Is the distinction between instinctive and learned behaviour a useful one?

4  Can studies of animals tell us anything useful about human behaviour?

### Practical exercises

1  Observe some animals in their natural habitat (e.g. nesting birds; wild horses; squirrels) or in a semi-natural habitat (e.g. cattle or horses at a farm; monkeys in a zoo). Document

the types of social interaction you see. Relate this to what you have learned in the chapter.

2   Watch the development of a domestic chick, or a duckling. Record how the following response develops. (You could try imprinting a chick or duckling to an artificial stimulus; but bear in mind the ethical issues involved, as once imprinted the chick will follow the object, and be distressed at its absence, for some some time.)

3   Ask people to rate the attractiveness of various facial stimuli, using figure 2.13 as a guide. Do you get the same results as Sternglanz et al? Is there a difference between parents and non-parents, or males and females?

Box 2.1

# The behaviour of free-living chimpanzees in the Gombe Stream Reserve

This study concerns the behaviour of chimpanzees in their natural habitat. Jane Goodall spent five years observing chimpanzees in the Gombe Stream area of Tanzania, in Africa. She spent much time approaching and following groups of chimpanzees, and letting them get used to her presence. She then made systematic observations and notes about what she observed. She established a base camp and at later stages in the project put out bananas at a feeding area near the camp to attract the chimpanzees and make observations easier.

She found that chimpanzees moved around singly or in small groups, looking for food such as fruits and leaves within a large home range area. Group composition varied. Infants (0–3 years) were carried by their mothers or followed them closely, and juveniles (3–7 years) usually travelled with their mothers as well. Subadults (8–12 years) and adults (12 up to around 40 years), however, seemed to join up or disperse quite freely. Chimpanzees live in forested areas and move around both on the ground and in trees. At night, they sleep in nests made from tree branches.

The newborn infant is dependent on its mother for food, transport and protection, but after 6 months or so begins to crawl around on its own while staying in the mother's vicinity. Soon it engages in play, both with mother, siblings and peers – tickling, wrestling and chasing play. Infants and juveniles watch and imitate when they see mother obtaining food, or making tree nests, and this is hypothesized to be important for their own acquisition of these skills. When the juvenile becomes a subadult, the frequency of play decreases and mutual grooming increases (box plate 2.2.1). Later observations have established that subadult females often leave their home range and may join a more distant group. Males, however, usually stay in the home range they were born in. Although older males do not stay with the mother all the time, they may still associate with her frequently. An older sibling may 'adopt' and care for an infant sibling if the mother dies.

There is a dominance hierarchy amongst the mature chimpanzees within a local group. Though most interactions are peaceful and friendly, long-term observations have shown how, at certain times, the dominance order is challenged and considerable conflict may ensue. Goodall and her co-workers documented how a 20-year-old chimpanzee called Figan came to dominate a 22-year-old, Evered, who was his main rival for being the most dominant, or alpha, male. Figan sought out fights with Evered when circumstances favoured him – especially when he was with his brother, Faben. Faben, a 25-year-old, had a paralysed right arm; he thus was not a serious contender for alpha male himself, but could help his brother. This example illustrates both the importance of dominance for individuals,

Based on material in J. Van Lawick-Goodall 1968: *Animal Behaviour Monographs* 1(3),161–311.

BOX PLATE 2.1.1   *Chimpanzees grooming*

and the way kinship (in this case, a sibling tie) can persist into adulthood. Dominance conflicts are usually between males, and the main benefit of being the alpha male is probably increased opportunity to mate with females.

Goodall's observations also revealed several instances of tool use in chimpanzees, and the first records of actual tool-making in a non-human species. Examples of tool use are: leaves for wiping the body; rocks to crack nuts; sticks to prise open the banana boxes; sticks and stones for throwing at baboons or other animals. Two examples of tool-making were documented; each involves some deliberate change in a tool to make it more suitable for its purpose. In one the chimpanzee wishes to drink water out of a crack or hollow. It gets some leaves, chews them in its mouth to make a spongy wad, then uses this to soak up the water and put back to its mouth again. In the other, the chimpanzee wishes to eat termites. This is difficult because they are in a termite nest, but it obtains them by poking slender branches or twigs down the entrance holes to the nest, pulling out the twigs with termites attached and licking them off (box plate 2.1.2). Chimpanzees prepare twigs for this by picking suitable small branches and breaking off the accessory stems which can be inserted readily (this is watched with fascination by younger chimpanzees, who then imitate the process).

Although primarily vegetarian, chimpanzees will eat insects (such as termites), birds eggs and will even hunt and kill small mammals such as young bushpigs or baby baboons. Several chimpanzees may cooperate in such a hunt. The kill is divided up rapidly amongst them, and other chimpanzees may then come up and form 'sharing clusters' around them, requesting a portion of the food.

Goodall's observations provided the first really substantial data on the natural behaviour of chimpanzees. Later research broadly confirmed her findings, with some minor changes. Territorial behaviour between local groups of chimpanzees has now been established, with some violent conflicts between groups and occasional instances of cannibalism. Further instances of tool use and tool-making have been found, with indications of 'cultural' differences amongst chimpanzees living in different parts of Africa.

This study did not have any prior hypothesis. It is thus not an experiment, and there are no dependent or independent variables. It is an observational study, designed to obtain basic data. Studies of a species based on observation in its natural habitat are often called 'ethological studies', and this is an example. Such studies can discover things not expected, such as chimpanzee tool-making. However, they cannot establish cause and effect. The

BOX PLATE 2.1.2 *A chimpanzee pokes a twig into a termite nest*

hypothesis that infants watching adults leads to learning, for example, would benefit from some more experimental confirmation. Ethological observation is also difficult and time-consuming – this is why Goodall started putting out bananas, even at the risk of changing the animals' behaviour.

# Box 2.2

# Food sharing by sibling vs nonsibling spiny mice

This experiment was designed by Porter and his co-workers to test the prediction, from kin selection theory, that related individuals will act in a more altruistic way to each other than will unrelated individuals. The experiment was carried out with the spiny mouse (*Acomys cahirinus*), a small rodent which lives in the Near East and has highly precocial offspring.

Tests were carried out on sibling and nonsibling pairs of spiny mice of around 30 days of age, after weaning. Sibling pairs were both related and familiar, as they had been raised in the same litter. Nonsibling pairs were unrelated and unfamiliar. The animals were put first in an exploration enclosure with a narrow passage to a food cage; and second, in an observation cage with a single food cup. Records were kept of several measures of behaviour, a number of which are shown in box table 2.2.1.

There were 12 sibling pairs and 12 nonsibling pairs. The scores were compared using independent groups *t* tests. As can be seen from box table 2.2.1 the sibling pairs spent more time together in the food cage in the first study, and spent more time simultaneously feeding from the cup in the second study. In the latter condition simultaneous feeding could only be done when in physical contact.

BOX TABLE 2.2.1  *Differences in behaviour between sibling and nonsibling pairs of spiny mice in food enclosures*

| Behaviour measure | Sibling pairs | Nonsibling pairs | Test of significance |
|---|---|---|---|
| Exploration enclosure: time(s) spent simultaneously in food cage | 180.5 | 62.8 | $t(22)=2.08$, $p<0.05$ |
| Observation cage: time(s) spent simultaneously feeding | 198.3 | 91.0 | $t(22)=2.09$, $p<0.05$ |
| Total time(s) spent feeding by dominant animal of pair | 560.7 | 548.8 | n.s. |
| Total time(s) spent feeding by less dominant animal | 389.5 | 193.4 | $t(22)=2.23$ $p<0.05$ |

R. H. Porter, J. D. Moore and D. M. White 1980: *Behavioral Ecology and Sociobiology*, 8, 207–12.

With two animals one is likely to be dominant over the other. In the nonsibling pairs the dominant animal took clear precedence, and sometimes chased the other animal away, or bit it if it approached the food cup. In the sibling pairs, the animals were more tolerant, and feeding time was more fairly distributed, as the remaining analyses in the table show.

The independent variable in this experiment is whether the mice are sibling or nonsibling pairs. The dependent variables are the behavioural measures, including those in box table 2.2.1. The hypothesis that kin selection would lead to more altruism (in this case more food-sharing) was confirmed. This conclusion only applies to the laboratory situation of the experiment. There is no reason to believe that spiny mice behave differently in this respect in their natural environment, but an ethological study of food-sharing in this species would nicely complement the experimental work.

The independent variable (sibling/nonsibling) confounded the two potentially separate aspects of (genetic) relatedness and familiarity. The sibling mice could be more altruistic either because they are more similar in appearance (because of genetic similarity) and recognize this, or because they have got used to each other through being reared in the same litter. In further work (Porter et al., 1980) these two factors were separated. Using huddling together in mice pups as a sign of recognition, they found that biological siblings reared apart by foster mothers did not huddle together. However, unrelated pups reared together by the same foster mother did huddle together in the test situation. Thus it seems that familiarity, rather than genetic kinship directly, influences recognition and, by inference, altruistic behaviour such as food-sharing. In this species, therefore, the mechanism by which siblings become altruistic seems to be the greater familiarity induced through being reared together. There is no evidence for direct recognition of genetic relatedness, though such evidence has been found in some other species.

# Part Two

# The Social World of the Child

# 3

# Parents and Families

The newborn baby has a lot to find out about the social world. If you pick her up, she will respond no differently to you than to anyone else. Yet some 9 months later the infant will discriminate familiar and unfamiliar persons, and will probably have developed one or more selective attachments. If you pick her up now she may well look anxious or cry; whereas if the mother or father picks her up, she will be reassured and pacified.

In this chapter we look first at the development of social interactions and attachment relationships between infants, parents, and other family members. The importance of such attachments for later development is considered, with its implications for policy issues such as institutional rearing, day care and childminding for young children. Finally we examine some of the factors affecting successful and less successful parenting.

## Early Social Behaviour and Social Interactions

The human infant is fairly helpless (or altricial) at birth. He or she depends on parents, or caregivers, for food, warmth, shelter and protection. For these reasons alone it is important for human infants, as for any other young mammal, that an attachment develops between the infant and the mother (or father, or other caregiver; we will use the term caregiver generically). In addition, human infants acquire something from this relationship that is largely absent in other mammals: the beginnings of symbolic communication and cultural meaning. The particular relevance of early caregiver–infant interaction for language development is considered in chapter 10.

Although fairly helpless, the human infant does have some reflexive (instinctive or highly canalized) abilities which assist the development of social interactions with caregivers. These are: (1) behaviours which operate primarily in social situations; (2) behaviours to which social responses are given; (3) an enjoyment of contingent responding by others; (4) an ability to learn, including discriminating social stimuli and attempting to imitate certain observed behaviours. Let us consider these in turn.

1    Behaviours that operate primarily in social situations. The types of auditory and visual stimulation which adults provide, are especially attractive to infants at or soon after birth (see also chapter 9). For example, infants orientate to (i.e. turn their head towards) patterned sounds rather than monotones, and especially to patterned sounds within the frequency range of human speech. They are interested in visual stimuli which move around, and which have a lot of contour information. The human face provides moving stimulation with much contour information, often at just the right distance for the infant to fixate easily. Infant reflexes, such as grasping, and rooting and sucking at the breast, are also used primarily with caregivers. None of these reflexive behaviours is directed only to adults, but all are well designed to operate with adults and to give the infant an initial orientation to social situations.

2    Behaviours to which social responses are given. Newborn babies will both smile and cry. In both cases this behaviour has no social meaning to the baby at first. She smiles apparently randomly from time to time, and cries if hungry or uncomfortable. However, caregivers respond to these signals as if they were social. They tend to smile and talk back if the infant smiles; and to pick up an infant and talk to her if she is crying (plate 3.1: one study found that picking up an infant reduced crying on 88 per cent of occasions, which is very rewarding for the adult). Gradually the infant will learn the social consequences of smiling, and crying, because of the social meaning and social responses which caregivers give to them. It is similar with babbling, which begins around two months of age.

3    An enjoyment of contingent responding by others. From quite early on it seems as though infants like to get 'contingent' stimulation – that is, stimulation which appropriately follows quickly on some action of their own; as it were, a 'reply' to their own action. An experiment which demonstrated this very neatly is described in box 3.1. Usually caregivers provide contingent responding when they react to the infant's smiling, crying, cooing or babbling in a rapid and appropriate fashion, or a bit later on engage in games such as peek-a-boo. Many studies of mother–infant interaction in the home have found that maternal 'sensitivity' (which is largely synonymous with contingent responsiveness) is correlated with good social development and attachment in the infant.

Enjoyment of contingent responsiveness can develop into turn-taking and into proper interactions such as conversations, or games. A games such as peek-a-boo is initially structured solely by the adult, who takes advantage of the infant's pleasure at the surprise generated by the sudden appearance and disappearance of the adult's face, or a teddy-bear: it becomes a more genuine turn-taking sequence as the infant comes to expect the next repetition of the game and thus take a more active part itself in the exchange (see Bruner and Sherwood, 1976).

4    An ability to learn. The development of perceptual abilities in infancy is discussed in detail in chapter 9. It is clear that infants learn to discriminate the sound of the mother's voice from that of a stranger within a few days of birth (p. 262), and learn to prefer pictures of faces to similar but scrambled up pictures by 2 months of age (p. 257; figure 9.4). Throughout the first months of life, infants are discriminating social stimuli and learning the consequences of social actions. By around 6 months of age they quite clearly discriminate between familiar and unfamiliar adults, for example in orienting and in ease of being comforted.

Another aspect of infant learning is imitation. Research by Kaye and Marcus (1978,

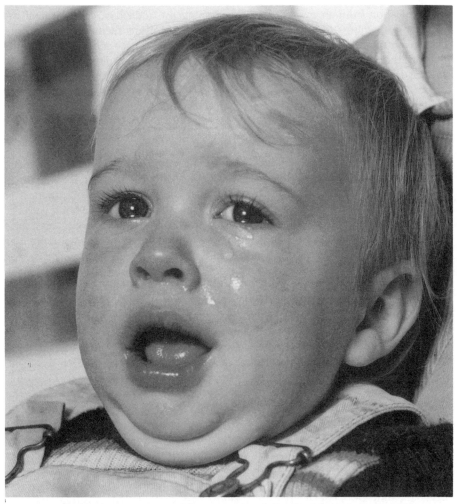

PLATE 3.1   *Crying is a very powerful message to adults about babies' needs; picking up a crying baby usually reduces the crying*

1981) shows that imitation of social stimuli is occurring between 6 months and 12 months of age. These investigators tried presenting infants with certain actions each time they got their attention. For example, they might open and close their mouth five times, like a goldfish; or clap hands in front of the infant, four times. Each action sequence was contingent on the infant re-establishing eye contact with the experimenter. Besides often establishing eye contact, the infants also tried to imitate the actions themselves, often trying to copy one feature at a time; the imitations improved over trials, and as the infants got older.

To summarize, these various features of infant behaviour assist in getting into social interaction sequences with adult caregivers. However, you can see that the adult has a vital role to play in this, by responding in appropriate ways and at appropriate times. Kaye (1982) calls this 'scaffolding' (see also chapter 12), and likens the infant to an apprentice who is learning the craft of social interaction and communication from an expert. At the beginning the adult has to do most of the work to keep things going: picking the infant up, putting their face at the right distance, responding whenever the infant makes a signal, perhaps having the 'illusion' that the infant is replying when it smiles or grimaces. Things get less one-sided as the infant develops her own social repertoire and begins to learn to take turns in social interaction. Even so, gearing one's behaviour at an appropriate pace and level to the child remains important through infancy and beyond.

### Very early bonding: the work of Klaus and Kennell

Although infants only gradually learn about their parents or caregivers, it has been claimed that the mother very quickly forms a bond with the infant, in the first hours or days after birth. In its strongest form it is claimed that the first 6–12 hours after birth are a sensitive period for the mother to form a strong emotional bond with her infant through physical contact. If absent, the bond is less strong, and later maltreatment or abuse more likely. This 'early bonding' hypothesis, if true, has profound implications for practices in maternity hospitals where, especially a decade or so ago, mothers were often separated from their infants with little contact for the first day or so.

The hypothesis was proposed by Klaus and Kennell (1979), on the basis of a study of 28 mothers in an American maternity hospital. Fourteen had the traditional treatment — 5 minutes' contact at delivery, then separation for some 6–12 hours followed by half-hour feeding sessions every 4 hours. The other 14 had extra contact — an hour of cuddling after birth, and then an extra 5 hours each day. One month later, and also one year later, there appeared to be some differences favouring the extra contact group. For example, the mothers were more likely to sooth the baby if it cried. This, and other studies, suggests that the extra contact in the first day or so makes a difference.

In the last decade, however, a number of similar studies have been carried out by other investigators, some with larger samples. Some have observed small effects, some none at all. Reviews of this evidence (Goldberg, 1983; Myers, 1984) suggest that while early contact is pleasurable for the mother and may have some short-term effects, the long-term effects are very small or non- existent. The positive results of the early studies are flawed by methodological drawbacks, small samples and focusing attention on a small number of significant results out of a very large number of measurements. Thus, the existence of this sensitive period is now thought to be very questionable; many other influences are important in the mother's relationship to the infant, and over a longer time period. The changes in hospital practice are probably beneficial; but parents who miss the first few hours or so of contact (some mothers, most fathers, and all adoptive parents) need not feel that they have lost out on a period crucial for later relationships with the baby.

## Temperament

Even from soon after birth, infants seem to vary considerably in their behavioural characteristics. Some will cry a lot, others will be equable; some will be active, others less so; and so on. In a longitudinal study in New York, Thomas and Chess (1977) interviewed mothers of young children at regular 3-month intervals, and found considerable consistency in what they call characteristics of *temperament*. Based largely on questionnaires, they identified nine main dimensions of temperament:

*Activity level* – the amount of physical activity during sleep, feeding, play, dressing, etc.

*Regularity* – of bodily functioning in sleep, hunger, bowel movements, etc.

*Adaptability* to change in routine – the ease or difficulty with which initial response can be modified in socially desirable ways.

*Response to new situations* – initial reaction to new stimuli, to food, people, places, toys, or procedures.

*Level of sensory threshold* – the amount of external stimulation, such as sounds or changes in food or people, necessary to produce a response in the child.

*Intensity of response* – the energy content of responses regardless of their quality.

*Positive or negative mood* – amount of pleasant or unpleasant behaviour throughout day.

*Distractability* – the effectiveness of external stimuli (sounds, toys, people, etc.) in interfering with ongoing behaviour.

*Persistence and attention span* – duration of maintaining specific activities with or without external obstacles.

On the basis of these dimensions, the researchers distinguished *difficult* babies (negative, irregular, and unadaptable), and *easy* babies (positive, regular and adaptable). Temperamentally difficult babies are more of a challenge for parents to cope with, and seem to be more at risk for later behaviour problems. The best outcome is if parents respond in a way suited to the baby or toddler – providing extra motor opportunities for active babies, for example, or specially encouraging approach in shy babies.

Thomas and Chess tend to see temperamental characteristics as inherent in the child; an alternative view is that since it is based on mother (or caregiver) ratings, it is a dyadic characteristic which much more reflects the mother's own psychological state and how she understands her child's behaviour (St. James-Roberts and Wolke, 1984). Temperament may be an important aspect to consider in parenting outcomes (see p. 86 and fig. 3.1).

## The Development of Attachment Relationships

Suppose you are watching a 1- or 2-year-old infant with his mother in a park. This is what you might observe. The mother sits down on a bench, and the infant runs off.

Every now and then he will stop to look around, point to objects or events, and examine things on the ground such as leaves, stones, bits of paper, or crawl or jump over grass verges. The infant periodically stops and looks back at the mother, and now and then may return close to her, or make physical contact, staying close for a while before venturing off again. Usually the infant does not go further than about 200 feet from the mother, who may however have to retrieve him if the distance gets too great or if she wants to move off herself.

The infant seems to be exploring the environment, using the mother as a secure base to which to return periodically for reassurance. This is one of the hallmarks of an 'attachment relationship'. The development of attachment has been described in detail by John Bowlby (1969). The observations of children in parks were made in London by J. W. Anderson (1972), a student of Bowlby's

Bowlby described four phases in the development of attachment, extended to a fifth in more recent work:

1   The infant orientates and signals without discriminating different people. We have already described this as characteristic of the infant in the first few months of life (excepting unusual laboratory situations).
2   The infant preferentially orientates to and signals at one or more discriminated persons. This marks the beginning of attachment. The infant is more likely to smile at the mother or important caregivers, for example, or to be comforted by them if distressed. Exactly when this occurs depends on the measures used, but it is commonly observed at around 5–7 months of age.
3   The infant maintains proximity preferentially to a discriminated person by means of locomotion and signals. For example, he crawls after the person, or returns periodically for contact, or cries or protests if the person leaves ('separation protest'). This is often taken as the definition of attachment to a caregiver. From 7–9 months usually brings the onset of attachment, in this sense. An important related criterion is that the infant becomes wary or even fearful of unfamiliar persons ('fear of strangers').
4   The formation of a goal-corrected partnership occurs between child and caregiver. Until now the mother has served as a resource for the child, being available when needed. The goal-corrected partnership refers to the idea that the child also begins to accommodate to the mother's needs, for example being prepared to wait alone if requested until mother returns. Bowlby saw this as characterizing the child from 3 years of age, though there is evidence that 2-year-olds can partly accommodate to verbal requests by the mother to await her return (Wienraub and Lewis, 1977).
5   Lessening of attachment as measured by the child maintaining proximity. Characteristic of the school-age child, and older, is the idea of a relationship based more on abstract considerations such as affection, trust and approval, exemplified by an *internal working model* of the relationship (p. 67).

Bowlby and other psychologists in an ethological tradition see attachment as a canalized developmental process, whose primary function is to provide the infant with protection, as in other mammals. Others put more emphasis on processes of learning in attachment development, and on the symbolic communication which occurs in its context. As we have seen, both the largely instinctive repertoire of the newborn, and certain perhaps constrained forms of learning, are important in early social interactions. Some aspects of cognitive sensori-motor development (chapters 9, 11) are also essential for attachment; until the infant has some idea of cause–effect relations, and of the continued existence of objects or persons when out of sight, he cannot consistently protest at separation and attempt to maintain proximity. Sensori-motor development is also a canalized process, and an ethological and a cognitive-learning approach to attachment development need not be in opposition.

Many of the characteristic behaviours in attachment have been described by Mary Ainsworth (1967, 1973). She observed babies both in the Ganda people of Uganda, and in Baltimore in the USA. She describes behaviours such as smiling and vocalizing preferentially to the mother, and being comforted; crying when the mother leaves, following her and greeting her by smiling, lifting arms, hugging or scrambling over her and burying the face in her lap; using the mother as a secure base for exploration, and as a haven of safety if frightened.

## The security of attachment

Ainsworth also went on to develop a method for assessing how well attached an individual infant is to her mother or caregiver (Ainsworth et al., 1978). This method is known as the 'strange situation', and has been used extensively with 12–24-month-old infants in the USA, and also in Britain, Germany, Holland, Israel and Japan. Essentially it is a method of checking out, in a standardized way, how well the infant uses the caregiver as a secure base for exploration, and is comforted by the caregiver after a mildy stressful experience.

*The strange situation*   The experiment involves seven short episodes, which take place in a comfortably equipped room, usually at a research centre where the episodes can be filmed. Besides caregiver or mother (M) and infant (I), there is a stranger (S) whom the infant has not seen before. The episodes are: (1) M and I in room, I explores 3 minutes; (2) S enters, sits for 1 minute, talks to M for 1 minute, and gets down on floor to play with I, 1 minute; (3) M leaves, S plays with I then withdraws if possible, up to 3 minutes; (4) M returns, S leaves unobtrusively, M settles I and then sits down for 3 minutes; (5) M leaves, I is alone for up to 3 minutes; (6) S comes in, attempts to settle I then withdraw if possible, up to 3 minutes; (7) M returns, S leaves unobstrusively, M settles I and sits down (session ends, after about 20 minutes).

In a well-functioning attachment relationship, it is postulated that the infant will use the mother as a base to explore (episodes 1, 2 and end of episode 4), but be stressed by the mother's absence (episodes 3, 5 and 6; these episodes are curtailed if the infant is very upset or the mother wants to return sooner). Especial attention is paid to the infant's behaviour in the reunion episodes (4 and 7), to see if he or she is effectively comforted by the mother. On the basis of such measures, Ainsworth and others distinguish a number of different attachment types, the primary ones being type A (anxious/avoidant), type B (secure) and type C (anxious/resistant).

*Type A*   These babies are characterized by conspicuous avoidance of proximity to or interaction with the mother in the reunion episodes. Either the baby ignores the mother on her return, greeting her casually if at all, or he mingles his welcome with avoidance responses such as turning away, moving past, or averting gaze. During separation, the baby is not distressed, or distress seems due to being left alone rather than to mother's absence.

*Type B*   These babies are characterized by actively seeking and maintaining proximity, contact or interaction with the mother, especially in the reunion episodes. He may or may not be distressed during the separation episodes, but any distress is related to mother's absence.

*Type C*   These babies are characterized by conspicuous contact- and interaction-resisting behaviour in the reunion episodes. Rather than ignoring the mother, this is combined with some seeking of proximity and contact, thus giving the impression of being ambivalent.

Some researchers have claimed that attachment type is related to other aspects of healthy development. For example, secure attachments at 12 months has been correlated with the quality and sensitivity of mother–infant face-to-face interaction at 6–15 weeks, with curiosity and problem-solving at age 2, with social confidence at nursery school at age $3\frac{1}{2}$ and with lack of behaviour problems (in boys) at age 6 (e.g. Lewis et al., 1984). Anxious/resistant attachment has been related to the likelihood of infant maltreatment or abuse (p. 85), and changes in attachment type have been related to changes in life events (such as financial or marital changes) of the mother (see Bretherton and Waters, 1985, for a review of this area of research).

In American studies, some 70 per cent of babies are classified as securely attached to their mothers (type B), some 20 per cent as type A and some 10 per cent as type C. However, there are variations between social and cultural groups. Some German investigators have found that some 40–50 per cent of infants were type A (Grossman et al., 1981), while a Japanese study found 35 per cent type C (Miyake et al., 1985). Such percentages must raise a question about the nature of 'anxious attachment'. Is it a less satisfactory mode of development, as Ainsworth and others allege, or are these just different styles of interaction?

Takahashi (1990) argues that the strange situation must be interpreted carefully when used across cultures. He found that Japanese infants were excessively distressed by the infant alone episode (episode 5), because normally in Japanese culture they are *never* left alone at 12 months. Hence, fewer Japanese infants scored B. Also, there was no chance for them to show avoidance (and score as A), since mothers characteristically went straight and without hesitation to pick up the baby. This may explain why so many Japanese babies were type C at 12 months (yet they are not at 24 months, nor are adverse consequences apparent). This distortion might be avoided by virtually omitting episode 5 for such babies.

*Criticisms of the attachment construct*

A number of criticisms have been made of these ideas concerning attachment. These have mainly concerned the way in which attachment is measured, and the use of the 'strange situation' to provide attachment types.

Some of the earlier work was justly criticized for being too loose in the definition of what were, or were not, attachment behaviours. For example, some behaviours, such as smiling, are directed at other persons as well as just the mother, or attachment figure. Attachment subsequently came to be defined in terms of behaviours shown very selectively, e.g. proximity maintenance and separation anxiety.

A concept closely related to attachment is the so-called 'fear of strangers'. At the time infants became attached to one or a few persons, they also seemed to show avoidance or protest at the appearance or proximity of unfamiliar persons. This was shown in laboratory studies where a 'stranger' might make a standardized approach to an infant in a high chair, who would often cry or protest. However, these studies have also been criticized for the unnatural way in which the stranger behaved, walking towards the infant and making physical contact at set time intervals without taking any notice of the infant's behaviour (very 'strange' behaviour, in fact!). We now know that this is just the sort of behaviour (non-contingent on the infant's own behaviour) which infants are not likely to find pleasurable. Later studies looked at how infants reacted to strangers in more natural environments, where the infant could approach the stranger when she wished. In such circumstances, infants do smile at and sometimes approach strangers (Rheingold and Eckerman, 1973). However, it is still the case that infants react differently to unfamiliar persons; some are wary, even in reassuring surroundings, and they do not usually want proximity in the same way as with the mother or caregiver. Some psychologists now talk of 'wariness of strangers' to describe this phenomenon (Sroufe and Waters, 1977).

Criticisms have also been made of the attachment typing resulting from the 'strange situation' procedure (Lamb et al., 1984). The typology was originally based on only 26 American infants (although since used with larger samples), and it has been suggested that the classification has been derived prematurely, on an inadequate sample base. The suggestion that type B attachment is 'normal' has been criticized, especially bearing in mind the cultural variations we saw earlier. It has also been pointed out that the procedure measures the relationship between mother and infant, not some characteristic of the infant. When father–infant attachment has been assessed, several studies have found that the attachment type is not related to that with the mother. Despite these criticisms and reservations, however, at present the 'strange situation' procedure is still a commonly and internationally used technique.

*Attachment beyond infancy and internal working models*

We have seen how, as the infant becomes older, the attachment relationship(s) become less dependent on physical proximity and more dependent on abstract qualities of the relationship, internalized in the child and also of course in the adult. Several studies have attempted to measure attachment quality in older children. For 3- up to 6-year-olds, variants of the 'strange situation' have been used with some success (e.g. Main and Cassidy, 1988). Another tool has been the 'Separation

Anxiety Test', in which children or adolescents respond to photographs showing separation experiences (Klagsbrun and Bowlby, 1976). A self-report questionnaire has been devised for adolescents (Armsden and Greenberg, 1987). There is considerable interest in the factors influencing stability or change in attachments, and also in the extent to which infant–parent attachment sets the pattern not only for later adult–parent relationships, but also for other attachments – for example to siblings, friends (see chapter 4) or marital partners, in later life (Ainsworth, 1989).

In considering the influence of early attachment on later relationships, several researchers have found it useful to think of internal representations of the relationship in the child's mind; the child is thought of as having an *internal working model* of his or her relationship with the mother (and similarly with other attachment figures) (Bowlby, 1988; Main, Kaplan and Cassidy, 1985). These are described as cognitive structures embodying the memories of day-to-day interactions with the attachment figure. They may be 'schemas' or 'event scripts' which guide the child's actions with the attachment figure, based on their previous interactions and the expectations and affective experiences associated with them.

Dyads of differing attachment type would be expected to have differing working models of the relationship. For example, a boy with a Type A anxious/avoidant relationship with his mother may have an internal working model of her which leads him not to expect secure comforting from her when he is distressed. She may in fact reject his approaches. His action rules then become focused on avoiding her, thus inhibiting approaches to her which could be ineffective and lead to further distress. This in turn can be problematic, as there is less open communication between mother and son, and their respective internal working models of each other are not being accurately updated.

Internal working models could normally be updated, or modified, as new interactions develop. It may be that for younger children, such change must be based on actual physical encounters. However Main et al. (1985) suggest that in older children or adults who have achieved formal operational thinking (chapter 11), it is possible to alter internal working models without having such direct interaction. They used an Adult Attachment Interview to probe adults' memories of their own childhood experiences. They found that adults who had an insecure relationship with their parents, tended also to have an insecure attachment relationship to their own child. However, some mothers who had had very negative experiences with their own parents seemed to have come to terms with this, and ascribed rational reasons to it (for example marital stress, or overwork). These mothers were more likely to have secure infants themselves; perhaps they had succeeded in updating their own working models of attachment relationships, even in retrospect, to the benefit of their relationships with their own children.

Main et al. (1985) report that the Adult Attachment Interview yields four main patterns. (1) Persons who can recall their own earlier attachment-related experiences objectively and openly, even if these were not favourable; these tended to be parents of securely-attached children. (2) Persons who dismissed attachment relationships as of little concern, value or influence; these tended to be parents of anxious/avoidant children. (3) Persons who seemed preoccupied with dependency on their own parents and still actively struggled to please them; these tended to be parents of anxious/ambivalent children. (4) Persons who had experienced the early death of an attachment figure and not worked through the mourning process; these tended to be parents of children who show an insecure-disorganized or disoriented pattern of behaviour in the strange situation, or type D, which Main and her colleagues believe to be a useful extension of the original Ainsworth classification (p. 66). Similar findings have been reported by Crowell and Feldman (1988).

*Who are attachments made with?*

In many articles and textbooks the attachment relationship is defined as attachment to the mother (e.g. Sylva and Lunt, 1981), thus assuming that it is only or primarily the mother with whom a baby forms an attachment. How true is this? Such studies as have been done suggest that early attachments are usually multiple, and although often the strongest attachment is to the mother, this need not always be so (see Smith, 1980, for a review).

One study was done in Scotland, interviewing mothers and asking to whom their babies showed separation protest (Schaffer and Emerson, 1964). It emerged that the proportion of babies having more than one attachment figure increased from 29 per cent when separation protest first appeared, to 87 per cent at 18 months. Furthermore, for about one-third of the babies the strongest attachment seemed to be to someone other than the mother, such as father, grandparent, or an older sibling. Generally attachments were formed to responsive persons who interacted and played a lot with the infant; simple caretaking such as nappy-changing was not in itself such an important factor. Cohen and Campos (1974) obtained similar results in a study in the USA.

Studies in other cultures bear out these conclusions. In the Israeli kibbutzim, for example, young children spend the majority of their waking hours in small communal nurseries, in the charge of a nurse of 'metapelet'. A study of 1- and 2-year-olds reared in this way used a modified version of the 'strange situation' to measure attachment to the mother, and the metapelet. It was found that the infants were strongly attached to both; either could serve as a base for exploration, and provide reassurance when the infant felt insecure (Fox, 1977).

In many agricultural societies mothers work in the fields, and often leave young infants in the village, in the care of grandparents, or older siblings, returning periodically to breastfeed. In a survey of data on 186 non-industrial societies, it was found that the mother was rated as the 'almost exclusive' caretaker in infancy in only five of them. Other persons had important caretaking roles in 40 per cent of societies during the infancy period, and in 80 per cent of societies during early childhood (Weisner and Gallimore, 1977).

## Relationships with Other Family Members

Although earlier researchers tended to focus rather exclusively on the mother when discussing the child's early social relationships and attachment, more recently attention has been paid to the child's relationships with other family members – father, siblings, grandparents.

## Fathers

How important is the other parent – the father? And has the role of the father changed in recent years, as is often suggested? Research in a number of societies has shown that fathers can fulfil a parenting role just as much as mothers, for example in single-parent father families; but that typically, fathers do not have such a large part in child-rearing and domestic tasks as do mothers (Lamb, 1987).

So far, the highest degree of father involvement in any human society seems to be amongst the Aka pygmies, a hunter-gatherer people in the Central African Republic. Fathers were found to be present with an infant or child for 88 per cent of the time, and to be holding an infant for 22 per cent of the time. This high degree of physical intimacy by fathers seems to be encouraged by the overlapping subsistence activities of men and women. Men don't just leave women in the campsite to look after children, while they go hunting with nets; women often assist in hunting, and men often carry infants back after the hunt. Nevertheless, even in this society mothers still engage in more child care than fathers (Hewlett, 1987). Another society where paternal care is encouraged is Sweden. Equality between the sexes has been encouraged since the 1960s, including legislation about work opportunities and parental leave, and an advertising campaign (see plate 3.2) to encourage fathers to take child care responsibilities seriously. While this has had some impact, it is still true that Swedish mothers do most of the housework and child care, even when both parents are working (Hwang, 1987).

In *Becoming a Father* (1986), Charlie Lewis carried out an interview study of 100 fathers of 1-year-old children in Nottingham, UK. One aspect which Lewis documented was that the majority of fathers (65 per cent) now attended all stages of the birth of their child. Many fathers were anxious about it, and had been encouraged to attend by their wives; but most found it a positive experience. As one father put it:

> I found it hard work and much more traumatic than I thought it would be ... I felt by the end of the experience that I had done a full day's work and was absolutely washed out, but nevertheless I wouldn't miss being there a second time. (Lewis, 1986, p. 70)

This has undoubtedly been a change since even three decades ago, when fathers were discouraged from attending hospital deliveries (it is also worth noting that up to the 1950s and 1960s many more deliveries took place at home anyway). However it was not the case that fathers who were present at the birth were also much more involved with child care after the baby was home; Lewis found no correlation between these two. Mothers predominantly did the child care, feeding, nappy changing, getting up at night if the baby was fretting. At least two factors seem to contribute to this. Firstly, the father will more often be in longer hours of employment. Lewis did find that fathers contributed more when the mother was also working. Secondly, it is easy for fathers to feel marginalized in baby care; mothers are seen as the 'experts' at this. Indeed it is only mothers who can breastfeed! However mothers may contribute to keeping their own areas of expertise, as the

PLATE 3.2   *A Swedish father cradles his young son. Photographs such as this were used in campaigns directed to increasing paternal involvement in child care (from Department of Information, Stockholm)*

following interview demonstrates:

> Interviewer:          How about changing him? Do you often change his nappies?
> Father (to wife):   Don't think I've done that, have I?
> Wife:                    In the first week when I weren't well.
> Interviewer:          Is there any reason why you haven't?
> Wife:                    Only 'cos I've always been there. They don't bother me in the slightest, you know.
> Father:                 Nappies don't bother *me*, you know. If Jan [wife] turned round to me and said, 'Could you do it for me, then?' ... Like I say, she's a very competent mother.
>
> (Lewis, 1986, p. 100)

Lewis was able to compare his data, obtained in 1980, with similar data obtained by the Newsons in interviews in 1960. Some results are shown in table 3.1. The most dramatic and significant changes are in the husband helping in the period after birth, and getting up for the baby at night; the changes for bathing and nappy changing are less clearcut and not significant. In the USA, Lamb (1987) similarly concludes that there have been some modest increases in paternal involvement over the last decade or so. The idea of the new, nurturant father is not entirely mythical, but it would be easy to exaggerate the changes which have taken place.

### Siblings

80 per cent of us have siblings – brothers or sisters. Usually, siblings only differ in age by a few years. Thus, while not exactly 'peers' (see chapter 4), they are

TABLE 3.1    *Changes in father involvement in child care, 1960 to 1980*

|  | 1960 (N = 100) | 1980 (N = 100) |
| --- | --- | --- |
| Husband helps in the period after birth? (Yes) | 30 | 77 $p < 0.001$ |
| Husband gets up to baby at night? (Yes) | 49 | 87 $p < 0.001$ |
| Husband involved in putting baby to bed/getting to sleep? | | |
| little/never | 29 | 26 |
| occasional | 35 | 24 |
| often | 35 | 48 n.s. |
| Husband involved in bathing baby? | | |
| little/never | 54 | 62 |
| occasional | 26 | 9 |
| often | 20 | 29 n.s. |
| Husband involved in nappy changing? | | |
| little/never | 37 | 40 |
| occasional | 43 | 32 |
| often | 20 | 28 n.s. |

*Source*: Lewis, 1986

generally close enough in age, and similar enough in interests and developmental stages, to be important social partners for each other in the home and family environment.

In many traditional societies with large families, older siblings may act in a caregiving role to younger ones, being asked to look after them while parents are busy. Weisner and Gallimore (1977) found that sibling caregiving was important in 57 per cent of their sample of 186 societies. Characteristically, older siblings can show great tolerance for younger ones, and can act as an important model for more competent behaviour. They can also show hostility and ambivalence, and this too has been observed in many different societies (Eibl–Eibesfeldt, 1989).

A study by Stewart (1983) in the USA showed that older siblings can act as attachment figures in a 'strange situation'. Stewart used an extended version of the procedure, with 54 family groups. At one point the older sibling (who was aged from 30 to 58 months) was left alone with the infant (who was aged from 10 to 20 months). Every infant responded to the mother's departure with some degree of distress. Within 10 seconds of the mother's departure, 28 of the older siblings had responded by showing some form of caregiving behaviour; for example approaching and hugging the infant, offering verbal reassurance of the mother's return, or carrying the infant to the centre of the room to distract him or her with toys. These actions were quite effective. The other 26 older siblings however ignored or moved away from the infant and did not show caregiving responses. This pattern of pronounced variation in the quality of sibling relationships is in fact a recurrent one in studies of siblings.

The 'strange situation' is of course just that — a strange situation! What is found in actual sibling relationships in the home? The most extensive research of this kind had been carried out by Judy Dunn and her colleagues (Dunn and Kendrick, 1982; Dunn, 1984). Dunn and Kendrick (1982) started making observations in the homes of 40 firstborn children living with both parents in or near Cambridge, UK. At first visit, a new sibling was due in a month or so, and the first child was in most cases nearing their second birthday. Subsequent visits were made *after* the birth of the sibling, when the second child was about 1 month old, and again at 8 months and at 14 months. Besides interviewing the parents, the natural behaviour between the siblings and with their parents was observed.

Naturally enough, many firstborns showed some signs of jealousy when the new sibling arrived. Previously they had been the centre of attention from mother, father or grandparents; now, the new brother or sister got the most attention. Parents do of course make some efforts to involve the firstborn in this, for example in feeding sessions, but inevitably rates of interaction with firstborns do decline overall (at times, fathers can play a more important role with the older child while the mother is undertaking primary caregiving responsibilities with the new baby). At this point, much of the jealousy and ambivalence of the firstborn is directed towards parents:

Mother: He keeps having tantrums and misery. Anything sets him off. He's just terrible.

(Dunn and Kendrick, 1982, p. 31)

Not many firstborns show much overt hostility to the infant, but some do; and some behaviour can be ambivalent. In the following example it is difficult to know if the behaviour is friendly, hostile, or more probably a mixture of both:

> Mother:   He wants to play with her but he's so rough. Lies on top of her. Then she cries. He wants to roll all over her. I have to keep her away from him 'cause I can't let her be bashed about yet.
>
> (p. 36)

Other children may express hostility in conversation, as the following extract shows:

> Child:    Baby, baby (caressing her). Monster. Monster.
> Mother:   She's not a monster.
> Child:    Monster.
>
> (p. 68)

However such hostility really is ambivalent. The great majority of the firstborns do show much interest and affection towards their new sibling:

> Mother:   He asks where she is first thing in the morning. He's happy when he can see her.
>
> (p. 34)

They may also show empathy and prosocial behaviour (see also chapter 7):

> Mother:   When she cries he's very concerned. Gets her dummy [pacifier], then comes and tells me.
>
> (p. 32)

There was considerable variation in the typical response when the infant was upset. Fourteen of the firstborns were themselves upset, like the boy just mentioned. Ten were neutral. Five were sometimes gleeful, while ten children actually increased their younger sibling's upset. Overall, Dunn and Kendrick feel that the sibling relationship is one in which considerable emotions may be aroused – both of love and of envy. (Incidentally, sociobiologists would not be surprised at finding sibling rivalry – see chapter 2).

However the title of Dunn and Kendrick's book, *Siblings – Love, Envy, and Understanding*, brings out another important feature; that of the enhanced understanding which this close and emotionally powerful relationship may generate. This may be an optimal situation in which to learn how to understand and hence influence others. Very early on (under two years of age) siblings seem to be learning how to frustrate, tease, placate, comfort or get their own way with their brother or sister. This is true not only of the older siblings, but of the younger ones as they grow up; consider the following observation of Callum, now 14 months, with his older sister Laura, aged 3 years.

> Callum repeatedly reaches for and manipulates the magnetic letters Laura is playing with. Laura repeatedly says NO gently. Callum continues trying to reach the letters. Finally, Laura picks up the tray containing the letters and carries it to a high table that Callum cannot reach. Callum is furious and starts to cry. He turns and goes straight to the sofa where Laura's comfort objects, a rag doll and a pacifier, are lying. He takes the doll and holds tight, looking at

Laura. Laura for the first time is very upset, starts crying, and runs to take the doll.

(p. 116)

The obvious interpretation here is that Callum has figured out how to annoy Laura so as to get his own back on her. These are interesting observations to consider in the light of ideas about children's 'theory of mind' (see chapter 5), as well as part of the critique of Piaget's ideas about egocentrism (chapter 11). Nevertheless it is also worth bearing in mind that children can learn these social cognitive skills with adults and peers, as well as with siblings. Research on only children appears to suggest that they do well on achievement and intelligence scores, and show no deficits in sociability or adjustment (Falbo and Polit, 1986). This, and other research on family size effects, does suggest that the adult–child relationship is still the most powerful so far as many aspects of development are concerned.

*Grandparents*

About 70 per cent of middle-aged and older people become grandparents. Since the average age of becoming a grandparent, in Western societies, is about 50 years for women, and a couple of years older for men, they are likely to remain grandparents for some 25 years or more; about a third of their life-span. Grandparenthood is thus an important part of the life-cycle for most people.

Only a small proportion of grandparents live in the same house as grandchildren, but many live fairly close, while those who are more distant characteristically keep contact via letters, phone calls and visits. Grandparents can have considerable influence on their grandchildren's behaviour. Tinsley and Parke (1984) described both *indirect* and *direct* influences. Indirect influence has its effect via some other person or agency, without there necessarily being any direct interaction. For example, the parent–child interaction will be influenced by the way the parent has been brought up and the experiences of child-rearing which the parent has had modelled by his or her parent, i.e. the grandparent. Grandparents can also provide emotional and financial support for parents, which will be especially valuable at times of emotional or financial stress.

Direct influences can also take many forms. Perhaps the strongest case is when a grandparent acts as a surrogate parent when the child is young (for example in a single parent family, or with a teenage pregnancy, or as a caregiver while both parents work). It is most often the maternal grandmother who fills this role. However grandfathers can be important too; Radin, Oyserman and Benn (1991) found that grandfathers can have a direct positive influence on young grandchildren of teen mothers, especially for grandsons.

Even if not acting as a surrogate parent, a grandparent who has contact with a grandchild can act as a companion and be an important part of the child's social network. Many grandparents enjoy conversations with grandchildren, asking them to run errands, and giving them small gifts. They can also act directly as a source of emotional support, acting as a 'buffer' in cases where a grandchild is in conflict with parents, or where the parents are in conflict with each other.

For example, Johnson (1983) analysed the responses of 58 US grandmothers to the divorce of one of their children. The younger grandmothers (below 65 years of age) generally maintained their level of contact with the grandchildren (usually weekly or more), and half of them actually increased their level of contact. One grandmother described how she filled a gap in the custody arrangements:

> I pick them up on Friday after work. We go to the Pizza Hut for dinner – then home to watch TV. I keep lots of goodies around for them. They fight, I shush them. Then they zonk out. The next morning, I fix breakfast – they watch TV. Then I take them to their dad's and dump them. It's kinda nice'
>
> (Johnson, 1983, pp. 553–4)

The older (over 65) grandmothers also usually maintained or increased contact after parental divorce, but the level of contact was noticeably less.

In not all situations is it easy for grandparents to see grandchildren of parental divorce. The issue of rights of access of grandparents of a non-custodial parent has been of recent concern in the UK and other countries. In the USA, all 50 states have passed statutes allowing grandparents to petition for legally enforceable visitation with their grandchildren (Thompson, Tinsly, Scalora and Parke, 1989), and the 1990 Children's Act in the UK should also facilitate this.

Another role of grandparents is to pass on information and values directly to grandchildren. They are particularly well placed to pass on the family history, and knowledge of times past. Sometimes the values of grandparents may conflict with those of the parental generation; for example, in an interview study of older people in London, Townsend (1957, pp. 106–7) remarked that 'the grandparents were notably lenient towards grandchildren'. As one informant put it, 'the grandmother can be free and easy. She [her daughter] has to be fairly strict wth them'. At other times grandmothers have been thought of as being too strict and punitive. Indeed in the 1930s and 1940s, some psychiatrists and social workers regarded the grandmother's influence very negatively. Vollmer, an American doctor, remarked (1937, pp. 378, 382) that 'every pediatrician ... will have made this discovery: grandmothers exert an extraordinarily pernicious influence on their grandchildren' and that 'the practical conclusion is that the grandmother is not a suitable custodian of the care and rearing of her grandchild'! Whatever grandmothers were really like in the 1930s, most present-day grandparents appear sensitive to the need not to interfere too much with parental rearing methods, and as we have seen the consensus of research is that the balance of their influence is overwhelmingly positive. Some negative stereotypes of grandparents still persist, however; many children's books portray grandparents as somewhat inactive persons in their eighties or nineties, rather than (as many grandparents are) actively employed and in their fifties or early sixties.

## Care outside the Family: Day Care and Childminding

In our society the standard expectation, at least until recently, has been that the mother of young children should stay at home to look after them until they are old enough to go to nursery or infant school, that is, 3–5 years of age. Nevertheless, it has always been the case that many mothers of young children have gone out to work, either through preference or through financial necessity. During the mid 1970s some 600,000 mothers of preschool children in the UK were in paid employment (and at that period most fathers were working full-time). Some parents manage to share care in their own home with grandparents, older siblings or neighbours; for example, a study of London working class homes found an average of more than four caregivers including parents (Tizard and Tizard, 1971). The alternatives are to place the child in a day nursery or creche, or with a childminder. Day nursery places have long been inadequate for demand, and it is difficult to know the numbers of children placed with childminders, as many childminders do not register. There are some 50,000 registered childminders in the UK, but the number of unregistered (illegal) childminders has been estimated at two to three times as many (Jackson and Jackson, 1979).

There has been recent controversy over both nursery-based day care and childminding (which Americans call 'home-based day care'). Most of the research on day care has been carried out in the USA, and suggests that day care does not have adverse effects provided that it is of high quality; that is, there are good staff-child ratios, low staff turnover and a stimulating, well-provided environment. In such circumstances, reviews have concluded that day care has no overall effects on intellectual development, and does not disrupt the child's attachment relationship with the mother (Belsky and Steinberg, 1978; Clarke-Stewart, 1982). It does increase the degree to which the child interacts, both positively and negatively, with peers.

The controversy over day care was reopened in the late 1980s by Belsky (1988) and others. Belsky (1988) pointed out that about half of US mothers with 1-year-olds were in employment. However, an analysis he made of some recent studies led him to conclude that 'a rather robust association emerges between extensive nonmaternal care experience initiated in the first year of life and insecure infant–mother attachment assessed in the Strange Situation' (Belsky, 1988, p. 401). Belsky concluded that initiating day care of more than 20 hours/week before the child is 1 year of age may be a risk factor for mother–infant relationships. Combining data from five studies, the risk of having insecure attachment to the mother was 43 per cent for infants experiencing high day care, but only 26 per cent for infants experiencing low (or no) day care.

The implications of this finding are controversial. Clarke-Stewart (1989) has queried whether the strange situation is a valid procedure for infants or working mothers (who experience many more routine separations); whether insecure attachment to mother can be generalized to general emotional security; and whether the differences may be due to other factors (e.g. differences in mothers choosing to work). However there is consensus that the issue deserves further urgent investigation; also that this new evidence does not affect the previous conclusions about day care starting *after* the first year. Interestingly, in Sweden either parent can take the first 12 months off, on full pay, to look after a new baby (on average, fathers take $1\frac{1}{2}$ months of this). Thus, this new concern arising from research does not worry the Swedes (Hwang, Broberg and Lamb, 1990).

There has been relatively little research on childminding, but such as there is has mostly been carried out in the UK. Several studies have been very critical of the effects of childminding, including one conducted in London (Mayall and Petrie, 1977, 1983) and one in Oxfordshire (Bryant et al., 1980). Both found that children often appeared insecure in the minder's home, and scored below expectations on tests of language or cognitive ability. These studies did not have proper control groups for comparison, however, so it is not clear that the children's problems were due to the minding, rather than home circumstances (Raven, 1981). There are certainly problems to be expected with some unregistered minders. Jackson and Jackson (1979) carried out a 'dawn watch' in Huddersfield, tracking down where mothers took their children to be minded before the early morning shifts in the factories. They found that some of the unregistered childminders provided a very poor emotional and material environment. Much can be done here by improving facilities for childminders, providing training courses and encouraging registration and resource back-up (Moss 1987).

Ideally, childminding (or in the USA, family-based day care) could provide an economic form of day care with high adult to child ratios; and perhaps best of all is when such care is provided by relatives, such as grandparents. Melhuish (1990) and his colleagues compared the progress of children in London, who (starting before 9 months of age) experienced either care with relatives, childminding, or private nursery care. The adult–child ratio was best for care by a relative, next for childminders, and lowest for nursery care. At 18 months, communication to children, and also some aspects of the children's language development, were highest for children cared for by relatives and lowest in the nursery group. (Contrary to Belsky's worries there were no apparent differences in attachment to mother.) By 3 years of age the children in nurseries continued to receive less language stimulation; their naming vocabulary was the least developed, though they did not differ on other language measures. There were no significant differences in cognitive development, however, and the nursery children did show more prosocial behaviour such as sharing, cooperation and empathy with others. These differences held even after controlling for measures of social class (such as mothers' education) which discriminated between the three groups.

## Bowlby's 'Maternal Deprivation' Hypothesis

There has been concern over day care and childminding for young children partly because of the hypothesis that children should not be 'deprived' of contact with the mother during a critical period when the primary attachment relationship is being formed. This hypothesis, which has come to be known as the 'maternal deprivation' hypothesis, was proposed by John Bowlby (1953, 1969). It carries strong practical policy implications. Many aspects of it have been strongly criticized, however (see Rutter, 1981). We aim to review both the hypothesis and the critiques in this discussion.

Bowlby first put forward his views publicly in a 1951 report to the World Health Organisation, published in paperback in 1953 as *Child Care and the Growth of Love*. The report was inspired by the needs of refugee or homeless children, separated from or without parents in the aftermath of the Second World War. At that time, as in the inter-war years, institutional care focused on the physical needs of the child – good food and a clean environment – but little on the child's emotional needs, which were poorly recognized. On the basis of psychoanalytic beliefs, contemporary ethological work and his own evidence, Bowlby proposed (1953) that 'mother love in infancy and childhood is as important for mental health as are vitamins and proteins for physical health'. This viewpoint provided a most important, indeed vital, corrective to the prevailing current of opinion. Bowlby went further, however. In a now notorious passage, he stated:

> What is believed to be essential for mental health is that the infant and young child should experience a warm, intimate and continuous relationship with his mother (or permanent mother- subsitute – one person who steadily 'mothers' him) in which both find satisfaction and enjoyment.

This statement, that the infant should have a continuous, unbroken relationship with one person (normally the mother), is backed up elsewhere in Bowlby's writings by assertions that mothers should not be separated from their young children, for example by work (even part-time), or hospitalization, and that if such separations do occur, there is a poor prognosis for social and cognitive development. The period of from about 6 months to 3 years was regarded as especially crucial. Even if not universally believed, this statement had a profound effect on a generation of mothers.

Why did Bowlby hold this belief? We can identify a number of sources of evidence which led him to these views:

1   The idea of a critical period for attachment formation came from the early work on imprinting and the following response (see chapter 2). The 9-month 'fear of strangers' was supposed to prevent subsequent attachment bonds being formed.

2   Observations of young children separated from parents – when placed for short-term stays in a hospital or institution, for example – showed that the children went through a characteristic sequence: first protesting, but able to be comforted; secondly despair, and being inconsolable; thirdly denial and detachment, with the child superficially unconcerned at the separation, but denying any affection or response to the mother on eventual reunion. These stages were vividly shown in a series of films made by J. and J. Robertson (1967–73), entitled 'Young Children in Brief Separation'.

3   Much research evidence suggesting that children in long-term institutional care were retarded in social, language and cognitive development; presumably as a result of the effects of maternal separation. Studies by researchers such as Goldfarb, and Spitz, documented the extreme retardation often found in orphanages and foundling homes, and the adverse long-term effects of institutional rearing (e.g. Goldfarb, 1947).

4   The adverse effects of long-term maternal separation were soon apparently further confirmed by research carried out with rhesus monkeys in the USA. Harry and Margaret Harlow (1958, 1969) reported a series of studies in which young rhesus monkeys were separated from their mothers and raised in isolation. Either they were placed in total isolation, in steel cages with diffused light and filtered sound; or they were placed in partial isolation, in wire cages where they could see and hear, but could not contact, other monkeys. Either way, when such an isolation-reared monkey was released and placed with other monkeys, it showed complete social maladjustment, usually being terrified of other monkeys, crouching, rocking

and biting itself, and occasionally being hyper-aggressive even to a play invitation. If isolated for only the first 3 months, a young monkey could recover, but isolation for 6 or 12 months seemed to produce irreversible effects. At adolescence these animals were unable to mate satisfactorily, and if a female did have a baby, she abused it rather than cared for it.

5    Evidence which linked delinquency or behaviour problems in adolescence to some form of separation experience in childhood, such as hospitalization, or a 'broken home' brought about by parental separation or divorce. The evidence came from retrospective studies: that is, those which started with adolescent children and then obtained certain data on their childhood experiences. Bowlby's interpretation was that the separation experience caused the later behaviour problems.

*Criticisms of the hypothesis*

Over the past ten years or so much further evidence has accumulated on the matters Bowlby addressed. As a result, the maternal deprivation hypothesis, at least in its strong form, has become largely discredited, although the debate continues (see Rutter, 1981). Let us consider the main reasons why the evidence cited above, does not necessarily lead to the conclusions which Bowlby reached.

1    The ethological evidence for critical periods is not so strongly stated now as in the 1950s; furthermore, the 'imprinting' characteristic of precocial birds and some mammals is not characteristic of primates (see chapter 2). The 'fear of strangers', which was thought to emerge as the primary attachment bond was formed, is also now seen as overstated. Recent evidence suggests that 1- and 2-year-olds can form new social relationships with adults and we have already seen how children at this age characteristically form several strong attachment relationships.

2    We have seen that Bowlby's idea of attachment to just one caregiver ('monotropism') seems incorrect. It follows from this that separation from the mother could be compensated for by the presence of another attachment figure. This does seem to be the case. Indeed, the Robertson's work referred to above found just this. Here, children were being placed in short-term care while the mother had a second baby and was to be in hospital for about a week. The Robertsons showed that institutional care led to the phases of protest, despair and denial, but that short-term foster care in a family, especially if the foster-mother got to know the child beforehand, very greatly alleviated the child's distress. Similarly, if a young child is in hospital, regular visits or stays by mother, father, and/or other attachment figures can prevent obvious distress.

3    The early work on the effects of institutional rearing has been re-evaluated. No one denies the terrible effects of the pre-war orphanages, which were poorly equipped and staffed by persons with little understanding of the psychological needs of the child. However, any effects of separation from the mother were confounded with the generally unstimulating environment provided. It is not surprising that children become linguistically and cognitively retarded if they are hardly spoken too and given few toys and little sensory stimulation. It is not surprising that they are socially immature, if they receive little social contact and few socially contingent responses. Such was often the case (see also chapter 14), but these are not necessary concomitants of institutional care. More recent research has

found that improved institutional care has fewer dramatically harmful effects (see box 3.2).

4    The Harlow's monkey research apparently gave experimental backing for the long-term and irreversible effects of maternal deprivation in another primate species. Yet these studies also confounded maternal deprivation with general social and sensory deprivation. Moreover, later research in this programme has shown how severe deficits can be ameliorated (Suomi and Harlow, 1972; Novak, 1979). The breakthrough came when the isolation-reared monkeys, instead of being released directly into a peer group, were first placed individually with a younger monkey. For example, 6-month isolates were paired with 3-month-old 'therapist' monkeys. The younger monkey approaches and clings to the older one, rather than attacking it, and seems to help it catch up on the sort of physical contact experiences it has missed. Even 12-month isolates can be helped by this method. This research has shown that deprivation effects may not be irreversible, if the right corrective treatment is used. It also shows that in many respects, peers can be as effective as mothers in reducing the effects of social isolation.

5    The retrospective evidence linking adolescent behaviour problems to early separation experience is open to various interpretations. No clear causal link can be inferred. For example, suppose a correlational link has been found between delinquency and a 'broken home' in early childhood. Parental separation may mean that there is increased discord at the time, or later, or perhaps less supervision of the child given by a single parent. These latter might be the real causes of the delinquency, not the separation itself. Rutter (1981) argued that it is the discord often present in separating or divorcing families which leads to later behaviour problems. It is not separation as such, since death of a parent, while obviously affecting the child, does not usually lead to the outcomes which were being ascribed to maternal deprivation.

In the long term Bowlby's work had some markedly beneficial effects. Together with other research it led to a marked improvement in the standard of institutional care (see box 3.2) and in many areas the phasing out of institutional care in favour of fostering arrangements. It also led to much easier access of parents to a child in hospital care. In general, a greater awareness of the child's emotional needs was stimulated. However, there were some effects which many people now see as detrimental, particularly a feeling of guilt amongst mothers who, perhaps out of necessity, went out to work while their children were young. In general, high-quality day care does not have adverse effects, although it may possibly do so if full-time in the first year; and the debate on childminding continues. On the other side of the coin, a mother who stays at home to look after young children full time can feel frustrated or isolated, particularly if she has little support from husband or relatives. Research on the causes of depression in women has identified a number of contributory factors, one of which is being at home full time with two or more children under five if other stresses are present (Brown and Harris, 1978). Sometimes the 'continuous relationship with his mother' which Bowlby advocated, can be more continuous than may be good for the mother, or the child.

Moderate shared care of young children seems to be very common, harmless and even perhaps beneficial. However, it does seem that extreme shared care, with tens of adults involved, can lead to immediate and long-term problems. A study by

Tizard (box 3.2) best documents this, but it is supported by independent research (see Rutter, 1981). The Tizard study also hints at the possibility that an early attachment bond is important for later adjustment, as the later adopted children in this study tended to share the same school problems as those who remained in institutional care.

There is also some evidence that repeated hospital admissions before 5 years of age can lead to later behaviour problems in adolescence, Two large-scale survey studies (Douglas, 1975: Quinton and Rutter, 1976) have found such a correlation. Does this also support the critical period idea? The opposite view is put by Clarke and Clarke (1976), who argue that repeated hospital admission is probably a symptom of inadequate parental care over a sustained period, with the latter being the causative factor. Nevertheless, the original studies did control for factors such as social class and parental interest in education, and the independent replication means that the findings cannot be dismissed lightly.

Thus, the overall assessment is that many of Bowlby's ideas on maternal deprivation are discredited. Nevertheless, it is a normal process for 1- and 2-year-olds to be forming strong attachments to a few persons, characterized by proximity seeking and separation protest. Bonds can be formed later, as studies of late adoption show, and many of the apparent adverse effects of maternal deprivation are now seen as due to other factors, perhaps not specific to the first 2 or 3 years of life. But, in certain much more limited senses than Bowlby first proposed, it may be that this early period is more crucial for social adjustment than are later years.

## Divorce and Step-Parenting

Divorce has become more common in modern Western societies; each year, between 1 and 2 per cent of marriages end this way (Richards, 1988). Thus, by the time a child is 16, there is something like a 1-in-4 chance that he or she will have experienced parental separation and divorce. What are the consequences of this for the child's development? In recent decades, several studies have been made to attempt to answer this question.

The effects of divorce have been found to vary considerably with the child's age when the separation occurs (Hetherington, 1988). Preschool children, although upset, are least able to understand what is going on. By middle childhood the changes are better understood, but there may be persistent wishes or fantasies of the parents reuniting. For early adolescents, the reaction may more often be one of shame or anger, perhaps siding with one parent or the other.

Wallerstein (1985) has described three phases in the divorce process. First is the acute phase, typically lasting about two years, in which the emotional and physical separation takes place. Second is a transitional phase, in which each parent experiences marked ups and downs while they establish separate lives. Third is a post-divorce phase, in which each parent has established a new lifestyle, either as a single parent or remarried. The impact on children varies through time as well; clearly longitudinal studies are vital to get any real understanding of the impact of divorce on children. Several such studies have been made in the USA.

One study commenced with 144 middle class white families in Virginia, USA. Half the children were from divorced, mother-custody families, and half from nondivorced families; their average age at separation was 4 years (Hetherington, Cox and Cox, 1982). After 1 year, most children from divorced families (and many parents) experienced emotional distress and behaviour problems associated with the disruptions in family functioning. This was much improved after 2 years; the main exception being that some boys had poor relations with their custodial mothers and showed more antisocial and noncompliant behaviour than boys from non-divorced families.

A follow-up was made after 6 years, when the children had an average age of 10 years, of 124 of the original 144 families. By now, 42 out of 60 divorced mothers had remarried (and 2 of these had redivorced); also 11 of 64 originally nondivorced families had divorced. A general finding was that children of divorced parents experienced more independence and power in decision making at an earlier age, and their activities were less closely monitored by parents. They 'grew up faster'. Mother–daughter relationships were generally not much different from those in non-divorced families. However mother–son relations continued to be rather tense for divorced mothers who had not remarried; even despite warmth in the relationship, sons were often noncompliant and mothers ineffective in their attempts at control.

Remarriage and the presence of a stepfather seemed to improve matters for sons, who perhaps responded well to a male figure to identify with; however the stepfamily situation often made matters worse for daughters, with the stepfather–stepdaughter relationship being a particularly difficult one. Step-parents are almost inevitably seen as intruders by stepchildren, and often try to tread an uneasy path between assisting their spouse in discipline problems (which may lead to their rejection by stepchildren), and disengagement. The difficulties facing some stepfamilies were also documented by a study in London by Ferri (1984), which still pointed out that many such families had successfully met the challenge. Remarriage does generally increase the life satisfaction of the adults, but forming strong relationships in the reconstituted family is often a gradual and difficult process.

Another study, starting in 1971, was of 131 children from 60 divorcing families in Northern California (Wallerstein, 1987). The children were between $2\frac{1}{2}$ and 18 years at the time of decisive parental separation. Initially, virtually all the children were very distressed at the separation. Things were not much better after 18 months; some of the younger girls had recovered somewhat, but some of the younger boys showed significantly more disturbance. A follow-up after five years showed a more complex picture. What was most important now was the overall quality of life within the post-divorce or remarried family. About one-third of the children, however, still showed moderate to severe depression.

At a follow up after 10 years, some 90 per cent of the original sample could still be located. Interviews with children now 16 to 18 years old, who had perhaps experienced the separation at the most vulnerable time, showed that many still felt sad and wistful about what had happened, while often accepting its inevitability. As one girl said,

I don't know if divorce is ever a good thing, but if it is going to happen, it is going to happen. If one person wants out, he wants out. It can't be changed. I get depressed when I think about it. I get sad and angry when I think about what happened to me. (Wallerstein, 1987, p. 205)

All the children had been in the legal and physical custody of their mothers; about 40 per cent had moved in for a while with their fathers during adolescence, but most had returned; visits to father varied greatly, but were not usually more than weekly due in part to geographical separation. However the quality of the father–child relationship was an important determinant of adjustment.

Although traditionally custody is given to one parent, usually the mother, joint custody is being increasingly advocated where possible (i.e. where both parents live fairly close and maintain a reasonable relationship). Luepnitz (1986) compared children who were in sole custody with the mother, sole custody with the father, or joint custody, 2 years or more after final separation. In fact, measures of child adjustment were found to be independent of custody type. Joint custody has the advantages of the child being able to develop two independent relationships, and of reducing financial and parenting pressures on a single parent. Luepnitz reported that 'the vast majority of children in joint custody were pleased and comfortable with the arrangement'. Single custody can however protect wives from possible abuse, and give more flexibility to relocation and remarriage.

Interestingly, Luepnitz found that only 11 per cent of her sample of children showed signs of maladjustment. This is less than one-third the level reported in Wallerstein's study, and may be due to sample differences. Wallerstein recruited subjects by promising counselling, and thus may have recruited particularly distressed families; whereas Luepnitz may have recruited rather non-distressed families who were willing to discuss custody arrangements and their outcome. Whatever the extent of maladjustment, however, all the major studies agree that experiencing good relationships with both parents, and an absence of continuing conflict, are generally conducive to the most positive outcome for the children involved. Hetherington (1989) describes 'winners, losers, and survivors' of parental divorce. Depending on circumstances, some children may continue to be damaged and insecure through to adulthood; others recover and 'survive'; yet others may develop particularly caring and competent ways of behaving as a result of coping with the experience.

## Child Neglect and Abuse

Usually, parents love and care for their children. No parent is perfect, but most provide 'good enough' parenting. Some conflict between parents and their offspring is inevitable (and indeed is predicted from evolutionary theory, see chapter 2), but generally such disagreements are kept within reasonable bounds.

In some cases however, parents or other caregivers may *neglect* a child, failing to give him or her the love, care and attention necessary for normal healthy development. Even more drastically, some may subject a child or children to physical or sexual *abuse*. Abuse can result in severe injuries, long-lasting psychological trauma, and even death. The extent of child abuse is very difficult to determine, as naturally parents are secretive about it, and children are often too young or too frightened to seek help. It also depends on the definition of abuse. *Physical abuse* has been defined as 'the intentional, non-accidental use of force on the part of the parent or other caretaker interacting with a child in his or her care aimed at hurting, injuring or destroying that child' (Gil, 1970). *Sexual abuse* has been defined as 'the involvement of dependent, sexually immature children and adolescents in sexual activities that they do not fully comprehend, to which they are unable to give informed consent or that violate the social taboos of family roles' (Kempe, 1980).

In the UK the National Society for Prevention of Cruelty to Children (NSPCC) has reported some 9,000 cases of physical abuse and 6,000 cases of sexual abuse per year (Creighton and Noyes, 1989). Some 200 children may die each year as a result of direct or indirect maltreatment by their parents; child abuse is in fact the fourth commonest cause of death in preschool children (Browne, 1989). The peak of physical abuse is in early childhood, with boys being more at risk than girls; the peak for sexual abuse appears to be later in middle childhood, with girls primarily at risk.

Diagnosis of abuse has its own set of problems. Questioning of young children has to be done carefully to maximize the accuracy and usefulness of children's testimony (Fundudis, 1989). In the case of sexual abuse, observation of unstructured play with anatomically correct dolls may be useful. Unlike conventional dolls, these dolls have sexual organs and characteristics. Some studies suggest that most children, while noticing the characteristics of the dolls, do not show sexually explicit play with them; when it is observed, such explicit play (for example, sucking a doll's penis) may well arise from the child's preoccupations based on previous exposure to explict sexual information or activity (Glaser and Collins, 1989). However the use of these dolls remains controversial (Westcott et al., 1989).

It can also be very difficult and distressing for victims of child abuse to speak out. At times they may not be believed and interviews by police and judges can seem very intimidating. In the USA and the UK it is increasingly possible to allow children to give evidence by means of a closed circuit television 'video link', so that they need not directly face their abuser (Davies, 1988) . Psychologists are closely involved in this work, and in attempts to help victims of abuse recover from their experiences (British Psychological Society, 1990).

The statistics we have indicate that child abuse tends to be more common in single-parent and low income families. Step-parents, who are not biologically related to the child, and may not have formed a close attachment to the child, are more apt to abuse children than natural parents. Nevertheless natural parents form a numerically larger category in statistics because they are most often the primary caregiver, especially the mother (Lenington, 1981). In cases of physical abuse, mothers and fathers are about equally likely to be involved (though there are obvious questions about who is willing to admit abuse – a mother may 'shelter' an abusing father or cohabitee). In cases of sexual abuse, some 95 per cent involve males as the perpetrators.

What leads a parent to abuse a child? Abusing parents have been found to very often have insecure attachment relationships with their children. In one study, 70 per cent of maltreated infants were found to have insecure attachments to their caregivers, compared to only 26 per cent of infants with no record of maltreatment (Browne, 1989).

Crittenden (1988) has examined the representations of relationships in abusing parents, using the idea of internal working models discussed earlier. She interviewed 124 mothers in Virginia, USA, many of whom had abused or maltreated their children, and gave them the Separation Anxiety Test (p. 68). She reported that adequate mothers generally had warm and secure relationships with both their children, and their partner. By contrast, abusing mothers appeared to conceptualize relationships in terms of power struggles. They tended to be controlling and hostile with anxiously attached children, and to have angry and unstable adult relationships. Another group, of neglecting mothers, appeared to conceive of relationships as emotionally empty. They were unresponsive to their anxiously attached children, and were involved in stable but affectless relationships with partners. These findings have implications for working with these families. Crittenden argues that 'the problem for those offering treatment to abused and abusing individuals is to find ways both to change their experience and also to change their conceptualization of it. Without a change in the representational model, the new experience will be encoded in terms of the old model and will be rendered useless' (Crittenden, 1988, p. 197).

However, it is not parents alone who should be held responsible for child abuse. Belsky (1984) has advocated a model of parental functioning which distinguishes three main influences on the quality of parental functioning. In order of suggested importance, these are:

1   personal psychological resources of the parent: this will include parental mental health, the quality of internal representations of relationships and their development history;
2   contextual sources of support: including the social network of support from partner, relatives and friends, and job conditions and financial circumstances;
3   characteristics of the child: in particular easy or difficult temperament (see p. 63).

Belsky's actual process model of factors influencing parenting is illustrated in figure 3.1. It clearly brings out the importance of a variety of factors, which in combination

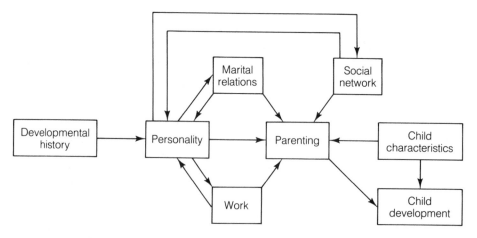

FIGURE 3.1   *Belsky's process model of the determinants of parenting*

can make child abuse much more likely than the presence of any single factor alone. While useful for conceptualizing abuse and neglect in the family, the model is also useful more generally for understanding how variations in family functioning, satisfactory as well as unsatisfactory, may come about.

**Further reading**

A useful and accessible introduction is R. Schaffer 1977: *Mothering*. Glasgow: Fontana/Open Books. There is a companion book in the same series by R. D. Parke 1981: *Fathering*, and one by J. Dunn 1984: *Sisters and Brothers*. K. Kaye 1982: *The Mental and Social Life of Babies*. London: Methuen, is a more advanced and argumentative text on early social development.

M. Rutter 1981: *Maternal Deprivation Reassessed*, 2nd edn. Harmondsworth: Penguin, is a thorough review of the controversy and later evidence bearing on Bowlby's views. J. Bowlby 1979: *The Making and Breaking of Affectional Bonds*. London: Tavistock Publications, is a collection of a number of Bowlby's articles, and his most recent book is 1988: *A Secure Base: Clinical Applications of Attachment Theory*, London: Tavistock/Routledge. A. Clarke-Stewart 1982 : *Day Care*. Glasgow: Fontana, is a readable review of the evidence on this issue which needs supplementing by more recent research.

**Discussion points**

1  How do infants becomes social?

2  What is meant by 'secure' and 'insecure' attachment? Are these culturally biased terms?

3  Do mothers, fathers, siblings and grandparents have different influences on a child's behaviour?

4  What did Bowlby mean by 'maternal deprivation'? How useful or valid has this concept proved to be?

5  What are the problems in diagnosing, and treating, child abuse?

**Practical exercise**

1  Visit some homes where there is a small child (aged about 3 months to 3 years of age). Ask if you can pick up the child, play with him or her, and/or be alone with him or her for a short while; behave in a natural, friendly way. Record what happened very soon afterwards. Did the child show wariness, friendliness, or mixed emotions at your interaction? Did this seem to vary with children of different ages?

2  Ask a mother, or primary caregiver, of a child below 3 years of age to keep a diary record through one week of who is looking after the child, and when. You could work out how many caregivers the child experiences in the week, and how many separations or reunions with mother or primary caregiver occur. You could combine this with an

interview about how the child usually reacts to the separations. The findings could be discussed in relation to Bowlby's theories.

3    Observe a young child in the home, when he or she is with (a) the mother, (b) the father, (c) an older sibling, or (d) a grandparent. Do these different caregivers behave differently towards the child? Does the child initiate different activities with them?

# Box 3.1

# Reactions to response-contingent stimulation in early infancy

The objective of this study was to examine the importance of contingent responsiveness on behaviour in 8-week-old infants. Forty infants were recruited from the San Francisco area in the USA and the study was carried out in the infants' homes.

A special apparatus, the 'contingency mobile', was designed for the study. It is shown schematically in box figure 3.1.1. The mobile was attached to the infant's cot so that it hung about 18 inches above the infant's head. The display consisted of three spheres or

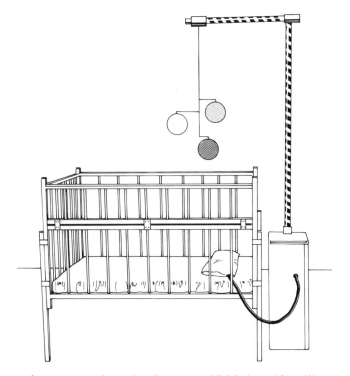

BOX FIGURE 3.1.1  *Apparatus used as a 'contingency mobile' (adapted from Watson and Ramey, 1972)*

Based on material in J. S. Watson and C. T. Ramey 1972: *Merrill-Palmer Quarterly*, 18, 219–27.

rectangles painted different colours. An electric motor, when activated, caused the display to rotate for one second, through 90 degrees. There were three conditions.

1   The 'contingency' condition (18 infants). A pressure-sensing pillow was put in the cot. Small changes in pressure on the pillow activated the electric motor and caused the display to rotate. When the infant was lying with her head on the pillow, she could cause the display to rotate by making small head movements.
2   The 'non-contingency' condition (11 infants). The pressure-sensing pillow was disconnected from the motor. The display rotated once every 3 or 4 seconds, independent of the infant's actions.
3   The 'stable' condition (11 infants). The pressure-sensing pillow was disconnected from the motor. The display did not rotate at all.

In all conditions the mothers were asked to hang the display and activate the system for 10 minutes a day, for 14 consecutive days, at times when the infant was peaceful but alert. The number of times the infant activated the pressure sensor in the pillow was recorded on an automatic counter.

The results are shown in box figure 3.1.2. The infants with the contingency mobile increased the number of pillow activations they made per session from about 90 (days 1 and 2) to 135 (days 13 and 14) (significant at $p < 0.01$ on a matched pairs $t$ test). For the non-contingency mobile and the stabile the changes were not significant. This showed that, as early as 8 weeks, infants can learn a simple response to produce contingent stimulation.

However, the investigators obtained another interesting result when they went to collect the equipment. One mother in the condition (1) group apologized that she had used the mobile additionally to the specified times, as a baby-sitter device to keep the baby happy. It turned out that almost all the mothers in this condition reported that their infants smiled and

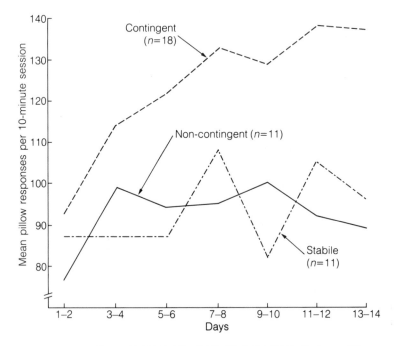

BOX FIGURE 3.1.2   *Mean response rate of infants in the three study conditions*

cooed at the mobile, after a few sessions. As one mother said,'You have to see it, when he's with his mobile, you can't distract him, he loves it'. Almost none of the mothers in the other two conditions reported this kind of strong positive emotional response.

This second result shows that contingent stimulation is enjoyed by the 8-week-old infant and produces or 'releases' socio-emotional behaviour such as smiling and cooing. These infant behaviours are normally used in social interactions with caregivers, and usually it is caregivers who provide response-contingent stimulation at this age. Watson and Ramey suggest that playful, game-like interactions are especially suitable for providing rapid contingent responses to infants, and thus eliciting positive social behaviours.

The independent variable in this study is the mobile condition; there is an experimental condition, a control for display movement and a control just for the presence of the display. The dependent variables are pillow activations and mothers' reports on socio- emotional behaviour. Obtaining the mothers reports was not planned in advance, and the authors report that this was recorded 'less systematically and objectively than would have been desirable'. Nevertheless, it would have been a pity not to have reported this information which, serendipitously, adds much to the interest of the results. The technique of this study is likely to be less useful in older infants, where the nature of the contingent stimulus and the infant's attempts at imitation are of more interest.

Box 3.2

# The effect of early institutional rearing on the behaviour problems and affectional relationships of 4-year-old children

The objective of this study was to see whether institutional rearing in early life resulted in behaviour problems and disturbances in affectional relationships. The research was carried out in London, and focused on 26 children aged $4\frac{1}{2}$ years who had been admitted to a residential nursery before 4 months of age and were still there. (In 17 cases the mother or putative father still spoke of reclaiming the child; the remaining nine had not been adopted, for various other reasons.) There were two comparison groups. One consisted of 39 children who had also been admitted to a residential nursery before 4 months, but had either been adopted (24 children) or restored to their mothers (15 children) before 4 years of age. The other group comprised 30 children from local working class homes who had not experienced any residential care. All the children were assessed at age $4\frac{1}{2}$.

The residential nurseries contained around 15–25 children, in small mixed age groups. They were well provided with books and toys. Owing to rota systems and high staff turnover, the average number to staff who had worked with each child for at least a week over the previous 2 years was 26 (range 4–45).

Each child was interviewed individually, usually with a familiar nurse or the mother present. An intelligence test was given, ratings made of the child's observed behaviour, and questionnaires given to the parent or nurse about the child's behaviour problems and attachments. Most comparisons of the three groups employed chi-squared tests of significance. On the ratings of the child's behaviour, the main differences were between the adopted/restored children, and the other two groups. The adopted/restored children were more friendly to the interviewer, and more cooperative and talkative during testing.

The institutional children had the highest score for behaviour problems, but only marginally. Their scores were significantly higher for 'poor concentration', 'problems with peers', 'temper tantrums' and clinging'. However, the home-reared children scored significantly higher for 'poor appetite or food fads', 'over-activity' and 'disobedience'. In the answers to the attachment questionnaire, the nurses reported that many of the institutional children (18 of the 26) did 'not care deeply about anyone'. While sometimes clinging and following, their attachments seemed shallow. Some of them, and some of the adopted/restored children (who otherwise had good attachments to natural or adoptive parents) were also described as being 'overfriendly' to strangers.

B. Tizard and J. Rees 1975: *Journal of Child Psychology and Psychiatry*, 16, 61–73.

The independent variable in this study is the early rearing experience; the dependent variables are measures of behaviour problems and social behaviour. The encouraging findings of the study are that the children who had experienced institutional rearing did not have very marked or severe behaviour problems (and a related study found quite good linguistic and cognitive development in this group, see chapter 12). Also, the adopted children generally did well and formed good relations with foster parents. However, most of the children still in institutional care had failed to form any strong attachments; this is not surprising as staff turnover was high and staff tended to discourage strong specific relationships from developing.

A real-life study such as this cannot be as neatly designed as a laboratory experiment. The children in the three groups differed in some respects (including sex and racial background), so rearing experience is confounded by these other factors. Ideally, also, the investigator would not know the background of each child interviewed, but this was not possible. Finally, the interview material relies on nurses' or mothers' reports, which may be less objective than actual observations of the child's behaviour.

A follow-up of the same children at 8 years of age was subsequently reported (B. Tizard and J. Hodges 1978: The effect of early institutional rearing on the development of eight year old children. *Journal of Child Psychology and Psychiatry*, 19, 99-118). Only 8 of the 26 children now remained in institutions. The late adopted children generally had good relations with their adoptive parents. The children all had reasonably good scores on IQ tests, and the early adopted children especially had high IQ and reading test scores. However the long-term effects of institutional rearing experience did show up in teacher's ratings. Compared to the home-reared controls, the children who had experienced some institutional rearing were rated as more attention-seeking, restless, disobedient and not getting on well with other children. The teacher's ratings, however, could be biased by negative stereotyping (i.e. if the teachers had negative beliefs about the effects of having been brought up in an institution, irrespective of the child's actual behaviour).

A further follow-up of the same children was made when they were 16 years of age (J. Hodges and B. Tizard, 1989: 'IQ and behavioural adjustments of ex-institutional adolescents'; and 'Social and family relationships of ex-institutional adolescents'. *Journal of Child Psychology and Psychiatry*, 30, 53–76 and 77–98). The sample available was now only about two-thirds of the original one, and a new comparison group of home-reared children was used, matched for sex, social class and family position. The findings were fairly clear. IQ scores were similar to those at 8 years, and the small variations were with family placement (adoptive/restored) rather than whether the child had or had not experienced early institutional care. However both parents and teachers rated the ex-institutional children higher on emotional and behavioural problems than the home-reared children. Ex-institutional children had more problems with social relationships, both inside the family (mainly for children restored to natural parents), and outside the family, with peers (for both adopted and restored children). The adopted children tended to score higher on symptoms of anxiety, while those who had been restored to natural families tended to score higher on antisocial behavior and school problems. These findings were supported by interviews with the young people themselves, suggesting they were not just due to stereotyped judgements by adults.

The careful follow-up of this subject group is an excellent example of the power of a longitudinal study, even with a relatively small sample size. The findings do indicate that experiencing extreme multiple caretaking in the first few years of life can be a noticeable risk factor for developing satisfactory social relationships, even by adolescence.

# 4

# Friends and School

In this chapter we look at how peer relationships change through childhood. We examine the factors influencing popularity and friendship, and the influences of peers and teachers on social behaviour and self-esteem in the school. We also look at aggression in children; and problems of school bullying and victimization.

A 'peer' is someone who is about the same age as yourself; for children, this is usually someone in the same year, class or age grade. Peers will usually be at similar stages of cognitive development. The contrast between adult–child and peer–peer relationships is also discussed in chapter 6, and is reviewed by Hartup (1989).

## Age Changes in Peer Relationships

From quite an early age, peers seem to be especially interesting to children. In one study of 12–18-month-old infants, two mother–infant pairs who had not previously met shared a playroom together. The investigations observed whom the infants touched, and whom they looked at. The results are shown in figure 4.1. The infants touched their mothers a lot (thus remaining in proximity to them, as we would expect from attachment theory, chapter 3). However, they *looked* most at the peer, who was clearly interesting to them (Lewis et al., 1975).

The interactions between under-2s have been examined extensively in the past 15 years, using video film. Video is very useful, since at this age range peer interactions are short, subtle and easy to miss. They often consist of just looking at another child and perhaps smiling, or showing a toy, or making a noise. In toddler groups an infant might make such overtures to another child once every minute or so, and each may last only a matter of seconds (Mueller and Brenner, 1977). This rather low level of peer interaction is probably because infants have not yet learnt the skills of social interaction, such as what are appropriate behaviours in certain situations, what behaviour to expect back and waiting to take one's turn. As we saw in chapter 3, adults can 'scaffold' social interactions with infants; but it takes young children some 2 or 3 years to become really competent at interacting socially with age-mates. There is some evidence that early peer experience (e.g. in toddler groups or day nurseries) can help this along (Mueller and Brenner, 1977; Rubin, 1980).

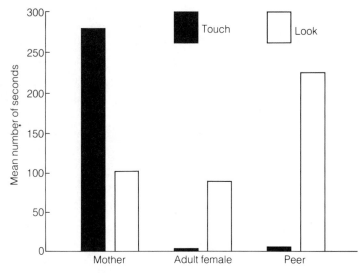

FIGURE 4.1    *Amount of time during a 15-minute period in which children aged 12–18 months touched and looked at mother, an unfamiliar adult female and an unfamiliar peer (from Lewis et al., 1975)*

There is also some evidence that infants who are 'securely attached' to their mothers are more confident and better able to explore both objects and peers, and to make new social relationships over the next year or so (Bretherton and Waters, 1985).

By 2 or 3 years of age a child is usually thought ready for nursery school. Certainly the period from 2 to 4 years sees a great increase in the skills children have with peers. As we shall see in chapter 6, socio-dramatic play and rough-and-tumble play with one or more partners become frequent in this age range. Parallel with this, the child is beginning to develop concrete operational thought and to be able to take the perspective of others in simple ways (chapters 5 and 11).

The increase in social behaviour in preschool children was documented by Mildred Parten at the Institute of Child Development in Minnesota in the late 1920s. She observed 2–4-year-olds and described how they might be 'unoccupied', an 'onlooker' on other's activities, or, if engaged in an activity, they could be 'solitary', in 'parallel' activity with others or in 'associative' or 'cooperative' activity with others. Parallel activity is when children play near each other with the same materials, but do not interact much – playing independently at the same sandpit for example. Associative activity is when children interact together at an activity, doing similar things, perhaps each adding building blocks to the same tower. Cooperative activity is when children interact together in complementary ways; for example, one child gets blocks out of a box and hands them to another child, who builds the tower. Parten (1932) found that the first four categories declined with age, whereas associative and cooperative activity, the only ones involving much interaction with peers, increased with age.

Subsequent researchers have used Parten's categories quite a lot, though they are often simplified to 'solitary' (including unoccupied and onlooker), 'parallel' and 'group' (comprising associative and cooperative). Studies in the UK and the USA

PLATE 4.1   *The beginnings of social relations and friendship between peers can be seen in toddler groups and nursery schools; these two 3-year-olds are very much aware of each other's behaviour*

have found that, very approximately, preschool children in free play divide their time equally amongst these three categories, with the balance shifting more towards 'group' activity as they get older (Smith, 1978). Most group activity involves just two or three children playing together, though the size of groups does tend to increase in older preschoolers. These trends continue in the early school years. According to a study of more than 400 Israeli children, group activity rises to about 57 per cent of the time in outdoor free play, while parallel activity falls to about 6 per cent; the number of groups comprised of more than five children increased from about 12 per cent to 16 per cent between 5 and 6 years of age (Hertz-Lazarowitz et al., 1981). The size of children's groups continues to increase through the middle school years, especially in boys, as team games such as football become more popular (Eifermann, 1970).

By the middle school years, sex segregation of children's groups is becoming very marked. In fact, children tend to choose same-sex partners even in nursery school, but by no means exclusively; typically, some two-thirds of partner choices may be same-sex, though this is influenced by such factors as the class size, toys available and the role of teachers in encouraging (or not) cross-sex play (Smith, 1986). However, by the time children are getting into team games, from about 6 or 7 years onward, sex segregation in the playground is very much greater.

In a study of 10–11-year-old children in American playgrounds, Lever (1978) found that there were distinct differences between boys' and girls' activities and friendships. Boys more often played in larger mixed-age groups, while girls were more often in smaller groups or same-age pairs. Boys tended to play competitive team games that were more complex in their rules and role-structure, and seemed to emphasize 'political' skills of cooperation, competition and leadership in their social relations. Girls seem to put more emphasis on intimacy and exclusiveness in their friendships (Berndt, 1982).

The nature of children's groups changes again as adolescence is reached. Large same-sex 'cliques' or 'gangs' become common in early adolesence, changing as heterosexual relationships become more important in later adolescence. A study of Australian adolescents aged 13–21 years (Dunphy, 1963) presents a picture of this process. Natural observations were supplemented by questionnaires, diaries and interviews in this study. At the younger end of this age range many teenagers went around in cliques comprising some three to nine individuals of the same sex. They would interact little outside their own clique. A few years later, however, adolescents would be participating in larger groups or 'crowds', made up of several interacting cliques. These would still be same-sex groups, but the more mature or higher-status members of the crowds would start to initiate contacts with members of the opposite sex. Gradually, other members of the crowd would follow their lead. This led to a stage where heterosexual crowds were made up of male and female cliques in loose association. Finally, young people associated most in heterosexual couples, going on dates, and loosely associated with other couples, prior to engagement and marriage.

## Conceptions of Friendship

Friendship is related to social participation, but it is not the same thing. While a solitary child obviously does not have friends, a child who interacts a lot with others may or may not have friends. Usually we take friendship to mean some close association between two particular people, as indicated by their association together or their psychological attachment and trust. It is quite possible to interact a lot with others generally, but not have any close friends.

The American psychiatrist Harry Sullivan (1965) theorized that children in the 4–9 age range had a uniquely important need for playmates and for friends. At this age, which he called the 'juvenile period', he suggested that friendships and peer relations were initiated mainly out of a need to enhance one's own status and popularity. The child seeks competitively to gain personal prestige in the eyes of his or her peers. However, a more genuine friendship, Sullivan thought, was more typical of the pre-adolescent period from 9 or 10 years onward. Now children needed one or more same age 'chums' or close friends, which involved greater intimacy and a more sincere concern for the other's well-being. Sullivan thought such relationships were crucial for feelings of self-esteem and self-worth. By developing awareness of others, the young person is accepted at a more intimate level by friends and consequently feels more sure of their own worth as a person.

How do children themselves conceive of friendship? In one research programme (Bigelow and La Gaipa, 1980), children aged 6–14 years were asked to write an essay in class about their expectations of best friends. Essays were obtained from 480 Scottish children and also 480 Canadian children, and analysed for their content. Results were similar in Scotland and Canada. At the earlier ages children mentioned sharing common activities, receiving help and living nearby; later, admiring and being accepted by the partner; and later still, such aspects as loyalty and commitment, genuineness and potential for intimacy. These last were found to be especially important in adolescence. Bigelow and La Gaipa have suggested a three-stage model for friendship expectations (table 4.1).

In similar research, Selman and Jaquette (1977) interviewed 225 persons aged from 4 to 32 years on their understanding and awareness of friendship relations. They documented five stages of understanding, also outlined in table 4.1, and linked to stages in perspective-taking abilities (chapter 11). Although different in detail, there are considerable correspondences between the two schemes. There clearly seems to be a shift towards more psychologically complex and mutually reciprocal ideas of friendship during the middle school years, with intimacy and commitment becoming especially important later in adolescence (Berndt, 1982).

TABLE 4.1    *Two analyses of stages of understanding friendship*

| | | |
|---|---|---|
| Bigelow and La Gaipa (1980) | Reward–cost stage<br>    Common activities, living nearby<br>    similar expectations | Around 7–8 years |
| | Normative stage<br>    Shared values, rules and sanctions | Around 9–10 years |
| | Empathic stage<br>    Understanding, self-disclosure,<br>    shared interests | Around 11–12 years |
| Selman and Jaquette (1977) | Momentary physical playmate<br>    Playing together, being in proximity | Around 3–7 years |
| | One-way assistance<br>    A friend helps you, but no notion<br>    of reciprocation | Around 4–9 years |
| | Fairweather cooperation<br>    Reciprocity focused on specific<br>    incidents rather than the friendship<br>    itself; conflicts may sever the<br>    relationship | Around 6–12 years |
| | Intimate; mutual sharing<br>    Awareness of intimacy and mutuality<br>    in a relationship which continues<br>    despite minor setbacks | Around 9–15 years |
| | Autonomous interdependence<br>    Awareness that relationships grow<br>    and change; rely on friends but<br>    accept their need for other<br>    relationships | Around 12–adult |

*The measurement of friendship: sociometry*

How can we record children's actual friendships? This has been done in three main ways: by direct observation of behaviour; by asking another person, such as a teacher or parent; or by asking the child.

If you watch a class of children, you can record which children are interacting together. If you do this at regular intervals, it is possible to build up a picture of the social structure in the class. For example, in a study of two classes in a nursery school, Clark, Wyon and Richards (1969) observed a child for 10 seconds to see whom he was playing with, then they observed another child, and so on through the class; this was continued over a five-week period. From this data the authors constructed a 'sociogram' for each class, as shown in figure 4.2. Each symbol represents a child; the number of lines joining two children represents the percentage of observations on which they were seen playing together. The concentric circles show the number of play partners a child has: if many, that child's symbol is towards the middle, if none, at the periphery. This enables us to see at a glance that in class A, for example, there is one very popular girl who links two large subroups; one boy and one girl have no clear partners. In class B there are several subgroups, and, unlike class A, there is almost complete segregation by sex; two boys have no clear partners. This is a very neat way of illustrating social structure, provided the class is not very large.

Observation gives a valid measure of who associates with whom, but this may not be quite the same thing as friendship. An alternative is to ask a teacher, for example, 'who are John's best friends in the class?', or to ask John himself 'who are your best friends?'. These nomination methods also give data that can be plotted on a sociogram. If John chooses Richard as a 'best friend', but Richard does not choose John, this can be indicated by an arrow from John to Richard; if the choice is reciprocated, the arrow would point both ways on the sociogram.

A common nomination method is to ask each child to name their three best friends. Other methods are to ask children to rate each child for liking (e.g. asking them to sort names into three pairs of 'like', 'neutral' and 'don't like'), or to ask them which they prefer of all possible pairs of children. For younger children who cannot read well, photographs of classmates can be used (see Hymel, 1983, for a review).

Some investigators have also asked children to say whom they do not like. There may be ethical objections to this; for example, such questions actually might bring about increased negative behaviour to unliked peers. So far such effects have not been found (Hayvren and Hymel, 1984). American researchers who have obtained both positive and negative nominations have not constructed sociograms (which would then look very complicated), but have rather categorized children as 'popular', 'controversial', 'rejected', 'neglected' or 'average', according to whether they are high or low on positive and on negative nominations (see box 4.1, and especially box figure 4.1.1).

In a study of 8- and 11-year-olds over a four-year period, Coie and Dodge (1983) looked at the stability of these sociometric status categories on a year-to-year basis. Was a child still in the same category after a four-year interval? They found that this stability was highest for 'rejected' children; 30 per cent of those rejected at the start of the investigation were still rejected four years later, and another 30 per cent were 'neglected'. By contrast, those merely 'neglected' at the start of the study tended to

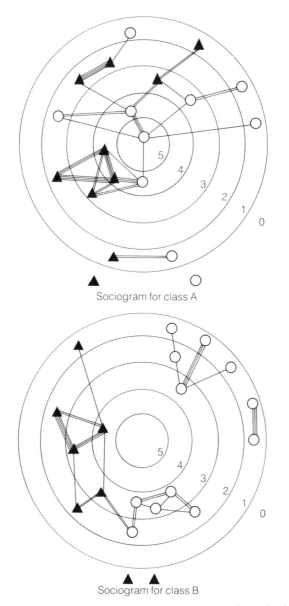

Sociogram for class A

Sociogram for class B

FIGURE 4.2   *Sociograms of association networks in two classes of preschool children: circles represent girls, triangles boys (from Clark et al., 1969)*

become 'average'. Thus, the researchers argued that children who were positively rejected in the middle school years were perhaps much more in need of help than those who simply kept a low profile and were ignored or neglected.

Other studies have found that 'rejected' children differ in their behaviour in what seem to be maladaptive ways. For example, Ladd (1983) observed 8- and 9-year-olds in playground breaks. Rejected children, compared to average or popular children, spent less time in cooperative play and social conversation, and more time in arguing and fighting; they tended to play in smaller groups, and with younger or with less popular companions. In another study, Dodge et al. (1983) looked at how 5-year-olds attempted to get into ongoing play between two other peers. They suggested that whereas popular children first waited and watched, then gradually got themselves incorporated by making group-orientated statements, and neglected children tended to stay at the waiting and watching stage, rejected children tended to escalate to disruptive actions such as interrupting the play. These sorts of findings can be taken to suggest that rejected children are lacking in some social skills. This is a widely held view, and has been developed by Dodge et al. (1986).

Dodge and his colleagues suggest that the social skills of peer interaction can be envisaged as an exchange model (see figure 4.3). Suppose child A is interacting with child B. According to this model she has to (1) encode the incoming information – perceive what child B is doing, (2) interpret this information, (3) search for appropriate responses, (4) evaluate these responses and select the best, and (5) enact that response. For example, suppose child B is running forward with arms raised, shouting and smiling. Child A needs to perceive all these actions, interpret their meaning (is this friendly or aggressive?), search for appropriate responses (run away? ignore? play fight?), select what seems best, and then do it effectively. Child B, or course, will be engaged in a similar process with respect to child A.

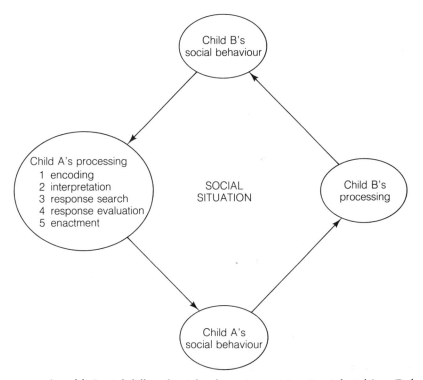

FIGURE 4.3   *A model of social skills and social exchange in peer interaction (adapted from Dodge et al., 1986)*

This model may be helpful in making the term 'social skills' more explicit. If a child has a social skills deficit, where is this located? Does an over-aggressive child misinterpret others' behaviour (stage 2), or just too readily select aggressive responses (stage 4), for example? (There is some evidence for both of these; Dodge and Richard, 1985).

However not all behaviour labelled as maladjusted may be due to *lack* of social skills. Some aggressive children may be quite skilled at manipulating others. And some rejected children may be simply reacting to exclusion by the popular cliques and would not necessarily be rejected or lacking in social skills in other situations outside the classroom.

## The importance of friendship

Does friendship carry the importance that theorists such as Sullivan have imputed to it? It is difficult to prove that having friends is developmentally important, since it is not something one can test experimentally. However, several sources of evidence support the general idea that friendship is a very important aspect of social development, both immediately and at a later time.

An interesting small-scale study at the preschool age range was carried out by Field (1984) in a US kindergarten. This class of 28 children had been together from the age of 6–12 months and half the children were now due to leave the kindergarten. Field noted in the two-week period prior to leaving that these children showed increased rates of fussiness, negative affect, aggressive behaviour, physical contact and fantasy play – possibly signs of anticipation and attempted coping with the separation from peers and their familiar environment. Also, this could be due to anxiety about attending a new school. However, in observing the children who stayed behind, Field found these children showed similarly increased agitated behaviour after the other children had left. This could have been, on a small scale, a 'grief' response to the friends they had lost.

This suggests that friendships are affectively important to a child, even at 3 or 4 years of age. Do they have other consequences, such as Sullivan hypothesized? In a study of pre-adolescents, Mannarino (1980) identified those who had 'chums' – close, stable best friendships – and compared them with those who did not, on measures of altruism and self-concept. Pre-adolescents with chums had higher levels of altruism, and higher levels of self-concept, than those who lacked chums. This is consistent with Sullivan's ideas, though being a correlational study, it does not prove that having a chum in itself caused the greater altruism or self-concept (rather than, for example, the other way round).

Is friendship in childhood important for later development? In one US study data were gathered on a large number of 8-year-olds in school, including IQ scores, school grades, attendance records, teachers' ratings and peer ratings. Eleven years later, when the subjects were nearly adult, the researchers checked mental health registers to see who had needed any psychiatric help during this period. Those who had were two-and-a-half times more likely to have had negative peer ratings at 8 years; indeed, the peer ratings were the best of all the earlier measures at predicting appearance in the mental health registers (Cowen et al., 1973).

A large scale review of all available studies was undertaken by Parker and Asher (1987). They looked at three measures of peer relationships: peer acceptance/

rejection (basically, number and quality of friendships); aggressiveness to peers; and shyness or withdrawal from peers. They examined the relationship of these to three main kinds of later outcome: dropping out of school early; being involved in juvenile and adult crime; and adult psychopathology (mental health ratings, or needing psychiatric help of any kind). Most, but not all, of the studies they reviewed were carried out in the USA (the study by Cowen et al. was one of these).

They found that the different studies were very consistent in linking low peer acceptance (or high peer rejection) with dropping out of school; and suggestive but not so consistent in linking it with juvenile/adult crime. Conversely, the studies were very consistent in linking aggressiveness at school with juvenile/adult crime; and suggestive but not so consistent in linking it with dropping out of school. The data on effects of shyness/withdrawal, and on predictors of adult psychopathology, were less consistent; while some studies found significant effects, others did not, and thus any links or effects remain unproven at present.

Most of the studies were 'follow-back' designs; that is, retrospective data on peer relations was sought for people who were currently dropping out of school, getting in trouble with the law, or seeking psychiatric help. A smaller number were 'follow-up' designs – taking a large sample of schoolchildren, obtaining data on peer relations, and seeing what happens later. The latter, while more costly to organize, are likely to provide more valid data for establishing predictive links. However, whichever design was used, the data is correlational in nature. We cannot be certain that low peer acceptance, for example, is a *causal* predictor of later problems. Two somewhat different causal models, discussed by Parker and Asher, are shown in figure 4.4. In (a) the low peer acceptance has a direct causal role; in (b), it is an outcome of more enduring traits such as aggressiveness, or shyness, rather than a cause in itself. (In both models, the original reasons for the deviant behaviour are not

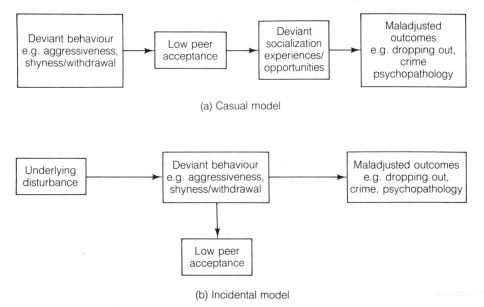

(a) Casual model

(b) Incidental model

FIGURE 4.4    *Two models of the role of peer acceptance in leading to maladjusted outcomes (from Parker and Asher, 1987)*

spelt out; you might consider whether some of the factors discussed in chaper 3 would be relevant in making the models more complete).

Most psychologists probably favour a version of model (a) over model (b), whatever the difficulties of proof are. Either way, many psychologists also believe that social skills training may be useful for those children who lack friends; this training is anyway usually directed to changing behaviours which are the correlates of peer rejection (such as high aggression, or high withdrawal).

*Social skills training*

Several attempts have been made by American psychologists to help improve social skills in neglected children. In one study (Furman et al., 1979), 4- and 5-year-olds who seldom played with other children were identified by observation. Some were given special play sessions with a younger partner, to see if this might give them more confidence in social interaction. This did seem to help, and more so than play sessions with a same-age peer, or no intervention at all. However, this study only used levels of social interaction as the measure of adjustment, so it does not directly address the issuee of friendship and rejection.

Other researchers, working with middle-school children, have used more direct means of encouraging social skills — modelling techniques, for example. A child might watch a film showing an initially withdrawn child engaged in a series of increasingly complex peer interactions. Watching such films has been shown to increase social interaction subsequently (O'Connor, 1972). A more instructional approach was used by Oden and Asher (1977). They coached 8- and 9-year-old children identified as socially isolated (neglected or rejected) on skills such as how to participate in groups, cooperate and communicate with peers; they did this in special play sessions with the target child and one other peer. These children improved in sociometric status more than those who had special play sessions without the coaching. This effect was present a year later at a follow-up assessment, and was also replicated by an independent study (Ladd, 1981). However another study with 9-year-olds found that academic skill training was even more effective than social skill training (Coie and Krehbiel, 1984). Thus, the hypothesis that rejected children are lacking in social skills, while promising, may not be the whole story.

## Factors Affecting Popularity in Children

We have seen how children differ in popularity and have discussed the theory that less popular children have less adequate social skills. We have also seen, however, that this theory is partly but not wholly confirmed by the available evidence and that therefore we should take account of other factors that may predict popularity.

One such factor is physical attractiveness. Children, like adults, differ in how physically attractive they are rated by persons who know them. In one study (Vaughn and Langlois, 1983) ratings of physical attractiveness were obtained for 59 preschool children. The correlation with sociometric preference using a paired-comparison method was 0.42 ($p < 0.01$); the correlation was higher for girls (0.66, $p < 0.01$) than for boys (0.22, n.s). Several other studies have found that ratings of physical attractiveness correlate with sociometric status (e.g. box 4.1). Around puberty, early physical maturation is also a variable affecting popularity and status (chapter 8).

Popularity may also be influenced by the composition of the peer group a child is in. Children tend to pick as friends peers similar to themselves (Hallinan, 1981). We have noted already how, through the middle-school years, children choose predominantly same-sex partners. Also children tend to choose friends of the same race or ethnic background as themselves, and children of similar intelligence or academic achievement. Thus, a child might tend to appear sociometrically 'neglected' or 'rejected' simply because he or she differs in such respects from most others in the class.

The factors affecting popularity may thus vary in different classes and different schools. That this was so was shown in a large-scale investigation by J. S. Coleman (1961), who looked at the factors influencing social status in teenagers in ten different schools in varying locations in the state of Chicago, USA. Coleman identified teenagers who were in the 'leading-crowd' or high-status clique in different classes. He found that prowess in sporting activities was usually the major factor affecting popularity in boys, though in one school having a car was very important, especially for popularity with girls. For girls, being a leader in activities and having nice clothes were important. For both boys and girls popularity with the opposite sex seemed an important component of being in the 'leading crowd'. Coleman argued that beauty was more important than brains for popularity in most high schools, and voiced concern that 'the adolescent subcultures in these schools exert a rather strong deterrent to academic achievement'. Given the individually competitive nature of academic achievement in the conventional school system. Coleman argued, it was difficult for a teenager to get social status and respect by intellectual achievement; whereas sporting or athletic achievement was displayed publicly and for the benefit of the whole class or school.

Critics have accused Coleman of exaggerating his case (Rutter et al., 1976). For example, even though athletic students were more popular than academic ones, the most popular of all were students who were both good scholars and good athletes. However, the issue was taken further by David Hargreaves (1967) in a study of social relations in a British secondary modern school for boys. This school had five streams in the fourth-year classes, of which Hargreaves observed all but the bottom, remedial stream. The A stream contained boys who would take CSE exams. They had largely positive views of the teachers, and popularity in this class correlated positively with academic achievement. In the lower streams, however, views of teachers and also of A stream 'swots' became increasingly negative. Popularity was not correlated with academic success, and the leaders of these cliques had anti-school values and were prone to delinquent behaviour. Hargreaves concluded that there were 'two subcultures' in the school, with radically different values. He thought the situation typical of many secondary schools among children approaching school-leaving age, and one exacerbated by streaming for academic ability.

## Aggression in Children

We have already mentioned children's aggressive behaviour several times, and its possible links to peer rejection. Many of the studies of childhood aggression have used observational methods. Some, mostly on preschool children, started in the late 1920s (see chapter 1). Like Parten's study of friendship discussed on p. 95, researchers systematically observed children unobtrusively in the nursery school. For example, Jersild and Markey (1935) observed conflicts in 54 children at three nursery schools. Many kinds of conflict behaviour were defined: for example *snatches* as 'takes or grabs toys or objects held, used, or occupied by another child; uses, tugs at, or pushes material away with hands or feet: all contacts with material which, if completed, would deprive the other child of the use and possession of material'; and *unfavourable remarks about persons* as comments like 'you're no good at it'; 'you don't do it right'; 'I don't like you'. Jersild and Markey recorded who was the aggressor and who the victim, what the outcome of the struggle was, and the role of the teacher. They found some decline in conflicts with age, and overall boys took part in more conflicts than girls. A follow-up was made of 24 children, after about 9 months. Conflicts had become more verbal, but individual differences between children in types and frequencies of conflict tended to be maintained. Very similar results were found in a recent observational study by Cummings et al. (1989); they reported that aggressive boys tended to stay aggressive between two and five years of age, even though the overall level of physical aggression declined over this period.

In another early study, Appel (1942) made observations in 14 different nursery schools. She delineated 15 kinds of adult responses to children's aggression. Five are 'ending techniques': *diverting; separating or removing; restraining; arbitrary decision; enforcing a rule*. Ten are 'teaching techniques': *explaining property rights; urging self-defence; suggesting a solution; suggesting children find solution; interpreting; encouraging friendly acts; making light of troubles or hurts; requiring good manners; disapproval; retaliation*. An evaluation of the effectiveness of these different techniques was made, by deciding whether the conflict continued or ended after the adult intervention. Some techniques were much more effective than others at ending the immediate conflict. Least effective was suggesting to the children that they find a solution themselves. Appel concluded that 'teachers should not intervene too readily in children's conflicts. Children will teach each other a great deal. Too much interference prevents self-reliance'.

Through the 1950s and early 1960s direct observation was neglected, and more constrained investigations in laboratories, often experimental in nature, were seen as the preferred method (see p. 4). Aggression was assessed by means of observing children punching inflatable dolls, and pressing buttons to supposedly deliver punishment to another child. These studies have subsequently been criticized as lacking ecological validity (p. 12).

By the late 1960s, direct observation had started to make a comeback. The impetus for his first came from ethology (see chapter 2). Blurton Jones observed the social behaviour of children in a UK nursery school (1967). Most aggressive behaviour occurred in the context of property fights. Another common action was a beating movement − an overarm blow with the palm side of the tightly clenched fist. Blurton Jones drew a clear distinction between aggressive behaviour, evidenced by beating or hitting at another with a frown or angry face, and rough-and-tumble play, where children chased and tackled each other, often smiling or laughing (see also chapter 6). These two kinds of behaviour can be confused because of their superficial similarity.

*Types and typologies of aggressive behaviour*

There are many types of aggressive behaviour, and it may be important to distinguish them. There are a number of ways in which distinctions can be drawn. These include *verbal* and *nonverbal* aggression (based on the presence or absence of verbal threats or insults); *instrumental* or *hostile* aggression (based on whether the distress or harm is inferred to be the primary intent of the act); and *individual* or *group* aggression (depending on whether more than one child attacks another).

The distinction based on intent was elaborated by Manning, Heron and Marshall (1978). They proposed a three-way classification. They defined 'specific hostility' as that which occurs in a specific situation which annoys or frustrates the aggressor: defending one's own rights, or keeping a toy, for example. The victim is almost incidental to the situation. In contrast, 'harassment' is more unprovoked, and is directed at a person. The aggressor gains nothing tangible from the act; the reward appears to be the victim's reaction. Finally, 'games hostility' is seen as rough, intimidating or restrictive activities which occur in a rough-and-tumble or fantasy game; for example very rough variants of rough-and-tumble, or bullying, intimidating or imprisoning against the victim's will in a fantasy game.

*Environmental effects on aggression*

Besides child characteristics, the nursery environment may encourage or discourage aggression. Smith and Connolly (1980) used observational methods, combined with an experimental design, to study this. They carried out a series of systematic environmental variations on two preschool playgroups, and made observations of the children's aggressive and social behaviour.

One study was on the effects of a 'free-play' nursery regime, compared with a 'structured activities' nursery regime. One playgroup in each condition was observed over an eight-month period. The two playgroups shared the same staff, premises, and equipment. Levels of aggression did not differ between the two groups initially. It did not change significantly in the children experiencing the free play regime, but aggression did increase steadily for the children in the structured activities regime (for all of Manning et al.'s categories of aggression), especially when the children were allowed back into free play in a final baseline assessment period. The authors concluded (similarly to Appel, as discussed earlier) that the decreased peer interaction which characterized the structured activities condition might have decreased the opportunities for the children to learn how to manage their own conflict situations without escalation.

Other studies examined the effects of numbers of children, space per child, and numbers of toys per child, by varying these systematically. A range of from 10 to 30 children in the group did not affect the level of aggression, provided that space and toys were increased in line with the number of children. Variations in space per child within a range of 7.0 to 2.3 sq.m./child did not affect aggression; but a further reduction to 1.4 sq.m./child did increase it, leading to a recommendation that 2.3 sq.m./child should be a minimum provision in preschool facilities. Finally, providing more toys per child did reduce the frequency of aggression between children, though it did also reduce the frequency of sharing and of children being together in large subgroups, due to the greater dispersal of the children amongst the available items of toys and equipment.

*Causes of high aggression*

For most children, while a certain amount of aggressive and assertive behaviour is normal, it is kept within reasonable bounds such that they are not disruptive of peer group activities and hence rejected by peers. However some children show high levels of aggression, often of a hostile or harassing nature, which can be quite stable over time and for which some adult intervention seems justified. If not dealt with at the time, such children who show persistent high aggressiveness through the school years are at greatly increased risk for later delinquency, anti-social and violent behaviour (Farrington, 1990).

There is considerable evidence that home circumstances can be important influences leading to aggressive and later anti-social behaviour. In a review, Patterson, DeBaryshe and Ramsey (1989) suggest that certain key aspects of parenting are involved. They argue that children who experience irritable and ineffective discipline at home, and poor parental monitoring of their activities, together with a lack of parental warmth, are particularly likely to become aggressive in peer groups and at school. Such children are experiencing aggressive means of solving disputes at home, and are not being given clear and effective guidance to do otherwise. Anti-social behaviour at school is likely to be linked to academic failure and peer rejection, according to this view; and in adolescence, especially if parental monitoring is lax, these young people are likely to be involved in deviant and delinquent peer groups. This hypothesis is shown in figure 4.5. (You may find it interesting to compare figure 4.5 with figure 3.1 and figure 4.4; all relate to different linked aspects of parenting and peer relations. Do you feel they can be linked together, or are some aspects in disagreement?)

Patterson's approach suggests that the social skills of *parenting* are very important in preventing anti-social behaviour; and his interventions focus on helping parents improve their child-management skills, for example via manuals and videotaped materials.

## Popularity, Leadership and Aggression

What is the relationship between popularity and leadership? How does aggressive behaviour relate to both of these? These are complex questions which have not yet

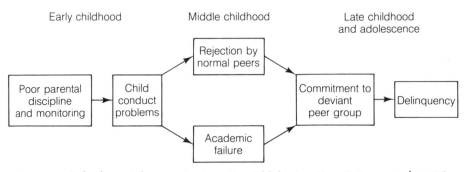

FIGURE 4.5   *A developmental progression for anti-social behaviour (from Patterson et al., 1989)*

been fully worked out. The answers may vary depending on the age of the child, the social context, and the way we define terms such as 'leadership' and 'aggression'.

One view is that aggressive children tend to be disliked and unpopular. We saw earlier that some American studies have linked 'rejected' sociometric status to disruptive behaviour with peers. Such studies usually make it clear that it is unprovoked aggression which causes such children to be actively disliked – they may push another child, or disrupt a game, with little or no reason or provocation. In their research Manning et al. (1978) found that specific hostility seemed to be characteristic of well-adjusted children (perhaps equivalent to 'popular' children in box figure 4.1.1), whereas the other forms of aggression were more characteristic of children who had poor peer relationships (perhaps like 'rejected' children in box figure 4.1.1).

Some children, however, are quite aggressive but not clearly disliked. These are the 'controversial' children in box figure 4.1.1. According to American researchers, such children are highly socially skilful and highly aggressive (box 4.1; Dodge and Richard, 1985). Peers describe them as good leaders, but also as starting fights – a pattern of behaviour which appeals to some peers but not to others. In other words, some children may use aggressive behaviour as a means of acquiring status in the peer group.

Again, some British studies confirm some aspects of this picture. One intensive study of playground behaviour in an Oxford first school and a middle school was made by Sluckin (1981). In the first school he describes how a boy called 'Neill' was known by his peers as the 'boss' of the playground. Neill was often observed in conflicts, although usually these were not overt fights (Neill was not particularly strong physically) but verbal conflicts by which Neill sought to enhance his prestige and manipulate social situations. Neill disliked losing, and would try to redefine or reinterpret situations so that it appeared he had won. For example, in a race with Ginny, where they finished at the same time, Neill cried out 'yes yes' (I'm the winner). Ginny called out 'draw', to which Neill replied 'no, it wasn't, you're just trying to make trouble'. In another example, playing football, Neill says 'I'm in goal, bagsee'. Nick replies 'no, I'm in goal'. Neill retorts 'no, John's in goal' and John goes in the goal. Here (perhaps avoiding a fight) Neill has kept the initiative and given the impression of being 'in charge' even though he did not get his own way entirely. Neill had a high dominance status in the playground, and was clearly a leader of sorts, but he does not seem to have been especially popular. His leadership was often distruptive, since he always insisted on winning games.

Another example comes from Hargreave's (1967) work, discussed earlier. In the delinquent clique of the lower streams a boy called 'Clint' was the best fighter and was described as the 'cock of the school'. Although an intelligent boy, he had rebelled against the academic values of the school and become the dominant member of the delinquent subgroup. He had done so by his reputation as a fighter. As his peers reported, 'he beat up a prefect last year ... Clint was hurt an' all, but he won'. His reputation was maintained because no one challenged him: 'Clint must be the best 'cos Don won't have him a scrap. Clint's the best fighter. Then Don comes next. They've never had a fight, but Clint's the best fighter 'cos Don won't have him.' Also, Clint's confidence was displayed publicly: 'People are afraid of you if you go swaggering around the playground threatening everybody.' However, although the leader of this clique, Clint was apparently too bigheaded and indiscriminately aggressive to be really popular: 'Everyone knows Clint 'cos he's cock, but he's not popular, 'cos no one likes him, you know what I mean? I don't see why he should go round bullying people like he does just 'cos you can fight them. Taking money off them and all that. He's bigheaded.' In fact, on a sociometric test of friendship, Clint received six choices, but Don, the second ranking 'cock', received 11. Don was more popular because he did not abuse his power: 'Don's smashing to get on with. You've no need to be frightened of him 'cos he won't touch you.' Whereas Clint would seem to be 'controversial' by the typology of box figure 4.1.1, Don would be 'popular'. Both are high on dominance status.

### Dominance

The quotes from the playground observations of Sluckin and Hargreaves suggest that school children can rank others for 'dominance' or 'fighting strength' in a consistent way. Several psychologists have confirmed that this can be done reliably from about 4 or 5 years of age onwards (Sluckin and Smith, 1977). They have used the concept of a 'dominance hierarchy' in children's groups, just as it has been used in the study of animal social groups (chapter 2). Winning fights is one criterion of dominance, but more generally it is taken as getting one's own way or influencing others. Thus, the concept is close to that of 'leadership'.

While some of this research has involved asking children for their rankings of peers, other researchers have used direct observation of which individuals win conflicts. Strayer and Strayer (1976), observing children in a Canadian preschool, separated out three kinds of conflict behaviours: 'threat–gesture', 'physical attack'; and 'objection/position struggles'. They then examined the usefulness of a dominance hierarchy for each of these three kinds of behaviour, separately, whenever there was a clear winner or loser. Strayer and Strayer looked at the linearity of the hierarchies (basically, how many reversals of expected position there were) to assess how descriptively useful the concept of a hierarchy was in each case. The values were very high, though slightly lower for 'object/position struggles' than for the other two behaviours.

Savin-Williams made studies of dominance formation in groups of American teenagers (aged 10–16 years), mostly previously unacquainted, who came together in five-week summer camps. In one report (Savin-Williams, 1976) he studied intensively one cabin group of six boys aged 12 and 13. It took about three days for a stable, ordered hierarchy to emerge; it then remained very consistent through the duration of the camp. Observational measures of dominance correlated highly ($r = 0.90$, $p < 0.05$) with a sociometric measure from the children themselves. The most frequently observed dominance behaviours were verbal ridicule (seen 235 times), giving a verbal command which was obeyed (seen 190 times) and ignoring or refusing to comply with another's command (seen 158 times). The most dominant boy also was usually the leader in hiking and athletics, and was well liked. However the least dominant boy, quiet, serious, but friendly, was also popular.

Another study (Savin-Williams, 1980) was of four groups of five girls (aged 12–14) at summer camp. Again dominance hierarchies formed, although they did not seem as clear-cut as in boy's groups, perhaps because girls more often formed smaller groups (pairs or threesomes). Verbal ridicule was again the most frequently observed indicator of dominance. The position in the dominance heirarchy correlated significantly with ratings of leadership. However, Savin-Williams distinguished between 'maternal leaders' who were perceived by peers as a source of security and support, and 'antagonists' who imposed themselves on others.

A related concept to that of social dominance has been that of 'attention structure'. This refers to the amount of visual attention (looking) directed to individuals by others in the group. Several studies have examined the relationships between dominance, and attention structure, in preschool groups. The correlations are generally quite high; children look a lot at other dominant children to see what they are up to. However the two constructs are not interchangeable. Not surprisingly, children also look a lot at their friends, irrespective of dominance.

Related to attention-structure is the phenomenon of 'showing-off' behaviour, discussed by Hold-Cavell (1985). These are ways by which a child can attract other's attention The most frequent forms she observed in a German kindergarten included calling out loudly to others, singing loudly, climbing on chairs, jumping around in the room, and wearing unusual headgear. Showing-off behaviour was found to correlate significantly with attention structure and with physical aggression. Hold-Cabell suggests that showing-off may serve as one strategy for getting high regard in the group.

*Summary*

A number of studies seem to present converging findings. Children are often popular, and some are leaders, because they are socially skilled and mature and, although they stand up for themselves, are not gratuitously aggressive. Another way of being a leader, or achieving high dominance status, is to be a good fighter (at least in certain groups, see also p. 120; and perhaps more in older children and in boys). This is a more 'controversial' way, which may not bring true popularity with all one's peers. High aggression without the social skill to go with it, however, leads to unpopularity and 'rejection'.

## Bullying in Schools

Bullying or harassment emerged as one of the three types of aggressive behaviour defined by Manning et. al (1978). Bullying can be carried out by one child, or a group. It is usually a repeated action against a particular victim. Also, the child(ren) doing the bullying is generally thought of as being stronger, or perceived as stronger; at least, the victim does not feel him/herself to be in a position to retalliate effectively. While some bullying takes the form of hitting, pushing, taking money, it can also involve teasing, telling stories, and social exclusion.

Bullying and victimization in schools has become a topic of considerable public concern in many countries. Research in western Europe suggests that bullying is quite pervasive in schools, and probably to a greater extent than most teachers and parents realize, since many victims keep quiet about it. It is difficult to observe bullying, for obvious reasons. It is often assessed by means of an anonymous questionnaire, which children or young people can fill in confidentially.

*The occurence of bully/victim problems*

A study of pupils in the South Yorkshire area of the UK showed that about 1 child in 10 reported being bullied 'sometimes', and about 1 in 15 'several times a week'. Altogether about 1 child in 6 seemed to be experiencing a bullying problem. Similarly about 1 child in 15 admitted to bullying others, at least 'sometimes' (Yates and Smith, 1989). These and other studies suggest that bully/victim problems in British schools are considerable, and similar figures have been reported from Dublin in Eire (O'Moore, 1989), and from Spain (Garcia and Perez, 1989). The incidence seems to be somewhat less in Scandinavian countries such as Norway (see box 4.2), but still considerable enough to justify remedial action.

Most of the children or young people who report being bullied say that it takes the form of teasing; but about a third report other forms such as hitting or kicking, or (more occasionally) extortion of money. These latter may seem the more serious forms, but some 'teasing', especially that related to some disability, or which takes the form of racial or sexual harassment, can be very hurtful to the victim.

It is a fairly consistent finding that boys report, and are reported as, bullying more than girls; whereas boys and girls report being bullied about equally. Girls' bullying more usually takes the form of behaviours such as social exclusion, or spreading nasty rumours, rather than the physical behaviours used more by boys. Victims are more likely to report being alone at break time, and to feel less well liked at school; having some good friends can be a strong protective factor against being bullied. Only a minority of victims report that they have talked to a teacher or anyone at home about it, or that a teacher or parent has talked to them about it.

The more serious forms of bullying, at least, can have very serious consequences. For children being bullied, their lives are made miserable often for some considerable period of time. Already probably lacking close friends at school, they are likely to lose confidence and self-esteem even further. Research by Gilmartin (1987), using retrospective data, suggests that these children and young people are at increased risk for relationship difficulties later in life, especially intimate heterosexual relationships.

Such long-term effects can be brought out by in depth case study interviews. The following extract, from a woman aged 28 who experienced being bullied through much of her school career, and was now engaged to be married, illustrates such long–term effects:

*Do you feel that's left a residue with you … what do you feel the effects are?*
… I'm quite insecure, even now … I won't believe that people like me. … and also I'm frightened of children … and this is a problem. He [fiancé] would like a family. I would not and I don't want a family because I'm frightened of children and suppose they don't like me? … those are things that have stayed with me. It's a very unreasonable fear but it is there and it's very real.

Those who bully others are learning that power-assertive and sometimes violent behaviour can be used to get their own way. We saw earlier how children who are aggressive at school are more likely to be involved in criminal activity later. A follow-up by Olweus (1989) of Norwegian secondary school pupils up to age 24, found that former school bullies were nearly four times more likely than non-bullies to have had three or more court convictions.

### Intervention strategies

A lot can be done to reduce bully/victim problems in schools (Besag, 1989; Tattum and Herbert, 1990). The most extensive intervention has been carried out in Norway, and is described in box 4.2. Other countries, notably the USA and Japan, are developing programmes about bullying in school. In the UK, the Kidscape organisation (1986) has particularly directed attention to role-playing techniques, and to 'bully courts' in which a children's court would arbitrate on bullying incidents. Schools can ensure that incidents are treated seriously, and recorded; and that playgrounds and corridors are effectively supervised. Cooperative group work in the classroom may also be helpful (Herbert, 1989).

## Popularity, Status and Conformity

As children get older they become more independent of parents and spend more time with peers, both in and out of school. Thus, the norms and values of their peer group are likely to become increasingly important, while those of parents may become less so. For example, a young child usually wears clothes chosen by parents. As older children begin to exert more choice over what clothes they wear, they are likely to choose clothes of a similar style to others in their peer group. If jeans are 'in', or short skirts are 'in', these are likely to be selected; similarly with shoes, hair style, choice of hobbies, ways of speaking, favourite pop stars, and so on. Imitating the attitudes and behaviours of other in a group is called 'conformity'. Children may feel a pressure to conform to peer group values or interest, to avoid feeling left out or being rejected. For example, in Hargreave's (1967) study, 'A' stream boys usually conformed to a set of values involving being tidily dressed, not wearing jeans in school, not smoking and having an 'interesting hobby' such as chess, table tennis, cycling, fishing or stamp collecting. Lower stream boys tended to conform to a set of values in favour of wearing jeans, having long hair, smoking, visiting cinemas and dance halls, and preferring long-haired pop groups. Thus, while the pressure to conform is probably very widespread, the actual values children conform to will vary in time and place.

Several studies have been made to try to assess whether such pressures to conform change with age. Most have used laboratory experiments. In one such study (Costanzo and Shaw, 1966) children and young people between 7 and 21 years of age were given a test of conformity whereby the subject looks at a display of three lines of differing length, with another line equal in length to the middle one of the others, placed nearby as a comparison. He or she is asked which of the three lines is the same length as the comparison line. It is fairly obvious what the answer is, but the subject is put off by first hearing three same-sex peers choose one of the longer or shorter lines (these peers had been asked to do this by the experimenter). Over many trials, the number of times that the subject chooses the wrong line so as to agree with his or her peers is taken as a 'conformity score'. The results of this experiment were that conformity was found to increase up to early adolescence, then decline again.

The lines task is of course an artificial one. In another study (Berndt, 1979), American students aged 9–18 years were presented with hypothetical situations in which peers suggest doing something the child is unwilling to do. Some of the hypothetical suggestions are for antisocial behaviours, such as cheating or stealing. One of Berndt's examples is:

> You are with a couple of your best friends on Halloween. They're going to soap windows, but you're not sure whether you should or not. Your friends all say you should, because there's no way you could get caught. What would you really do?

Some of the hypothetical suggestions were about neutral activities such as choice of sports, or places to eat (for example, peers might ask a child to go bowling when he or she wanted to go to the cinema). Finally, some suggestions concerned positive or 'prosocial' activities, such as helping other children or doing charitable work (for example, peers might ask a child to help his brother with homework, when he wanted to visit a sick child). The results are shown in figure 4.6.

As with the previous study, conformity with peers increased at first, then decreased with age. This was much more marked with conformity to antisocial peer suggestions which, while less likely than in neutral or prosocial situations, clearly peaked at around 14 years. Conformity to antisocial suggestions was greater for boys than for girls. In a follow-up study, the findings shown in figure 4.6 were

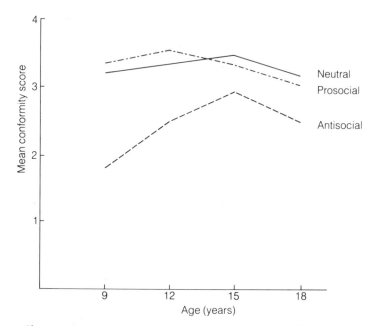

FIGURE 4.6    *Changes in mean conformity score with age for prosocial, neutral and antisocial behaviour (from Berndt, 1979)*

replicated on a different sample of children. In addition, using similar measures of hypothetical conformity but to parents, it was found that children conformed more to parents than peers at 8 years. However, conformity to parents declined with age, so that there was little difference between conformity to parents and peers by 14 years.

Psychologists have examined many different influences on the extent to which people conform. One relevant to us here is status in the peer group. Some studies have found that conformity is highest amongst those of intermediate status in a group, or dominance hierachy. For example, Harvey and Consalvi (1960) measured conformity amongst cliques of delinquent boys. Conformity was lowest in the group leaders, and also in those of lowest status. Perhaps children of intermediate status are particularly anxious to remain accepted by their group. Group leaders need not conform in this way – they can set the trend; whereas very low status children have little to lose from not conforming.

### Self-concept and self-esteem

Investigators of children's social relationships are often concerned with how children see themselves, and how they think that others see them (a topic we return to in chapters 5 and 8). A general term for how someone thinks about themselves is self-concept, or identity. This can refer to all aspects of the self – appearance, personality, ability, as well as gender, nationality, ethnic group. Some aspects of one's self-concept are evaluative; we all compare ourselves with others and think that we are good at some things, not so good at other things. These evaluations we make are called by psychologists self-esteem.

It is possible to measure self-esteem in children by means of questionnaires. For example, in the Harter Self-Perception Profile for Children (Harter, 1985), designed for 8- to 13-years-olds, children read a series of paried items such as

> some kids find it hard to make friends
> BUT
> some kids find it's pretty easy to make friends

They decide which statement is true for them, and whether it is 'sort of true' or 'really true'. There are 36 such statements, and the answers give scores for the child's own perception of their 'global self-worth', as well as for more specific aspects of self-esteem such as scholastic competence, social acceptance, athletic competence, physical appearance, and behavioural conduct.

## Teachers as Models

What influence do teachers have on their pupils? In this section we shall look not so much at the academic acheivement of young people as at the social context in which learning takes place. Why do some children thrive in the school setting? Why do others internalize a feeling of inadequacy and inferiority? Are working class children at a disadvantage? How do teachers respond to children from ethnic minorities? Does teaching style affect the learning and behaviour of children in the class room?

*Teaching style*

One approach to this issue focuses on the teacher's style in the classroom. Teaching style has been variously categorized, but one major distinction has been made between a 'formal', 'teacher-centred' or 'traditional' style on the one hand, and an 'informal', 'child-centred' or 'progressive' style on the other.

A classic study by Lewin et al. (1939) provided useful insights into the effects on the behaviour of young people of different kinds of leadership style. In their study, 11-year-old boys, involved in activities such as making *papier mâché* masks, were allocated at random into three groups, each with a different type of leader. The authoritarian leaders directed activities, were highly critical of work, kept distance from the boys, made all the decisions and gave few explanations about mask-making or how it should be carried out. The democratic leaders, by contrast, talked about the aims of the course, encouraged participation by the boys in decision-making, allowed them to choose their working groups and facilitated dialogue and discussion during classes. *Laissez-faire* leaders allowed the boys to do as they pleased, gave little guidance or direction about the mask-making activity and provided scarcely any feedback on the quality or quantity of output.

The boys responded very differently to the three leadership styles. Classes run in an authoritarian style displayed more tension and aggressive behaviour, there was more damage to materials and a general feeling of dissatisfaction among the participants. Output was high if the leader was present, but discipline lapsed when he left the room. In the democratically run classes there was much less hostility, more group satisfaction and a high level of enthusiasm for the project. Productivity was lower than in the authoritarian class room but the quality was better and showed more imaginativeness on the part of the boys. When the leader left the room the boys continued to work on their masks; they seemed to be self-motivated and to rely less on direction from the teacher. The *laissez-faire* group fared worst of all. There was a great deal of apathy among the class, the productivity was low and the quality of masks poor. The boys were not happy working in these circumstances and seemed confused by the lack of direction. This approach was clearly not satisfactory by any standards.

The authoritarian approach was most successful in terms of sheer quantity of output, while the democratic approach was less efficient in terms of output but the gains were apparent in the creativity and enthusiasm of the boys. Furthermore, boys in the democratic group showed the capacity to continue working even when not being supervised.

This experiment took place in a youth club setting and was concerned with a specific task. Can lessons be drawn from theses findings for teachers and pupils in normal school settings? A more recent study (Bennett, 1976) plotted the relationship between teaching styles and pupils attainment in British schools. Bennett aimed to explore the strengths and weaknesses of the range of teaching styles from formal, teacher-centred classrooms at one end of the continuum to informal, child-centred ones at the other. Formal teachers, in his study, were those who dominated, controlled and directed their pupils; lessons were teacher-centred, criticism of the teacher was discouraged and there was a low noise level in the classroom. These teachers tended to emphasize skills and academic attainment. Informal teachers, by contrast, were child-centred and encouraged children to take responsibility for their own learning. There was more interaction and communication among members of the class, questioning and inquiry were common. These teachers were more likely to stress the value of self-expression and creativity.

Bennett found that children in the formal classrooms attained more in reading and mathematical skills than children in informal settings. Surprisingly, the children in informal classrooms did not perform any better on a test of imaginative writing than those in formal classrooms. Further, he found that anxious or insecure children felt more threatened in informal classrooms since, in his view, they could not cope with the emphasis on autonomy and self-directed learning, and were more likely to be distracted by the time-wasting activity that was more in evidence in such classrooms. Thus Bennett's study did not confirm the theory that the informal teaching style was most supportive of social and emotional development in children, although some timid children did seem to become more *socially* at ease in the informal classrooms.

Bennett concluded that his findings indicated a complex network of interaction effects between pupil personality, behaviour and teaching style. In some areas of behaviour teaching style had a general influence – for example, on the relative incidence of chatting and playing in formal and informal classrooms. In others, children's approach to their work for example, there was a clear interaction between the personality of the child and teaching style. In formal classrooms conformist pupils tackled work alone while anxious pupils consulted peers; in informal classrooms this trend was reversed.

Bennett's study produced bitter debates between advocates of traditional, formal teaching methods and those who advocate progressive, child-centred methods. The debate continues today and will not be easily resolved. Examination subjects are more likely to be taught in a formal, teacher-centred way; moreover pupils expect this style of teaching and tend to feel threatened by its absence. Areas of the curriculum which emphasize creativity, social skills and personal development are more likely to be taught in an informal way. But the distinction between the two approaches is by no means clear-cut.

*Teacher expectations*

We have looked at teaching style and the effect it might have on pupils. A second approach focuses on the expectations and even prejudices which teachers bring to the class situation. These expectations, it is argued, which are reflected in the pupil–teacher interactions of the classroom, produce differential responses in the children, thus fulfilling the teacher's predictions. For example, if the teacher believes in the academic potential of a child and responds positively to that child, the child will come to behave like a successful pupil and fulfil the teacher's expectations.

In the literature on this subject the terms 'self-fulfilling prophecy' and 'teacher expectation' are widely used. It is assumed that the self concept is a social product which arises out of interaction with others, and is influenced by the interpretation which the individual makes of the perceptions which other people have of him or her.

Let us look at two statements from a girl in an inner city comprehensive about the effect which the expectations of two teachers has on her capacity to learn and on her feelings about herself.

Mr F. – he's great. He treats you as if you were a person. He gives us the responsibility for our own learning. We feel as if he trusts us.

Mrs S., she's like Hitler. Her voice is so stern it makes you want to die of embarrassment. She doesn't trust us. She makes you feel stupid so you are afraid to open your mouth.

It is clear that this girl behaves quite differently with the two teachers. With Mr F., who believes that his pupils can take initiative and be responsible for their own learning, she responds with enthusiasm, does extra work on her project at home and feels very positive about her learning experience; she has fulfilled his expectation of her. By contrast, she perceives that Mrs S sees her as stupid and inarticulate; in turn, she behaves in this way and again fulfils her teacher's expectations of her.

It is a widely held belief that the personal factors, attitudes and beliefs which a teacher brings to the classroom affect not only the intellectual development of children but also their personal and social development. However, the area is extremely difficult to investigate. The 'hidden curriculum' of the classroom, as it has sometimes been called, is an elusive phenomenon which the very presence of a researcher can destroy. This probably explains why the research studies there are have come up with conflicting findings. In a famous and controversial study, Rosenthal and Jacobson (1968) investigated the extent to which the performance of children at school reflected their teachers' expectations of them. Their subjects, disadvantaged children aged 5–10 years, were given intelligence tests. It was suggested to teachers that the tests would identify those students who would be 'academic spurters', making rapid intellectual gains during the next academic year. The names of these children were given to the teachers. In reality the names of the spurters were selected at random from the class and the only difference between the experimental and control subjects was thus in the minds of the teachers, who now had higher expectations of them. When Rosenthal and Jacobson retested the children after eight months, they reported that the IQs of the spurters were significantly higher than those of the controls. Furthermore, the teachers described the experimental children as more curious, happier, more interesting and livelier than controls.

Rosenthal and Jacobson (1968) hypothesised that the teacher may have communicated to the children of the experimental group that she expected improved intellectual performance by what she said, by how and when she said it, by her facial expressions, postures, and perhaps by her touch. In other words, the 'reality' which the teachers made through their positive expectations of the children became a reality for the children in their increased sense of self-worth and confidence.

The Rosenthal and Jacobson study stimulated widespread reaction in educational circles. At one extreme teachers were angry that they should be portrayed as being so easily biased. At the other extreme, the study seemed to provide confirmation of the view that children from certain backgrounds or with certain characteristics were made to fail by the very nature of the classroom environment. However, a closer look at the data revealed serious flaws in the research design of the experiment; for example, some of the tests had been administered by teachers and some by researchers so that test conditions were not standardized; the norms which were used were not adequate for younger children in the sample or for children of low socioeconomic status. Repeat analysis of the data by Elashoff et al. (1971) showed no treatment effect on children in grades 3 and 4 (8 and 11 year olds). Significantly, too, in a follow-up interview the teachers could in many cases not remember the names of the 'spurters'.

Some later studies have in fact failed completely to replicate the expectancy effect (Claiborn, 1969; Wilkins and Glock, 1973). But despite criticisms research into effects of teacher expectations has continued. This is probably because the concept seems credible and there is widespread belief in the idea that teachers, like other significant persons in a child's environment, play an important role not only in a child's capacity to learn, but also in the development of social factors such as self-esteem and confidence. One researcher, for example, (Kehle, 1974), has found that physical attractiveness of children can be a factor that seems to influence the number and quality of verbal contacts made by teachers.

Other studies have shown more precisely how teachers favour some pupils at the expense of others by, for example, making allowances for mistakes, or facilitating and encouraging some pupils, while others are ridiculed, put down or ignored. An early study (Becker, 1952) of 60 teachers in Chicago schools found that teachers favoured those children who were cooperative, hard-working and docile; these children also were usually from middle class backgrounds. Working class children, by contrast, were more often perceived as difficult, hostile, lazy and stupid. Children's backgrounds were thus found to be an important factor in the judgements which teachers made of them (see also chapter 14). Brophy and Good (1970) found that high-achieving first grade children got more praise than low-achieving children. The teachers were more likely to praise them, to prompt them when they made a mistake and to build up their confidence through praise. Low-achieving children received a higher proportion of discouraging or critical responses. In the words of Brophy and Good (p. 373), 'the nature of this differential treatment is such as to encourage the children to begin to respond in ways which would confirm teacher expectations'.

There is some evidence to support the idea that the pattern of pupil–teacher and pupil–pupil interaction influences how both teachers and pupils perceive the individual pupil in the class. Nash (1973) observed that primary school pupils who had been judged unfavourably by their teachers were more likely to have a low opinion of their ability to succeed in the school system, and other studies (Barker-Lunn, 1970; Ferri, 1972) have found a relationship between the self-concept of the child and the judgements which teachers make of them. But Ferri also found that low ability children with a low self-concept often developed higher self-esteem when they transferred to secondary school, and a number of studies have found that older children do not necessarily respond in the same way to teacher expectations.

In a study of working class boys in a British midlands comprehensive school, Willis (1977) found what he called 'an alternative culture of dignity'. He argued that in many British schools children are valued for their intellectual abilities. Those who cannot match up to this standard are judged as inferior, as the terms 'low ability', 'less able', 'non-academic' etc. imply. Thus many children in this framework are bound to be labelled as failures. As a defence of their own self-worth, he argued, some pupils in his sample developed an alternative set of values. This 'counter-culture' stresses qualities such as masculinity and aggressiveness; academic boys were despised and labelled as effeminate; fighting and causing trouble were valued as positive virtues. As Willis wrote:

> There is a positive joy in fighting, in causing fights through intimidation, in talking about fighting, and about the tactics of the whole fight situation. Many important cultural values are expressed through fighting. Masculine hubris, dramatic display, the solidarity of the group, the importance of quick, clear and not over-moral thought, comes out time and again.

The traditional explanation for this behaviour is that working class boys behave aggressively because they bring these values and behaviour patterns from home; they become a part of the counter-culture because the values of their background are incongruent with the values of the school. But Willis puts forward an alternative explanation. The aggressiveness and rowdy behaviour appear only as a defence against the assault on their dignity which constant failure provides; the boys turn to these values because the school system undermines their own feelings of self-worth by labelling them as failures.

Hargreaves (1982) explored the implications of such a hypothesis. (We have discussed Hargreaves' (1967) work on peer group networks earlier.) He suggested that for pupils who have a traditional set of working class values to fall back on, the counter-culture of dignity emerges in the form which Willis described. However, he also considered the problems facing low ability young people who do not have this pool of values on which to draw. These children, belonging neither in the culture of the school, unless they accept the label of failure, nor in the aggressive counter-culture, may, Hargreaves suggested be the ones who withdraw psychologically. Deprived of the physical outlets which their more aggressive, acting-out peers possess, they may be the ones who are most damaged by the school system, since they lack dignity in any context. In addition, they are more likely to be overlooked by teachers since the withdrawn child presents less of an immediate threat to the organization of a lesson.

Willis (1977) suggested that an area of agreement between members of the counter-culture and teachers was that both groups felt resentful of ethnic minority pupils. What effect does this have on black pupils – on their self-concept, on their aspirations and perceptions of themselves as learners? In her book *The Education of the Black Children in Britain*, Stone (1981) argued that Afro-Caribbean pupils reciprocate these negative feelings towards teachers. Furthermore, she claims that as far as Afro-Caribbean parents and children are concerned, 'the schools do not even begin to offer anything like equal opportunity; they [the children] suffer all the disadvantages of the urban working class and the additional ones of prejudice and racism'. This issue is dicussed further in chapter 14.

Clearly, there are no quick solutions to the difficulties engendered by low expectations on the part of teachers towards certain types of pupil. Teachers, like all human beings, form impressions of others, and research work indicates how important it is to be aware of the effects these have on children. Perhaps the research findings can be used to help teachers and other significant adults to get the best out of young people by setting them realistic goals and then encouraging them to attain them. Teachers need to be aware of the factors identified in research studies as being influential in the formation of the self-concept of the growing child, so as to have some control over the cycle which can lead to success or failure in the school context.

## Further reading

A readable introduction to peer relationships is Z. Rubin 1980: *Children's Friendships*. Glasgow: Fontana. A more advanced collection is S. R. Asher and J. M. Gottman (eds) 1981: *The Development of Children's Friendships*. Cambridge: Cambridge University Press. A fascinating account of the social life of a school playground is in A. Sluckin 1981: *Growing up in the Playground*. London: Routledge & Kegan Paul.

D. Tattum and G. Herbert 1990: *Bullying: A Positive Response*. Cardiff: South Glamorgan Institute of Higher Education, is a short booklet for parents and teachers. A more comprehensive survey is V. Besag 1989: *Bullies and Victims in Schools*, Milton Keynes: Open University Press.

Interesting case studies of teacher–pupil relationships are provided by R. Nash 1973: *Classrooms Observed*. London: Routledge and Kegan Paul. The experience of schooling from the perspective of the black child is put in M. Stone 1981: *The Education of the Black Child*. Glasgow: Fontana.

## Discussion points

1   Are friendships important for children? How can we find out?

2   Why are some children popular, and others not?

3   What would be the best ways of tackling bullying in schools?

4   How does teaching style affect pupil behaviour?

5   How could teachers overcome negative expectations they may have of certain children?

## Practical exercises

1   Ask children of different ages what they mean by 'a friend', or 'friendship'. Write down their answers, and look for changes with age. Compare with the trends shown in table 4.1.

2   Observe a group of preschool children in a nursery school or playgroup. What kinds of conflicts occur? Are certain children consistent winners (or losers)? How do adults intervene, and how effective are they?

3   Interview young people from different social class or ethnic minority backgrounds about their experiences at school. How do their responses relate to research findings on teacher attitudes and self-concept?

# Box 4.1

# Dimensions and types of social status: a cross-age perspective

Two studies were carried out in this investigation of the types of social status in children's groups, and the kinds of behaviours which correlated with them.

In the first study approximately 100 children at each of three age levels (8, 11 and 14 years) were interviewed at two schools in North Carolina, USA. Each child was seen individually, and asked to name the three classmates whom he or she liked most, and the three classmates whom he or she liked least. Then, he or she was asked to name the three children who best fitted each of 24 behavioural descriptions, such as 'disrupts the group' or 'attractive physically'. The interview was repeated 12 weeks later to check that the data were reliable.

The scores used were the total nominations each child received for each of the 26 questions (liked most, liked least, and 24 behavioural descriptions). The correlations between the liked most and liked least scores, and some of the behavioural descriptions, are shown in box table 4.1.1. (The results were similar when each age group was treated separately.) The interesting thing about these results is that different behavioural descriptions correlate significantly with the 'liked most' and 'liked least' ratings. The two measures are not simply opposites of each other. 'Liked most' children tend to be supportive, cooperative, leaders and attractive physically; 'liked least' children tend to be disruptive, aggressive and snobbish.

If 'liked most' is not just the opposite of 'liked least', the researchers argued that it made sense to think of them as independent measures (in fact the correlation between them was

| POPULAR | CONTROVERSIAL |
|---|---|
| High on 'liked most' | High on 'liked most' |
| Low on 'liked least' | High on 'liked least' |
| AVERAGE | |
| NEGLECTED | REJECTED |
| Low on 'liked most' | Low on 'liked most' |
| Low on 'liked least' | High on 'liked least' |

BOX FIGURE 4.1.1   *Five types of sociometric status*

Based on material in J. D. Coie, K. A. Dodge and H. Coppotelli 1982: *Development Psychology*, 18, 557–70

BOX TABLE 4.1.1  *Correlations between nominations for 'most-liked' and 'least-liked' and behavioural descriptions for 311 children aged 8 to 14*

|  | Liked most | Liked least |
|---|---|---|
| Supports peers | 0.63* | −0.24* |
| Leads peers | 0.51* | −0.08* |
| Cooperates with peers | 0.51* | −0.31* |
| Attractive physically | 0.57* | −0.25* |
| Remains calm | 0.43* | −0.28* |
| Defends self in arguments | 0.37* | 0.03 |
| Acts shy | −0.12 | −0.05 |
| Gets rejected by peers | −0.28* | 0.30* |
| Acts snobbish | −0.04 | 0.66* |
| Starts fights | −0.02 | 0.70* |
| Gets into trouble with teacher | −0.03 | 0.71* |
| Disrupts the group | −0.07 | 0.78* |

* $p < 0.001$.

−0.21, which is quite a small value). In that case, there are four possible status outcomes shown in box figure 4.1.1 and mentioned in the text above (see p. 99) with a fifth if 'average' children are included.

In the second study the differences between these five status groups were examined more closely. More children of the same ages were interviewed at the same schools over the next two years. They were asked to nominate the three peers whom they liked most, liked least and who best fitted the descriptions 'cooperates', 'disrupts', 'shy', 'fights', 'seeks help' and 'leader'. Out of a total of 848 children, 486 were selected who clearly fitted one of the five social status groups. It was then possible to calculate the average 'behavioural profile' for children of each social status in terms of the six behavioural descriptions obtained from

BOX TABLE 4.1.2  *Behavioural profiles associated with five types of sociometric status in 486 children*

|  | Leads peers | Cooperates | Acts shy | Seeks help | Fights | Disrupts group |
|---|---|---|---|---|---|---|
| Popular | HIGH | HIGH |  | Low | Low | Low |
| Controversial | HIGH |  | Low | High | HIGH | HIGH |
| Rejected | Low | LOW |  | HIGH | HIGH | HIGH |
| Neglected | Low | Low |  | Low | Low | Low |
| Average |  |  |  |  |  |  |

Use of upper case denotes a stronger difference than lower case; a blank cell implies the score was near the average for all the children.

peers. Box table 4.1.2 shows the results. Children who lead in a cooperative way are 'popular'. Children who lead but fight and are disruptive are 'controversial', liked by some but disliked by others. Disruptive children who lack any cooperative or leadership skills are 'rejected'. Children who lack cooperative or leadership skills and are not aggressive either are 'neglected'. The pattern of results was similar across the three ages, for both sexes, and for different ethnic groups.

The strengths of this study are the large pool of participants and the attempt to make important distinctions in types of sociometric status. The authors speculate, for example, that 'controversial' children, high on both leadership and aggression, may become leaders of delinquent peer groups in adolesence. A weakness is that no direct observational measures were taken; we do not know that 'rejected' children really fight a lot, for example, only that other children (who do not like them) say they do. Some subsequent work (see p. 100) has linked the status groups to more direct behavioural measures.

## Box 4.2

# Bully/victim problems among schoolchildren: basic facts and effects of a school based intervention programme

Norway has seen the most active research and intervention on problems of school bullying. Local and then nationwide surveys of the extent of the problem revealed that some 9 per cent of the school population were fairly regular victims of bullying, and some 7–8 per cent engaged in bullying others. Often, these children and young people did not tell teachers or parents about their involvement in bullying.

In 1982 two young people in Norway took their own lives because of bullying at school. This and the associated media interest and public concern, combined with the previous research findings, led to the Ministry of Education supporting a nationwide Norwegian Campaign Against Bullying. This commenced on 1 October 1983.

The intervention programme, aimed at students, teachers, and parents, had a number of components:

- a 32-page booklet for school personnel, giving detailed suggestions about what teachers and school can do to counteract bullying
- a 4-page folder with information and advice for parents
- a 25-minute video cassette showing episodes from everyday lives of two bullied children, a 10-year-old boy and a 14-year-old girl. Child actors were used in making this video, which could be used as a basis for class discussion.
- a short inventory or survey given to pupils, to ascertain the level and nature of bully/victim problems in each school.

In an evaluation carried out by Dan Olweus in the Bergen area of Norway, the effects of this intervention programme were assessed in 42 primary and junior high schools, with some 2,500 students. Children only start school at 7 years in Norway; these students were aged around 11 and 14 years. A cohort-sequential design was used (cf. pp. 7–8 and figure 1.2), and is illustrated in box figure 4.2.1. The four grade(age) cohorts started at grades 4, 5, 6 and 7 (ages 11, 12, 13 and 14) in May 1983, shortly before the intervention campaign was started. Measurements were taken at this point (time 1), and again in May 1984 (time 2), and May 1985 (time 3).

Based on material in D. Olweus, in K. Rubin and D. Pepler (eds), *The Development and Treatment of Childhood Aggression*. Hillsdale, N.J.: Erlbaum, 1989.

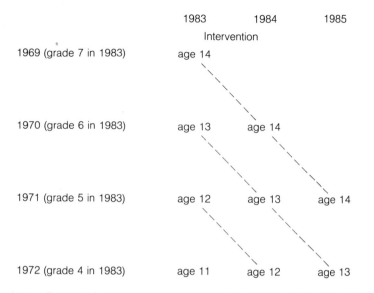

BOX FIGURE 4.2.1   *Design of cohort-sequential study of effects of an intervention pro-gramme against school bullying. Year of assessment is shown horizontally, and cohort (year of birth/initial grade level) vertically. The approximate ages of each sample of children from each cohort and at each year of study are shown in years*

This cohort-sequential design was important for interpreting any results. Suppose that there was some improvement in bullying problems with time. This could be due to the intervention programme; or it could be due to age or historical changes. Usually in a study of this kind we would control for these by comparing the results for other children who did not experience the intervention, or 'treatment'. However, as the intervention campaign was on a national basis, there could not be any 'no-treatment' control groups. What could be done was to make 'time-lagged contrasts between age-equivalent groups'. For example, the children who were grade 6 at time 2, and had experienced one year of intervention, could be compared with those who were grade 6 at time 1, before the intervention started. Later, the same comparison could be made with children who were grade 6 at time 3, after two years of intervention. Altogether, five such time-lagged comparisons can be made (see box figure 4.2.1).

These comparisons are matched for age, obviously an important factor. The children are different, but in the same schools, and given the large sample size this should not matter. Also, you will be able to see from the design that the same children, starting in grades 5 and 6, serve as both baseline groups and treatment groups in different comparisons.

The measurements made at the 3 time points were based on anonymously filled in questionnaires from the students. These indicated the frequency of being bullied and bullying others, and of spending playtime alone; self-ratings of anti-social behaviour; ratings of satisfaction with school life; and ratings of the number of peers in the class being bullied or bullying others.

The results were encouraging. There were substantial reductions in the levels of both being bullied, and bullying others, reported by both boys and girls. Box table 4.2.1 shows the changes for the two time 1–time 3 comparisons (shown in box figure 4.2.1), on the questionnaire scores for 'How often have you been bullied in school?', and 'How often have you taken part in bullying other students in school?' Similar reductions were found for ratings of peers involved in being bullied or bullying. The bullying was not just displaced

BOX TABLE 4.2.1   *Effects of intervention programme: questionnaire scores for (a) being bullied, and (b) for bullying others, for boys and girls, for each of the two time 1–time 3 comparisons (at grade 6, and grade 7)*

| (a) | How often have you been bullied in school? | | | |
| | BOYS | | GIRLS | |
| | Grade 6 | Grade 7 | Grade 6 | Grade 7 |
| Time 1 | 0.36 | 0.47 | 0.46 | 0.19 |
| Time 3 | 0.19 | 0.18 | 0.11 | 0.07 |
| (b) | How often have you taken part in bullying other students in school? | | | |
| | BOYS | | GIRLS | |
| | Grade 6 | Grade 7 | Grade 6 | Grade 7 |
| Time 1 | 0.49 | 0.47 | 0.26 | 0.23 |
| Time 3 | 0.33 | 0.31 | 0,10 | 0.04 |

elsewhere; there were no changes in reports of bullying on the way to and from school. There were some decreases in the self-reports of anti-social behaviour, and some increases in student satisfaction with school life such as liking playground time.

This research programme provides a convincing account of the application of psychological research to diagnosing a social problem, helping devise an intervention programme, and then assessing the results of such an intervention. The independent variable is time of assessment, while the dependent variables are the questionnaire measures. The data does depend largely on self-reports, which could be open to distortion or to effects of repeated testing; but is supported by ratings of peers.

The cohort-sequential design overcomes the absence of conventional no-treatment control groups. However the comparisons do not control for historical effects. For example, suppose some other events had happened in 1984, such as severe economic depression, or increased racial tension such as the Rushdie affair in the UK in 1989; these might influence the comparisons. In effect, the comparisons are measuring the effects of the intervention programme (itself an historical effect!) and any other large-scale effects felt in 1983–5. Nevertheless, there were no other such obviously important effects in Norway in the period concerned.

Another study carried out on 37 schools in the Rogaland area of Norway around Stavanger, did not obtain such encouraging findings (Roland, 1989). Here assessments were made in 1986; preliminary results showed that levels of bullying had remained largely stable for girls, but had actually increased for boys. Nevertheless the schools which had implemented the intervention programme most thoroughly did have better results. The discrepancy between this study and the one based in Bergen remains to be explained.

# 5

# Becoming Socially Aware

So far, we have looked at the child developing in the context of the family, the peer group, and the school. In this chapter we shall retrace our steps and look at how the child develops an understanding of him- or herself, and of others; and discuss various influences on this process. There is an important body of research which makes links between the child's social world (the focus of Part Two of this book) and the child's thinking and language abilities (the focus of Part Three). We will start by considering children's developing sense of self; their understanding of their own emotions: and their ability to symbolize and to 'meta-represent'. This will lead on to a discussion of how the child learns to categorize others and understand their emotional expressions, and the developing awareness of other's mental states, beliefs and desires: what has been called a 'theory of mind', or skills in 'mindreading'. The particular case of autistic children, and whether they are deficient in a 'theory of mind', will be discussed.

The second part of the chapter examines the development of gender and ethnic differences—how children understand these, as well as what behavioural differences are found. Finally, we shall look at the effects of television on sex stereotyping and on social behaviour.

## How Children Begin to Understand Self and Others

One basic step the infant must take in understanding about others is to realize that he or she is distinct from other people, who have a separate continuing existence. In other words, they must acquire a sense of self as distinct from others.

One early landmark of this is referred to as 'person permanence'. It has been assessed in terms of infants' recognition of particular others, and search for them when that person disappears from view. Person permanence implies an internal representation of a social being, corresponding to that person's continuity in time and space. Closely related to the concept of person permanence is that of 'object permanence', applied to non-social objects, and discussed in chapter 11. Both are achieved during the sensorimotor period (up to about 18 months of age), with major progress in the degree of permanence achieved (measured by the success of the infants' search stategies) towards the end of the first year.

## The infant's recognition of self

While person permanence experiments show that an infant can recognize particular others and expect them to continue existing, they do not tell us specifically about the infant's own sense of self. The development of self-recognition has been discussed in detail by Lewis and Brooks-Gunn (1979). They found that infants aged as early as 9 to 12 months were capable of some differentiation between pictorial representation of themselves, and others; for example, they would smile more and look longer at pictures of themselves than at pictures of other same-age babies. By 15 to 18 months, children are using verbal labels such as 'baby', or their own name, to distinguish pictures of themselves and others. One ingenious technique to assess self-recognition has been the 'Mirror test', also used with primates (chapter 2). In a study of this kind, Lewis and Brooks-Gunn (1979) used 16 infants at each of six age groups – 9, 12, 15, 18, 21, and 24 months. Each infant was first placed by the mother in front of a fairly large mirror, and their behaviour observed for about 90 seconds. Then, the infants' nose was wiped with rouge discreetly, on the pretence of wiping the infants' face (only one of the 96 infants immediately felt for his nose after this). The infant was subsequently placed in front of the mirror again and observed for another 90 seconds. How would the infant react?

At all ages, most of the infants smiled at their image in the mirror (see table 5.1), and many pointed to the mirror or reached out to touch it. However in the first, 'no rouge' condition, very few touched their own nose, and not many touched their own body at all. When the rouge had been applied, the effect depended markedly on the infants' age. The 9- and 12-month-old infants never touched their own nose, despite being able to see their unusually red nose in the mirror; a minority of 15- and 18-month-olds, and most 21- and 24-month-olds, did reach for their own noses. This suggests that after about 18 months, an infant has a pretty good idea that the reflection in the mirror is a representation of him- or her-self.

## The relationship between sense of self, and understanding others

A sense of self can be used as a reference point for understanding others, and some psychologists regard the two as inextricably linked. The idea goes back to an American child psychologist, J. M. Baldwin (1861–1934). It is supported by Lewis

TABLE 5.1   *Percentages of infants smiling, and touching own nose, on viewing their reflection in a mirror*

| Infants' behaviour | | Age (months) | 9 | 12 | 15 | 18 | 21 | 24 |
|---|---|---|---|---|---|---|---|---|
| Smiling | No rouge | | 86 | 94 | 88 | 56 | 63 | 60 |
| | Rouge | | 99 | 74 | 88 | 75 | 82 | 60 |
| Touching own nose | No rouge | | 0 | 0 | 0 | 6 | 7 | 7 |
| | Rouge | | 0 | 0 | 19 | 25 | 70 | 73 |

*Source*: Lewis and Brooks-Gunn, 1979

and Brooks-Gunn (1979), who advanced three principles regarding early social awareness:

1   any knowledge gained about the other also must be gained about the self.
2   what can be demonstrated to be known about the self can be said to be known about the other and what is known about the other can be said to be known about the self.
3   social dimensions are those attributes of others and self which can be used to describe people.

Related ideas are developed by Paul Harris (1989) in his theory of how children come to understand others, which we shall discuss shortly.

The link between knowledge of self, and others, is also supported by recent empirical work. Bischof-Kohler (cited in Perner, 1991) carried out the mirror test on infants aged 16 to 24 months; she also assessed their level of empathy when playing with an experimenter who is 'sad' when the arm of a teddy bear falls off. There was a high correlation between a child's level of self-recognition, and their level of empathic behaviour, irrespective of the child's age. In general, it seems as if the beginnings of a truly empathic understanding of others emerges at around 20 months (see also chapter 6), at the same time as other aspects of understanding others (for example jealousy, and deception, chapter 3), and as self-recognition as assessed by the mirror test.


## How Children Categorize Others

We have seen how infants achieve person permanence through the sensorimotor period, often ahead of object permanence. As concepts of particular persons become more stable, persons can begin to be categorized along social dimensions. Lewis and Brooks-Gunn (1979) argued that the three earliest social dimensions learned are *familiarity, age* and *gender*. They argue that these are concurrently developed in relation to oneself and to other persons.

The importance of *familiarity* is apparent from the research which shows that infants behave differently to familiar and to strange adults by around 7 to 9 months of age (when attachment relationships have usually formed), if not earlier (see chapter 3; and Sroufe, 1977). A bit later, infants respond differently to familiar and unfamiliar peers. Jacobson (1980) found that wariness of an unfamiliar peer (compared to a familiar peer) developed between 10 and 12 months. Greater previous experience with the familiar peer predicted an earlier onset of wariness of the unfamiliar peer.

Age and gender are also used very early on in a categorical way. Infants aged 6 to 9 months of age discriminate in their behaviour between the approach of a child and of an adult, and infants aged 9 to 12 months can differentiate between photographs of baby and adult faces. Lewis and Brooks-Gunn (1978) suggest that height, movement, voice, and extreme differences in facial and hair characteristics (in baby and adult photographs) are the cues which infants use to catagorize by age. Verbal age labels (e.g. baby, mummy, daddy) begin to be used correctly by 18 to 24 months of age. By the preschool years, age can be used as an explicit criterion for classification. Edwards and Lewis (1979) found that $3\frac{1}{2}$ year-olds could successfully sort head-and-shoulders photographs of persons into four categories: little children, big children, parents and grandparents.

Differentiation of people by gender also occurs early. Nine to 12-month-olds respond differentially both to photographs of female and male strangers (Brooks-Gunn and Lewis, 1981) and to direct approach by male and female strangers (Smith and Sloboda, 1986). Verbal gender labels (e.g. mummy, daddy, boy, girl) begin to be used correctly after 18 months of age. The development of gender identity is considered further, later in this chapter.

## Emotional Development

### Producing emotions

From birth onwards, babies start signalling their emotional state (see also chapter 3, p. 60; chapter 10, p. 283. Perhaps the earliest distinction one can make for babies is between positive and negative affect – whether they are contented and happy, as indicated by smiling; or discontented and distressed, as indicated by pursing the lips and crying. A study by Ganchrow, Steiner and Daher (1983) showed that at the time of the very first feed, newborns would produce distinct facial expressions to a sweet liquid (slight smile) or bitter liquid (mouth corners down, purse lips). Observers who watched the babies without knowing which liquid was being given, could judge whether the babies liked or disliked the liquid, and also the intensity of response.

Interviews with mothers suggest that they can distinguish a variety of emotions in their infants in the first few months of life (Campos et al., 1983). Some basic emotions, which may be discernible from the first few weeks onwards, are happiness, interest, surprise, sadness, fear, anger, and pain. For example, surprise is indicated by wide open eyes and mouth, together with a startle response by the trunk and limbs. Fear responses increase considerably after about 7 months of age, when infants become wary and fearful of unfamiliar persons and objects (see chapter 3, p 67); and sadness can occur in periods of separation from a familiar caregiver. (The balance of different emotional expressions is crucial in scoring the 'strange situation' procedure, see chapter 3, p. 65, where anger as well as happiness may occur in reunion episodes).

Anger and pain also become increasingly easily distinguished from each other, especially after about 7 months. This was shown in a study by Izard et al. (1987). They looked at babies' facial expressions when they were given routine inoculations. The babies were aged from 2 to 8 months. For younger babies the reaction was one of generalized distress, but for older babies a distinctly angry expression (brows compressed together, eyelids tensed, mouth compressed or squared) became progressively more frequent.

One of the earliest descriptions of emotional development comes from Charles Darwin (1877), who published an article about the early development of one of his own children. Here is his description of the development of anger:

It was difficult to decide at how early an age anger was felt; on his eighth day he frowned and wrinkled the skin round his eyes before a crying fit, but this may have been due to pain or distress, and not to anger. When about ten weeks old, he was given some rather cold milk and he kept a slight frown on his forehead all the time that he was sucking, so that he looked like a grown-up person made cross from being compelled to do something which he did not like. When nearly four months old, and perhaps much earlier, there was no doubt, from the manner in which the blood gushed into his whole face and scalp, that he easily got into a violent passion. A small cause sufficed; thus, when a little over seven months old, he screamed with rage because a lemon slipped away and he could not seize it with his hands. When eleven months old, if a wrong plaything was given him, he would push it away and beat it: I presume that the beating was an instinctive sign of anger, like the snapping of the jaws by a young crocodile just out of the egg, and not that he imagined he could hurt the plaything.

Darwin's account is interesting for several reasons. It brings out clearly both his skill as an observer, and also the difficulty in interpreting emotions especially at younger ages. Darwin's account is an example of the diary method (p. 13); though in this case Darwin actually wrote up the article 37 years after keeping the diary on which it is based! Finally, you will see that Darwin suggests that some emotional displays are 'instinctive', in children as well as in animals. The very early development of emotional display in infants does seem to suggest that some of the mechanisms for producing emotion are 'innate', or strongly canalized in development (p. 37). The main alternative view would be that infants learn emotional expression from others, through observation and imitation; this seems less plausible in early infancy, but more plausible later, for example in explaining cultural differences in emotional expression.

### Recognizing emotions in others

If infants were to learn aspects of emotional expression from others, they would have to understand something of their meaning. How early does this occur? We will look at two kinds of evidence, both suggesting that during the first year infants can distinguish and react appropriately to different emotional expressions by caregivers.

Some studies have looked at dialogues between mother and baby (cf. pp. 60, 283). Usually mother and baby are interacting happily. What would happen if the mother adopted a sad face, or an angry face? Haviland and Lelwica (1987) asked mothers to do this for a short while with their 10-week-old babies, adopting appropriate facial expressions and tone of voice. The babies did react differently. If the mother appeared happy, so did the baby. If the mother appeared angry, so did the baby. If the mother appeared sad, the baby did not particularly look sad, but did engage in chewing, mouthing and sucking.

These studies show that babies can discriminate emotions in others early on. Their reactions seem broadly appropriate, but it could be misleading to say that the baby 'understands' the mothers' angry emotion; they might for example simply find the angry tone of voice (loud and harsh) unpleasurable in itself. However evidence that infants can sensibly interpret the emotional expression of their mother comes from studies of 'social referencing'.

*Social referencing*

Sometimes, an infant will look carefully at his or her mother (or familiar caregiver), as if to gauge their emotional expression, before as it were deciding how to react themselves to a situation. This kind of behaviour is referred to as 'social referencing', and has been defined as a 'process characterized by the use of one's perception of other persons' interpretation of this situation to form one's own understanding of the situation' (Feinman, 1982, p. 445). Not surprisingly, it is more likely in ambiguous situations, where some extra 'advice' is needed by the infant. Two well-studied examples are: reactions to strangers; and behaviour on the 'visual cliff'.

From about 7 months of age, we have seen that infants do tend to be wary of strangers, even if overt fear is rare except in unusual laboratory situations (p. 67). The infants' reaction to the stranger is known to be quite strongly affected by context, and part of this context is now known to be the mothers' reaction to the stranger. Feiring, Lewis and Starr (1984) observed how 15-month-olds would respond to a stranger. They would often turn to the mother when the stranger entered, as if to ascertain her reaction. The experimenters asked the mother to either interact positively with the stranger, or ignore the stranger. The reaction of the infants to the stranger was less positive when the mother ignored the stranger. Similar results have been obtained with the reactions of 12-month-old infants to toys, depending on the facial expression of the mother (Klinnert, 1984).

Another experiment was carried out using the 'visual cliff' (illustrated on p. 260). In the visual cliff, infants generally refuse to move onto a glass surface when it appears that there is a large drop at the boundary (see p. 261). The situation can be made more ambiguous by making the apparent drop smaller. This was done by Sorce et al., (1985) with a sample of 12-month-olds. The mother was opposite the baby (see the right-hand photo on p. 260) and some mothers were asked to adopt a happy face, others a fearful face.

The results were clear. Of 19 infants whose mother had a happy face, 14 crossed the visual cliff; of 17 whose mother had a fearful face, none crossed. This strongly suggests that the infants are interpreting the mother's expression appropriately, as a commentary on the situation. This is particularly well illustrated by this experiment, as a mother's fearful expression would normally cause an infant to approach the mother for safety; but in this experiment, the mother's fearful expression actually prevents approach across the apparent cause of danger, the visual cliff.

*Talking about mental states*

By about 9 to 12 months, it seems as though infants can produce, and discriminate, a variety of emotional expressions; and begin to respond appropriately by interpreting the emotional expressions of others as a commentary on the situation. We also saw earlier that by 18 months (the completion of sensorimotor development, see chapter 11), the infant has a well-developed sense of self and others, and is able to start responding appropriately to others as a result of their emotional state; for example, showing empathy and comforting someone in distress.

From about 18 months, further insight can be obtained into emotional development by looking at how infants talk about emotions – how they use 'emotion words' in natural conversation (Bretherton et al., 1986). Both diaries of child speech, and observations in the home, show that use of words which label emotions (such as 'have fun', 'surprised', 'scared', 'yucky', 'sad'), while rare at 18 months, are common by 24 months. Interestingly, although these words are used somewhat more frequently by children to refer to themselves than to refer to others, the use of these words for self and others goes very much in parallel; this supports the ideas discussed earlier of the interdependence of concepts of self and other (p. 131).

By 28 months, children are using language to comment on and explain their own feelings, for example:

'I see tiger. That too scary'
'Me fall down. Me cry'

and the feelings of others, for example:

'Grandma mad. I wrote on wall'
'You sad Mommy. What Daddy do?'

They can also use them to guide or influence someone else's behaviour, for example:

'No not angry. Not nice' (age 19 months; parents are quarrelling)
'Baby crying. Kiss. Make it better' (age 22 months; to mother, in shop where child noticed other child crying)
'I hurt your hair. Please don't cry' (age 24 months; to child victim, after being scolded for hair-pulling).

(from Bretherton et al., 1986).

From this and other evidence, Wellman (1990) argues that by 2 years of age, children can already be considered 'desire psychologists'. That is, they can understand that other people have emotions and desires, and that a person's desire may lead them to a certain action. By 3 to 4 years, however, they can be considered 'belief-desire psychologists'. That is, they can understand that someone's desire will interact with that person's belief about things, to result in a certain action.

### Emotional deception

One way to see whether children can think about the links between beliefs, desires and actions in others is to see if they can deliberately manipulate emotions to achieve a certain effect on others. For example, can they deceive others by hiding or changing a facial expression of emotion? It looks as though they can do this by 3 or 4 years of age.

In one study, Cole (1986) looked at how 3- and 4-year-old girls would react when given a disappointing present. The girls were given picture-story tasks to do. Before the tasks, each girl had rated ten possible gifts from best to worst. After the first set of tasks, the children were given their 'best' present; but after the second set of tasks, they were given their 'worst' present (a broken toy, or some raisins). How would they react? Cole found that when the interviewer was not present, the children (filmed by a videocamera) would show disappointment to the 'worst' toy, but that when the interviewer stayed present, many would hide their disappoint-ment with a half-smile. (The children were subsequently given the opportunity to trade in their 'worst' toy for another one).

Another study (Lewis et al., 1989) was done with children who were just 3 years of age (33–37 months). The child sat at a table with the experimenter (and the mother in the background), and was told that the experimenter was going to put out a surprise toy (actually, a Fisher-Price zoo), but that they must not peek while the experimenter left the room; they could play with the toy when the experimenter returned. The experimenter then left the room, and the children were observed and filmed through a one-way mirror. The experimenter returned and asked 'did you peek?' before playing with the child and reassuring them that it was alright if they did peek.

Of 33 children taking part, 29 did peek at the toy when the experimenter left! Of these, 11 admitted to peeking, 11 denied it, and 7 gave no answer to the question. Besides the verbal deception of many children, there was evidence of facial deception. The children who peeked tended to put on a smile when the experi-menter re-entered and looked at them (unlike the few children who did not peek, who did not smile), and when questioned, these children continued smiling; those who denied peeking had the most relaxed and positive facial expression!

As we saw in chapter 2 (p. 45), there can be different levels of deception. The above examples would seem to indicate level four deception, that is a deliberate intent to deceive. In the Lewis et al. (1989) study, it could admittedly be argued that the child's response 'no', to 'did you peek?' may have been just an avoidance reaction, or a stereotyped denial strategy; but this would hardly explain the manipulation of facial expression which occurred as well.

## Understanding Others' Beliefs, Desires and Emotions

We have seen that there is considerable evidence that children can understand other people's beliefs, desires and emotions by 3 or 4 years of age, and indeed that the beginnings of this can be seen by 2 years of age. How does this understanding come about? One theory has been put put forward by Paul Harris in his book *Children and Emotion* (1989). Harris believes that it is a child's awareness of his or her own mental state which allows them to project mental states on to other people using an 'as if' or pretence mechanism; understanding someone else results from imagining yourself in their position. (This is in fact similar to the argument by Humphrey, chapter 1, p. 3.) On this basis, Harris argues that there are three important precursors, or preconditions, for the child to be able to understand another person's mind. These are (1) self-awareness; (2) the capacity for pretence; and (3) being able to distinguish reality from pretence.

1   Self-awareness: as we saw earlier, children are aware of themselves by about 18–20 months of age and can verbally express their own emotional states by 2 years.

2   The capacity for pretence: in chapter 6 (pp. 173–4) we see that the ability to pretend that something in the world is something else emerges in pretend play

during the second year. Specifically, children start acting out scenes with dolls or stuffed animals, for example feeding teddy 'as if' he were hungry. By 2 and 3 years of age, children are conjuring up animate beings in their pretend play, with emotions and desires of their own.

3   Distinguishing reality from pretence: when children are in pretend play, they do not usually confuse this with reality. Admittedly this can happen sometimes. When an adult joins in with a 1- or 2-year-old's play, the child can be confused as to whether the adult is in 'pretend' or 'real' mode; for example if a child knocks an empty cup over in play and mother says 'you spilled your tea, better wipe it up', the child may actually pick up a cloth to wipe it. However more usually, and especially by 3 or 4 years, the pretence-reality distinction is a stable one. Things would be difficult if it was not! Suppose a child pretends a wooden block is a cake, for a tea party. If they confused pretence and reality, they would actually try to eat the wooden block. By 3 years, children often signal the pretend mode in their play, for example 'let's pretend to be families. You be daddy ... '. Direct interviews with 3-year-olds also confirm that they can distinguish real from imaginary situations, and understand the use of the words 'real' and 'pretend'.

How do all these precursors come together in Harris's theory? He supposes that once a child is aware of his or her own emotional state, he or she can use the ability to pretend in order to project this emotional state on to inanimate beings (in pretend play), or on other people; and to realize that the other person's imagined reality may differ from their own reality. Let's take as an example the child who said 'You sad Mommy. What Daddy do?', cited earlier. We can suppose that previously this child has experienced sadness herself; and perhaps has experienced sadness because her Daddy was nasty to her. Her ability to imagine things in an 'as if' or pretend mode enable her to suppose that Mummy too may be sad, because Daddy was nasty to her also. Furthermore, she does not confuse this with her own emotional state; the child does not have to be sad herself, in order to imagine that Mummy is sad, for a certain reason.

There is one obvious alternative interpretation which would dispense with Harris's 'as if' mechanism. That is that young children learn to link common situations with common emotions (compare the discussion of Borke's results in chapter 11, p. 328). Perhaps they just have learnt that mummies are usually sad because daddies have been nasty to them, and it doesn't require any imaginative projection of one's own emotional state.

One way to distinguish this alternative explanation from Harris's theory is to see whether children can understand that someone else's emotion in a given situation depends on what they desire or want. To ascertain this, Harris and his colleagues asked children to listen to stories about animal characters, for example, Ellie the elephant and Mickey the monkey. Ellie the elephant is choosy about what she likes to drink. Some children were told that she likes milk to drink and nothing else; others that she likes coke to drink and nothing else. Mickey the monkey is mischievous and mixes up the drink containers; for example, he might pour all the coke out of a coke can, fill it with milk, and offer it to Ellie. How would she feel when she tastes the drink? 4-year-olds are able to answer correctly that (if she likes milk) she will be pleased, or that (if she likes coke) she would be sad, and explain why in terms of Ellie's desires.

This does tend to suggest that, at least by 4 years, children are taking account of someone's desires in predicting their emotional state; they are not just basing their judgement on a stereotyped situation–emotion link (such as: you are pleased if you are given a drink). In a subsequent study, the experimenters also asked children how Ellie would feel before she tasted the drink. How would she feel if she likes coke, and is given a coke can (which Mickey has secretly filled with milk). By 6 years (though in this study, not at 4 years), children correctly judge that Ellie would be happy when given the can, though sad when she tasted the contents. Here, belief and desire of another are being successfully linked in the prediction of emotion, even when the belief is different from the child's own belief (the child knows the coke can has milk, but Ellie has a 'false belief'), and the desire may be different from the child's desire; not all children like coke (or milk).

### Theories of Mind

From the above account, we might say that children are developing hypotheses about other persons' emotions, desires, and beliefs. This could be described as developing a 'theory of mind' or skills in 'mindreading'. As we saw at the end of chapter 2, there are similar ideas about the evolutionary origins of intelligence in the higher primates.

Indeed, Harris (1988, p. 77) argues that

> Children can be credited with a theory-like understanding of the mind. They explain and predict people's behaviour and emotion by considering the relationships that hold between concepts such as beliefs and desires.

However Harris explicitly uses the term 'theory' in a different way from how it is used in the physical sciences. According to him, 'children do not invoke unobservable entities ... [they] do not "postulate" such states when they explain someone's behaviour. They simply imagine wanting or believing a particular state of affairs' (1988, p. 76).

There is currently a lot of debate about how 'theory of mind' develops in children (see Astington, Harris and Olson, 1988; Perner, 1991; Wellman, 1990). Harris's approach is only one of several. Leslie (1987), for example, agrees with Harris that pretence is important, but takes it as being only one, though an early, example of deploying what he calls second-order representations, or 'metarepresentations' (cf. p. 46), which appear at around 18 months. A metarepresentation is 'decoupled' from a primary representation; with this ability, primary representations can be manipulated. A 'primary representation' could be a representation of someone else's emotional state. When these can be manipulated via metarepresentation, a 'theory of mind' can be said to develop. Thus, Leslie regards the cognitive ability to 'metarepresent' as the common factor underlying 'theory of mind', this ability being evidenced in such phenomena as pretend play, talking about mental states, and understanding false beliefs.

Another position is taken by Perner (1991), who uses terms such as 'metarepresent' rather differently, and disagrees with Harris's view on the importance of pretence. Perner suggests that up to 12 months, the infant is acquiring a 'knowledge base' – a straight reflection of reality. After the first year, 'representations' or 'mental models' begin to be used, as shown in language. The child attributes mental states to others but has little understanding of the underpinnings of these mental states (what causes them, how beliefs and desires are related). Only by 3 or more likely 4 years do children 'metarepresent' in Perner's terms of modelling mental models. They then do have a 'theory of mind', and can for instance succeed on 'false belief' tasks. Perner does not believe that role-playing, or the emotional projection postulated by Harris, is critically important, but rather that by 4 years children really do postulate mental states as theoretical constructs in a theory which integrates internal information with externally observable facts.

### The Understanding of False Beliefs

Several times, we have come across the idea of being able to understand that someone else has a false belief about something; and there has been mention of 'false belief' tasks. Such tasks have been of particular interest, as they seem to provide a test case for finding out if children really understand how beliefs interact with desires and emotions; if it can be understood that someone else has a false belief, this could not be explained in terms of stereotyped knowledge, linking common emotions to common situations.

A standard format of false belief task has evolved, which involves someone looking for an object they have previously hidden. The child being tested has seen someone else move the object to a different place. So where does the child think the first person will look for the object? In the place they previously hid it, or in the place where the child now knows it is? The former answer is correct, but the child can only give this answer if they can realize that the first person has a 'false belief' about the object's location.

This test format was first developed by Wimmer and Perner (1983) from a study made with children in kindergartens and summer camps in Salzburg, Austria. In their version of the story, a boy called Maxi comes back with his mother from shopping. Mother lifts Maxi up to help him put some chocolate away in a blue cupboard. Then Maxi goes out to play. His mother later takes the chocolate out, and puts it back in a green cupboard. She leaves. Maxi returns. 'Where will Maxi look for the chocolate?'

Wimmer and Perner found that 3-year-olds could not succeed on this task by saying correctly that Maxi would look in the blue cupboard (instead, they often said that Maxi would look in the green cupboard). Some 4- and 5-year-olds succeeded, but only by 6 years were almost all children correct. Those children who failed had not just forgotten the story, as most answered correctly the 'reality' question, 'Where is the chocolate really?' Some variants of the task were also tried. For example, if mother uses up all the chocolate in cooking, so that the chocolate disappears, most 4- and 5-year-olds correctly say that Maxi will look in the blue cupboard. Further variants were used by Perner, Leekam and Wimmer (1987) to confirm that 3-year-olds could really not succeed on the false belief task. For example, one problem might be that young children interpret 'Where will Maxi look for the chocolate?' as meaning 'Where *should* Maxi look for the chocolate?' (after all, he should look in the green cupboard if he is to find it!). To check for this, they asked instead 'Where does he think the chocolate is?' Most 3-year-olds still failed the task. (Another version of the false belief task is given in box 5.1).

These findings have parallels with the work on conceptual role-taking, such as that of Marvin, Mossler and Greenberg, 1976, discussed in chapter 11 (p. 328–9). As in that debate, there is continuing discussion on exactly when children can start to succeed on such tasks. Perner believes that because children do not succeed on false belief tasks until 4 years, this metarepresentational ability must be at a different level to those abilities (which he calls representational) which underlie pretend play and the pretend-really distinction, which are achieved earlier. However, as in the work on egocentrism (chapter 11), it is possible that, notwithstanding all the precautions taken and test variants used, some aspects of the test situation may be inadvertently tricking children into giving the wrong answer. After all, children aged 2 and 3 years do seem able to practise high-level deception in natural situations.

Lewis and Osborne (1990) wondered whether too much was being asked of a child's language skills, in the standard false belief test. In particular, when the child is asked 'Where will Maxi look for the chocolate?' does the child understand that his question refers to a time before Maxi finds out where the chocolate really is? They used a sample of 131 3- and 4-year-olds from nursery schools in the UK. In their variant of the task (used also by Perner et al., 1987), the child is first shown a Smartie box, and asked what they think is inside. Children expect Smarties (small chocolates) to be inside (incidentally, you may notice that false belief tasks focus a lot on chocolate! This is no doubt to encourage children's interest).

However the box is then opened, and in this Smartie box there is only a pencil. The lid is put back, and the child is questioned to ensure that they remember what is now in the box. In the 'standard' version of the task, the child is then asked

'What did you think was in the box?' (own false belief)

and then told that a friend was going to come in and asked

'What will [name of friend] think is in the box?' (others' false belief)

and Lewis and Osborne replicated the findings of Perner et al. (1987) that most 3-year-olds fail at these questions, though most 4-year-olds succeed. However simply changing the questions to

'What did you think was in the box before I took the top off?'

and

'What will [name of friend] think is in the box before I take the top off?'

improved children's performance, such that a clear majority of 3-year-olds now succeeded at the task.

PLATE 5.1  *A child being tested on the 'hide-and-seek' version of the false belief task*

The 'false belief' task can also be presented in a simplified form, as a hide-and-seek game. This has been done by Freeman, Lewis and Doherty (1991). The hide-and-seek game is illustrated in plate 5.1. A small playperson doll represents Sarah, a larger one her Daddy. Sarah runs off to hide down the yellow coloured pathway while Daddy counts to ten. But Daddy cheats and peeps at Sarah halfway through the counting (the experimenter angles the Daddy doll to look at Sarah) and sees her going into the yellow shed. Daddy finishes counting; meanwhile Sarah finds a little doorway and crawls into the red shed. Then Daddy says 'Coming!'.

'Where do you think Daddy will look for Sarah?' (Belief question: correct answer is yellow shed, see plate 5.1a)
'Where is Sarah?' (Reality question: correct answer is red shed, see plate 5.1b)
'Where did Sarah hide in the beginning?' (Memory question, correct answer is yellow shed.)

Using this hide-and-seek test, many 3-year-olds pass all the questions, including the first, critical Belief question, even when they fail a standard 'Sally' test as in box 5.1. They are more successful when they are asked to 'take Daddy to find Sarah'. This 'action' format seems to help; in addition perhaps the design of the test is simpler, or the hide-and-seek game is familiar even to quite young children and maximally engages their interest and competence. The kind of belief-desire reasoning measured by the false-belief task is probably a cultural universal. It is present in young children of the Baka, a pygmy people living in the rain forests of south-east Cameroon (Avis and Harris, 1991). Using an adapted task of hiding mango nut kernels, almost all 4-year-olds and many 3-year-olds passed the standard questions of the test.

### Do Autistic Children Lack a Theory of Mind?

Autism is a rare disorder, which can be readily diagnosed from about 3 years of age onwards, and is very disabling. It is characterized by severe social and communicative impairments. Autistic children seem uninterested in social contact and interaction, often playing alone and using eye contact with others very oddly. If they do interact with others they do so in a mechanical and repetitive way, as if people were like objects. This social deficit is usually seen as the primary diagnostic symptom, but autistic children also often have deficits in language; many are mute, others often repeat words over and over again, or use words in idiosyncratic ways. They don't seem to communicate very effectively with others, either verbally or non-verbally. They also usually have some cognitive deficits, but these seem to be more patchy and variable. Finally, they seem unable to show much of the pretend or symbolic play normally seen in young children.

There has been a lot of debate over the causes of autism, and whether these lie in social, language or cognitive impairments (see Rutter, 1983; Gillberg, 1990). In this section we will look at two recently debated hypotheses. One is that autistic children have an inability to respond emotionally to others (Hobson, 1990); the other is a more cognitivist view that autistic children lack a theory of mind (Leslie and Frith, 1990).

Hobson believes that a primary disability in autism is that such children cannot understand the emotional states of other people. We saw earlier that this ability emerges in the first two years of life in normal children, and that the early stages of emotional expression and recognition appear to be highly canalized. Perhaps there is some 'innate' disability which autistic children have in this developmental process? An experiment by Hobson (1986) lent some support to this idea. He asked children to match exaggeratedly drawn facial expressions of emotion (figure 5.1) with videotaped sequences of actors showing emotions such as anger, unhappiness, happiness, and fear. The task was given to 23 autistic children with a mean age of 14 years, and a mental age (see p. 374) of 7 to 10 years. For comparison, the task was given to normal children, whose mental and chronological age was about 7 years. The results were quite clear — the autistic children did poorly on the task while the normal children performed most of the matches correctly. The deficit of the autistic children was not just a problem of understanding the task, as Hobson found that

FIGURE 5.1    *Exaggeratedly drawn facial expressions of emotion (from Hobson, 1986)*

they could match pictures of things such as trains, dogs, birds and cars with appropriate videotape sequences. He concluded that the deficit was in recognizing how different expressions of emotional states (for example, different expressions of happiness, in the photo or video) are associated with each other.

Hobson (1990) expanded this and other findings to suggest that autistic children have a difficulty right from the start in distinguishing people from objects and attributing emotional states to other people. They may remain only dimly aware that other people have feelings and mental states. He believes that the other disabilities in autism, including deficits in pretend play, follow from this.

A somewhat different hypothesis is advanced by Baron-Cohen (1989), Frith (1989), and Leslie and Frith (1990). They take a more cognitivist view, that autistic children cannot engage in second-order or meta-representations (pp. 46, 138) and as a result they cannnot develop a proper theory of mind. Part of their argument hinges on the finding that autistic children do not seem to show pretend or symbolic play. For example, Baron-Cohen (1987) gave children toys such as stuffed animals, a toy kitchen stove, and playpeople. Four-year-old normal children engaged in much pretend play with these, but autistic children matched for mental age mostly engaged in functional and sensori-motor play. Leslie (1987) argued that pretend play was an early indication of the ability to decouple representations, or use metarepresentations; therefore, the autistic child's deficits in pretend play might indicate a general deficit in metarepresentational ability. If so, this could also explain their social disabilities (as an inability to represent mental states in others). Also, it would predict that they would fail on false belief tasks.

Baron-Cohen, Leslie and Frith (1985) established that, compared to normal and to Down's syndrome children matched for mental age, autistic children did indeed have a specific disability on a standard false belief task; very few could succeed at it (see box 5.1). Unlike Down's syndrome children who have a rather general developmental delay, they argued that autistic children show a specific developmental delay in theory of mind (Baron-Cohen, 1989), or metarepresentational ability (Leslie and Frith, 1990).

These theories are the subject of much debate, and it has been disputed whether autistic children are really unable to show pretend play (Boucher, 1989). More funadmentally, one study carried out on autistic children in Australia (Prior et al., 1990) found that autistic children could perform as well as normal children on Hobsons's (1986) emotional expressions task, and that many could succeed on the false belief task of Baron-Cohen et al. (1985). The success of the autistic children correlated with their language ability. If substantiated, this could cast doubt on both the hypotheses discussed above (of Hobson; and of Baron-Cohen, Leslie and Frith) and focus attention again on language deficits and the difficulty of adequately matching autistic and normal children for mental age and linguistic ability. Quite what the relationship between language and theory of mind ability is, remains to be seen.

## Later Developments

We have reviewed in detail the development of the sense of self, emotional development, and theory of mind, in the preschool years, since it is up to the age of 4 years that some of the most basic developmental changes occur in normal children. However further changes take place in the school years. A number of advances in emotional development are discussed by Harris (1989).

Although young children can understand the more straightforward emotions such as anger, happiness or fear, some emotions are more complex and depend on one's own behaviour in the light of the behaviour or expectations of others; for example, pride or shame, or guilt. A child will feel pride when they have done something which gains someone else's approval, or shame if it gains their disapproval. Such approval or disapproval can be directly forthcoming from others, but older children can internalize such reactions in terms of social and cultural norms and obligations. 7-year-olds, but not 5-year-olds, are able to describe situations which would bring about pride or shame. From about 7 years, they are also able to describe situations where they could experience mixed feelings – for example, feeling both angry and sad if their brother hit them.

In general, by 6 or 7 years children seem able to understand and manipulate emotions in a more complex way. It would appear that, as well as being able to understand that someone else can feel a different emotion (metarepresentation), they can begin to operate recursively on such understanding (Harris, 1989). Consider, for example, how children might respond to the following story:

> Diana falls over and hurts herself. She knows that the other children will laugh
> if she shows how she feels. So she tries to hide how she feels.

What will Diana do, and why? Many 6-year-olds (but not 4-year-olds) are able to say that Diana will look happy, and explain why; for example 'she didn't want the other children to know that she's sad that she fell over'. This is an embedded sentence with a recursive structure of the form 'I may not *want* you to *know* how I *feel*'. We've seen that 4-year-olds can cope with 'I *know* how you *feel*', but only by 6 years does this further recursion seem to become possible.

This is also born out by experimental studies of false belief tasks. The standard false belief task involves understanding that 'Sally *thinks* that the marble is in the basket because she doesn't *know* that Anne moved it to the box' (box 5.1). In a higher-order false belief task, children must solve problems of the form 'John *thinks* that Sally *thinks* that ...', which children cannot solve until 6 or 7 years. This ability to think recursively thus marks another step forward in understanding emotion and in social-cognitive development gradually.

## Early Sex Differences

We saw earlier how infants use sex, or gender, as one way of categorizing people. We will now look further at sex differences in behaviour and the development of children's awareness of these differences. Then some hypotheses about why sex differences develop are compared. Incidentally, some authors prefer to use the term 'gender' rather than 'sex' when referring to differences which may have been produced by upbringing, reserving 'sex' for purely biological differences. In practice, the distinction is not always that easy. Here we refer to 'sex differences', but to 'gender identity', these being the most common usages.

### Sex differences among children in Western societies

Many studies have been carried out in the UK and the USA on sex differences in infants and young children, most involving observations of behaviour in the home or in nursery classes. Individual studies often have rather small samples, say 20 children or so, and measure a large number of behavioural categories; so even by chance one or two measures may give apparently 'significant' differences. (Remember a result significant at the 0.05 level occurs by chance 1 in 20 times.) Thus, it is important to look for replication of findings over a number of studies. There are many reviews of this subject area in the literature (e.g. Huston, 1983; Archer and Lloyd, 1986; Hargreaves and Colley, 1986) .

The results of research in the infancy period (up to 2 years) do not reveal many consistent differences between boys and girls. The similarities certainly outweigh the dissimilarities. However, the replicated findings include: girl infants may be more responsive to people, staying closer to adults, whereas boy infants may be more distressed by stressful situations which they cannot control (such as the 'strange situation' separations discussed on p. 65). Girls also seem to talk earlier.

Among 2-year-olds and in older children some sex differences in toy choice are apparent. Observations of 2-year-olds at home, and of 3- and 4-year-olds in nursery classes, show that boys tend to prefer transportation toys, blocks and activities involving gross motor activity such as throwing or kicking balls, or rough-and-tumbling; girls tend to prefer dolls, and dressing-up or domestic play. Many activities, however, do not show a sex preference at this age.

School-age children tend to select same-sex partners for play, and more so as they get older. Also, boys tend to prefer outdoor play and, later, team games; whereas girls prefer indoor, more sedentary activities, and often play in pairs. Boys more frequently engage in both play-fighting and in actual aggressive behaviour. Girls tend to be more empathic, and remain more orientated towards adults (parents and teacher) longer into childhood. There are also some differences in verbal and visuo/spatial abilities (see chapter 13). All these differences refer to overall trends, with much overlap between boys and girls in general. Many differences, while statistically significant when tests are carried out on large samples, are actually quite small in magnitude.

*Awareness of gender identity and sex differences*

If you ask a 2-year-old 'are you a boy or a girl?', quite a few will not know the answer or will be easily confused, although many will answer correctly. The easiest task seems to be to show pictures of a male and female of stereotyped appearance (such as figure 5.2). In one such study, Thompson (1975) found that 24-month-old children gave 76 per cent correct identification of sex; this rose to 83 per cent by 30 months and 90 per cent by 36 months. By 3 years most children can correctly label their own, or another person's sex or gender, and are said to have achieved 'gender identity'.

The next stage, called 'gender stability', is achieved by 4 or 5 years. This is when a child realizes that gender is normally constant; for example a girl will answer that she will be a mummy when she grows up. A bit later the child reaches 'gender constancy', a mature awareness that biological sex is unchanging, despite changes in appearance. This is tested by questions such as 'could you be a girl if you want to be?' (to a boy), or 'suppose this child (picture of boy) lets their hair grow very long; is it a boy or a girl?'. This is reported to be achieved around 7 years of age, at or soon after the child can conserve physical quantity (see chapter 11); but may be achieved earlier if children understand the genital difference between the sexes (Bem, 1989).

Sex-role stereotypes are also acquired early; these are beliefs about what is most appropriate for one sex, or the other. In one study (Kuhn et al., 1978), preschool children were shown a male doll and a female doll, and asked which doll would do each of 72 activities, such as cooking, sewing, playing with trains, talking a lot, giving kisses, fighting or climbing trees. Even $2\frac{1}{2}$-year-olds had some knowledge of sex-role stereotypes (see table 5.2). This sex-stereotyping increases with age and is

FIGURE 5.2    *Stereotyped female and male figures (adapted from Emmerich et al., 1976)*

TABLE 5.2    *Beliefs about boys and girls, held by both boys and girls aged 2½ and 3½*[a]

| Beliefs about girls | play with dolls |
| | like to help mother |
| | like to cook dinner |
| | like to clean house |
| | talk a lot |
| | never hit |
| | say 'I need some help' |
| Beliefs about boys | like to help father |
| | say 'I can hit you' |

[a] Only results at or approaching statistical significance are recorded.
*Source*: Kuhn et al., 1978

well established by the middle school years. In a study of 5- and 8-year-old children in England, Ireland and the USA (Best et al., 1977), the majority of boys and girls, of both ages and in all countries, agreed that females were soft-hearted whereas males were strong, aggressive, cruel and coarse. Many more characteristics were stereotyped in the 8-year-olds only.

By 8 years of age children's stereotypes are very similar to those obtained with adults. Several studies have shown that adult stereotypes are quite consistent across a variety of ages and social backgrounds. They are also reflected in the mass media, such as books, comics, films and TV programmes (see later in this chapter). By and large, of course, such stereotypes correspond to actual differences in behaviour. Nevertheless, they often seem to exaggerate such differences, especially at a time when sex roles may be changing quite rapidly. For example, few children's books have depicted working mothers, even though about one-third of mothers of young children have been in employment for decades.

### Cross-cultural studies

The sex differences in behaviour and sex-role stereotypes so far discussed apply to Western urban societies such as the UK and the USA. But how widely do they apply in other societies? Much of what we know here comes from the work of anthropologists. One study made a survey of the anthropological literature on child-rearing in 110, mostly non-literate, societies (Barry et al., 1957). They found that in more than 80 per cent of those societies where accurate ratings could be made, girls more than boys were encouraged to be nurturant, whereas boys more than girls were subject to training for self-reliance and achievement. In many societies responsibility and obedience was also encouraged in girls more than boys (table 5.3). The degree of pressure for sex-typing does vary with the type of society, and appears to be especially strong in societies where male strength is important for hunting or herding, and less strong in societies with small family groups, where sharing of tasks is inevitable.

A more detailed study of child-rearing was made in the 'Six Cultures Study' (Whiting and Edwards, 1973; Whiting and Whiting, 1975) in which direct observations were made on samples of children in Kenya, Japan, India, the

TABLE 5.3    *Incidence among different cultures of training girls or boys more strongly for certain characteristics*

|  | Girls trained more % | Boys trained more % | No difference % |
|---|---|---|---|
| Nurturance (*n=33*) | 82 | 0 | 18 |
| Responsibility (*n=84*) | 61 | 11 | 28 |
| Obedience (*n=69*) | 35 | 3 | 62 |
| Self-reliance (*n=82*) | 0 | 85 | 15 |
| Achievement (*n=31*) | 3 | 87 | 10 |

*n* = number of cultures rated.
*Source*: Barry et al., 1957

Phillipines, Mexico and the USA. In the majority of these societies girls were more nurturant and made more physical contacts while boys were more aggressive, dominant and engaged in more rough-and-tumble play. Differences among the six cultures could often be related to differences in socialization pressures, e.g. the extent to which older girls were required to do 'nurturant' tasks such as looking after younger siblings.

## Theories of Sex-role Identification

Why do boys and girls come to behave in different ways, and have certain beliefs about sex-appropriate behaviour? There are several theories about this process of acquiring a sex-role, or 'sex-role identification'. Here we consider biological factors, social learning theory and the cognitive-developmental approach.

### Biological factors

Boys and girls differ in one chromosome pair; girls have two linked X chromosomes, whereas boys have one X and one Y chromosome. This genetic difference normally leads to differential production of hormones, both in the fetus and later in adolescence (chapter 8). These hormones lead to differentiation of bodily characteristics, such as the genital organs, and may also influence brain growth and hence behaviour patterns.

Most of the evidence linking sex hormones to behaviour comes from animal studies, although there have been several studies on human children who have accidentally received unusual amounts of sex hormone early in life, for example while in the uterus. A well-known study was reported by Money and Ehrhardt in 1972. They examined girls who had been exposed to unusually high levels of the male sex hormone androgen before birth. (At the time this hormone treatment was given to some mothers for problems such as repeated miscarriages; it has now been discontinued.) Any malformation of the genitals was corrected surgically and the children were reared as girls. Compared to a matched group of girls who had not been exposed to excess androgen, these girls and their mothers reported themselves as being more tomboyish and less likely to play with other girls and like feminine clothes. In evaluating this study the parent's knowledge of the hormonal abnormalities must be borne in mind; this could have affected their behaviour towards the children. However, it may seem unlikely that the parents actually encouraged these girls to be tomboyish, for example.

These and similar studies do suggest that sex hormones may have some effect on behaviour. In normal fetal development male sex hormones perhaps predispose boys to become more physically active and interested in rough-and-tumble play, for example. Such effects are consistent with evidence that some sex differences appear early in life, and in most human societies (such as boys' preference for rough-and-tumble). However, while biological factors are probably important in any comprehensive explanation of sex differences, they do not in themselves explain the process of sex-role identification, and they do not explain the variations in sex roles in different societies. Nor do Money and Ehrhardt (1972) ignore the influence of social learning. In related studies they have looked at what happens when a child's sex is reassigned at some point after birth (for example, if a girl exposed to excess androgens is raised first as a boy, before the mistake is realized). Whatever the biological sex, the child can normally be raised according to the assigned sex without major difficulties; the major aspects of sex-role identification are acquired by learning. However, as might be expected, reassignment of sex becomes very difficult once a child has got some way in establishing its own gender identity, as has happened by 3 years of age. Money and Ehrhardt (1972) conclude that there is a critical period between 18 months and 3 years when gender identity is being established. Before this period, gender reassignment is easy; after it, it is very problematical.

*'Social' learning theory*

One approach to the learning of sex-role identification, espoused by psychologists such as Bandura (1969) and Mischel (1970), is that children are moulded into sex-roles by the behaviour of adults, especially parents and teachers – the social learning theory approach. The idea of reinforcement is particularly important in this theory, which postulates that parents and others reward (or 'reinforce') sex-appropriate behaviour in children. Parents might encourage nurturant behaviour in girls, and discourage it in boys, for example. This theory also supposes that children observe the behaviour of same-sex models, and imitate them; for example, boys might observe and imitate the behaviour of male figures in TV films, in their playful and aggressive behaviour.

Do parents behave differently towards boys and girls? The answer seems often to be yes. For example, Fagot (1978) studied children aged 20–24 months in American homes. She found that girls were encouraged by their parents to dance, dress up, follow them around, and play with dolls, but were discouraged from jumping and climbing; boys however were encouraged to play with blocks and trucks, but discouraged from playing with dolls or seeking help. Thus, even many of the earliest sex differences could be explained by parental reinforcement. In a similar study of 3-5-year-olds (Langlois and Downs, 1980), mothers, fathers and also same-age peers reinforced sex-appropriate behaviour and discouraged sex-inappropriate behaviour in children. Other studies have found direct evidence that reinforcements or punishments by same-age peers can affect the child's behaviour (Lamb et al., 1980).

The role of observation and imitation in sex-role identification is less clear-cut. If observation in itself were important, we would expect most children to acquire a female sex-role identity, as the great majority of caregivers of young children, and nursery and infant school teachers, are female. Imitation of same-sex models may be important, but probably only by middle childhood, by which time gender constancy is achieved. In fact, it is the influence of the child's own gender awareness which many psychologists now consider to be the missing element in the social learning approach to sex-role identification.

*Cognitive-developmental theory*

The cognitive-development approach in this area stems from the writings of Kohlberg (1966, 1969). He argued that the child's growing sense of gender identity is crucial to sex-role identification. Children attend to and imitate same-sex models, and follow sex-appropriate activities, because they realize that this is what a child of their own sex usually does. This process has been termed 'self-socialization' by Maccoby and Jacklin (1974), since it does not depend directly on external reinforcement. The difference between the cognitive-developmental and social learning viewpoints is summarized in figure 5.3.

What evidence is there for the cognitive-developmental view? In a number of studies the development of gender identity and constancy has been found to correlate with the degree of sex-typed behaviour. For example, in a study of 2- and

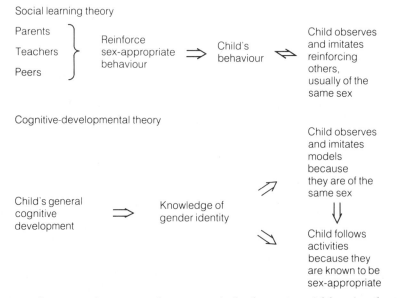

FIGURE 5.3    *Summary of two approaches to sex-role development: social learning theory and cognitive-developmental theory*

3-year-olds by Weinraub et al. (1984), it was found that the children who had achieved gender identity more securely were also the ones who were observed to make more sex-stereotyped toy preferences. In another study of 4–6-year-olds (Ruble et al., 1981), the level of gender constancy was measured, and each child was shown a film of either same-or opposite-sex children playing with a new toy. Only children high on gender constancy were influenced by the film; if a child high on gender constancy saw opposite-sex children playing with the toy, that child avoided playing with it subsequently.

A second source of support is that reinforcement theory in itself seems insufficient to explain sex-role development. For example, several studies have found that nursery school teachers tend to reward 'feminine' type behaviours (e.g. quiet, sedentary activities near an adult) in both boys and girls equally, yet this does not prevent boys engaging more in noisy, rough-and-tumble play. The limited importance of reinforcement by teachers is also brought out in a study by Serbin et al. (1977). They asked teachers in two preschool classes to praise and encourage cooperative play between boys and girls for a 2-week period. This did increase the level of cooperative cross-sex play, but as soon as the special reinforcement was discontinued, cross-sex play declined to just as low a level as before.

A detailed study by Fagot (1985) has shown how reinforcement theory must be augmented by other considerations. She observed 40 children aged 21–25 months in playgroups, looking at what activities were reinforced (e.g. by praise or joining in) and by whom. As in other studies, she found that the teachers reinforced 'feminine' activities in both boys and girls. She also looked at the effectiveness of the reinforcement (in terms of continuation of the activity). This varied with who was reinforcing, and with what was being reinforced. Girls were influenced by teachers and by other girls, but not much by boys. Boys were influenced by other boys, but not much by girls or teachers. Furthermore, boys were not influenced at all by girls or teachers whilst they were in 'masculine' activities such as rough-and-tumble or transportation toys.

In summary, while reinforcement does seem to have some effect, it looks as though its effects are being 'filtered' through other factors. From some studies it seems that the child's own gender identity is important here. In Fagot's (1985) study, however, the children were so young that gender identity was unlikely to have been achieved. The effects of reinforcement must have been mediated either by some early, non-verbal awareness of gender not tapped by the usual tests (figure 5.2), or by some canalized processes of activity preference and behavioural compatibility between the sexes. It appears that any complete understanding of sex-role development will require an integration of biological factors, reinforcement and social learning provided by others, with the cognitive-developmental view which provides an active role for the child himself or herself. Recent work on the way children grow into gender roles is summarized by Archer (1989).

## Ethnic Awareness, Identity, Preference and Prejudice

Besides differing by gender, people differ in terms of their racial or ethnic group; both are usually obvious from physical characteristics such as hair and skin colour, and facial appearance. There is not universal agreement on how people should be classified by ethnic group. In the UK, for example, some people whose (grand)-parents come from the Indian subcontinent might wish to be called by the general term of British Asian, others might wish to be called Indian, Pakistani or Bangladeshi from the country of origin of their (grand)parents, while yet others might wish to be called Black, in common with Afro-Caribbeans and other ethnic minority groups seen as being in an underprivileged position in a predominantly white society. The UK government census of 1991 asks people to identify themselves into one of nine ethnic groups: white, black (African), black (Caribbean), black (other), Indian, Pakistani, Bangladeshi, Chinese, and other. In North America, main ethnic groups would include white, black, American Indian, Chinese. An inclusive group such as white could be broken down into finer ones, e.g. Anglo-Saxon, Celtic, Hispanic. Other important dimensions are language (e.g. English Canadian and French Canadian) and religion (e.g. Muslim Indian and Hindu Indian). In this section we will look at how children become aware of ethnic differences and identify with an ethnic group; and how this affects their behaviour.

*Ethnic awareness*

As a child grows up he or she will become aware that people differ by ethnic origin. This ethnic awareness can be assessed by, for example, showing a child photographs of different persons and saying 'show me the Afro-Caribbean person', 'show me the Chinese person', and so on. By the age of 4 or 5 years children seem able to make basic discriminations, for example between black and white; and during the next few years more difficult ones, such as Anglo and Hispanic.

PLATE 5.2    *Part of a test for understanding that a child's ethnic identity does not change with superficial attributes such as clothes (from Aboud, 1988)*

A bit later, at around 8 or 9 years, children understand that ethnic identity remains constant despite changes in age, or superficial attributes such as clothing. For example, in one study children were shown a series of photos of an Italian Canadian boy, labelled as such, putting on native Indian clothes (plate 5.2). When asked to identify the boy in the final photo, half the 6-year-olds thought that he was different from the boy in the first photo and that he really was Indian. By 8 years, none made this mistake (Aboud, 1988). This development is similar to that of gender awareness and gender constancy (p. 146), though it seems to occur a year or so later.

## Ethnic identity

Ethnic identity can be thought of as awareness of one's ethnicity. It closely parallels the developing awareness of ethnicity in others. It is usually assessed by using dolls, or photographs, and asking the child to point to one that looks most like them. Generally, children of 4 years and above choose the doll or photograph of someone from their own ethnic group, though there are variations in different studies (Aboud, 1988). Of course, a child might quite well use other (non-ethnic) criteria to decide which is most like them, such as facial expression; so it is best to provide several examples for each ethnic group, for the child to choose from.

## Ethnic preference

How do children react to, and evaluate, the ethnic differences which they become aware of from about 4 years? We can look at this in several different ways.

Firstly, we could use similar test situations to those used in assessing ethnic awareness and idenity, with dolls or photographs representing different ethnic groups. This time, however, we could ask the child which they would like to be themselves; or which they would like to play with.

A number of studies of this kind have found that most white children choose or prefer the white doll (or photo) from 4 years, whereas black and other ethnic minority children are more divided, with (in some of the earlier studies) most of them choosing the white doll too. These preferences strengthen up to about 7 years. Beyond 7 years, black children tend to choose the black doll or photo more frequently. These studies were mostly carried out in North America or the UK, where whites form the dominant and more privileged social group; and this probably influences the results. Effects of historical period are likely to be very important here (cf. p. 6). With the rise of ethnic minority group consciousness and pride in their own culture which has characterized recent decades in North America and the UK, the extent to which minority group children choose their own group has increased, at least among 7 to 11-year-olds (Davey, 1983; Milner, 1983).

Another way of looking at ethnic preference is more naturalistic; we could observe whom children actually choose as play partners, in playgroup or playground situations. We saw earlier (p. 145) that children tend to segregate by sex; do they segregate by race?

The answer from available studies seems to be a definite 'yes'. For example, Finkelstein and Haskins (1983) observed black and white kindergarten children in the USA. They found that even these 5-year-olds showed marked segregation by

TABLE 5.4    *Mean percentage of White and Asian play-mates, by gender, summed for 8- and 9-year-olds in two UK middle schools to 1980*

|  | White playmates | Asian playmates |
|---|---|---|
| White boys | 62.9 | 19.9 |
| White girls | 84.4 | 7.0 |
| Asian boys | 16.2 | 79.9 |
| Asian girls | 9.4 | 89.6 |

*Source:* Boulton and Smith, 1991

race, and that this increased over the kindergarten year. However, neither black nor white children behaved differently to other-colour peers from same-colour peers.

In older children too, segregation by race is noticeable, whether in the US (e.g. Schofield and Francis, 1982), or in the UK (e.g. Boulton and Smith, 1991). However, segregation by race seems to be less marked than segregation by sex, at least in the middle school period. Table 5.4 shows choice of playground partners from two UK middle schools with a mixture of white and British Asian children. Amongst these 8- to 9-year-old children, segregation is marked by both sex and race, in that order of priority. It may be noticed that segregation by race is less marked amongst boys than by girls, a finding consistent with that of Schofield and Francis (1982). This may be because boys play in larger groups than girls; when playing football, for example, ethnic group may be ignored in order to fill up a team with the requisite number of good players.

*Ethnic prejudice*

Preference is not in itself the same as prejudice. One might choose to play with same-sex or same-race partners, but still regard other-sex and other-race children as being just as good or able as oneself and one's friends. Indeed, the limited evidence from Finkelstein and Haskins (1983) study is that their kindergarten children showed preference, but not necessarily prejudice; when a white child played with a black child his or her behaviour did not change (and visa versa).

Prejudice implies a negative evaluation of another person, on the basis of some general attribute (which could be for example sex, race, or disability). Thus, racial prejudice means a negative evaluation of someone as a consequence of their being in a certain racial or ethnic group. If a white child dislikes a black child because of some individual attribute, this is not prejudice. But if a white child dislikes a black child (and black children) because of his or her colour, this is racial prejudice. It may not always be easy to be sure whether an action is racial prejudice in individual cases, but the experience of prejudice can be very damaging and at times tragic. The disastrous effects of racial prejudice in the school system is illuminated in a case study of a British school, *Murder in the Playground* (MacDonald, 1989) (and see also chapter 14).

Many children do seem to show racial prejudice from 4 or 5 years of age, as they become aware of ethnic differences. For example, children can be asked to put photos of children from different ethnic groups along a scale of liking (Aboud, 1988). Or, children can be asked to assign positive adjectives such as 'work hard' and 'truthful', or negative adjectives such as 'stupid' or 'dirty', to all, some, one or none of photos representing different ethnic groups (Davey, 1983). The results are rather similar to those of ethnic identity; prejudice seems to increase from 4 to 7 years, mainly at the expense of minority ethnic groups. During middle childhood, white children tend to remain prejudiced against black or minority group children, while the latter show a more mixed pattern but often become more positive to their own group.

Aboud (1988) argues that there are definite stages in children's development of prejudice. Before about 3 or 4 years of age, ethnic awareness is largely absent and prejudice is not an issue. From 4 to 7 years, she argues, children perceive other ethnic groups as dissimilar to themselves, and because of this tend to have negative evaluations of them. From 8 years onward, children can think more flexibly about ethnic differences, and in terms of individuals rather than groups. Thus, the rather natural prejudice of the younger child against dissimilar others can be modified, especially from around 7–8 years onwards. (This theory however has some difficulty in explaining why some minority group children prefer the majority group up to 7 years of age.)

Schools have been a focus for work to reduce racial prejudice in children. This can be assisted by a multi-racial curriculum approach which emphasizes the diversity of racial and cultural beliefs and practices and gives them equal evaluation. Procedures such as Cooperative Group Work (Cowie and Rudduck, 1991) may help to bring children of different race (and sex) together in common activities, and thus reduce ethnic preference and prejudice in the classroom.

## The Influence of Television

The mass media exert an important influence on children's awareness of their world, and their behaviour. The influence of television has attracted most attention among the mass media over the past 20 or 30 years. This is probably because of the relative newness of television, compared to radio, books and magazines, and also because of the degree of exposure to it which the average child receives. More recently still the influence of computer and video games has received considerable attention. Patricia Greenfield's *Mind and Media* (1984) is a useful study which looks at and compares the impact of these various media forms. However, most research has been done on television, and it is this we will discuss in this section.

Television has only been available since the late 1940s, but the television set is now a commonplace in the great majority of homes. We also know that children watch a great deal of television. When it was first introduced, children in Britain watched about two hours a day (box 5.2). This has tended to increase, perhaps as transmission hours have been extended. A survey in Britain made in 1971 (Greenberg, 1976) found a peak of exposure in working class boys aged 12–14 years (table 5.5). More recently figures show exposure in most Western societies to be

TABLE 5.5    *Daily amount of television viewing (in hours and minutes) by British adolescents in 1971*

|         | 12–14 years | | 15–19 years | |
|---------|-------------|--------------|-------------|--------------|
|         | *Middle class* | *Working class* | *Middle class* | *Working class* |
| Male    | 3.01        | 3.22         | 2.01        | 2.06         |
| Female  | 2.48        | 2.48         | 1.56        | 2.13         |

*Source*: Greenberg, 1976

between two and four hours, with surveys generally agreeing that there is a rapid rise through middle childhood to a peak in viewing in early adolescence, followed by a slower decline (Murray,1980). A survey by Cullingford (1984) found that most children (well over 80 per cent at all ages from 7 to 12) reported watching television the previous evening, and typically watching three to six programmes each evening. Many 9-year-olds and almost all older children had watched television after midnight, at some time. Thus, children do not only watch children's programmes. Even from the early surveys (e.g. box 5.2) evidence is that crime thrillers, dramas and comedies have been popular from middle childhood onwards.

Children then spend a great deal of time watching television. So how does it affect them? In Britain an early report by Himmelweit et al. (1958) looked for changes in children's behaviour as television started coming into most people's homes (see box 5.2). Much research has also been carried out in the USA. The effect of television probably depends on many factors, such as the child's age, sex and background, and of course the nature of the programmes shown. There has been considerable concern in the USA at the use of children's television advertising to promote 'war toys' such as GI Joe, Transformers, or Teenage Mutant Ninja Turtles, linked to corresponding programmes (Carlsson-Paige and Levin, 1987). There is also concern that violence on television may make children more aggressive, and that many programmes portray stereotyped images of sex roles, or of ethnic minorities. Conversely, some social scientists think that television can be used to encourage prosocial and cooperative behaviour, or reduce stereotyped views (Greenfield, 1984). Other researchers think that television does not have nearly as much effect, either way, as most people fear (Cullingford, 1984).

There are different theoretical perspectives on this issue. One point of view is that watching violence on television might be 'cathartic' – a Greek word referring to the purging of emotions which was supposed to result from watching classical drama. Perhaps children watching 'The A Team', James Bond films or any programmes featuring violence, have their emotions purged or drained in a similar way. A more prevalent view is that watching television violence may encourage aggression. This could be so because the child may imitate actions seen on television, especially if they are associated with admired figures, or if aggression seems to have successful outcomes. The issue is certainly an important one: it has been estimated that the average child in the USA, by the age of 16, will have spent more time watching television than being in school, and will have seen 13,000 killings on television!

There is certainly some evidence favouring the latter theory rather than the former. For example, one study looked at how young children respond to actual violence between others (Cummings et al., 1985). Two 2-year-old children and their mothers were brought to an apartment-type room in a research laboratory. After settling in, two actors entered a kitchenette area at the far end of the room. Following a script, they simulated first a friendly exchange, then a period of angry verbal conflict, then a reconciliation of their differences. It was observed that the children typically responded to the conflict episodes with signs of distress, and also increased aggression to the other child. Furthermore, some of the children who experienced the simulation the second time, a month later, showed still higher levels of aggression and distress. The witnessing of anger on the part of others seemed to arouse emotion in these children and release aggression, rather than purge it vicariously.

The children in Cumming's study were 2 years old. At that age children do not watch much television, rather paying attention to actual people. But from 3 years of age onwards children seem to watch and imitate people on television as much as actual persons. Do we have direct evidence that television violence produces aggression?

There have been a number of laboratory studies which have suggested this. Typically, children would be shown aggressive or non-aggressive films, and then placed in situations where they could hit a punch bag or inflatable doll, or push buttons which supposedly 'helped' or 'hurt' another child. Children who watched aggressive films punched the bag or doll, or pushed the 'hurt' button, more. However, these experiments have been criticized as very artificial. Hitting the punch bag might have been playful, not aggressive; and some of the experiments seem so contrived that the main effect being measured may be obedience to the experimenter (Cullingford, 1984). We will look in detail at two more naturalistic studies: one is a 'field experiment', while the other has a correlational, longitudinal design.

### A field experiment on nursery school children

Friedrich and Stein (1973) studied 4-year-old children enrolled in a nine-week summer nursery school programme. After three weeks of baseline observations, the 100 children were assigned to 'aggressive ($n = 30$), 'prosocial' ($n = 30$), or 'neutral' ($n = 40$) conditions. For the next four weeks, children saw a total of 12 television programmes. The children in the aggressive condition were taken as a group to see 'Batman' or 'Superman' cartoons; those in the prosocial condition saw 'Misterogers neighbourhood', which prompted themes of cooperation, sympathy and friendship; while those in the neutral condition saw factual films with little aggressive or prosocial content. During the four-week period, and also the final two weeks, the children's behaviour was closely observed.

Some of the results are shown in table 5.6. It seems that the children who watched the prosocial programmes were scored as more patient ('tolerance of delay') than the children who watched the aggressive programmes, and tended to be more persistent at tasks and more spontaneously helpful or obedient ('rule obedience'). However, the findings on aggressive and prosocial behaviour were complicated. Aggressive behaviour decreased amongst those children who were initially high in aggression, and watched the prosocial or neutral programmes, but there was no

TABLE 5.6    *Mean changes in rates of behaviour (per minute) in preschool children exposed to television programmes with aggressive, neutral or prosocial content*

|  | Aggressive | Neutral | Prosocial | |
|---|---|---|---|---|
| **Aggression** | | | | |
| initially low | 0.039 | 0.079 | 0.046 | n.s. |
| initially high | −0.019 | −0.123 | −0.088 | $p<0.05$ |
| **Prosocial** | | | | |
| lower social class | −0.007 | −0.026 | 0.093 | $p<0.05$ |
| higher social class | 0.071 | 0.047 | −0.017 | $p<0.05$ |
| Tolerance of delay | −0.016 | 0.036 | 0.019 | $p<0.05$ |
| Task persistence | −0.039 | −0.068 | 0.014 | n.s. |
| Rule obedience | −0.039 | −0.014 | 0.014 | n.s. |

*Source*: Friedrich and Stein, 1973

significant effect for children intially low in aggression. For prosocial behaviour, it was found that this increased in children from lower social class families who watched the prosocial programmes; but it also increased in children from higher social class families who watched the aggressive programmes!

The results of this study are rather mixed. They do suggest some positive effects from watching programmes with prosocial rather than aggressive content, but some effects are not statistically significant or even go in the opposite direction. The researchers carried out many analyses and clearly tried to emphasize the 'desired' findings in their report, which is often cited. Nevertheless, the results of these and similar studies leave scope for sceptics (Cullingford, 1984).

### A longitudinal, correlational study on adolescents

Quite a different research strategy is exemplified in a study by Lefkowitz et al. (1977). These researchers interviewed the parents of 8–9-year-old children (184 boys, 175 girls) to find out their favourite television programmes, and hence constructed a measure of exposure to television violence. This score was higher for boys than for girls. The children were also asked to rate the others in their class for aggressiveness. They found that the correlation between the two measures was 0.21 for boys, but only 0.02 for girls. The correlation for boys, while small, was significant ($p < 0.01$); but this correlation could mean either that viewing television violence caused aggression, or that aggressive boys liked watching violent television programmes. Yet another explanation could be that some other factor, parental discord in the home for example, led a child both to watch violent television programmes and also to be aggressive himself.

The same measures were taken ten years later, when the children were 19 years old. The correlations between the same two measures at this time, and the correlations between the two time periods, are shown for both boys and girls in figure 5.4. The results for the boys are the most interesting and the most quoted. They show that watching a lot of violent television at age 9 is significantly

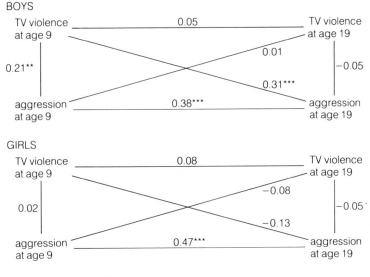

FIGURE 5.4    *Cross-lagged correlations between amount of television violence viewed at ages 9 and 19 and peer-rated aggression at ages 9 and 19, for 184 boys and 175 girls (from Lefkowitz et al., 1977)*

correlated ($r = 0.31$) with peer-rated aggression at age 19; however, peer-rated aggression at age 9 is not correlated ($r = 0.01$) with watching violent television at age 19. This certainly suggests that watching violent television leads to aggression, rather than visa versa. A similar, though less strong, association was found when aggression was measured by self-ratings, or personality questionnaires. Some other factor or factors might still be responsible for the associations, but this technique (known as 'cross-lagged correlations') does give more weight to the findings than a simple correlation would do. The researchers felt they had identified a small but statistically reliable influence of television violence on aggressive behaviour in boys.

The findings for girls (figure 5.4) are much weaker, and tend to go in the opposite direction. The researchers attempted to explain this by arguing that, first, there were few aggressive females portrayed on television (this was in the 1960s), and secondly, that since female aggression was less socially approved of, then 'for girls, television violence viewing may actually be a positively sanctioned social activity in which aggressive girls may express aggression vicariously since they cannot express aggression directly in social interactions' (Lefkowitz et al., 1977, p. 122). It seems that the researchers have resorted here to a 'cathartic' explanation, despite there being no direct evidence to support it.

### A continuing controversy

Although the studies we have looked at, and others, do tend to support the hypothesis that television can affect social behaviour, the evidence is not clear-cut. Some findings are small, or not significant. Some are present only for certain measures, or for one sex or for children initially high in aggression. Some reviewers feel the case is not proved (e.g. Freedman, 1984). After all, they would argue, much television violence involves fantasy figures (such as Batman and Superman films in the Friedrich and Stein study) which older children certainly distinguish from real violence. Also children may be 'desensitized' to violence in serials such as 'The A Team' which are viewed basically as entertainment. In his survey, Cullingford (1984) found that many children could not remember much of what they had viewed the evening before, and that the more programmes they had watched, the fewer details they could remember. He argued that children 'see that television is not to be taken seriously, that the murders are there as stunts, that shooting is a part of entertainment. Thus the violence on television passes them by'. This may seem a bland and complacent view, but the research evidence so far, while suggestive that television does have some effects on aggression or prosocial behaviour, is not of sufficient weight for us to be really certain how important the effect is. We know from case studies of a few abnormal individuals that television violence can on occasion provide a stimulus or model for some violent crime. But it may be that for most children, most of the time, the impact of television is rather small.

If we are considering aggression, then other influences may be much more important. For example, actual aggression in the home between parents might be a more potent influence than fictitious aggression on television. Parental discord has been consistently found to predict later conduct disorders (Rutter, 1981). We saw the impact of actual (though simulated) aggression on young children in the study by Cummings et al. (1985). The latter state that viewing actual discord in the home could be a powerful influence on aggression in the home, an influence that is not so easily turned off as a television set (cf. p. 108).

## Television Programmes as a Source of Social Stereotypes

The other major concern of social scientists in connection with the content of television programmes is that they may present a stereotyped picture of real life which may encourage undesirable prejudices. These might be, for example, about female roles (in what is arguably still a male-dominated society), about minority ethnic groups or other nationalities, and about people with disabilities.

Television programmes, like many children's books, do seem to present a one-sided view of sex-roles. Researchers in both the UK and the USA have carried out 'content analyses' of television programmes, seeing how many male and female characters there are, and what sort of roles they have. These studies have found that there are two or three times as many male as female characters, and that the males are usually portrayed as more powerful, dominant, rational and intelligent. Females are often depicted as weak and passive, watching admiringly while the males have most of the action (Sternglanz and Serbin, 1974; Durkin; 1985). There has been increasing awareness of the imbalance, and some attempt to redress it with programmes such as 'WonderWoman' to parallel 'Superman' and other popular male-dominated programmes. Nevertheless, many programmes present a stereotyped and sometimes prejudiced or 'sexist' view of sex roles.

We saw earlier how parents, and later peers, are probably very important in sex-role learning, so how important is television viewing in this process? In *Television, Sex Roles and Children* (1985), Kevin Durkin has reviewed the evidence. He concludes that there is little to suggest that the more television children watch, the more sex-stereotyped are their views. The few studies which did report this seem to have been methodologically unsound (as with some of the work on television violence and aggression). Durkin emphasizes that the child or young person is an active agent in interpreting television programmes, not just a passive recipient of a 'dose' of sex-role stereotyping. Thus, it is important to consider the age of the child, his or her understanding of gender, as well as the family and sociocultural context.

A related topic is whether television programmes can be used effectively in 'counter-stereotyping' — presenting sex roles of a deliberately non-traditional kind. This has been attempted in the British children's programme 'Rainbow', and in an American programme called 'Freestyle'. There is some evidence that 9- to 12-year-olds who watched 'Freestyle' did have less stereotyped views of sex roles, especially when viewing at school was followed by teacher-led discussion. There are, however, important ethical issues to consider in such attempts to 'manipulate' attitudes, which are discussed in Durkin's book.

Other ethnic groups or nationalities may also be portrayed adversely in the mass media. Table 5.7, taken from the Himmelweit et al. (1958) (see box 5.2) shows how 'villains' were much more often foreigners than 'heroes' and 'heroines' were (and also of lower social class, though the upper/middle class bias of British television programmes in the 1950s may have lessened somewhat and does not now get so much attention). Until recently there were few programmes which showed people from ethnic minorities, such as people of Asian or Afro-Caribbean origin, in ordinary roles, or which presented their cultural background. There are now some programmes for young children, such as 'You and Me' in Britain, or 'Sesame Street' (first made in the USA), which have tried to remedy this. Some research has indicated that these programmes do have positive effects on inter-racial attitudes and encourage greater cultural pride and self-confidence among ethnic minority children (Greenfield, 1984). Similar findings have also been made concerning the portrayal of disabled persons in a more realistic and positive light, for example in 'Sesame Street' (Greenfield, 1984).

Most reviewers agree that parents have an important role to play in the effects television may have on their children. Besides encouraging responsible viewing

TABLE 5.7   *Percentage of heroes/heroines and villains having certain characteristics in 13 television plays*

|  | Heroes/heroines (n = 27) | Villains (n = 11) |
|---|---|---|
| British nationality | 60 | 37 |
| Upper or upper/middle class | 93 | 55 |
| Glamorous and high-powered occupations | 70 | 55 |

*Source*: Himmelweit et al., 1958

habits, parents can talk about programmes with their children, discussing information or attitudes which are being transmitted. From the beginning (e.g. box 5.2)
research has indicated that children are influenced most by television portrayals
which are not counteracted or put in perspective by anything in their immediate
environment. Thus besides influencing the educational value of television programmes, parents and teachers can probably have an appreciable effect on how
programmes influence children's social attitudes and behaviour (Greenfield, 1984;
Collins et al., 1981).

### Further reading

The best introduction to emotional development in children is P. Harris 1989: *Children and
Emotion.* Oxford: Basil Blackwell. Also useful is J. Dunn 1988: *The Beginnings of Social
Understanding.* Oxford: Basil Blackwell. For more advanced reading, A. Whiten (ed.) 1991:
*Natural Theories of Mind: Evolution, Development and Simulation of Everyday Mindreading.*
Oxford: Basil Blackwell, is a good source both for this chapter and the relevant parts of
chapter 2. For more on autistic children see U. Frith 1989: *Autism: Explaining the Enigma.*
Oxford: Basil Blackwell.
     A useful review of sex differences in children (and adults) is J. Archer and B. Lloyd 1986:
*Sex and Gender.* 2nd edn. Harmondsworth: Penguin. A more advanced collection is D.
Hargreaves and A. Colley (eds) 1986. *The Psychology of Sex Roles.* London: Harper and Row.
The development of racial awareness in children is reviewed by F. Aboud 1988: *Children and
Prejudice.* Oxford: Basil Blackwell.
     A readable review of the effects of television and other mass media on behaviour is in
P. M. Greenfield 1984: *Mind and Media: the Effects of Television, Computers and Video Games.*
Aylesbury: Fontana. More sceptical views of the impact of television are in D. Howitt 1982:
*Mass Media and Social Problems.* Oxford: Pergamon; and C. Cullingford 1984: *Children and
Television.* Aldershot: Gower. The impact of television on sex roles is reviewed by K. Durkin
1985: *Television. Sex Roles and Children.* Milton Keynes: Open University Press. The war toys
issue is discussed by N. Carlsson-Paige and D. E. Levin 1987: *The War Play Dilemma:
Balancing Needs and Values in the Early Childhood Classroom.* New York: Teachers College,
Columbia University.

### Discussion points

1    When can a child understand someone else's emotional state?

2    What deficits do autistic children show, and what might be the cause?

3    What causes sex differences in behaviour?

4    How does awareness of race develop?

5    How good is the evidence relating television violence to aggressive behaviour in
     children?

**Practical exercises**

1    Try the 'rouge' experiment of p. 130 with one or more babies aged 9 to 24 months. You will need the parents' cooperation, and a mirror, as well as the rouge or lipstick. Observe the baby's responses. Do your results agree with Table 5.1? If it is easier for you to find older participants of 3 to 5 years, try one or more of the 'false belief' tasks described in the text. When do you find children can succeed in these tasks?

2    Make a list of toys, or activities. Ask people to state for each item on the list whether it is predominantly chosen by males, by females, or about equally by both sexes. Do different people agree on this? Are there clear male and female stereotypes? Are these stereotypes stronger in people of certain ages, or from certain social groups?

3    Watch a sample of fictional drama or crime thriller television programmes which children might watch, for example any such programmes screened between 7 and 9 pm, each night for a week. Make a list of the main characters, their sex and ethnic background, and whether they are portrayed as strong or weak, active or passive, kind or evil, etc. Construct a table similar to table 5.7. Do your results suggest that stereotyping is still occurring in such programmes?

---

Box 5.1

---

# Does the autistic child have a 'theory of mind'?

The aim of this study was to examine whether autistic children have some specific deficit in the area of 'theory of mind'. The authors used an adaptation of the 'false belief' task, originally used by Wimmer and Perner (1983), and illustrated schematically in box figure 5.1.1.

In this task there are two dolls, Sally and Anne (picture 1). With the child watching, the experimenter causes Sally to place a marble in her basket (picture 2). Sally then leaves (picture 3), and Anne transfers the marble to her own box (picture 4). Sally then returns (picture 5). The experimenter now asks the child three questions.

*Reality question*   'Where is the marble really?'

*Memory question*   'Where was the marble in the beginning?'

*Belief question*   'Where will Sally look for her marble?'

The first two questions are control questions to ensure that the child has attended, knows the current location of the object, and remembers where it was before. The crucial question is the third. To pass the third question correctly, the child has to understand that someone else (in this case the doll, Sally) can hold a different belief from oneself, and indeed a belief that is *false*. For this reason, the task is known as a 'false belief task'. It involves understanding that 'Sally *thinks* that the marble is in the basket because she doesn't *know* that Anne moved it to the box'; Baron-Cohen, Leslie and Frith believe that this ability involves what they call second-order or meta-representations, which are necessary for a theory of mind and which autistic children may have great difficulty acquiring.

Two trials were done with each child; first as shown in the figure, and secondly with the marble being hidden in a new location (the experimenter's pocket).

The experiment was done with 20 autistic children, aged 6 to 16 years. Based on standard tests (see chapter 13), their mental age was around 5 years on verbal IQ tests and about 9 years on non-verbal IQ tests. Two comparison groups were used. One was a group of 27 normal children, between 3 and 5 years (that is, similiar or slightly lower in verbal ability). The other was a group of 14 Down's syndrome children, aged 6 to 17 years, whose IQ levels were somewhat below those of the autistic children; this group provided a control for mental retardation *not* specifically involving autism.

Based on material in S. Baron-Cohen, A. M. Leslie and U. Frith 1985: *Cognition*, 21, 37–46.

FIGURE 5.1.1  *The Sally–Anne experiment (from Frith, 1989)*

All the children passed the Reality question, and the Memory question, on both trials. Thus, they had understood and remembered what had happened. The results for the Belief question were striking. As can be seen in box table 5.1.1., most of the normal children and most of the Down's syndrome children passed the Belief question on both trials. (This was to be expected, certainly for the normal children, as 4-year-olds can usually solve such false belief tasks). Most of the autistic children (16/20) did not, and in fact failed on *both* trials.

BOX TABLE 5.1.1    *Numbers of children, in each group, who passed the Belief question on both trials*

| Number of children | Normal | Down's | Autistic | Significance of group differences |
|---|---|---|---|---|
| Passing both trials | 23 | 12 | 4 | $\chi^2 = 25.9$, $p < 0.001$ |
| Not passing both trials | 4 | 2 | 16 | |

These children, when asked 'Where will Sally look for her marble?', pointed to where the marble really was. The authors claimed that this result supported the hypothesis that autistic children as a group fail to employ a theory of mind, and specifically that they are unable to represent mental states and impute beliefs to others.

This study has an experimental design with the different groups of children as the independent variable, and the 3 questions (especially the Belief question) as the dependent variables. Some criticisms have been made of details of the experimental design. For example, de Gelder (1987) suggested that using dolls to represent people might make the task especially hard for autistic children, since they have difficulties with pretend play. Leslie and Frith (1987) acknowledged this, but reported similar results when actual children were used instead of dolls. Another problem is whether the groups of children were well matched for language ability; the authors used the British Picture Vocabulary Scale, which is a simple measure of object-naming ability, not a measure of understanding complex grammatical questions which the actual experiment involves (Boucher, 1989). Much less dramatic differences were reported in a replication of the false belief tasks (both with dolls, and with people), by Prior, Dahlstrom and Squires (1990). Nevertheless, other replications have confirmed the severity of this deficit.

It can be seen from box table 5.1.1 that 4 autistic children *did* succeed on both trials. In a subsequent study, Baron-Cohen (1989) showed that these, and other autistic children who could pass this false belief test, nevertheless failed a higher order test involving understanding how another person understands a third person's knowledge or beliefs (e.g. John *thinks* that Sally *thinks* that the marble is in the box because she doesn't *know* that Anne moved it to the box). In this study, autistic children of mental age 7 to 10 years failed the task, even though both normal and Down's syndrome children of mental age 7 years succeeded. The hypothesized impairment of autistic children is therefore not absolute for all such children, but according to these findings does seem to continue to be noticeable relative to other children (normal or Down's syndrome) of comparable mental age.

Box 5.2

# Television and the child: an empirical study of the effect of television on the young

The objective of this research study was to assess the impact of television on children and young people. The study was funded by the Nuffield Foundation, at the suggestion of the Audience Research Department of the BBC. Television sets were only just becoming common in households during the 1950s, thus there was considerable interest and concern about what the effects might be. At this time there was also still the opportunity to compare large numbers of children who both did, and did not, have a television set in their home.

The researchers carried out both a 'main survey' and some subsidiary studies, in particular a 'before-and-after study'. The main survey was carried out in London, Portsmouth, Sunderland and Bristol, from May to July 1955. Questionnnaires were given to children aged 10–11 and 13–14 years. In addition, children filled in diaries of their activities after school for one week; and measures of personality and teachers' ratings were obtained.

The design compared children who had television at home ('viewers') with those who did not, and were not regular guest viewers ('controls'). Viewers and controls were matched individually for age, sex, intelligence score and social class; altogether 1,854 matched viewers and controls were tested. The results of this comparison could give an indication of how television viewing affected children; but a critic might still raise objections. The design is not tightly controlled (for which participants should be assigned randomly to conditions) but is correlational in design, taking advantage of the fact that many homes did not yet have television. Despite the matching on some criteria, viewer children and their families might differ from controls in other respects – as they clearly did in so far as viewers' parents had chosen to acquire a television set while control families had not, despite having similar incomes. In other words, there might be pre-existing differences between children from homes which bought a television set early, and those which did not. These, rather than the effects of television *per se*, might be responsible for any findings from the main study.

As a check on this, the researchers carried out a before-and-after study (a quasi-experiment, p. 11) in Norwich, where a new television transmitter was being introduced. They gave questionnnaries to 10–11 and 13–14-year-olds both before the installation (when hardly any family there had a television set) and one year later (when many, but not all, had). At the later point in time they matched viewers and controls as in the main study, with 370 children in all. They could then see whether differences found later were already present in families before a television set had been acquired. In some cases this was so: for example, the main study found that viewers attended Sunday School less regularly. The

Based on material in H. T. Himmelweit, A. N. Oppenheim and P. Vince 1958: *London: Oxford University Press.*

before-and-after study revealed that this, and a generally lower level of religious interest and observance, was a characteristic of families who bought television sets early and not an effect of television as such.

The main findings were that both age groups watched television for about two hours a day; more than any other single leisure activity. There were no sex or social class differences in this, but more intelligent children did spend less time viewing. Also, more active, outgoing and sociable children spent less time watching. Children settled down to a routine within about three months of their family acquiring a set. Many children watched, and preferred, 'adult' programmes, particularly crime thrillers, comedies, variety programmes and family serials. Viewers spent less time than controls listening to the radio, going to the cinema and reading. The findings for reading were complex, however; acquisition of a television caused an initial decline in the time spent reading books and comics, but book-reading tended to recover, especially as some television programmes such as serials encouraged children to read the books on which they were based.

There were small but consistent differences in values and outlook. Viewers were more ambitious about jobs and more 'middle class' in their values. Adolescent girl viewers were more concerned about growing up and marrying than controls. Viewers made fewer value judgements about foreigners, though where stereotypes were given, they tended to reflect those offered by television. In general, television had most impact where the child could not turn for information to parents, friends and the immediate environment. Effects tended to be greatest in older children of least intelligence.

Many children spoke of being frightened by certain programmes, and sometimes of how these caused nightmares or difficulties in falling asleep. Such reactions seemed accentuated by viewing in the dark. Children enjoyed exciting programmes and being a little frightened, but not being really scared. Aggression on television upset them if they could identify themselves with the situation; the sheer amount of physical violence was less important. Viewers were no more aggressive or maladjusted than controls.

There was little difference in general knowledge between viewers and controls, except for less intelligent or younger children unable to read well, where the stimulus of television did give them an advantage. Viewing seemed to have little effect on school performance, or teachers' rating of concentration; teachers did say that they felt television viewing was a cause of tiredness in the morning, but this stereotype was not borne out by the comparison of viewers and controls.

This research has strengths in its scope and its large number of subjects. It is in some ways of historical interest, as both the nature of television programmes and children's behaviour may have changed in the 30 intervening years. At the time there were no programme transmissions between 6.00 pm and 7.30 pm; only one or two channels were available, programmes were in black and white; and the content was probably more 'middle class' and certainly contained less for ethnic minorities than at present. Probably levels of violence on television were lower than now, although it was already a cause for concern. It is also possible that 'second generation' television viewing families have adapted to television in a way that affects its impact on their children. However, the study is virtually unrepeatable in that it took advantage of a time when genuine comparisons of viewers and non-viewers in Britain could still be carried out.

# 6

# Play

Three sequences of behaviour are described below. Study them and think what they have in common.

*Example 1* A 2-year-old lies in his cot, babbling to himself: 'Big Bob. Big Bob. Big Bob. Big and little. Little Bobby. Little Nancy. Little Nancy. Big Bob and Nancy and Bobby. And Bob. And two three Bobbys. Three Bobbys. Four Bobbys. Six.' [All with giggles and exaggerated pronunciation.]

*Example 2* Helen, a 4-year-old, is sitting in a play house, by a table with a plastic cup, saucer and teapot. She calls out 'I'm just getting tea ready! Come on, it's dinner time now!' Charlotte, also 4, answers 'Wait!'; she wraps up a teddy in a cloth in a pram, comes in and sits opposite Helen, who says 'I made it on my own! I want a drink.' [She picks up teapot] 'There's only one cup – for me!' [pretends to pour tea into only cup]. Charlotte pretends to pour from the teapot into an imaginary cup, which she then pretends to drink from. Darren, a 3-year-old, approaches. Charlotte goes and closes the door, shutting a pretend bolt and turning a pretend key; but Helen says 'No, he's daddy; you're daddy aren't you?' [to Darren]. Charlotte 'unbolts' and 'unlocks' the door, and Darren comes in.

*Example 3* Some 6- and 7-year olds are in a school playground. A boy runs up to another, laughing, and grabs his shoulders, turns and runs off. The second boy chases the first, catches him by the waist and pulls him round. They tussle and swing around, then fall and roll over on the ground, grappling. They get up and run off, laughing and chasing again.

Most observers would agree in saying that, despite their differences, all three are examples of play, or playful behaviour. Respectively they could be described as language play, fantasy or pretend play and rough-and-tumble play. This chapter first discusses why we consider such behaviour sequences to be playful, what are the defining characteristics of play, and how it differs from the related behaviour of exploration. The next section examines the development of various kinds of play in childhood. The ideas of leading play theorists are then discussed, before the final section examines what empirical studies can tell us about the significance of play in children's development.

## The Characteristics of Playful Behaviour

Attempts to characterize or define play are legion; a concise definition seems almost impossible. Different authors tend to list different selections of criteria, or to give definitions which embody some of these criteria. There is probably less agreement between researchers as to the definition of play than there is between observers as to whether an episode of behavior is playful or not.

Some generally agreed features of play are worth noting but fall short of being defining criteria. For example, play is often described as an 'active' behaviour (yet, not all play is physically active, see example 1 above); it is described as characteristic of infancy and childhood (yet adults play, even if it is often with children); and as behaviour which is easily suppressed by other motivations, such as hunger, fear or anxiety, curiosity, or fatigue.

The last feature is related to the idea that play does not have an end in itself,or external goal. Thus, if an external goal is present (such as a need to eat, or to seek comfort) then play ceases. This has led to a functional definition of play, that the behaviour has no clear immediate benefits or obvious goal. Symons (1978) advanced this sort of definition for monkey social play, but it can equally apply to human play (Smith, 1982). If you look at examples 1 to 3 above, it is not clear when an episode is completed, or obvious what the purpose of the behaviour is. In fact, most theorists believe the child gets benefits from playing, but they are not clear, immediate ones. Indeed, there is considerable disagreement about exactly what the benefits of play are (see pp. 27, 182–5).

Another ethologist, Fagan (1974), has made a distinction between the functional approach just outlined, and a structural definition of play. The latter attempts to describe the sorts of behaviour that only occur in play, or the way in which behaviours are performed playfully.

The main examples of behaviours that only occur in play, are play signals. In mammals they often take the form of an open-mouthed play face (as in monkeys grappling), or a bouncy gambol (as in puppies or kittens initiating a chase). In children similarly laughter and the associated 'open mouth play face' (see figure 6.1) usually signals play. Such play signals are especially useful in rough-and-tumble play (example 3 on p. 169), where they can indicate that no aggressive intention is implied in a chase or wrestle.

Not all play is indexed by play signals, however. Often play is made up entirely of behaviours familiar in other contexts – running, manipulating objects, etc. According to the structural approach, we think of these behaviours as being done playfully if they are 'repeated', 'fragmented', 'exaggerated' or 're-ordered'. For example, a child just running up a slope may not be playing; but if she runs up and slides down several times (repetition), runs just halfway up (fragmentation), takes unusually large or small steps or jumps (exaggeration) or crawls up and then runs down (re-ordering), we would probably agree that it was playful.

This structural approach is not in opposition to the functional one. After all, the child running up and down the slope has no immediate purpose, apart from enjoyment. The two approaches are logically distinct, however.

Another approach which can encompass both the previous ones, is to say that observers identify play or playfulness by a number of different play criteria. No one

FIGURE 6.1   *Play signals: (a) 'open mouth face' in a chimpanzee (from Hooff, 1972); (b) 'play face' in a human child (from Smith, 1974)*

criterion is sufficiant, but the more criteria are present, the more agreement we will have that the behaviour is play. A formal model along these lines, proposed by Krasnor and Pepler (1980), is shown in figure 6.2. 'Flexibility' sums up the structural characteristics of play – variation in form and content. 'Positive affect' refers to the enjoyment of play, especially indexed by signals such as laughter. 'Nonliterality' refers to the 'as if' or pretend element (see example 2 on p. 169 above). 'Intrinsic motivation' refers to the idea that play is not constrained by external rules or social demands, but is done for its own sake.

An empirical test of Krasnor and Pepler's model was made by Smith and Vollstedt (1985). They used the four criteria above, and a fifth – means/ends, i.e. the child is more interested in the performance of the behaviour than in its outcome. They made a video film of nursery school children playing and designated short, discrete episodes which they asked 70 adults to view. Some scored each episode as to whether it was playful or not, others as to the applicability of the play criteria. Analyses showed that the episodes seen as playful were often seen as nonliteral, flexible and showing positive affect. Furthermore, the more of these were present, the higher the ratings for playfulness. Means/ends also correlated with play, but did not add anything to the first three criteria. Interestingly, the intrinsic motivation criterion did not correlate with play judgements, despite its common occurrence in definitions of play. Observers often rated non-playful activities (such as watching others, or fighting) as intrinsically motivated; equally some play episodes were externally constrained, e.g. by the demands of others in social play.

The play criterion approach seems a promising one: it does not attempt a one-sentence definition – a seemingly hopeless task. It does acknowledge, however, the continuum from non-playful to playful behaviour, and seeks to identify how observers actually decide to call a behaviour sequence 'play'. The main criteria so far identified for young children, as we have seen, are enjoyment, flexibility and pretence.

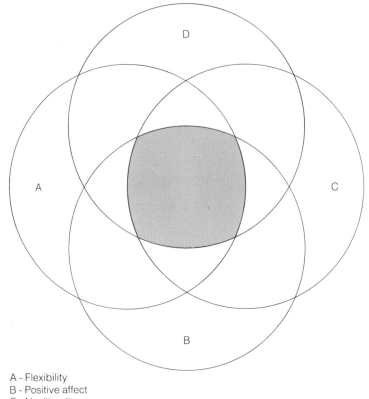

A - Flexibility
B - Positive affect
C - Nonliterality
D - Intrinsic motivation

FIGURE 6.2    *A model of play criteria. The shaded area is that most likely to be considered as playful (from Krasnor and Pepler, 1980)*

*Exploration and play*

A behaviour that is sometimes confused with play is exploration. These were often subsumed together in the 1950s and 1960s, perhaps because of the influence of behaviourism and learning theory. Both exploration and play were awkward for traditional learning theorists, as neither was obviously goal-seeking or under the control of reinforcers. It is also true that with very young children, during sensori-motor development (see chapter 11), the distinction between exploration and play is difficult to make, as for young infants, all objects are novel. By the preschool years, however, the distinction is clearer.

An experiment which made the difference clear was carried out by Hutt (1966). This is detailed in box 6.1. Using a novel toy, Hutt suggested that children typically proceed from specific exploration of the object to more playful behaviour. A slightly more elaborated, cyclic scheme was proposed by Nunnally and Lemond (1973) (see figure 6.3). In their scheme 'specific exploration' facilitates convergent learning, leading to play which consolidates learning and fosters creativity (ideas we shall

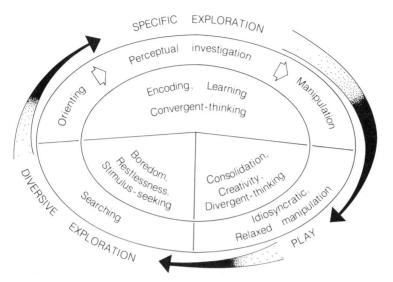

FIGURE 6.3    *The exploration–play cycle (from Nunnally and Lemond, 1973)*

return to); 'diversive exploration' refers to the searching for new forms of stimulation when the potential of the present situation is exhausted.

## The Development of Play

*Fantasy and sociodramatic play*

The beginnings of fantasy play can be seen from about 12–15 months of age. In the course of his extensive observations of his own children, Piaget (1951) recorded the following behaviour on the part of his daughter Jacqueline:

> every appearance of awareness of 'make-believe' first appeared at 1;3(12) in the following circumstances. She saw a cloth whose fringed edges vaguely recalled those of her pillow; she seized it, held a fold of it in her right hand, sucked the thumb of the same hand and lay down on her side, laughing hard. She kept her eyes open, but blinked from time to time as if she were alluding to closed eyes. Finally, laughing more and more she cried 'Nene' [Nono]. The same cloth started the same game on the following days. At 1;3(13) she treated the collar of her mother's coat in the same way. At 1;3(30) it was the tail of her rubber donkey which represented the pillow! And from 1;5 onwards she made her animals, a bear and a plush dog also do 'nono' (p.69).

The development of pretend play is well documented by Fenson and Schnell (1986), who distinguish three parallel trends; decentration, decontextualization and integration.

Decentration
(a)   child pretends to drink from empty cup
(b)   child pretends to feed doll from empty cup
(c)   child makes doll feed itself from empty cup
Decontextualization
(a)   child uses empty cup to drink from
(b)   child uses object such as shell as pretend cup to drink from
(c)   child pretends to drink from imaginary cup
Integration
(a)   child pretends to feed doll
(b)   child feeds one doll, then another
(c)   child feeds doll, then washes it, and puts it to bed.

The earliest pretend play tends to involve the child directing actions towards herself – in Jacqueline's case, pretending to sleep on a cloth. It is clear from Piaget's records that a month or so later Jacqueline directed the same actions to a toy bear and a stuffed dog. This is what is meant by decentration – incorporating other participants into pretend activities. The others may be parents (e.g. the child tries to feed parent with an empty cup), or stuffed animals or dolls. By around 24 months the child can get the doll itself to act as an agent, rather than have things done to it (see above).

Early pretend play also depends heavily on realistic objects – actual cups, combs, spoons, etc., or vey realistic substitudes. Decontextualization refers to the ability to use less realistic substitute objects – for example, a wooden block as a 'cake', or a stick as a 'gun'. Experiments have shown that the more different the object from its referent, the more difficulty children have in using it in a pretend way. It has also been shown that adults can help the process, by modelling or prompting the pretend use. In one study (Fein, 1975), after modelling by an adult, some 93 per cent of 2-year-olds would imitate making a detailed horse model 'drink' from a plastic cup; however, only 33 per cent would imitate making a horsey shape 'drink' from a clam shell. The less realistic objects made the pretence more difficult, especially as two substitutions were needed (the horsey shape, and the clam shell). If the horse alone or the cup alone were realistic, 79 per cent and 61 per cent of the children respectively could imitate successfully.

By 3 years of age this kind of decontextualized pretence occurs much more spontaneously in children's play. Here we also begin to get quite imaginary objects or actions, without any real or substitute object being present (example 2 on p. 169 has several examples). While possible for 3- and 4-year-olds, this is easier still in middle childhood. When asked to pretend to brush their teeth, or comb their hair, one study (Overton and Jackson, 1973) found that 3- and 4-year-olds used a substitute body part, such as a finger, as the brush, or comb; whereas most 6–8-year-olds (and indeed, adults) imagined the brush or comb in their hand. The ultimate in imagination in the preschool/early school years is perhaps the imaginary companion, who may follow the child around, or need to be fed at mealtimes, or tucked up in bed with him. Some one-quarter to one-third of children have some form of imaginary companion, judging from parent's reports (Partington and Grant, 1984).

Finally, play sequences become more integrated with age. Initially, one action is involved; then variations on a single theme, such as stirring the spoon in the cup,

PLATE 6.1    *Preschool children acting out a pretend sequence of preparing a meal*

then drinking; or feeding two dolls in succession. By 2 years of age multischeme combinations are in evidence. Mini-stories begin to be acted out, following 'scripts' such as shopping, or bedtime (plate 6.1). Language plays an increasing role in maintaining the play structure.

All these developments come together in sociodramatic play, prominent in 3- to 6-year-olds. Here, two or more children act out definite roles, such as mummy and daddy, spacemen and monsters, doctors and patients. Roles can be inferred from behaviour, but are often assigned verbally (see example 2 on p. 169 where Darren is labelled 'daddy').

### Language play

The most well-known examples of language play come from Weir's book *Language in the Crib* (1962). Weir left a tape recorder on under her 2-year-old son's crib at night-time. At this age toddlers often talk to themselves a lot before going to sleep, or waking up. Sample extracts are shown on p. 169 and p. 287. A similar study (Keenan and Klein 1975) recorded social play, with syllables and words, between twins aged 21 months. Children appear to use these presleep monologues or dialogues to play with and practise linguistic forms they are in the process of acquiring (Kuczaj II, 1986; and p. 288).

Language is often used playfully in sociodramatic play episodes. Several examples have been given by Garvey (1977); 'Hello, my name is Mr Elephant!'; 'Hello, my name is Mr Donkey!'. In school-age children rhymes and word play are common, and have been documented by Opie and Opie (1959). The repetition of well-known verses, with variations, has more in common with the rule-governed games common by the age of 6 or 7 years (see below and also chapter 10).

*Rough-and-tumble play*

The origins of play fighting and chasing may lie in the vigorous physical play which parents often engage in with toddlers – tickling, throwing and crawling after them, for example. Actual play fighting between peers is common from 3 years on through to adolescence. Wrestling generally involves some struggle for superior position, one child trying to get on top of another and pin him or her down; though roles quickly reverse themselves. More fragmentary episodes involve pushing, clasping, leg play and kicking. Chasing play is generally included in rough-and-tumble as well (example 3, p. 169).

The friendly intent in play of this kind is typically signalled by smiling and laughter. At the preschool age play fighting seems distinct from serious fighting, at least in the great majority of cases. The former is carried out with friends, who often stay together after the episode. The latter is often not between friends, involves different facial expressions and the participants usually do not stay together after the encounter. Preschool children themselves seem to be aware of the difference. However, there is some evidence that towards adolescence strength and dominance become more important in the choice of partners in play fighting, and the distinction from real aggressive intent is possibly not always so clear (Humphreys and Smith, 1984).

*Games with rules*

The play of preschool children often has some rule structure; for example, if someone is role-playing 'doctor' to a 'patient', there are some constraints on what he or she is expected to do, exerted by the other participants. Nevertheless, any rules or constraints are largely private to that particular play episode, and can be changed at any time ('I'm not the doctor now, I'm a policeman'). By the time children are 6 or 7 years old, rule-governed games like hopscotch, tig, or football take up much more playground time. These are games with public rules, sometimes codified, with much less latitude for change. The transition from play to games is nevertheless a gradual one (see also chapter 7, and Piaget's study of the game of marbles).

*Play sequences*

Piaget (1951) described a developmental sequence from practice play, through symbolic play, to games with rules, while acknowledging that these were overlapping stages. By 'practice play', Piaget mainly meant early sensori-motor play in infants, and most animal play. As others have pointed out, if practice play means play that is neither symbolic nor rule-governed, then it can occur well beyond the sensori-motor period. Indeed rough-and-tumble would seem to count as practice play, unless it has symolic elements (as in monster play), or is rule-governed (as in tig).

Smilansky (1968) postulated a four-fold sequence, from functional play (similar to practice play,) to constructive play, then dramatic play and finally games with rules. She thus suggested that constructive play (making something, e.g. from Lego bricks) was intermediate between functional and dramatic play (plates 6.2, 6.3 and 6.4).

PLATE   177

PLATE 6.2   *'Practice' or 'functional' play in a 1-year-old infant; simple actions like mouthing, banging or pushing are performed with one or two objects*

Some American play researchers have used this scheme as a 'play hierarchy'. Piaget (1951), however, thought that 'constructive games are not a definite stage like the others, but occupy . . . a position halfway between play and intelligent work, or between play and imitation'. The goal-directed nature of much constructive activity, for Piaget, made it more accommodative than purely playful behaviour (see later, and chapter 11). Either it was work-like, or some symbolic element might be present.

PLATE 6.3   *These 3-year-olds are engaged in 'constructive play' – making things from objects*

PLATE 6.4   *This child is engaged in a simple pretend sequence – putting a doll to sleep in a pram*

The distinct, sequential nature of constructive play in Smilansky's scheme is thus questionable (Smith et al., 1986).

### Factors affecting play

The role of adults, the influence of the environment, and the personality and sex of the child are all factors thought to have an effect on play.

As has been mentioned in the development of fantasy play, adults often have a part in encouraging play in children. Parents often encourage pretend play when it starts to appear in their young children, but there may be a social class difference in this. Newson and Newson (1968), in a longitudinal interview study of child-rearing in Nottinghamshire families, found that for most social class groups more than 70 per cent of mothers reported that they sometimes joined in play with their 4-year-olds; this fell to under 50 per cent in social class V (labourers, cleaners, long-term unemployed). Similarly, there was a social class difference in whether children talked about their fantasies to their mothers. Family size was also important: mothers joined in less, and children talked to them about fantasies less, in larger families.

Social class differences have also been reported in children's sociodramatic play in nurseries and playgroups. Several studies have suggested that children from disadvantaged backgrounds show less frequent and less complex fantasy and sociodramatic play, starting with a large-scale study by Smilansky, in Israel, published in 1968. These studies have been criticized by McLoyd (1982) for poor methodology. Some failed adequately to define social class, or confounded it with other variables such as race, or school setting. McLoyd claims that the general pattern is one of marginal and conflicting findings. Nevertheless, others would argue that there are large variations among children and among cultural groups in the amount of fantasy play that is readily observed. Global statements about social class may be unwarranted, since any such effects will vary with historical time, cultural group and even location within a country. For example, the results of the Newsons' study may be valid for white children in the Nottinghamshire area around 25 years ago, but not for other groups, in other times and other places. If nothing else, the number and type of families placed in social class V (as 'persistently unemployed') would be different in a period of continuing high unemployment.

Even children from similar backgrounds seem to vary greatly in their play preferences. Singer (1973) devised a short questionnaire to give to children about their tendency to engage in fantasy activities. On this basis he identified children of 'high-fantasy' and 'low-fantasy' disposition. He claimed that high-fantasy children were in some respects more creative, and more able to tolerate delays (e.g. by day-dreaming).

If children, for whatever reason, do not engage in much fantasy or sociodramatic play in nursery school, it does seem that nursery staff can encourage it by play tutoring. This technique was pioneered by Smilansky (1968), and has been summarized by Christie (1986). Such intervention at its least intrusive involves verbal guidance or suggestions; alternatively, more direct involvement in the play may be made by acting as a model for roles and actions, or by giving deliberate training in imaginative activities or fantasy themes. Play tutoring can be made even more effective if appropriate toys are provided (e.g. dressing-up clothes, hospital props), and if children are taken on visits (e.g. to a zoo, hospital, or factory).

Immediate environmental factors can also facilitate or hinder play. This was shown, for example, by a series of experimental studies on playgroup environments carried out by Smith and Connolly (1980). Fantasy play was more frequent in groups of children who were well acquainted with each other. Rough-and-tumble play occurred more often in large groups, with plenty of space and not too many toys provided.

Several investigators have studied sex differences in children's play. Differences in the frequency of fantasy play are inconsistent, but there are sex differences in the choice of roles in sociodramatic play. Naturally enough, girls tend to act out domestic scenes – shopping, washing the baby, etc. Boys less often imitate male roles, as they have usually not been able to observe their father at work; rather, they rely on roles familiar from books (e.g. police, fireman), or act out film or television characters such as Spiderman.

There does appear to be a reliable sex difference in rough-and- tumble play; this has almost always been found to be preferred by boys. A predisposition for boys to engage more in this activity may be related to the influence of sex hormones during the period of fetal growth, as indicated by Money and Ehrhardt (1972; see pp. 148–9). However, social factors are likely to be very important too; fathers engage in more rough-and-tumble play with boys, even by 2 years of age, and this kind of play is very much socially stereotyped as a male activity (Humphreys and Smith, 1984; see also chapter 5).

## Play Theorists

Theoretical perspectives on the nature of play and on its role in development cover a wide range. Several influential ideas can be traced back to the late nineteenth century and early twentieth century. The views of a number of earlier play theorists and educators are summarized here.

*Friedrich Froebel*   The ideas of Froebel, as expounded in *The Education of Man* (published posthumously in 1906), were influential in the start of the kindergarten and nursery school movement. 'Kindergarten' translates from German as 'child-garden', and this aptly sums up Froebel's ideas about play and development: 'Play, truly recognized and rightly fostered, unites the germinating life of the child attentively with the ripe life of experiences of the adult and thus fosters the one through the other.' On this view play exemplifies development from within the child, but can be nurtured by adult guidance and the provision of appropriate materials. Froebel's influence, following that of Pestalozzi (with whom he studied for two years), encouraged a positive evaluation of the educational significance of play, as compared to the rote-learning approach which nevertheless became characteristic of many infant schools at the end of the nineteenth century (Whitbread, 1972).

*Herbert Spencer*   In his book *The Principles of Psychology* (1878, final edition 1898), Spencer proposed a less enthusiastic view of play. He believed play is carried out 'for the sake of the immediate gratifications involved, without reference to ulterior benefits'. He suggested that the higher animals are better able to deal with the immediate necessities of life, and that the nervous system, rather than remaining inactive for long periods, stimulates play. 'Thus it happens that in the more evolved creatures, there often recurs an energy somewhat in excess of immediate needs ... Hence play of all kinds – hence this tendency to superfluous and useless exercise of faculties that have been quiescent.' Spencer's approach has been labelled the 'surplus energy' theory by subsequent writers, who have noted that the idea can be traced back further to the eighteenth-century philosopher, Friedrich von Schiller.

*Karl Groos*   At the turn of the century, Groos published two influential works, *The Play of Animals* (1898), and *The Play of Man* (1901). Groos criticized Spencer's theory on a number of grounds. He thought that surplus energy might provide 'a particularly favourably condition for play', but was not essential. He also thought play had a much more definite function than in Spencer's theory. Groos argued that a main reason for childhood was so that play could occur: 'perhaps the very existence of youth is largely for the sake of play.' This was because play provided exercise and elaboration of skills needed for survival. This has been called the 'exercise' or 'practice' theory of play, and in its modern form it has many adherents.

*G. Stanley Hall*   In his volume on *Adolescence* (1908) and elsewhere, Hall argued that Groos' practice theory was 'very partial, superficial, and perverse'. This was because Groos saw play as practice for contemporary activities. By contrast, Hall thought that play was a means for children to work through primitive atavisms, reflecting our evolutionary past. For example, 'the sports of boys chasing one another, wrestling, making prisoners, obviously gratify in a partial way the predatory instincts'. The function of play was thus cathartic in nature, and allowed the 'playing out' of those instincts that characterized earlier human history. This became known as the 'recapitulation theory' of play. In the form proposed by Hall, it has had little or no recent support.

*Maria Montessori*    The work of Montessori has been another major influence in the education of young children (see Kramer, 1976). Like Froebel, Montessori saw the value of self-initiated activity for young children, under adult guidance. She put more emphasis on the importance of learning about real life, however, and hence on constructive play materials which helped in sensory discrimination and in colour and shape matching. She did not value pretend or sociodramatic play, seeing pretence as primitive and an escape from reality. She preferred to encourage children actually to serve meals, for example, and to clear up around the house themselves, rather than play at mealtimes in a 'play house'. This particular aspect of her philosophy however, did not find favour in Britain in the 1920s and 1930s.

*Jean Piaget*    The place of play in Piaget's theory of cognitive development has often been misunderstood (see Sutton-Smith, 1966; Piaget, 1966; and Rubin and Pepler, 1982 for reviews). Piaget saw adaptation as depending on the two processes of accommodation and assimilation (see chapter 11). Play 'manifests the peculiarity of a primacy of assimilation over accommodation'. Children acted out their already established behaviours, or schemata, in play, and adapted reality to fit these. For example, referring to episodes such as his daughter Jacqueline's pretending to sleep (p. 173), Piaget wrote

> It is clearly impossible to explain this symbolic practice as being pre-exercise; the child certainly does not play like this in order to learn to wash or sleep. All that he is trying to do is to use freely his individual powers, to reproduce his own actions for the pleasure of seeing himself do them and showing them off to others, in a word to express himself, to assimilate without being hampered by the need to accommodate at the same time.

Here is a criticism both of some aspects of Groos's approach (play as pre-exercise), and of play as being important in learning. For Piaget learning was related more to accommodation to reality. This emphasis may be linked to Montessori's influence, for Piaget carried out his early research at a modified Montessori school, and for many years was president of the Swiss Montessori Society. The functions of play in Piaget's framework are two-fold. Play can consolidate existing skills by repeated execution of known schemas, with minor variations. Also, it can give a child a sense of 'ego continuity', that is, confidence and a sense of mastery. It does this because failure is largely circumvented in fantasy play, where the real properties of the materials are not at issue, and no external goal is aimed for.

*Sigmund Freud*    Freud himself did not write a great deal about play, but it has come to have an important role within the psychoanalytic movement, and especially in play therapy. Freud thought that play provided children with an avenue for wish fulfilment and mastery of traumatic events. As Peller (1954) put it, 'play ... is an attempt to compensate for anxieties and depression, to obtain pleasure at a minimum risk of danger and/or irreversible consequences'. Thus play provided a safe context for expressing aggressive or sexual impulses which it would be too dangerous to express in reality. In addition play could, within limits, help achieve mastery of traumatic events; 'Small quantities of anxiety are mastered in play, but anxiety of high intensity inhibits play.' Both aspects are important in play therapy.

First, play expresses the child's wishes and anxieties (Peller relates the development of fantasy play themes to Freud's psychosexual stages). Second, play can help overcome such anxieties, by catharsis or by working through.

*Susan Isaacs*   The view of play as essential to both emotional and cognitive growth of young children, strong in the British educational tradition, owes much to Susan Isaacs and to her successor at the Institute of Education at London University, Dorothy Gardner. Isaacs combined a belief in the emotional benefits of play (deriving from the psychoanalytic tradition) with a wider view of its benefits for physical, social and cognitive development generally, echoing the evolutionary perspective that animals that learn more, also play more: 'Play is indeed the child's work, and the means whereby he grows and develops. Active play can be looked upon as a sign of mental health; and its absence, either of some inborn defect, or of mental illness' (Isaacs, 1929).

*Lev Vygotsky*   Another combination of the affective and cognitive aspects of development occurs in Vygotsky's approach to play (1966; from a lecture given in 1933). Like psychoanalysts, Vygotsky saw the affective drive behind play as being 'the imaginary, illusory realisation of unrealisable desires'; not with very specific or sexual impulses, but in a much more general sense, to do with the child's confidence and mastery (for example in attitudes to authority in general): 'Play is essentially wish fulfilment, not, however, isolated wishes but generalized affects.' Furthermore, Vygotsky saw play as being 'the leading source of development in the preschool years'. Essentially, this was because the nature of pretend play meant that the child was liberating itself from the immediate constraints of the situation (e.g. the actual object), and getting into the world of ideas (e.g. what that object might become): 'The child is liberated from situational constrains through his activity in an imaginary situation.'

*Recent theorists*   In recent decades, theorists have tended to argue the benefits of play for cognitive development and creative thinking. Jerome Bruner (1972) suggested that play in the advanced mammals, and especially in human children, serves both as practice for mastery in skills, and as an opportunity for trying out new combinations of behaviour in a safe context. Sara Smilansky (1968) and Jerome Singer (1973) have advanced the value of fantasy and sociodramatic play in particular. Brian Sutton-Smith (1967) initially supported the importance of play for creative processes; but more recently (Sutton-Smith and Kelly-Byrne, 1984) has come to argue against what he sees as the 'idealization' of play. In sharp contrast to the other theorists we have considered, he now concludes that many theories about play, and even the way we define play, reflect the needs of adults in organizing and controlling children, rather than the actualities of children's behaviour.

## Empirical Studies

Most of the theorizing about the importance of play has been carried out in the absence of any real evidence that play does, or does not, have the effects or benefits postulated. Much can be learned by examining the nature of play, but hypotheses about its importance should then be tested out in a more controlled way. Experimental studies of play and non-play curricula were carried out by Gardner (1942), but by and large the empirical study of play was neglected until the past decade.

Here we will review the evidence about the importance of play from three different perspectives; the form of play, or 'design studies' – does the actual nature of play behaviour reveal something of its value?; correlational studies – what tends to go with playfulness in children?; and experimental studies – attempts to compare the value of play experiences in controlled conditions.

*The form of play*    If we look closely at what goes on in playful episodes we may form hypotheses as to what uses the behaviour has. Indeed, it is this approach that Piaget used, and which led him to his own theory of play (p. 181). Similar observations of the flexibility present in play led Bruner (1972) to postulate its role in problem-solving and creativity. Working with Bruner, an extensive study of Oxfordshire nursery schools was made by Sylva, Roy and Painter (1980). They documented which activities of nursery school children resulted in what they considered to be complex or challenging activities. They concluded that activities with some sort of goal, and the means to achieve it, were the most challenging – activities such as building, drawing, doing puzzles. They called these 'high-yield' activities. Depending on one's exact definition, these might be considered less playful (i.e. more constuctive, or goal-directed), than what they thought of as 'medium-yield' activities – pretending, play with small-scale toys, manipulating sand or dough. Finally, 'low-yield' activities comprised informal and impromptu games, gross motor play and unstructured social playing and 'horsing around' (i.e. rough-and-tumble play).

The Sylva, Roy and Painter study actually suggests that the unstructured, free play kinds of activities may be less cognitively useful than more structured activities. A similar philosophy lies behind the 'structuring play in the early years at school' programme (Manning and Sharp, 1977). It would seem though that the emphasis in Sylva and colleagues' study is on cognitive, rather than social, challenge or complexity. Observations of sociodramatic play suggest there is sometimes considerable negotiation about social roles, while observations of rough-and-tumble have shown that coordination with a large number of partners is often involved. The importance of such kinds of play can only really be decided on the basis of other forms of evidence.

*Correlational studies*    If playful behaviour has useful developmental consequences, then we would expect that children who practise a lot of a certain type of play should also be more advanced in other areas of development for which play is supposed to be beneficial. We have already seen that children do vary considerably in their play preferences (p. 179).

One study, by Hutt and Bhavnani (1972), used data from the novel toy experiment we have mentioned earlier (see box 6.1 and p. 172). They traced 48 children who had been observed with the novel toy at around 4 years of age, when they were four years older. From the earlier data they had recorded those children who, after investigating the toy, used it in many imaginative ways (15 of the 48).

Four years later they gave the children some tests designed to measure creativity (see also chapter 12). The imaginative players scored significantly higher on these tests than did the children who at 4 years had not played much with the novel object.

This is consistent with the idea that imaginative play fosters creativity; but no more than that. An alternative explanation would be that another factor (for example, shyness with adults) was responsible for the poor performance both with the novel object, and later in the tests. Or, perhaps the playfulness of the imaginative children is just a by-product of their creativity, not a cause of it. As discussed elsewhere (chapter 1), correlations may be due to extraneous factors, and we cannot infer causal relations from them.

Many other correlational studies have been reported in the literature. In one (Johnson et al., 1982), 34 4-year-olds were observed in play and also given cognitive and intelligence tests. The researchers found that constructive play, but not sociodramatic play, was positively and significantly correlated with intelligence scores. This finding would be congruent with the position of Sylva's group (above). In another study (Connolly and Doyle, 1984), 91 preschoolers were observed in social fantasy play, and measures of social competence were obtained from observation, role-taking tests (see chapter 11) and teacher ratings. It was found that the amount and complexity of fantasy play significantly correlated with several measures of social competence. This would be congruent with the point made above that the benefits of sociodramatic play may be social more than cognitive. These and other studies are nevertheless subject to the same caveats about drawing conclusions from correlational evidence.

*Experimental studies of play*   In all the experimental studies of play carried out the benefits of some form of extra play experience have been compared with the benefits of some non-play experience. Since subjects are randomly allocated to the play or non-play conditions, it should be more possible to make causal inferences than is the case in correlational studies.

Some experiments have used short sessions, often of about 10 minutes' duration. Children, usually of nursery school age, are given some play experience with objects; others are given an instructional session, or an alternative materials condition (e.g. drawing), or are put in a no-treatment control group. After the session is over, they are then given an assessment; for example of creativity (e.g. thinking of unusual uses for the objects they have played with), problem-solving (e.g. using the objects to make a long tool to retrieve a marble), or conservation. A number of such studies claimed some form of superiority for the play experience, but more recent work has not always borne these claims out. In a review, Smith and Simon (1984) argue that the earlier studies are methodologically unsound due to the possibility of experimenter effects (see p. 13). When the same experimenter administers the conditions and tests the subjects immediately after, some unconscious bias may come in. Some studies were criticized for inadequate control for familiarity with the experimenter. When these factors are properly taken account of, there is little evidence that the play experience helps, or indeed that such sessions have any real impact. Smith and Simon conclude that either the benefits of play in real life occur over a longer time period, or they are not substantial enough to measure by this sort of experimental procedure (for a critical reply, see Dansky, 1985).

A more ecologically valid approach is to look at the effects of play over periods of weeks, or perhaps a school term. This has been done in a number of studies, especially those that looked at the effects of play tutoring (see p. 179) in preschool classes. Several studies on disadvantaged preschool children in the USA found that play tutoring, besides increasing children's fantasy play, also had benefits in a variety of areas of cognitive, language and social development. The problem with these studies was that the play tutored children were compared with children who received little or no extra adult intervention. Thus, general adult involvement and conversation might have caused the gains, rather than fantasy play *per se*. This alternative idea has become known as the 'verbal stimulation' hypothesis.

Some play tutoring studies since then have embodied controls for 'verbal stimulation', or more generally, adult involvement. Box 6.2 discusses one in detail. This, and some similar studies, found little superiority for the play tutoring condition. This does not mean that play tutoring is not worth while, but it does imply that it is no more value than some other kinds of adult involvement. The particular benefits of play have still not been pinned down, though again, the most likely benefits may be social ones (box 6.2).

*Summary*    Considerable empirical investigation has now been made into the benefits of play, but 'the jury is still out'. Most of the investigations have concentrated on the supposed cognitive benefits of play, and have been made in an explicitly educational framework. Yet as we have seen, the evidence for strong cognitive benefits, either from theory, observation, correlational or experimental studies, is not convincing. If anything, the evidence is better for the benefits of play for social competence. This has been less thoroughly studied; while the postulated benefits of play for emotional release and catharsis (see p. 181) have scarcely received any well-controlled experimental study at all.

According to a Department of Environment report in 1973, 'the realisation that play is essential for normal development has slowly but surely permeated our cultural heritage'. This, like the words of Isaacs quoted on p. 182, embodies a prevalent view which Sutton-Smith and Kelly-Byrne (1984) have called 'the idealisation of play'. Yet, in some societies children seem to play little, but develop normally. As we have seen, the empirical evidence is mixed. Another view emerging from studies of both animal and human play is that, while play is likely to have benefits, it is unlikely that they are essential. Rather, these benefits could be achieved in a number of ways, of which play would be one: for example, children can acquire social competence by playing, but by other activities as well. Whatever the final verdict, it will not detract from the enjoyment of play, both on the part of the participant and the observer. This in itself gives an enduring value to play, whatever the extent of its developmental consequences may be.

### Further reading

An excellent overview, especially for those interested in education, is J. R. Moyles 1989: *Just Playing*. Milton Keynes: Open University Press. A collection of articles accessible to the general reader is P. K Smith (ed.) 1986: *Children's play: Research Developments and Practical*

*Applications.* London: Gordon & Breach. Another collection is edited by T. D. Yawkey and A. D. Pellegrini 1984: *Child's Play: Developmental and Applied.* Hillsdale, NJ: Erlbaum.

P. K. Smith (ed.) 1984: *Play in Animals and Humans.* Oxford: Basil Blackwell, is a more advanced collection covering both animal play, children's play, and games. A reference source is K. H. Rubin, G. G. Fein and B. Vandenberg 1983: Play, in P. H. Mussen and E. M. Hetherington (eds), *Handbook of Child Psychology*, 4th edn, vol. 4. Chichester: Wiley.

### Discussion points

1 How important is it to define play? Does play at different ages require different definitions?

2 Are exploration and play really distinct?

3 How useful is it to distinguish stages in the development of play?

4 Have theorists been too ready to speculate about the value of play, without sufficient evidence?

5 Are experimental studies of play worthwile?

### Practical exercises

1 Watch preschool children in a playgroup or nursery class. Try to categorize the different types of play, and assess the amount of time spent in each; or describe the different roles you see acted out in sociodramatic play.

2 Observe children in a school playground, or in an outdoor area with play equipment. Estimate the amount of social interaction going on in different types of activity, or on different items of play equipment

3 Watch a young child when it is given a new toy which it has not come across before. See if you can distiguish exploratory behavior from play.

# Box 6.1

# Exploration and play in children

The aim of Hutt's study was to see how a novel object elicited exploratory behaviour in young children, and how this behaviour changed with repeated exposure. The main participants were 30 nursery school children, aged 3–5 years. Each child had eight ten-minute sessions in a room in the nursery school. The first two sessions were for familiarization, and five toys were provided. For the ensuing six experimental sessions a novel toy was also available – a red metal box with a lever, whose movements could be registered on counters and could result in a buzzer sounding and a bell ringing (see box figure 6.1.1)

There were two independent variables. One was the complexity of the novel object; the other was exposure to the object, measured over the six successive sessions. The object

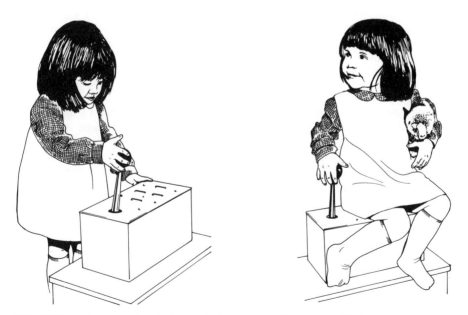

BOX FIGURE 6.1.1    *A child exploring and later playing with a novel object*

Based on material in C. Hutt 1966: *Symposia of the Zoological Society of London*, 18.

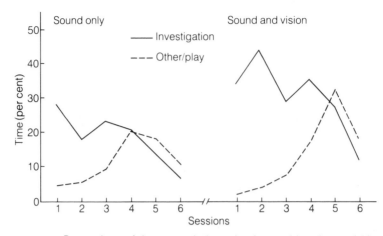

BOX FIGURE 6.1.2 *Proportions of time spent in investigating and in other activities, including play with the novel object, when sound, or sound and vision, were available*

complexity was varied through 'no sound or vision' (bell and buzzer switched off; counters covered up), 'vision only', 'sound only', to 'both sound and vision' available. The dependent variables were taken from counter readings (showing how much lever manipulation had taken place) and observations of the children, especially the amount of time spent exploring (visually or tactually) the novel object.

The results showed that children looked at the object immediately on entering, and often approached it or asked the observer what it was. They would then examine the object visually and manually, holding and manipulating the lever. For the 'no sound or vision' and 'vision only' conditions, this exploration and manipulation declined rapidly over sessions. However for the 'sound only' and 'both sound and vision' conditions, manipulation of the lever increased over the first five sessions. More detailed analysis of the observations showed that in these conditions, although exploratory behaviour declined, more playful or game-like behaviours increased (see box figure 6.1.2), for example, running around the object with a truck and ringing the bell each time; or using the object as a seat and pretending it was a car.

These observations led Hutt to suggest that exploration could lead on to play, and to characterize the two behaviours distinctly. Exploration was characterized as relatively serious and focused, essentially asking 'what does this object do?'. Play was characterized as relaxed, and by a diversity of activities essentially asking 'what can I do with this object?'.

This study combined an experimental design with some degree of natural observation of the child's behaviour. Note that the less structured observations allowed for the distinction between exploration and play to be made; an outcome not expected in the initial aims of the study. The results are shown as graphs of changes over sessions, as in box figure 6.1.2, and the exploration/play distinction is reported qualitatively. No statistical tests are used, though some might have been appropriate. No control group is really necessary for this study as exploration of the novel object could not occur in its absence.

The exploration/play distinction is considered further by Weisler and McCall (1976) and Wohlwill (1984). It has been noted that the particular novel object used in this study probably makes the distinction clearer than some situations might do. In other reports Hutt (1970) stated that boys were much more exploratory than girls in this setting, but this sex difference has not been well replicated in other studies of exploratory behaviour (McLoyd and Ratner, 1983).

Box 6.2

# A comparison of the effects of fantasy play tutoring and skills tutoring in nursery classes

This study was set up to discover whether fantasy play tutoring had any different, or more beneficial, effects than skills tutoring which involved an equal amount of extra adult involvement. The participants (mean age 4 years) were mainly from economically disadvantaged backgrounds. They comprised classes of about 20 children, two from each of two nursery schools.

At each school one class experienced extra 'play tutoring', the other extra 'skills tutoring'. Recordings of the tutoring sessions confirmed that the amount of verbal interaction by the tutor was similar in the two conditions but that a fantasy element was prominent only in the play tutoring. The research design is shown in box figure 6.2.1. The independent variables were tutoring condition and time when assessments were made (both before, and at two time points after, the intervention period). The dependent variables were scores on a variety of social, cognitive and language assessments, obtained by test and by observation.

Statistical analyses were made of the changes in scores on the various measures using a technique known as analysis of variance. In all classes the children improved on most of the measures, but with little difference between the two tutoring conditions. There were no differences between conditions for changes in play complexity, verbalizations, attention span, role-taking, creativity, or intelligence test subscales. The only differences found consistently at both schools, and remaining at follow-up, were that the play tutored children showed a greater interest in fantasy play, social participation, subgroup size and physical activity.

In most respects this study supported the 'verbal stimulation' hypothesis concerning the effects of play tutoring (see p. 185). It suggested that different forms of structured adult involvement had similar educational benefits. Play turoring did, however, additionally foster social participation.

It may be noted that there was no 'no treatment' control group in this study. Thus it is assumed that the interventions do have some effect, i.e. that they are to a significant degree responsible for the gains at post-assessment. The author based this assumption on several previous studies which showed that play tutoring did have a greater effect compared with

Based on material in P. K. Smith, M. Dalgleish and G. Herzmark 1981: *International Journal of Behavioural Development*, 4, 421–41.

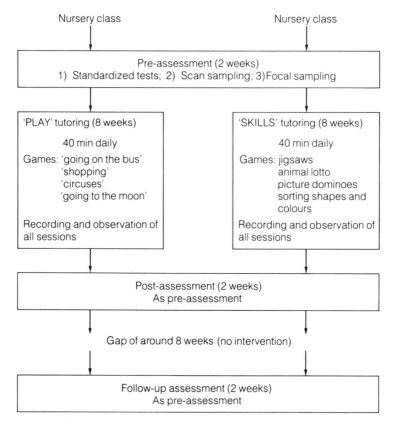

BOX FIGURE 6.2.1  *Design of a study conducted by Smith et al. (1981) of play tutoring and skills tutoring.*

control groups with little or no extra adult involvement; in this study they wished only to compare play tutoring with a non-fantasy tutoring of equal intensity. Nevertheless, use of a no treatment control group would have enabled stronger conclusions to be drawn about whether either kind of intervention was worth while from an educational viewpoint.

# 7

# Helping Others and Moral Development

## The Development of Prosocial Behaviour

Prosocial behaviour is taken to mean helping, comforting, sharing or altruistic behaviour on the part of one person to another. In a standard text on the subject, Mussen and Eisenberg-Berg (1977, pp. 3–4) define it as 'actions that are intended to aid or benefit another person or group of people without the actor's anticipation of external rewards. Such actions often entail some cost, self-sacrifice or risk on the part of the actor'. The following are some examples of prosocial behaviour in young children, taken from mothers' reports.

1  *Bobby, at 19 months*  As I was vacuuming I began to feel a little faint and sick ... I turned off the vacuum and went to the bathroom kind of coughing and gagging a little. Bobby followed me to the bathroom door, and the whole time that I was in there he was pounding on the bathroom door saying 'OK Mommie?' And I finally came out and picked him up and he looked at me with a very concerned, worried look in his eyes, and I said 'Mommie OK'. Then he put his head on my shoulder and began to love me (Zahn-Waxler and Radke-Yarrow, 1982, p.116).

2  *Todd, almost 2 years*  Today there was a little 4-year-old girl here, Susan. Todd and Susan were in the bedroom playing and all of a sudden Susan started to cry ... I said 'What happened?' and she said 'He hit me'. I said 'Well, tell him not to hit you', and I said, 'Todd!' He didn't seem particularly upset, he was watching her cry. I said 'Did you hit Susan? You don't want to hurt people.' Then they went back in the bedroom and there was a second run-in and she came out. That's when I said sternly 'No, Todd. You musn't hit people'. He just watched her sniffle as she was being stroked by her mum ... on the table right by us were some fallen petals from a flower and he picked up one little petal and smiled and handed it to her and said 'Here'. She kind of reached out and took it and then he searched for other petals and gave them to her (Zahn-Waxler et al., 1979, p. 322).

3  *Cynthia, at 4 years*  We were getting ready to go to friends for the rest of the day and preparations were becoming rather frantic. Cynthia said to Richard (her

younger brother) 'Come on, I'll read you a story and we'll stay out of Mum and Dad's way'. They sat together on the couch and Cynthia 'read' (memorized) two books to him. When they were finished I said 'It was great being able to get ready without any interruptions' (Grusec, 1982, p. 140).

Comforting occurs in example 1, helping in example 3, and a form of sharing in example 2. These behaviours occurred when the child saw someone else in difficulty or distress, either through some event to which the child was a bystander (e.g. examples 1 and 3), or because the child itself had caused the distress (e.g. example 2).

Example 1, of a child only 19 months old, suggests that prosocial behaviour can occur very early on. However, we might question whether the action is intended to aid another person, as our initial definition stipulated. Did Bobby intend to help his mother, or was he just reacting to her behaviour? It is difficult to tell at such an early age, whereas it is clear from what she herself says that Cynthia, aged 4, did intend to help her parents. There is another problem with our definition, when it stipulates that no external reward is anticipated. We can see that Cynthia was rewarded (verbally at least) for her behaviour; did she anticipate this, and therefore was hers not prosocial behaviour after all? Some researchers are greatly concerned about such definitional matters, whereas others are happy to label helping and sharing behaviours as prosocial, largely irrespective of intent or reward. The related concept of altruistic behaviour is often used in a more restricted sense, however, as referring to behaviour that does entail some self-sacrifice to the person performing it (Underwood and Moore, 1982, discuss definitional matters further). You may like to compare these definitions of prosocial and altruistic behaviour with the definitions of mutualism and altruism used by ethologists and given in chapter 2: they are similar.

*Observational studies*

The origins of prosocial behaviour in the young child have been the subject of several studies. Zahn-Waxler and Radke-Yarrow (1982) have described a study of 24 children which used a combination of cross-sectional and longitudinal design to span the age range from around 12 to 30 months. These researchers relied on mothers' recordings. Mothers were asked to report on children's response to events in which negative emotions were expressed (A subset of this investigation is highlighted in box 7.1, and examples 1 and 2 above are from their studies.) Two noticeable changes were found between the younger children (aged up to about 20 months) and the older children (20–30 months). The younger children often orientated to someone's distress, and often cried, fretted or whimpered themselves, but only seldom acted prosocially. Such prosocial behaviour as there was usually took the form of simply touching or patting the victim, or presenting objects. Prosocial behaviour was much more likely in the older children, however, and occurred in about one-third of all incidents reported. It took a variety of forms, such as reassurance ('you'll be all right'), combative altruism (hitting an aggressor), giving objects (e.g. bandages, comfort object), or getting help from a third party. This developmental pattern was similar whether the child was a bystander to the distress or had caused it. From this study it is clear that children below 3 years of age can show some forms of prosocial behaviour. This is especially so after about 20 months, which is when sensori-motor development is completed (Chapter 11), and thus when children understand cause–effect relations and the distinction between themselves and other people (chapter 5). Before this age children often seek comfort as much for themselves as for the other person, but after about 20 months they are increasingly aware that the distress is in the other person (and, somewhat later, of whether they have caused it or not), and act more appropriately.

Other examples of early prosocial behaviour have been reported by Harriet Rheingold. In one study (Rheingold et al., 1976) she watched children aged 12–18 months in a laboratory situation. She described sharing behaviour with mothers and fathers, and to a lesser extent with unfamiliar persons. Sharing was defined as showing or giving objects, or playing (jointly manipulating an object) with a partner. In another study (Rheingold 1982), children aged 18–30 months were watched in a laboratory setting that simulated a home. Parents and other adults were asked to perform houshold chores, such as clearing up wastepaper, putting away books, folding up clothes. It was observed that many of the children helped in many of these tasks. The likelihood of helping increased from around 63 per cent in the 18-month-olds, to 89 per cent in the 30-month-olds. Most of these actions were spontaneous, in the sense that the parents did not directly suggest that the child helped, although they often elicited the child's attention and proximity.

Other researchers have documented prosocial behaviour by children in nursery school. Eisenberg, Berg and Hand (1979) for example watched 35 children aged 4 and 5 years in preschool classes. They found that a child showed sharing, helping or comforting behaviour about once every 10–12 minutes, on average. There were few age or sex differences. In an Israeli study, Bar-Tal, Raviv and Goldberg (1982) observed 156 children aged 18 months to 6 years. Prosocial behaviours made up some 10–20 per cent of all social contacts. Again, there were no sex differences and no very prominent age changes.

Grusec (1982) used the same technique as Zahn-Waxler and Radke-Yarrow (1982), namely mothers' reports, to examine prosocial behaviour in children aged 4 and 7 years (example 3 p. 191 above is from her study). She asked mothers to record, over a four-week period, any act in which their child intended to help another (excluding regular duties). Mothers recorded about one such act every day or so. No difference was found between boys and girls. Some interesting results from this study are shown in table 7.1. The top half of the table shows it was rare for mothers not to respond when they observed an act of helpfulness by their child. The great majority of such acts were 'rewarded' verbally, by thanking or praising, or physically by smiling or hugging. Similarly, the lower half of the table shows that if a child was not helpful when the mother thought that help was appropriate, it was very rare for the mother to accept this. Usually she encouraged the child to be helpful, either directly ('altruism requested') or in general terms ('moral exhortation'), or by expressing disapproval ('scolding, frowning'). More rarely, she would explain to the child how his or her lack of helpfulness might affect others ('empathy training'), or directly instruct or coerce the child to behave appropriately.

Many researchers have been concerned with the consistency of prosocial behaviour. For example, are children who are prosocial in one way, also likely to be so in others? Are children who are helpful at one age, likely to remain so at a later age? By and large the evidence suggests moderate consistency in these respects (Underwood and Moore, 1982). Some quite striking age consistencies were reported in a longitudinal study on siblings (Dunn and Kendrick, 1982; see p. 73): for

TABLE 7.1    *Mothers' reports of reactions to their child's behaviour*

|  | Child spontaneously helpful (% of incidents) | |
|---|---|---|
|  | *4-yr-olds* | *7-yr-olds* |
| Acknowledge, thank, express personal appreciation | 33 | 37 |
| Smile, thank warmly, hug | 17 | 18 |
| Praise act or child | 19 | 16 |
| No outward response | 8 | 9 |

|  | Child fails to be helpful (% of incidents) | |
|---|---|---|
|  | *4-yr-olds* | *7-yr-olds* |
| Moral exhortation | 26 | 30 |
| Request altruism | 22 | 30 |
| Scold, frown | 18 | 15 |
| Empathy training | 6 | 5 |
| Direct or force behaviour | 6 | 5 |
| Accept lack of altruism | 8 | 5 |

*Source*: Grusec, 1982

example, they found that children (aged 1–3 years) who showed friendly interest and concern for a new baby in the first three weeks after birth were also likely to respond with concern if their younger sibling was hurt or distressed at a follow-up six years later (the correlation was 0.42, significant at the 0.05 level).

## Factors Influencing Prosocial Behaviour

We have seen that mothers do not stand by idly when their child does, or does not, show helpful or altruistic behaviour; the evidence is that they often intervene. Fathers, teachers and peers are also likely to respond to a child's prosocial behaviour. What effect do such interventions have? We have also seen that interventions may take the form of reinforcement (e.g. praise) or punishment for not being helpful, modelling of altruistic behaviour, or moral exhortation. Are some techniques more effective than others? And what does the child contribute to this process?

One attempt to look at the effectiveness of different parental techniques in a naturalistic way is documented in box 7.1. This study suggests that (for 2-year-olds) affective explanation as to the consequences of their action (moralizing or prohibition with reasons), perhaps combined with some power assertion by the mother, is associated with prosocial behaviour by the child. However, being an uncontrolled correlational study, cause-and-effect relations cannot be deduced with confidence. Many researchers have attempted experimental studies to elucidate more clearly the causes of prosocial behaviour.

A technique that many researchers focused on in the 1970s was reinforcement (verbal or material reward). We have seen from Grusec's (1982) study that children do often receive reinforcement for prosocial behaviour, but has this actually been shown to be an effective technique? Let us look at a typical experimental study. Gelfand et al. (1975) reported a study with 21 children aged 5–6 years. The children came to a research caravan where they played a marble-drop game to earn pennies. The pennies accumulated could be spent on a prize at the end, but periodically the child was told that he or she could donate a penny earned to help another child in a nearby room win a prize (in fact there was no other child; this was simulated by a tape recording of an adult and child in conversation). Over a series of trials, the effects of both prompts by the experimenter ('maybe it would be nice if you helped the other boy/girl once or twice'), and praise for donating ('very good! Think how that boy/girl must feel now') was evaluated in terms of the subsequent rate of donations. It was found that both prompts, and praise, were effective in increasing donation rates – temporarily for some children, more permanently for others. The authors concluded that this was a clear 'demonstration of reinforcement effects on donating' (p. 983). Other studies have suggested that material reinforcement may be more powerful than social reinforcement for young children, and that the nature of the person giving the reinforcement is an important factor (see Rushton, 1982 for a review).

Other experimental studies have attempted to see whether modelling is a useful technique. Here, an adult models a helpful or altruistic act, which the child observes. One study (Grusec et al., 1978), has compared this with moral exhortation (preaching) for its effectiveness as a technique. The participants were 96 boys and girls aged 8–10 years. Children came individually to a research caravan in a school yard to play a marble-bowling game in which they could win marbles (the game was fixed so that all the children won the same number of marbles). Nearby was a poster reading 'Help poor children: Marbles buy gifts' over a bowl with some marbles already in it. An adult (of the same sex as the child) played the game first; she then either exhorted the child to give half her marbles, or said nothing (two preaching conditions), and then either gave, or did not give, half her own marbles (two modelling or performance conditions). The child was then left alone to play, but was observed through a one-way mirror to see how many marbles she donated. It was found that most children who saw the adult give marbles did so themselves, irrespective of preaching; whereas few children who saw the adult not giving marbles did so, although preaching did have some effect here. The children were asked to play the game again three weeks later and, irrespective of previous condition, few of them donated any marbles. This, and other studies, suggest that the behaviour children actually observe in others may be more important than moral exhortations from them though both do have some effect.

The experimental design of these studies is such as to enable us to make fairly certain inferences; for example, that modelling (performance) by an adult does increase the likelihood of altruism in a child who is watching. However, one could criticize these experiments for being rather artificial. The experimenters are unfamiliar, the situations are contrived and some deception is involved. Is it really helpfulness and altruism that is being measured in these settings, or is it just some kind of conformity to adult demands? For instance, in the study by Grusec et al. (1978) is it the case that modelling (performance) causes altruism in the child, or is it simply that the child is trying to puzzle out what is going on, and that the more compliant children, or perhaps the more uncertain children, tend to go along with what the adult seems to be suggesting? The fact that there was no effect of modelling at the three week follow-up would be consistent with this explanation.

An experimental study on 6–10-year-olds suggests just this sort of interpretation as regards age differences in generosity. Several experimental studies (unlike some naturalistic studies, see above) have found that generosity or altruism increases with age. However, Zarbatany et al. (1985) found that older children were only affected by experimenter obtrusiveness, not by other factors such as whether peers would know how generous the child was. The authors concluded that 'the finding that older children were more generous than younger children only under conditions of experimenter obtrusiveness provides some justification for concerns that laboratory analogue investigations of age differences in children's generosity may assess age differences in conformity to adult expectations rather than age differences in altruism' (p. 753). This critique could apply to other inferences made from laboratory studies, too. Of course, it could be argued that such compliance is similar to, or involved in, altruistic behaviour; but if so, it does seem different from the kind of 'genuine' helpfulness envisaged in our original definition, or seen in very young children who have as yet little notion of what is socially expected of them.

So far we have considered effects which other people can have on the child – reinforcing, punishing, modelling or exhorting. Can we ascertain what the child is thinking about all this? One study (Eisenberg, 1983) found that school-children (aged 7–17 years) clearly differentiated among people whom they might help. When posed with hypothetical moral dilemmas, they indicated that they would be more likely to help family than non-family members; friends rather than non-friends; people they knew rather than people they did not know; people more similar to themselves in race or religion; and non-criminals rather than criminals. These are not surprising findings, but they do put helping behaviour in a social context. Similarly, other studies have suggested that techniques such as reinforcement, exhortation or modelling are most effective when done by an adult whom the child loves or respects, e.g. a parent.

Other studies have looked at whether the level of moral reasoning in a child relates to that child's helpfulness or altruistic behaviour. Moral reasoning, or moral judgement as it is often called, is discussed in the next section, which is concerned with what the child *thinks* about a moral issue rather than what a child *does*, but we might expect the two to be related. There does seem to be some connection, with children at higher moral reasoning levels tending to be more altruistic (see Underwood and Moore, 1982, for a review). Amongst the studies we have considered here, Eisenberg-Berg and Hand (1979) found that the frequency of spontaneous sharing in nursery school did correlate with measures of moral reasoning (though the frequency of helping/comforting did not); while Eisenberg (1983) found that children at higher levels of moral reasoning were more likely to say that they would be helpful to other people who were not immediate friends or relatives.

It may well be that the most effective promoters of prosocial and altruistic behaviour are those who both provide some social reward or praise for the child, and also appeal to the child's developing sense of reasoning or justice. Box 7.1 shows that affective explanation by mothers is associated with prosocial behaviour in 2-year-olds. So far as the more general topic of discipline is concerned, Hoffman (1970) reviewed a large number of correlational studies relating parental rearing techniques with measures of either moral reasoning or moral behaviour. He categorized the dominant parental techniques into 'love-oriented discipline' (which threatened withdrawal of affection or approval), 'power-assertive discipline' (physical punishment or withholding privilages), and 'induction' (explaining the consequences of actions). As can be seen from table 7.2 (based on many studies), it seems that 'induction' is associated with moral maturity, whereas 'power-assertive discipline' tends to be associated with moral immaturity. Is 'induction' similar to 'affective explanation' in box 7.1? Quite probably, as it is in the context of a close parental relationship. Thus the evidence suggests that providing cognitive explanations enhances positive exhortation or reward in inducing prosocial behaviour, and is also effective as a disciplinary technique. Similarly, experimental studies have suggested that the most effective way to induce resistance to temptation is to combine the threat of punishment with an explanation or cognitive rationale (Parke, 1977).

TABLE 7.2   *Research studies reporting positive or negative correlations between disciplinary strategies and measures of children's moral reasoning or behaviour (from Hoffman, 1970)*

| Type of parental discipline | Positive correlation | Negative correlation |
|---|---|---|
| Power-assertive | 7 | 32 |
| Love-orientated | 8 | 11 |
| Induction | 38 | 6 |

## The Development of Moral Reasoning

Moral reasoning refers to how we reason, or judge, whether an action is right or wrong: it is different from moral behaviour. Often, of course, we do follow our moral reasoning when we decide on a course of behaviour. For example, we might reason that it is right to give some money for overseas aid, and then do so. It is equally clear that we do not always follow our moral reasoning. For example, if we are incorrectly given extra change in a supermarket, we might reason that it is wrong to keep it, but still do so.

We are concerned here with the way in which moral reasoning (often referred to as moral judgement) develops. Since this is about how we think about morality in the first place, and only indirectly about how we act, it is not surprising that moral reasoning is seen by many psychologists as closely linked to cognitive development. Such an approach is called 'cognitive developmental'. Work in this area was pioneered by Piaget, and this tradition has been carried on in the USA by Kohlberg and others.

### Piaget's theory

Piaget turned his attention to moral reasoning in children early in his career. He spent time in the suburbs of Geneva watching children at play and also posing them moral dilemmas. The results of his investigations were reported in *The Moral Judgement of the Child* (first English publication in 1932).

Piaget describes how he studied the boys' game of marbles. He was interested in how children acquired the rules of the game, where they thought the rules came from, and whether the rules could be altered. Here, the 'rules of the game' are taken as corresponding to the 'rules of society' for adults – you should follow the rules, you can break them, but there are sanctions if you do so. Piaget used four methods here: he asked the children directly ('teach me the rules'); he played with a child, pretending to be ignorant so that the child had to explain the rules – though not too ignorant in case the child gave up in frustration!; he watched the child play with others; and he interviewed children about where rules came from and whether they could be changed.

From his results Piaget distinguished three stages in children's awareness of rules. In the first (up to 4 to 5 years), rules were not understood. In the second stage (from 4–5 to 9–10 years) the rules were seen as coming from a higher authority (e.g. adults, God, the town council) and could not be changed. In the third (from 9–10 years onwards) rules were seen as mutually agreed by the players, and thus open to change if all the players agreed. (Piaget also distinguished corresponding stages in how the child's awareness of rules was put into practice. He also examined a girls' game, a version of hide-and-seek, in much less detail and described similar stages, occurring somewhat earlier, perhaps as the game was simpler.)

Here are two protocols (slightly edited) from Piaget's book, which illustrate the second two stages, and also Piaget's method of interview (called the 'clinical method', see p. 317).

1    B.E.N. (10 years, but still at the second stage)

| | |
|---|---|
| Piaget | Invent a rule. |
| B.E.N. | I couldn't invent one straight away like that. |
| Piaget | Yes you could. I can see that you are cleverer than you make yourself out to be. |
| B.E.N. | Well, let's say that you're not caught when you are in the square. |
| Piaget | Good. Would that come off with the others? |
| B.E.N. | Oh, yes, they'd like to do that. |
| Piaget | Then people could play that way? |

| B.E.N. | Oh, no, because it would be cheating. |
|---|---|
| Piaget | But all your pals would like to, wouldn't they? |
| B.E.N. | Yes, they all would. |
| Piaget | Then why would it be cheating? |
| B.E.N. | Because I invented it: it isn't a rule! It's a wrong rule because it's outside of the rules. A fair rule is one that is in the game. |

(Piaget, 1932, p. 58)

2   From G.R.O.S. (13 years, and at the third stage)

| Piaget | Are you allowed to change the rules at all? |
|---|---|
| G.R.O.S. | Oh, yes. Some want to, and some don't. If the boys play that way you have to play like they do. |
| Piaget | Do you think you could invent a new rule? |
| G.R.O.S. | Oh, yes ... you could play with your feet. |
| Piaget | Would it be fair? |
| G.R.O.S. | I don't know. It's just my idea. |
| Piaget | And if you showed it to the others would it work? |
| G.R.O.S. | It would work all right. Some other boys would want to try. Some wouldn't, by Jove! They would stick to the old rules. They'd think they'd have less of a chance with this new game. |
| Piaget | And if everyone played your way? |
| G.R.O.S. | Then it would be a rule like the others. |

(Piaget, 1932, p.63)

The difference between these two stages was thought of by Piaget as being that between a 'heteronomous' morality of coercion or restraint, and an 'autonomous' morality of cooperation or reciprocity. As the child's conception of rules changes, from their being absolutely fixed to their being mutually agreed, so a unilateral respect for adult or higher authority changes towards an equality with peers. These are cognitive changes, which in Piaget's later theory can be linked to the decline in egocentrism and the growth of operational thought. Important other factors are the growing independence from parents, and especially interaction with same-aged peers. Different children may have acquired slightly different versions of the rules, and through playing together these discrepancies will come to light and have to be resolved. This contact with divergent viewpoints, Piaget thought, was a crucial element in evolving the autonomous morality of reciprocity.

It is surprising that this ingenious, semi-naturalistic study was not followed up for decades. Despite its impact, it was only based on an unspecified but small number of subjects. A large-scale follow-up was made some 50 years later by a Spanish psychologist, Jose Linaza (1984). He interviewed several hundred children, in England and Spain, about a number of games. He confirmed the main aspects of Piaget's sequence, and elaborated it. No difference was found in the sequence between English and Spanish children, or between boys and girls playing the same game, though different games did vary in the age at which certain stages were usually attained.

Piaget also reported the results of another study in his 1932 book. In this he presented children with several pairs of short episodes or stories which posed a problem of moral judgement. An example is given below:

(A) A little boy who is called John is in his room. He is called to dinner. He goes into the dining room. But behind the door there was a chair, and on the chair there was a tray with fifteen cups on it. John couldn't have known that there was all this behind the door. He goes in, the door knocks against the tray, bang go the fifteen cups and they all get broken!

(B) Once there was a little boy whose name was Henry. One day when his mother was out he tried to get some jam out of the cupboard. He climbed up on the chair and stretched out his arm. But the jam was too high up and he couldn't reach it and have any. But while he was trying to get it he knocked over a cup. The cup fell down and broke.

Piaget would tell a child this pair of stories, and get them to repeat each to make sure that they remembered them. Then he would ask them to make a judgement as to which child in the two stories was the naughtiest. He found that before 9 or 10 years children often judged on the basis of the amount of damage, whereas after this age the child judged by motive or intention. Here are two short extracts from the protocols:

1. From S.C.H.M.A. (aged 6)

| | |
|---|---|
| Piaget | Are those children both naughty, or is one not so naughty as the other? |
| S.C.H.M.A. | Both just as naughty. |
| Piaget | Would you punish them the same? |
| S.C.H.M.A. | No. The one who broke fifteen plates. |
| Piaget | And would you punish the other one more, or less? |
| S.C.H.M.A. | The first broke lots of things, the other one fewer. |
| Piaget | How would you punish them? |
| S.C.H.M.A. | The one who broke the fifteen cups: two slaps. The other one, one slap. |

(Piaget, 1932, p.120)

2. From C.O.R.M. (aged 9)

| | |
|---|---|
| C.O.R.M. | Well, the one who broke them as he was coming isn't naughty, 'cos he didn't know there was any cups. The other one wanted to take the jam and caught his arm on a cup. |
| Piaget | Which one is the naughtiest? |
| C.O.R.M. | The one who wanted to take the jam. |
| Piaget | How many cups did he break? |
| C.O.R.M. | One. |
| Piaget | And the other boy? |
| C.O.R.M. | Fifteen. |
| Piaget | Which one would you punish the most? |
| C.O.R.M. | The boy who wanted to take the jam. He knew, he did it on purpose. |

(Piaget, 1932, pp. 123–4)

In the first of these stages, children judge by the objective amount of damage, and also tend to see punishment as inevitable and retributive. Piaget called this stage 'moral realism', as compared with the 'moral subjectivism' of the following stage, in which subjective intent is taken account of, and punishment is seen more as a lesson suited to the offence. Piaget related these stages to his idea of heteronomous and autonomous morality from the marbles study. A summary of his stages is given in table 7.3

There are problems with Piaget's dilemma method, many pointed out in a critique by Karniol (1978). Characteristically, Piaget makes it difficult for the child by having unequal consequences in the two stories (15 cups versus one cup broken), thus in effect tempting the child to ignore intention. The stories are badly designed: for example, it is not clear that Henry was being naughty in going to get the jam, and he probably didn't intend to break the cup, he was just careless. So the 'bad intention' in this story has to be inferred. There are also considerable memory demands made on young children (Kail, 1979). Several studies have shown that when methodological improvements are made (e.g. contrasting intent and accident when there is equal damage) children as young as 5 years will judge on the basis of intent.

Further research has shown that young children do not have a monolithic conception of rules as constraints. They distinguish between behaviours that violate purely social conventions (e.g. not putting your belongings in the right place), and those which violate moral conventions (e.g. not sharing a toy; hitting a child). A study by Smetana (1981) of children aged $2\frac{1}{2}$–5 in two American nursery schools found that children distinguished between these two kinds of behaviour in terms of whether it was dependent on context (home, or school), and on the amount of punishment it deserved.

Despite limitations, the approach of presenting children and young people verbally with moral dilemmas has been pursued by a number of psychologists in the USA. It has been used especially by Kohlberg, over a longer age span than Piaget and on a more ambitious scale.

TABLE 7.3    *Summary of Piaget's stages of moral judgement*

| Up to 4 or 5 yr | From 4–5 yr to 9–10 yr | After 9–10 yr |
| --- | --- | --- |
| *Premoral judgement* | *Moral realism* (Heteronomous morality of constraint) | *Moral subjectivism* (Autonomous morality of cooperation) |
| Rules not understood | Rules come from higher authority and cannot be changed | Rules are created by people and can be changed by mutual consent |
| | Evaluate actions by outcomes | Evaluate actions by intentions |
| | Punishment as inevitable retribution | Punishment as chosen to fit crime |

*Source*: Based on Piaget, 1932

*Kohlberg's theory*

Kohlberg researched on the development of moral reasoning for some 30 years, and his theory has proved influential in education and criminology, as well as psychology. The work started with, and extended from, research for his doctoral thesis, in which he commenced in 1955 a longitudinal study of 50 American males initially aged 10–26 years. These subjects were re-interviewed every three years. Kohlberg asked these subjects questions, such as 'why shouldn't you steal from a store?', and also posed them story dilemmas. Of a number of dilemmas, the most famous is that of Heinz and the druggist (Kohlberg, 1969, p. 379).

> In Europe, a woman was near death from a special kind of cancer. There was one drug that the doctor thought might save her. It was a form of radium that a druggist in the same town had recently discovered. The drug was expensive to make, but the druggist was charging 10 times what the drug cost him to make. He paid $200 for the radium and charged $2,000 for a small dose of the drug. The sick woman's husband, Heinz, went to everyone he knew to borrow the money, but he could only get together about $1,000, which is half of what it cost. He told the druggist that his wife was dying, and asked him to sell it cheaper or let him pay later. But the druggist said 'No, I discovered the drug and I'm going to make money from it.' So Heinz got desperate and broke into the man's store to steal the drug for his wife.

> Should Heinz have done that? Why or why not?

On the basis of these questions and dilemmas, Kohlberg postulated three levels of moral reasoning, each subdivided to make six stages in all. These levels and stages are defined in table 7.4. We look briefly at each level in turn.

*Level one: precoventional morality*   This is similar to Piaget's morality of constraint. Kohlberg (1976) thinks of it as 'the level of most children under 9, some adolescents, and many adolescent and adult criminal offenders' (p.33). On this level the individual reasons in relation to himself and has not yet come fully to understand and uphold conventional or societal rules and expectations. Here is a level one response from Joe, aged 10 years, one of Kohlberg's original longitudinal sample:

Kohlberg    Why shouldn't you steal from a store?
Joe         It's not good to steal from a store. It's against the law. Someone could see you and call the police.
                                                            (Kohlberg, 1976, p.36)

*Level two: conventional morality*   This is 'the level of most adolescents and adults in our society and in other societies' (p.33). At this level the individual thinks of what is right as conforming to and upholding the rules, expectations and conventions of

TABLE 7.4    *Kohlberg's stages of moral judgement*

| Level | Stage | What is right |
|---|---|---|
| Preconventional | Stage 1 Heteronomous morality | To avoid breaking rules backed by punishment, obedience for its own sake, avoiding physical damage to persons and property |
| | Stage 2 Individualism, instrumental purpose, and exchange | Following rules only when it is to someone's immediate interest; acting to meet one's own interests and needs, and letting others do the same. Right is what's fair, an equal exchange, a deal, an agreement |
| Conventional | Stage 3 Mutual interpersonal expectations, relationships and interpersonal conformity | Living up to what is expected by people close to you or what people generally expect of people in your role. 'Being good' is important and means having good motives, showing concern about others and keeping mutual relationships, such as trust, loyalty, respect, and gratitude |
| | Stage 4 Social system and conscience | Fulfilling the actual duties to which you have agreed. Laws are to be upheld except in extreme cases where they conflict with other fixed social duties. Right is contributing to society, the group, or institution |
| Postconventional or principled | Stage 5 Social contract or utility and individual rights | Being aware that people hold a variety of values and opinions, that most values and rules are relative to your group but should usually be upheld in the interest of impartiality and because they are the social contract. Some non-relative values and rights like life and liberty, however, must be upheld in any society and regardless of majority opinion |
| | Stage 6 (hypothetical) Universal ethical principles | Following self-chosen ethical principles. Particular laws or social agreements are usually valid because they rest on such principles. When laws violate these principles, one acts in accordance with the principle. Principles are universal principles of justice: the equality of human rights and respect for the dignity of human beings as individual persons |

*Source*: Adapted from Colby et al., 1983

society. Here is a level two response from Joe, now aged 17 years:

Kohlberg     Why shouldn't you steal from a store?
Joe          It's a matter of law. It's one of our rules that we're trying to
             help protect everyone, protect property, not just to protect a
             store. It's something that's needed in our society. If we didn't
             have these laws, people would steal, they wouldn't have to
             work for a living, and our whole society would get out of kilter.
                                                         (Kohlberg, 1976, p. 36)

*Level three: postconventional morality*     This level 'is reached by a minority of adults
and is usually reached after the age of 20' (p.33). Someone at this level broadly
understands and accepts the rules of society, but only because they accept some
general moral principles underlying these rules. If such a principle comes in conflict
with society's rules, then the individual judges by principle rather than by
convention. Here is a level three response from Joe, now aged 24 years:

Kohlberg     Why shouldn't you steal from a store?
Joe          It's violating another person's rights, in this case to property.
Kohlberg     Does the law enter in?
Joe          Well, the law in most cases is based on what is morally right so
             it's not a separate subject, it's a consideration.
Kohlberg     What does 'morality' or 'morally right' mean to you?'
Joe          Recognising the rights of other individuals, first to life and then
             to do as he pleases as long as it dosen't interfere with
             somebody else's rights.
                                                       (Kohlberg, 1976, pp. 36–7)

As a cognitive-developmental theorist, Kohlberg supposed that the level of moral
reasoning was dependent on having achieved a level of cognitive development, and
also of social perspective or role-taking (chapter 11). He thought that someone still
at the concrete operational stage would be limited to preconventional moral
judgement (stages 1 and 2). Someone at early formal operations would be limited to
conventional morality (stages 3 and 4). Postconventional morality would be
dependent on late formal operations being achieved.

Kohlberg hypothesized that in all societies, individuals would progress upwards
through these stages, in sequence (stages would not be skipped, and subjects would
not regress). He also hypothesized that an individual would be attracted by
reasoning just above their own on the scale, but would not understand reasoning
more than one stage above; if true, this would have obvious implications for moral
education.

### Early criticisms

A substantial number of criticisms of Kohlberg's methodology were made by
Kurtines and Greif (1974). They pointed out that the moral judgement score of an
individual was assessed from his or her scores on a number of dilemmas, yet the

different dilemmas were derived intuitively and did not intercorrelate very highly. The scale was critisized as being unreliable, and the 'clinical method' of interview (similar to Piaget's) as being subjective. The vadility of the scale was also called into question, since the invariance of sequence could not be properly proved from Kohlberg's sample if that was the sample from which he derived the sequence in the first place.

Damon (1977) elaborated the criticism that the original dilemmas were intuitive, and in many ways unrealistic. How does the 'Heinz' problem appear to a 10- or 17-year-old? Damon listened to actual moral debates among children, and made up a number of interview items, such as:

All of these boys and girls are in the same class together. One day their teacher lets them spend the whole afternoon making paintings and crayon drawings. The teacher thought that these pictures were so good that the class could sell them at the fair. They sold the pictures to their parents, and together the whole class made a lot of money.

Now all the children gathered the next day and tried to decide how to split up the money.

What do you think they should do with it? Why?

Kathy said that the kids in the class who made the most pictures should get most of the money. What do you think? [More probe questions follow.]

From using these more realistic items, Damon derived a six-step 'positive-justice sequence', which describes children's reasoning about sharing, fairness and distributive justice. Other scales and sequences have also been published.

Another criticism has been that Kohlberg's original subjects were all male, and that the consequent sequence of stages reflects the development of male morality and is male-biased. This viewpoint has been put most strongly by Carol Gilligan in her book *In a Different Voice: Psychological Theory and Women's Development* (1982). In fact, Gilligan argues quite widely for a 'female psychology' to complement the predominantly 'male psychology' so far developed. So far as moral reasoning is concerned, Gilligan described a short-term longitudinal study in which she interviewed 29 women, aged 15–33, who were attending abortion and pregnancy counselling services. These women were faced with a very real moral dilemma – whether to have an abortion or go through with the pregnancy. Gilligan found that these women considered their dilemma in somewhat different terms from what she calls the 'justice' orientation of Kohlberg; rather they focused more on 'responsibility'. Instead of abstract, principled judgements which are universally applicable, as in Kohlberg's stages 5 and 6, these women made rational, context-dependent judgements which were more concerned about the impact of behaviour on people's actual feelings. Put simply, it is a question of whether you put principles before people (a 'male' characteristic), or people before principles (a 'female' characteristic). On this basis, Gilligan suggested an alternative ethic of care and responsibility as being more representative of women's moral reasoning development.

*Recent revisions*

Kohlberg and his co-workers, especially Anne Colby, revised some aspects of the theory. This, and independent replications, go some way to answering earlier criticisms. A new scoring system, called Standard Issue Scoring, was published in 1978. This scores separately and with clear referents, the responses to the issue chosen by the subject for each dilemma; in the Heinz dilemma, for example, this would be the law issue if the subject says Heinz should not steal, the life issue if Heinz should save his wife. High reliabilities are reported for this scoring method. A rescoring of the original American longitudinal sample produced the results shown in figure 7.1. The stage sequence model is well supported for the first four stages. The low incidence of stage 5 is noticeable. Stage 6 is absent. Kohlberg therefore considered this to be a hypothetical stage, which has not been established empirically (Colby et al., 1983).

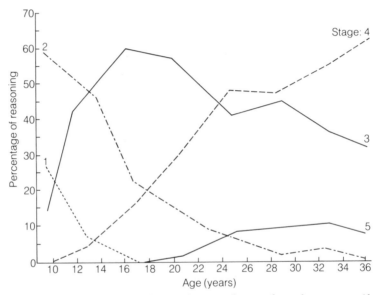

FIGURE 6.1    *Mean percentage of moral reasoning at each stage for each age group (from Colby et al., 1983)*

This sequence of stages has now been broadly confirmed in many other societies. A review by Snarey (1985) lists studies in 27 different cultural areas; most are cross-sectional, but there have been longitudinal studies in the Bahamas, Canada, India, Indonesia, Israel, Turkey and the USA. Naturally the dilemmas are adapted slightly for different cultures; the Turkish version of the Heinz dilemma, for example, involves a man and his wife who have migrated from the mountains, and are running out of food so that the wife becomes sick; there is only one food store in the village, and the storekeeper charges so much that the man cannot pay. Here is an example of a level one (stage two) response from Turkey (Snarey, 1985, p.221):

> Should the husband have stolen the food?
> Yes. Because his wife was hungry ... otherwise she will die.

Suppose it wasn't his wife who was starving but his best friend; should he
steal for his friend?
Yes, because one day when he is hungry his friend would help.
What if he doesn't love his friend?
No, [then he should not steal] because when he doesn't love him it means
that his friend will not help him later.

In his review Snarey found that almost all the studies in different societies agreed
in finding a progression from stages 1 through to 4, at reasonably appropriate ages.
There was some discordance about stage 5, however. Very few studies found true
stage 5 reasoning, and even transitional stage 5 reasoning was only found in urban
societies. It was not found at all in rural or village societies (e.g. Alaskan eskimos,
Guatamala, rural Kenya, New Guinea, rural Turkey). Rather than argue that
individuals in these societies are in some sense inferior in moral reasoning, Snarey
and other psychologists argue that Kohlberg's level three (stage 5) is significantly
culturally biased. It reflects the individualistic, capitalistic orientation of middle class
Western urban society. Other religions, such as Hinduism, may put less value on
individual human life than does the Christian religion. Other societies, socialist or
rural, may put more emphasis on collectivist values based on reciprocity and on
conflict resolution by interpersonal means. This is illustrated by an extract from an
interview with an Israeli kibbutz male (Snarey, 1985, p.222):

Should Moshe steal the drug? Why or why not?

Yes ... I think that the community should be responsible for controlling this
kind of situation. The medicine should be made available to all in need: the
druggist should not have the right to decide on his own ... the whole
community or society should have the control of the drug.

In this example the subject is somewhat at cross-purposes with the assumptions of
the interviewer. Such responses may be difficult to score on Kohlberg's scheme, but
(Snarey and others argue) should not therefore be devalued.

## Conclusion

The cognitive-developmental approach to moral reasoning has been very influential. It has definite implications for moral education, supporting the general view of
the educational philosopher John Dewey that education is not instruction, but
providing the right conditions for development. An approach such as Kohlberg's
suggests that instruction in moral reasoning may not be very helpful; rather,
methods such as peer interaction or conflict, and/or exposure to reasoning at a
slightly higher level, should be especially effective ways of developing moral
reasoning. The empirical evidence on this is so far fairly mixed; for example, in
training young children to use intention as a criterion for moral judgement, simply
telling them in a didactic fashion had more impact than peer interaction or training
in role-taking skills (Lickona, 1976). An example of an empirical study that did find
evidence to support the effectiveness of peer interaction is discussed in box 7.2. A

review of 55 studies of moral education programmes has found that techniques such as dilemma discussion can produce modest effects on moral reasoning scores over a 3–12 week-period (Schaefli et al., 1985).

### Further reading

P. Mussen and N. Eisenberg-Berg 1977: *Roots of Caring, Sharing, and Helping*. San Francisco: W. H. Freeman, provides a useful introduction to the development of prosocial behaviour. A more advanced collection is in N. Eisenberg (ed.) 1982: *The Development of Prosocial Behavior*. New York: Academic Press.

J. Piaget 1977 [1932]: *The Moral Judgement of the Child*. Harmondsworth: Penguin, is worth reading for an insight into Piaget's style and methods; the theoretical excerpts are however rather dated and heavy going. Unfortunately, there is not a good, simple primer on Piaget's and Kohlberg's theories. Good advanced collections are in T. Lickona (ed.) 1976: *Moral Development and Behavior*. New York: Holt, Rinehart and Winston; H. Weinreich-Haste and D. Locke (eds) 1983: *Morality in the Making*. Chichester: John Wiley & Sons; and W. M. Kurtines and J. L. Gewirtz (eds) 1984: *Morality, Moral Behavior, and Moral Development*. New York: Wiley.

### Discussion points

1   How should we define prosocial behaviour? What implications does the definition have for the way in which prosocial behaviour is studied?

2   Contrast the use of naturalistic and experimental designs for studying what influences prosocial behaviour and altruism.

3   Compare Piaget's two methods of studying moral reasoning.

4   Is Kohlberg's way of obtaining levels of moral reasoning biased towards male, upper/middle class, urban, Western-educated respondents?

5   How can either moral reasoning, or moral behaviour, be encouraged?

### Practical exercises

1   Observe children, either in a home or a school setting. Watch one child at a time, record all instances of prosocial behaviour, and the way in which other persons respond to it. Compare your findings with the tables in the text. Do you find any age or sex differences in your results?

2   Try out some of Piaget's story tasks (e.g. the stories of the broken cups) on children of different ages. See if you can replicate his findings.

3   Ask a range of people of different ages questions on moral issues, such as 'why is it wrong to steal from a shop?' Record their answers, and see how well they fit with Kohlberg's stages of moral reasoning.

# Box 7.1

# Child rearing and children's prosocial initiations toward victims of distress

The objective of this study was to examine the relationship between a mother's behaviour and her child's willingness to help others in distress. Particular attention was paid to mothers' reactions when their child observed or caused distress in another child. An intensive study of a small sample was used. Sixteen mothers of children aged between $1\frac{1}{2}$ and $2\frac{1}{2}$ years volunteered to take part. For a nine-month period they kept diary records of all incidents of distress in which someone in the child's presence expressed painful feelings, whether due to the child's own actions or not. The child's responses, and the mother's own behaviour, were recorded as soon as possible after the event, on a tape recorder. Mothers received initial training and an investigator visited the home every third week to check on the observations. At these visits the investigator also rated the mother on empathic caregiving (defined as anticipating difficulties, or responding promptly to child's needs).

The analysis distinguished between those distress incidents which the child did not cause ('bystander incidents'), and those which the child did cause ('child-caused distress'). The children's prosocial behaviour took the form of physical or verbal sympathy ('all better now?'; hugs victim), providing objects such as food, toys or bandages, finding someone else to help, protecting the victim, or giving physical assistance. In bystander incidents children were altruistic on 34 per cent of occasions (range 5–70 per cent), and in child-caused distress they made reparations on 32 per cent of occasions (range 0–60 per cent). There were clearly large individual differences between children, and these are fairly consistent over the two types of incident; the correlation between the two was 0.55, $p < 0.05$.

The mother's behaviour was categorized into various techniques, and the use of each technique calculated (more than one technique could be used in any incident). In bystander incidents, more frequent maternal techniques were 'no reaction' (56 per cent), 'reassurance' ('don't worry, it's OK') (36 per cent), and 'modelling altruism to victim' (e.g. picks up and pats crying child) (21 per cent). In child-caused distress the most frequent maternal techniques were 'no reaction' (31 per cent); 'affective explanation' often involving moralizing ('You made Doug cry. It's not nice to bite') or verbal prohibition ('Can't you see Al's hurt? Don't push him') (22 per cent); 'neutral explanation' ('Tom's crying because you pushed him') (18 per cent); 'unexplained verbal prohibition' ('Stop that!') (15 per cent); 'suggestion of positive action' ('Why don't you give Jeffy your ball') (13 per cent); 'physical restraint' ('I just moved him away from the baby') (13 per cent); and 'physical punishment' ('I swatted her a good one') (9 per cent).

Based on material in C. Zahn-Waxler, M. Radke-Yarrow and R. A. King: 1979 *Child Development*, 50, 319–30

BOX TABLE 7.1.1   Average percentage of incidents in which child shows altruism in bystander incidents and reparation for child-caused distress incidents when mothers are high or low in use of different techniques

| Mother's technique | Altruism | | | Reparation | | |
|---|---|---|---|---|---|---|
| | High use | Low use | t test | High use | Low use | t test |
| No reaction | 29 | 40 | n.s. | 28 | 33 | n.s. |
| Affective explanation | 42 | 21 | 2.60 p<0.05 | 44 | 13 | 4.77 p<0.01 |
| Neutral explanation | 37 | 31 | n.s. | 37 | 23 | n.s. |
| Unexplained verbal prohibition | 24 | 42 | 2.41 p<0.05 | 18 | 40 | 3.37 p<0.01 |
| Suggestion of positive action | 32 | 37 | n.s. | 30 | 31 | n.s. |
| Physical restraint | 41 | 27 | n.s. | 31 | 29 | n.s. |
| Physical punishment | 29 | 28 | n.s. | 27 | 42 | n.s. |

Was the way in which mothers reacted to child-caused distress related to the likelihood that a child behaved in a prosocial way in distress incidents? The investigators took the mothers scores for each technique, found the median and grouped mothers into those above or below the median (high or low on that technique). Then, the child's likelihood of prosocial behaviour was compared for 'high' and 'low' mothers on each technique, using independent groups $t$ tests. The results are shown in box table 7.1.1, giving the analysis for the likelihood of children showing altruism in bystander incidents, and the corresponding analysis for the child showing reparation in child-caused distress incidents. It can be seen that mothers who gave affective explanations to their children when they caused distress are likely to have children who spontaneously show altruism to others, and also make reparation for distress they have caused themselves. On the other hand, mothers who gave more unexplained verbal prohibitions were likely to have children who showed less prosocial behaviour in both situations. Other techniques gave non-significant correlations. Physical methods (restraint, or punishment) were neither strongly effective nor ineffective, but they were positively correlated with some aspects of affective explanation; that is, many mothers combined affective explanation with some physical action.

The mothers' empathic caregiving ratings were also split into 'high' and 'low' groups. Mothers high in empathic caregiving had more prosocial children than did mothers low in empathic caregiving. For altruism in bystander incidents, the respective percentages were 46 per cent and 24 per cent; for reparation, the figures were 47 per cent and 17 per cent; both comparisons are significant at the 0.01 level on the $t$ test.

The investigators conclude that 'the prototype of the mother whose child is reparative and altruistic is one whose communications when her child transgresses are of high intensity and clarity both cognitively and affectively ... [it] is not calmly dispensed reasoning, carefully designed to enlighten the child, it is emotionally imposed, sometimes harshly and often forcefully. These techniques exist side by side with empathic caregiving.'

This study has noticeable strengths and weaknesses. The strengths are that it examines prosocial behaviour in real-life situations, and over some considerable time period. One weakness is the small sample, composed only of volunteer mothers. It would certainly be problematic to generalize very widely, without a replicative study on a different sample. Another weakness might be the use of the mothers' records: how objective were they? The training procedures, and investigators' recordings, went some way to alleviate this concern. Finally, the authors are tempted to infer causation from the correlations they discovered. They suggest that maternal techniques are influencing the child's behaviour. However, it could be that child characteristics influence the mother's behaviour. All we can be sure about is that, in this sample, empathic and affectively explaining mothers have prosocial children. We cannot be sure whether one causes the other, although we can generate plausible hypotheses from the data of this study.

Box 7.2

# Peer interaction and the process of change in children's moral reasoning

Damon and Killen sought to discover, first, whether peer interaction in a moral debate would increase levels of moral reasoning; and secondly, whether certain kinds of peer interaction could be linked to such change. The study was carried out on 147 children, aged about 5–8 years, from public schools in an urban centre in the USA. The experimenters used Damon's positive-justice interview, rather than Kohlberg's scale, as a measure of moral reasoning. The interview was given both at pre-test, and about three and a half months later at post-test.

About two months after the pre-test the children in the experimental condition participated in a peer debate, in groups of three. First, together with a fourth, younger child, they were given a task of making bracelets from beads and string. Then, the youngest child (who always made the fewest bracelets) was called away. After some further comments on the participants' efforts the experimenter then asked the three children to decide how ten sweet bars should be distributed between them and the fourth child. This peer debate was videotaped and scored for the content of discussion made by each participant.

The children in the first control group came individually to the laboratory and discussed a hypothetical justice problem of a similar nature. This controlled for the effect of practice in reasoning which was not in a peer context. The children in a second control group received no extra intervention; this controlled for changes in moral reasoning due to age and general experience over the three and a half months between pre-test and post-test.

A first analysis was done to see how many children had changed their modal level of moral reasoning. Very few had done so. However, many children had increased the proportion of their reasoning which was above their modal level, and these results are shown in box table 7.2.1. Here, the independent variable is the experimental condition, and the dependent variable is the change in moral reasoning. The experimental group display more change in moral reasoning than the control groups, ($\chi^2(2) = 14.4$, p. $< 0.001$).

A second set of analyses considered only the children in the experimental condition. Whether or not there was a change in moral reasoning was now the independent variable, and the dependent variables examined were the kind of verbal interaction made in the peer debates. Chi-square analyses were used again. Children initially at low reasoning levels, who both initiated and received a lot of statements indicating acceptance and clarification or elaboration, were especially likely to show a change in moral reasoning, $\chi^2(3) = 8.5$, $p < 0.05$, but this finding did not apply to children already at a high reasoning level. However, many verbal contributions involving disagreements, rejection or ridicule predicted that moral reasoning would not change, $\chi^2(1) = 5.1$, $p < 0.05$).

Based on material in W. Damon and M. Killen 1982: *Merrill–Palmer Quarterly*, 28, 347–67

BOX TABLE 7.2.1   *Number of experimental and control participants whose percentage of reasoning above the modal value advanced from pre-test to post-test*

|  | Advanced | Did not advance |
|---|---|---|
| Experimental group ($n=78$) | 32 | 46 |
| Control group 1 ($n=44$) | 5 | 39 |
| Control group 2 ($n=25$) | 4 | 21 |

A problem with small-scale intervention studies is that any convincing effects are likely to be small, and thus difficult to detect against general variation due to error and to random factors. In this study the peer debate only lasted about 10–11 minutes, so one might question what impact this could possibly have in a three-month period. In fact, sufficient numbers of participants were employed that some increase in moral reasoning does seem to have been detected. While such changes are admittedly small (since they are only changes within a level), any larger changes would surely be suspect. The experimental design means that any change can be ascribed to the impact of peer interaction over a moral issue. The main objection would be that the peer debate was 'stage-managed' in an artificial situation (what did the children think was going on?) and might not be representative of real-life peer interaction.

# 8

# Adolescence

Adolescence is the period of transition between childhood, and life as an adult – it covers basically the teenage years. Biologically, it is marked by the onset of puberty. After puberty, a person is sexually mature and could potentially become a mother or father of a child. Socially, adolescence is marked by an increasing independence from parents as the young person prepares to leave home, to complete his or her education, to form sexual partnerships and to seek some vocation or employment.

Adolescence has generally been thought of as a difficult period, as indeed times of transition often are. This has been emphasized, and perhaps overemphasized, by writers from both psychoanalytic and sociological traditions. Phrases such as 'the identity crisis of adolescence', the 'generation gap' between teenagers and their parents, and the turmoil or 'storm and stress' of the adolescent period have become well worn if not hackneyed. In this chapter we will look at the nature of adolescence and examine how well the evidence supports these views. In doing so we shall note again the importance of the social and historical context in considering development in adolescence. We need to keep a balance between the cultural variations in different societies and the relatively invariant features which may always character-ize adolescence. The most obvious universal feature is the onset of puberty, and we will start with an overview of the biological and physical changes which this involves.

## The Biological and Physical Changes of Puberty

The precise timing of puberty depends on the measure taken, but in girls the onset of menstruation (menarche) provides a fairly definite marker, and in boys the time of first ejaculation. There are great variations between individuals, and puberty comes slightly later for boys. The typical age sequence of physical changes is shown in table 8.1.

The physical differences between the boys and girls are examples of *sexual dimorphism* (discussed in chapter 2). During puberty hormonal changes greatly exaggerate these differences. The reproductive organs become fully funtional at puberty. In girls both the external genitalia (the vulva, including the clitoris) and the

TABLE 8.1   *Approximate age and sequence of appearance of sexual characteristics during puberty*

| Age (yr) | Boys | Girls |
|---|---|---|
| 9–10 | | Growth of bony pelvis<br>Budding of nipples |
| 10–11 | First growth of testes and penis | Budding of breasts<br>Pubic hair |
| 11–12 | Activity of prostate gland producing semen | Changes in lining of vagina<br>Growth of external and internal genitalia |
| 12–13 | Pubic hair | Pigmentation of nipples<br>Breasts fill out |
| 13–14 | Rapid growth of testes and penis | Axillary hair (under armpits)<br>Menarche (average: 13.5 years; range 9–17 years). Menstruation may be anovulatory for first few years |
| 14–15 | Axillary hair (under armpits)<br>Down on upper lip<br>Voice change | Earliest normal pregnancies |
| 15–16 | Mature spermatozoa (average: 15 years; range: 11.25–17 years) | Acne<br>Deepening of voice |
| 16–17 | Facial and body hair<br>Acne | Skeletal growth stops |
| 21 | Skeletal growth stops | |

*Source*: Adapted from Katchadourian, 1977

internal genitalia (the ovaries, fallopian tubes, uterus and vagina) become enlarged. The clitoris becomes more sensitive to stimulation, and the lining of the uterus and the vagina are strengthened. Menarche follows these changes. In boys, the testes and penis become larger, and so does the prostate gland, which is important for the production of semen. This is followed by the first ejaculation.

Other sexually dimorphic features are linked to these (for example, they may also be caused by sex hormones), but are not directly part of the reproductive system. In both sexes there is a growth of body hair, especially under the armpits and in the pubic areas. In boys there is more coarse body and facial hair, and the beginnings of beard growth. There are skin changes, and the sweat glands become more active, often leading to acne. The voice deepens, especially in boys. In girls, breast development occurs.

Another feature of the pubertal period is the adolescent growth spurt. Throughout the school years growth is fairly steady, averaging about 5 or 6 cm per year.

This increases early on in puberty reaching about 9 cm per year in girls and 10 cm per year in boys before falling off sharply at adulthood (figure 8.1 shows these changes in growth velocity for an average boy and girl). The extent of this growth spurt is largely independent of the child's previous height and some 35 per cent of the variation in adult height is due to these rapid changes in adolescence.

All of the physical changes at puberty are linked to biological changes in the body. These are summarized in figure 8.2. The key role is played by the hypothalamus, as it controls the action of the pituitary gland which produces the necessary hormones. The action of the hypothalamus resembles that of a thermostat regulating temperature – it 'shuts down' when high enough levels of sex hormones are circulating in the body. These sex hormones (especially androgen, testosterone, estrogen and progesterone) are produced by the adrenal cortex, and by the gonads (the testes and ovaries). The growth of the latter is in turn stimulated by hormones released by the pituitary gland. At puberty there is a change in the 'setting' or

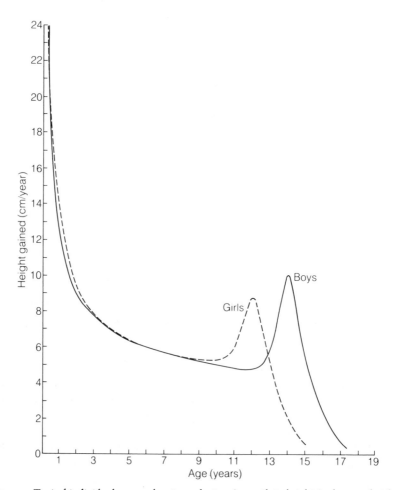

FIGURE 8.1    *Typical individual curves showing velocity of growth in height for boys and girls (from Katchadourian, 1977)*

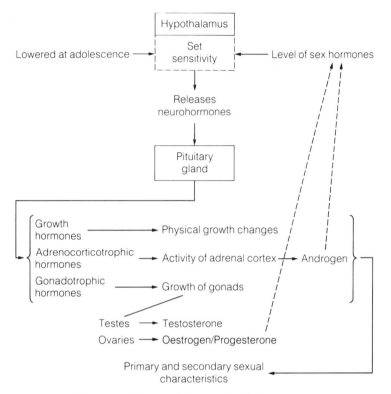

FIGURE 8.2    *Summary of hormonal changes at puberty*

sensitivity of the hypothalamus. As a result, the pituitary gland works harder, and sex hormone levels are raised resulting in the physical changes we have summarized.

*Variations in physical maturation rates*

The age of pubertal development can vary a great deal between individuals. This is dramatically shown in figure 8.3, which shows the growth and sexual development of three boys, each aged 14 years and 9 months, and of three girls, each aged 12 years 9 months. To some extent this variation may be genetic. For example, two randomly chosen girls will differ in age of menarche by, on average, 19 months; for two sisters, however, the average difference is only 13 months, and for identical twins, less than 3 months (Tanner, 1962). The variation is also linked to general body build. Children who are short and stocky tend to mature earlier than children who are slimmer and more linear in body shape (Katchadourian, 1977).

Environmental factors can also have very pronounced effects on maturation. Undernourishment or malnutrition can slow down growth and retard the onset of puberty. This is not surprising, as caloric requirements increase with puberty. Although it is difficult to prove, it is highly likely that nutritional differences are largely responsible for social class and cultural differences in the timing of puberty. In less wealthy countries especially, social classes may differ by about a year in the

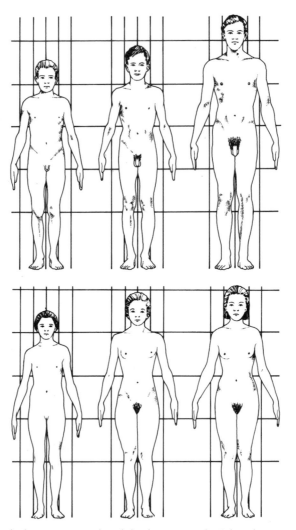

FIGURE 8.3    *Individual variation in pubertal development: each of the 3 boys is 14¾ years old, and each of the 3 girls is 12¾ years old (from Tanner, 1973)*

age of menarche; the difference is less marked or absent in richer countries, where perhaps almost all young people get adequate nourishment (Katchadourian, 1977).

A fascinating phenomenon in Western Europe and North American has been the secular trend in the age of menarche, illustrated in figure 8.4. This is based on records from the Scandinavian countries, going back to the mid-nineteenth century, and more recent records, including those in the UK and the USA. Figure 8.4 indicates that the age of menarche in girls declined over a hundred-year period from an average of around 16 or 17 in the 1860s to around 13 in the 1960s. The change averaged about 0.3 years per decade. There have been similar secular trends in height. Over the same period the average height of 12-year-olds increased by about 1.5 cm per decade; the trend for adult height was less – about 0.4 cm per

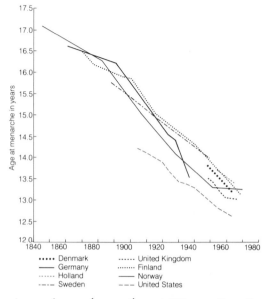

FIGURE 8.4   *Changes in age of menarche over the past 120 years (from Tanner, 1973)*

decade – since some 'catching up' occurs in later maturers in early adulthood. Since the 1960s these changes in height and in age of menarche seem to have ceased, as one would presume they had to do eventually (Roche, 1979).

Figure 8.4 has been extensively reproduced in textbooks, but in fact it seems that some of the earlier data is in error. Bullough (1981) re-examined available data from the nineteenth century, which suggests that menarche occurred between 14 and 16 years of age. The data for the nineteenth century in figure 8.4 suggesting an age of 17 years are based on very small samples from Scandinavia which are not representative. Nevertheless no-one denies that there has been a secular trend. The historian Herbert Moller (1985, 1987) has looked at available evidence for still earlier periods, and for males. One source of evidence was records of Bach's choirboys in Leipzig for 1727–47. Their voices broke distinctly later, at around 17 years, than would be the case nowadays (15–16 years, table 8.1). An analysis of beard growth in males, from writings and portraits, suggests that before the nineteenth century many young men did not grow a beard until their twenties; for example, the series of Rembrandt self-portraits only show him with a beard by age 24. Nowadays beard growth happens at around 17 years (table 8.1).

The secular trend is believed to have been due to improving nutritional and health standards. Decreases in mean family size may have been a contributing factor (see Malina, 1979 and Frisch, 1988, for a discussion).

## Psychological Effects of Puberty

We have seen how the onset of puberty produces marked physical changes. These in their turn have psychological effects on the young person. The adolescent is becoming aware of his or her sexual development, and of associated changes in body size and shape, depth of voice, skin texture and facial and body hair. Many writers on adolescence have ascribed the awkwardness or self-consciousness which is often thought to characterize this period to awareness of these changes. We should also bear in mind the cognitive changes which are thought to occur in this period (chapter 11). Entering the period of formal operational thought, adolescents are increasingly able to think about abstract issues and hypothetical situations. Thus, they may well reflect on how they are perceived by hypothetical others, and have problems adjusting to their changing physical appearance. David Elkind (1967) suggests that adolescents often imagined how their appearance or behaviour would seem to an 'imaginary audience' of others, hence their own self-consiousness. Elkind also argued that adolescents often thought that their own actions were very important in the eyes of others, and that they become bound up or obsessed with their own feelings, constructing a 'personal fable', an imaginary story of their own life, perhaps containing fantasies of omnipotence or immortality. These concepts of the 'imaginary audience' and the 'personal fable' led Elkind to postulate that a new kind of egocentrism appeared in adolescence (cf. chapter 11). In this 'adolescent egocentrism' young people are unable to differentiate their own feelings about themselves from what others might be feeling. Elkind was writing at a time when the 'storm and stress' view of adolescence was popular and empirical work on his concepts has yielded rather mixed results (Buis and Thompson, 1989). However it does seem that the onset of puberty tends to decrease the closeness the young person feels to their parents, and increase conflict with parents, (Steinberg, 1988).

How do adolescents react to the physical changes associated with puberty? One area of research has been the attitude of girls to the onset of menstruation. A number of studies on the psychological impact of menarche have been reviewed by Greif and Ulman (1982). Retrospective studies, in which women are asked to recall their menarcheal experience, suggest that it remains a clear and vivid event in the memory; it is recalled in rather negative terms, as an unplesant experience for which social support was lacking. These conclusions are limited by the samples (mainly middle class American) and historical period studied (occurrence of menarche in the first half of the twentieth century). A few studies have looked at recent attitudes in pre-and post-menarcheal girls. After menarche girls tended to report more negative emotions or experiences than they had expected, despite some educational preparation and support, usually from mothers. In a longitudinal study of 120 girls through menarche, Ruble and Brooks-Gunn (1982) confirmed that menarche did initially create some inconvenience, ambivalence and confusion, but that typically it did not seem to be a traumatic experience. The negative feelings were greater for early maturers, and also for girls who thought themselves poorly prepared for the experience. There can be positive features to menarche as well. Some studies have found that menarche can serve as a focal reference point, bringing a girl closer to her mother and heightening an awareness of and interest in her femininity. Menarche, or at least general changes associated with menarche, may be correlated with greater maturity on some personality characteristics (Greif and Ulman, 1982).

Nevertheless, some authors believe that the experience of menarche is better handled in other, traditional, cultures, in which there are well-defined rituals surrounding menstruation which gave it a symbolic meaning and importance (Mead, 1928, 1949; Greif and Ulman, 1982). In the village of Lesu in Melanesia, for example, the focus of a well-known anthropological study by Powdermaker (1933), the onset of menstruation is an important ritual event for the women in the community. The girl is washed in the sea before sunrise by an old woman, who dips the leaves of a branch in the water and over the girl, saying

Leaf, leaf I wash her
Soon her breasts will develop
I take away sickness of blood.

The leaves are then mixed with white lime and rubbed over the girl's body. This ritual is thought necessary if the girls' breasts are to develop, and full womanhood be achieved. A feast is held later the same day.

In many traditional societies boys also go through initiation ceremonies, often grouped together into an 'age set' spanning some five years. For example, in the Karimojong, a cattle herding people of Uganda, boys to be initiated first have to spear an ox. Semi–digested food from the stomach sack of the slaughtered animal is smeared over the initiate's body, while the elders call out. 'Be well. Become wealthy in stock. Grow old. Become an elder.' After further rituals, the boy has become a man and is allowed to grow his hair long in the fashion of men in the tribe (Dyson-Hudson, 1963).

These rituals are important in signalling the transition point from child to adult. Some anthropologists believe that they also reinforce the authority of the elders of the tribe, who perform the ceremonies. Another idea is that male initiation rites serve to break the close link children have with the mother. One study found that elaborate initiation rites were especially likely in societies where mothers nursed infants and shared the same bed with their child for a long period (Whiting et al., 1958). However other explanations are possible. It may simply be that in male-dominated societies men may have several wives (so prolonged nursing and post-partum sex taboos are tolerated) and, independently, male initiation rites are important in forging male solidarity (Young, 1965).

*Effects of early and late maturation*

At 11 years a girl would be early in experiencing menarche; at 14 she would be late. Similarly a 12-year-old boy would be early, a 15-year-old late, in reaching puberty. Do these differences have important psychological consequences?

Early maturing boys tend to be at an advantage socially, as their growth spurt favours strength and sport achievement, usually highly valued in boys' groups (chapter 4). A boy who is late in reaching puberty may feel less confident socially and be rated as less mature, attractive, or popular (Mussen and Jones, 1957).

A study in Sweden found a more complex picture for girls (Magnusson, Stattin and Allen, 1985). Data on 466 girls was obtained before puberty, after puberty at 14 years, and in a follow-up at 25 years. At 14 years it was clear that girls who had reached puberty early (before 11 years) were much more likely to be involved in drinking alcohol, smoking hashish, playing truant, and generally breaking social norms more than girls who matured on time or late. However this was found to be the case because these girls were more likely to mix with an older peer group who were more likely to engage in these activities. In other words, early maturation often led to associating with older peers, and if and when this happened the norm-breaking followed. This was a temporary effect; by age 25 the differences between early and late maturers in drinking alcohol had vanished. Nevertheless there was a more permanent effect of early maturation on education. Early maturing girls tended to engage in sexual activity earlier, get married and have children earlier, and were less likely to be in tertiary education than late maturers (2 per cent compared to 15 per cent).

Data on academic achievement in the UK come from a longitudinal study reported by Douglas and Ross (1964) and based on the National Survey of Health and Development, which followed the fortunes of 5,000 boys and girls born in Britain in one week in March, 1946. When followed through secondary school, it emerged that both boys and girls who were early maturers scored higher than late maturers on tests of mental ability and performance while at school. Some other studies have reported similar results. However, the superior performance of early maturers might not be due to the physical changes of puberty and greater physical maturity. First, the effect seems to interact with social class, being larger in lower social class groups. Also, family size may explain much of the effect. Puberty tends to be later in large families, and being a member of a large family also tends to depress intelligence and school achievement in a slight but consistent fashion. When children of similar family size are compared, the differences between early and late maturers are small (Douglas and Ross, 1964).

A study of this topic was made in Sweden with a random sample of 740 children followed from 9 to 14 years of age (Westin-Lindgren, 1982). In relation to achievement in Swedish, English and mathematics, the effects of social class were generally much greater than effects of early or late maturation. Thirteen-14-year-old early maturers did score better in Swedish and English if they came from families of manual workers, but there was little effect for children from families of salaried workers or employers. There were no effects of early or late maturation on mathematics scores. The possibly confounding effects of family size were not looked at in this study.

## Identity Development and the 'Identity Crisis'

Who are you? What sort of a person are you? All of us have some sense of identity, of who or what we are. Try heading a blank sheet of paper 'Who am I?', and providing 20 short answers on the rest of the sheet. This 'Twenty Statement Test' is the kind of test some psychologists use in looking at identity development. Other methods are to see whether a subject agrees with statements such as 'I take a positive attitude to myself', or to ask a subject to rate his or her 'characteristic self' against adjective pairs such as relaxed–nervous, happy–sad, or valuable–worthless. These latter assessments measure self-esteem (see also p. 115), or how one evaluates oneself, a very important aspect of overall identity.

In the earlier half of the twentieth century many theorists thought of adolescence as a time of acute identity crisis and turmoil. One influence here was that of psychoanalysis. Freud, at the turn of the century, was elaborating his views on human psychosexual development. On this view much of an individual's psychic energy was hypothesized as being taken up with trying to cope with unacceptable sexual impulses early in childhood. In the 'oral', 'anal' and 'oedipal' stages the very young child experiences frustration and anxiety at his or her developing sexual impulses, resulting in psychological defences and repression of these impulses during a 'latency period' from about 5 years of age to puberty. However, at puberty there was a renewed upsurge of sexual 'instincts' which reawakened old conflicts. The psychoanalytic approach was developed by Peter Blos (1962) in his book *On Adolescence*. Blos likened the adolescent transition to independence, to the earlier transition that the infant went through to become a self-reliant toddler; in both, ambivalence and regression were likely. Blos called adolescence a 'second individuation process', because of this parallel.

Freud's and Blos's theories have received much criticism. The 'instinct' model is outdated (chapter 2), and the emphasis on sexual concerns is generally felt to be exaggerated. However, a revision of the psychoanalytic approach made by Erik Erikson has attracted a lot of support. Erikson realized that Freud emphasized innate impulses too strongly; he gave a much larger role to cultural influences in personality formation. He accepted Freud's insight into the importance of sexual desires, but regarded other concerns as equally, or more, strong at various stages of the life cycle; he therefore described 'psychosocial' rather than 'sexual' stages of development. Finally, he thought that adolescence (rather than early childhood) was the most decisive period in the formation of adult personality. A summary of Erikson's eight stages in the life cycle is shown in table 8.2. In each stage there is a 'normative crisis' – the area in which Erikson considered conflict to be most characteristic.

Erikson elaborated his ideas about role confusion and identity in adolescence in his influential book *Identity: Youth and Crisis* (1968). Erikson argued that while identity was important throughout the life cycle, it was in adolescence that the most turmoil in this area could normally be expected. He thought that adolescents typically went through a psychological or psychosocial 'moratorium', in which they could try out different aspects of identity without finally committing themselves. For example, a young person might temporarily adopt different religious beliefs, or changed views about their vocation, without adults expecting this necessarily to be a final choice. After this period of crisis, a more stable, consolidated sense of identity would be achieved.

There are of course good reasons why one's sense of identity might change considerably through adolescence. We have seen how marked physical changes occur, which will affect one's body image or sense of physcial self. At this time also a pattern of sexual relationships needs to be decided upon. Society expects a young person to make some choice of vocation by around 18 years, and in many countries they also get the vote at this age and have to decide on their political preferences. Nevertheless, it must be borne in mind that Erikson's ideas were not obtained from any large-scale survey; they were based on his own observations, and on his clinical practice. As such, they certainly needed to be tested against empirical findings.

The most thorough attempt to do this has been made by James Marcia (1966, 1980). Marcia developed an interview technique to assess 'identity status' in certain areas, notably those of occupation, religion, political belief and attitudes to sexual behaviour. He would ask questions such as 'Have you ever had any doubts about

TABLE 8.2   *The eight developmental stages proposed by Erikson (1968)*

| Normative crisis | Age (yr) | Major characteristics |
|---|---|---|
| Trust vs mistrust | 0–1 | Primary social interaction with mothering caretaker; oral concerns; trust in life-sustaining care, including feeding |
| Autonomy vs shame and doubt | 1–2 | Primary social interaction with parents; toilet training; 'holding on' and 'letting go' and the beginnings of autonomous will |
| Initiative vs guilt | 3–5 | Primary social interaction with nuclear family; beginnings of 'oedipal' feelings; development of language and loco-motion; development of conscience as governor of initiative |
| Industry vs inferiority | 6–puberty | Primary social interaction outside home among peers and teachers; school age assessment of task ability |
| Identity vs role confusion | Adolescence | Primary social interaction with peers, culminating in heterosexual friendship; psychological moratorium from adult commitments; identity crisis; consolidation of resolutions of previous four stages into coherent sense of self |
| Intimacy vs isolation | Early adulthood | Primary social interaction in intimate relationship with member of opposite sex; adult role commitments accepted, including commitment to another person |
| Generativity vs stagnation | Middle age | Primary social concern in establishing and guiding future generation; productivity and creativity |
| Integrity vs despair | Old age | Primary social concern is a reflective one: coming to terms with one's place in the (now nearly complete) life cycle, and with one's relationship with others; 'I am what survives of me' |

your religious beliefs?'. Depending on the answer to these and other questions, a subject would be characterized as in 'diffusion' (or 'confusion'), 'foreclosure', 'moratorium', or 'achievement of identity' (Marcia, 1966).

Someone in diffusion (confusion) status has not really started thinking about the issues seriously, yet alone made any commitment. Thus in answer to the above question, they might answer 'Oh, I don't know. I guess so. Everyone goes through some sort of stage like that. But it really doesn't bother me much. I figure one's about as good as the other!'. By contrast, someone in foreclosure status has formed a commitment, but without ever having gone through a crisis or seriously considered alternatives. They probably accept unquestioningly parental or conventional beliefs. They might answer 'No, not really, our family is pretty much in agreement on these things' to the question about religious doubts.

Someone in moratorium status is going through the crisis predicted by Erikson. They are going to form a commitment, but at present are still considering various alternatives. They might answer 'Yes, I guess I'm going through that now. I just don't see how there can be a god and yet so much evil in the world or ...'.

Finally, someone in achievement status has been through the crisis and has reached a resolution. They have consolidated their identity in this respect. Thus, they might answer 'Yeah, I even started wondering whether or not there was a god. I've pretty much resolved that now, though. The way it seems to me is ...'.

In this scheme diffusion is seen as the least mature status, and achievement as the most mature. The most likely transitions in identity status are shown in figure 8.5. A number of studies have been made using this scheme, and have been reviewed by Waterman (1982). In a cross-sectional study of 11- to 17-year-olds, it was found that the diffusion and foreclosure statuses were most frequent, at all age levels (Archer, 1982). Identity achievement is very infrequent in 11- to 13-year-olds but does indeed increase through adolescence. The results of another cross-sectional study (Meilman, 1979) on 12- to 24-year-old males are shown in figure 8.6. It can be seen that only just over half the subjects interviewed had reached identity achievement at 24 years. Thus, identity achievement may go on well into adulthood. This is borne out by a study by O'Connell (1976), who carried out retrospective interviews with married women who had school-aged children. Most of the women said that they had experienced an increasingly strong sense of identity as they moved from adolescence through to when they married, then had their first child, then had their children going to school. Such findings suggest that identity development is not so strongly focused in adolescence as Erikson suggested.

FIGURE 8.5 *Most likely predicted changes in identity status*

Another study (Waterman and Waterman, 1975) compared identity status in a number of male college students and their fathers. The students were mainly of diffusion or moratorium status, while the fathers (aged 40–65) were mainly in the foreclosure status and had not reached identity achievement. These men had grown up in the 1930s to 1950s, and it could be that social expectations favoured a more conforming, 'foreclosure' kind of identity development at that time. Alternatively, of course, both Erikson and Marcia may be exaggerating the maturity of 'achievement' compared to 'foreclosure', or we may not be measuring these statuses as well as we think. Indeed, some subjects have been found to change from identity achievement back to foreclosure status, which should not theoretically be possible.

The most definite evidence on identity development would come from longitudinal studies, following the same subjects. Few have been done, but one is described

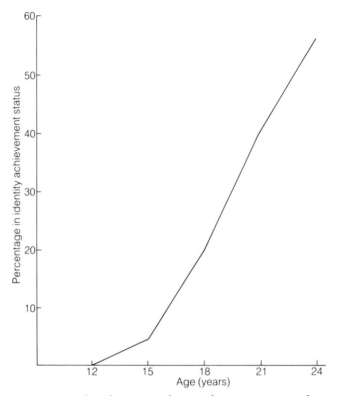

FIGURE 8.6  *Percentage of males who were in identity achievement status at five age levels (from Meilman, 1979)*

in box 8.1. As with the great majority of the studies in this area, American college students were the subjects. But college subjects are not typical of the whole population. One study found that identity achievement was much higher in working youths than in a sample of college students of equivalent age (Munro and Adams, 1977); the researchers suggest that 'college attendance might be seen as an extended moratorium period'.

We can have more confidence in identity status measures if they correlate with, or predict, other variables. Sex differences in identity status are not very marked (Archer, 1982), except in the area of sexual attitudes (which we shall discuss shortly). Identity status has been related to family background. Those in foreclosure report close relationships to parents, those in moratorium and achievement more distant or critical ones. Possibly related to this, children from divorced families tend to score 'higher' on identity status than those from intact families.

Amongst other findings, persons in moratorium for vocation are indeed more likely to change their academic plans (box 8.1). Students in identity achievement have a wider range of cultural interests and express more interest in expressive writing and poetry (Waterman, 1982). Identity status has also been found to relate to Kohlberg's level of moral reasoning (chapter 7). In one study the percentage of college students reasoning at the postconventional level was 51 per cent for those in identity achievement, 31 per cent for moratorium, 12 per cent for foreclosure and 9 per cent for diffusion.

The work on identity status is an interesting attempt to try to pin down Erikson's ideas, but it is clear there are problems. Some criticism has been made of how useful the status categories are and how adequately they assess identity (Matteson, 1977; Côte and Levine, 1988). Also, the idea of an 'identity crisis' seems suspect on at least three counts. First, adolescents do not experience the moratorium status in different topic areas at the same time; at one particular time one content area may be stable while another of life decisions is in crisis. A second point is that crisis can occur throughout adult life, and identity development can be quite prominent in the early adult years. Finally, we have a lot of evidence that for most young people, most of the time, changes in identity and self-esteem are gradual. We will conclude this section by looking at a couple of studies which show this, neither making use of the Marcia identity status categories.

Montemayor and Eisen (1977) used the Twenty Statements Test on about 50 young people each in the ages 10, 12, 14, 16 and 18. They found that there were indeed significant age changes, but without any dramatic crisis at say 14 or 16 years. Many of the changes were from a more concrete to a more abstract way of describing oneself: for example, responses in terms of one's address or citizenship (e.g. 'I live in the High Street'), possessions ('I own a bike'), or physical self ('I am 5 feet high') declined with age. Responses in terms of occupation ('I hope to be a doctor'), ideological beliefs ('I am a pacifist'), sense of self-determination ('I want to succeed in life') and interpersonal style ('I am a friendly person') increased with age. Some kinds of response showed a curvilinear trend, for example one's name ('I am called Fred'), or judgements and likes ('I like swimming'). These trends are given in table 8.3 and sample answers below, also from Montemayor and Eisen's study, from a boy of nearly 10, and a girl of nearly 18, illustrate some of them.

TABLE 8.3  *Percentage of participants in each age group who used each category at least once in the Twenty Statements Test*

| Category | Age (yr) | | | | |
|---|---|---|---|---|---|
| | 10 | 12 | 14 | 16 | 18 |
| Address/citizenship | 48 | 16 | 21 | 13 | 11 |
| Possessions | 53 | 22 | 24 | 14 | 8 |
| Physical self | 87 | 57 | 46 | 49 | 16 |
| Occupational | 4 | 12 | 29 | 28 | 44 |
| Ideological | 4 | 14 | 24 | 24 | 39 |
| Self-determination | 5 | 8 | 26 | 45 | 49 |
| Interpersonal style | 42 | 76 | 91 | 86 | 93 |
| Name | 50 | 10 | 8 | 11 | 31 |
| Judgements, likes | 69 | 65 | 80 | 45 | 31 |

All are significant at $p<0.001$ on chi-square tests.
*Source*: Montemayor and Eisen, 1977

Boy nearly 10: My name is Bruce C. I have brown eyes. I have brown hair. I love! sports. I have seven people in my family. I have great! eye sight. I have lots! of friends. I live at Pinecrest Dr. I'm going on 10 in September ... I have an uncle who is almost 7 feet tall. My teacher is Mrs V. I play hockey! I'm almost the smartest boy in the class. I love! food. I love fresh air. I love! school.

Girl, nearly 18: I am a human being. I am a girl. I am an individual. I don't know who I am. I am a Pisces. I am a moody person. I am an indecisive person. I am an ambitious person. I am a very curious person. I am not an individual. I am a loner. I am an American (God help me). I am a Democrat. I am a liberal person. I am a radical. I am a conservative. I am a pseudoliberal. I am an atheist. I am not a classifiable person (i.e. I don't want to be). (Montemayor and Eisen, 1977, pp. 317–18.)

Savin-Williams and Demo (1984) examined changes in self-esteem in a longitudinal sample of about 40 young people from 12 to 15 years of age. They used a variety of different measures of self-esteem. They found that changes were gradual, both on a daily and on a yearly basis. Feelings of self-esteem increased slowly but gradually through the early adolescent years. There were a few exceptions – a small number of young people who did experience very fluctuating feelings. The authors' general conclusion however is that there is 'a gradual process whereby adolescents' developing cognitive abilities permit greater self-awareness ... adolescence appears more to be a stage of development, in the true sense, than of disruption'.

*The transition to work*

For school leavers one of the main areas of identity achievement has traditionally been through the normal transition from school to work. But in the wake of widespread economic recession in many developed countries the majority of early school leavers experience unemployment at some stage in the 16- to 19-year age period. A number of studies now point to the personal consequences of youth unemployment in terms of psychological distress, anxiety, unhappiness, dissatisfaction, stigma and lowered self-esteem (for a review see Banks and Ullah, 1986). One study attempted to apply Erikson's developmental model to the experience of employment or unemployment (Gurney, 1980). Students were interviewed just before, and four months after, leaving school. Obtaining a job was a significant factor in perception of identity for females only. This research did not find unemployment to have traumatic effects, perhaps because of the short period of unemployment. However, later research does suggest that for most young people continued unemployment is a particularly distressing experience.

**Sex-role Identity**

We examined the development of gender identity in children in chapter 5, where we saw that this referred primarily to the awareness of oneself as a boy or girl. Many writers use the term 'sex-role identity' to refer to the acquisition of a set of standards for appropriate masculine or feminine behaviour, in a particular culture. This develops through middle childhood, but many aspects are likely to become much more significant at adolescence.

According to Douvan (1979), the development of sex-role identity is most difficult for adolescent females in modern urban societies. This is because schools encourage girls (like boys) to be independent, competitive and achieving, but on leaving school these traits are not valued for girls as they are for boys. Young women are conventionally expected to be non-assertive, and give up any financial independence by assuming a domestic and motherly role on marriage. This conclusion is largely based on an extensive interview study carried out in the 1950s (Douvan and Adelson, 1966). This study has been criticized, however, for bias in the way the interviews were conducted (Hopkins, 1983). For example, boys were asked more questions about jobs, and girls were asked more questions about marriage. Furthermore, social attitudes have undoubtedly changed over the past 30 years, and greater assertiveness, independence and job-orientation in younger women is now relatively more accepted.

It could be argued that young men have less choice of different routes to establish sex-role identity (Conger, 1977). Female roles may at present be more changeable and varied (i.e. a young women can readily choose to be either career-orientated, or a mother). Also, research has generally found that cross-sex interests or behaviour (e.g. boys doing needlework; girls doing metalwork) are more tolerated in girls than boys. Overall, it is difficult to draw conclusions about whether boys or girls find sex-role identity a more difficult process.

Many young men and women develop attitudes and behaviours conforming to conventional stereotypes of masculine and feminine behaviour. For example, the majority of caring for young children is still done by women; the majority of car repair tasks are done by men. Using questionnaires it is easy to obtain measures of sex-role orientation in terms of tasks such as these. In the USA especially there has been interest over the past decade in the concept of 'androgyny' — an androgynous person is someone, male or female, who scores fairly equally on both masculine and feminine items of sex-role orientation. For example, an androgynous person might enjoy both baby-minding and car-repairing. Some researchers have argued that androgyny is more psychologically healthy, and leads to higher levels of self-esteem (Bem, 1975; Spence and Helmreich, 1978). In part such arguments and findings may reflect a current questioning of conventional sex-roles, and the restrictions of choice and inequality of opportunity which they are thought by some to embody.

Sex-role conventions, besides changing with time, also vary between different societies (see also chapter 5). Margaret Mead documented many instances of such cultural variations. For example, from studies of three tribes living close to each other in New Guinea (Mead, 1935), she reported that amongst the Arapesh, both men and women were sensitive and non-aggressive and had 'feminine' personalities; amongst the Mundugamor, both men and women were ruthless, unpleasant and 'masculine'; amongst the Tchambuli, women were dominant and men more emotional and concerned about personal appearance, an apparent reversal of our own conventions. The pattern seems almost too neat to be believed, and indeed Mead has been criticized for being selective in her presentation of results (Harris,

1968; Blurton Jones and Konner, 1973). For example, in all three tribes men seem to have shown the most violent behaviour, and in all three societies men did the hunting. In her later writing Mead did recognize a possibly greater importance of biological factors in sex roles (Mead, 1949). However, her demonstration of cultural differences, while perhaps exaggerated, is in many respects a valid indication of how society can powerfully influence sex-role development, which has been borne out by many other studies (Archer and Lloyd, 1986).

### Sexual Knowledge, Attitudes and Behaviour

Adolescence is a time when knowledge of the processes of reproduction and of sexual intercourse assumes great importance. We have seen earlier how an understanding of menarche, for example, can ease the pubertal transition in adolescent girls. But how much do adolescents know about these matters? A large-scale study of children's sexual thinking has been carried out, in four different countries, by Goldman and Goldman (1982), and their results show that knowledge of sexual matters does increase greatly in early adolescence, but that surprising areas of ignorance remain.

The Goldmans interviewed children aged 5–15 in schools in Australia, England, North America (Canadian/US border area) and Sweden. About 30–40 children were interviewed in each country, at each age. Amongst many other items, the children were asked to explain the meaning of certain words such as 'pregnancy' and 'puberty'. Some of the results, for the three older age bands, are shown in table 8.4. This shows the percentage of participants who gave 'fully appropriate' answers (for example for 'puberty', some mention that having children became possible).

TABLE 8.4   *Children's understanding of sexual terms: percentages of 'fully appropriate' responses at 11, 13 and 15 years of age in four different countries.*

|  | Age | Australia | England | N. America | Sweden |
|---|---|---|---|---|---|
| Rape | 11 | 25 | 38 | 10 | 47 |
|  | 13 | 73 | 65 | 64 | 87 |
|  | 15 | 100 | 87 | 87 | 86 |
| Virgin | 11 | 8 | 15 | 0 | 13 |
|  | 13 | 48 | 38 | 39 | 70 |
|  | 15 | 83 | 63 | 61 | 93 |
| Pregnancy | 11 | 20 | 18 | 13 | 50 |
|  | 13 | 27 | 45 | 30 | 77 |
|  | 15 | 38 | 50 | 52 | 87 |
| Venereal disease | 11 | 0 | 0 | 0 | 0 |
|  | 13 | 3 | 0 | 0 | 3 |
|  | 15 | 20 | 10 | 20 | 20 |
| Puberty | 11 | 0 | 0 | 0 | 17 |
|  | 13 | 3 | 3 | 9 | 20 |
|  | 15 | 5 | 3 | 3 | 43 |

*Source*: Goldman and Goldman, 1982

It can be seen that early adolescence sees a rapid increase in understanding of terms such as 'rape' and 'virgin'. Some terms remain poorly understood at 15, however, notably 'venereal disease' and 'puberty' itself. This is taken by the Goldmans to point to the importance of increased sex education in schools. They consider this argument strengthened by the greater understanding shown by the Swedish children (e.g. for 'pregnancy', and 'puberty'). Sweden does have compulsory courses in sex education and personal relationships for 7–16-year-olds; in the other countries studied sex education is largely confined to late in the secondary school. In all countries most children said they would have liked more sex education in school, and at an earlier age. The home remained the most cited source of information on sexual matters.

An interesting feature of the Goldmans' study is that they had difficulty gaining access to many North American schools, simply because they wanted to ask questions with a sexual content. For many people sex is still a 'taboo' area. However, the Goldmans might have encountered even more difficulties if they had been doing their research 50 years ago. Attitudes to sexual matters generally seem to have been much more restrictive then, and to have changed markedly through the 1960s and 1970s.

This shift in attitudes can be gauged from such sources as parents' manuals on how children should be brought up and educated; teachings of the churches on sexual matters; articles in the mass media; and direct attitudinal surveys by social scientists. As an example from parents' manuals, consider the following extract on masturbation from *What a Boy Should Know*, published in 1909:

> The results on the mind are the more severe and more easily recognised ... A boy who practises this habit can never be the best that Nature intended him to be. His wits are not so sharp. His memory is not so good. His power of fixing his attention on whatever he is doing is lessened ... The effect of self-abuse on a boy's character always tends to weaken it, and in fact, to make him untrustworthy, unreliable, untruthful, and probably even dishonest.

These stern warnings have scarcely lessened in the *Mothercraft Manual* of 1928 (Liddiard, 1928):

> This is a bad habit ... The habit, if left unchecked, may develop into a serious vice. The child's moral nature becomes perverted; one such child has been known to upset a whole school.

Current medical opinion, however, is that masturbation is normally harmless, and we also know that it is the usual way in which young males first reach orgasm following puberty. Masturbation has become much more socially acceptable, especially in adolescents. Dr Spock's 1976 manual stated that:

> Some conscientious adolescents feel excessively guilty and worried about masturbation ... If a child seems to be generally happy and successful, doing well in school, getting along with his friends, he can be told that all normal young people have these desires and that a great majority do masturbate. This won't take away all his feeling of guilt, but it will help. (p. 413)

Attitudes to premarital sexual intercourse have also changed. Over the 1960s and 1970s surveys have shown that older generations have less permissive attitudes on such matters than younger people. This is not just a matter of age – it is not the case that everyone gets less permissive as they get older. Rather, it seems to reflect a genuine historical trend which has been working its way through the population as people socialized in earlier decades get older and eventually die. For example, in a general survey in the USA in the 1969, only 21 per cent of Americans judged premarital sex to be 'not wrong'; yet by 1979, this had risen to 55 per cent (Reinhold, 1979). Similar changes have occurred in the UK and other Western socities.

How have these general changes in attitudes affected the sexual behaviour of adolescents? What we know of sexual behaviour in young people, and adults also, comes from questionnaire and interview studies. The first modern large-scale survey was by Kinsey and his co-workers in the USA (Kinsey et all., 1948, 1953). There have been a number of other studies in the USA, and two notable studies in the UK, by Schofield (1965) and Farrell (1978). Most of this work was done in the late 1960s and early 1970s; the interest shown by social scientists in sexual attitudes and behaviour at this time probably reflects the considerable change attitudes and behaviour were undergoing. There was less interest up to the mid-1980s but this is changing again as the spread of AIDS has its impact on sexual attitudes and behaviour.

Obviously there are problems with interview studies in which adolescents are asked questions about their attitudes to sexual behaviour, whether they have had sexual intercourse, if so how many partners they have had, and so forth. These are usually considered very personal matters only to be revealed to a close confidant, if at all. Problems of truthful responding, which will always qualify interview studies, are likely to be particularly strong for sexual matters. There may also be problems in understanding terms (see table 8.4), as illustrated by the question and answer 'Are you a virgin?' 'Not yet' obtained in one study! The interviewer must obviously try to obtain rapport with the person being interviewed, stress the confidentiality with which the answers will be treated, make sure questions are properly understood, and make clear the reasons for carrying out the survey. Some assurance that replies are reasonably truthful can be obtained when systematic trends are found in the results, for example an increase in sexual experience with age (see figure 8.7). Finally, if results are to be generalized, a representative or random sample must be obtained, and not too many participants should refuse to answer or drop out of the survey.

In the UK, the Schofield report of 1965 was based on a sample of 2,000 unmarried adolescents aged 15–19. The sample was a random one across different parts of the country. Interviews took about an hour. The main qualification to the results of this thorough survey is that about 15 per cent of teenagers approached refused to take part. The interviews showed that young people went through successive stages of sexual experience. Dating was usually the first form of independent contact with a member of the opposite sex, often leading to kissing. This was usually lip kissing; deep kissing or 'French kissing' (where one partner's tongue enters the mouth of the other) was less common at this stage, and was usually preceded by breast stimulation over clothes. Further forms of petting included breast stimulation under clothes, and direct touching or stimulation of the partner's genitals. These heavier forms of 'petting' usually preceded full sexual intercourse, which only a minority of

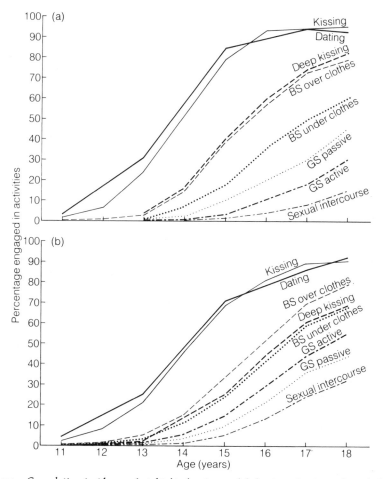

FIGURE 8.7  *Cumulative incidence of eight kinds of sexual behaviour for (a) girls and (b) boys.*
*BS = breast stimulation  GS = genital stimulation (from Schofield, 1965)*

the sample reported having had. The age trends in these various forms of sexual behaviour are shown in figure 8.7.

A similar survey in the UK was reported by Farrell in 1978. This showed clearly that the increased permissiveness in sexual attitudes had been reflected by an increased incidence of sexual behaviour in young people. Table 8.5 shows how the proportion of teenagers reporting having had sexual intercourse at 17 and 19 years of age approximately doubled in males and tripled in females over the period between the two studies. A similar change between the mid-1960s and mid-1970s has been found in American studies, as figure 8.8 shows. In another study, in Sweden, people were asked to recall when they had first had intercourse. In 1967 people in their 50s recalled an average age of 18.6 years; this fell to an average of 17.0 years in people in their early 20s. A study ten years later found that this had fallen further, to 16.0 years.

TABLE 8.5    *Percentage of participants reporting having had sexual intercourse in two UK studies of adolescents*

|  | At 17 yr | | At 19 yr | |
| --- | --- | --- | --- | --- |
|  | *Males* | *Females* | *Males* | *Females* |
| Schofield (1965) | 25 | 11 | 37 | 23 |
| Farrell (1978) | 50 | 39 | 74 | 67 |

What do we know of the factors influencing whether a young person engages in sexual behaviour and sexual intercourse? In the Schofield report there was little effect of social class, religious background or family background. However, lack of discipline or restraint from parents was associated with early sexual experience, especially in girls. Early physical development, conformity to teenage rather than adult norms, and a lively gregariousness were also associated with early sexual experience. Studies in the USA have confirmed the influences of the peer group and of physical attractiveness on sexual behaviour. They also suggest that sexually inexperienced adolescents are more likely to describe themselves as religious. Social class effects seem to be complicated and to vary with historical epoch. The Kinsey report of the late 1940s indicated greater sexual experience in lower social class groups, but this was not found in the 1960s. Some recent studies suggest greater sexual experience in students from higher social class groups (Hopkins, 1983; Griffitt and Hatfield, 1985).

Another influence is the nature of the relationship with one's partner. Most people, including adolescents, regard intercourse as more acceptable if there is affection for and emotional commitment to one's partner – if it is a 'steady'

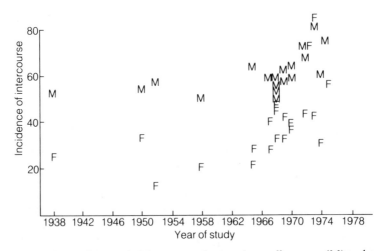

FIGURE 8.8    *Incidence of premarital intercourse in American college men (M) and women (F) from 1938 to 1975 (from Hopkins, 1983)*

TABLE 8.6   *Four standards concerning premarital sexual intercourse, according to Reiss (1967)*

| | |
|---|---|
| Single standard: | no sexual intercourse before marriage |
| Double standard: | no sexual intercourse before marriage, for women; permitted for men |
| Permissiveness with affection: | premarital sexual intercourse allowed if partners have some emotional commitment to each other |
| Permissiveness without affection: | premarital sexual intercourse allowed or encouraged even without emotional commitment |

relationship. Reiss (1967) identified four standards of sexual behaviour in the USA, shown in table 8.6. Some form of the 'single standard' or 'double standard' seems to have been most common up to the 1950s, but the 'permissiveness with affection' standard seems most common now. The figures in table 8.7 show how 'permissiveness with affection' has been endorsed by a majority of American college students since the late 1960s, while 'permissiveness without affection', although more tolerated recently, remains less approved of. The double standard of attitudes to premarital intercourse in males and females is not so strong in recent surveys, as can be seen by comparing the attitudes to males and females in table 8.7. As figure 8.8 and table 8.5 show, not only has sexual experience increased in adolescents, but this increase has been more marked in females; as a result, the difference between males and females in sexual experience has markedly decreased.

No doubt many factors contributed to the changes in attitudes and behaviour in the 1960s and 1970s. Probably increased affluence and also a greater availability of effective contraceptives played a part. Sexual attitudes and behaviour will continue to change. The possibility of contracting venereal disease has always been a deterrent to more permissive or promiscuous sexual behaviour, and the outbreak of new strains of sexually transmitted diseases, such as the herpes virus, and the spread of AIDS in the 1980s, may (unless effective antidotes are found) lead to futher changes in the next decade. Considerable publicity is being given to the risks of

TABLE 8.7   *Percentage approval of premarital sexual intercourse by college students in the USA for different levels of affection between partners*

| | Early 1960s | Later 1960s | Early/mid-1970s |
|---|---|---|---|
| If no strong affection for partner | | | |
| approved for males | 21 | 51 | 50 |
| approved for females | 11 | 28 | 38 |
| If strong affection for partner | | | |
| approved for males | 37 | 65 | 73 |
| approved for females | 27 | 50 | 70 |
| If engaged to partner | | | |
| approved for males | 52 | 76 | 85 |
| approved for females | 44 | 70 | 75 |

AIDS and the ways in which it is transmitted. It is thought likely that the possibility of contracting AIDS will lead many people to restrict the number of partners with whom they have sexual intercourse.


## Relations with Parents and Peers

As adolescents become independent from their parents, they may spend more time with peers and turn to peers more for social support and identity. One view of adolescent social development is that there is a transition from 'parent orientation' to 'peer orientation' during this period. This view was especially prevalent in the 1960s and early 1970s. We saw in chapter 4 how researchers such as J. S. Coleman in the USA and David Hargreaves in the UK documented the importance of peer groups or cliques in secondary schools, and how the values of such peer groups might diverge greatly from those of teachers and parents. Also, some evidence suggests that conformity with peers, especially in antisocial situations, does increase up to early adolescence before declining again. Anxieties about friendships with peers also peak at about this age, according to a study by J. C. Coleman (1980). Coleman asked adolescents to complete unfinished sentences about friendships in a small group, and analysed the results for their emotional content. Themes of anxiety and fear of rejection by friends increased from 11 to 13 and then to 15 years, but declined by 17 years (the effect being stronger for girls than boys).

A number of studies during this period attempted to compare the relative importance of parents and peers to the adolescent by placing them in opposition. For example, the adolescent might be asked to agree or disagree with statements such as 'I prefer to wear the kind and style of clothing that my parents suggest, regardless of what type of clothing my friends and schoolmates think are best'. Based on a 20-item scale of this kind, an American study by Floyd and South (1972) found a shift from 'parent orientation' to 'peer orientation', shown in figure 8.9, with a crossover at around 15 years of age. In another kind of assessment, called the 'cross-pressures test', adolescents are presented with hypothetical situations or dilemmas in which one course of action is favoured by parents and another by peers (Brittain, 1963).

Research using these methods has tended to support the view that adolescents become more peer-orientated and less parent-orientated as they get older, though with the qualification that the content area or situation is of great importance. For instance, parents have been found to remain more influential than peers in areas such as educational plans and future life goals. However, peers are more influential in everyday and peer-status-linked issues such as choice of clothes and use of leisure time. Studies in the USA also find that peers can have considerable influence on the use of drugs; college students with a high 'peer orientation' are much more likely to use marijuana than those with a high 'parent orientation', for example (Stone et al., 1979; Hopkins, 1983).

In fact, the nature of an adolescent's social relationships with his or her parents may be substantially different from that with peers. Through childhood the parental relationship is often characterized as one of 'unilateral authority', in which parents strive to impart an already constructed set of knowledge and attitudes to their

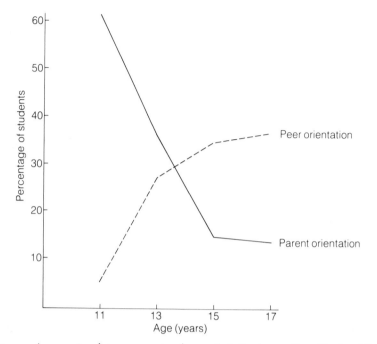

FIGURE 8.9   *A comparison between parent and peer orientation by age (from Floyd and South, 1972)*

children. Friendship, however, is a form of mutually reciprocal relationship in which divergent opinions may be expressed and new ideas discussed. We have come across these conceptions previously, in discussing the development of friendship (chapter 4) and Piaget's views of the development of moral reasoning (chapter 7). While parent–child relations may become more mutual during adolescence, it is thought that they do not become as truly mutual or reciprocal as peer relationships (Youniss, 1980).

In one American study of 180 adolescents aged 12–20 years, subjects were asked to check on a questionnaire how father, mother or friend might react when a disagreement arose, or when they were being consulted about an important decision (Hunter, 1984). Responses such as 'he points out where I'm wrong for my own good', or 'he tells me that I would realize his ideas are right when I get more experience', were considered representative of unilateral influence, while responses such as 'he tries to figure out with me whether or not I'm right', or 'he tells me he wonders about the same thing' were considered representative of mutual influence. It was confirmed that parents were seen as more unilateral, and friends as more mutual, in their influence. This difference was greater for females than for males. There was not much effect of age, although parents were at their most unilateral with the 14–15 year age group.

Hunter's study tells us how young people perceive their parents and peers, which is not necessarily the same as how parents perceive events, or what an outside observer might record as happening if they could watch family interactions. Another study which tried to examine more directly the influence of parents and peers, and also came up with distinct differences, is detailed in box 8.2. If parents and peers do have distinctively different styles of social influence, it may be rather meaningless directly to oppose them in strength, as some of the earlier research we looked at attempted to do.

Obviously the influence that parents retain over adolescents may vary appreciably with the kind of parenting style adopted. We saw in chapter 7 how, with young children, different styles of parenting had different outcomes for moral development and altruism. An influential study by Elder (1963), in the USA, identified three styles of parental authority. 'Permissive' parents allowed adolescents virtually unlimited freedom; 'autocratic' parents told adolescents what to do and tended to use physical punishment as a means of discipline; 'democratic' parents discussed matters with adolescents and encouraged them to participate in decision-making. A democratic style of authority, and any attempts to explain decisions to adolescents, fostered not only good relationships with parents, but greater independence and confidence in self-direction, and a likelihood of choosing friends approved of by parents. Rebellious adolescents were more likely to come either from highly permissive, or highly autocratic, family backgrounds.

These findings, once again, suggest that opposing parental and peer values may be too simple. After all, parents and peers may share very many common values. Rather than giving tests which force adolescents into choosing one or the other, it can be more informative to assess the values or attitudes of parents or peers directly, and see how convergent or divergent they are. Orloff and Weinstock (1975) conducted a study in which both adolescents and their parents were asked to fill in a 36-item 'Contemporary Topics Questionnaire' which assessed attitudes to areas such as drug use, sexual behaviour, choice of clothing, racism and war. It was found that parents and adolescents agreed on about 80 per cent of these items; thus, while there may be differences in attitude, they should not be exagggerated.

It seems the idea of the 'generation gap', so popular in the 1960s, is an example of a concept that contains some truth, but which has been greatly exaggerated. This is borne out by what we know of the incidence of direct conflicts between parents and adolescents. For most adolescents, at least, these seem to be mainly about minor matters. A study by Douvan and Adelson (1966) in the USA, in which 3,000 teenagers were interviewed, found that most conflicts were about such matters as use of make-up, dating, playing music and choice of leisure activities; there was usually agreement on more major issues, such as political or religious beliefs (the more recent study in box 8.2 confirms this). The picture seems to be similar in the UK. A book called *Britain's Sixteen-Year-Olds* (Fogelman, 1976) gives the results of questionnaires administered to more than 11,000 teenagers and their parents as part of a continuing longitudinal study organized by the National Children's Bureau. The majority of parents, and their 16-year-old children, reported the relationship between them as being satisfactory. Eighty-six per cent of the teenagers reported that they 'got on well with' their mother, and 80 per cent that they 'got on well with' with their father. Only a minority of parents had conflicts with their children. These were highest in areas such as dress or hairstyle, and time of coming in at night, but even so only about 10 per cent of the sample reported that they often disagreed about these matters.

Such results cast doubts on the straightforward identification of adolescence as a time of storm and stress, characterized by a generation gap between parents and children. Another major British study has made a further contribution to putting this hypothesis into a more realistic perspective. This is the 'Isle of Wight' study carried out by Michael Rutter and his colleagues, which we should consider in detail.

## Conflict and Turmoil – the 'Isle of Wight' Study

This research study attempted to avoid the problems of selective sampling which are the pitfall of small-scale studies. The Isle of Wight, in the English Channel off the coast of Hampshire, provided a bounded area of population living in small towns and villages. Behavioural questionnaires were completed by parents and teachers for all the 14- to 15-year-olds on the island, numbering 2,303. The most detailed results, however, were obtained from two subsamples. One, of 200 teenagers, was a random sample of the total population; the other, of 304 teenagers, was of those with extreme scores from the parent and teacher questionnaires which pointed to 'deviant' behaviour. The adolescents in both these subgroups were given further questionnairses and tests, and were interviewed individually by psychiatrists. Their parents and teachers were also interviewed. Two main areas are explored in the report (Rutter et al., 1976): one is the extent of conflict between adolescents and their parents (the 'generation gap'); the other, the extent of inner turmoil and of observed behavioural or psychiatric disorder ('storm and stress'). A selection of the results are shown in tables 8.8 and 8.9, based on the random sample of 200.

Regarding the extent of conflicts, only about one parent in six reported any altercations or arguments with their children about when and where they went out, or about their choice of activities (table 8.8). About one parent in three however said they disapproved of their youngster's clothing or hair styles. The great majority of

TABLE 8.8 *Percentages of parents and 14-year-old children in the Isle of Wight study reporting conflicts and feelings of inner turmoil*

|  | Boys | Girls |
|---|---|---|
| Parental interview |  |  |
| any altercation with parents | 18 | 19 |
| physical withdrawal | 12 | 7 |
| communication difficulties | 24 | 9 |
| Adolescent interview |  |  |
| any altercation with parents | 42 | 30 |
| any criticism of mother | 27 | 37 |
| any criticism of father | 32 | 31 |
| any rejection of mother | 3 | 2 |
| any rejection of father | 5 | 9 |
| Often feel miserable or depressed (questionnaire) | 21 | 23 |
| Reported misery (psychiatric interview) | 42 | 48 |
| Observed sadness (psychiatric interview) | 12 | 15 |

*Source*: Rutter et al., 1976: based on the random sample of 200

parents approved of their children's friends, and nearly all had discussed with them their plans after leaving school. Rather more of the teenagers themselves reported having altercations with parents. However, only about one-third made any criticism of their mother or father during the interview; and only a small percentage expressed outright rejection of either parent.

By and large these results, like those we have already discussed in this chapter, confirm that the average adolescent is not in a state of crisis and conflict with parents. Nevertheless, this is true of a minority (for example 9 per cent of girls expressed outright rejection of their father, table 8.8). These difficulties are much greater in the children with some behavioural or psychiatric disorder (the second subgroup). Altercations with parents, physical withdrawal of children from the rest of the family, and communication difficulties or problems parents had in 'getting through' to adolescents, were all some three times more common in this sample.

What about experiences of inner turmoil, sadness and misery? Only about one-fifth of the adolescents reported on the questionnaire that they often felt miserable or depressed; from the psychiatric interview, nearly a half were diagnosed as reporting miserable feelings, though a much smaller proportion actually looked sad in the interview (table 8.8). It would seem that severe clinical depression is rare, but that some degree of inner turmoil may well characterize many adolescents.

In making judgements about adolescence as a stage, it is obviously necessary to compare with other groups and stages of development. In the Isle of Wight study such comparisons were made for the prevalence of psychiatric disorder, as based on parental interview. Table 8.9 shows the rates of disorder for the teenagers at 14–15 years, for the same children at the age of 10, from a previous survey of psychiatric disorder, and for adults (the parents of the teenage sample). There is a rather modest peak in adolescence (though the adolescent interview data gave a slightly higher figure for disorder of 16.3 per cent at this age). Again, this suggests that adolescent turmoil is not a complete myth, but that it should not be over-exaggerated. As Rutter et al. (1976) conclude, 'adolescent turmoil is a fact, not a fiction, but its psychiatric importance has probably been over-estimated in the past'.

TABLE 8.9   *Percentages of those interviewed in the Isle of Wight study having any psychiatric disorder, at different ages*

|         | 10 yr | 14–15 yr | Adult (parent) |
|---------|-------|----------|----------------|
| Males   | 12.7  | 13.2     | 7.6            |
| Females | 10.9  | 12.5     | 11.9           |

*Source*: Rutter et al., 1976

## Adolescence in Another Culture: Margaret Mead and Samoa

So far we have looked mainly at adolescents in modern Western society – the UK and the USA especially. We have seen that the view of adolescence as a difficult period does have some validity, even if it has probably been exaggerated by some writers (perhaps especially by psychoanalytic or clinical authors, such as Blos or Erikson, who would have come into most contact with the minority of adolescents who are particularly disturbed). The question arises however as to whether such difficulties are an inevitable part of puberty, sexual maturity and gaining independence from parents, or are merely a product of our particular kind of society, and the way we treat adolescents. Different cultures vary widely in the treatment of adolescents, as we have noted earlier in connection with puberty rites (p. 221).

One study in particular has often been quoted to support the view that adolescence can be a tranquil and conflict-free period. This is Margaret Mead's book *Coming of Age in Samoa* (1928). In this report Mead described adolescence as 'the age of maximum ease', with 'an absence of psychological maladjustment'. Indeed, Samoan society as a whole was described as 'replete with easy solutions for all conflicts'. This picture of an island paradise was supported by drawing attention to two important differnces between Samoan and American society. The first related to the context of child-rearing. Compared to what, at its extreme at least, can be the oppressive and confining atmosphere of the Western nuclear family, the Samoans had a more open and extended family-rearing system, in which 'the child is given no sense of belonging to a small intimate biological family'. As a result, an adolescent who might be in disagreement with parents could easily go and stay with another relative. Human relationships were thus warm, but diffuse.

The second point related to methods of child-rearing. There was little physical punishment of children by parents, and little repression or sense of guilt. Therefore, there was little for teenagers to rebel against. According to Mead, Samoan society 'never exerts sufficient repression to call forth a significant rebellion from the individual'. There was 'no room for guilt'. In particular, there was no guilt about sexual behaviour and experimentation before marriage. According to Mead, adolescents had 'the sunniest and easiest attitudes towards sex', and promiscuity and free love were the norm in the adolescent period.

Samoan society would thus seem to be about as different from the 'storm and stress' model of adolescence as one could imagine. Mead's work, and that of other anthropologists such as Ruth Benedict, suggested that the adolescent experience was entirely a matter of social structure and cultural pressures. The biological impact of puberty was of little consequence. As Franz Boas, the eminent anthropologist who supervised Mead's work in Samoa, put it: 'much of what we ascribe to human nature is no more than a reaction to the restraints put upon us by our civilisation'.

Mead's work was influential for a long time, but not all writers on Samoa agreed with her interpretations. These disagreements were brought to a head by Australian anthropologist Derek Freeman in his book *Margaret Mead and Samoa: the Making and Unmaking of an Anthropological Myth* (1983). He attempted to refute Mead's work, arguing that her methodology was poor and that she had simply found what she was looking for. The study was Mead's first (in a long and distinguished career) and at the age of 23 (as Mead said) she did not 'really know much about fieldwork'. Although Mead reported that she had spent nine months in Samoa, 'speaking the language and living in the conditions in which they lived', she only spent six weeks learning Samoan, and only three months on her study of adolescence. She did not live in the native way, but stayed with the only white family on Ta'u, the island where her interviews were carried out. Thus, it is not clear how much trust or rapport she had with the adolescents whom she interviewed (often about very personal matters such as sexual experience). Mead interviewed 50 girls and young women, but only half of these (aged 14–20) were past puberty. In fact only 11 of these reported having heterosexual experience. Thus, Freeman suggested that Mead was selective in the way she interpreted her results, and was also perhaps misled by some female adolescents who, taking advantage of her naivety and poor understanding of the language, fooled her about the extent of their sexual adventures.

We cannot now know how well Mead's inteviews were carried out, but Freeman's other argument is that both earlier and later studies of Samoa give a different overall picture. Certainly, recent studies (and reports by older Samoans of their society in the 1920s) suggest that family bonds are strong, that physical punishment is used, that brides are expected to be virgins (in one survey Freeman found that about three-quarters are), and that strong emotions including sexual jealously and competitiveness are common.

Not all researchers agree with all Freeman's conclusions. He bases many of his contentions on his own work in Samoa in the 1940s and the 1960s; yet, due to the influence of Christian missionaries and American military bases, Samoan society may have changed greatly even since the 1920s. His criticisms are probably sufficient to bring a verdict of 'not proven' against Mead's Samoan evidence. The picture of an adolescent paradise may have been more a wish-fulfilment dream, than a reality.


## Overview

Adolescence is not the only period of transition in our lives, but it is one in which several transitions occur in a relatively short period. The biological impact of puberty is common to all adolescents. Also, in most societies adolescents are becoming independent of parents, and in Western societies especially are faced with choices about career and about political and religious beliefs.

We have seen that these changes can lead to some stresses which are probably particularly high in adolescence; for example, anxieties about friendships, or feeling miserable or even clinically depressed, Severe difficulties, however, only seem to characterize a minority of adolescents. An important point here is that the various changes (such as puberty, choice of career, leaving home) are not exactly synchronous; over the six-year period from say 14 to 20, different issues may be focused on and coped with at different times. J. C. Coleman (1980) has termed this a 'focal theory' of adolescence. This acknowledges the real adjustments that adolescents do have to make, while at the same time being more consistent with the notions of gradual change and adjustment that the opponents of the 'storm and stress' view have suggested are more characteristic of adolescent development, as indeed of development throughout the life-span.

Finally, we should remember the importance of historical factors in considering the position of the adolescent. We have seen how the age of puberty has declined in Western societies from the 1840s up to the 1960s. Also, sexual attitudes and behaviour have changed, especially in the 1960s and 1970s. These changes can be expected to impact on the parent–adolescent relationship. For example, in the 1960s the gap between parent and adolescent values (e.g. about sexual permissiveness) might well have been wider than in the 1980s and 1990s (when the 1960s adolescents themselves became parents of adolescents). Thus, a supposed characteristic of adolescence (the 'generation gap') might actually be due mainly to a particular historical change in attitudes. While consideration of such historical factors is important in all of psychology, it is perhaps especially so in adolescence, as one generation is 'handing on' its knowledge, attitudes and experience to the next.

## Further reading

J. M. Tanner 1973: Growing up. *Scientific American*, gives a succinct overview of the physical aspects of adolescence. More detail is available in Tanner's books (e.g. *Fetus into Man* (1978), Cambridge, Mass: Harvard University Press; *A History of the Study of Human Growth* (1981), Cambridge: Cambridge University Press) and in H. Katchadourian 1977: *The Biology of Adolescence*. San Francisco, Freeman.

An excellent general overview is J. C. Coleman and L. Hendry 1990: *The Nature of Adolescence*, 2nd edn. London: Routledge. J. R. Hopkins 1983: *Adolescence: The Transitional Years*. New York and London: Academic Press, is a thorough and readable American textbook. A comprehensive sourcebook for reference purposes is J. Adelson (ed.) 1980: *Handbook of Adolescent Psychology*. New York: Wiley.

## Discussion points

1    Does the biological phenomenon of puberty have any direct psychological effects?

2    Is there an 'identity crisis' at adolescence?

3    How have attitudes to sexual behaviour changed over the past 50 years? Why might this have happened?

4    Are adolescents switching from a 'parent orientation' to a 'peer orientation?'

5    Is adolescence inevitably a period of 'storm and stress'?

## Practical exercises

1    Give the 'Twenty Statements Test' to children and young people of different ages that you know, or from a secondary school. Sort the responses into different categories and compare the results with those of Montemayor and Eisen (1977).

2    Attempt to document the change in attitudes to sexual behaviour over the past few decades. For example (a) compare statements on similar topics, in books or parenting manuals from different decades of this century which may be available in libraries; or (b) give a simple attitude questionnaire, for example on attitudes to premarital sexual intercourse, to persons of different ages (e.g. from 20 to 70).

3    Ask teenagers of different ages (say, 14–18) how much time they spend per day with mother, father, peers or alone, in different types of activity. Compare with the study described in box 8.2.

---

# Box 8.1

---

# A longitudinal study of changes in ego identity status from the freshman to the senior year at college

This study focused on the pattern of change in identity status through the college years and the stability of the various identity categories during this period. The study was carried out in the framework of Marcia's (1966) categorization of identity status. The authors used an identity status interview covering the areas of ideology and occupation. Interviews were carried out at a polytechnic institute, in spring 1969 (during the first or 'freshman' year) and in spring 1972 (during the third or 'senior' year). Scorable data were obtained for 47 students for occupational status, and for 45 for ideological status. The ages of participants were not reported, but were presumably 17/18 to 20/21 years.

The number of students assigned to each of the four identity statuses, for the two topic areas and at the two times of interview, is shown in box table 8.1.1. The results are fairly similar for the two topic areas. Few students had reached identity achievement in their freshman year, but this had increased significantly by the senior year. This increase was significant both in occupational area ($\chi^2 = 9.00$, p < 0.01) and for ideological area ($\chi^2 = 15.00$, p < 0.001).

BOX TABLE 8.1.1   *Identity status of college students in occupational and ideological areas*

| Identity status | Number in each identity status | | | | Stability[a] | |
|---|---|---|---|---|---|---|
| | Occupational | | Ideological | | | |
| | F | S | F | S | Occupational | Ideological |
| Achievement | 7 | 19 | 5 | 20 | 71.4 | 100.0 |
| Moratorium | 8 | 0 | 4 | 1 | 0.0 | 0.0 |
| Foreclosure | 17 | 14 | 19 | 7 | 70.6 | 31.6 |
| Diffusion | 15 | 14 | 17 | 17 | 46.7 | 70.6 |

[a] Percentage stability over a 3-year period.
F = Freshman; S = Senior.

Based on material in A. S. Waterman, P. S. Geary and C. K. Waterman 1974: *Developmental Psychology*, 10, 387–92.

In the occupational area there was a significant decrease in the number of students in moratorium status ($\chi^2 = 8.00$, $p < 0.01$). Presumably, some students in crisis about their future occupational role had decided what to do towards the end of their course. In the ideolgical area, the significant decrease was in the number of students in foreclosure status ($\chi^2 = 10.28$, $p < 0.01$). Presumably, some students who had uncritically accepted ideological positions, perhaps from parents, at the time of entering college, had rethought their position during the college years; they either changed their beliefs, or reaffirmed their original beliefs but on a fully considered basis. It would be expected that these students would have passed through a crisis, or period of moratorium identity; but the study does not prove this. It is usually supposed that the moratorium status is relatively short-lived, so more frequent interviews would have been necessary to detect the passage through this status.

The results confirm that, over the three-year period, the moratorium status is the least stable of the four identity statuses. The percentage of students who changed out of each status is also shown in box table 8.1.1. Identity achievement is the most stable, and moratorium status the least stable, in both content areas.

The trend toward identity achievement, and its stability once achieved, conform with the expectations from Erikson's theory. However, it is surprising that a relatively high proportion of students were still in the identity diffusion status shortly before graduating.

The study is limited by the number of participants and by a lack of further insight into why certain changes did or did not occur. The authors themselves admit that their sample was too small to allow any measures of personality or family background to be related to changes in identity status in a meaningful way. Also, findings are limited to the kind of college studied (this institute had a strong vocational orientation), and of course the historical period investigated (in this case, one of intense political and ideological debate).

Sample limitations are often a problem in longitudinal studies, and this study is no exception. The initial sample consisted of 92 male undergraduates who entered the institute in 1968. However, 22 of these had dropped out by the senior year. Of the 70 remaining, seven declined to participate, one failed to keep an appointment and nine could not be contacted. In addition, some eight participants provided partially unscorable data from the interview (i.e. data that could not be reliably coded).

These participant losses mean we must exercise care in generalizing the results obtained from the remaining participants, who are those who stayed at college, were willing to participate and provided scorable interview data. How different are these participants from the others? Interestingly, in this study we do have some informtion on this, as all 92 students had been interviewed in the freshman year. Comparing those who had left the polytechnic with those still in the follow-up study, it was found that those who had left were more likely to have been in moratorium status in the freshman year ($\chi^2 = 5.15$, $p < 0.05$) and less likely to be in foreclosure ($\chi^2 = 5.27$, $p < 0.05$), so far as occupational area was concerned. In other words, those who had left had been uncertain about their vocation on entry. There were no differences of identity status in the area of ideology.

There have been only one or two other longitudinal studies looking at identity change through the college years and their results are quite similar (Waterman, 1982). Good longitudinal investigations should be a prerequisite for accepting any validity for Erikson's theory of identity development and crisis in adolescence, and Marcia's method of measuring this.

# Box 8.2

# The relationship between parent–adolescent conflict and the amount of time adolescents spend alone and with parents and peers

Raymond Montemayor's aim in this study was to examine the belief that among adolescents there is an inverse relationship between parent and peer involvement, and that those in conflict with parents are likely to have a greater peer orientation. The author felt that asking general questions about the quality of relationships with parents would not be the best way, as answers might be inaccurate or designed to please the interviewer; also, he wanted to avoid presenting stereotyped situations in which parents and peers were in opposition. He therefore decided to carry out interviews with adolescents about how they had actually spent the day prior to the evening they were interviewed. Interviews were carried out by telephone with high school pupils who agreed to take part following a letter of invitation. Each participant had three such interviews at about one-week intervals. They were asked to recount how they had spent their time during the day, who they were with, and to describe any conflicts which occurred with parents. Out of 150 students contacted, 64 (30 males, 34 females) agreed to take part. Their mean age was 15 years; all were in intact families, white, predominantly middle class.

Time spent was coded as 'free time' if engaged in leisure activities such as sports, reading, watching television, and 'task time' if little choice was involved, as in home chores,

BOX TABLE 8.2.1   *Time (minutes) per three-day period spent by adolescents in different social contexts*

|  | With mother | With father | Both parents | With peers | Alone |
|---|---|---|---|---|---|
| **Free time** |  |  |  |  |  |
| males | 50 | 95 | 108 | 431 | 246 |
| females | 83 | 33 | 128 | 465 | 239 |
| **Task time** |  |  |  |  |  |
| males | 27 | 63 | 115 | 71 | 336 |
| females | 92 | 18 | 108 | 78 | 387 |

Based on material in Raymond Montemayor 1982: *Child Development*, 53, 1512–19.

BOX TABLE 8.2.2   *Correlations between free time spent with either parent, and free time spent with peers or alone*

|  | *With peers* | *Alone* |
|---|---|---|
| Males | | |
| with mother | n.s. | −0.37 ($p<0.05$) |
| with father | n.s. | −0.36 ($p<0.05$) |
| Females | | |
| with mother | −0.43 ($p<0.05$) | n.s. |
| with father | n.s. | n.s. |

eating, attending church. It was also coded as being with mother, father, both parents together, peers, or alone (it was very rare for acitivities to be with both parents and peers at the same time). The means for the sample are shown in box table 8.2.1. This shows that these adolescents spent about the same amount of time with parents as with peers, but in different ways. About half the time spent with parents was in 'task time', but most of the time spent with peers was in 'free time'. Also, it is clear that male adolescents spent more time with father than mother, but female adolescents spent more time with mother than father. These differences were all found to be significant, using analysis of variance.

Correlations were carried out between time spent in free time and task time in different social contexts. It was found that adolescents who spent more time with one parent also tended to spend more time with the other parent; so there was a general 'parent' orientation. But was it the case that adolescents who did not spend much time with parents were more peer-orientated? An interesting sex difference was found here, shown in box table 8.2.2 for the free time measures. For males, those who spent little time with parents spent more time alone; for females, those who spent little time with the mother spent more time with peers. Montemayor suggests that this and other research points to different development pathways for males and females in the process of separating from parents, with males spending more time in hobbies and sports, females more time in interpersonal relations with peers.

The data on reported conflicts gave a three-day mean of 0.85 conflicts for males and 1.21 for females (range 0–7). Altogether males reported 17 conflicts with mothers and 11 with fathers, females reported 34 conflicts with mothers and six with fathers. This was a significant male–female difference on a chi-square test, $\chi^2 = 5.18$, $p < 0.05$. The mother–daughter relationship seemed especially conflict-ridden, perhaps because mothers and daughters spend more time together (box table 8.2.1) and may be in conflict *vis-à-vis* status in the house. However, it can be seen that the rate of conflicts is not high (overall about once every three days), and all were about everyday matters such as home chores rather than about life-style issues such as sex, drugs, religion or politics.

Correlation coefficients were also calculated between the frequency of conflicts with either parent, and different ways of spending time. Few significant correlations were found; it was not the case in this study that conflicts with parents predicted time spent with peers. There was, however, some indication that adolescents who conflicted a lot with the mother spent more time with the father.

This study has strengths in the probable validity and reliability of the data obtained relative to other research on this topic. However, the findings are obviously limited to the white, middle class American subjects who took part. Even then, the participation rate was small (64 out of 150), and we cannot be sure that those who declined to participate were similar to those who did take part.

## Part Three

# Children's Developing Minds

# 9

# Perception

The sensory capacities of very young babies have for long posed many questions for psychologists. What can a newborn infant perceive? How early does she begin to interpret the stimuli which surround her? And how active a part does the infant herself play in the process? To what extent can environmental influences modify perceptual development? These are but some of the intriguing issues.

Psychologists make an important distinction between sensation and perception. 'Sensation' refers to the process through which information about the environment is picked up by sensory receptors and transmitted to the brain. It is known that babies have certain sensory abilities at birth since they respond to light, sound, smells, touch and taste. 'Perception' refers to the interpretation by the brain of this sensory input. It is through perception that we gain knowledge about the events, objects and people who surround us. As Gibson and Spelke (1983, p. 2) write, '[perception] is the beginning of knowing, and so is an essential part of cognition'.

As adults we can discriminate speech from birdsong, a distant tree from a nearby flower. But can infants, with their limited experience, understand the variety of stimuli which their sensory receptors detect? Are they born with certain perceptual capacities or must these be acquired through learning and experience?

The debate about the relative influence of heredity and environment in perception has a long history. *Empiricists*, following the tradition of the philosopher John Locke (1690/1939), argued that the baby was a 'tabula rasa', a blank slate, upon which experiences were imprinted. For example, the psychologist William James (1890) is famous for his assertion that, to the infant, sensory inputs become fused into 'one blooming, buzzing confusion' and that it is only later, through experience, that the child can discriminate amongst them. In other words, the child's ability to perceive develops as the result of a long learning process. A contrasting view was proposed by the *nativists*, who claimed that many perceptual abilities were present at birth. Philosophers such as Descartes (1638/1965) and Kant (1781/1958) argued that infants' capacity to perceive space, for example, was innate. Later, psychologists of the Gestalt school (early 20th century) lent support to the idea that certain perceptual abilities were present at birth because of the structural characteristics of the nervous system. Furthermore, they argued that the baby, far from being a tabula rasa, actively tried to create order and organization in his perceptual world.

In recent years experimental psychologists have been able to make a great contribution to our knowledge of perceptual development in the infant. Research has revealed that babies are born with a wider range of perceptual capabilities than the empiricists had suggested; on the other hand, however, their capacity to learn from experience is greater than the nativists would have allowed. Thus the evidence we have of the perceptual competence of the infant must be balanced against the mistakes which young babies make, revealing the long learning process that has to be undertaken during the early years.

Gibson and Spelke (1983), in a useful review of theory and research in the development of perception, point out that even the neonate (newborn infant) possesses some capacity for exploring events and objects in her world. This is enough to form the basis for a long process of gaining understanding about the environment. Through exploration, the infant discovers about invariant (unchanging) aspects of her surroundings, and about the properties of objects and people under different conditions. As a result the child goes through a progressive process of differentiation, that is, she perceives 'progressively more deeply embedded structure and more encompassing superordinate relations' (p. 59). In other words, exploration of the environment appears to be directed from the start, but as the child grows this exploration becomes more systematic: 'Perceiving becomes more efficient as exploratory skills increase and as the critical, minimal information for guiding action is detected ... There is continuity even here, for the youngest infant appears to search for invariants – the information for persisting structure over the maelstrom of change' (pp. 59–60).

Let us begin by considering the development of visual perception, since this is an area which has been widely researched. Also, psychologists have considered vision to be normally the most dominant sense modality. We will then consider auditory perception and the transfer of information between different sensory modalities.

## Visual Perception

There are obvious difficulties in using babies in research, but ingenious techniques for discovering the development of visual capacities have been devised. These include monitoring the eye movements of babies, looking at their behaviour in response to visual stimulus patterns, examining which visual stimuli they look at longest, conditioning a head-turning response to particular visual stimuli, looking at habituation to stimuli and measuring response such as heart rate. We shall describe some of these techniques in more detail shortly.

By such means we know that the newborn infant does not have the visual acuity or very high resolution of visual detail which adults have. This ability improves rapidly during the first year of life, though adult levels of acuity are not reached until about 10 years of age. Also, the neonate focuses best on objects which are near, that is at about the distance of the adult's face when being cradled. Objects further away than 19 cm seem to be perceived as blurred. Babies can detect moving lights and objects, and indicate sensitivity to brightness. There is some evidence (Bornstein et al., 1976) that infants can distinguish colours and that their attention to various colours parallels the preferential ratings of those colours by adults. Infants younger than 2 months cannot track a moving object smoothly. Instead they seem to follow the object in a series of jerky eye-movements (Salapatek and Banks, 1978) and it is only from around 8 weeks onwards that the infant is able continuously to track a moving object against a stationary background.

We shall examine two areas of research in some detail: these are pattern perception, and especially the perception of the human face, and the perception of space, especially depth perception and size constancy of objects at varying distances.

## Pattern perception

In the 1960s Fantz carried out pioneering research into the visual abilities of babies. His series of experiments into pattern perception revealed the ability of infants to discriminate among patterns at a very early age. Babies lay in a specially designed 'looking chamber' and were presented with two patterned stimuli (plate 9.1). An observer then recorded the length of time the baby spent looking at each pattern. This is known as the 'preference' technique.

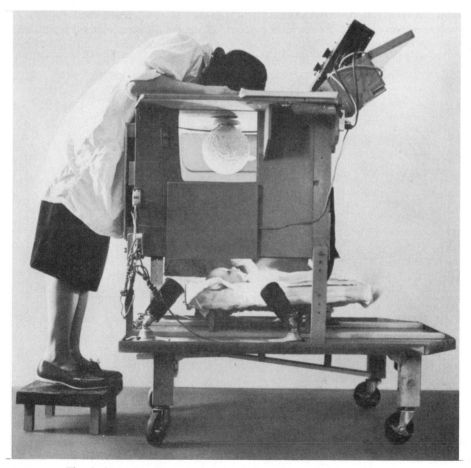

PLATE 9.1  *The 'looking chamber' used by Fantz (from Fantz, 1961)*

Fantz found that babies as young as 2 days could discriminate between patterned and unpatterned shapes. For example, they preferred striped, bulls-eye or checkerboard patterns to plain discs or squares. He also found, in a sample of 49 infants aged from 4 days to 6 months, that babies preferred face-like patterns and stimuli containing scrambled facial characteristics to an unpatterned stimulus which contained the same amount of light and depth shading (see figure 9.1 and Fantz, 1961). Furthermore, in this and other experiments, Fantz and his colleagues showed that infants can differentiate among patterns; they prefer curved forms to linear ones, and prefer symmetrical to asymmetrical patterns.

Fantz's results suggested that pattern perception in humans is innate, and he concluded that 'the early interest of infants in form and pattern in general, as well as in particular kinds of pattern, plays an important role in the development of behaviour by focusing attention on stimuli that will later have adaptive significance'.

Later research has revealed an interesting change in infants' pattern preferences. Fantz and Fagan (1975) presented 1- and 2-month-old infants with two stimuli which each had identical amounts of light and dark on them; the only difference was in the complexity of the patterns (figure 9.2). In this study, the 1-month-old babies preferred the less complex stimulus (eight 1-inch squares) while the 2-month-old babies preferred the more complex pattern (32 smaller squares). Thus it seems that,

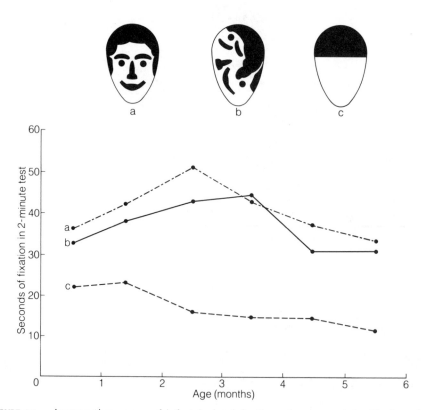

FIGURE 9.1    *Average time scores of infants' visual fixation when presented with three face-shaped objects paired in all the possible combinations (from Fantz, 1961)*

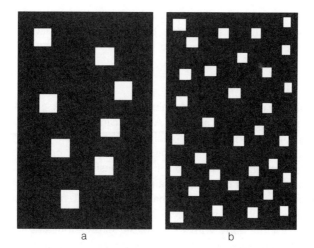

FIGURE 9.2 *Stimuli similar to those used by Fantz and Fagan*

although babies are born with a preference for patterned over plain stimuli, this liking for complexity develops during the first few months of life.

Salapatek (1975) developed a photographic technique to record the eye-movements of babies as they scanned geometric shapes such as triangles, circles and squares. He noted that at 1 month babies tended to focus on a single, or limited, number of features in a figure or pattern, e.g. the boundary of the shape in figure 9.3. By 2 months, the babies focused on the central areas of figures.

Salapatek's results suggested that at under 2 months of age infants did not see the entire figure but focused on regions which had high contrast contour, such as boundaries. This, he thought, was due to neural immaturity in the central visual system, especially in the visual cortex. After 2 months, infants changed to scanning the whole figure; this change was thought to be due to maturation of central, visual pattern-decoding mechanisms and suggested a developmental trend in the extent of scanning by infants during the first 3 months. More recent work (Hainline and Lemerise, 1982) has challenged Salapatek's findings and suggested that infants of all ages show variability in the extent of their scanning of geometrical forms. The topic remains controversial. However, the research indicates quite clearly that the newly

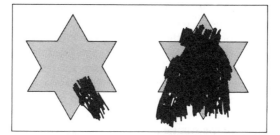

FIGURE 9.3 *Visual scanning of a geometrical figure by 1- and 2-month-old children (from Schaffer, 1985)*

born baby does respond in a directed exploratory manner to visual stimuli. The baby shows the capacity to attend selectively to certain aspects of a geometrical pattern, and prefers complex patterns to plain ones, at least by 2 months of age.

### Perception of the human face

Fantz's early findings led some researchers to conclude that babies' preference for face-like patterns is an innate capacity. As you can see in figure 9.1, the babies in Fantz's sample spent slightly longer gazing at the real face than at the scrambled face. Fantz (1961, p.70) wrote at the time: 'The degree of preference for the "real" face to the other one was not large, but it was consistent among individual infants. The experiment suggested that there is an unlearned primitive meaning in the form perception of infants'. Fantz suggested that the baby's interest in pattern was related to the social uses which vision has for the child. The human face would have an intrinsic interest for the baby with its changing expressions and contours and this interest would be adaptive in facilitating the development of attachment relationships (chapter 3).

There are limitations to Fantz's early study, however. Even if the infants did prefer the real face to the scrambled face in figure 9.1, this could be because the scrambled face is asymmetrical rather than because it is not a real face (we saw earlier that young infants prefer some symmetrical to asymmetrical non-facial patterns). In fact, the difference between the time spent looking at the real and scrambled faces is not significant. But this reveals another limitation of the study. The 'preference' techinque which Fantz developed is useful for seeing what infants actually like to look at, but not so useful for finding out what infants are able to discriminate. Admittedly a preference must mean an ability to discriminate; but a lack of preference (as between real and scrambled faces) does not necessarily mean the infant does not discriminate between them – she might just find both equally interesting.

Maurer and Barrera (1981) used both the 'preference' technique and an 'habituation' technique to look further at infants' perceptions of face-like stimuli. They used the three stimuli shown in figure 9.4. One is a natural face, the second a symmetrical scrambled face, the third an asymmetrical scrambled face; all had the same facial features, and thus the same brightness and contour information.

In the first experiment Maurer and Barrera used a preference technique somewhat similar to that of Fantz, with babies aged 1 month and 2 months. Rather than pairing stimuli, as Fantz did, however, they timed how long an infant fixated a stimulus before looking away. The mean fixation times over many trials are shown in figure 9.4. For 1-month-old babies there was no significant difference; they did not show a preference for any of the stimuli. At 2 months, however, the natural face was significantly preferred. This shows that by 2 months of age, at least, a preference for faces involves something more than the fact that faces are complex and symmetrical visual stimuli.

In a second experiment Maurer and Barrera looked further at whether the infants could actually discriminate amongst the stimuli which they did not show a preference for, namely all the stimuli at 1 month of age, and the two scrambled faces at 2 months of age. To do this they used an 'habituation' technique. First, they presented an infant with the asymmetrical scrambled face pattern lots of times, until

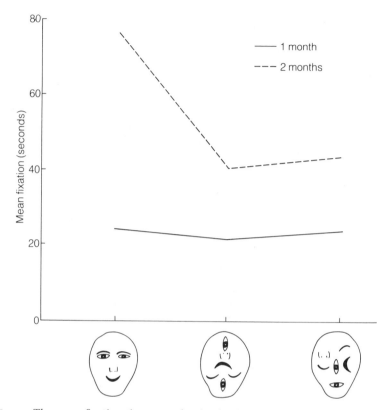

FIGURE 9.4    *The mean fixation time on each stimulus by infants (from Maurer and Barrera, 1981)*

the infant was sufficiently bored with the stimulus, or habituated to it, that fixation time was less than half what it was at the beginning. Then, they presented one of the other stimuli. If the infant's fixation time 'recovers', that is shows a significant increase again, this is evidence that the other pattern is discriminated from the first, habituated one.

This did not happen with the 1-month-olds, who did not look for any longer at the new stimuli. However, the 2-month-olds did. Out of 18 infants tested, 17 looked longer at the natural face and 16 looked longer at the symmetrical scrambled face, compared to the asymmetrical scrambled face they had been habituated to. (In addition, most looked longest at the natural face.) This confirms that 1-month-olds neither discriminate nor prefer any of the stimulus patterns; at 2 months they discriminate all three, though they only significantly prefer the natural face.

The difference between 1- and 2-month-old infants has also received support from eye-movement studies. Maurer and Salapatek (1976), using the same photographic technique as had been used in pattern perception research, recorded the eye-movements of babies aged 1 and 2 months as they scanned drawings of real faces. The 1-month-old babies tended to scan only a small part of the face, usually at its boundaries: the 2-month-old babies were more likely to scan the internal aspects of the face and focused on features such as the nose, the mouth and particularly the eyes. The authors concluded that the younger babies scanned faces in the same way as they scanned geometrical forms, i.e. by focusing on the edges. In other words, they responded as they would to a non-social stimulus. Thus babies do not have an innate preference for face-like stimuli, but show a preference as they become able to identify faces from non-faces at about 2 months of age.

There remains some controversy about what infants below 2 months of age are capable of. Maurer (1983) found that newborns and 1-month-old babies do spend some time looking at the internal properties of faces and do not focus simply on the boundaries as Salapatek suggested. Maurer also found that infants under 2 months fixated on a drawing of facial features more than they did on a picture of a square within a frame, a result which may be due to the complexity and contrast information which is given out by the human face. By 2 months, however, the babies definitely showed an interest in facial features.

In the period from 3 to 6 months infants show an increasing ability to discriminate between and respond to different facial patterns. At 3 months Barrera and Maurer (1981a) found that infants could discriminate a smiling face from a frowning face (see figure 9.5). They did this best when posed by the mother, but could also do it when posed by a female stranger. Furthermore, Samuels and Ewy (1985) found that babies at 3 months prefer attractive to unattractive faces and that these preferences correspond to adults' judgements of attractiveness. They suggest that some kind of aesthetic sensibility to the attractiveness or otherwise of a human face begins early in life.

Barrera and Maurer (1981b) found that 3-month-old babies were able to recognize photographs of their mothers and that they preferred to look at pictures of their mothers rather than strangers. They concluded that the babies' concept of 'faceness' is definitely established by this age but that the babies need time to take in the information about a new face. By contrast, 5- and 6-month-old babies seem to see the face as a whole rather than as a collection of separate features (Cohen et al., 1979). They can quickly distinguish between a familiar and a strange face. Fagan

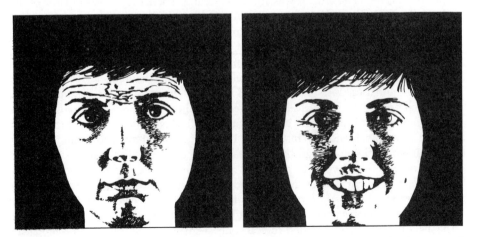

FIGURE 9.5    *Stimuli of a frowning and a smiling face, such as those used by Barrera and Maurer (1981a)*

(1979), using the habituation technique, showed that at this age infants can remember a face even after a two-week time lapse

What these experiments suggest is that the ability to perceive faces follows a similar developmental trend to the perception of non-social, geometrical forms and patterns. From scanning boundaries of faces at 1 month, the child at 2 months can focus on particular features inside the faces; he progresses to a concept of 'faceness' by around 3 months; between 3 and 6 months he develops an ability rapidly to discriminate and remember different faces. By around 6 months of age it seems as though the infant has developed stable representations or 'schemas' (sometimes called 'schemata') (see p. 318) for the faces of particular individuals. They are also learning to discriminate facial expressions of emotion, and their meaning (discussed further in chapter 5).

*Spatial perception, size constancy and the object concept*

By 3–6 months of age then, babies seem to be developing mental representations, or schemas, of visual stimuli such as faces or face-like patterns. However, there is more to developing a representation of a person, or object, than merely discriminating a static visual stimulus, such as a photograph. As an actual person or object moves relative to the viewer, the visual size, shape and colour information it projects on the eye will change also. Yet we perceive a given object as the same, even though its apparent size, shape and colour change in this way. These consistencies of perception are called 'constancies'. For example, if we observe a car driving away from us along a road, the image of the car on the retina becomes smaller but we do not perceive the car as getting smaller. We perceive that the car remains the same size but is actually getting further away. To perceive this way is to display 'size constancy'; in other words, to understand that the size of an object remains constant even though the object may be at a different distance. This is an observation that seems obvious to the adult, but does the infant have the same knowledge at birth or must she learn to respond to the approriate cues? There is some evidence that infants between 2 and 4 months of age have some degree of shape constancy and colour constancy (Bower, 1966; Bornstein et al., 1976). Most research, however, has been carried out on size constancy, and on the related topic of depth perception.

For infants depth perception is an essential part of size constancy, and is also vital for the normal activities of reaching out for objects to grasp. If this task is to be done properly the baby must have some capacity to judge depth. Several kinds of cues can be used to estimate depth or distance. They include (i) texture gradients – patterns become more closely spaced, and less definite, the further away they are (ii) motion parallax – as we move, nearer objects seem to move in an opposite direction relative to more distant objects (like trees against the moon, as we walk through a wood); and (iii) retinal disparity – each eye has a slightly different view of the world (as you can see if you close one eye, then the other); this disparity is greater for nearer objects.

At what age then does this capacity to perceive depth appear? Bower, (1970) investigated the responses of 6- to 20-day-old babies to a cube which 'loomed' towards their face. He found that as the object came close to the babies, they showed movements such as throwing up their arms, moving their heads back and opening their eyes very wide. Bower interprets these responses as defensive

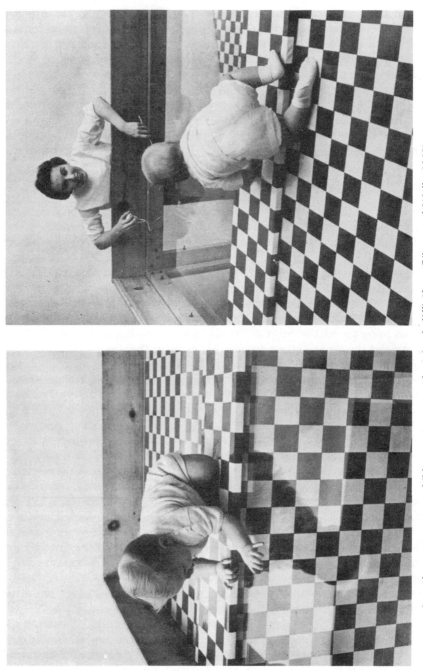

PLATE 9.2  *A mother encourages a child to venture over the 'visual cliff' (from Gibson and Walk, 1960)*

movements, which indicated that the babies did have the capacity to perceive distance and the approach of an object (the cube). However, a criticism of this conclusion is that the infants may only have been tracking the top edge of the object, which appeared higher as the object approached; hence the backward movement of the head. Later experiments have only succeeded in showing an eye-blink response to looming stimuli in infants at 1 month of age (Yonas, 1981).

Accurate depth perception would be indicated by infants' accurately reaching for objects which they can see. This 'visually directed reaching' is only achieved at about 5–6 months. Clearly, infants have some depth perception by this age. Before the age of 5–6 months, reaching is not systematic or accurate, though some experiments have found evidence that by $3\frac{1}{2}$–$4\frac{1}{2}$ months some adjustment to distance is being made (see Harris, 1983). An early study which succeeded in showing depth perception in older infants was the ingenious 'visual cliff' experiment of Gibson and Walk (1960). This used a glass table with a checkerboard pattern underneath the glass; at one side the pattern is immediately below the glass, at the other side, the pattern is several feet below (see plate 9.2). Gibson and Walk argued that if the baby had no depth perception he would readily crawl over the 'cliff' part of the table; on the other hand, if he did have depth perception, he might be unwilling to go over the edge. The subjects used by Gibson and Walk were 6-month-old babies, that is babies old enough to crawl. For the most part they were happy to crawl on the shallow side of the table but would not crawl over the 'cliff', even when encouraged by their mothers to do so.

Later researchers devised techniques to measure the responses of younger babies. Campos and his colleagues (1970) looked for heart rate responses in babies as they were lowered on the 'deep' and 'shallow' sides of the visual cliff apparatus. Two-month-old babies showed a lowered heart rate when they were placed on the cliff side but a normal heart rate over the shallow side. It seemed that the deep side of the apparatus was more interesting to them and they had not yet learned to be afraid of depth. However, 1-month-old babies showed no differences in their reactions to the two sides. It could be concluded that they did not yet have the ability to perceive depth or at least that they did not have the capacity to discriminate the depth cues in the visual cliff context.

Finally, some experimenters have investigated directly whether infants show size constancy. One such experiment by Bower (1965), is described in box 9.1. Bower's experiment indicated that babies as young as 6–12 weeks could demonstrate size constancy by responding to the real size of a cube rather than the size of its retinal image. This is the earliest that evidence for some perception of depth has been found. Day and McKenzie (1981) have found evidence for size constancy in infants aged $4\frac{1}{2}$ months, using an habituation procedure.

Altogether the evidence from Bower's work and the visual cliff experiments suggests that some degree of depth perception and size constancy may be operating from about 2 months onward. This also seems to be the age period when infants' focusing and ability to use the two eyes together is reaching the level where retinal disparity may be an available cue to depth perception. Some of this improvement is due to maturation of the visual system; a great deal may also be attributable to the learning which occurs as the baby explores her environment, reaches out for objects and manipulates them. As the infant develops size constancy and the other constancies, and becomes increasingly able to discriminate different stimuli, she can be thought of as developing internal representations of objects, which can be called 'schemas'. We know this because at around 5 or 6 months infants reach for any object they can see, whereas towards the end of the first year they show some wariness, or delay, in reaching for novel objects. (Similarly, they show some wariness of new persons, chapter 3.) Towards one year of age they may also search for objects, or persons, who have moved out of sight. The development of this sense of 'object permanence' was considered in detail by Piaget and is discussed further in chapter 11.

A further source of sensory information about objects comes from auditory cues, and we consider this in the next section.

## Auditory Perception

For adults, vision is the most important of the senses. For young infants, this may not be so. Relative to adults, the auditory acuity of neonates is much better than their visual acuity. Newborns will turn their heads towards a sound, which suggests they can locate sounds very soon after birth. Although there has not been such extensive investigation of infants' auditory ability, some interesting observations have been made in recent years. Here we shall look especially at the infant's response to voices and speech sounds, since these are very significant auditory stimuli both for the development of attachment relationships (chapter 3) and language (chapter 10).

To examine when infants can first discriminate the mother's voice from that of others an ingenious technique was devised utilizing the infant's sucking response. Sucking on a teat can be used to operate an electrical circuit and cause an adult's voice to be heard. The method can thus be used to assess what sounds or voices infants prefer to hear. In one study (Mills and Melhuish, 1974) infants 3–4 weeks old sucked more in order to hear the mother's voice than the voice of a female stranger which was equated for loudness. In a similar study (DeCasper and Fifer, 1980) such a discrimination was obtained in the first day or so of life, after only about 12 hours of post-natal contact with the mother. This suggests very rapid learning (though some learning is known to be possible while the fetus is in the uterus).

Such results suggest that infants can discriminate their mother from a stranger by auditory stimuli, well before they can do so visually. Other studies have indicated very early responses to the speech-like nature of sounds. Babies prefer patterned sounds, at the frequency range of human speech, to monotones. In addition, Condon and Sander (1974) made observations of very fine synchronization between the sound patterns of adult speech and the body movements of newly born babies. Even as young as 2 days, infants matched the movements of their hands, legs, heads and elbows to the structure of spoken language. The synchronization did not occur in response to tapping sounds or random vowel sounds but seemed to be specifically elicited by speech.

There is also evidence that very young babies can distinguish vowel and consonant sounds. Eimas (1985) exposed infants of 1 and 4 months to pairs of sounds like 'pah' (voiceless) and 'bah' (voiced). He measured the babies' responses to the stimuli by a method known as the 'high-amplitude pacifier' which was wired to recording instruments. Whenever the baby sucked, one sound of a stimulus pair was played. As the sucking rates of the participants fell (because of habituation to the sound), the experimenters switched to the other sound of the stimulus pair. A sharp increase in sucking ensued, indicating that the babies noticed the change. These researchers concluded that the discrimination occurs because babies are 'born with perceptual mechanisms that are tuned to the properties of speech'. They see these mechanisms as underlying the phonemic categories which will enable the child later to acquire language.

In another experiment (Kuhl, 1985), 6-month-old babies were trained to turn their heads towards a loudspeaker whenever contrasting vowel sounds interrupted background noise. (A colourful toy appeared on top of the loudspeaker to reward successful responses.) The babies were able to identify the vowel 'i' (as in 'peep') against a background noise of 'o' (as in 'pop'); these vowels were heard in a variety of voices and intonations. Success averaged 80 per cent. Even with less clear- cut differences like 'a' and 'o' (as in 'paw'), the babies were successful 67 per cent of the time. Kuhl concluded that infants are sensitive to the acoustic dimensions of speech long before they understand language. As Eimas (1985, p. 34) puts it, infants are 'richly endowed with innate perceptual mechanisms, well adapted to the characteristics of human language, that prepare them for the linguistic world they will encounter'.

As they get older children lose some of their ability to discriminate sounds which are not actually used in their native language. They seem to sharpen their perceptions or phonemes in their own language and lose the ability to make distinctions which are not needed. For example, Japanese adults find it difficult to distinguish 'r' and 'l' even though Japanese infants are sensitive to differences between these consonants. Werker and Tees (1985) found that babies of 6–8 months from an English-speaking community could distinguish consonantal contrasts in Hindi. By 12 months, the same infants could no longer detect the differences. The Hindi infants retained their ability to perceive consonantal contrasts that occurred in their own language (see figure 9.6). These findings suggest that babies are born with the underpinnings of language but that these perceptual abilities are modified by the environment in which the child is developing.

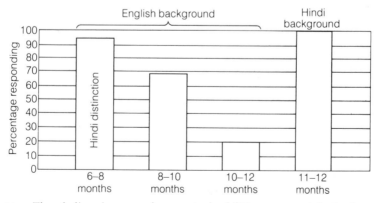

FIGURE 9.6 *The decline in unused perceptual abilities among infants from English backgrounds compared with those from Hindi backgrounds (adapted from Eimas, 1985)*

**Intersensory Perception**

So far we have examined visual and auditory perception separately. In everyday life, however, it is unusual to receive perceptual information from one source only. Normally we coordinate information from a number of senses – vision, audition, touch, taste and smell. We see a bus approaching and hear its engine sound getting louder; we see, taste and smell our food as we eat. This coordination of information from different sensory modalities is called 'intersensory perception'.

Adults use their knowledge of intersensory perception in a number of ways. For example, it can be used to direct a person's attention. The increasing sound of the engine round the corner from the bus-stop results in a visual search for the approaching bus. Also it means that an object familiar in one sensory mode may be recognized when presented in another mode. As adults, we can often recognize an object by touch which previously we have only identified visually. This ability is called 'cross-modal perception'.

But do infants understand these intersensory relationships? When does stimulation in one sensory mode lead to exploratory searching or expectation in another? At what point do babies become capable of cross-modal perception? Put another way, are the neonate's senses integrated at birth and differentiated through learning and experience, or are they separate at birth and only later integrated? There is still disagreement among psychologists on this question.

One line of argument is that the senses already show some integration at or soon after birth. We have seen that newborns look in the direction of sounds: this could be just an orienting reflex, but it could also suggest that the newborns are looking for something they have heard. Similarly, at a fairly early age infants make reaching movements when they see an object. Does this suggest some sort of expectation that they should be able to touch the object?

One way of examining this is to see whether, when given a choice between two or more stimuli in one sensory modality, infants choose that which matches with information in another sensory modality. For example, Spelke (1981) found that if a 3- or 4-month-old baby could see both mother and father, and hear a tape-recorded voice of one of them, the infant would look at the parent whose voice he heard. In another study Spelke showed films of two events side by side on a screen directly in front of a baby. Only one of the two sound tracks was played. The babies spent more time looking at the film whose actions related to the sound track. Studies such as these (see plate 9.3) show that, by the age of 4 months, infants have some definite expectations about the links between visual and auditory stimuli.

Another way of answering this question is to produce situations of intersensory incongruity – clashes between information from two sensory modalities – and then to see how babies respond. Aronson and Rosenbloom (1971) examined the effects of incongruities between vision and audition on infants' behaviour. Three-week-old babies were seated so that they could see their mothers through a sound-proof screen but only hear them through two loudspeakers. When the two speakers were equally loud, the mother's voice was perceived as coming from the mother's mouth, as would be expected. But when the speakers were imbalanced there was separation of sight and sound, with the mother's voice appearing to come from the left or right. When this happened the babies were very upset, suggesting that even at that age

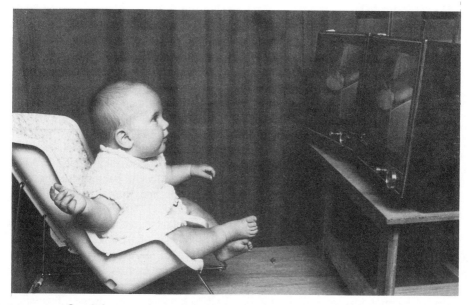

PLATE 9.3   *One infant experiences two visual inputs*

babies expected there to be coordination between auditory and visual stimuli. These results are controversial since other investigators have not been able to replicate them (McGurk and Lewis, 1974). Therefore we cannot be absolutely certain that such very young babies use auditory information to guide the direction in which they look.

Other experiments have examined the incongruities between vision and touch (Bower et al., 1970). Bower and his colleagues presented infants with an object which they could easily reach. The object was in fact a 'virtual object', that is, a visual illusion; when the baby reached out for it, there was nothing there. The authors argued that, if the baby expected to touch an apparently solid object which he saw, he should show surprise when his hands passed through it. Younger babies in this study, aged from 8 days to 6 months, were extremely upset when their hands grasped nothing, despite a number of attempts to take hold of the object. Older babies, however, showed a different pattern of behaviour. At 6 months the babies were still startled by the virtual object but quickly stopped making the grasping movements with open hands typical of the younger babies. Instead, they rubbed their hands or banged their heads as if trying to verify that their hands were still in working order! These responses were usually followed by exploratory visual behaviour, e.g. swaying their heads as if to check normal motion parallax. After that, the babies would stop reaching; they seemed to realize that this virtual object did not have normal properties and saw no need to continue their efforts, unlike the younger babies.

To Bower, this experiment suggested that younger babies have an integrated awareness, responding with all sensory modalities at once to a stimulus; by 6 months, however, vision and touch have become differentiated modalities. Bower's results seem to indicate a high level of intersensory competence amongst babies, but again we cannot be absolutely certain about this conclusion. Other experimenters (Gordon and Yonas, 1976) have not been able to replicate Bower's findings; they reported that 5-month-old babies made fingering movements but gave no indication of emotional upset when they reached out for a virtual object.

A related line of research has focused on cross-modal perception. Experimenters have looked to see whether an object that is known already through one modality can be recognized when it can only be sensed in another modality. One study suggests that this is possible very early in life. Meltzoff and Borton (1979) found that 1-month-old babies showed visual preference for an object which they had only previously experienced by touch. An object (either a smooth sphere or a nubbed sphere) was placed directly into the mouth so that the babies could not see it. When larger versions of these objects were later presented to the babies visually, they showed a clear preference for the object they had mouthed, thus showing that they can coordinate information gained through touch with visual information. Other work, however, places the acquisition of cross-model perception from touch to vision in the 6-month to 12-month period (Rose et al., 1981).

Altogether research in this area does not give an entirely clear message. There is still uncertainty about what very young babies can do in integrating information from different sensory modalities. By about 4–6 months of age, however, infants do seem to be showing some understanding that two sources of sensory information (for example, the sound of a voice and the sight of a face) can be part of one object in the environment. Again, this supports the idea that from this period on the baby is starting to develop internal representations or 'schemas'.


**Environmental Influences**


We have seen that some aspects of visual perception seem to be present very early on in life. These could be described as 'innate', or more correctly as 'highly canalized' processes (see chapter 2). However, we know from a variety of sources of evidence that environmental influences are also important for the way in which perceptual abilities develop. We will look at two sources of evidence: one involves the experimental manipulation of visual rearing environment in non-human species; the other involves the comparison of humans who have naturally experienced different visual rearing environments, either through illness or through cultural differences.

There have been a number of case studies of people who have been blind for much or all of their lives, but have had their sight restored as adults, for example, by removal of congenital cataracts. Such people find it difficult at first to identify objects or shapes, though this ability usually improves slowly with time. The prognosis is highly variable, depending probably on how completely blind the patient had been, for how long, and whether there are any associated visual abnormalities (see Mitchell, 1978). Because of the difficulty of generalizing from this data, some investigators decided to use animal species in studies of artifically deprived rearing environments.

An early series of studies was carried out by Reisen (1950). He reared a number of young chimpanzees with bandages over their eyes, or (on finding that the chimpanzees removed the bandages) in a completely darkened room. He found that when reared in this way and tested at 16 months of age, chimpanzees were visually incompetent. Although their pupils were sensitive to light, and they were startled by sudden changes of illumination, they did not respond to approaching objects or visually track moving objects in a systematic way. In fact, they showed little response to objects (such as a feeding bottle) unless touched by them.

In part, these deficits were found to be due to deterioration or degeneration of the optic nerve and retinal cells. Such degeneration was irreversible if the dark experience lasted more than about seven months. When chimpanzees were reared with diffuse, unpatterned light, however, this seemed to avoid physiological deterioration of the retina; yet the difficulties in visually recognizing objects remained. Improvement in this area was very slow to develop. Such difficulties seemed to be similar to those of the humans who had been operated on for congenital cataracts.

This work led researchers to investigate which visual inputs were important for certain visual abilities, and whether there were critical or sensitive periods (see chapter 2) for such input. As an example of how this research has developed, we will consider work on binocular vision.

### Critical periods in the development of binocular vision

Many visual cortical cells respond binocularly, that is, they will fire if a visual stimulus is shown to either eye. However, this is not so if one eye is covered or occluded early in life. In such circumstances most cells will only fire in response to stimuli presented to the non-deprived eye.

This was shown to be the case for kittens in an experiment by Weisel and Hubel (1963). They covered one eye on each of several kittens, soon after birth, for periods of 2 or 3 months. After this period the kittens had very defective vision in the deprived eye, and recordings from the visual cortex showed that very few cortical cells would respond binocularly. Subsequent research has shown that there is a critical period between about three weeks to three months after birth for binocular connections to be made in the kitten's visual cortex. Subsequent experience cannot reverse the effects of deprivation through this period. A similar phenomenon has been found in monkeys, though with a critical period extending up to about 18 months.

What relevance does this have for human infants? The parallels seem to be quite close. An interesting study by Banks, Aslin and Letson (1975) was carried out on 24 human participants who had suffered abnormal binocular experience due to squint in childhood, later corrected. The degree of binocularity was assessed in these people by means of the tilt after-effect. This visual illusion is shown in figure 9.7. Staring between the tilted gratings and then between the vertical grating leads to the latter being perceived as tilted in opposite directions. Bank's team asked participants to stare at the tilted gratings with one eye, then at the vertical gratings with the other eye. The amount of transfer of the after-effect from one eye to the other (called interocular transfer) was used as a measure of binocularity.

Amongst 12 people with congenital squint (with onset at or near birth), six had had surgery between the ages of 14 and 30 months. These people had levels of interocular transfer not greatly below those of normal persons. The other six had

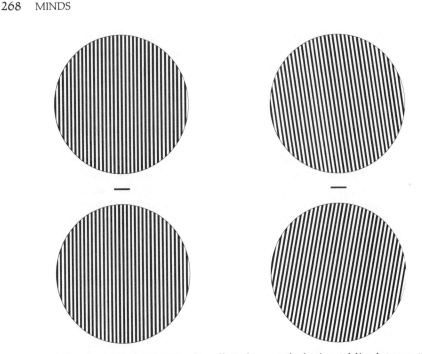

FIGURE 9.7   *Demonstration of the tilt after-effect. Stare at the horizontal line between the two gratings on the right for one minute, allowing the eyes to wander along the line. Then quickly transfer fixation to the line between the two left-hand gratings. Instead of appearing vertical they will briefly appear to be tilted in opposite directions to each other (from Mitchell, 1978)*

not had surgery until between the ages of 4.5 years and 20 years. None of these people showed any appreciable interocular transfer. These results suggest that there may be a critical period before about 3 or 4 years in human infants for the development of binocular vision.

For a true critical period, the length of deprivation itself is not as important as at what stage in development the deprivation occurs. Banks and his colleagues checked that this was the case. Some of their other participants had a late onset of squint: for example, several had squint diagnosed at between 2 and 7 years of age, but were not operated on until two or three years later. These individuals achieved reasonably good levels of binocularity. The experimenters concluded from this and related evidence that the critical period for binocularity in humans was from a few months after birth to between 1 and 3 years of age. This finding has clear practical implications: early corrective surgery is important for congenital cases of squint, but is not so urgent when the squint is of late onset.

*Depth perception and the effects of movement*

Binocular vision is useful in depth perception, but as we have seen, it is not the only cue for depth. Motion parallax, for example, is also useful from very early on (see box 9.1). Some evidence has suggested that active rather than passive visual experience is important for visually guided behaviour, such as responding to the visual cliff (p. 260), blinking at approaching objects, or extending arms or limbs when placed on a surface, which rely on perceiving depth accurately.

This argument was advanced by Held and Hein (1963) on the basis of research with kittens reared in the dark for 8–12 weeks and then given three hours a day in a lighted environment under conditions shown in figure 9.8. The apparatus consisted of a cylindrical container with vertical stripes. One, active, kitten moved around, while the other, passive, kitten was in a holder and pulled around by the movements of the first kitten. After about ten days of this, the kittens were tested for visually guided behaviour. In general, the active kittens showed evidence of depth perception at this point; the passive kittens did not and required some further experience of running around in a normal enviroment before their visually guided behavior recovered.

Held and Hein argued that for each pair of kittens the two animals had experienced similar visual input, but had differed in activity. They argued that active movement in a visual environment, together with sensory feedback accompanying this movement, was important in perceptual adaption. However, they may have been wrong in assuming that the pairs of kittens had equivalent visual experience.

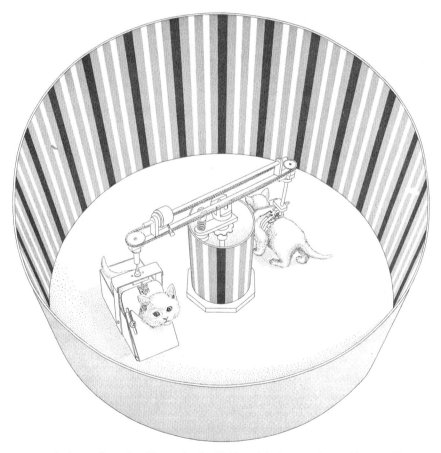

FIGURE 9.8 *Active and passive kittens in the Held and Hein experiment (from Held, 1965)*

Orientation

90

180

45

135

FIGURE 9.9 Autodemonstration of the 'oblique effect'. While holding the book at a comfortable reading distance, count how many gratings can be resolved in each row. Readers who possess the classical 'oblique effect' will be able to see further along the row of vertical and horizontal gratings than along either of the two rows of oblique gratings (adapted from Mitchell, 1978)

The passive kittens might have dozed off more, or paid less attention to the visual environment. Subsequent research by Walk (1981) found that kittens that were constrained in their movements, but had interesting visual stimuli to watch (such as toy cars moving on a racetrack), showed good depth perception. Thus attention, rather than activity, may have been the crucial variable in Held and Hein's results. Studies of human infants who have been restricted in motor activity in the early years of life (for example, infants reared on cradleboards; or thalidomide victims without limbs) have not found deficits in depth perception, which would also suggest that activity may not be as crucial as Held and Hein believed.

## Horizontals, verticals and the 'carpentered world' hypothesis

We have seen that the presence of patterned visual input can be important for the development of binocular vision and depth perception. It also seems that there may be effects, some gross and some subtle, depending on the kind of patterned information that the early visual environment provides. This has been investigated particularly for the response of the visual cortex to horizontal, vertical and diagonal lines or contours.

We know that in adult cats some cells in the cortex respond mainly to barlike stimuli at a certain orientation. However, the response of these cells may be only weakly specified at birth and the nature of the early visual environment may greatly affect how the responsiveness of such cells develops. This was shown for kittens in an experiment by Blakemore and Cooper, described in box 9.2. Later work has confirmed the general nature of their findings, even though some details are disputed. It seems that, in both the cat and the monkey, the development of cells that fire to certain visual stimuli is facilitated if such stimuli are experienced early in life. However, there is also some bias or canalization (chapter 2) to this. Some cells that fire to horizontal or vertical contours are found following exposure to horizontal, vertical or diagonal lines or stripes in early life (although the distribution between horizontal and vertical may vary, as Blakemore and Cooper suggested). However, cells firing to diagonal lines are found *only* when the animals are exposed to diagonal lines early in life; thus, a more specific visual input is required for these cells (Leventhal and Hirsch, 1975). The visual cortex seems to be biased more towards responding to horizontal and vertical contours, perhaps because they often contain the most information for the animal.

In humans, too, the visual system shows some preference for horizontals and verticals over diagonals, for example in visual acuity. If you look at figure 9.9 you can experience this so-called 'oblique effect'. By looking from left to right, you will probably find that you can still resolve horizontal or vertical gratings of a particular frequency or spacing, while corresponding diagonal (oblique) gratings have become a homogeneous blur.

An ingenious study by Leekey et al. (1975) suggests that the oblique effect is present in infants. We saw earlier that infants prefer looking at patterned to plain stimuli. Leekey's group presented infants with pairs of gratings of the same frequency; one was horizontal or vertical, the other diagonal. They used the preference technique to assess infant looking. They found that if the spacing was very wide (clearly resolvable) or very fine (obviously appearing blurred) the infants did not prefer either kind of stimulus. At intermediate spacing, however, the horizontal or vertical grating was preferred to the diagonal, suggesting that the former could be resolved but the latter could not (the spacing at which this happened decreased with age, as infant visual acuity improved).

The youngest infants Leekey tested were 6–13 weeks age. These findings suggest that, as for kittens, some bias to responding to horizontal and vertical contours is present in the structure of the visual cortex. However, it could be that subsequent visual experience may also have an effect (as it seems to have in kittens, box 9.2). Evidence has been put forward to support this from studies of people in different societies who have experienced characteristically different visual environments. For example, it has been proposed that in urban or 'Westernized' societies people see mainly vertical or horizontal contours, in houses, tables, books, trucks, and so on. If you look around you, or make a drawing or look at a sample of drawings or pictures, you are likely to find that vertical or horizontal contours predominate over diagonals.

Those who argue that this is largely an artefact of modern civilization, advocates of the 'carpentered world' hypothesis, believe this may not be true of people in traditional societies. Such peoples might not experience the 'oblique effect' (figure 9.9), for example. Annis and Frost (1973) tested this hypothesis by measuring the visual acuity of participaants for gratings of different orientation. They examined two groups of participants: a sample of urban Euro-Canadians, and a sample of Cree American Indians living in a traditional setting. The Cree lived in tents which presented many diagonal contours, as shown in plate 9.4. The prediction was that the Cree would show a less strong 'oblique effect' than the Euro-Canadians.

The results, shown in figure 9.10a supported their prediction. The figure shows the threshold acuity for gratings at different orientations, averaging data for all participants. The oblique effect was significantly less strong for the Cree Indian subjects.

Nevertheless, other interpretations of these results are possible. One is that there are genetic differences between racial groups in the strength of the bias of the visual cortex, as measured by the oblique effect. This interpretation was supported by

PLATE 9.4    *A Cree Indian summer cook tent (from Annis and Frost, 1973)*

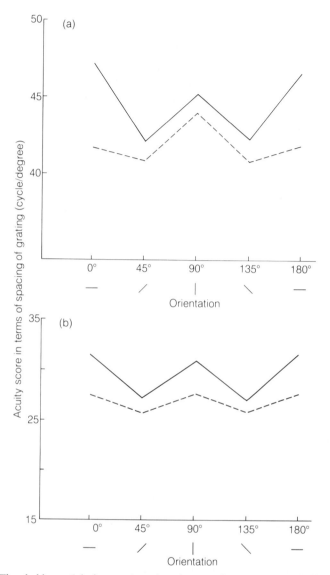

FIGURE 9.10   *Threshold spatial frequencies plotted as a function of grating orientation: (a) comparing Euro-Canadian (solid line) and Cree Indian (broken line) subjects (from Annis and Frost, 1973); (b) comparing Caucasian (solid line) and Chinese (broken line) subjects (from Timney and Muir, 1976)*

Timney and Muir (1976), who carried out a study similar to that of Annis and Frost, but with Caucasian subjects from North America and Chinese subjects from Hong Kong, which they considered an equally urban and 'capentered' environment. They found that the oblique effect was stronger in the Caucasian subjects, even though no obvious difference in visual environment had been postulated (figure 9.10b). They also found very considerable individual differences, within each group, in the strength of the effect. They suggest that genetic differences would be a plausible explanation of these findings.

Cultural differences are often very difficult to interpret because of the multitude of factors that may be involved – genetic, experiential and even the response of the participant to the test situation. We saw earlier that culture can influence auditory development, in the case of discriminating consonantal contrasts (see figure 9.6). However, whether cultural experience significantly affects visual development, and if so how it does so, is still a matter of controversy.

### Further reading

T. Bower 1979: *The Perceptual World of the Child*. Glasgow: Fontana/Open Books, provides an accessible introduction to these and other issues in perceptual development. Some more advanced texts are R. D. Walk 1981: *Perceptual Development*. Monterey, Ca: Brooks/Cole, and R. D. Walk and H. L. Pick Jr (eds) 1978: *Perception and Experience*. New York and London: Plenum Press.

For general texts on perceptual and cognitive development, try J. G. Bremner 1988: *Infancy*. Oxford: Basil Blackwell; J. H. Flavell 1985: *Cognitive Development*, 2nd edn. Englewood Cliffs, NJ: Prentice-Hall; and J. McShane 1991: *Cognitive Development*. Oxford: Basil Blackwell.

### Discussion points

1 How early does the young child recognize her mother's face? Discuss the evidence to support your answer.

2 What evidence is there for canalization in visual development?

3 Compare the methods used to assess visual and auditory abilities in infants.

4 Can infants integrate information from different sensory modalities?

5 To what extent do environmental factors influence aspects of perceptual development?

### Practical exercises

1 Try to replicate Bower's study of infants' responses to an object which looms towards them. Use as participants infants of different ages from a few days onwards, preferably reclining slightly in a chair. Bring an object up fairly suddenly from some distance away to within a few inches of the infant's face, taking care not to hit the baby. Record the infant's reactions. Note the difficulties you experience in making precise observations using babies as participants.

2 Make some cardboard face-size models, like those in figures 9.1 or 9.4. Hold them, one at a time, above the head of a small baby (under 6 months old) while she is awake and lying in a cot. Hold each model about 18 inches above the baby's head for two minutes. Using a stopwatch, see how long the baby looks at each model. Is there a difference? Does the

baby smile at any of the models? Does movement make any difference? Does the baby smile more at your face, if you put it where the model was?

3   Examine individual differences in the 'oblique effect'. You could use figure 9.9, or make a copy of your own using white card and Indian ink. Ask your participant to stand still and look at the figure while you approach slowly from a distance. The participant informs you when they can resolve (say) the fourth vertical grating from the left. Record (i) which other gratings they can resolve at that distance, and (ii) what the distance is. This gives you a rough measure of both the 'oblique effect' and of general visual acuity. You could see if there are age and sex differences in subjects from different cultural backgrounds.

Box 9.1

# Stimulus variables determining space perception in infants

The aim of this study was to assess the age at which infants show size constancy (perceiving an object at varying distances as the same even though it projects different sizes of retinal image). Bower used a procedure in which he rewarded babies aged between 40 and 60 days for turning their heads to one side. The reward was a peek-a-boo response by an adult who popped up in front of the baby and then disappeared again (see box figure 9.1.1). As we saw in chapter 3, infants enjoy contingent responses from adults, such as the peek-a-boo response. If an infant turned his head to the left, this operated a sensitive pressure switch on a pad behind his head. This in turn alerted the adult, who popped up to give the peek-a-boo reward. Once Bower had firmly established the head-turning response, he rewarded the baby only when it occurred in the presence of a 30 cm cube placed at 1 m distance from the baby. After training the baby to respond only to the cube, the schedule was gradually changed to one in which every fifth response was rewarded with the peek-a-boo.

In order to determine whether the baby possessed size constancy, Bower next presented four stimuli in a counterbalanced order for four 30-second periods each. The four stimuli were

1   The original cube on which the infant had been rewarded, or 'conditioned', placed 1 m away.

2   The same 30 cm cube placed 3 m away.

3   A 90 cm cube 1 m away.

4   The 90 cm cube placed 3 m away.

As box table 9.1.1 shows, stimulus 4 projected on to the baby's retina the same size image as stimulus 1, the original cube.

Bower predicted that if the baby does not have depth perception or size constancy, he should continue to display head-turning in response to stimulus 4, since it projected the same retinal image as stimulus 1. If the infant possesses depth perception or size constancy, however, then he will respond to stimulus 3 (at the same distance as stimulus 1) or stimulus 2 (the same object as stimulus 1), rather than stimulus 4 (a different object, at a different distance).

Nine infants were tested. The results are presented in box table 9.1.1 (top line) and show that stimulus 2 and stimulus 3 each elicited two to three times as many responses as

Based on material in T. G. R. Bower 1965: *Science*, 149, 88–9.

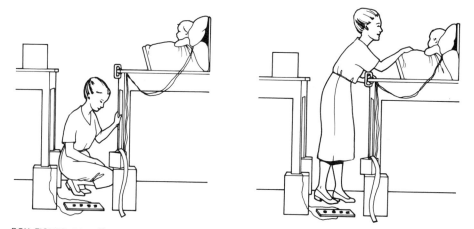

BOX FIGURE 9.1.1 *The apparatus used in Bower's experiment (from Bower, 1982)*

stimulus 4. The babies were affected by the real distance or size of the object; they did not seem to use the size of the retinal image as a guide.

What cues might the babies have been using to gauge the depth (distance) of the stimuli? We saw on p. 259 that possible cues include texture gradients, motion parallax and retinal disparity. Bower therefore conducted further studies to investigate this (see also Bower, 1966), using three new conditions as variants of the first. Nine infants were in each condition. In one of the new conditions Bower covered one eye of the infants with a patch; this prevented them using retinal disparity as a cue. In another, he projected slides of cubes rather than putting real cubes in front of the infant; this removed both retinal disparity and motion parallax as cues. In a third condition, infants wore stereoscopic goggles and viewed projected stereograms; this removed motion parallax but not the other cues. The three conditions, the cues infants could use in each to gauge depth, and the results obtained are also shown in box table 9.1.1.

It can be seen that when texture gradient cues only were available (the projected slides condition), infants responded to retinal size and not to real size or distance. This means that the infants could not use texture gradient cues as a guide to distance. The best performance, equal to that of the original group, was achieved by the infants with a patch over one eye. If they could not use texture gradients (as we have just concluded) then they must have been using motion parallax. They did not need retinal disparity cues for depth perception. However, the results of the group viewing projected stereograms (who could not use motion parallax but could use retinal disparity), being intermediate between the results for the other two groups, suggest that infants can make some limited use of retinal disparity in depth perception.

Bower concluded that infants of 6–8 weeks have some depth perception and size constancy, and that this depends primarily on motion parallax, to some extent aided by retinal disparity. Texture gradients did not seem to be used as a cue.

This study has an experimental design with the different conditions as the independent variable, and the head-turning response as the dependent variable. The ingenious arrangements allow strong conclusions to be drawn about infants' perceptual abilities. Working with infants so young is difficult, however, since they can be fussy, fidgety or drowsy. Such difficulties can be made worse by requiring such young children to wear stereoscopic goggles! Getting a conditioned response is not easy with infants of this age. Behaviour can be difficult to interpret and studies difficult to repeat. Not surprisingly, some researchers have questioned the reliability of Bower's findings.

BOX TABLE 9.1.1   Number of responses elicited by conditioned stimulus and three test stimuli when shown to babies aged 6–8 weeks under different conditions

| Condition and cues available | Stimulus 1 (conditioned) Size: 30cm Distance: 1m Retinal image: — | Stimulus 2 (test) Same (30cm) Diff. (3m) Diff. | Stimulus 3 (test) Diff. (90cm) Same (1m) Diff. | Stimulus 4 (test) Diff. (90cm) Diff. (3m) Same |
|---|---|---|---|---|
| Normal | | | | |
| Retinal disparity; texture gradients; motion parallax | 98 | 58 | 54 | 22 |
| Patch over one eye | | | | |
| Texture gradients; motion parallax | 101 | 60 | 53 | 22 |
| Projected slides | | | | |
| Texture gradients | 94 | 52 | 44 | 96 |
| Projected stereograms | | | | |
| Retinal disparity; texture gradients | 94 | 44 | 40 | 32 |

## Box 9.2

# Development of the brain depends on the visual environment

Blakemore and Cooper were interested in how the visual rearing environment might affect both the development of cells and the visual cortex, and thus visually guided behaviour. They conducted their study in an experimental fashion, using kittens.

The kittens were housed from birth in a completely dark room. From the age of 2 weeks each kitten was put into a special apparatus for five hours a day. This was a tall cylinder, without visible corners or edges, covered with high-contrast black-and-white stripes. The kitten was also prevented from seeing its own body by a wide black collar round its neck. Some kittens were put in cylinders with vertical stripes (an example is shown in box figure 9.2.1) and some were put in cylinders with horizontal stripes. Their different rearing environments constituted the independent variable of the experiment.

After five months of experiencing these environments, all the kittens were put in a small, well-lit room containing tables and chairs for several hours a week. The experimenters then recorded the visually guided behaviour of the kittens in this new environment.

BOX FIGURE 9.2.1   *A kitten in a cylinder with vertical black-and-white stripes (from Blakemore and Cooper, 1970)*

Based on material in C. Blakemore and G. F. Cooper 1970: *Nature*, 228, 447–8.

At first the kittens were visually inept. They did not show a startle response when an object was quickly brought up close to their eyes, nor did they show visual placing, i.e. putting out their paws to land on when put down on a table top. These abilities rapidly improved, however, after about ten hours of normal visual experience. But other visually guided behaviour remained poor. These kittens used clumsy, jerky head movements in following objects, and tried to reach out for things which were well out of reach on the other side of the room. They also frequently bumped into table legs.

These deficits applied to all the kittens. In addition, it seemed that the kittens reared with vertical stripes were effectively blind for horizontal contours in the room, while those reared with horizontal stripes were effectively blind for vertical contours. As the authors put it, 'The differences were most marked when two kittens, one horizontally and the other vertically experienced, were tested simultaneously with a long black or white rod. If this was held vertically and shaken, the one cat would follow it, run to it and play with it. Now if it was held horizontally the other cat was attracted and its fellow completely ignored it.'

The visual rearing environment had clearly affected the kittens' visual behaviour. An explanation for this became apparent when the experimenters looked at another dependent variable, the nature of cells in the visual cortex. When the kittens were 7.5 months old they were anaesthetized and recordings were made from single-nerve cells (neurons) in the primary visual cortex at the back of the brain. The researchers found that most of the cells were binocular, that is, they would fire to stimuli presented to either eye. However, in a kitten that had been reared with vertical stripes, it was found that almost all the neurons responded most to stimuli which were at or near vertical, and none responded to horizontal stripes. The reverse was true for a kitten reared with horizontal stripes.

It seems that the vertically reared kitten may have been effectively blind to horizontal stimuli, because it lacked visual cortical neurons to respond to such stimuli (and vice versa for the horizontally reared kitten). Thus, the nature of the visual cortex had been changed by the rearing environment; visual neurons had developed to respond to the kinds of visual features encountered during early rearing.

Relatively little quantitative data was presented in the report, and not all the conclusions reached have been accepted. While Blakemore and Cooper claimed that the response of cortical cells was changed in response to the visual environment, another possibility is that cells not stimulated by the visual environment atrophied or decayed. Also, one replication study in which the experimenters did not know the rearing experience of the kitten they were recording from, failed to find the same effect in cortical cells. It seems clear that the visual rearing environment can have an effect in kittens, but the details are still subject to debate.

# 10

# Language

Communication systems exist within almost all species. As we saw in chapter 2, amongst mammals and birds sexual, territorial and threatening messages can be expressed through specific displays, gestures and calls. The Nobel prize-winning scientist Von Frisch showed that bees can convey detailed information about food sources through a series of dance-like movements. But these communication systems fall far short of the flexibility of human language. With a small number of signals which are in themselves meaningless, a person has the potential for creating an infinite number of meaningful statements. That person can generate completely new utterances which will nevertheless make sense to an audience. Besides communicating intentions and ideas in detail to others, a person can share others' thoughts on a topic, and can speculate about themes remote in time and space. Young children, as we shall see, have the capacity to communicate and to negotiate meaning at a prelinguistic level. But through language the child gains access to the shared consciousness of her culture – its concepts, its metaphors, its frames of reference, its values.

Such a complex, abstract system must, one might speculate, take many years to master. But in fact by the age of 5 children from all cultures understand and use most of the grammatical rules of their language, communicate effectively with peers and adults and demonstrate inventive ways of expressing themselves in words.

The relative speed with which children acquire this complex system is not yet fully understood. It may be that children are in some way programmed to learn language (canalized development, see chapter 2) but psychologists also emphasise the role of dialogue between child and significant others in the achievement of meaning. A number of questions have intrigued developmental psychologists. Do children go through identical stages as they learn to talk? Is there any connection between the non-verbal sounds and gestures which the baby produces and later speech? What part do adults play in creating a context in which child language will flourish? How important is it to examine the child's growing competence in a socially meaningful context? These and other issues will be explored in the following sections as we examine the sequences of language development through which children progress and the contexts where this happens. We will look at some research findings in the field and major theoretical explanations of the processes involved in learning language.

## The Aspects of Language Development

There are four main areas of language competence which the child must acquire. These are the rules of sounds (*phonology*), grammar (*syntax*), meaning (*semantics*) and knowledge of social context (*pragmatics*).

*Phonology* is the system which governs the particular sounds (or *phonemes*) used in the language of a child's community. For example, an English speaker treats the sounds 'I' and 'r' as two separate phonemes; to a Japanese speaker they are one (p. 263). Scottish people use the speech sound 'ch' (as in 'loch') which many English people cannot pronounce.

*Syntax* refers to the form in which words are combined to make grammatical sentences. The child progresses, for example, from saying 'Anna cup' to saying 'Anna please pass me the the red cup on the table'.

*Semantics* refers to the meaning of words and utterances. Phonemes, which are by themselves meaningless, are combined to form *morphemes*, the smallest meaningful units of language. These may be whole words ('dog' in English, 'chien' in French) or grammatical markers, such as '-ed' at the end of a verb to make the past tense. The child learns that words refer to events, people, objects, relationships, in short, that they convey meaning.

Finally *pragmatics* is knowledge about how language is used in different contexts. The young child has already developed some competence in making interpretations of her social setting. She must also learn to adapt her language to the situation in which she finds herself. A toddler may shout out loudly on the bus, 'That man's got a bald head': the sentence shows understanding of phonology, syntax and semantics, but lacks sensitivity to others. This ability to understand social constraints and the needs of the listener grows throughout childhood and helps the child to become more effective as a communicator.

## Sequences in Language Development

There seem to be great similarities in all human societies in the sequence of language development, as children progressively master the rules of sounds (phonology), of words (syntax) and of meaning (semantics), and learn to combine words in ways which are acceptable and understandable within their linguistic community (pragmatics). For example, whether the child speaks pidgin, dialect, patois, Japanese, French or English, he constructs a grammar with rules and strategies. Let us start with the newborn baby to see how this complex process of acquiring language begins.

### The first year

*Sounds: cries, gasps, grunts*   From birth to one month sounds arise merely from the child's physiological state of the moment, but even at this stage they can convey different kinds of information. For example, parents are often sensitive to differences between cries of hunger and cries of pain, and research has shown that babies with physical difficulties have more piercing cries than normal. Psychologists have identified three distinct types of crying:

1   A basic crying pattern, arising usually from hunger which is at first quiet and intermittent but which gradually becomes louder and more rhythmical.
2   An angry cry, which follows the same sequence as the basic crying pattern but which is characterized by differences in the length of the sound and in the length of pauses between sounds.
3   A pain cry which is sudden and loud from the onset; it consists of a long cry followed by a long silence and a series of short gasping sounds.

It would seem that the temporal characteristics of crying patterns have an important communication function which enables babies to pass on vital information about their needs to parents and other caregivers.

Kaye (1984) uses the argument of 'evolved fit' between infant and parent behaviour to explain the universal adult reactions to a child's cry. This 'good fit', he claims, has arisen from mutual natural selection. However, he also acknowledges that there are wide differences across cultures in the *time* which it takes for mothers to respond to their babies' crying. Western mothers can take 5 to 10 minutes before they attend to a crying baby; hunter-gatherer mothers will typically take a few seconds. Again, he indicates the range of responses to crying on the part of parents from 'feeding to murdering the baby' (Kaye, 1984, p.26) as an example of cultural change coming into conflict with biology. We clearly need to look beyond the individual child to the social system of which she is a part, and recognize that infant behaviour and parent behaviour are contingent upon one another.

*Cooing*   From around 1 month babies produce the vowel 'ooo', a sound which seems to grow out of pleasurable social interactions, especially out of the dialogues which occur spontaneously during normal caregiving activities like nappy-changing and bathing. Here is one example of a mother talking to her baby before feed-time; the interaction shows how much meaning the mother imputes to the baby's sounds and gestures.

Baby      (smiles)
Mother   What a good girl. That's a lovely smile.
Baby      Oooo
Mother   There you are. Ready for your dinner now?
Baby      (grunts)
Mother   Yes, I knew you were. Here's your milk.

Videotapes of these apparently one-sided conversations show that the baby will often stare intently at the adult and display signs of enjoyment. Trevarthen (1974) and Snow (1977) argue that early parent–child interactions of this kind serve as a basis for the acquisition of speech later on (plate 10.1), a view developed later by Bruner with his idea of the Language Acquisition Support System (LASS), discussed at the end of the chapter.

PLATE 10.1  *A mother and her 9-month-old baby engage in 'turn-taking' during their 'conversation'; although he cannot talk, he responds to her with speech-like rhythms, gestures and facial expressions*

This is the period of 'shared rhythms and regulations' (Kaye, 1984, p.66) where the parent builds on the biological rhythms of the baby to develop a mutual 'dialogue' which will form the basis for the communication patterns which characterize the adult world.

*Babbling and echolalia*  From 6 to 9 months, the baby produces more vowels and some consonants. She no longer confines herself to cries and cooing sounds. Echolalia is the frequent repetition of sounds – like 'dadadadad' or 'mummummum-mum' – in which the baby engages. She can also shout for attention or scream with rage; she spends time making noises when alone. During this stage infants begin to develop a whole range of behaviours some of which are directed only at familiar people. For example, certain gestures, facial expressions and sounds seem to be reserved only for the mother, or primary caregiver (see chapter 3).

Parents seem to spend a lot of time guessing at the intentions which underlie the baby's actions and sounds. The fact that they often go beyond the actual meaning of the baby's actions (as far as we can determine) plays a crucial part in the parents' integration of the young child into their social system. This is an example of *scaffolding* (see chapter 12). At around 9 months a new pattern appears. The baby produces strings of utterances which have the intonations of language even though they do not yet contain any meaningful words. Some psychologists have called this the 'jargon' period. Certainly before the first words appear the baby shows signs of understanding some of what is said to him. He can obey simple instructions (for example, respond correctly to 'come here' or 'stop it') and identify objects or pictures by pointing. Thus the child is beginning to share the adult's intentions and this becomes characterized by what Kaye (1984, p. 67) calls 'a shared memory'.

Snow's (1977) study of conversations between mothers and babies and the development of *turn-taking* in these exchanges gives insight into this process. If you observe adult conversations, you will find that as one person talks, the other listens and responds with gestures, head-movements, eye-contact etc.; then the listener will take his or her turn to talk while the speaker listens. Snow examined in detail the speech of two mothers to their babies at points between 3 and 18 months of age. She argues that these interactions are best described as *conversational* in nature. In other words, mothers are not only communicating information to their babies, but they are also trying to elicit information *from* them. The process, as in a conversation, is two-way. At the beginning this is of course hard work for the mothers since very young babies are not aware of the need to take turns.

The mothers in Snow's study used a variety of techniques to fill in the conversational gaps – repetition, a high frequency of questions and making a response to any sound, gesture or facial expression on the part of the baby. Furthermore, the fact that the mothers tended not to talk when the babies were actually feeding suggests that the mothers' speech arose from a 'turn-taking model'; when the baby's mouth was full, there was no point in talking. Towards 7 months the frequency of speaker-switching or turn-taking increased dramatically as the mothers became more likely to respond to 'high-quality' vocalizations and the babies played a more active part in responding. The baby's behaviour was consistently seen as intentional and communicative. By 12 months, mother and baby had a repertoire of shared activities some of which lasted several minutes – imitation of sounds, hiding and finding objects, looking in a mirror. The mothers now explained or expanded baby's babbles, as if they were words. Here is an example:

Baby      abaabaa
Mother    Baba. Yes, that's you. What you are.

By 18 months, the mother expected the child not only to take turns but also to reply in an appropriate way:

Mother    (picks up cup of coffee)
Child     Hot
Mother    Hot, Hot! Ooh, it's hot!
Child     Tea.
Mother    No, it's not tea. It's coffee.
Child     Coffee.
Mother    It's lovely. Mmm.
Child     Coffee!
Mother    Coffee's not nice for you. You're having your dinner now.

In fact, almost any word from this toddler was responded to by her mother as part of a conversation. As Snow concludes: 'The way mothers talk to their babies is one reflection of their belief that the babies are capable of reciprocal communication'.

It would seem that adults have been anticipating the baby's first meaningful words long before they actually appear. The importance of parental responsiveness to children's language will be discussed in more detail later in this chapter when we examine the Baby Talk Register (BTR) or, as it used to be called, the 'motherese hypothesis'.

*First words*

It is easy to miss the first words a baby utters since they are often sounds not to be found in the dictionary! However, they can be considered as words if the child uses them consistently in the presence of a particular object or situation. One 12-month-old baby, for example, said 'da' every time he pointed at something which he wanted, and 'oof' whenever he saw animals. These first words have the function of naming or labelling the people and objects in the child's environment. But they also condense meaning. 'Milk' can mean 'I want milk' or 'My milk is spilt'. Even though the child can only say one word at a time, variations in context, intonation and gesture can convey a richer meaning. Single words used in this way are known as *holophrases* since the one word can be interpreted as expressing a whole idea.

It can take three or four months after the emergence of the first words before vocabulary increases very much, but after that the acquisition of new words is rapid. Vocabulary typically grows from around 20 words at 18 months to around 200 words at 21 months. New words are mainly object names ('Daddy', 'car', 'cat') but also include action names ('Look', 'gone'), state names ('red', 'lovely', 'sore') and some 'function' words referring to types of events ('there', 'more', 'bye-bye'). The vast majority of object names refer to objects which the child is able to manipulate (e.g. shoes, toys, foodstuffs etc.) or which are spontaneously dynamic (e.g. people, animals, vehicles etc.) (Nelson 1981).

*Sentences*

At around 18 months the child starts to combine single words into two-word sentences. Of course single word utterances continue to be used for some time, but they gradually give way to more complex word combinations. The child's first sentences are often described as *telegraphic speech*, i.e. speech in which the meaning is highly condensed. 'Ben shoe' means 'That is Ben's shoe' or 'Put on my shoe'. The child may also have a characteristic way of asking for more information – 'Who dat?' – or of making observations – 'Ju ju gone'; 'mummy gone'; 'Sammy gone', often repeated. By this age, children are quite skilled at monitoring the responses of other people even though they have much to learn about the grammatical rules of the language. Wilcox and Webster (1980) found that children from 12 to 24 months of age could adapt their language if they failed to communicate properly. If the message implied by 'Bikkit' did not come through, they could change to 'Give' or 'Want it!'. It seems that children are actively trying to use a rudimentary language system for the purposes of already relatively sophisticated communicative needs.

*From 2 to 3 years*

By 24 to 27 months the child is regularly producing three- and four-word utterances. There are many sentences which are in a strict sense 'ungrammatical' but which reveal that the child is in fact using grammatical rules of syntax. These errors are 'logical errors'. The child will produce sentences like: 'Mouses gone away' in which the normal rule for plurals is extended to exceptions like 'mouse'. These 'errors' are made *because* the child is applying a set of rules. Idiosyncratic words are also common. For example, one child called a chocolate biscuit a 'choskit', a word which he had invented himself. Grammatical rules are applied to such words; for example the plural is formed by adding 's' – choskits.

After the three- and four-word linking stage, there is a rapid increase in grammatical rules. Prepositions and irregular verb endings appear. Now the child can begin to *re-order* the words of a sentence, for example to make questions or negative statements. Thus, 'John is swimming' becomes 'Is John swimming?'

'Wh-' questions are formed, though often in an unorthodox form – 'Where my glove?' or 'Why John is eating?' – in which the 'wh-' form is just tacked on to the beginning of the sentence. The negative is used more, though also in unusual forms initially: 'Not my daddy work'; 'I no want it'; 'Not shut door, no!'. In these sentences, 'no' or 'not' is put in to express negation. Later, the child will re-order the sentence in a more 'adult' way, e.g. 'My daddy not working'.

Children at this age show a great interest in rhymes and will sing songs they have learned, though sometimes in a distorted form. Imaginative play, too, reflects developing language and may also act as a stimulus for further growth (see chapter 6). Conversations acted out in play or commentaries which accompany actions contribute greatly to the expression of ideas and experience.

Weir (1962) studied her child Anthony as he talked himself to sleep each night between the ages of 28 and 30 months (see also chapter 6). The monologues which she recorded took the form of social exchanges even though he was alone. Anthony asked questions, responded to an imaginary companion, invented words and created rhythmical songs. It seems that his language served three purposes. First he seemed to be practising new words and grammar forms which he had recently learned. Secondly, he was playing with sounds for their own sake and creating poetic rhythms. Thirdly, he seemed to be trying to make sense of his world by ordering events in a systematic way.

Here is an example of one of Anthony's monologues (Weir, 1962 pp. 138–9); another was given on p. 175.

That's for he
Mamamama with Daddy
Milk for Daddy
OK
Daddy dance
Daddy dance
Hi Daddy
Only Anthony
Daddy dance
Daddy dance
Daddy give it
Daddy not for Anthony
No.

Weir argues that Anthony is practising language as well as trying to make sense of the non-linguistic world of which he is a part – the sharing of his attachment between Mama and Daddy is one theme, his offer of milk 'for Daddy' another.

Another example shows sound play with no clear meaning at all. You will notice the use of rhyming and alliteration, a skill which will have implications for the future process of learning to read (see p. 255) (Weir, 1962 p. 105):

Bink
Let Bobo bink
Bink ben bink
Blue kink.

Weir notes that Bobo was a doll which had no particular significance for Anthony during the day time. At night, Bobo became an imaginary audience during the pre-sleep monologues.

### From 3 to 4 years

The 3-year-old's speech is largely understandable to adults, even outside the family. Her vocabulary is now around 1,000 words; length and complexity of utterances has increased, and she can carry on reasonable conversations, though these still tend to be rooted in the immediate present.

By 3 years children begin to use complex sentences containing relative clauses. Progress is gradual through the preschool and early school years. Sentences like 'See the car that I got' appear before 'The car that I got is a red one'. The second sentence is more difficult for children since the relative clause 'that I got' is embedded. Children also begin to understand the passive form of the verb. Even this understanding only comes gradually, Brown and Fraser (1963) gave 3-year-olds a comprehension test of the passive form. When asked to point to the picture of 'The boy pushes the girl' or 'The girl pushes the boy', 3-year-olds had no difficulty. But when they were asked to point to the picture where 'the boy is pushed by the girl' (i.e. the passive form of the verb) they indicated the picture where the boy pushed the girl. At this stage 3-year-olds almost always put the subject before the verb and indicate that they have difficulty in understanding the passive form, let alone using it in their own speech.

### The early school years

By the time a child enters school his use of language is very similar to that of an adult. He can understand and express complex sentences and is even able to adjust his speech in a number of ways to suit listeners of different ages with whom he is communicating, as Gelman and Shatz (1977) found when they tape-recorded 4-year-olds introducing younger children and adults to a new toy. The 4-year-olds used longer sentences with more complex grammatical constructions when they spoke to adults than they did to 2-year-olds. They had clearly learned the importance of adjusting their language to suit the level of their listeners. Despite these skills, however, the child is still perfecting various linguistic systems, such as pronouns and auxiliary and irregular verbs. She will still produce logical errors like: 'That one's the bestest'. Some specific aspects of syntax continue to pose difficulties. Carol

Chomsky (1969) tested young children's ability to understand *semantically* complex sentences which resemble simpler forms at the surface level. Take the following example:

John is eager to please.
John is easy to please.

John has different functions in the two sentences. In the first, he is the *subject* – the person doing the pleasing. In the second, he is the *object* – the person being pleased. Carol Chomsky presented children aged from 5 to 9 years with a blindfolded doll and asked, 'Is the doll easy to see or hard to see?' She then asked the children to make the doll hard or easy to see (the opposite to the child's response). The 5-year-olds misinterpreted the question and often took off the blindfold in order to make the doll 'easy to see'. All the 9-year-olds said that the doll was easy to see and hid her in order to make her hard to see. The 6-, 7- and 8-year-olds showed intermediate levels of understanding. Chomsky concluded that children's use of aspects of syntax continues to develop throughout the school years.* In general, however, by the time children enter school their language use is correct, and their basic sentence types are similar to those used by adults.

## The Playful and Humorous Use of Language in the Preschool and Early School Years

We saw earlier how 2-year-old Anthony used language in a playful way in his pre-sleep monologues. The humorous use of language becomes very prominent in the older preschool child. Chukovsky (1963) reports examples of rhyming poems created by 3- and 4-year-old children:

I'm a whale
This is my tail

I'm a flamingo
Look at my wingo.

Preschool children will spontaneously express a whole range of humorous responses, including interactive 'pre-riddles', conventional riddles and joking behaviours. However what they find amusing changes with age and cognitive development. By about age 2, incongruous language and labelling of objects and events appear humorous:

J. aged 3 years while drawing a picture of her mother put hair all round the circle face and then called it 'Mommy porcupine' with shouts of glee.

By about age 4 conceptual incongruity appears humorous:

C. aged 5 said to her mother 'I can play a piano by ear'. Then she banged her ear on the piano keyboard and laughed.

*You might like to return to this experiment after you have read the chapter on Piaget and consider why the 5-year-olds had difficulties with the question in the context which Carol Chomsky created.

By about age 6, children begin to understand and enjoy humour with multiple meanings (McGhee, 1979); however they usually cannot do so when younger, and often laugh inappropriately or make up 'pre-riddles':

> L. aged 3 years: after her older sister told the riddle 'Why does the turtle cross the road? To get to the Shell station', L. insisted on telling a 'riddle' also. Her riddle was 'Why does the dog cross the road? To get to the station' (she laughed at the 'riddle').
> B. aged 5 years: asked 'What's red and white? A newspaper' and laughed at his 'riddle'.
> S. aged 6: asked his uncle and father this riddle, 'Why was 6 afraid of 7? Because 7, 8, 9!' Everyone laughed at this joke.
>
> (Examples adapted from Bergen, 1990)

Other imaginative activities also play a part in language development. Sociodramatic play (chapter 6) is common in the preschool years, and may provide an opportunity for children to practice language and the skills of story-telling.

Scarlett and Wolf (1979) showed that, whereas children under the age of 3 demonstrate play which is mainly carried out by actions, by the time the children are ready to enter infant school at 5, the meaning of their stories is much more likely to be expressed in *linguistic* ways – though the recounting of a narrative, through the dialogue of the characters in the story, and through communications which reveal a growing sense of audience. How does this happen? It seems that the 2- or 3-year-old can only sustain a story when she is in direct contact with concrete props. She cannot create an imaginary world if she loses touch with objects in the real world. With the help of toys, blocks and model people, a kind of story language emerges in play which fuses speech and action. Scarlett and Wolf gave children props – a castle, a dragon, king and queen, prince, animals, toy trees – and observed the stories they told. The changes they observed through the preschool years are illustrated in table 10.1. They concluded that the emergence of the different types of story language and the resolution of problems within the story itself are major advances which preschool children make as they gradually free themselves from concrete props and actions and rely more on the language itself. In addition, the children are becoming aware of the pragmatics of language – the rules which govern the most effective ways of communicating with others.

The child's concept of story develops further with the understanding that the story-teller can stand outside the narrative. Children will now say, 'Let's pretend' or interrupt the flow of a story in order to clarify a point: 'I wonder what the lion will do next? I know! He'll go back through the trees to his home.' They will also show awareness that they have control over the events and characters of their narratives. Stories are now more structured; Applebee (1978) has shown that, in stories told by 5-year-old children, the narrative has a central episode around which the story is built; there is more audience awareness, incidents in the story are linked and they lead to a climax; in addition, there is a hero or heroine who holds the story together. Examples of two stories illustrate the great changes which take place during the preschool years. Here is how Warren, aged $3\frac{1}{2}$, responds to the invitation to tell a story:

> A girl and a boy, a mummy and maybe a daddy. And then a piggy. And then a horse. And maybe a cow and a chair. And food and a car. Maybe a painting.

TABLE 10.1    *Stories told by one child at different ages*

| Age (yr.mth) | Story | Commentary |
|---|---|---|
| 2.10 | C. picks up the dragon prop and makes a hissing noise while having the dragon's mouth touch the king's crown. The dragon touches the queen and goes on to the forest where he touches, while hissing, the prince and all the animals. The story ends when the dragon knocks over the trees and the castle all the while saying 'Bang!' | The meaning of the story depends almost entirely on the actions. The hissing sounds and bangs only embellish what is being enacted |
| 3.3 | C. uses a toy lion, man and house. While putting the man outside the house facing a window, she says, 'Him looks in window'. Next, putting the lion in the house, she says, 'This one's in'. Finally, putting the lion on its side, C. says 'Him lay down' | Language is emerging as an important aspect of the story presentation. The language outlines the basic structure of events in the story. Notice that the action is all in the present |
| 3.8 | C. takes the dragon and says, 'He's gonna killed them'. She then has the dragon fly up to the king and queen and knock them off the turret. She then says, 'And the dragon killed them'. C. then has the dragon knock over all the other props | The narrative refers to past enactments and forecasts future events. This time-split gives the story some independence from the immediate actions |
| 3.11 | C. moves the dragon towards the king and queen. C. says, 'He huffed and puffed and he blew, then the king and queen runned [C. moves king and queen to the forest.] Then he goes to the forest [C. moves the dragon to the forest] and scares the prince so he [the prince] goes home' [C. moves the prince to the castle] | Story language goes beyond the action. This is shown when C. conveys information which is not obvious from the enactment. This gives C. freedom to express feelings and intentions on the part of her characters. Without her narrative, we could not understand why the royal family move between castle and forest |
| 4.00 | C. makes a purple elephant walk up to and stand outside a toy house containing a girl prop. Without moving the props, C. says, 'And he [the elephant] says there's no one there. And he says, 'Knock, knock, knock! Who's there?' Then C. says for the girl prop, 'No-one', 'no one who?' [speaking for the elephant] 'There's not a little girl who lives here' [speaking for the little girl] | C. begins to speak for the characters so the language tells far more than the action. The dramatic speech and the voice intonations (deep for the elephant, squeaky for the girl) carry the meaning of the story event. Without changes in the props, the story moves on |

*Source*: Adapted from Scarlett and Wolf, 1979

Maybe a baby. Maybe a mountain stone. Somebody threw a stone on the bear and the bear's head broke right off. A big stone, this big. And they didn't have glue either. They had to buy some at the store. You can't buy some in the morning. Tomorrow they're gonna buy some. Glue his head on and the baby will look at a book. (Applebee, 1978, pp. 58-9)

There are parallels between this kind of story and the verbal play shown in the pre-sleep monologues of Anthony noted by Weir (1962). The story, Applebee suggests, is a 'heap' of unconnected perceptions with only a rudimentary plot which does not get off the ground.

Tracy, at $5\frac{1}{2}$, produces a more structured story:

There was a boy named Johnny Hong Kong and finally he grew up and went to school and after that all he ever did was sit all day and think. He hardly even went to the bathroom. And he thought every day, and every thought he thought up his head got bigger and bigger. One day it got so big he had to go and live in the attic with trunks and winter clothes. So his mother bought some goldfish and let them live in his head – he swallowed them – and every time he thought, a fish would eat it up until he was even so he never thought again, and he felt much better. (Applebee, 1979, p. 66)

It can be seen that a theme develops in the course of telling this narrative. Stories like these show the development of children's sense that language can capture events and delineate characters with motives and feelings and that to tell a story effectively you need to take account of the needs and interests of your audience. It is an example of the pragmatics of language use, and of the decline of egocentrism (see chapter 11).

### Pre-reading and Pre-writing Skills

By 6 or 7 years of age most children have begun the process of learning to read and write. Obviously some perceptual skills are needed, but other aspects of language development in the preschool years may also be important or necessary if a child is to become a proficient reader and writer a few years later. These are called 'pre-reading skills' and 'pre-writing skills'. As well as the usual skills of perception and discrimination, these include the understanding of reading conventions and the concept of story, and the awareness of rhyming and alliteration. From an early age the child can be helped to develop these skills.

When a child begins to read and write he needs to consider *visual* information as well as the sound and sense of words. During the preschool years the child's perceptual skills can be sharpened by encouraging him to observe specific aspects of his environment.

Training in visual discrimination can be done in an enjoyable way through games; for example, jigsaws, picture-matching games, exercises in grading shapes and objects by size or by colour, or the experience of noticing differences and similarities between objects can give the child useful preparation for discriminating among words and letters. It is also useful if the child understands concepts of 'up', 'down', 'forwards', 'backwards'.

Children's drawing seems to form a useful basis for later skills in reading and writing. In fact, to Vygotsky (1978) the squiggles produced by preschool children are 'the first precursors of future writing'. Gardner (1980) observed that as early as the age of 2 some children have catergorized certain activities as 'writing' and will try to imitate the flow of a script. In fact, he suggests that although they do not understand that particular graphic units correspond to particular sounds, many children do seem to have grasped that some 'marks' represent words. Ferreiro (1978), working in Mexico with 3- to 5-year-olds, found that children have simple hypotheses about writing which change with experience. One sequence made by a girl over a period of time was:

Writing has shape (she drew a circle)
Shapes can be separated (she drew several circles)
Shapes go in lines (she drew several circles in linear arrangement).

Other hypotheses included the idea that a word must have three or more letters before it is 'readable', that 'readable' text should be made up of different letters, and even that the length of a word is related to the size of the object it describes!

Ferreiro argues that concepts like these need to appear before the alphabetic principle of letter – sound relationships can begin to take place. These observations held good with children from both literate and non-literate families. (See figure 10.1 for an example of a child's attempt to make written representations of the singular, 'cat', and the plural, 'cats'.)

FIGURE 10.1 *Writing by Javier, aged 5 years 5 months. Top row, 'Gatito' (little cat); bottom row, 'Gatitos' (three little cats in the picture). He explains as he is writing: 'One little cat' (the first three letters); 'the little cats here' (six letters); 'another cat' (the three remaining letters). You can see that the plural is obtained by repeating the original word as many times as there are cats to be represented (adapted from Ferreiro, 1985)*

### The conventions of reading and the concept of story

We have seen how children invent stories in the preschool years, and many contemporary researchers into reading argue that we need to build on this spontaneous creation of narrative if we are to sustain children's interest in actually reading stories for themselves (Root, 1986).

The experience of being read to by adults and taking part in mutual story-telling during the preschool years creates conditions that facilitate the transition to independent reading by the child (plate 10.2).

PLATE 10.2   *The child's interest in books develops throughout the preschool years; parents and other adults have a key role to play in facilitating pre-reading skills*

Moon (1986) describes a study where children in a nursery class were given a book which showed individual animals, each with a single word caption accompanying it:

Page 1   Elephant
Page 2   Lion
Page 3   Tiger
Page 4   Crocodile
Page 5   Giraffe

The children had no difficulty in 'reading' the book, though none read the words as printed. There were two broad categories of response. Some children described each page:

There is an elephant
This is a lion
This is a tiger

Others created a narrative based on the pictures:

Once upon a time there was an elephant who lived in a forest. One day the elephant went out and met a lion ... etc.

These nursery school children, argued Moon, had brought to the pre-reading task an expectation that the words would be meaningful; already they seemed to have formed concepts 'about how print works and what it is used for' (p. 40).

Moon and Wells (1979) found that a highly significant factor in determining success at reading at the age of 7 was the child's knowledge about conventions of reading at the time he or she entered school (for example, knowing that words are read from left to right). Confirmation comes from a longitudinal study (Tizard et al., 1988) which showed a strong association between the child's ability to identify letters at the preschool stage and reading level at age 7.

Re-telling stories can enable children to become familiar with the convention of written stories, thus providing motivation and a framework for help with reading. Wade (1984) suggests that parents have a crucial part to play in the period before the child begins to read by making stories an enjoyable, shared experience. He describes the role of turn-taking, sharing and empathizing in this experience and argues that these form a natural basis for later learning experiences, including reading. (The basis for this model of reciprocity between adult and child was described on pp. 284–5). Such ideas confirm the view that an activity should be intrinsically interesting if it is to be sustained and enjoyed in the future.

### Rhyming and alliteration

Bryant and Bradley (1985) argue that young children's awareness of rhyming and alliteration indicates a skill in analysing words into their constituent sounds which is essential for learning to read. Young children usually respond with delight to nursery rhymes such as 'Ring a ring o' roses' which contain rhyming ('Roses' and 'posies') and alliteration (the recurrence of the letter 'r' in 'ring a ring o' roses' and 'p' in 'a pocket full of posies') and will often create their own rhymes, as we saw in the rhyming couplets created by 3-year-olds (Chukovsky, 1963) and the alliteration in some of the presleep monologues produced by 2-year-old Anthony (Weir, 1962).

Bryant and Bradley (1985, p. 47–8) quote (from Chukovsky) jingles by 3-year-olds which also demonstrate the children's ability to change words to suit the rules of rhyme:

> The red house
> Made of strouss
> The duckling and the big goose
> Sat on the broken sail-oose.

Bradley and Bryant argue that 'all these children know a great deal about how to spot the common sounds in different words. They show this every time that they produce rhyme'. In the process of becoming familiar with rhymes and alliteration they are also developing an awareness of speech sounds which will have an influence on their later ability to read and spell. Bradley and Bryant hypothesize a direct link between sensitivity to sounds (as shown in responses to rhyming and alliteration games) and competence in learning to read. The backward reader is likely to be a child who has not developed this skill in detecting speech sounds during the preschool years. Some support for this hypothesis is found in the study reported in box 10.1.

### Theories of Language Development

Our brief review of sequences in language development has outlined the remarkable achievements that can be made during the preschool years. The child masters the phonology of her language. She has acquired grammatical morphemes (e.g. pluralizing nouns or adding modifiers such as '-ed' to verbs to indicate past tense) and learned how to produce declarative statements (e.g. 'I have a cup'), 'why-' questions (e.g. 'Where is my cup?' or 'Why is my cup on the floor?') and the negative ('I do not have a cup'). Sentences have become more complex and relative clauses appear ('The cup, which is on the table, is red'). Semantic development has progressed in that children can express quite subtle meanings in their language. Their skill as tellers of stories, jokes and riddles is increasing as they realize the layers of meaning embedded in language. The pragmatics of communication have improved and there is growing awareness that they need to adapt language to particular contexts and adjust speech to suit the requirements of different people.

How does the child achieve this? As yet, there is no one theory which successfully encompasses all aspects of language development. Explanations, as opposed to description, of the course of language development vary in emphasis. For a time, the principles of *learning theory* seemed to provide a logical explanation; while other theorists have suggested that there is a *biological basis* for language acquisition with innate mechanisms underlying it. Still others take the *interactionist approach* and argue that the development of linguisitic competence needs to be studied within its social context. We will consider each of these broad approaches in turn.

*Learning theory*

Skinner (1957) argued that children acquire language because adults *reinforce* correct usage. The baby's random coos and babbling sounds are progressively shaped into words by adults rewarding those which are most 'word-like'. Later the adults reinforce word combinations into sentences. Successive approximations are rewarded or reinforced until finally the child's language is similar to the adult's. Other learning theorists have suggested that *imitation* also plays an important part in language acquisition (Bandura, 1971).

At face value learning theory sounds plausible. The environment must be responsible for differences in learning one language or another, or one particular dialect. How else can we explain why one child speaks Russian and another Japanese, or why 'I were stood there while six' is said by one speaker and 'I was standing there until six o'clock' by another? But the empirical evidence suggests that the process is more complicated. Brown, Cazden and Bellugi (1969) tape-recorded mothers talking to their young children. They found that as far as syntax was concerned there was very little evidence that mothers *shaped* their children's grammar. Statements like, 'Want milk' or 'Ben cup' were accepted. For the most part mothers responded to the *content* of what their children said rather than the grammatical structure. Thus they only corrected sentences which were untrue. For example, if the child said, 'That pig' (indicating a sheep), the mother would say, 'No, that's a sheep'. If the child said 'That sheep' the mother might then say, 'Yes'.

Findings like these gave no support for reinforcement or reward as an explanation for syntactic acquisition. What about the role of imitation? Clearly it must have some effect on language acquisition since children learn the same language and accent as members of their social group. They often learn new words by reproducing the words of other people. Furthermore, in terms of sheer quality of language, it has been found that children whose mothers talk a lot to them have larger vocabularies than those who do not (Clarke-Stewart, 1973).

However, imitation alone could not account for the way the child creates words and sentences he has never encountered before; and studies of young children's *syntax* reveal that children's spontaneous speech is not a direct reflection of the adult speech they hear since they seem to use different rules.

Research into Baby Talk Register, and the recasting of sentences (see box 10.2), indicate that adults and peers do play an important role in children's language learning, but the principles of reinforcement and imitation are not in themselves able to explain how the process occurs.

*Baby Talk Register (BTR) (Motherese)*

Adults talking to young children typically talk differently from they way they speak to adults. The simpler speech style which adults use with young children used to be called 'motherese', but now psychologists consider this term to be sexist and prefer to call it Baby Talk Register (BTR). Gelman and Shatz (1977) found that utterances in BTR are shorter than the sentences spoken to adults, are spoken in a high-pitched voice and emphasize key words. Moreover, the adults adjust the length and complexity of their sentences to fit the level of difficulty with which the child can cope. From two years onwards there is a steady reduction in the adjustments which parents make to their children's speech, but even at five years there are still differences between parents' speech to children and their speech to adults. The process, in which the child is gradually introduced to more complex language, is a form of modelling but is not direct teaching. In fact, the main purpose of verbal exchanges between adult and child is communication, not the teaching of correct grammar. Shatz and Gelman (1973) found that even 4-year-olds had the capacity to modify their language to adapt to their younger listeners. The mother–child dialogues in Snow's (1977) study would also support the finding that the mother closely adapts her language to the child. The *motherese hypothesis* suggested that these special properties of the mother's or caregiver's speech play a causal role in the child's acquisition of language.

Some controversy has arisen over the precise way in which this process might take place. Some argue that the sentences which parents use to children are 'finely-tuned' to the child's needs as a learner (e.g. Furrow et al. 1979); others disagree (e.g. Gleitman et al. 1984). One aspect of BTR is that short sentences are used. A measure of this is the MLU – the 'mean length of utterances'. Basically, this is the number of words (or sometimes morphemes) in a sentence. One study, made in naturalistic settings, of maternal language style (including MLU) and its specific influence on child language (Gleitman et al., 1984) failed to find consistent effects of MLU across the age-range of 18–25 months. By contrast, another study (Furrow et al., 1979) found positive effects on child speech associated with lower MLUs on the part of mothers.

Some of the conflicting results may be due to the different age levels of the children. Sample sizes were small, and clearly more empirical work remains to be done. However, the motherese hypothesis itself has not been very precisely stated. How short should the mother's MLU be, for example? No one has suggested that mothers should speak in one-word utterances! One theory might be that optimal MLU should be longer, but only a bit longer, than child MLU, a process of scaffolding. This would predict a positive correlation between maternal MLU and child MLU, not a negative one as Furrow's team found. The controversy can only be resolved by further painstaking analyses of real conversations carried out in naturalistic settings, preferably on representative samples of children, but so far research into BTR has been disappointing in its results.

Other aspects of BTR may be important as well as MLU. For example, Newport, Gleitman and Gleitman (1977), Furrow et al. (1979), and Wells (1980), have all found that if adults often use sentences in which the auxiliary verb appears at the beginning (e.g. 'Have you finished?') young children seem to learn the use of auxiliaries more quickly. Another aspect of adult speech which has been examined is the recasting of sentences.

*Recasting of sentences*   Nelson et al. (1973) compared the effects of *expanding* children's incomplete sentences (that is, putting them in their complete form) and *recasting* them (that is, keeping the topic the same but giving the child a new way of talking about it). For example:

| Child's incomplete sentence | Adult expansion | Adult recasting |
|---|---|---|
| Doggy eat | Doggy is eating | What is the doggy eating? |

Children whose sentences were recast performed better in a sentence imitation task than children whose sentences were only expanded. Furthermore, the children whose utterances were recast used more complex grammatical forms in their spontaneous speech than those whose sentences were simply expanded. An even more specific effect was found when an experimenter recast children's utterances into questions or into complex verb constructions: each treatment group showed growth in the use of negative 'wh-' questions or complex verb constructions depending on the type of adult intervention. Box 10.2 gives the details of this study.

As the painstaking analysis of real-life conversations between parents and their children has shown, children do not directly imitate adult language and adults do not normally use reinforcement techniques to teach their children to speak. The presence of involved adults and children who use a form of BTR closely adapted to the child's level, and who recast sentences in a form to which the child has access, seems to provide an environment in which language will flourish.

## The biological basis theory

With the publication of Chomsky's (1959) critique of Skinner's account of language development came a new focus for linguistic research – a biological theory of language development. Lenneberg (1967) proposed that there are specific biological mechanisms which underlie language development and that there is a critical period (see chapter 2) for language learning. The lower limit of this critical period was set by motor control of the speech organs and the upper limit was set by the onset of puberty.

It was argued that language has certain universal properties. The sequences of language acquisition are broadly similar in all societies; language occurs in all human cultures, and all languages have certain features in common (Chomsky, 1965; McNeill, 1970). Chomsky proposed that humans have an innate 'language acquisition device' (LAD), without which language could not develop. The LAD is so constructed that it can 'perceive' regularities in the utterances which the child hears. The LAD generates hypotheses about those regularities (for example, that the plural is formed by adding -s to the noun). These are then tested against new utterances and so come to be rejected or accepted as appropriate. The LAD can acquire any language and faced with the utterances of a particular language, it developes a grammar. To do so, however, one must suppose that all human language (and hence too the LAD) must share some common, universal constraints as to the types of language that may occur. This theory, then, encompasses not just specific languages but the general form of human language, and proposes that 'the theory of grammar and its universal constraints describes the internal structure of LAD, and, thus, of children' (McNeill, 1970, p. 151).

What, then, are these universal characteristics of language? First they refer to phonological aspects of language, since every language has consonants, vowels and a syllabic structure. They also apply to syntax. All languages have sentences, noun phrases, verb phrases and a grammatical structure underlying them. Chomsky (1965) argued that there are *deep structures* and *surface structures* in all languages as well as *rules of transformation* which connect the two. The surface structure – that is the ordering of words in a sentence – can vary but still reflect the same deep structure, that is the underlying meaning. For example:

The dog bit the man
The man was bitten by the dog.

These two sentences have the same deep structure in the sense that they are about the same occurrence, but the surface ordering of words is different. The relationship between deep and surface structures is achieved through the rules of transformation. These rules make the connection between sound and meaning in a language. Table 10.2 shows sentences which, by contrast, show differences in deep structure but a similar surface structure.

TABLE 10.2 *Examples of sentences with similar surface structure but a different deep structure*

| Sentence | Paraphrase | Non-paraphrase |
|---|---|---|
| They are buying glasses | — | — |
| They are drinking glasses | They are glasses to use for drinking | They are glasses that drink |
| They are drinking companions | They are companions that drink | They are companions to use for drinking |

*Source*: McNeill, 1970

We understand that, although the three sentences have the same surface structures, different relationships among the words are implied and thus different meanings. Finally, some sentences can have two meanings: for example, 'The peasants are revolting'. It is the rules of transformation which enable us to understand whether the peasants 'are in revolt' or 'revolt us'. As McNeill (1970) writes: 'Every sentence, however simple, has some kind of underlying structure related to some kind of surface structure by means of certain transformations'.

The essence of Chomsky's argument is that the relationship between speech sounds and meaning is not a simple one of association (as the behaviourist school of psychology and the learning theory approach suggested). Instead, we need to distinguish between the surface structure of the language and its deep structure, that is, between the arrangement of words in the utterance and the logical, grammatical relationships among the elements in that utterance. The connection between the two is specified by the transformational procedures or rules of grammar. Different languages use different transformational rules but the universal features are to be found in deep structure. The ability to infer such transformational rules from surface structure utterances was, Chomsky and McNeill both thought, embodied in the LAD.

*Research findings*

Chomsky's theory of transformational, generative grammar provided the impetus for a great deal of research into child language. His own work investigated grammars in which deep structure or 'meaning' had transformational rules applied to it in order to change it to surface or spoken utterance. This he called 'generative grammar' because the application of rules generates actual sentences. Chomsky's research focused on examples of child grammars; he argued that the child was involved in the creative process of generating language, as utterances like 'two sheeps' or 'all done milk' seemed to show.

If this theory is right, then children should possess an initial knowledge of the transformational rules of language, embedded in the LAD. In order to examine this theory, we need to analyse the speech produced by the child at different stages. For example, Menyuk and Bernholz (1969) tested the hypothesis that a holophrase could have a more differentiated meaning than simple labelling. They recorded the speech of a child between 18 and 20 months and found that listeners reached 81 per cent agreement over different uses of a single word, 'door', by this child:

| | | | |
|---|---|---|---|
| Declarative | 'door' | = | 'That's a door!' |
| Question | 'door' | = | 'Is it a door?' |
| Emphatic | 'door' | = | 'Shut the door.' |

The use of a sound spectrograph – a device for analysing the frequency and amplitude characteristics of sound – confirmed these differences. The authors concluded:

> Although the data are extremely limited, there appear to be indications that the child's single utterances are not simply names of objects and events and

that the child uses prosodic features generatively, productively or creatively according to rules to create sentence types. (1969, p. 218)

This seems to support the theory that quite young children are using the transformational (or generative) rules even at the one-word stage. However Menyuk and Bernholz's study only shows that *adults* can use these prosodic features to interpret children's utterances, not that children themselves actually use these features generatively to signal these distinctions.

The picture becomes clearer when children produce sentences. Brown and Fraser (1963), studying telegraphic speech in children, concluded that the utterances could all be classified as grammatical sentences from which certain words had been omitted. For example, 'Mummy hair' only omitted the possessive inflection (Mummy's hair'); 'chair broken' was an acceptable sentence if 'is' was added. Similarly, McNeill (1966) noted other grammatical relationships in the telegraphic speech of young children. Ordering was important in the structure of children's speech even though it was not in direct imitation of the order of adult language. The child might say 'Me want that coat', but phrases like 'Want that coat me' did not appear. Brown and Bellugi (1964) analysed the early speech of two children, Adam and Eve, and noted the over-generalization of inflections described earlier. For example, the use of -s to form plurals was observed as 'deers', 'sheeps', 'knifes', 'tooths'. Use of -ed to form past tense was observed as 'comed', 'doed', 'growed', 'hurted', 'swimmed', 'caughted', drinked'.

The child's innate propensity to use rules, argued Brown and Bellugi, led to 'errors' from which the linguist can infer the grammar being used. The incorrect grammatical constructions made by Adam and Eve did not come from adult models; it seemed that the children had produced them themselves on the basis of simple grammatical 'hypotheses'. This would be consistent with the LAD theory.

Linguistic research has also investigated transformational rules in child language. We will look at one kind of transformation, the question. Menyuk and Bernholz, as we saw, observed the question form in the single-word utterances of an 18-month-old child. Table 10.3 gives examples of an older child using telegraphic speech, and showing the gradual development of the correct form of question. This is one type of transformation; there are many others (e.g. use of the past tense, the negative, the use of plurals) which also seem to demonstrate that the child, from an early age, acts as though she expected language to be governed by a set of rules.

The analysis of children's utterances in terms of deep structure, surface structure and the transformational rules which relate the two (Brown, 1973; Slobin, 1973; McNeill, 1970) has greatly enriched our understanding of early language development. Children's language does seem to be governed by rules and does seem to develop in a systematic way. Children do seem to progress through similar stages in the acquisition of language. However, many contemporary psychologists question the notion of an inborn LAD which operates most efficiently during a critical period between birth and puberty. As we have seen, Chomsky and his colleagues suggest that the child has an innate knowledge of the basic rules and constraints of language, and of her community. But some psychologists have suggested that the rule-bound nature of children's speech arises not so much from an innate LAD as from the child's *prelinguistic knowledge*, since the child, it is argued, already has some ability to categorize her world even before she can communicate with others in language.

TABLE 10.3  *Stages in the development of question forms*

| Ages for Adam | Questions | Commentary |
|---|---|---|
| 28 months | Sit chair?<br>Ball go? | Expressed by intonation only |
| | What that?<br>Where mummy go?<br>What mummy doing? | The child has developed a routine form of the question |
| 38 months | Will you help me?<br>Does the kitty stand up? | The child has developed the use of *auxiliary verbs* |
| | What I did yesterday?<br>Why the Christmas tree going?<br>How he can be a doctor? | For questions expecting the answer yes or no, there is inversion of the verb but not for 'what' and 'why' questions |
| 42 months | Are you thirsty?<br>Why can't we find it? | Inversion of the verb in 'why' questions |
| | I have two turn, huh?<br>We're playing, huh?<br>That's funny, isn't it? | Development of 'tag' questions, e.g. tags on 'huh?' at the end of a sentence |
| | Why can't they put on their swimming suits? | Later, inversion of auxiliary verbs appears too |

*Source*: Adapted from Cazden, 1972

From this perspective, the investigator focuses on the precursors of early language, for example, gestures, facial expression, actions. This approach, which has been called the 'interactionist approach', moves in emphasis away from *grammatical* competence to the study of *understanding* and *communication*. We turn now to an examination of two aspects of this approach – the relationship between language and cognition and the relationship between language and social interaction.

*The interactionist approach*

*Language and cognition*    The interactionist action to child language is often viewed within the framework of Piaget's theory. As we see in chapter 11, Piaget claims that during the first two years of life the child's intellectual skills do not rely on symbols, such as words and images, but are rooted in sensori-motor experiences, such as seeing, hearing and touching. Symbolic actions do not appear until the end of the sensori-motor period. Although interactionists would accept that children develop a system of rules, they would not accept that the rules grow out of an innate LAD but rather from a much wider cognitive system. Children talk alike because they share many similar experiences and their language is facilitated by the sensori-motor schemas of early infancy. This hypothesis – called the 'cognition hypothesis' (Cromer, 1974) – argues that: (i) we understand and use particular linguistic structures only when our cognitive abilities enable us to do so (for example, the child can gesture that he wants an apple before he uses the holophrase 'Apple'); (ii) even once our cognitive abilities allow us to grasp an idea, we may say it in a less complex way because we have not yet acquired the grammatical rule for expressing it freely. Thus the child may not be able to say 'Have you looked?' but he can express the same meaning in the less complex sentence 'Did you look yet?'

What Piagetians are suggesting therefore is that children form schemas to explain events in their lives and *then* talk about them. Language development *reflects* the stages of cognitive development through which the child is progressing. They agree with other theorists that, as children develop intellectually, they produce more elaborate sentences which are expanded by the adults and older children who are close to them. Out of these interactions arise even more sophisticated utterances which in turn prompt a more complex response from others in the child's environment. This is a reciprocal relationship, in which the child plays an active part. However, the child is not applying an innate LAD to the talk which he hears. Instead, his understanding arises out of his existing knowledge of the world.

Many observations support this interactionist approach. In chapter 11, we examine Piaget's work on the object concept which shows that by the end of the first year the child understands that objects exist independently of herself, whether in her sight or not. In Piaget's view, the child needs to have this sense of object performance before she can begin to understand that words can represent things. Observations of first words show that children usually focus on familiar objects or actions. They are using words to express aspects of their environment which they already understand and there seem to be regularities in the ways in which children combine their early one- and two-word utterances with gestures or with knowledge of the context in which the word occurs. From this perspective, the child's early combinations of words are based on an existing understanding of the relationships among objects, people and events in the real world. If the child did not have this understanding the first words would be like random unconnected lists. In fact, as we have seen, the child's one- and two-word utterances are combined in a rule-bound way.

There is some empirical evidence to support this argument. Brown noticed that if he considered the four concepts Agent, Action, Object and Location then the *actual* number of pairings in the child's language was fewer than the *possible* number of pairings. There are 12 *possible* pairings of the four concepts (e.g. Agent–Action, Action–Agent, Action–Object, Object–Action etc.), but Brown observed that children at the two-word stage used only six such combinations

| | |
|---|---|
| Agent–Action | 'Daddy run' |
| Action–Object | 'Eat biscuit' |
| Agent–Object | 'Mummy sock' ( = Mummy is putting on her sock) |
| Action–Location | 'Put table' |
| Agent–Location | 'Baby table' |
| Object–Location | 'Cup table' |

Furthermore, they all kept to the order in the following structure:

Agent–Action–Object–Location

Thus the child would not say 'biscuit eat' (which would be Object–Action) but preferred to put this sentence in the form that the Action preceded the Object (Brown, 1973). The order of the two-word utterances provided evidence for an underlying structure in the child's understanding of events in her world:

Some psychologists have argued that concepts like Agent, Action, Object, Location have all been grasped during the sensori-motor period and suggested that these familiar concepts were the ones which children first chose to express in language. De Villiers and De Villiers (1979) note that older children rarely use hypothetical sentences like 'If it had rained, we would have been soaked' before they are 4 or 5. Is this because the grammatical construction is complex or because the statement requires the ability to shift from the past to a hypothetical future? In fact, in Russian this particular grammatical structure is much simpler, yet children in Russia do not use hypothetical statements until they are the same age as English-speaking children. It would seem that the use of hypothetical statements depends on the child's grasp of the concept rather than the grammatical complexity of the sentences. In short, children need to have congnitive skills as well as linguistic skills if they are to use their language properly.

This cognitive approach to children's language development was very influential in the 1970s, until some psychologists began to suggest that it gave a rather narrow view of the child. It ignored, for example, the child's social skills and the effect of the social environment on a child's capacity to learn. It is this shift of emphasis towards the child as communicator in a social world that we will consider next.

*Language and social interaction*   Piaget's theory emphasizes the child's knowledge of the world as a precursor of language and demonstrates the role of language in representing objects and events in the child's physical world. A second interactionist approach places greater emphasis on the child's early experiences of communicating and interacting *socially* with the people in his surroundings; the baby masters a social world on to which he later 'maps' language.

But how does this happen? One powerful factor according to this theory is the adults' tendency to give meaning to the sounds and utterances of infants. As we have seen (Snow, 1977), observations of parents interacting with very young babies indicate that burps, gurgles and grunts are interpreted as expressions of intention and feeling on the part of the baby: 'You really enjoyed that, didn't you?', or 'Will you please make up your mind?' Many infants experience extensive verbal exchanges with their mothers, during which the mother actively interprets, comments upon, extends, repeats and sometimes mis-interprets what the child has said, in a 'conversational' format.

Another important development, according to this viewpoint, is the development of joint attention, and mutual understanding of gestures. As early as 6 months, infants will follow the mother's gaze to see what she is looking at (Butterworth, 1987); and by 9 or 10 months, they will start pointing at objects in a communicative way. It is communicative because the infant clearly wants to direct the mother's attention to the object, and is not satisfied until this is achieved. Nonverbally, it is the equivalent of saying 'look at this!' A good response of the adult is to name the object or say something about it.

By this age, too, reaching for objects changes and becomes more social. At 6 months, a baby reaching is really trying to get the object herself. By 9 months, she may make a more ritualized gesture of reaching, and look at the mother. This is the nonverbal equivalent of 'give me this!'. At about this age infants will show or give objects to a parent or adult, as well.

The crucial development at this age, shortly before first words appear, is *joint attention*; both adult and infant are jointly giving their attention to a particular object, and are communicating about this by shared understanding of gestures such as looking, pointing, reaching and showing. The adult often names the object in these situations; and one can see that it is a relatively small step for the infant to start naming objects also. In this view, joint attention, together with the experience of turn-making or 'conversational' formats of interaction, are crucial precursors of early language development.

Ryan (1974) argues that the psycholinguist's emphasis on grammar obscures the function which these interactions have in preparing the infant for language. Infants and adults *together* create a range of *formats*, that is habitual exchanges which form the basis for interpreting what both parent and child mean. In the course of these dialogues or pre-speech 'conversations', the child is developing skills which are 'as essential to speaking and understanding language as the mastery of grammar is supposed to be'. Furthermore, the skills are extended by ritualized games such as peek-a-boo, and joint picture book reading.

Bruner (1983) calls these interactive precursors and later supports for language the Language Acquisition Support System (LASS). These social formats or rituals, and experience of social reciprocity are important parts of the environmental context which structures the child's understanding of the world and hence her early language utterances. The distinctions between subject and object, or between nouns and verbs, for example, may be facilitated in this way. In fact, Bruner argues, adult conversation would be impossible if this prior shared meaning and reciprocity between speakers had not been established.

This socio-cognitive perspective traces the child's competence in language back to her experience as a communicator in the pre-verbal stage – a time when the responsiveness of adults is a key factor. It considers both social *and* cognitive functioning, with particular reference to the adult's sensitivity to the child's early capacity to perceive and understand experiences. Where infants do not experience this reciprocity and shared social interaction, or where the parents fail to give feedback to the baby's early vocalizations and gestures (as happens with children reared in restricted environments), then later linguistic development is likely to suffer.

Some reservations about this interpretation of child language development come from work with blind children, who learn to speak without mutual eye-gaze and peek-a-boo games. Furthermore, there seem to be cultural differences in the types of pre–linguistic interactions that occur between adults and babies. For example, the Kaluli children of New Guinea develop language despite the fact that mothers and babies do not appear to engage in mutal eye-contact as is customary in Western society (Schieffelin and Ochs, 1983).

However, joint attention seems to develop whatever the means of achieving it may be. Blind babies obviously do not 'look', but they learn how to direct their parents' attention and may even use the work 'look'. Transcripts of Kaluli children and parents talking indicate that they also develop mutual points of focus. It could be that interactions between adults and babies do not occur according to one particular 'biologically designed choreography' (Schieffelin and Ochs, 1983, p. 127).

The child's language, it would seem, is rooted in earlier social experiences out of which arise both the desire to communicate with other people, and the opportunity to develop increasingly complex grammatical structures which will enable the child to communicate more effectively.

## Further reading

A readable introduction to basic concepts in child language development is P. De Villiers and J. De Villiers 1979: *Early language*. London: Fontana. Another useful book is C. Garvey 1984: *Children's Talk*. London: Fontana. This shows how the study of children's talk gives us rich insights into ways in which they understand their social world. Garvey discusses turn-taking in conversation and shows how young children learn to adapt their speech to different social contexts. An up-to-date review is A. Garton and C. Pratt 1989: *Learning to be Literate: the Development of Spoken and Written Language*. Oxford: Basil Blackwell.

A clear introduction to Chomsky's ideas is provided by J. Lyons 1985: *Chomsky*. London: Fontana.

Amongst more advanced books, C. G. Wells 1981: *Learning Through Interaction: the Study of Language Development*. New York: Cambridge University Press, is a collection of papers analysing the relationship between language structure and language use. Wells is also author of 1985: *Language Development in the Preschool Years*. Cambridge: Cambridge University Press. For more on theories, see R. Stevenson 1988: *Models of Language Development*. Milton Keynes: Open University Press.

On the subject of story development, A. N. Applebee 1978: *The Child's Concept of Story*. Chicago: University of Chicago Press, argues that through hearing and telling stories children are enabled to understand more deeply the people and events in their lives. He examines language use, the development of the concept of story and responses to literature in young children.

D. Wood 1988: *How Children Think and Learn*. Oxford: Basil Blackwell (chapter 4, 'Language and learning') describes competing views on the relationship between language, learning and educational achievement.

## Discussion points

1   To what extent do adults interpret babies' sounds and gestures as if they were part of a meaningful dialogue?

2   What is the developmental importance of pre-linguistic communication between adult and baby?

3   Discuss how research findings on BTR can help parents to talk more effectively with their young children.

4   How important is it to take semantic (or meaning) aspects into account when examining the language of young children?

5   Does the study of child 'grammar' in the preschool years help us to understand the process through which children acquire language?

## Practical exercises

1   Tape-record an adult talking to a 2- or 3-year-old child. Note any examples of the following:

> The child's imitation of adult speech. Grammatical but 'logical' errors on the part of the child.
> Adult corrections of child grammar.
> Expansions or re-castings by the adult.

> How do your findings relate to the theories of language development discussed in the chapter?

2   Tape-record a parent talking to a toddler. Next, tape-record the same adult talking to an adult friend. Note differences in the forms of speech which the adult uses in the two conversations. Is the parent adopting BTR when talking to the child? Are there differences in intonation and gesture? How frequent are repetitions and elaborations?

3   Ask a 4-year-old to introduce a new toy to (a) a 2-year-old child and (b) an adult. Note differences in:

> Length of sentences.
> Complexity of sentences
> Style of introducing the topic.

Relate your findings to those of Gelman and Shatz (1977).

# Box 10.1

## Categorizing sounds and learning to read: a causal connection

The investigators in this study wished to test the hypothesis that the experience a child has with categorizing sounds, as in rhyming and alliteration, has a considerable effect on later success in learning to read and spell. To do this, they used two methods – a large-scale correlational study, and a small scale experimental study.

The correlational study started with 118 4-year-olds and 285 5-year-olds. None could yet read. The children were tested on their ability to categorize sounds, by detecting the odd word out, i.e. the one that did not share a common sound, in a series of words. This common sound could be at the end of the word (e.g. bun *hut* gun sun), the middle (e.g. *hug* pig, dig, wig) or the beginning (bud bun bus *rug*). Where it came at the end or the middle of the word, the task was to spot words which *rhymed*. Where it came at the beginning of the word, the children's awareness of *alliteration* was tested.

In addition, each child was given a test of verbal intelligence (the English Picture Vocabulary Test, or EPVT), and a memory test.

Four years later, when the children were 8 or 9 years old, Bradley and Bryant gave them standarized tests of reading and spelling. They also tested their IQ, using the WISC-R, and their mathematical ability on a standarized test. (By this time, 368 of the original 403 children remained in the project sample.)

BOX TABLE 10.1.1 *Correlations between initial sound categorization, EPVT and memory scores, and final reading and spelling levels*

| | | Initial scores | | | | | |
|---|---|---|---|---|---|---|---|
| | | Sound categorization | | EPVT | | Memory | |
| | Age (yr) | 4 | 5 | 4 | 5 | 4 | 5 |
| Final reading score (Schonell test) | | 0.57 | 0.44 | 0.52 | 0.39 | 0.40 | 0.22 |
| Final spelling score (Schonell test) | | 0.48 | 0.44 | 0.33 | 0.31 | 0.33 | 0.22 |

*Source*: Bradley and Bryant, 1983

Based on material in L. Bradley and P. E. Bryant 1983: *Nature*, 301, 419–21.

There were high correlations between the intial sound categorization scores (at ages 4–5 years) and the children's reading and spelling scores four years later (box table 10.1.1). This in itself does not prove the hypothesis that the ability to categorize sounds has a causal connection with reading success. Some third factor might lie behind both abilities. For example, general intelligence, or perhaps memory for words, might help in both. However, as can be seen in box table 10.1.1, the correlations of reading and spelling scores with sound categorization are a bit higher than with the EPVT or memory scores. This means that while intelligence and memory may explain some of the association between sound categorization and reading and spelling, it is unlikely that they can explain all of it.

BOX PLATE 9.1.1 *Children receiving training in sound categorization skills: (a) selecting pictures with names which have common sounds (e.g. bat, mat, hat); (b) identifying sounds with the aid of plastic letters*

To provide more definite evidence for the causal relationship which this suggested, the investigators carried out a training study with an experimental design (a field experiment, see chapter 1), using 65 children from the larger sample. They were selected from those whose orginal scores on sound categorization were at least two standard deviations below the mean.

Two experimental groups received training in sound categorization skills for 40 individual sessions over two years. In Group 1 ($n = 13$) coloured pictures of familiar objects were used to teach the children that the same word could share common beginning (hen, hat), common middle (hen, pet) and common end (hen, man) sounds with other words. This training experience was purely concerned with increasing awareness of rhyming and alliteration. For Group 2 ($n = 13$), in addition to the rhyming and alliteration training, the children were shown plastic letters and taught how to identify the sounds which the names of the pictures had in common with particular letters ('c' for 'cat' and 'cup'). The relationship between common sounds and letters of the alphabet which represented them was made clear (plate 10.1.1).

Two control groups were also used. Group 3 ($n = 26$) were taught over the same period of time to categorize the same pictures in a *conceptual* way, (e.g. hen and bat are animals: hen and pig are farm animals) but received no tuition in sound categorization. Group 4 ($n = 13$) received no training at all. All four groups were matched for age, initial EPVT scores and initial scores on sound categorization. The results are shown in box table 10.1.2. Group 1, the experimental group which had been trained on sound categorization only, was ahead of Group 3 (the group trained to categorize conceptually) by 3–4 months in reading and spelling levels. The second experimental group, Group 2, which had been trained on sound categorization and alphabetic letters as well, performed best of all in reading and spelling. The authors conclude that not only does training in sound categorization have an influence on reading and spelling, but that if it is combined with alphabetic teaching, it will be even more effective. They also argue that the effect is specific to reading and spelling since the differences among the four groups in scores in the mathematics test were considerably smaller and not statistically significant.

The drawbacks of this training study are that the numbers in the experimental groups are small, and some differences are not statistically significant (for example, the scores for Group 1 in themselves do not differ significantly from those in Group 3). Also, as the investigators point out, we do not know how well such experimental results would

BOX TABLE 10.1.2   *Mean final reading, spelling and mathematics levels, and intelligence test scores, in groups from the training study*

|  | Experimental groups | | Control groups | | Significance of group differences |
|---|---|---|---|---|---|
|  | 1 | 2 | 3 | 4 |  |
| Reading age in months (Schonell test) | 92.2 | 97.0 | 88.5 | 84.5 | $p<0.01$ |
| Spelling age in months (Schonell test) | 86.0 | 98.8 | 81.8 | 75.2 | $p<0.001$ |
| Mathematics score | 91.3 | 91.1 | 88.0 | 84.1 | n.s. |
| Final IQ (WISC-R) | 97.2 | 101.2 | 103.0 | 100.2 | n.s. |

*Source*: Adapted from Bradley and Bryant, 1983

generalize to a wider spectrum of children in real-life teaching conditions. This is where the strength of combining two methods comes in. The original correlational study strongly suggests that the relationship between sound categorization skills and later reading and spelling abilities is an ecologically valid one. Taken together, these results provide strong evidence for a moderate degree of causal influence along the lines the investigators hypothesized. The educational implications are considered further in P. Bryant and L. Bradley 1985: *Children's Reading Problems*. Oxford: Basil Blackwell. In view of the large number of children who do experience reading difficulties, this study offers practical guidelines for identifying specific problem areas and intervening to overcome them.

# Box 10.2

# Facilitating children's syntax development

Nelson had already shown (Nelson et al., 1973) that the recasting of children's incomplete sentences by adults had a positive effect both on performance on a sentence-imitation task, and complexity of grammar use in spontaneous speech. In this experiment he aimed to discover whether these effects were specific. Would children whose utterances were recast into complex questions show improvement in the use of question forms? Would children whose utterances were recast into sentences that contained complex verbs show greater use of verbs? To answer these questions he devised an experimental intervention study.

His sample was 12 children (six boys and six girls), aged 28–29 months, who all lacked two categories of syntactic structures in their spontaneous speech. These were complex questions and complex verbs of the type given:

*Complex questions*

| | | |
|---|---|---|
| 1 | Tag questions | For example 'I changed them round, didn't I?' where 'didn't I?' is tagged on to the end of a statement. |
| 2 | 'Wh-' negative questions | Negative questions beginning with 'what', 'why', 'where', 'who' etc., e.g. 'Why can't I go?' |
| 3 | Other negative questions | For example, 'Doesn't it hurt?' or 'It won't fit?'. |

*Complex verbs*

| | | |
|---|---|---|
| 1 | Single verbs in future or conditional tense | For example, 'He will help me' or 'He would help me': |
| 2 | Sentences in which two verbs were used | For example, 'He will run and jump' or 'The bear ate the girls who visited'. |

Two one-hour sessions with each child were taped to determine initial language levels. Assignment of children in groups was based on mean length of utterance (MLU) in words. Three boys and three girls were assigned to an intervention schedule focused on complex questions; the remaining six children were assigned to receive an intervention designed to facilitate the use of complex verbs. Each group had an average MLU of 3.69 words per utterance (range 3.09–4.29). Both groups were closely comparable in terms of the presence

Based on material in K. Nelson 1977: *Developmental Psychology*, 13, 101–7.

or absence of complex verbs and complex questions in their spontaneous speech during these two sessions.

Five one-hour sessions of intervention were scheduled for each child. Three women were the experimenters, each one working with four children (two assigned to question intervention and two to verb intervention).

In question intervention sessions the experimenter frequently recast the child's sentences in the form of tag or negative questions. For example, when one child said, 'You can't get in', the researcher replied, 'No, I can't get in, can I?' If recastings did not come readily, the experimenter constructed new examples. When one child said, 'And you're a girl', the experimenter replied, 'Right! And aren't you a little girl?'

Similarly in verb intervention sessions both recastings and new constructions were used. If the child said, 'Where it go?', the adult replied, 'It will go there'. When one child said, 'I got it, I reached it', the adult said, 'You got under the bed and reached it'.

The children's utterances during the fourth and fifth sessions (the last two intervention sessions) were recorded. Each child's transcript was scored for presence or absence of sentences containing complex questions or complex verbs, using the measures shown in box table 10.2.1. Analysis of the data revealed clear-cut effects of the interventions. Complex questions which had been lacking before intervention were used by all six children in the question intervention group: only one of the children in this group (subject 6) also showed use of complex verbs. The opposite pattern held for the acquisition of new verb forms. All the children in the verb intervention group used complex verbs which they had not

BOX TABLE 10.2.1   *Type of sentence structure used by each participant (numbered) after intervention but not prior to intervention*

| Sentence type | Question intervention | | | | | | Verb intervention | | | | | |
|---|---|---|---|---|---|---|---|---|---|---|---|---|
| | 1 | 2 | 3 | 4 | 5 | 6 | 1 | 2 | 3 | 4 | 5 | 6 |
| Tag questions | + | | | + | + | + | | | | | | + |
| 'Wh–' negative questions | | | + | | | | | | | | | |
| Other negative questions | | + | | | | | | | | | | |
| Future tense (one verb) | | | | | | + | | | | + | | |
| Conditional tense (one verb) | | | | | | + | + | + | | | | + |
| Future tense (two verbs) | | | | | | | + | + | | | | + |
| Conditional tense (two verbs) | | | | | | | + | | | | | |
| Past tense (two verbs) | | | | | | + | | + | + | | | + |

Sign tests show the results to be significant ($p<0.01$) for both question and verb intervention. MLU for both groups was not affected. Examples of sentences with complex questions or verb structures which appeared after intervention are given in the text.

expressed before intervention; only one (subject 6) also used new complex questions. Sign tests showed the results to be significant for both question and verb intervention. MLU was not affected for either group. Examples of sentences with complex questions or verb structures which appeared after intervention were:

*Newly acquired question forms*

Tag       'He's shaking, isn't he?
          'It does fit, doesn't it?'
          'Look, I changed them round, didn't I?'

Negative   'You don't see it?'
           'No more, OK?'
           'Can't it go through?'

*Newly acquired verb forms*

One-verb   'I could take mine.'
           'He'll bite my finger.'
           'I could make a ball.'

Two-verb   'He fell and he broke.'
           'And mummy didn't do it, I did it.'
           'Member [remember] that ugly dinosaur, he would just bite.'
           'I will get up, hide it.'

Nelson concluded that this experiment increases our understanding of how children get information from adults about syntax. In comparing the experimenters' recasting with normal parental responses, he noted that in real life adults do use negative and tag questions, and complex verbs when they talk to their children, but they do not use them frequently. So why did recastings of children's sentences have the effect shown by this experiment?

Nelson suggested that the experimental recasting probably drew the child's attention to the new forms. The experience of hearing complex questions and verbs was not a wholly new one to the child but the researchers, by reworking the child's own sentences, pointed attention to a more complex form which was close to the child's existing language use and which made immediate sense to the child. The experimenter's response to 'Donkey ran' of 'The donkey did run, didn't he?' was more complex but also entirely appropriate in a playful, conversational content. The child was thus able to make a direct comparison between her own utterances and the sentence structure of the adult's reply. The introduction of new grammatical forms which are still closely tied to the child's language use thus seems to be one way of extending language development.

# 11

# Cognition: Piaget's Theory

Jean Piaget (1896–1980) was born in Neuchâtel, Switzerland. At an early age he showed a keen interest in observing animals in their natural environment. At the age of 10 he published his first article, a description of an albino sparrow which he had observed in the park; before he was 18, journals had accepted several of his papers on the subject of molluscs. During his adolescent years a second major intellectual interest grew from his study of philosophy, in particular the branch of philosophy concerned with knowledge – 'epistemology'. His undergraduate studies, however, were in the field of biology and his doctoral dissertation was on molluscs.

He then worked for a period at Bleuler's psychiatric clinic in Zurich where he became interested in psychoanalysis. As a result, he went to the Sorbonne University in Paris in 1919 to study clinical psychology. Here he could also pursue his continuing interest in epistemology. While in Paris, he worked at the Binet Laboratory with Theodore Simon on the standardization of intelligence tests (see chapter 13). Although his task was to examine children's correct responses to test items, Piaget became much more interested in the mistakes the children made and in the mental processes they brought to bear on these test items. Binet was a French psychologist who had pioneered studies of children's thinking, and his method of observing children in their natural settings was one which Piaget followed himself when he left the Binet Laboratory to begin his own research programme.

The discipline of psychology seemed to Piaget to offer the opportunity for forging links between epistemology and biology. By integrating the disciplines of psychology, biology and epistemology, Piaget aimed to develop a scientific approach to the understanding of knowledge – the nature of knowledge and the ways in which the individual acquires knowledge. Although the *quantitative* methods of the French intelligence testers did not appeal to Piaget, he was strongly influenced by the developmental work of Binet. As a result, he integrated his experiences of psychiatric work in Bleuler's clinic with the questioning and observational strategies which he had learned from Binet. Out of this fusion emerged the 'clinical interview' – an open-ended, conversational technique for eliciting children's thinking processes. His interest was in the child's own judgements and explanations. He was not testing a particular hypothesis, but rather looking for an explanation of how the child comes to understand his or her world. The method is not easy, and Piaget's researchers were trained for a year before they

PLATE 11.1 *Jean Piaget in 1936 (courtesy of the Archives J. J. Rousseau)*

actually collected data. They learned the art of asking the right questions and testing the truth of what the children said.

Piaget's life was devoted to the search for the mechanisms of biological adaptation on the one hand, and the analysis of logical thought on the other. He wrote more than 50 books and hundreds of articles, revising many of his early ideas in later life. In essence Piaget's theory is concerned with the human need to discover and to acquire deeper knowledge and understanding. Piaget's prolific output of ideas suggests that he was constantly constructing and reconstructing his theoretical system, but this, as we shall see, was quite consistent with his philosophy of knowledge. His major theme is that adaptation is based on the achievement of a successful equilibrium in the interactions between the organism and the environment. This concept grew out of his early interest in biology, and near the end of his life he wrote in the foreword to the anthology of his writings by Gruber and Vonèche (1977, p. xi) that he had always viewed the mechanisms of biological adaptation as the source for *epistemology*, that is, for knowledge itself.

In Piaget's view, the individual is always in the process of reconstrucing reality: the only way in which we come to have knowledge of our world is through a process of continual construction of it. There is no point at which we can say 'I have arrived. I *know*'; there is always something else ahead:

> In epistemology ... I am happy with what I have been able to glimpse, although very conscious of the gaps to be filled. (Piaget, 1977, p. xi)

In this chapter we describe the model of cognitive structure developed by Piaget. We will also take notice of modifications and re-interpretations which subsequent researchers have made to Piaget's ideas. Although many aspects of Piaget's theory are now questioned, no one denies the valuable contribution he made to our understanding of the thinking processes of both children and adults.

Piaget argued that in order to understand how children think we have to look at the qualitative development of their ability to solve problems. Let us look at an example from one of Piaget's dialogues with a 7-year-old:

| Adult | Does the moon move or not? |
| Child | When we go, it goes. |
| Adult | What makes it move? |
| Child | We do. |
| Adult | How? |
| Child | When we walk. It goes by itself. |

(Piaget, 1929, pp. 146–7)

On the basis of many observations such as these, Piaget described a period during childhood which was characterized by *egocentrism*. Because the moon appears to move with the child, she concludes that it does indeed do so. But later, with the growth of logic, she makes a shift from her own egocentric perspective and learns to distinguish what she *sees* from what she *knows*. Gruber and Vonèche (1977, p. xix) quote an observation by Anne Roe of a child – later to become a scientist – as he tackled this problem. He sent his little brother down to the garden to find out what each of them saw when one was moving and the other standing still. What was self-evident to the younger child – that the moon moved with him – was seen by the older boy as an inconsistency which could be solved by logic.

Another example is adapted from Piaget's famous 'conservation' experiments, which are concerned with how children come to realize that, for example, the *amount* of liquid is conserved despite changes in the shape of the container holding it. John, aged 4, and Mary, aged 7, are given a problem. Two containers, A and B, are of equal capacity but A is wide and B is narrow. A is filled to a certain height and the children are each asked separately to pour the same quantity of liquid into B. In spite of the striking difference in the proportions of the two containers, John cannot grasp

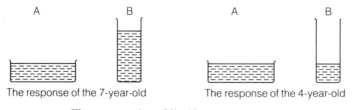

FIGURE 11.1   *The conservation of liquid*

that the smaller diameter of B requires a higher level of liquid. To Mary, John's response is incredibly stupid: of course you have to add more to B (figure 11.1).

From Piaget's perspective both responses are revealing. John cannot 'see' that A and B are not equal, since he is using a qualitatively different kind of reasoning not yet having the mental operations (or schemas) that will enable him to understand conservation. Mary finds it difficult to understand why John cannot see his mistake.

Piaget proposed that the essence of knowledge is activity. This may refer to the baby directly manipulating objects and so learning about their properties; it may refer to the child rearranging pebbles in different ways and so learning about the conservation of numbers (see p. 330); it may refer to the adolescent forming hypotheses in order to solve a scientific problem. In all these examples, the child is learning through action, whether physical (e.g. exploring a wooden brick) or mental (e.g. thinking of different outcomes and what they mean). This has been an important idea in forming the child centred approach to education (see p. 340). However, Piaget did not advise that, in order to learn, children only need to manipulate objects; they also need to manipulate ideas.

## Underlying Assumptions: Structure and Organization

Using observations, dialogues and small-scale experiments such as those just described, Piaget suggested that children progress through a series of stages in their thinking each of which corresponds to broad changes in the structure or logic of their intelligence (see table 11.1). These stages occur in a fixed order – sensori-motor, pre-operational, concrete operational and formal operational.

Piaget's structures are sets of mental operations which can be applied to objects, beliefs, ideas or anything in the child's world. Such a mental operation is called a schema (plural, schemas or schemata). Mary, in the example above, had developed a set of operations which enabled her to understand the conservation of liquid quantity. The schemas are seen as evolving structures, i.e. structures which grow and *change* from one stage to the next. We will look at each stage in detail in the next section, but before we do so, we need to look at Piaget's concepts of the unchanging (or 'invariant', to use his term) aspects of thought, that is those broad characteristics of intelligent activity which remain the same *at all ages*. These are the *organization* of schemas and their *adaptation* through assimilation and accommodation.

TABLE 11.1  *The stages of intellectual development according to Piaget*

| Stage | Age (yr) | Characteristics |
|---|---|---|
| Sensori-motor | 0–2 | The baby knows about the world through actions and sensory information. She learns to differentiate herself from the environment; the child begins to understand causality in time and space; internal mental representations emerge as shown in imaginative play and symbolic thought |
| Pre-operational | 2–7 | The further development of the symbolic function, e.g. through the symbolic use of language and intuitive problem-solving; the child begins to understand about classification of objects but thinking is still characterized by egocentrism, irreversibility, centration. By the end of this stage social perspective-taking skills are emerging and the child is beginning to grasp conservation of number |
| Concrete operational | 7–12 | The child understands conservation of mass, length, weight and volume; she can more easily take the perspective of others; can classify and order, as well as organize objects into series. The child is still tied to the immediate, concrete experience but within these limitations can perform logical mental operations |
| Formal operational | 12 | Abstract reasoning begins. The child can now manipulate ideas in her mind as well as actual objects and people; she can speculate about the possible; she is now able to reason deductively, to formulate and test hypotheses |

*Organization* to Piaget means the inborn capacity to coordinate existing cognitive structures, or schemas, and combine them into more complex systems. For example, the baby of 3 months has learned to combine looking and grasping with the earlier reflex of sucking. She can do all three together when feeding, an ability which the newborn baby did not have. Or at 2 years, Ben has learned to climb downstairs, to carry objects without dropping them and to open doors. He combines all three operations in order to deliver the newspaper to his grandmother in the basement flat. Each separate operation combines into a new action which is more complex than the sum of the parts.

Organization also grows in complexity as the schemas become more elaborated. Piaget noted his son, Laurent, at 6 months as he developed a particular *action schema*, that of striking a hanging object. What had been initially a random movement became quite deliberate. Laurent now possessed the mental structure which guided the action involved in hitting a toy. He also learned to accommodate his actions to the toy's weight, size, shape and distance from him.

This leads us to the other invariant function identified by Piaget – *adaptation*. By adaptation he means the striving of the organism for balance (or equilibrium) with the environment; this is achieved through the complementary processes of *assimilation and accommodation*.

Through *assimilation* the child 'takes in' a new experience and fits it into an existing schema. For example, a child may have learnt the words 'dog' and 'car'. For a while all animals are called 'dogs' or all four-wheeled vehicles 'cars'. This process is balanced by *accommodation*, in which the child adjusts an existing schema to fit in with the nature of the environment. He begins to perceive that cats can be distinguished from dogs, and discriminates lorries, cars, vans and trucks.

Through the twin processes of assimilation and accommodation the child achieves a new state of equilibrium. This equilibrium, however, is not permanent. The balance will soon be upset as the child assimilates further new experiences or accommodates his existing schemas to another new idea. In a sense, equilibrium only prepares the child for *disequilibrium*, that is further learning and adaptation; the two cannot be thought of separately. It is through the constant interplay between them that both stability and change occur. Assimilation helps the child to consolidate mental structures; accommodation results in growth and change. Thus all adaptation contains components of both processes. If accommodation occurred without assimilation, the result would be disorganized, unpredictable behaviour; by contrast, assimilation without accommodation would lead to rigid and unchanging behaviour patterns. The striving for balance between assimilation and accommodation results in the child's intrinsic motivation to learn, says Piaget. When new experiences are close to the child's capacity to respond, the conditions are at their best for change and growth to occur. Through the child's developing capacity to regulate her own actions, she moves progressively from states of lesser to greater stability in her understanding.

## The Stages of Cognitive Development

Piaget considered intellectual development to be a continuous process of assimilation and accommodation. Although we go on here to describe the four stages he identified, there is no sharp dividing line between each. The order of stages is the same for all children, but the ages at which they are achieved vary widely from one child to another.

## The Sensori-motor Stage

During the sensori-motor stage the child changes from a newborn, who focuses almost entirely on immediate sensory and motor experiences, to a toddler who possesses a rudimentary capacity for symbolic thought. Piaget described in detail the process by which this occurs, by carefully documenting his own children's behaviour. On this basis of such observations, carried out over the first two years of life, Piaget divided the sensori-motor period into six substages (table 11.2) through

TABLE 11.2    *Substages of the sensori-motor period according to Piaget*

| Substage | Age (mth) | Characteristics |
|---|---|---|
| Reflex activity | 0–1 | The infant practises the innate reflexes, e.g. sucking, looking. Behaviour largely, but not entirely, assimilative |
| Primary circular reactions | 1–4 | The behaviour is primary in the sense that it is basically made up of reflexes or motor responses; it is circular in the sense that the child repeats it. The primary circular reactions centre on the baby's own body. There appears to be no differentiation between self and outside world |
| Secondary circular reactions | 4–10 | The infant now focuses on objects rather than on his own body. He now begins to make interesting things happen, e.g. moving a hanging toy by hitting it. He has begun to change his surroundings intentionally |
| Coordination of secondary schemas | 10–12 | He begins to combine schemas in order to achieve goals, or to solve problems in new situations. For example, he will use the hitting schema in order to knock down a barrier between himself and a toy |
| Tertiary circular reactions | 12–18 | He actively uses trial and error methods to learn about objects. Increased mobility enables him to experiment and explore. Learns new ways of solving problems and discovers more about the properties of the environment |
| Internal representation | 18–24 | The beginning of mental action, and insightful solutions to problems. Objects and people can be represented symbolically; behaviour can be imitated from previous observations |

which the child gradually progresses, starting with the innate reflexive abilities and spontaneous rhythmic activity of the newborn (see also chapters 3 and 9).

Let us look at some of the transitions from one stage to the next. Between *primary circular reactions* and *secondary circular reactions* the child begins to understand that there is a difference between herself on the one hand and other objects and people in the environment on the other. At this point too she will show signs that she *intends* things to happen, by, for example, repeating actions that have interesting outcomes (see plate 6.2). Here is Piaget's observation of Jacqueline, aged 5 months, kicking her legs in the air – in itself a primary circular reaction.

Jacqueline looks at a doll attached to a string which is stretched from the hood to the handle of the cradle. The doll is at approximately the same level as the child's feet. Jacqueline moves her feet and finally strikes the doll, whose movement she immediately notices ... The activity of the feet grows increasingly regular whereas Jacqueline's eyes are fixed on the doll. Moreover, when I remove the doll Jacqueline occupies herself quite differently; when I replace it, after a moment, she immediately starts to move her legs again. (Piaget, 1936, p. 182).

Jacqueline seemed to have established a general relation between her movement and the doll's and was, in effect, engaged in secondary circular reaction. A little later, at 8 months, Jacqueline's response to a cigarette case exhibits the fourth substage of coordination of secondary schemas, as she incorporates the new object into several different schemas of assimilation:

Jacqueline grasps an unfamiliar cigarette case which I present to her. At first she examines it very attentively, turns it over, then holds it in both hands while making the sound *apff* (a kind of hiss which she usually makes in the presence of people). After that she rubs it against the wicker of her cradle then draws herself up while looking at it, then swings it above her and finally puts it into her mouth. (Piaget, 1936, p.284)

If we turn to the final (sixth) substage of the sensori-motor period, we see the emergence of internal or symbolic representation in which the child shows the ability to use images, words or actions to represent objects. Piaget observed the emergence of internal representations in the following areas:

The acquisition of language (see also chapter 10).

The appearance of symbolic play (see also chapter 6).

Deferred imitation, that is, the ability to imitate behaviour which has been observed on a previous occasion.

The first manifestations of representation in intelligent acts (i.e. symbolic thought).

Here is Jacqueline at 1 year 8 months trying to solve the problem of opening a door while carrying two blades of grass at the same time.

She stretches out her right hand towards the knob but sees that she cannot turn it without letting go of the grass. She puts the grass on the floor, opens the door, picks up the grass again and enters. But when she wants to leave the room things become complicated. She put the grass on the floor and grasps the door knob. But then she perceives that in pulling the door towards her she will simultaneously chase away the grass which she placed between the door and the threshold. She therefore picks it up in order to put it outside the door's zone of movement. (Piaget, 1936, pp. 376-5)

Piaget regarded this sequence of operations as very characteristic of the first intelligent acts founded upon representation of the awareness of relationships. Jacqueline shows that she can manipulate the mental images of door and grass in order to work out a solution to the problem. She is using mental combinations rather than the sensory and motor explorations of the previous five substages. The child at this point is able to solve problems without the trial and error behaviour characteristic of younger babies.

### The emergence of object permanence

As adults we take it for granted that an object continues to exist even when it is no longer in sight. The object's existence is quite independent of our own. Piaget argued that the child in the earlier sensori-motor substages does not understand this. When an object disappears or a person goes out of the room, they cease to exist. The baby only gradually acquires what Piaget calls 'the object concept'.

To the adult, an 'object' has a reality regardless of whether it is directly perceived. If I put a plate away in the cupboard one evening I can assume that it will still be there next morning when I need it for breakfast. To Piaget, the beginning of object permanence occurs when the child actively looks for an object which has been hidden or which has slipped out of view. The act of searching for objects which are out of sight is seen as one of the first intelligent behaviour patterns which the child shows. It is an enormous intellectual breakthrough since it provides evidence that the child has developed an internal representation of objects even when they are not present. The child is no longer dependent on the immediate environment since she can retain a mental image of things which are not present. Out of this is to grow the understanding not only that things are permanent, but also that, in Piaget's words, 'the universe becomes objectified and is detached from the self' (1936).

Piaget used both observation and contrived situations or 'experiments' to substantiate his view of object permanence. He observed that if a child of 4–5 months is playing with a toy which is then covered by a cloth, she responds as if the toy no longer existed. If the object is only partly covered, the baby can retrieve it. At a later age the baby can recover an object which has been totally hidden, but still makes 'place' errors. For example, if an object has previously been hidden two or three times in succession under the same cloth, but is then hidden under a second cloth, the baby will continue to look for it under the first cloth. She still does not entirely understand that if an object is hidden under a particular cloth, it remains in the same place. Babies do not seem to learn this until 10–12 months. Even at 10 months the baby can still be tricked. If two cloths are put on a table and an object hidden under one of them, and the adult then changes the cloths round, the baby will reach out for the object in the place where it was *first* placed, even though the cloths were changed over in full view of the baby (plate 11.2). The baby is not totally confident about this until 18 months. The stages which Piaget observed babies go through in the attainment of object permanence can be summarized thus (ages are approximate):

| | |
|---|---|
| 0–4 months | No response to hidden object |
| 4–8 months | Baby looks for partly hidden object |
| 8–12 months | Baby searches for completely hidden object |
| 12–18 months | Searches after he sees object being displaced |
| 18 months and over | Searches for object even when it has been displaced unseen by baby |

(a)

(b)

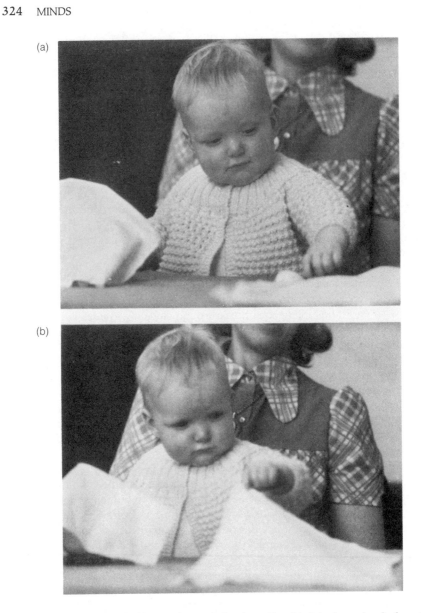

PLATE 11.2   *An infant looking under a cloth where the object had previously been hidden, although it is now under the other cloth (from Bower, 1982)*

*Re-interpretations of Piaget: the sensori-motor stage*

Although Piaget's observations of babies during this first stage have been largely confirmed by subsequent researchers, in some areas he seems to have under-estimated children's mental capacity to organize the sensory and motor information they take in. As we have seen in chapters 3 and 10 young babies show the ability to imitate much earlier than Piaget would suggest (Trevarthen, 1975; Meltzoff and Moore, 1983). Evidence of internal representation has been found in babies during the first year of life and parents play a critical role in presenting the world of objects, space and time in a socially structured way (Kaye, 1984; more of this in chapter 12).

Perhaps the sharpest criticism has come from work by Bower on the development of the object concept. Bower (1981) describes several experiments designed to test Piaget's hypotheses. In one, infants aged 5–6 months are presented with an object which is then made to vanish by dropping a screen over it. When the screen is removed, the object has gone. If the babies think that the object has gone when it is shielded by the screen, they should show no surprise to see nothing there when the screen is removed. If, however, they think that the object *does* exist behind the screen, they should be surprised if it does not reappear when the screen is removed. In Bower's experiment the babies showed more surprise (as measured in change of heart rate) at the *non-reappearance* of the object than by its reappearance. Piaget's hypothesis was thus not confirmed; the infants responded as if they believed the object did continue to exist behind the screen and would reappear when the screen was removed.

A second experiment by Bower tested infants' ability to track an object as it moved behind a screen and reappeared at the other side. Bower found that infants as young as 8 weeks turned their eyes to follow the expected movement of an object as it passed behind a screen. However, further experiments with babies' responses to moving objects suggest that babies under 5 months seem to think that the same object seen in different places is in fact a number of objects. Bower showed this by getting babies to watch a toy train moving from point A to point B stopping at each point for 10 seconds. After the babies had learned this sequence, the train was moved from point B to point C, yet the babies continued to stare at point B, appearing to be surprised that the train was not there, even though it was clearly visible at point C.

What do all these results add up to? Bower suggests that between 12 and 20 weeks infants do not know that place and movement are linked. If an object is moved from place to place, it becomes a series of different objects. However, by 5 months, the infant does know that when an object moves around, it remains the same object. Bower also made this interpretation from experiments using multiple mirror images of the infant's mother. Below 5 months of age, the infants responded happily to seeing three mirror images of their mother. After 5 months this experience was very upsetting to the baby. Bower suggests that the younger baby is happy thinking he has many mothers, whereas the older baby knows he has only one and is upset at the triple image.

Bower and Piaget are each approaching the same issue from different standpoints. Together, their empirical findings and theoretical interpretations give richer insights into the perceptual and conceptual world of the child. Bower's findings that babies have difficulty in relating the movement of objects with their identity has important implications. The study of babies seeing multiple images of their mothers, and certain other investigations, suggest that 'person-permanence' is a concept that may be acquired slightly earlier than object permanence. The mother's importance to the baby and her frequent movements around him probably are a factor in this sequence of development. Movement in relation to appearance and non-reappearance is clearly part of the babies' growing capacity to coordinate the identity of an object and its permanence despite disappearance and reappearance in different places. Bower's experiments showed that babies have to grasp these ideas *before* they can solve the problem posed by Piaget in his experiments with covered objects.

The age at which certain sensori-motor abilities are first acquired does seem to be earlier than Piaget suggested. Almost all psychologists agree, however, that by the end of the sensori-motor period, the child has changed from being ruled by reflex actions and motor behaviour into a person who has begun to use internal mental representations to solve problems. This capacity for symbolic thought, which grew out of the actions of the sensori-motor period, is the basis for the changes that take place in the next stage, the pre-operational stage.

### The Pre-operational Stage

Piaget divided this stage into the preconceptual period (2–4 years) and the intuitive period (4–7 years).

*The preconceptual period*   Towards the end of the sensori-motor stage we saw the emergence of symbolic thought. The preconceptual period builds on this capacity. One example is the rapid increase in language which, in Piaget's view, results from growth of the symbolic function. In this Piaget differs from other theorists who argue that thought grows out of linguistic competence. However, as we saw in chapter 10 Piaget maintained that thought arises out of action and this idea is supported by research into the cognitive abilities of deaf children who, despite limitations in language, are able to reason and solve problems. Piaget argued that thought shapes language far more than language shapes thought, at least throughout the preconceptual period.

Symbolic thought is also expressed in imaginative play (see chapter 6), in deferred imitation and in activities with an end goal, including constructive activities such as using lego or building bricks, representational drawing or completing simple jigsaws. However, Piaget identified two severe limitations in the child's thinking capacity at this stage – *animism* and *egocentrism*.

Children at this stage attribute feelings and intentions to inanimate objects: the moon follows them, teddy has a sore head, the table can kick them. Piaget called this *animistic* thinking. Similarly, at times the child finds it hard to distinguish between fantasy and reality, and nightmares may be responded to as if they had really happened.

To Piaget, the pre-operational child is still very centred in his or her own perspective and finds it difficult to understand that other people can look at things differently. Piaget called this 'self-centred' stance *egocentrism* – that is, the inability to understand that another person's thoughts, feelings or perceptions are different from one's own.

*Egocentric* thinking occurs because of the child's view that the universe is centred on him. He finds it hard to 'decentre', that is, to take the perspective of another person. The following dialogue illustrates a 3-years-old child's difficulty in taking the perspective of another:

| Adult | Have you any brothers or sister? |
| John | Yes, a brother. |
| Adult | What is his name? |
| John | Sammy. |
| Adult | Does Sammy have a brother? |
| John | No. |

John's inability to decentre makes it hard for him to realize that from Sammy's perspective, he himself is a brother.

One of Piaget's most famous experiments, and one which he took as illustrating egocentric thought, is the three mountains experiment (see figure 11.2). Piaget and Inhelder (1956) asked children between 4 and 12 years to say how a doll, placed in various positions, would view an array of three mountains from different perspectives. This perceptual role-taking ability was measured in three ways:

1   A child was given a series of pictures of the three mountains from different viewpoints and asked to select the correct one from the doll's point of view.
2   A child chose one picture and placed the doll in the appropriate place.
3   A child arranged three identical cardboard mountains in the way the doll would see them.

Four and five-year-olds in this test usually made a choice based on *their* perspective, not that of the doll. It was not until the age of nine that they were sure of the doll's

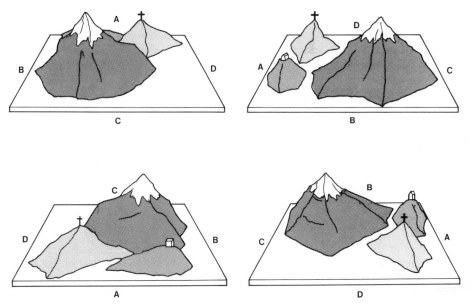

FIGURE 11.2   *The model of the mountain range used by Piaget and Inhelder viewed from four different sides*

perspective of the scene. Piaget and Inhelder concluded that the younger children were rooted in an egocentric viewpoint.

However, severe doubts have been raised about Piaget's interpretation of the three mountains task. It seems that the nature of the task can greatly affect the child's ability to demonstrate perspective-taking skills (see Donaldson, 1978, and Borke's study described in box 11.1).

Research findings also indicate that there are different kinds of perspective-taking skills, some involving empathy with other people's feelings (Borke, 1971) and some involving the ability to know what other people are thinking (Marvin et al., 1976; and see also chapter 5). The context within which these skills are expressed is clearly an important factor, and Piaget may well have under-estimated the ability of the preconceptual child in this area. Let us look first at a study that investigated the child's ability to respond empathically to the feelings of another.

Borke (1971) found that children as young as 3 or 4 years are aware of other people's feelings and *can* take the perspective of others. Using a series of short stories she asked children between 3 and 8 years to indicate how the child in each story felt by selecting a picture of a 'sad', 'happy', 'angry' or 'afraid' face. Even 3-year-olds showed that they could empathize with the feelings of another child in some situations, a result which challenges Piaget's position that the child between the ages of 2 and 7 years is primarily egocentric. Young children could, it seemed, show awareness that 'other people have feelings and that these feelings vary according to the situation in which the individual finds herself' (Borke, 1971, p. 269).

Borke's study was open to the criticism that it did not differentiate clearly enough between the child's *own* response to the situation in the story and that of the character. Most children are happy at birthday parties (the scene of one story), so the child might be giving her own (egocentric) viewpoint rather than empathizing with the child in the story.

With this criticism in mind, Mossler, Marvin and Greenberg (1976) investigated the ability of young children to take the perspective of another person using a task based on the notion of a secret. Their subjects were 80 children ranging in age from 2 to 6 years, tested at home with their mothers. The children were shown two video-taped stories and asked to make an inference about another person's restricted viewpoint. (In all cases, the stories were about children of the same sex as the subject.) Here is one of two stories:

> The Cookie Story: A 5-year-old child is shown sitting at a kitchen table. The child stands up and walks over to his/her mother. In the sound track, the child asks, 'Mummy, can I have a cookie?' and the mother replies, 'Sure'.

Each subject was shown one of the video tapes while the mother was out of the room and was questioned to make sure that he or she remembered what had happened in the story. Then in the company of the mother, each child saw the videotape again, only this time the sound was turned down. Then the child was questioned about the mother's knowledge of the story.

For the cookie story, the child was asked, 'Does your mummy know what the boy/girl wanted?' and (depending on the answer) 'How does your mummy know that?' or 'How come she doesn't know?'. The answers were scored as egocentric or non-egocentric. A non-egocentric score was given if the child stated that her mother did not know what the child in the cookie story wanted.

Children of different ages performed differentially with regard to perspective-taking. Sixty per cent of the 2-year-olds could not understand the question at all and none answered non-egocentrically. Only one (5 per cent) of the 3-year-olds answered non-egocentrically, as compared to 12 (60 per cent) of the 4-year-olds and 17 (85 per cent) of the 5-year-olds. All of the 6-year-olds answered non-egocentrically. The authors conclude that 4- and 5-year-old children can engage in conceptual perspective taking.

Piaget's work had suggested that the ability to make inferences about another person's thoughts, feelings and motives does not appear until around the age of 7, but studies such as these by Borke and by Marvin, Greenberg and Mossler suggest that Piaget's results could have been caused by the use of tasks that were too strange to the child and too complex to allow a valid measurement of their perspective-taking abilities.

The specific task used to measure perspective-taking abilities appears to be a crucial factor in determining whether the children will demonstrate them in an experimental situation. If the experiences and cognitive abilities of the child are not taken into account, the child will not perform at the level of his or her true capacity.

*The intuitive period*   A further shift in thinking was claimed by Piaget to occur at around the age of 4, when the child begins to develop the mental operations of ordering, classifying and quantifying in a more systematic way. Piaget applies the term *intuitive* to this next period since the child is largely unaware of the principles that underlie these operations and cannot explain why she has done them, nor can she carry them out in a fully satisfactory way.

For example, if a pre-operational child is asked to arrange sticks in a certain order, this poses difficulties. Piaget gave children ten sticks of different sizes from A (the shortest) to J (the longest), arranged randomly on a table. The child was asked to seriate them, that is put them in order of length. Some could not do the task at all; some arranged a few correctly but could not sustain the complete ordering; others would put all the small ones in a group and all the larger ones in another; another more advanced response was to arrange the sticks so that the tops were in the correct order even though the bottom was not (figure 11.3). In short, the child at this stage is not capable of ordering more than a very few objects.

FIGURE 11.3   *The pre-operational child's ordering of different-sized sticks. One arrangement in which the child has solved the problem of seriation by ignoring the length of the sticks*

Similarly, the child has problems with *part–whole relations*. Suppose she is given a box that contains 18 brown beads and two white beads; all the beads are wooden. When asked 'Are there more brown beads than wooden beads?', the pre-operational child will typically reply that there are more brown beads. She cannot at the same time focus on the whole and the parts.

Cross-cultural research has replicated Piaget's results. Investigators found that Thai and Malaysian children gave responses very similar to Swiss children and in the same sequence of development. Here a Thai boy, shown a bunch of seven roses and two lotus, states that there are more roses than flowers when prompted by the standard Piagetian questions:

Child:          More roses.
Experimenter:   More than what?
Child:          More than flowers.
Experimenter:   What are the flowers?
Child:          Roses.
Experimenter:   Are there any others?
Child:          There are.
Experimenter:   What?
Child:          Lotus.
Experimenter:   So in this bunch which is more, roses or flowers?
Child:          More roses.

(Ginsburg and Opper, 1979, pp. 130–1)

The area where the pre-operational child's thinking processes have been most investigated is *conservation*. According to Piaget the child at this age finds it hard to understand that even when an object is changed in shape or superficial appearance certain qualities remain the same, for example weight, length, volume or number. There is a series of conservation tests; examples are given in figure 11.4 and plate 11.3. If the child is given two identical balls of clay and asked if they are the same size, she will agree that they are. But if one is rolled into a sausage shape, the child will say that one or other of the balls is larger. When asked why, she will say 'Because it is larger'. The pre-operational child can only focus on one attribute at a time (for example, the length of the clay sausage in figure 11.4b). She cannot coordinate both the length and the cross-sectional area; she can only centre on limited aspects of the information given.

Similarly, if the row of flowers in figure 11.4a is made shorter by bunching them closely together, the pre-operational child thinks that there are fewer flowers. Even though she knows that when the flowers are moved back to the first position there will be one flower for each vase, she still thinks that when the appearence of the row alters, the number of objects in it changes. The child at this stage has failed to conserve; she does not really understand that the two sets are numerically equivalent.

There are three aspects of such failure. In our last example the child cannot grasp that there is a relation between the length of a row and the density of the arrangement of flowers. Piaget called this the knowledge of *compensation*, that is, the understanding that the length of the row is compensated for by the increase in density of the flowers. In other words, the child cannot yet attend to the two relevant dimensions – length and density – at the same time.

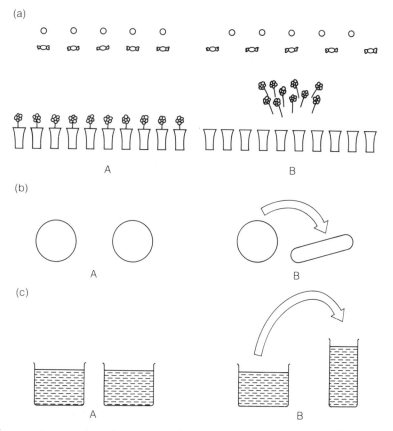

FIGURE 11.4    *Some tests of conservation: (a) two tests of conservation of number;*
*(b) conservation of mass; (c) conservation of quantity*

Another aspect is a failure to understand the *reversibility* of the operations. The pre-operational child cannot yet understand that changes in the density of a row of flowers can be negated by by reversing the process; in other words, that the flowers can be put back where they were in the first place.

Finally, the pre-operational child cannot yet reason that the arrangement must still be the same since nothing has been added or taken away – they are still the same flowers. She lacks what Piaget calls the *identity* operation.

The ability to conserve according to Piaget is gradually acquired by the child as a result of decentration and the development of these three operations: compensation, reversibility and identity.

### Re-interpretations of Piaget: the pre-operational stage

We have seen how Piaget claims that the pre-operational child cannot cope with seriation, with part–whole relations and with conservation, but his interpretation of

(a)

(b)

PLATE 11.3   *A 4-year-old puzzles over Piaget's conservation of number experiments; he says that the rows are equal in number in arrangement (a), but not in arrangement (b) 'because they're all bunched together here'*

all three has been challenged. Let us look first at seriation. The ability to make transitive inferences is a necessary part of the seriation. Bryant and Trabasso (1971) investigated these 'transitive inferences', for example, the ability to infer that because A > B and B > C, A must be bigger than C. According to Piaget, the young child cannot infer that A > C from the information that A > B and B > C because he cannot coordinate the two pieces of information.

Bryant and Trabasso claim that the pre-operational child *can* cope with a transitive inference task provided he remembers the necessary information. The failure of the pre-operational child to make inferences about number, they argue, could be due to a failure in memory. Bryant and Trabasso presented 60 children aged from $4\frac{1}{2}$ to $6\frac{1}{2}$ years with a set of five coloured rods each of a different length and colour. (The colours were red, white, yellow, blue and green and the lengths 3, 4, 5, 6 and 7 inches.) The rods were presented in pairs in such a way that each protruded from a box by one inch. The task was to say which was 'taller' or 'shorter'. When the child made a choice, the experimenter pulled out the rods and showed them to the child so that a direct comparison could be made. The children were trained until they responded correctly to six successive presentations of each pair. The training period was followed by a test period in which the children were tested for their ability to make transitive judgements *and* to remember the initial comparisons.

Children at all age levels were able to make the transitive inferences very well. The authors conclude that it is a failure of memory on the part of the younger children rather than a lack of ability to make transitive inferences which causes the usual poor performance. Even the 4 year olds in the sample showed that they could combine separate quantity judgements quite competently.

If we turn to the study of part–whole relations, we also find a challenge to Piaget's conclusions coming from recent research findings. The pre-operational child seems unable to understand the relationship between the whole and the part, and will happily state that there are more brown beads than wooden beads in a box of brown and white wooden beads 'because there are only two white ones'. The contradiction in such a statement does not appear to be recognized by the pre-operational child.

However, a variation in the wording of the questions can have dramatic effects on the child's performance. McGarrigle (quoted in Donaldson, 1978, pp. 43–50) showed children four toy cows, three black and one white, lying asleep on their sides. If the children are asked 'Are there more black cows or more cows?' (as in the standard Piagetian experiment) they tended not to answer correctly. If the question was rephrased 'Are there more black cows or more *sleeping* cows?', then pre-operational children were significantly more likely to respond correctly. McGarrigle found that in his sample of children (mean age 6 years) 25 per cent answered the standard Piagetian question correctly. When it was re-phrased, 48 per cent of the children were correct, a significant difference. It was the wording of the question rather than an inability to understand the part–whole relations which had caused the difficulty.

Similarly, McGarrigle and Donaldson (1974) questioned Piaget's interpretation of the conservation experiments and asked whether the form of questioning actually influences the child's responses. By introducing a character called 'Naughty Teddy' who muddled up the experimental displays 'accidentally', McGarrigle and Donaldson found that many more 4–6-year-old children *were* capable of conserving than in the classical Piagetian condition (box 11.2).

Donaldson (1978) suggests an alternative explanation for the young child's failure to conserve. She argues that children build up a model of the world by formulating hypotheses which help them anticipate future events on the basis of past experience. The child, therefore, has expectations about any situation. The child's interpretation of the words she hears is influenced by the expectations she brings to the situation. When the experimenter clearly points out the change in the array of counters (figure 11.4a), it is probably quite logical for the child to think that there is some link between that action (changing the display) and the next question ('Are there more counters or are they both the same?') Her point is that we normally interact within a context, and that the child negotiates meaning through social interaction with significant others.

Other researchers (e.g. Gelman, 1969) have attempted with some success to train children to conserve at an earlier stage than Piaget would say was possible. Training focuses on aspects like height, shape and length, which in the original study seem to have distracted the children from arriving at the right answer. These training procedures improve children's performance on the specific conservation task, and can sometimes be generalized to other areas.

Piaget was right to point out difficulties that pre-operational children have with conservation and with decentring. But more recent research suggests that, given appropriate wording and context, the child seems capable of demonstrating at least some of the abilities which, in Piaget's view, would not appear until later. In the right social context, the child emerges as a more competent being than Piaget's work would suggest. Furthermore, from an early age, as some developmental psychologists maintain, children's understanding grows within a wider framework of meaning (see chapter 12).

### The Concrete Operational Stage

From around the age of 7 the child's thinking processes change again as she develops a new set of strategies which Piaget calls *concrete operations*. These strategies are *concrete* because the child can still only apply them to immediately present objects; Piaget calls them *operations* because they are *mental* actions. Thinking becomes much more flexible because of her understanding of reversibility. Operations like addition and subtraction, multiplication and division become easier. The child succeeds on conservation tasks such as quality and number since for each mental action the child can perform its opposite. She ceases to focus only on the immediate visual qualities of an object or on just one dimension of the situation. Rather, she can simultaneously coordinate two aspects. For example, she can deal with length *and* density in the conservation of number; she can consider height *and* width in the conservation of quantity. Thus she understands transformations and can reverse her thinking processes. When the round ball of clay is transformed into a sausage shape, she can now say, 'If you change it back, it will be the same'. Conservation of number seems to come first (around 5 or 6 years), then conservation of weight (around 7 or 8 years); finally conservation of volume is fully understood at 11 years.

Another major shift comes in the concrete operational child's ability to classify and order, and, in particular, to understand the principle of class inclusion which the pre-operational child found so difficult.

There are still some limitations on thinking, since the child is reliant on the immediate environment and has difficulty with abstract ideas. Take the following question: 'Edith is fairer than Susan. Edith is darker than Lily. Who is the darkest?' This is a difficult problem for the concrete operational child, yet faced with dolls to rank in order, the child would solve the problem immediately. What the child at this stage cannot do is speculate abstractly. This type of reasoning is not found until the child has reached the stage of formal operations.

Finally, the egocentrism typical of the younger child changes in the concrete operational child. The ability simultaneously to coordinate two aspects of a situation enables the child to coordinate his own perspectives with that of another. Thus, the capacity to realize that someone else's viewpoint is different from one's own develops as egocentrism declines.

### Re-interpretations of Piaget: the concrete operational stage

Many of Piaget's observations about the concrete operational stage have broadly been confirmed by subsequent research. Tomlinson-Keasey (1978), for example, has noted that conservation of number, weight and volume are acquired in the order stated by Piaget. The fact that conservation does not occur in all areas at once is an example of what Piaget describes generally as *horizontal décalage*; that is, the development of related concepts at different points in time. However, Piaget has given no explanation for it, and this may be an area for future research.

Horizontal décalage may occur elsewhere in development. Another example would be the possible earlier occurrence of person permanence than object permanence, discussed earlier. It may also occur in abstract thinking processes, and indeed Tomlinson-Keasey argues that some such abstract abilities are available to children in the concrete operational period. The following study provides an example.

Jahoda (1983) showed that 9-year-olds in Harare, Zimbabwe, had a much more advanced understanding of economic principles than British 9-year-olds. The Harare children, who were involved in their parents' small businesses, had a strong motivation to understand the principles of profit and loss. Jahoda set up a mock shop and played a shopping game with the children. The British 9-year-olds could not explain about the functioning of a shop, did not understand that a shopkeeper buys for less than he sells, and did not know that some of the profit has to be set aside for purchase of new goods. The Harare children, by contrast, had mastered the concept of profit and understood about trading strategies. These abstract principles had been grasped by the children as a direct outcome of their own active participation in the running of a business. The experiment, like Donaldson's studies (1978), indicates the important function of context in the cognitive development of children. We discuss this major issue – that the child learns to make sense of the world in a shared, social context – in chapter 12.

## The Formal Operational Stage

We have seen that during the period of concrete operations the child is able to reason in terms of objects (e.g. classes of objects, relations between objects) when the objects are present. However, it is only during the period of formal operations, Piaget argues, that the young person is able to reason hypothetically. He no longer depends on the 'concrete' existence of things in the real world. Instead, it is possible to reason in terms of verbally stated hypotheses, considering the logical relations among several possibilities or deducing conclusions from abstract statements.

For example, consider the syllogism 'all green birds have two heads'; 'I have a green bird at home called Charlie'; 'How many heads does Charlie have?'. The young person who has reached formal operational thinking will give the answer which is correct by abstract logic: 'two heads'. The younger child will usually not get beyond protesting about the absurdity of the premise.

Another example of a formal operational task is to generate all possible combinations or permutations of events, for example: make up all the possible words from the letters A, S, E, T, M. At the formal operational level this will be done systematically, in a logically ordered way, for example considering first all combinations of two letters, then three letters, and so on. Below this level, the attempt will be unsystematic and disorganized.

The major description of this stage of development comes in a book by Inhelder and Piaget called *The Growth of Logical Thinking from Childhood to Adolescence* (1955, translated into English in 1958).They describe the process of logical reasoning used by young people when presented with a number of natural science experiments. An example of one of their tasks – the pendulum task – is shown in figure 11.5. The person is given a string, which can be shortened or lengthened, and a set of weights, and is asked to find out what determines the speed of swing of the pendulum: possible factors are the length of the string, the weight at the end of the string, the height of the release point and the force of the push. Although in this problem the materials are concretely in front of the person, the reasoning, to be successful, involves formal operations: a systematic consideration of the various possibilities, the formulation of hypotheses (e.g. 'what would happen if I tried a heavier weight?'), and logical deductions from the results of trials with the materials. Indeed, the whole process of scientific inquiry has a close resemblance to the characteristics of formal operational thinking in Piaget's theory. Other tasks considered by Inhelder and Piaget included the flexibility of metal rods, balancing different weights around a fulcrum, and the combination of coloured and colourless chemicals.

On the basis of his original work, carried out in schools in Geneva, Piaget claimed that formal operational thinking was a characteristic stage which children or young people reached between the ages of 11–12 years and 14–15 years, having previously gone through the earlier stages.

### Re-interpretations of Piaget: the formal operational stage

Piaget's claim has been modified by more recent research. Work carried out in Britain and the USA has found that the achievement of formal operational thinking

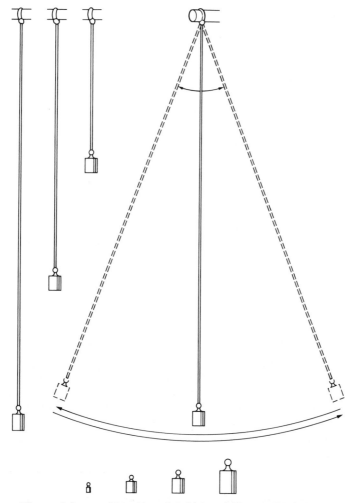

FIGURE 11.5    *The pendulum problem (from Inhelder and Piaget, 1958)*

is gradual, haphazard, dependent on the nature of the task and often limited to certain domains.

For example, Shayer et al. (1976; Shayer and Wylam 1978) gave problems such as the pendulum task (figure 11.5) to large numbers of British schoolchildren. His results (figure 11.6) showed that by 15 or 16 only some 30 per cent of young people had achieved 'early formal operations'. Indeed, from their data it would seem that the period from 11–12 to 14–15 years is actually that when late concrete operations are consolidated. In a study in the USA, Martorano (1977) gave ten of Piaget's formal operational tasks to girls and young women aged 12–18 years. At 18 years success on the different tasks varied from 15 per cent to 95 per cent; only two children out of 20 succeeded on all ten tasks.

These results are in Western urban societies, where scientific, logical and thus formal operational thought is fostered in secondary schooling. In non-literate

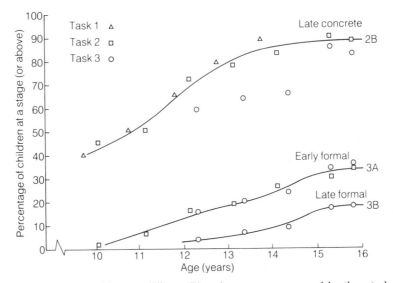

FIGURE 11.6 *Proportion of boys at different Piagetian stages as assessed by three tasks (from Shayer and Wylam, 1978)*

societies some studies have found considerable delay of formal operational thinking, or even an absence in adults. So can formal operational thought really be considered a proper developmental stage? This problem was discussed by Piaget (1972). He entertained three possibilities. One was that everyone proceeded through the same stages, but at different speeds depending on the amount of cognitive and social stimulation they received. Thus, in poor environments formal operations might be delayed to between 15 and 20 years, or 'perhaps in extremely disadvantageous conditions, such a type of thought will never really take shape' (1972, p. 7). A second possibility was that aptitudes became more diversified with age, so that abilities in older children could not be considered within one single general framework such as formal operations; in other words, 'our fourth period can no longer be characterized as a proper stage' (p. 9). A final possibility, which Piaget favoured, was a combination of the previous two; 'all normal subjects attain the stage of formal operations or structuring if not between 11–12 to 14–15 years, in any case between 15 and 20 years. However, they reach this stage in different areas according to their aptitudes and their professional specializations (advanced studies or different types of apprenticeships for the various trades)' (p. 10). This third possibility is consistent with evidence that secondary schooling does promote formal operational thinking in natural science tasks, while allowing also that non-literate persons may well use formal operational thought in domains familiar in their culture (for example, Kalahari bushpeople use hypothetical and logical reasoning in hunting and tracking animals, as reported by Blurton Jones and Konner, 1976).

Several studies have shown that formal thinking can be trained. For example, figure 11.7 shows the results of a study by Danner and Day (1977). They coached students aged 10, 13 and 17 in three formal operational tasks. As can be seen, training had limited effect at 10 years, as would be expected, but it had very marked

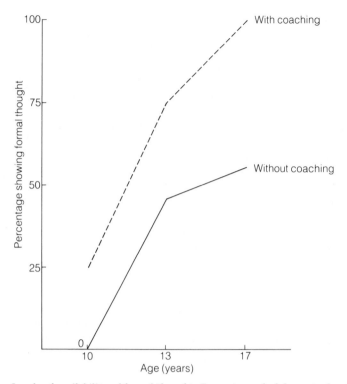

FIGURE 11.7    *Levels of availability of formal thought. Percentage of adolescents showing formal thought, with and without coaching (from Danner and Day, 1977)*

effects at 17 years. In summary, it seems that the 11–15 age period signals the start of the possibility of formal operational thought, rather than its achievement. Formal operational thought is only used some of the time, in certain domains we are familiar with, are trained in, or which are important to us. Often formal thinking is not used. After all, we all know of areas of life where we should have thought things out logically, but in retrospect realize we did not do so.

## Piaget's Theory: an Overview

Piaget's theory was elaborated over many decades throughout his long life. At first, it was slow to make an impact in the UK and the USA, but by the 1950s and 1960s its ambitious, embracing framework for understanding cognitive growth was becoming the dominant paradigm in cognitive development. The 1970s and 1980s have seen more critical evaluation, such that many aspects of Piaget's theory, and indeed its whole basis, are now subject to debate and dispute.

No one denies the stature of Piaget's achievement, beginning his work as he did in the 1920s, when scientific psychology was in its infancy. However, several objections have been raised as to his methods. He seldom reported quantitative information on the number of subjects tested, or the percentage who passed a certain test (although this was compensated for by investigators who replicated his findings in the 1950s and 1960s). He used a flexible method of interviewing children, the 'clinical method', which meant that he adapted his procedure to suit the child rather than following a standardized approach. This has advantages, but it puts a heavy premium on the interviewer's skill and makes replication difficult. Piaget also relied on cross-sectional data (with the exception of the observations of his own children, during the sensori-motor period); ideally, longitudinal data would give a better insight into stage progressions. Piaget has also been criticized for putting too much emphasis on the child's failures rather than successes.

As we have seen, in many domains recent research has found that children can perform tasks earlier than Piaget predicted (for concrete operations), or only later (for formal operations). His stage model has clearly been 'stretched' well away from its original periods. So is the stage model still useful? Only if certain abilities go hand-in-hand, linked by similar processes of thinking. For example, concrete operational thought might occur earlier and still be a stage, but only if the various aspects (conservation, classification, seriation, decline of egocentrism) still remain linked together. Unfortunately, the evidence for this kind of linkage is not strong, either for concrete or formal operations. For example, different measures of egocentrism do not correlate together strongly (Ford, 1979). Also, Piaget himself admitted that formal operational thought is achieved in a limited, patchy way. Only for the sensori-motor period (which seems to be a much more canalized or maturational process, see chapter 2) is the stage model holding up reasonably well.

## Educational Implications

Whatever its shortcomings, Piaget's approach has provided the most detailed, comprehensive account of cognitive growth to date and as such has had considerable implications for education, notably in the child-centred methods of the nursery and infant school, the mathematics curriculum in the primary school and the science curriculum at the secondary school level.

Piaget argued that the young child thinks quite differently from the adult and views the world from a qualitatively different perspective. It follows that the teacher must make a strong effort to adapt to the child and not assume that what is appropriate for adult learning is necessarily right for the child. At the heart of this child-centred approach to education lies the idea of active learning. From the Piagetian standpoint, children learn from actions rather than from passive observations; for example, telling a child about the properties of materials is less effective than creating an environment in which the child is free to explore, touch, manipulate and experiment. The teacher must recognize that each child needs to construct knowledge for himself; active learning results in deeper understanding.

How can the teacher promote active learning on the part of the pupil? First, it is the child rather than the teacher who initiates the activity. This does not mean that the children are free to do anything they want, but rather that the teacher sets tasks which are finely adjusted to the needs of their pupils and which, as a result, are intrinsically motivating to the young learners. Secondly, the teacher is concerned with process rather than end-product. For example, the nursery school classroom provides children with play materials such as climbing frames which give the opportunity to gain a knowledge of the spatial properties of objects; smaller toys, which encourage the practice of sorting, grading and counting; play areas, like the Wendy House, where children can develop role-taking skills through imaginative play; and materials like water, sand, bricks and crayons which help children make their own constructions and create symbolic representations of the objects and people in their lives.

From these varied experiences the child constructs knowledge and understanding for herself. The teacher's role is to create the conditions in which this learning may best take place, since the aim of education is to encourage the child to ask questions, try out experiments and speculate, rather than accept information unthinkingly. From this it follows that the teacher should be interested in the reasoning behind the answer a child gives to a question rather than in the correct answer alone. Conversely, mistakes should not be punished but treated as responses that can give the teacher insights into the child's thinking processes at one time.

The idea of active learning has meant a radical change in attitudes towards education. The teacher's role is not to impart information; in Piaget's view, knowledge is not something to be transmitted from an expert teacher to an inexpert pupil. It is the child, according to Piaget, who sets the pace; the teacher's part in the educational process is to create situations which challenge the child to ask questions, to form hypotheses and to discover new concepts. The teacher is the guide in the child's process of discovery, and the curriculum is adapted to each child's individual needs and intellectual level. In the mathematics and science lessons at primary school, children are helped to make the transition from pre-operational thinking to concrete operations through carefully arranged sequences of experiences which develop concepts of, for example, reversibility and conservation.

The Nuffield Science materials work on the principle that children begin with practical and experimental work before moving on to abstract deductive reasoning. In this way, the teacher provides the conditions which are appropriate for the transition from concrete operational thinking to the stage of formal operations. Shayer's work on formal operational thought (see p. 337) also has strong implications for teaching, especially science teaching, in secondary schools. Teaching techniques and syllabuses can be analysed in terms of the logical abilities required to fulfil them, and adjusted to the age and expected abilities of the children accordingly.

Ideally, much of this learning should be individualized in view of the wide range of activities and interest which appear in any class of children. However, Piaget did not ignore the importance of social interaction in the learning process. Through interaction with peers, the child is also enabled to move out of an egocentric viewpoint (see also chapter 7, p. 199). This occurs through cooperation with others, arguments and discussions. By listening to other children's opinions, having one's own view challenged and experiencing through others' reactions the illogicality of certain concepts, the child learns about perspectives other than her own. Communication of ideas to others also helps the child to sharpen concepts by finding the appropriate words. Piaget recognized the social value of interaction but also viewed it as an important factor in cognitive growth. Thus, another implication of Piaget's theory is that interaction with other children and adults has an important part to play in a child's education.

### Further reading

An excellent exposition of Piaget's ideas, including applications to education, is H. Ginsberg and S. Opper 1979: *Piaget's Theory of Intellectual Development: an Introduction*. Englewood Cliffs, NJ: Prentice Hall.

A clearly written student's introduction to the basic concepts of Piaget's theory, including its educational implications, is B. Wadsworth 1979: *Piaget's Theory of Cognitive Development*. New York: Longman. It also has a chapter on Piaget's work on moral judgement.

H. E. Gruber and J. J. Voneche 1982: *The Essential Piaget*. London: Routledge and Kegan Paul, is more advanced reading. The authors have made an anthology of Piaget's own writing accompanied by a lucid commentary. As Piaget himself wrote in the introduction to this book, 'in reading the explanatory texts, I came to understand better what I had wanted to do'. What better recommendation could there be!

There are a number of useful critiques of Piaget. These include M. Donaldson 1978: *Children's Minds*. London: Fontana. This is a very readable book which argues forcefully that Piaget has greatly under-estimated the logical powers of young children. It makes practical suggestions about ways in which parents and teachers can help children make transitions from one stage to the next, and has strong views on the teaching of reading. J. Bruner and H. Haste (eds) 1987: *Making Sense*. London: Methuen, also challenge Piaget's model and stress instead that making sense of the world is a *social* process. M. A. Boden 1979: *Piaget*. London: Fontana, discusses the biological and philosophical issues which influenced Piaget. It makes links between Piaget's ideas and current work on artificial intelligence.

### Discussion Points

1   Why did Piaget consider the development of the object concept to be important in a child's cognitive development?

2   What does Piaget mean by egocentrism? How have his ideas on egocentrism been challenged?

3   Discuss ways in which Piaget seems to have over-estimated the age at which formal operations are acquired. Illustrate with examples from your own experience.

4   What are the implications of Piaget's theory for education? Discuss in relation to your own experiences in school.

5   In what ways did Piaget consider that peer interactions were important with respect to cognitive development? Can you think of ways in which conceptual development can be facilitated by making use of peer activities, such as games, role-play, arguments etc.?

### Practical exercises

1.   Replicate the classic object concept experiment. Place an attractive object in front of a baby within reach. Before the child can grasp it, cover the object or place a screen between it and the child. Observe the child's behaviour and judge whether he or she seems to be aware of the hidden object. Repeat the experiment, if possible, with a number of babies aged between 4 and 12 months. Consider responses in the light of Piaget's stages in the development of the object concept.

2. Explore the level of conservation ability among preschool or infant school children. Take some Plasticine, divide it in half and form two identical balls. Ask the child, 'Are these the same?' Make sure that the child thinks that the two quantities are the same. Take one ball and form it into a sausage shape in front of the child. Ask, 'Now do these two have the same amount of Plasticine?' Record the child's answer and ask him or her to explain it. Reform the sausage shape into a ball in front of the child. Again ask, 'Do these two have the same amount?' Record the child's answer, and explanation, again. Repeat this procedure with a number of children of different ages. Compare the level of conservation achieved, and reasons given, with those Piaget found.

3 Investigate the child's understanding of classification. Arrange coloured paper circles, triangles and squares randomly in front of the child. Ask the child to put the ones that belong together in separate piles. Observe what the child does and ask why that particular arrangement was made. See whether the child is able to classify objects by more than one characteristic, e.g. shape *and* colour. Repeat this procedure with children of different ages and note their responses.

## Box 11.1

# Piaget's mountains revisited: changes in the egocentric landscape

Borke questioned the appropriateness for young children of Piaget's three mountains task (described on p. 327). She thought it possible that aspects of the task not related to perspective-taking might have adversely affected the children's performance.

Perhaps viewing a mountain scene from different angles was not an interesting problem for young children. Also, photographs might be difficult for young children to interpret. Finally, some simple practice or training might improve performance. With those points in mind, Borke, in the USA, repeated the basic design of Piaget and Inhelder's experiment but changed the content of the task, avoided the use of photographs and gave some initial

| Practice display | Display 1 |
|---|---|
| a large fire engine (1) | a lake with a boat on it (1); a horse and cow (2); a house (3) |
| Display 2 | Display 3 |
| Piaget's three mountains: the mountain with a cross on top (1); the mountain with a snowcap (2); the mountain with a house on top (3) | a variety of toy animals and people, all in natural settings, e.g. cowboys, Indians and trees (1); a woman feeding chickens (7) |

BOX FIGURE 11.1.1  *A schematic view of Borke's four three-dimensional displays viewed from above*

Based on material in H. Borke 1975: *Developmental Psychology*, 11, 240–3.

practice. She used four three-dimensional displays (box figure 11.1.1): these were a practice display and three experimental displays.

Borke's participants were eight 3-year-old children and fourteen 4-year-old children attending a day nursery. Grover, a character from the popular children's television programme 'Sesame Street', was used instead of Piaget's doll. Each display had two identical scenes, one for the child to look at, the other for Grover to drive around. The children were tested individually. Each was first shown the practice display, a large fire engine. An exact duplicate of the fire engine appeared on a revolving turntable to the left of the child. Borke then told the child that Grover was going to play a game: 'He will drive his car along the road. Sometimes Grover likes to stop and look out of his car. Now the fire engine on this other table turns so you can look at it from any side. When Grover stops to look out of his car, I want you to turn the scene that moves so you are looking at it in the same way Grover is'. Then Borke parked Grover in turn at each of the three sides which presented a view different from the child's.

If necessary, Borke helped the children to move their turntable to the correct position and also walked the child round to where Grover was to show how Grover saw things. Only after this practice period was the child ready to move on to the experiment itself. Here the procedure was the same, except that no help was given by the experimenter. Each child was shown the three experimental displays one at a time (see box figure 11.1.1). Grover drove round his display, and, when he stopped, the children rotated the replica displays on their turntables to give Grover's point of view.

The analysis of responses showed statistically significant differences in the children's perceptual role-taking ability on the three displays. Using analysis of variance, it was found that the difference was significant at $p < 0.001$. All subjects showed a high ability to take Grover's perspective for Display 1 (3- and 4-year-olds were correct 80 per cent of the time) and Display 3 (3-year-olds were correct 79 per cent of the time and 4-year-olds, 93 per cent). For Display 2, however (the three mountains task) the 3-year-olds were correct only 42 per cent of the time and 4-year-olds 67 per cent of the time. As far as errors went, there were no significant differences in the children's responses for any of the three positions – 31 per cent of errors were egocentric (i.e. took the child's perspective rather than Grover's) and 69 per cent were random.

Borke thus demonstrated clearly that the task itself had a crucial influence on the perspective-taking skills of young children. Where toys which are interesting to the children are used, even a complex problem like taking Grover's perspective in Display 3 can be solved by a high proportion of 3- and 4-year-olds after a brief practice session. Furthermore, asking the children to rotate a turntable with a replica of the scene presents much less difficulty for young children than selecting a photograph or building a model, as Piaget and Inhelder asked their subjects to do.

Faced with the more difficult display similar to that which Piaget and Inhelder had used, the children seemed to fall back on their egocentric perspective rather more, even though they still performed at above chance levels.

Borke's conclusion was that the potential for understanding another's viewpoint is already present in children as young as 3 and 4 years of age – a strong challenge to Piaget's assertions that children of this age are egocentric and incapable of taking the viewpoint of others. It would seem that young children make egocentric responses when they misunderstood the task, but given the right conditions show that they are quite capable of decentring. Further confirmation of these results comes from Hughes's study reported by Donaldson (1978), in which children are asked to hide a doll from a toy policeman – a task which requires coordination of different points of view. Again 3-year-olds succeed at this task because, in Hughes's opinion, the task 'makes sense' to them in a way that the three mountains test does not. The reasons for hiding from the policeman are clear, even to children as young as 3!

# Box 11.2

# Conservation accidents

This study set out to discover whether children as young as 4–6 years could succeed at conservation tasks when a different procedure from Piaget's was used. Altogether 80 children, aged between 4 years 2 months and 6 years 3 months, were tested in two situations involving conservation of number (equal and unequal) and two involving conservation of length (equal and unequal). In addition, each child performed each conservation task under two conditions:

IT    *intentional transformation* where the transformation of materials was clearly intended by the experimenter.

AT    *accidental transformation* where the materials were disarranged 'accidentally' by a mischievous teddy bear.

The children were divided into two groups of 40 subjects each balanced for age and sex. Group 1 made all their conservation judgements in the AT condition before encountering the IT condition. Group 2 made all their conservation judgements in the IT condition before the AT condition. Within each of the two groups, half of the children were given the number conservation task first and half were given the length conservation first (thus counter-balancing for the order of the conservation tasks).

In the *number equal* situation, four red and four white counters were arranged in a one-to-one correspondence into two rows of equal length (see box figure 11.2.1).

Transformation occurred when the counters of one row were moved until they touched one another. In the IT condition, the experimenter did this deliberately. In the AT condition, 'Naughty Teddy' swooped over the counters and pushed them together; the child, who had already been warned that Teddy might 'mess up the toys', helped to put Teddy back in its place. Before and after the transformation the child was asked: 'Is there more here or more here, or are they both the same number?'

In the *number unequal* situation, rows of four and five counters were used and the child was asked: 'Which is the one with more – this one, or this one?' (box figure 11.2.2). A similar procedure was carried out for the conservation of length, using lengths of black and red string. In this study the independent variables are the equal and unequal conditions, the IT and AT conditions, and the order of presentation of IT and AT (Groups 1 and 2). The dependent variable is the number of correct responses.

As you can see in box table 11.1.1, the largest effect is between the IT and AT conditions. Correct responses were more frequent when the transformation was accidental: 71.9 per

Based on material in J. McGarrigle and M. Donaldson 1974: *Cognition*, 3, 341-50.

Before transformation                After transformation

BOX FIGURE 11.2.1  *Transformation of counters in the number equal situation, either intentionally or accidentally*

Before transformation                After transformation

BOX FIGURE 11.2.2  *Transformation of counters in the numbers unequal situation, either intentionally or accidentally*

cent of the responses were correct when the display was moved accidentally, whereas only 33.7 per cent were correct in the intentional transformation condition (which corresponds to the normal Piagetian procedure). There was little difference between the equal and unequal conditions; this was found in the experiments that investigated conservation of number (using counters) and those that investigated conservation of length (using pieces of string).

However, the order in which the displays were presented did have an influence on the children's responses. When the authors compared performance in the AT condition of Group 2 (where IT came first) with that in Group 1, the difference was significant ($\chi^2 =$ , $p < 0.05$). In other words, if children are given the 'Naughty Teddy' task first and then the traditional task second, they perform significantly better than children who do the tasks in the reverse order. The authors conclude that the experimenter's behaviour towards the task materials can influence the interpretation the children make of the situation since the child is trying to make sense of the situation, and of what the experimenter wants. Unless the setting is considered, the child's ability to conserve may be greatly under-estimated – something which traditional tests of conservation seem to do.

For example, traditional experiments in number conservation seem to make the child think that the experimenter is asking about the *length* of the row of counters rather than the number. If the misleading clues are removed (by a 'Naughty Teddy' in this case), the child's

BOX TABLE 11.2.1  *Total of correct responses given by Groups 1 and 2 under AT and IT conditions*

|  | Group 1 (n=40) | | | Group 2 (n=40) | | |
|---|---|---|---|---|---|---|
|  | AT | then | IT | IT | then | AT |
| Number equal | 32 | | 19 | 14 | | 22 |
| Number unequal | 36 | | 18 | 13 | | 22 |
| Length equal | 34 | | 15 | 8 | | 24 |
| Length unequal | 37 | | 12 | 9 | | 23 |
|  | 139 | | 64 | 44 | | 91 |

ability to conserve improves dramatically. This implies that the social setting of the conservation experiments and the actual words used by the experimenter may be very important factors.

As McGarrigle and Donaldson conclude:

> It is possible that the achievements of the concrete operational stage are as much a reflection of the child's increasing independence from features of the interactional setting as they are evidence of the development of a logical competence (p. 349)

This study has been widely cited to support the view that Piaget under-estimated the abilities of the pre-operational child. However, not all subsequent investigators have replicated the main findings, and queries have been raised about the reliability of the main conclusions. Eames, Shorrocks and Tomlinson (1990) used interviews with the children themselves to see if McGarrigle and Donaldson's explanation was supported, but failed even to replicate the contextual effects of the naughty teddy experiment. They suggest that the inconsistency among findings may be explained by experimenter effects (see also p. 13), in effect challenging what they call a 'new orthodoxy' about the reinterpretation of Piaget's experiments.

# 12

# Learning in a Social Context

## The Challenge of Vygotsky

We saw in chapter 11 Piaget's account of how children develop as thinkers and learners. Essentially the Piagetian model shows us children as individual 'scientists' who formulate and test increasingly complex hypotheses about their world and about their own experiences and interactions. By and large, it is the inanimate world of objects which Piagetian psychologists have paid most attention to. But developmental psychologists have also explored the idea of the child as someone who negotiates meaning and understanding in a *social* context. Margaret Donaldson and her colleagues, for example, have demonstrated young children's competence at taking the perspective of another person in tasks which are socially meaningful to them (chapter 11). Developmental psychologists are also increasingly interested in the critical role which language plays in enabling children to enter into their culture (chapter 10). The child develops repertoires of shared meanings even before the emergence of language, starting with such phenomena as 'joint attention' (p. 305). But with language the child gains a much more powerful entry point into the images, the metaphors, the ways of interpreting events, which are distinctive about her own culture.

The point is that these are *social representations* which give to the child a framework for constructing knowledge.

A major challenge to Piaget's theory comes from this more recent emphasis within the field of developmental psychology on the intricate and reciprocal relationship between the individual person and the social context. One influential strand in this shift of perspective comes from Russian psychologists; in particular from the writings of Vygotsky (1896–1934), whose work was unknown in the West until it began to be translated in the 1960s and 1970s. Vygotsky, like Piaget, saw the child as an active constructor of knowledge and understanding. But he differed from Piaget in his emphasis on the role of direct intervention by more knowledgeable others in this learning process. Vygotsky argued that it is as a result of the social interactions between the growing child and other members of that child's community that the child acquires the 'tools' of thinking and learning. In fact, it is out of this cooperative process of engaging in mutual activities with more expert others that the child becomes more knowledgeable. Instruction, according to Vygotsky, is at the heart of learning.

Vygotsky (plate 12.1) created an ambitious model of cognition with a socio-historic approach at its centre. During his short life, despite poor health, he worked intensely and productively. Yet much of his work was censored or simply hidden by his colleagues out of fear. *The Psychology of Art* which led to the award of his Ph.D. in 1925 was not published even in Russian until 1965; *Thought and Language*, his best-known work, was first published in 1934 but was suppressed by the Stalinist authorities in 1936 and did not reappear until 1956. We only have the barest information about his personal life — that he came from a Jewish family; that his father was a bank official; that he was a brilliant student of law, literature and cultural studies at the University of Moscow, and at Shaniavskii People's University (an

PLATE 12.1  *L. S. Vygotsky*

unofficial university that appeared in Moscow when the authorities expelled staff and students from Moscow University on suspicion of being involved in anti-tsarist activities). Vygotsky's colleagues have been unforthcoming about his path through the stormy years of the Russian Revolution, but we have to remember how dangerous it was for social scientists during the Stalinist era to express views which did not conform to party doctrine. We do know that for a period Vygotsky was disgraced for exploring the changing mentality of peasant farmers as they experienced collectivization. At this time a reductionist model of mind predominated in Russia, as in the USA, derived from a distorted interpretation of the physiologist Pavlov's work (which Pavlov himself never endorsed). This was that higher mental processes, such as reasoning, and even consciousness itself, could be accounted for within the conditioned reflex approach. Vygotsky distanced himself from this dominant view:

Vygotsky distanced himself from this dominant view:

> A human being is not at all a skin sack filled with reflexes, and the brain is not a hotel for a series of conditioned reflexes accidentally stopping in. (Vygotsky, quoted in Joravsky, 1989, p. 260)

By contrast, he argued that consciousness is central to the science of mind and that human beings are subject to 'dialectical interplay' between biological and cultural factors.

Vygotsky's psychology was consistent with Marxism, but it was far more sophisticated than the psychology favoured by Stalinist party ideologists. He had to tread a minefield and, for the most part, managed to avoid head-on conflict with the authorities while stating his own views with integrity:

> Our science will become Marxist to the degree that it will become true, scientific; and we will work precisely on that, its transformation into a true science, not on its agreement with Marx's theory. (Vygotsky, quoted in Joravsky, 1989, p. 264)

It says a great deal for him that he was able to separate himself from the Stalinist pressure to reject 'bourgeois' aspects of science and to address himself to the study of the self-directed, conscious mind.

## The Role of Instruction

Whereas Piaget's view of the child's intellectual growth was as 'a manifestion of the child's largely unassisted activities' (Wood, 1988, p. 24), Vygotsky's view was quite different. He saw thought and language as instruments for planning and carrying out action. Through language, the person comes to organize his or her perceptions and actions:

> Children solve practical tasks with the help of their speech, as well as with their eyes and hands. This unity of perception, speech and action ... constitutes the central subject matter for any analysis of the origins of uniquely human forms of behaviour. (Vygotsky, 1978, p. 26)

Vygotsky places a greater emphasis on language than does Piaget, but in addition he stresses that this process must also be seen in the context of the person's culture, and the tools and aids which exist in that culture.

Vygotsky's view highlights three points. First, Vygotsky argues that before this conscious, self-directed control develops, *action* is the way in which the child responds to the world. Second, it is the process of 'turning round and reflecting on one's own thoughts', using *language*, that enables one to see things in a new way. Third, that learning is achieved through cooperation with others in a whole variety of *social settings* — with peers, teachers, parents and other people who are significant to the child. Learning also comes through the 'symbolic representatives' of the child's culture — through its art and language, through play and songs, through metaphors and explanations. Development as a learner reflects the child's cultural experience; in turn, significant cultural experiences become internalized into the structure of the child's intellect (see box 12.1). Vygotsky's theory stresses the role of interpersonal processes and the role of society in providing a framework within which the child's construction of meaning develops. The interactions between the individual child, the significant people in her immediate environment and her culture can be represented diagrammatically (figure 12.1)

A central concept of Vygotsky's is the *zone of proximal development*, or ZPD, which provides an explanation for how the child learns with the help of others. The ZPD is the distance between the child's actual developmental level and his or her potential level of development under the guidance of more expert adults or in collaboration with more competent peers. To Vygotsky the child is initiated into the intellectual life of the community and learns by *jointly* constructing his or her understanding of issues and events in the world. Unlike Piaget, Vygotsky did not

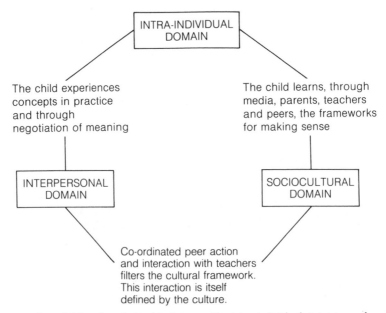

FIGURE 12.1  *A model for the relationship between the intra-individual, interpersonal and social domains (adapted from Haste, 1987)*

LEVEL OF POTENTIAL DEVELOPMENT

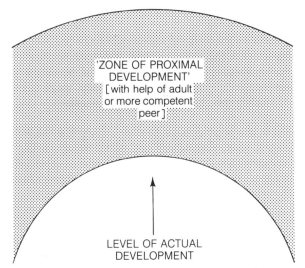

'ZONE OF PROXIMAL DEVELOPMENT'
[ with help of adult or more competent peer ]

LEVEL OF ACTUAL DEVELOPMENT

FIGURE 12.2   *Vygotsky's concept of the zone of proximal development (ZPD)*

wait for the child to be 'ready'. Instead, he argued, children learn from other people who are more knowledgeable than themselves (figure 12.2).

How does this 'expert intervention' enable the child to learn? It should be at a level beyond the child's existing developmental level so that it provides some challenge; but not too far ahead, so that it is still comprehensible. This is then within the ZPD and the child can accomplish something he or she could not do alone, and learn from the experience.

An example from a contemporary description of a session in a nursery class will perhaps make this point clearer. The teacher, Mrs Morgan, has given the children a box of cardboard toilet roll centres and invites them to explore the possibilities of this material. Amongst other things, some of the children spontaneously make sounds with their new-found toilet-roll trumpets. When she judges the moment to be right, Mrs Morgan intervenes to build on the children's ideas:

She stood back – she watched – she thought – and then acted in a manner which did not destroy the validity of the children's work, but contributed to it. She produced other cylindrical and tubular items which, in turn, produced new effects. The children who seemed keen on the sound idea sorted amongst the items – selected – tried out – rejected – found others – combined watering cans with tubes – plastic pipes and bowls of water – teapots with rubber hose. It looked rather chaotic, and sounded terrible, but the five children were feverishly excited. After ten minutes Mrs Morgan once again stepped into the situation together with her tape recorder, and a new event evolved. Listening – not just hearing, but really listening.
   'What is this sound?'
   'Who else thinks that's Jill's cardboard tube we can hear?'

'Who thinks it is Robert's watering can with the tube on it?'

'Who would like me to play it again so we can listen more carefully?'

Edward's device with the screwed up ball of paper squashed into the end of a washing machine hose was generally acclaimed to be the funniest, and Jo's the shrillest. Jill's was easily the longest sound, but it seemed impossible to agree as to whose was lowest ... Gerald's offering was impossible to record due to the fact that he had gone outside and pushed his piece of plastic piping into the spout of the drainpipe. (Dixon, 1988, pp. 21–22)

What is happening in this short episode? For one thing, the children are discovering more about their own 'noise-making devices' by listening, sorting, categorizing the tape recorded sounds. They build on the teacher's intervention and introduce objects and tubes for sound-making; for example, a drainpipe, hoses, bicycle pumps, ballpoint pens, straws all become wind instruments. The children exercise their own potentiality and desire to learn, but the teacher's sensitive intervention has played a significant part in the process. The children have been encouraged to look rather simply see; to listen rather than simply hear; to feel rather than simply touch. The teacher is engaging with the children as they make sense of their experience, and it is through this interplay of words, actions and shared experiences that Mrs Morgan guides each child through his or her ZPD.

The process of collaborating with another person who is more knowledgeable not only gives the child new information about a topic but also confirms those aspects of the issue which the child does understand. Furthermore, this cooperation between the child and more expert others helps the child to move on (Vygotsky, 1978; Wood, 1988). The intervention is at its most effective when it is contingent upon the child's existing repertoire of skills and knowledge, that is when it is within the ZPD. When the child's level of understanding is deliberately challenged (but not challenged too much), then he or she is more likely to learn new things effectively without experiencing failure.

Vygotsky wrote a lot, but seldom reported detailed empirical studies. However one such study (by a student of his) is highlighted in box 12.1. It brings out both the importance of cultural experiences, and of the ZPD, in his thinking.

## The Impact of Bruner

Vygotsky's ideas have been extensively developed and applied in educational settings by the American psychologist Jerome Bruner (plate 12.2). Central to Bruner's thinking is the conviction that the process of learning is the same whether we are talking about the pioneer at the frontier of knowledge or the child engaged in making a construction of wooden blocks:

If one respects the ways of thought of the growing child, if one is courteous enough to translate material into his logical forms and challenging enough to tempt him to advance, then it is possible to introduce him at an early age to the ideas and styles that in later life make an educated man. We might ask, as a criterion for any subject taught in primary school, whether, when fully

PLATE 12.2   *Professor Jerome Bruner*

developed, it is worth an adult's knowing, and whether having known it as a child makes a person a better adult. If the answer to both questions is negative or ambiguous, then the material is cluttering the curriculum. (Bruner, 1963, p. 52)

Bruner described the child's cognitive development as made up of distinct ways of representing the world. The earliest to appear is the *enactive* mode of representation in which the child represents the world through action. Events are portrayed through appropriate motor responses (e.g. building with bricks, riding a bicycle). Between the ages of 2 and 6 years the child begins to represent the world through images or spatial schemas. Bruner called this the *iconic* mode of representation which enables children to use images to stand for objects. Last and most important to emerge is the *symbolic* mode of representation which, appearing at around the age of 7 years, frees children from the immediate context and enables them to symbolize (Bruner, 1966). Children at this stage are beginning to be able to 'go beyond the information given' and represent their world symbolically. This ability to symbolize, depending to a large extent on language, is at the heart of the child's capacity to think abstractly and to make knowledge her own.

These modes of representation lie at the heart of Bruner's concept of *the spiral curriculum*. By this Bruner means that the principles of a subject come to be understood by the person at increasingly sophisticated levels. He too was not happy with the Piagetian view that educators should wait for the child to be ready to learn. Instead he proposed a much more active policy of intervention. He is famous for his dictum that 'any subject can be taught effectively in some intellectually honest form to any child at any stage of development' (Bruner, 1963, p. 33). The idea behind this statement is that true knowledge arises out of a process of deepening understanding. Ideas, Bruner claimed, need to be 'revisited'. Bruner's concept of the *spiral curriculum* implied that even quite young children can grasp ideas in an intuitive way which they can return to later at progressively more complex levels of difficulty. For example, children can intuitively understand the concept of tragedy as represented in story or myth. As adults they will understand the concept in a more abstract way. Each level of understanding is valid; each can be taught in a way which is intellectually honest. In fact, he argued, the school curriculum should be built around the important issues and values of society.

Bruner argued forcefully that educators need to be concerned with the role of *structure* in learning. Teachers must address the issue of enabling students to grasp the structure of a discipline rather than simply mastering facts. The structure of a body of knowledge is as important as its mode of representation. By structure he means the principles and concepts of a discipline – relative and related to the needs of the learner. The mastery of structure gives the learner purpose and direction; it is a process which enables the child to go beyond the information given in order to generate ideas of her own. Bruner also stressed the need to encourage students to make links and to understand relationships between and across subjects. Curriculum planning should be concerned to enhance learning as an active and problem-solving process.

There are some similarities here with Piaget's theory (chapter 11). Both Bruner and Piaget view *action* as important in cognitive development. There are also similarities in the ways in which the two psychologists consider that abstract thinking grows out of action and perception. Both would agree that competence in any area of knowledge must be rooted in active experience and concrete mental operations. Where the two theorists differ, and where Bruner has been greatly influenced by the work of Vygotsky, is first in the part which language and interpersonal communication plays in this process; and secondly in the need for active intervention by expert adults (or more knowledgeable peers) for the child at a suitable level (as in the spiral curriculum) so enabling him or her to develop as a thinker and problem-solver. So, like Vygotsky, Bruner argues that instruction is an essential part of learning.

### Scaffolding

Vygotsky's *Thought and Language* was not translated into English until 1962. Bruner (1986, p. 72) describes how he welcomed the invitation to write an introduction to the book and how he read the on-going translation with 'astonishment'. Vygotsky's ideas on thought and speech as instruments for planning out action were in tune with Bruner's views. He was intrigued by Vygotsky's suggestion that society provides the tools which enable the child to become more advanced as a thinker. Bruner was especially interested in the concept of the ZPD and the role which other people play in helping the child to learn and reflect on things. Bruner called this help 'the loan of consciousness'.

However, Vygotsky had not actually spelt out in any detail how the more expert adult might 'lend' consciousness to the child who did not already have it. Bruner's metaphor of *scaffolding* is illuminative here. Imagine the tutor has erected scaffolding which could help the child to climb to a higher level of understanding. To be more effective, scaffolding has to be constructed so that the child is not asked to climb too much at once. It has to take account not only of the child's existing level, but of how far she can progress with help; essentially the idea of Vygotsky's ZPD.

Bruner and his colleagues initiated a number of research studies to investigate the role of scaffolding in learning. For example, Wood, Bruner and Ross (1976) decided to look at what happens when a tutor tries to pass on her knowledge to a child. Scaffolding, they concluded, has distinctive aspects:

*Recruitment*   The tutor's first task is to engage the interest of the child and encourage the child to tackle the requirements of the task.

*Reduction of degrees of freedom*   The tutor has to simplify the task by reducing the number of acts needed to arrive at a solution. The learner needs to be able to see whether he has achieved a fit with task requirements or not.

*Direction maintenance*   The tutor needs to keep the child's motivation up. Initially the child will be looking to the tutor for encouragement; eventually the solution of the problem should become interesting in its own right.

*Marking critical features*   A tutor highlights features of the task that are relevant. This gives information about any discrepancies between what the child has produced and what he would recognize as a correct production.

*Demonstration*   Modelling solutions to the task involves completion of a task or explanation of a solution already partly done by the young learner. The aim is that the learner will imitate this back in a better form.

(Adapted from D. Wood, J. S. Bruner and G. Ross, 1976, p. 98)

Details of an experimental study by these researchers are given in box 12.2. Here the tutor acknowledged the ZPD by being aware of what the children could recognize and then guiding them towards what they could do on their own. This kind of tutoring skill can in itself be learned. It is a skill which demands that the tutor be acting contingently upon the child's abilities. Parents do it routinely through the rituals and games which are part of normal adult-child interaction (see chapter 3) and clearly language plays a critical part in the scaffolding process.

Scaffolding appears in a whole variety of forms. It may appear when the parent responds to the child's first attempts at speech (see the section on the baby talk register in chapter 10). We might see it when the adult, closely in tune with the child's on-going monologues, helps to solve a problem. We might see it when the child, frustrated by inability to convey the excitement of a new experience, is guided by the adult to use appropriate words and images. Dunn (1984) describes the scaffolding process in operation when mothers in her study structured the feeling states of 2-year-olds, so giving the child a framework for interpreting emotions (see chapter 3).

Butterworth's (1987) studies highlight the scaffolding processes at work when the mother builds on the infant's capacity to adjust his or her own line of gaze to that of the mother, by commenting on the object of joint attention; and through the enjoyable experience of turn-taking in ritual language games and rhymes (see chapter 10, pp. 285, 305).

These examples, commonplace in family life, show the collaborative nature of the learning process and suggest that language, foremost among the social representations, provides a framework within which the growing child comes to interpret and understand experience.

## Talking and Thinking

Vygotsky held that meaning is socially constructed, and that social reality is what we achieve in the process of sharing human cognition. We *negotiate* the meaning of what we need to know. This view has strong implications for education and differs quite sharply both from the child-centred model of education which sprang from Piaget's theory and from traditional, didactic models of education. From the Vygotskian standpoint children do not operate in isolation but make knowledge their own in a community of others who share a common culture. Language plays a key part in this process. Vygotsky suggested that it was through speech – which had been formed through the processes of social interaction as outlined above – that the child develops as a thinker and learner.

To Vygotsky language reflects our culture and its forms, whether in story, folklore, fiction, films. The person as a conscious thoughtful being could accomplish very little without the aids and tools which are provided by his or her history and culture. Piaget, by contrast, had not stressed the importance of language as the principal source of cognitive development. Piaget, as discussed in chapter 11, maintained that language was strongly influenced by the underlying cognitive structures in the child. We have already examined one of his major theoretical constructs – egocentrism. Piaget made extensive observations of children at the Rousseau Institute in Geneva and, on that basis, concluded that up to half of the utterances made by children under the age of 7 years are examples of *egocentric speech*; in other words, they show no sign that the children have attempted to communicate with another person or adapted their speech so that another might understand it. Piaget observed further that young children often did not seem to care whether anyone else could understand them or not. He noticed that young children would often talk at length to themselves while engaged in solitary activity; these *monologues* were like commentaries on the children's own actions rather than forms of communication. They might also carry out *collective monologues* where children were close to one another and spoke in pairs or a group, but where the utterances were not made in response to other children's speech.

Piaget interpreted this behaviour as a sign of the child's inability to take account of the perspective of another. With maturity, the child comes to decentre and also becomes more logical. She is then able to take the perspective of others and engage in socially meaningful verbal exchanges. This process of decentration, according to Piaget, unfolds between the ages of 4 and 7 (see also chapter 10). By 7 the child's speech would become more fully socialized.

Vygotsky's view was quite different. He did not accept that the young child's language is largely egocentric and that monologues have no part to play in cognitive development. 3-year-old Ben, for example, talks to himself as he cuts out a paper figure:

'Now I'm going to make a man. Cut round here. This is his magic wand. He's a wizard now. Oops! Too far. Oh! Start again.

The monologues of younger children were to Vygotsky highly social and represented the transition between language as *a tool for regulating action and communicating needs* to language as *a tool for thought*. In fact, he argued that the

TABLE 12.1  *The contrasting views of Piaget and Vygotsky on pre-schoolers' private speech*

| Piaget's model | Vygotsky's model |
|---|---|
| *Repetition:* the child merely repeats sounds | *Social dialogue* between adult and child: children and adults engage in joint activities, e.g. peekaboo play |
| *Monologue:* the child alone speaks to herself as if she were thinking aloud | *Monologues or overt inner speech:* these are internalized to regulate a child's activity, and originate from social dialogues |
| *Collective monologue:* the child uses monologue in social settings but does not take the listeners' viewpoint into consideration. True dialogue does not emerge until around age 7 | *Inner speech:* utterances internalized in private speech to guide behaviour. Inner speech is internalized by the end of the preschool period |

monologues show children's development in their capacity to regulate their own activities – already a social and culturally formed process. The monologues help children to plan and organize their behaviour – they are a form of communication with the *self*. Vygotsky suggested that monologues become internalized at around 7 years to become *inner speech*, the dialogue with ourselves which we all have and which helps us to guide our actions. Once the meaning of words is understood, it is internalized as inner speech and then becomes thought. Inner speech makes the link between *thought* on the one hand and *the meaning of overt speech*. However, when tasks are too challenging, older children will still revert to externalized monologues. Vygotsky's and Piaget's contrasting views are summarized in table 12.1.

In Vygotsky's words, language reflects 'the organizing consciousness of the whole culture'. He argued that the child's development as a thinker arises both from the dialogue with parents and other adult carers, and in relation to the wider society of which the parents are a part. His perspective encompasses the use of language as a framework for thought and the use of language as a representation of the culture. The two are inextricably intertwined.

## The Implications for Education

This chapter has been concerned to present an alternative explanation of the development of cognition in the child from that of the preceding one. The key point has been that children's growth as thinkers cannot be understood outside the social context in which they exist and that the social context is an intrinsic part of the learning process itself. Developmental psychologists working from this perspective have become increasingly critical of the lack of emphasis on social and cultural context in Piaget's model, with its concentration on the child as an individual progressing through developmental stages. The debate continues in the field of academic developmental psychology but it is of more than academic significance. There are important practical implications for the ways in which we educate our children.

Educators influenced by the Vygotskian tradition would not be content to view the child as an individual who develops mental operations through her own actions, important though that perspective is. In addition they would propose that concepts develop in a collaborative process through interaction with others, in particular through interaction with more knowledgeable others. Bruner pointed out that the invention of 'schooling' itself has had a great impact on the nature of thinking since schooling creates particular ways of looking at problems and of acting on the world. Teachers are not, he argues, simply handing on knowledge but actively recreating distinctive ways of thinking.

This can be enabling or inhibiting. Donaldson's research has shown how children's will to learn may be unwittingly crushed by the educational experience. Competence, where not recognized or fostered, can wither. Failure to scaffold on the part of teachers, failure to build on the knowledge which the child brings to the classroom, may well lead the child to learn to fail in school settings. The committed involvement of parents and teachers is important if interventions are to be effective. Follow-up research on the impact of compensatory programmes like Project

Headstart (see chapter 14) highlight the need for active links to be forged between home and school in order that the child's learning may be experienced as meaningful and relevant. Indeed there is evidence (Tizard and Hughes, 1984; Wells, 1985) that some of the best conditions for learning may well be in the home where talk is an enjoyable, reciprocal activity in which both parent and child jointly engage and where the goals are likely to be shared ones.

The teacher in the Piagetian tradition is a facilitator who provides the right materials for the child's level of development and helps the child to 'discover' by herself, through the conflict between her existing schemas and the evidence facing her. The teacher does not confront the child with these discrepancies but stands back and allows the child to find out for herself. The view of Vygotsky and of Bruner is that the adult and child can work together to construct new schemas, and that the intervention by the more expert adult is positively helpful in moving the child's thinking on. The adult's expertise is actively harnessed to the child's level of competence and to the ZPD. Concepts are 'jointly constructed through interaction with those who already embody them, together with the ways of doing and thinking that are cultural practices, recreated with children through processes of formal and informal teaching'. (Wood, 1986, p.195). It is important, from this standpoint, to give help to the child which is contingent on her failure to give a correct response. If the child succeeds, it is important to give less help. The more the teacher's behaviour is contingent on the child's behaviour in these sorts of ways the more able the child becomes to work independently.

Even if children do not properly understand something, they may know enough for the adult to be able to direct them to relevant activity. If this activity is within the ZDP, then the scaffolding function supports the young learners. 'Contingent control helps to ensure that the demands placed on the child are likely neither to be too complex, producing defeat, nor too simple, generating boredom or distraction'. (Wood, 1988, p. 201). In fact, the commentary from more expert people helps the child integrate existing knowledge into a wider framework. Thus it supports existing understanding while giving the opportunity to branch out into new regions.

Children may also need help in having their attention directed towards significant features of a task or a situation. Left alone they might not make the right connections. The interventions by the knowledgeable adult give the child a structure within which to formulate meaning. By helping the young learner to use language as an instrument of thought, the adult frees the child from the world of immediate perceptions and enables her to 'go beyond the information given'.

It would appear, then, that the ideal situation for learning is the one-to-one context where the child can have the undivided attention of an expert. But how is this feasible in the school context? Child-initiated encounters upon which the teacher can be immediately contingent are difficult to establish and sustain in the classroom. In sharp contrast to the home, teachers are much more likely to control the learners and to ask questions which require a specific answer. There is less opportunity for exploratory activity in which the teacher can find out the individual child's ZPD. Ideally what the adult seeks to 'show and tell' children should be contingent on what they know already; more frequently, however, in classroom settings questioning highlights children's *lack* of knowledge. Wood (1988) argues that this kind of questioning strategy is counter-productive. So how can the teacher, managing a class of 30 pupils, create conditions in which to become more aware of each child's existing thoughts and tentative ideas on a topic and then respond to them contingently?

The work on *play-tutoring* described in chapter 6 gives one example of how this may be achieved in normal nursery class conditions. There is also a growing literature on the role of *peer-tutoring* in the learning process. Here the expert tutor is a fellow pupil. Foot, Morgan and Shute (1990) stress the appropriateness of Vygotsky's model in explaining how peer-tutoring works. One child (the tutor) is more knowledgeable than the other (the tutee) and each is aware of the distinctiveness of their roles as expert and novice; it is clear to each child that the aim is for the expert to impart his or her knowledge to the novice. However the 'expert' is not likely to be that much ahead of the 'novice', and so more readily appreciates the latter's difficulties and thus can scaffold effectively within the latter's ZDP.

Peer-tutoring provides a good example of interaction as a necessary condition for cognitive growth since it is through the processes which are involved in this interaction between tutor and tutee that the less expert child masters a new skill. Note that it is not simply the encounter between child and child that brings about the change but the impact of communication and instruction from the more capable peer. Learning occurs when this joint intellectual activity becomes internalized. The instruction is effective when it is slightly ahead of the tutee's actual level and when the assistance from the peer tutor lies within the ZDP.

Research enquiries have begun to investigate ways in which pupils in the classroom can explore and negotiate meaning through the processes of dialogue, active participation and engagement in issues of significance to themselves (e.g. Barnes, 1976; Cowie and Rudduck, 1988; 1991; Salmon and Claire, 1984). *Cooperative group work* can offer an effective alternative means of enabling children to act contingently upon one another. Bennett and Dunne (1989), investigating the effect of three types of grouping arrangement on primary school children's talk, note the increase in the quality of children's language and thinking when they are given the opportunity to work in small, interactive cooperative groups. The children who participated in cooperative group work showed less concern for status, less competitiveness and were significantly more likely to express evidence of logical thinking. This was particularly so when the children were encouraged to engage in an exchange of views, often conflicting, and to explore a range of possible perspectives. Even the most stilted discussions, write Bennet and Dunne, are characterized by talk in abstract modes, rarely found in individualized work. Ironically, these authors note, much of what is called 'group work' in classrooms is simply individual work carried out by children who happen to be seated round a table. The opportunity for the children to learn from active interaction, especially through dialogue and shared problem solving, is seldom used.

These studies, set in real classroom contexts, place central importance on the idea that the learning process is about the negotiation of meaning rather than its transmission, and that it is firmly rooted in personally significant issues, human contexts and social relationships. Central too is the view that in education it is essential to give pupils opportunities to acknowledge multiple perspectives on complex issues.

Advances in technology also offer support to the model of instruction outlined in this chapter. The recent development of computer assisted learning (CAL) enables teachers to harness the educational potentialities of computers to the specific needs of the child. The computer can present a series of information and tasks to the child. In *intelligent tutoring systems*, the student does not just go through a rigid linear sequence of tasks, but (depending on his or her prior responses) is taken down a branching route suited to the student's ability; for example being given more detailed help or prompts when required. Also computers can increase opportunities for socially interactive learning. Pupils, knowledgeable in this area, often become a valued resource in the classroom, thus also increasing the opportunities for genuine peer-tutoring.

## Conclusion

As we have seen, there are a number of ways in which Piaget's and Vygotsky's theories differ. They have contrasting views on language and thought. Piaget argues that thinking develops out of *action* rather than out of language. Language does not create thought but enables it to emerge. Before the age of around 7, that is before the onset of concrete operations the child, in Piaget's view, is unable to think or discuss things rationally. Preschoolers' language and thought is primarily egocentric since the child is unable to enter into the perspective of another person. Children do not enter into discussions with one another since there is no real reciprocity or attempt at mutual understanding.

Vygotsky, by contrast, did not view children's speech as egocentric but as highly social. Vygotsky saw the collective monologues in which preschoolers typically engage as representing a transition between the communicative function of language and its function as a tool of thought, that is between the social and the intellectual. The child who talks to herself, then, is involved in a process of regulating and planning ongoing activity. This overt commentary will later be internalized as inner speech or thought. Vygotsky proposed that language arises out of social interaction.

With regard to learning and thinking, Piaget claimed that children pass through a series of stages of intellectual development before they are able to reason and think logically. Teaching, from this standpoint, is only effective if the child is 'ready' to assimilate the new idea or experience. Piaget emphasized the key part of action for the child's learning. Vygotsky agreed that action underlined thinking and learning but placed much more emphasis on the role of language, and of direct intervention, and help by others more skilled in a task. However, it is sometimes overlooked that Piaget too valued peer interactions as playing a significant part in facilitating children's intellectual development (see also chapter 7).

Recently, developmental psychologists have begun to examine ways in which the insights from both Piaget's and Vygotsky's perspectives might be synthesized. Piagetian researchers such as Doise and Mugny (1984) have documented the types of cooperative context in which children progress in their understanding. Conflict of views and perspectives can encourage children to re-think (see also box 7.2). Doise and Mugny have shown that children, working in pairs or in small groups, come to solve problems more effectively than when they work alone. The reason seems to be that it is through social interaction that they came to see the solution. When the child encounters conflicting views this stimulates internal disequilibrium which the child is motivated to resolve. The social process of negotiating with peers erects a 'scaffold' which helps each child to reconstruct his or her ideas. This interpretation by Doise and Mugny starts from a Piagetian standpoint but takes account of the social context of peer interaction within which the child operates.

Research in the field of cooperative group work also offers ideas on integrating the approaches of Piaget and Vygotsky. The Jigsaw method (Aronson, 1978) is designed in such a way that children work interdependently by splitting a task into four or five sections. Each pupil has access to only part of the material to be mastered and must work with others to fit together all the pieces of the 'Jigsaw'. The pupils work in groups where they become expert in one section; the expert pupils then return to their home groups where they tutor other members of their team in the material which they have mastered. Slavin, a proponent of similar methods, asserts that:

> Under the right motivational conditions, peers can and, more important, *will* provide explanations in one another's proximal zones of development and will engage in the kind of cognitive conflict needed for disequilibration and cognitive growth. (Slavin, 1987, p. 1166)

Group learning environments, if properly structured, encourage questioning, evaluating, and constructive criticism, leading to restructuring of knowledge. For example, in these learning settings a child may need to explain something to another, defend his or her own viewpoint, engage in debate or analyse a disagreement. This can result in learning with understanding, and, many proponents claim, in fundamental cognitive restructuring.

Such possibilities do depend on structuring the learning environment correctly. Not all social interaction in cooperative learning leads to cognitive growth. Slavin (1987) emphasizes the importance of motivation, and encourages inter-group competition in learning. Brown and Palenscar (1989) suggest that the effect of collaboration depends on key factors such as the initial ability of the child and the child's social status. They argue that cooperative learning will be most helpful to a child who has only partial grasp of the situation, and who, while not overruled by another more dominant child, is faced with a view that not only conflicts with theirs but is also one they can take seriously.

### Further reading

D. Joravsky 1989: *Russian Psychology*. Oxford: Basil Blackwell, gives a fascinating historical analysis of the social and political context in which Russian psychologists, including Vygotsky, developed their theories of the human mind. For a scholarly and insightful psychological analysis of Vygotsky's cultural-historical approach to human development read J. Wertsch 1985: *Vygotsky and the Social Formation of Mind*. Cambridge, Mass.: Harvard University Press. For another overview see A. Kozulin 1990: *Vygotsky's Psychology: A Biography of Ideas*. New York and London: Harvester-Wheatsheaf.

J. Piaget 1959: *The Language and Thought of the Child*. London: Routledge and Kegan Paul, was originally written in 1923. It contains his ideas on childrens egocentric speech, which Vygotsky disagrees with in L. Vygotsky 1962: *Thought and Language*. Cambridge, Mass.: MIT Press. This actually dates from 1934, and was the first of Vygotsky's writings to be widely available in English (though in truncated form).

In *How Children Think and Learn* Oxford: Basil Blackwell, 1988, David Wood compares Piaget's ideas with those of Bruner and Vygotsky. He also considers practical implications for teachers and gives useful perspectives on the emergence of the mathematical mind and the literate mind. A very useful and readable text strongly in sympathy with the ideas of Vygotsky and Bruner. *Making Sense*, London: Methuen, 1987, edited by Jerome Bruner and Helen Haste, explores how the developing child comes to make sense of experience and understand ideas in a *social* context. The authors draw on topical research in areas such as the emergence of planning skills in young children, the social representation of gender and how children grow into rules. *Children of Social Worlds*: 1986 edited by Martin Richards and Paul Light (Polity Press in association with Blackwells) looks at children's development through the process of communication with others. The authors are strongly critical of the individualistic approach to the study of child development. They also look at ways in which children come to understand social phenomena such as the threat of nuclear war.

## Discussion Points

1 Vygotsky argued that instruction is at the heart of developing and internalizing new ideas. How can the adult most effectively help children to do this?

2 Think of the strategies which teachers might use to scaffold children's learning in the classroom. Can you think of examples from your own experience as a student?

3 Bruner claimed that 'any subject can be taught in some intellectually honest form to any child at any stage of development' (Bruner, 1963, p. 33). Do you agree?

4 How do the views of Piaget and Vygotsky differ? In what ways might they be reconciled?

5 Does language structure our thinking, or thinking structure our language?

## Practical Exercises

1 Observe nursery school children as they play, and record their speech. Do you observe the kinds of solitary or collective monologues which Piaget described? How much evidence is there of the child's adapting his or her speech to the needs of others?

2 Compare the experience of working (a) *individually* and (b) *in a small discussion group* on a learning task such as reading a new chapter of this book. The discussion group should be organized in such a way that each individual has the opportunity to express ideas, however tentative and unformed they may be. The emphasis should be on non-judgemental, supportive commentary from peers. How useful is it to explore ideas in a small cooperative group? Ask group members in turn to describe how they felt in the group and what they learned from one another. Are there other ways in which the group might be structured in order to facilitate learning?

3   Working in pairs devise a peer-tutoring lesson. One will take on the role of *expert*, the other the role of *novice*. Identify some aspect of a skill which the expert can impart to the novice (e.g. knowledge of a foreign language; understanding of a computer programme; ability to play a musical instrument). See how effectively the expert can structure the session so that the intervention is challenging but not discouraging to the novice. Make sure to allow time at the end for debriefing so that each partner can evaluate the experience.

# Box 12.1

# The development of [social] scientific concepts in childhood

Vygotsky and his colleague Shif designed a study to investigate 'the relationship between instruction, learning and the processes involved in the internal development of [social] scientific concepts in the child's consciousness'. The first aim of this research was to *describe* the unique characteristics of the ways in which concepts about social science, as opposed to everyday concepts, developed in school-age children. The second aim was to examine the relationship between instruction and development. This posed a much broader question. In Vygotsky's words,

> Does the process involved in the internal development of concepts follow instruction like a shadow follows the object which casts it, not coinciding with it but reproducing and repeating its movement, or do both processes exist in a more complex and subtle relationship which requires special investigation?

Using a series of pictures, the experimenter told Grade II and Grade IV children (that is 7- and 9-year-olds) a story that ended with a sentence broken off at the word 'because' or 'although'. This procedure was supplemented by interviews with the children (Vygotsky calls them 'clinical discussions') in order to establish levels of conscious reflection on 'cause–effect relationships with both social scientific and real-world material'. The pictures illustrated a sequence of events based either on materials from social science lessons (e.g.

BOX TABLE 12.1.1   *Percentage of completed sentences, illustrating understanding of scientific and of everyday concepts, at two grade (age) levels*

| Sentences with the conjuction: | | Grade 2 | Grade 4 |
|---|---|---|---|
| | | Percentage completions | |
| Because | Scientific concepts | 79.7 | 81.8 |
| | Everyday concepts | 59.0 | 81.3 |
| Although | Scientific concepts | 21.3 | 79.5 |
| | Everyday concepts | 16.2 | 65.5 |

*Source*: Vygotsky, 1987

Based on L. S. Vygotsky 1987: The development of scientific concepts in childhood. In R. W. Rieber and A. S. Carton (eds) *The Collected Works of L. S. Vygotsky*, Vol. I. New York: Plenum Press.

'Planned economy is possible in the USSR because...' to which one correct answer was ' ... there is no private property') or common occurrences in everyday life (e.g. 'Kolya went to the cinema because ... ', 'The train left the tracks because... ' or 'Olya still reads poorly although ... '. In addition, Vygotsky and his colleague observed the children during their social science lessons.

An analysis of the results for each age-group (see box table 12.1.1) showed that the development of social scientific concepts, that is those which develop through instruction, outstrips the development of everyday concepts, that is those that develop through the child's practical activity and immediate social interaction. This suggested to Vygotsky that instruction plays a critical role in the development of thinking in the school-age child. It also appears that the children's understanding of concepts following the conjunction 'although' developed much more slowly than for those following the conjunction 'because'.

The data also showed that, whereas the younger children have more understanding of social scientific concepts than everyday concepts, there is a progressive development of social scientific thinking which is followed by a rapid increase in levels of performance with everyday concepts by the older age range so that the gap between the understanding of the two kinds of concepts has narrowed.

Vygotsky concludes that the accumulation of knowledge in the educational context leads directly to an increase in the level of scientific thinking and that this, in turn, influences the development of spontaneous, everyday thinking. To Vygotsky this confirmed his view that instruction plays a leading role in the development of thinking abilities in the school-age child. How does this happen? Vygotsky explained it in this way:

> The development of scientific concepts *begins with the verbal definition*. As part of an organised system, this verbal definition descends to the concrete; it descends to the phenomena which the concrete represents. In contrast, the everyday concept tends to develop outside any definite system; it tends to move upwards towards abstraction and generalization. The development of the scientific ... concept, a phenomenon that occurs as part of the educational process, constitutes a unique form of systematic cooperation between the teacher and the child. The maturation of the child's higher mental functions occurs in the cooperative process, that is, it occurs through the adult's assistance and participation .... The earlier maturation of scientific concepts is explained by the unique form of cooperation between the child and the adult that is the central element of the educational process; it is explained by the fact that in this process knowledge is transferred to the child in a definite system. This is also why the level of development of scientific concepts forms a zone of proximal possibilities for the development of everyday concepts. The scientific concept blazes the trail for the everyday concept. It is a form of preparatory instruction which leads to its development.

The actual methodological details of Vygotsky's and Shif's study are sketchy, to say the least! There are also some problems in translation; for example, the Russian word 'obuchenie', translated here as 'instruction', actually has a different shade of meaning in Russian a bit closer to 'learning'. (There are analogous problems in translating Piaget.) Nevertheless, Vygotsky's ideas have an influence even 60 years later.

# Box 12.2

# The role of tutoring in problem solving

This study aimed to investigate the nature of the tutorial role of the adult expert in helping the less expert child to solve a problem. The tutor was to teach 3-, 4-, and 5-year-old children to build a 3-dimensional structure, a task which on their own they would not have been able to do. The researchers proposed that, in order to benefit from help, the learner has to be able to *recognize* a solution before he is able to produce a good strategy for solving the problem alone. The investigators, therefore, were looking at the behaviour which young children engage in when they are trying to identify the nature of the problem; and they were also interested in the way in which the adult tutor 'scaffolded' the children's steps towards the completion of the task. The method was observational. They were not testing a hypothesis about the tutoring process, but giving a systematic description of children's responses to different kinds of help from the adult tutor.

30 children were equally divided into groups of 3-, 4- and 5-year-olds; the age-groups contained equal numbers of boys and girls. The researchers had designed a task which, in their view, would be interesting and challenging to young children. David Wood had designed a wooden toy consisting of 21 blocks which combined to form a pyramid 9 inches high on a 9 inch square base. The pyramid had six levels. The top block was a solid square with a circular depression in its bottom. The other five layers were composed of four equal-sized blocks made up of two interlocking pairs. Each pair fitted together by a hole and peg system. Each four-block layer had a round depression in its base and a matched elevation on top. These could only be formed by putting the pairs together in the correct orientation. (See box figure 12.2.1.).

It was agreed in advance that the tutor, Gail Ross, working with individual 3-, 4- and 5-year-olds, was to allow the children (here referred to as 'he' or 'they') to do as much as possible by themselves. When she had to intervene she would do so verbally before she demonstrated what to do. She was 'led' by each child in the sense that his success or failure at the task determined the next level of instruction.

After the initial period of free play with the jumbled blocks, the tutor began to show the child how to connect a pair. If he succeeded in doing this spontaneously, then she would invite him to 'make some more like that one'. The tutor then began to respond systematically to three types of response from the child. The tutor's interventions were classified into three categories:

1   *Direct interventions* e.g. joining and positioning two blocks to make a pair; if the child ignored her and continued with play then she would join two blocks to form a correct pair.

Based on material in D. Wood, J. S. Bruner and G. Ross 1976: *Journal of Child Psychology and Psychiatry*, 17, 89–100

BOX FIGURE 12.2.1 *Stages in the construction of a pyramid. Source: Wood, D. (1988). How Children Think and Learn. Oxford: Blackwell (p. 68, Figure 3.3)*

2 *Verbal corrections* e.g. 'Does this (a mismatched construction) look like this (a matched one)?' If the child picked up the blocks which she had assembled and manipulated them then she would verbally tell the child that the pieces were not correctly joined.

3 *General verbal direction* to remind the child of the task requirements, e.g. 'Can you make any more like this?' If the child tried to do something with the blocks (e.g. putting pegs into holes) similar to the tutor but had overlooked an aspect, she would ask him to compare his with hers.

Box table 12.2.1 shows that there were significant age-related differences in the amount and type of help which the children required. The 5-year-olds received significantly less help than the 4-year-olds ($p < 0.05$) and the 3-year-olds ($p < 0.05$). If we look at the ratio of 'showing' and 'telling' we can see that both 5-year-olds ($p < 0.002$) and 4-year-olds ($p < 0.0002$) received significantly higher proportions of verbal assistance than the 3-year-olds.

Box table 12.2.1 shows that the main kind of interaction between tutor and 4-year-olds was verbal. As the researchers point out, 'with the youngest ones, the tutor is principally concerned with luring them into the task either by demonstrating it or providing tempting material. Consequently, the tutor intervenes directly twice as often with the 3-year-olds as with the 4-year-olds, and four times more often than with the eldest group. The tutor, then, is both intervening more and being ignored more when working with 3-year-olds than with older children'. So the tutor seems to be principally a lure to the younger children but takes on the role of 'verbal prodder and corrector' for 4-year-olds. When we come to the 5-year-olds, the median number of tutorial interventions drops by half. The tutor seems to have become a 'confirmer or checker of constructions' since the children are clearly aware of the point of the task. For older children verbal interventions are more successful (Box table 12.2.2).

This experiment demonstrates the function of scaffolding. The youngest children in this study can *recognize* a correct solution but they have to be induced to try the task in order to *learn* through recognition. These children had other ideas about what to do with the blocks. The tutor had a hard task in keeping the goal before their eyes. By the age of four, the children now know about constructing, so the role of the tutor has changed. She now has to help them recognize the discrepancy between what the task requires and what they have achieved so far. This shifts the balance from showing to telling. The 5-year-old needs the

BOX TABLE 12.2.1 *Median instances of direct interventions, verbal corrections and general verbal directions*

| | Age | | |
|---|---|---|---|
| | *3* | *4* | *5* |
| Direct intervention | 12.0 | 6.0 | 3.0 |
| Verbal corrections | 3.0 | 5.0 | 4.5 |
| Verbal directions | 5.0 | 8.0 | 3.0 |
| Total verbal intervention | 8.0 | 13.0 | 7.5 |
| Total help received | 20.0 | 19.0 | 10.5 |
| Ratio: $\dfrac{\text{'show'}}{\text{'tell'}}$ | $\dfrac{12.0}{8.0} = 1.5$ | $\dfrac{6.0}{13.0} = 0.46$ | $\dfrac{3.0}{7.5} = 0.40$ |

BOX TABLE 12.2.2 *Relative successes of each group with 'showing' and 'telling'*

|  | Age | | |
| --- | --- | --- | --- |
|  | 3 | 4 | 5 |
| Showing succeeds | 40 % | 63 % | 80 % |
| Telling succeeds | 18 % | 40 % | 57 % |

tutor in a still different way. He knows what he wants to do and only asks for help when he is having problems or needs to check on a particular construction. The tutor is becoming superfluous. The child is becoming self-controlling and can do the task on his own.

What can these results tell us about the effect which adult help can have on the child's capacity to solve a problem? The results suggest that the tutor became 'consciousness for two' (Bruner, 1986, p.75) for the children she tutored. She directed their attention to the task, kept them on task, kept the segments of the task appropriate to the child's capacity, she set things up so that the child could recognize a solution before he could solve the problem or even understand a verbal explanation of it. She operated within the ZPD which existed between what children can recognize when shown them and what they can do on their own. She did what the child could not do, but she then enabled the child to do with her what he could not do alone.

As the children acquired mastery of the task requirements, they became able to be self-regulating. At this point the tutor handed over those parts of the task where she was no longer needed. This demonstrated the transactional nature of the learning process. The study provides in microcosm an illustration of the way in which the adult can help the child through the ZPD.

One of the limitations of this study was that, whilst identifying tutoring functions, it had little to say about the actual processes (e.g. when and how each function should be realized). In part, the notion of contingent control of learning was an attempt to specify at least some aspects of the processes involved. The next step would be an examination of how the tutor could learn to do it most effectively. Case studies documenting in detail the interactions which take place between tutor and child would make a useful complement to this kind of study. In fact, it is instructive to look at Wells (1985) in the analysis of pupil-teacher talk to see examples of good and bad practice.

# 13

# Intelligence and Attainment

Psychologists studying cognitive development are interested in the *processes* of intellectual growth, as we saw in chapters 11 and 12. A rather different tradition has been the 'psychometric' one. Here psychologists have devised tests to measure a person's *aptitude* or *attainment*. Generally, the emphasis has been on comparing individuals for their performance, in a quantified way.

Aptitude or ability tests are designed to predict what a person can accomplish, given further training. The most well-known aptitude tests are intelligence tests. 'Intelligence' is usually taken as the ability to cope with one's environment (we discuss the definition of intelligence in more detail later), and intelligence tests are meant to measure this general kind of aptitude. In practice, however, intelligence tests have been used to predict educational ability and, later, achievement. There can also be more specific aptitude tests, for example, for musical ability or for pilot training.

Attainment tests, by contrast, measure what a person has achieved after training. Conventional examinations are attainment tests, as would be, to use the previous examples, an examination in music or a test of competence after completing a course of training as a pilot. The UK Education Reform Act (1988) specifies attainment targets for three core subjects – English, Mathematics and Science. Here a single assessment system is used to inform schools and teachers in planning the progress of their pupils, to report individual achievements to parents and other teachers, and to contribute to published statistics for local and national use. The Task Group on Assessment and Testing (TGAT) in the context of the National Curriculum explicitly makes a distinction between the assessment of *ability* and the assessment of *attainment*:

> Ability tests ... provide a general impression of which children are more or less successful. Such norm-referenced assessment has the advantage that overall performance can be reported as a single letter or number and that each child's performance can be compared with that of other children. Yet any aim to increase 'ability' is probably too general a concept to guide teaching. TGAT proposed that teachers should assess only that which is observable. Teaching decisions ... should always be based on an assessment, no matter how informal, of the children's responses to the current activity. (School Examinations and Assessment Council, 1990, p. 5).

In this chapter we shall first discuss the nature of intelligence tests and their history. Then we will consider the educational needs of both gifted children and children with special needs. We move on to examine other methods of assessment used in the educational system and finally more recent theories of the structure of intellect.

## The Early History of Intelligence Tests

Galton, in the 1880s was one of the first to attempt the scientific measurement of intelligence with a series of tests of reaction time and memory acuity. His view that intelligence, like physical variables of height and weight, was distributed systematically in the general population was an influential one, but his tests turned out to have little predictive value with regard to adult success or school performance, and were abandoned.

Early in the twentieth century, two French psychologists, Binet and Simon (1905), published tests which, they claimed, could identify children who were failing to make progress within the normal school system. Their aim was to give these children the special education which the overcrowded Paris schools were unable to provide. The battery of tests which Binet and Simon had devised represented the kinds of abilities which, in their view, children typically used during the school years, and included word definitions, comprehension, tests of reasoning and knowledge of numbers. Their assumption was that children who could not perform these tasks were unlikely to be able to cope with the normal level of school work. Binet and Simon had a very practical assignment – to differentiate between those who were failing at school and those who were successful; their intention was not to measure an abstract cognitive quality.

When they published their definition of intelligence in 1916 the emphasis was still on adaptation to real life situations; they called it 'judgement'.

> It seems to us that in intelligence there is a fundamental faculty, the impairment or the lack of which is of the utmost importance for practical life. This faculty is *judgement*, otherwise called good sense, practical sense, initiative, the faculty of adapting oneself to circumstances. To judge well, to reason well, these are the essential activities of intelligence. (Binet and Simon, 1916)

Binet and Simon developed age scales of mental ability by selecting items characteristic of what children of different ages could begin to succeed at. For example, a younger child might be able to repeat three numbers; an older child might not only be able to do this but also repeat five numbers in reverse order. Any particular child would then attempt test items of increasing difficulty until he/she consistently failed them, at which point the tester could calculate the child's 'mental age'. The average 5-year-old, for example, would complete test items at the 5-year-old level; a retarded 5-year-old might fail to solve test problems beyond the 4-year-old level, and would then have a mental age of 4. Later, these age scores were expressed as a ratio of mental age (MA) to chronological age (CA), and this formed the basis for the 'Intelligence Quotient' (IQ):

$$\frac{\text{Mental age}}{\text{Chronological age}} \times 100 = \text{IQ}$$

The average child's IQ by this calculation would be 100 and the IQs of children above or below the average could be calculated accordingly. The numerical scores of the IQ were less cumbersome than the original age scores and made it possible to compare the relative intellectual capability of individuals, even at different ages. The IQ assessment also made it easier to calculate correlations between intelligence and a whole range of variables.

## The Stanford–Binet Intelligence Scale

After Binet and Simon had produced their scale of items for measuring mental age, it was adopted by Terman at Stanford University, California, for use in the USA. Terman increased the original 54 tests to 90, and age graded the items on 1,000 children and 400 adults. This process of age grading items on a large representative sample is called *standardizing*. The scale, published in 1916, was called the First Revision of the Stanford–Binet. It produced mental age scores, like the original Binet test, and IQ was calculated as the ratio of MA to CA.

There were two main types of test item – verbal and non-verbal. Verbal tests relied on language abilities, e.g. general knowledge, comprehension, understanding similarities between things, vocabulary. Non-verbal or performance tests aimed to measure the child's perceptual skills and non-verbal reasoning, such as the ability to arrange pictures in a logical sequence to make a coherent story, to copy designs using a set of coloured blocks, or assemble pieces of a jigsaw-type puzzle into the right arrangement as quickly as possible.

In 1937, Terman and a colleague, Merrill, produced a substantial extension and revision of the scale. This Second Revision was made up of two similar but separate scales, each comprising 192 tests; these were called the L and M scales, and could be used as alternate forms of the test. The Second Revision was standardized on nearly 3,200 persons and, as before, was used to calculate mental age and from that, IQ.

In 1960 a Third Revision was published. This revision was necessary because some of the earlier items were clearly becoming dated or inappropriate for certain groups of subjects. The two separate L and M scales were recombined into a single L–M scale, taking the best from each and dropping some items. The test was standardized on nearly 4,500 persons.

Another change in the 1960 revision was in the calculation of IQ. The formula using mental age had two important drawbacks. First, it had been assumed that mental age did not increase after age 16 – an arbitrary assumption since found to be false. Secondly, the variation in IQ across individuals was different, depending on age level. Therefore, it was decided to calculate IQ in terms of the deviation or *standard score* of the subject from others of his or her own age. The final test was designed so that at each age level from 2 years to 18 years, the mean score was 100, but the standard deviation was 16. Thus someone with an IQ of 100 is at the mean for his or her age level; an IQ of 116 means a score one standard deviation above the mean, and so on.

## The reliability of the scale

If a test is said to be *reliable*, this means it can be used consistently to measure something. One way of assessing whether a scale is reliable is to give it twice to the same persons within a short time interval and see if the same result is achieved. Unfortunately, there is some familiarity or practice effect if the time gap is very short. An alternative is to use two versions of the same test. This was available in the L and M scales of the 1937 revision and when these were given within a week of each other, correlations ranging from 0.83 to 0.98 were obtained (depending on the age and intelligence of subjects). This remains the best evidence of reliability, even for the 1960 scale.

## The validity of the scale

If a test is *valid*, then it should be measuring what it is designed to measure, in this case, intelligence. How do we know that the Stanford–Binet scale is doing this?

Three sources of validity are cited in the manual (Terman and Merrill, 1960):

1 The items are based on the 1937 scale, in turn based on the 1916 scale, in turn based on Binet's items.
2 The items were such that performance on them improved with age.
3 Performance on individual items agreed well with performance on the total scale. Those items with poor correlations were dropped. The average item correlation with the total scale was increased from 0.61 in the 1937 scale to 0.66 in the 1960 scale.

As can be seen, the evidence for validity is limited. The evidence that the scale comprises a large number of subtests which correlate reasonably together (3, above), and that performance improves with age (2, above), does not tell us much. These criteria could hold for a test of physical dexterity or social confidence, as much as intelligence. Thus, a lot hinges on the nature of the items, being traced back to the earlier scales (1, above), and thus to the strengths and limitations of the beliefs of the first investigators – Binet, Simon and, later, Terman.

Binet devised his test for educational purposes, and other researchers have generally found that intelligence test scores do give a reasonable prediction of academic achievement. This is another possible source of validity. It does not prove that the tests measure 'intelligence' in a very general sense, but it does suggest they provide some measure of conventional academic ability, or ability to profit by the conventional educational system. This was the basis of the later use of the tests to select children for different kinds of educational provision.

## Later Uses of Intelligence Tests

The Binet test was initially used simply to differentiate between 'normal' children and those with learning difficulties; an IQ of 70 was taken as the cut-off point below which the child needed special education. However, in the UK Cyril Burt went on from there to argue that in any group of normal children, the variations in mental ability would be so wide as to make it impossible to teach them all at the same level. Since he had observed that the gap between the bright and dull children became even wider at the secondary school, he recommended the organization of classes on the basis of mental ability rather than chronological age. It was this view that the individual should be assigned a place in society according to his or her intellectual ability which was to have far-reaching effects on the educational system in Britain.

During the First World War, when large numbers of people were being assigned into categories to meet the requirements of different work roles, there was a proliferation of group intelligence and aptitude tests. After the war, the large industrial companies also demanded batteries of selection tests which could measure specific aptitudes in skills such as engineering, typing, dressmaking. This type of selection procedure, it was claimed, provided an effective means of assigning individuals to occupations appropriate to their abilities. Burt was one of the first psychologists in the newly formed National Institute of Industrial Psychology, and with his strong commitment to the idea that intelligence was innate, static throughout life and measurable, he proposed that intelligence tests also be used in schools with the aim of providing all children with an education appropriate to their level of mental ability. In his day Burt was highly respected as an educational psychologist, although he is now discredited because of his fraudulent research into the heritability of intelligence (see chapter 1).

With hindsight it is easy to see that the hierarchical concept of intelligence presented by these pioneers in the field of psychometrics reflected the hierarchical structure of society, and so was readily accepted as a means of assigning individuals to 'suitable' roles in that society. At that time, however, it was believed that intelligence tests were objective and accurate means of assessing mental ability. The tests, in fact, appeared to offer a fairer measure of the potential ability of children from differing backgrounds than did conventional examinations and school reports; for example, they were thought to be less susceptible to social biases which might affect teachers' evaluations. Unfortunately, insufficient weight was given to the effects of a child's environment on test performance, due to Burt's unfounded assumption that the tests measured 'innate ability'.

What then were the implications of the psychometric approach for educational practice? If, as Burt and many psychometrists believed, intelligence is an innate, stable factor, then it would follow logically that once suitable measures had been devised, children could be grouped according to ability levels for educational purposes. In the years following the First World War, when the Hadow Report (1926) recommended the establishment of secondary education for all children after 11, current psychological thinking had a very strong influence. Previously the majority of children had remained at the same elementary school until they were old enough to leave; only those bright enough to win a scholarship at 11 went on to 'grammar schools'. The Hadow Report suggested that for all children there should be a definite change of school at the age of 11 and that there should be a range of post-primary schools available – technical, selective and non-selective modern schools as well as traditional grammar schools.

In order to assign each child to the appropriate school, some form of assessment would have to take place; by implication, the classification of children through some form of grading or streaming was to begin during the primary school years. This official approval of selection and streaming was extended in the Hadow Report on Primary Education (1931) and the Handbook of Suggestions for Teachers (1937). The Spens Report (1938), also strongly influenced by psychometric thinking, advocated three-track streaming in primary schools and a selective tripartite system for the secondary years of schooling. (In practice, the number of technical schools was very few so the system was a *bipartite* one of allocating children to either a 'grammar' or 'secondary modern' school at the age of 11.)

Thus, by the late 1930s it was standard practice to select children at 11+ on the basis of attainment in English and arithmetic, and performance on an intelligence test. Furthermore, it was widely believed that children could be accurately categorized into different groups, each with particular educational needs (see table 13.1). Thus, children were not only selected at 11, but, once in the secondary schools, were further streamed into even narrower ability groups, the A, B and C streams. A hierarchical attitude to the curriculum grew up, with children in the A streams following academic courses, while C stream children studied practical subjects like domestic science, art, crafts etc.

By the end of the Second World War, attitudes were changing again. A Labour government came to power with a large majority and popular support for an attack on inequality in society. IQ tests themselves were coming to be seen as a less objective measure of mental ability than the psychologists claimed. There was also greater awareness of the detrimental effects which selection and streaming had on children, and the way in which the selective system discriminated against children from under-privileged backgrounds. However, despite the reaction against streaming in schools, the 11+ and the tripartite system, the Labour government failed to make the establishment of a comprehensive system of secondary education a high priority. The 1944 Education Act aimed to provide equality of opportunity for all children 'according to age, aptitude and ability', but it left the implementation of this policy to the local education authorities. Official sanction had been given to egalitarianism, but so firmly entrenched was the selective system that the changeover to a comprehensive system of secondary education was a very gradual one.

TABLE 13.1   *The categorization of children on the basis of IQ, as envisaged during the 1930s*

| IQ | Educational category | % of population |
|---|---|---|
| 50 | Ineducable idiots: occupation centres | 0.2 |
| 50–70 | Mentally defective: special schools | 2.0 |
| 70–85 | Dull and backward: 'C' classes in schools | 10.0 |
| 85–115 | Normal pupils: 'B' and 'A' classes in senior schools | 76.0 |
| 115–30 | Bright pupils: selective central schools | 10.0 |
| 130–50 | Scholarship pupils: secondary schools | 2.0 |
| 150+ | Scholarship pupils: ultimately university honours | 0.2 |

Source: Adapted from Evans and Waites, 1981

Burt and his colleagues continued to support the use of tests in the selective system and to defend the psychometric position against the hostile political climate of the post-war years. Although the 11+ as a selection procedure had, by the 1970s, been abolished in most parts of Britain, many of the arguments concerning selection, streaming, equality of opportunity and maintenance of standards continue in educational debate today; the controversies have not been resolved. Even this brief review of intelligence testing indicates the enormous influence the psychometric movement has had on educational thinking in this century.

The use of IQ tests may, however, still have application to some areas of educational psychology. In particular, the tests may be used as part of the assessment process in considering children at the extremes of the normal educational distribution – children with learning difficulties and gifted children.

## The Child with Special Needs

Children with special needs are usually considered as those who are failing within the normal educational system or who are, in some way, performing below the average which can be expected of children from their age group. In the past these children were categorized according to their handicaps, e.g. as educationally subnormal (ESN) pupils with IQs below 85, maladjusted pupils, or physically handicapped pupils (Ministry of Education, 1959); three to four children in every 1,000, labelled 'the mentally handicapped', were considered to be 'ineducable' and either remained at home or were placed in training centres or hospitals. In 1970 the Education (Handicapped Children) Act allowed the mentally handicapped to be educated in separate schools or institutions. At this point, the terms ESN(M) (where M stood for 'moderate') and ESN(S) (where S stood for 'severe') came into use; an IQ of 50 marked the dividing line between the two. More recently, the Warnock Report (1978) has suggested a radical change in procedure by recommending that 'statutory categorization of pupils should be abolished' and that educational provision should arise from a detailed description of the special needs of each child.

The Education Reform Act (1988) explicity states that the National Curriculum should be broad enough to cover 'the substantial majority of the ability spectrum' at each level. Furthermore, the Act requires local education authorities to ensure that pupils with special educational needs have their statements amended, if necessary, to take account of the National Curriculum. The aim is that each pupil should be 'stretched' to reach his or her potential.

How has this change in perspective come about? At the extremes, there is usually little disagreement about the meaning of a label attached to a particular child but there is also a large area in which it is difficult to know where the cut-off point between 'normal' and 'abnormal' behaviour or attainment occurs. When can it be said that a child's behaviour is so disturbed that he or she can be labelled 'maladjusted'? How far below the norm for his or her class does a child have to fall to be called 'a slow learner'? How do we take into account the variety of factors that may contribute to educational failure?

Some learning difficulties have been ascribed to general intellectual impairment.

Others, however, may be due to an unstimulating or stressful home background, to emotional disturbance, to a physical condition, to poor diet, or to a combination of factors. For example, Down's syndrome ('mongolism') results from a chromosomal abnormality and can be labelled as a distinct category of disability, yet for the individual so classified there can be a wide range of social, emotional and educational possibilities, and the attitudes of those who interact with him or her may be crucial factors. Similarly, Galloway (1979, p. 7) pointed out an even wider range of abilities encompassed in the category ESN(M):

> assessment as ESN(M) may mean that a child is very backward in all areas of development and needs specialized teaching of a sort that no ordinary school can be expected to provide; or that he is seriously retarded educationally due to prolonged illness; or that his educational retardation is due to learning difficulties associated with some specific perceptual problem; or that he comes from a problem family and is performing at the same level that one should expect of any child in similar circumstances.

Particular concern arose over the observations that ethnic minority children were disproportionately over-represented in the ESN category, and the use of intelligence tests as an accurate means of selection came under heavy criticism.

Intelligence tests are not now used routinely as they were in the past to assess low-attaining children. Educational psychologists try instead to assess children in the context of their home background, medical history of life events and in relation to the problems which the children, their parents or their teachers are experiencing. For example, if a child has had prolonged periods of illness or a traumatic event such as the loss of a parent, then these circumstances are taken into account when assessing present levels of attainment.

Methods of assessment are chosen which best answer the questions raised and which are linked to intervention procedures, such as specialist tuition. These methods may include IQ tests, but many other measures are also used. For example, naturalistic observation of the child's behaviour systematically recorded by parents and teachers can lead to a greater understanding of language capacity, performance on cognitive tasks and attention span. This approach can bypass formal testing and provide useful baselines for future progress. Educational tests can also give measures of attainment in specific areas, such as mathematics and reading. Diagnostic tests can help unravel reasons for a child's poor performance (for example, reading disabilities). Social assessment can be helpful, especially when linked with training programmes. These can cover self-help, communication and social skills, emotional adjustment and health.

The method of provision for the educational needs of these children remains a controversial one. If children with special needs continue within the normal school system, they have the advantages of sports facilities, laboratories, library and other school resources, as well as the possibility of choice from the full range of school subjects; there are also opportunities to mix with ordinary children and to learn the social skills they will need for survival in adult life. The task of educating the child with special needs can stimulate teachers to develop more creative and flexible methods. Additionally, the presence of these children in the ordinary setting gives staff and other pupils the opportunity to develop positive attitudes towards disability, based on familiarity and understanding rather than prejudice and ignorance.

There are also disadvantages. Lessons may not always be designed to cater for these children's needs. There may be a frequent sense of failure and inadequacy, and other children may not always be tolerant. Resentment may arise from the extra time and tuition which children with special needs require. To some educationalists there remain strong arguments in favour of special schools staffed by people trained to meet the social, emotional, physical and educational needs of these children. Even the Warnock Report (1978) recognized that there are some very severely disabled individuals for whom special schools are a necessity.

However, the main recommendations of the Warnock Report were that most children with special needs should not be segregated into special schools or classes. The 1981 Education Act has required in Britain that local authorities integrate children with special needs into mainstream education. The implementation of the Act is taking time, with wide variations from region to region but the Education Reform Act (1988), while acknowledging that a statement of special educational needs may specify some modification in the ranges of levels appropriate at different key stages for the individual child, requires that 'any departure from the National Curriculum be decided in the light of educational, medical, psychological and other evidence about the pupil including the views of the pupil's parents' (DES, 1989, paragraph 56). However, the present concern with accountability in school performance may discourage teachers from devoting their energies to children who have extreme learning difficulties. Clearly there is a great need for training and support for teachers in this task and such major changes cannot take place without considerable financial outlay; integration cannot happen overnight, and it is necessary to create a climate in which acceptance of the child with special needs can take place.

## The Gifted Child

Gifted children also have special needs. A child may be described as 'gifted' who is outstanding in either a general domain (such as exceptional performance on an intelligence test), or a more specific area of ability, such as music, or sport. Some researchers have attempted to identify the characteristics of gifted children at an early age, drawing up checklists such as the two shown in table 13.2. Such checklists are of limited value: they avoid the issue of whether general or specific abilities are the criteria for giftedness. In practice, most research studies of giftedness are concerned with the high IQ child, and these offer the most cohesive group of investigations.

Even if we identify criteria of giftedness, we still have the problem of where to set the borderline between gifted children and others. Terman (1925) defined the gifted child as one who had an IQ of over 140; Ogilvie (1973) set the borderline at 130. DeHaan and Havighurst (1960) set it at 120. The figures shown in table 13.3 indicate the approximate numbers cut off by different borderlines on a standard intelligence test such as the Stanford–Binet or the Wechsler (WISC-R) test (see below). These figures refer to a total school population and will vary considerably from one

TABLE 13.2  *Signs of giftedness according to Bridges, and Tempest*

| Bridges (1969) | Tempest (1974) |
|---|---|
| 1  They read as early as 3 years old | 1  Exceptionally good reader |
| 2  High powers of abstraction | 2  Ability to deal with abstract problems |
| 3  High qualitative level of questioning | 3  High level of curiosity expressed through perceptive questions |
| 4  Speed of thought | 4  Quickness of response |
| 5  Do not want to write as this breaks up oral communication | 5  Ability to work quickly, although sometimes inaccurately |
| 6  Withdraw to work on their own | 6  Work on their own |
| 7  Enormous energy | 7  Likely to be physically superior |
| | 8  Likely to be highly competitive |
| | 9  More selective in interests |

neighbourhood to another as well as from chance fluctuations. Thus, while the average school class should contain one child with an IQ of 130 or over, the number might fluctuate from none in many classes to say six in a few.

The most famous study of giftedness is Terman's (1925–59) *Genetic Studies of Genius*. This embodies a longitudinal study which has not yet been completed even though Terman himself is dead and the participants are now in their 70s and 80s. At the beginning of the study the participants ranged in age from 6 to 12 years and represented roughly the brightest 1 per cent of children in the State of California at that time. Almost all had IQs of 140 and over as measured by the Stanford–Binet, and the average score was 151. They excelled in reading, language and general information. Physical health and growth were superior from birth on. According to mothers' reports, they walked and talked early. Teachers' reports on maladjustment indicated that only 13 per cent of the gifted were 'nervous' as compared to 16 per cent of controls; thus common sense views that gifted children were likely to be more disturbed than other children were not confirmed in Terman's sample.

A follow-up in 1947 when the mean age was 35 indicated that the initial level of intelligence had been maintained. Health statistics were superior; death rate was low

TABLE 13.3  *Percentages of gifted children at different cut-off points*

| IQ | Approx. numbers |
|---|---|
| 150 and over | 0.1 (1 in 1000) |
| 140 and over | 0.5 (1 in 200) |
| 130 | 2.5 (1 in 40) |
| 120 and over | 10  (1 in 10) |

and only 5 per cent admitted serious maladjustment. Sixty-eight per cent had graduated from college. Many had been outstanding in their professions; for example, they had produced a large number of publications and patents.

In 1959 another follow-up indicated that they had continued to maintain their high achievements in occupational level; 71 per cent were in professional, semi-professional or managerial positions compared with 14 per cent of the Californian population as a whole, and their average income was higher than that of the average college graduate.

Most of the subjects in Terman's sample appeared to be exceptionally well-integrated, healthy and well-adjusted individuals. Unfortunately, as Terman's selection procedure was partly based on teachers' ratings, home background factors may have confounded his criterion of high intelligence. For example, working class and ethnic minority children might well have been under-represented from the start of the study. Certainly, social environment and home upbringing played an important part in the success of Terman's sample, even though, true to the psychometric tradition, he initially emphasized genetic influences.

Some of the literature on giftedness stresses problems and difficulties which gifted children experience, or that giftedness, especially where it is not recognized, can become a handicap. Hitchfield (1973) found that teachers were not good at identifying the gifted child. Sixty per cent of the children with an IQ of 140 + were *not* rated by teachers as being in the top 5 per cent in areas such as use of books, mathematical ability, general knowledge and oral ability; 45 per cent were not rated as being exceptionally good in any of these areas.

Torrance, writing of highly creative children, argued that 'society in general is downright savage towards creative thinkers' (1970, p. 361) and accused teachers of misunderstanding gifted children's unusual questions and answers. He argued that 'when teachers fail to understand highly creative children, refusal to learn, delinquency or withdrawal may be a consequence'. Joan Freeman tackled the question of whether this is an accurate picture of gifted children in her study, described in box 13.1.

There have been fears that the educational needs of children of high ability cannot be met by lessons pitched at the level of the middle range of ability. Ogilvie (1973), in the Schools Council Report on gifted children in primary schools, suggested that many local education authorities were not making any provision for gifted children. We can distinguish three broad categories of method which have been used in practice:

1   Acceleration: the bright child is promoted to a higher class or admitted to school at a younger age than usual. Ultimately, this can mean admission to university at a very young age. Many teachers are against this, as, they claim, the child may be *intellectually* at a level of older children but not sufficiently mature *socially* or *emotionally* to adjust well.

2   Segregation: the brighter children are selected for particular schools on the basis of their ability, and the curriculum adjusted accordingly. Opinions are divided on the effectiveness of this method. Some point to the academic success of selective schools; some argue, too, that special abilities such as musical or dance talents are best catered for in specialized schools, such as the Menuhin School or the Royal

Ballet School. Others argue that segregation is unfair, socially divisive and hard to implement.

3    Enrichment: an enriched education is provided for gifted children within the normal classroom. There are a number of ways in which this method can be implemented. Extra-curricular activities can give interesting opportunities to brighter children, especially if these are organized by specialist, enthusiastic teachers and provide opportunities for such children to spend time with others of similar ability. Withdrawal from the normal class can also give the gifted child the stimulus to work independently. Finally, individualized learning programmes offer another approach. Enrichment could avoid the negative aspects of the previous two methods and have the advantage that it can also be made available to moderate-ability children if they are interested.

## Different Methods of Assessing Intelligence

In this section, we describe in more detail the techniques psychologists have devised to measure intelligence and attainment. We saw earlier that the first intelligence test to be used widely was the Stanford–Binet Intelligence Scale. Table 13.4 shows the type of test items used in the scale. (The examples are similar but not identical to the original test items.) From the child's responses to age-standardized items of these types, the psychologist can obtain an overall IQ score.

The revisions of the Stanford–Binet scale tried to take account of cultural and educational changes in children's experiences, but the test is quite heavily loaded with verbal items, especially for older age groups. Verbal tests may under-estimate the intellectual capacity of children who speak a different dialect, or for whom the language of the test is not their mother tongue; furthermore, some backgrounds do not stress the language skills measured by intelligence tests. Thus, children who have language difficulties or who come from another cultural background may be at a disadvantage when taking the test.

However, many educational psychologists treat the Stanford–Binet test as a clinical interview in which they can gain insights into the child's personality, self-image, attention-span and motivation as well as level of intelligence. Thus, in the hands of an experienced clinician, it can be of diagnostic value. From this point of view, it is as well to remember Binet's original brief, which was to assess scholarship attainment in normal and retarded children and not to assess an abstract intellectual quality.

Another series of widely used intelligence tests was devised by Wechsler. In contrast to the Stanford–Binet, the Wechsler tests give a verbal IQ and a performance IQ as well as a full-scale IQ. As in the 1960 revisions of the Stanford–Binet, Wechsler did not estimate intelligence from mental age as Binet did, but related a child's score to the distribution of scores for other children of the same age. Raw scores are changed into standard scores within the subject's age group; subtest scores are then added and converted into an IQ with a mean of 100 and a

TABLE 13.4   *Items similar to those used in the Stanford–Binet Intelligence Scale*

| | |
|---|---|
| Vocabulary: | the child is asked to give the meaning of words; these increase in difficulty – 'What is an apple?'; 'What is harmony?' |
| Verbal analogies: | the child is asked to explain differences and similarities between things – 'a rabbit is timid, a lion is ...?'; 'in what way are spring and autumn alike?' |
| Arithmetic: | the child is given a series of arithmetical problems to solve |
| Memory: | the child may be asked to repeat a series of numbers: 4–7–3–8–5–9; the child copies a bead chain from memory |
| General information: | the child is asked questions on topics of general knowledge; 'What is the capital of France?', 'How many pennies are in a pound?', 'Who wrote *Macbeth*?' |
| Absurdities: | the child is asked to say what is silly about a picture in which the characters are doing something silly like sunbathing in the rain; older children are asked to say what is silly about an absurd sentence |
| Missing parts picture: | the child is asked to say what is missing in a picture: a door without a handle, a table without a leg |
| Spatial problems: | the child traces a path through a maze |
| Comprehension: | the child is asked questions that test adaptiveness and practical judgement; 'What is the thing to do if you are lost in a strange city?' 'What should you do if a child younger than you hits you?' |

standard deviation of 15. The correlation between full-scale Wechsler IQ scores and Stanford–Binet IQ scores of the same children is high, at around 0.80.

The main Wechsler test is the Wechsler Intelligence Scale for Children (WISC-R) designed for children from 6 to 16 years. In addition, there are tests for the preschool and early school years – the Wechsler Preschool and Primary Scale of Intelligence (WPPSI) (see Plate 13.1) – and also for adults of 16 and over – the Wechsler Adult Intelligence Scale (WAIS). Examples of items from the verbal and the performance subscales of the WISC-R are given in table 13.5. (Again, the examples are similar to but not identical to the actual test items.) Although the performance scale places very little emphasis on verbal skills, there is, in fact, a high correlation between the verbal and performance scales of the test.

The Stanford–Binet and the Wechsler tests are individually administered. However, for reasons of speed and efficiency, psychologists have devised tests that can be given to groups of people. While individual tests are mainly used in clinical settings for help in the diagnosis of learning difficulties, group tests are used largely for selection purposes in education (as the 11 + test was), or at work. Correlations between individual and group tests are fairly high and it is felt that they are each measuring the same kinds of ability. However, the group test has certain

PLATE 13.1   *A preschool child is tested on one of the subscales of the WPPSI*

disadvantages. The examiner may not notice signs of anxiety in the testee which would be more obvious in a one-to-one testing situation; furthermore, once the test has begun there is no opportunity for the psychologist to reassure the candidate. People with language difficulties or people for whom English is a second language are at a disadvantage since they may find it hard to read the instructions for each item. This criticism applies, for example, to the AH-6 test, a group test designed to discriminate among highly intelligent adults; the instructions for items are deliberately complex and require a good command of the English language.

One example of a non-verbal group test is Raven's Progressive Matrices. This is a test for adults and children which requires testees to complete matrices in which every square but one has been filled in according to a certain pattern (figure 13.1). When the testee has worked out the principle, he or she can then select the missing part of the design from a number of possible alternatives. Raven designed the test as a measure of Spearman's 'g' factor (see below), that is, the ability to understand relations among abstract items. The most commonly used version is in black and white but a brightly coloured version is also available to make the test more interesting to younger children and to testees who are not accustomed to test situations (for example, in cross-cultural research). For people of above average intelligence, there is a more difficult version, the Advanced Progressive Matrices; there is also a tactile version for the visually impaired. Although it is a non-verbal test, it has not been found to be completely culture-free, but it is less influenced than many verbal tests by the subject's social and educational background.

TABLE 13.5    *Items similar to those used in the WISC-R Intelligence Scale*

*Verbal scale items*

| | |
|---|---|
| Information: | the child is asked a series of general knowledge questions |
| Comprehension: | the child explains why certain courses of action are appropriate: 'What should you do if you break a friend's toy by mistake?' |
| Digit span: | the child is asked to repeat a series of numbers which increase in length, either in the same order or backwards |
| Similarities: | the child is asked to say in what way two things are alike, e.g. a pear and a plum |
| Arithmetic: | the child answers a series of arithmetical problems |
| Vocabulary: | the child is asked to define words of increasing difficulty |

*Performance scale items*

| | |
|---|---|
| Picture arrangement: | the child is shown a series of cartoon pictures which are out of order and asked to arrange them correctly |
| Picture completion: | the child is asked to say which part is missing in a picture; a dog with one ear, a cup with no handle |
| Block design: | the child is shown blocks which have some sides all white, some all red and some half white and half red; the child is asked to reproduce a series of designs using first four blocks and later nine |
| Object assembly: | the child has to assemble a jigsaw of parts into a whole shape; e.g. a dog, a human foot |
| Coding: | the child matches symbols with numbers according to a given code |
| Mazes: | the child traces a route on a series of mazes |

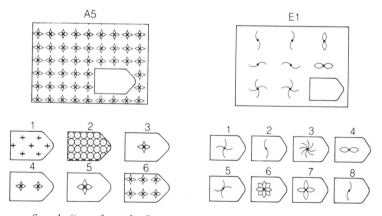

FIGURE 13.1    *Sample items from the Progressive Matrices (from Raven, 1958)*

*'Culture-free' and 'culture-fair' tests*

The tests described so far have often been criticized on the grounds that they discriminate against individuals from minority cultures. Within our society, children who do not speak English at home, or whose cultural background is different, or who speak non-standard English (see pp. 423–5), tend to score less highly than children from the dominant culture. Cross-cultural studies of intelligence also indicate that tests that have been standardized in one culture are not necessarily appropriate in another. Even the non-verbal items in traditional intelligence tests may be culturally loaded. Several attempts have been made to devise tests that are 'culture-free' but they have been largely unsuccessful; it is difficult to evaluate their validity, and anyway a realistic concept of intelligence must be based in a cultural context (see pp. 399–401).

'Culture-specific' tests represent one attempt to design tests that measure the abilities of people from minority cultures. One example is the Black Intelligence Test of Cultural Homogeneity (BITCH), which uses non-standard English and slang expressions. Items in the test (Williams, 1973) include:

1  *Nose opened* means (A) flirting; (B) teed off; (C) deeply in love; (D) very angry.
2  *Blood* means (A) a vampire; (B) a dependent individual; (C) an injured person; (D) a brother of colour.
3  *Mother's day* means (A) black independence day; (B) a day when mothers are honoured; (C) a day the welfare cheques come in; (D) every first Sunday in church.

Black children more often than not get the right answers (1, C; 2, D; 3, C) than white children, but although they score more highly on BITCH than on standard tests of intelligence, the BITCH tests does not predict academic attainment in the way that standard intelligence tests do.

Mercer (see Rice, 1979) has devised an alternative method for testing children from minority cultures by adjusting the norms from standard tests. Her System of Multicultural Pluralistic Assessment (SOMPA) is a battery of tests especially developed for ethnic minority children aged from 5 to 11. These include: the WISC (p. 385) as an assessment of the child's performance in the school environment; an interview with parents covering health, family background and the child's social competence in his or her own cultural environment; and a medical examination to check whether physical, perceptual or dietary factors might be impairing the child's performance in school. The aim of this battery of tests is to measure potential ability and to recognize the social competence which the child already has, even if this is not usually acknowledged in standard intelligence tests.

## Assessment of Attainment

Very commonly *attainment* tests are used in schools as a means of measuring performance in a particular subject, or in the basic skills of reading, comprehension and numeracy. This kind of test aims to give both teacher and student feedback about the effectiveness of a particular course of instruction and acts as a check on how much has actually been learned. The form which tests of attainment take varies widely from informal observation to standardized tests.

## Examinations

The examination can be a test devised by the class teacher or a public examination produced by one of the official Boards of Examiners, for example, the General Certificate of Secondary Education (GCSE). At the time of writing, all syllabuses and examinations which the UK Examining Boards produce have to meet general and subject-specific *national criteria* which have been approved by the Secretary of State for Education. At present formal selection takes place for the majority of pupils at 16+. Just as the 11+ examination was used to predict a child's potential for particular types of secondary education, so formal examination results often form the basis for judgements about an individual's potential for a particular career or for entry into further and higher education. Public examinations also serve the function of maintaining and monitoring national standards of performance.

There are a number of drawbacks, however, to this type of selection procedure. First, how *reliable* are examination results? Research into standards of marking indicate that wide fluctuations in allocation of marks can occur, particularly in the marking of essay-type answers. The public Boards of Examiners have attempted to overcome such unreliability by adopting marking schemes and devising systems of checking and re-checking scripts so that greater consistency among examiners is achieved. Furthermore, the national criteria (see above) for GCSE require an element of teacher involvement in assessment (e.g. in coursework and project work). But in less formal examinations there is greater possibility of bias and subjectivity in marking.

Another area of concern is *validity*. The examination should represent a valid selection of topics from the syllabus which candidates have followed, and should test the extent to which they have realized the aims of a particular course of study. However, the conventional three-hour examination may not be the most appropriate means of evaluating a candidate's understanding and achievement in a subject area. Furthermore, individuals vary in the extent to which they do themselves justice in examination settings. Anxiety, stress, lack of motivation, language or reading difficulties may hamper candidates in their capacity to express what they know. Attempts to overcome this problem, e.g. through the required use in GCSE examinations of orals, project work and continuous assessment, are now much more common than they were in the past, but the emphasis continues to be largely on written work.

How far do examinations succeed in predicting future performance? Their *predictive validity* is highly valued by colleges, universities and employers; but there are reasons to be cautious in placing so much weight on examination results. The success of the Open University in Britain, which requires no entry qualifications, indicates a large pool of people who have the capacity to benefit from higher education despite having failed to obtain conventionally required examination grades at school. Furthermore, many occupations require skills, aptitudes and personal qualities which are not measured by conventional examinations.

*Standardized tests of attainment*

Standardized attainment tests, which are published commercially and restricted in their availability to registered users, are different from examinations. The National Foundation for Educational Research (NFER) supplies a wide range of tests to measure attainment in reading, verbal reasoning, English, numeracy and comprehension. Attainment tests have been pre-tested on large numbers of children in order to eliminate badly worded questions or items that fail to discriminate among candidates. The instructions for administering the tests are usually standard so that candidates will all have taken the test under broadly similar conditions. This enables the teacher to make a meaningful assessment of an individual's performance in comparison with others of the same age.

Performance may be expressed in terms of an age; children at primary school, for example, are often given a reading age which helps parents and teachers evaluate the child's progress. Alternatively, attainment may be expressed as a quotient: a child may be given a Verbal Reasoning Quotient or an English Attainment Quotient. The child's performance can then be easily compared with the norm. Hence, these are sometimes called *norm-referenced* tests. Since the school curriculum is always changing, these tests must be kept up to date; the norms, too, need to be recent ones since norms for one generation may be inappropriate for another.

Many attainment tests correlate quite highly with IQ, but their primary function is to measure achievement within a particular subject area rather than general intelligence. They are of use to the teacher for assessing pupil progress in basic skills and they have the advantage over informal class examination results that they have been properly standardized on large representative samples. Thus they play a useful part in the on-going record of children's progress throughout the school years.

*Criterion-referenced tests*

In recent years there has been a move away from norm-referenced standardized tests towards criterion-referenced tests which set definite levels of performance to be achieved by pupils. In this system the person passes or fails a test regardless of the percentage of individuals of the same age who perform at that level. Criterion-referenced tests focus on a form of assessment which is closer to the school-based learning process since the emphasis is on what pupils 'know, understand and can do' (DES, 1985, p. 2). From this standpoint they may be viewed as tests which take into account aspects of attainment which are less easily assessed by conventional 3-hour examinations. Furthermore, criterion-referenced tests are currently associated with curriculum reform, especially in the growing concern with oral and practical work.

The tester decides on criteria which it is expected that the individual should have achieved. For example, a teacher might want to know whether a pupil understood how to do long division. The criterion would be reached if the child successfully solved 20 long division problems. The criteria need not be based on age norms, although frequently educators *do* have expectations about what a child should be able to do by a particular age. Rather, the teacher is using absolute criteria in assessing a skill. An example would be whether or not you pass the driving test. You either pass or not; the test is the same whatever your age. The Associated Board of the Royal School of Music sets standards of attainment in musical performance; this system of Grades is another example of a criterion-referenced test.

The British Abilities Scale is a criterion-referenced intelligence test designed by Elliot and his colleagues (1979) for use with subjects between the ages of 2 and 17. The subtests measure, for example, reasoning, spatial imagery, short-term memory, problem-solving; there is also a test for measuring social reasoning. The test can be used in a flexible way by educational psychologists not only to calculate IQ, but also to measure *changes* in particular abilities and to examine an individual's profile of abilities.

It has been claimed (ILEA, 1982) that the use of criterion-referenced tests in school is highly motivating to students at all levels of ability since they are able to see progress and achieve success at their own pace. In principle, all pupils could pass a criterion-referenced test if they could demonstrate that they had met the objectives of the particular course of study in question. The *principle of readiness* refers to the strategy of only entering pupils for such tests when they are likely to succeed. In practice, however, most children are still taught in mixed-ability, same-age classes and this places constraints on the organization of testing each pupil when he or she is 'ready'. The fact that criterion-referenced tests involve competition against targets rather than against peers may play a part in creating a cooperative classroom atmosphere. They also have the advantage that objectives are clearly stated so that pupils are aware of what is expected of them.

## National standards of attainment

A wider function of attainment tests is their role in the evaluation of *national* standards. The Assessment of Performance Unit (APU) was set up by the Department of Education and Science (DES) in 1975 with the general objective of promoting 'the development of methods of assessing and monitoring the achieve-ment of children at school, and to seek to identify the incidence of underachieve-ment in the areas of Language, Mathematics, Science as well as personal, aesthetic and physical development at primary and secondary levels'. Critics point to the narrowly quantitative nature of the research results and argue that much of the quality of learning is missed in such large-scale surveys. In addition, there are fears that this type of monitoring procedure may impose constraints on the curriculum and hinder imaginative teaching, which does not lend itself to quantitative evaluation. An example of an APU study is given in box 13.2.

Educators have also expressed concern about the role of nationally prescribed tests done by all pupils at the ages of 7, 11, 14 and 16 as required in the National Curriculum in the UK. (See table 13.6.)

All National Curriculum subjects have Attainment Targets, or goals showing what children should know or do at each stage. Pupils are measured on a 10-point scale with an average child reaching Level 2 by age 7, Level 4 by age 11, Level 5 or 6 by age 14, and Level 6 or 7 by age 16. Children are assessed by a series of national tests (or Standard Assessment Tasks) given at four key stages, at ages 7, 11, 14 and 16). In table 13.6 you can see examples of attainment targets in maths (using and applying maths) at Levels 3, 6, 8 and 10.

## Alternative approaches to assessment

There has been a radical shift on the part of psychologists and educators away from standardized tests towards more flexible types of assessment which are directly

TABLE 13.6 *Testing at the four key stages in mathematics in the National Curriculum*

| Level | Statements of attainment | Example |
|---|---|---|
| 3<br>(Keystage 1) | Pupils should:<br>–select the materials and the mathematics to use for a task; check results and consider whether they are sensible | Estimate the distance around the school hall; select appropriate method for measuring and units to be used; measure and compare the results |
| | –explain work being done and record findings systematically | Sketch a plan of the school hall and enter measurements made |
| | –make and test predictions | |
| | | |
| | | Predict the number of cubes needed to construct this figure and test the prediction |
| 6<br>(Keystage 2) | –design a task and select appropriate mathematics and resources; check there is sufficient information and obtain any that is missing; use 'trial and improvement' methods | Design and make a device to measure accurately a given period of time, e.g. two minutes |
| | –use oral, written or visual forms to record and present findings | Plot Cartesian coordinates to represent simple function mappings:<br>$x \rightarrow 2x + 3$, (or $y = 2x + 3$). |

—make and test generalizations and simple hypotheses; define and reason in simple contexts with some precision

Explore the pattern:

Stage 1
1 square

Stage 2
5 squares

Stage 3
13 squares

Stage 4
25 squares

Use the difference method to extend the pattern; determine a rule for the sequence and test the rule

8
(Keystage 3)

—devise a mathematical task and make a detailed plan of the work; work methodically, checking information for completeness; consider whether the results are of the right order

Decide where to put a telephone box in the locality

—make statements of conjecture using 'if ... then ...; define, reason, prove and disprove

In exploring decimals and fractions with a calculator or microcomputer make statements of the type. 'If the denominator has prime factors other than 2 or 5, then the decimal will recur'; offer justifications, explanations and proofs of such statements

10
(Keystage 4)

—design, plan and carry through a mathematical task to a successful conclusion; present alternative solutions and justify selected route

Investigate and design traffic light and 1-way systems for a city centre, given the street plan and traffic flows; present an analysis of the effects of the systems and suggest a best solution

—give definitions which are sufficient or minimal; use symbolization with confidence; construct a proof including proof by contradiction

Rearrange the equation $x^3 - 5x + 3 = 0$ to obtain the iterative formula

$$x_{n+1} = \frac{(x_n^3 + 3)}{5}$$

and test whether it converges or diverges for different initial values of $x$

*Source:* DES, 1990

related to the individual's needs in a particular context. More weight is being given to teacher-assessment and self-assessment; personal and social qualities are being taken into account. Significantly, it has been recommended that records of achievement be used as a means of recording progress and attainment within the National Curriculum assessment system.

Several factors account for this change. First, we have seen how educational psychologists have become more sceptical about the practical usefulness of the concept of IQ. With regard to learning failure, for example, the present-day psychologist is more likely to focus on specific areas of difficulty with a view to diagnosis and remedial education than on an overall intelligence test score. Secondly, the cultural bias in standardized tests and in test situations seems to be a major obstacle which stands in the way of accurate assessments of a child's level of performance. Rigidity in the scoring and administration of tests can too easily result in the under-rating of the child's ability. Thirdly, the narrow range of abilities measured by traditional intelligence tests often fails to do justice to the complex nature of a child's cognitive development, and there is the danger of concluding that an aptitude that cannot be quantified in some way is not worth considering. Although careful use of intelligence tests may still have some part to play in assessment, it should be part of a wider assessment of the individual's specific achievements, needs and strengths, home environments, relationships with peers and teachers, motivation, interests, imagination, sensitivity to others and intellectual independence.

One recently-adopted procedure is *profiling* or *records of achievement* in which teachers and pupils collaborate to produce a profile of individual achievements, interests and social skills. In prevocational courses, e.g. in Youth Training Schemes (YTS), the Certificate of Pre-Vocational Education (CPVE) and the Technical and Vocational Education Initiative (TVEI), which cover a broad range of work experience, profiling is felt to be the only means of assessing performance. Murphy and Torrance (1988) give a useful evaluation of profiling as an alternative to traditional tests of achievement, but note the difficulties which face teachers as they attempt to develop a policy for profiling in schools and colleges. They recommend certain conditions as being essential for promoting the change which the DES recommends:

- a review of school aims and curricular intentions;
- a review of existing assessment, recording and reporting practices;
- the establishment of a school assessment policy;
- appropriate training for testers;
- more flexible teaching methods, such as small group work;
- more flexible timetabling to facilitate the integration of teaching, observation, assessment and discussion.

(Murphy and Torrance, 1988, pp. 65–6)

A key feature is the process of negotiation and regular dialogue between pupil and teacher. Clearly this can be difficult to achieve when teachers are working with large numbers of pupils, and there is a real danger of bias in such assessments even when there is a framework, such as checklists, systematic observation and personal self-assessment information. This flexible method of gathering information about individuals must also be judged on its capacity to deal with issues concerning the competence of assessors and bias in the measures.

## Concepts of Intelligence and Ability

Our review of methods of assessment leads back to a basic question – what do tests, be they of intelligence or attainment, measure? Binet, it will be remembered, had devised his intelligence tests in order to identify those children who would be unsuccessful in school, and investigations have shown that intelligence tests correlate fairly well with academic attainments. But a difficulty which has persisted throughout the history of intelligence testing has been a lack of agreement as to the definition of intelligence itself. A famous symposium in 1921 produced 13 different definitions by psychologists and the concept remains controversial to this day.

### The psychometric approach

Spearman (1927) proposed that there was a common factor – which he called 'g' – of general intelligence, to be found in a wide variety of mental skills. He distinguished 'g' from those abilities specific to a particular skill. Thus a person's score on an arithmetic test would result from general mental as well as a specific numerical ability. The more intellectually demanding the task, the more it involved the grasping and application of relationships, and the more it depended on the 'g' factor.

By contrast, Thurstone (1938) claimed to have identified eight primary factors of intelligence. These were: verbal; numerical; spatial; rote memory; perceptual speed; word fluency; inductive reasoning and deductive reasoning. His eight factors have been criticized for their narrowness and for the fact that they are to some extent determined by the particular tests which he chose. He later conceded that a 'second-order factor', a form of 'g', ran through the eight primary abilities.

More recently, many psychologists have become dissatisfied with the psychometric model on the grounds that it focuses too much on individual abilities without taking enough account of the testing situation or, at a wider level, the social and educational context within which the assessment takes place. In the following sections we look at attempts by psychologists to break free from the straitjacket of the psychometric tradition of intelligence testing by acknowledging a wider range of cognitive abilities in the individual and by taking into account the social context as an integral part of the child's development as a thinker.

### Cognitive style

Some psychologists have chosen to look at the 'cognitive style' of the individual, i.e. the characteristic way in which he or she approaches the world. Cognitive style is often viewed along one dimension, such as convergence/divergence, or field-dependence/field-independence (see below). Guilford (1967) distinguished *convergent* and *divergent* thinking. The converger, he suggested, is good at dealing with problems that require one correct answer and will tend not to go beyond the information given; the converger, therefore, can cope well with the kinds of tasks that are commonly presented in intelligence tests. *Divergers*, by contrast, are in their element with open-ended situations that call for a variety of responses involving fluency, flexibility, originality and elaboration of ideas. Since these two approaches to tasks seem to represent two distinct cognitive styles, educators have been interested in implications of research in this area. For example, Hudson (1966)

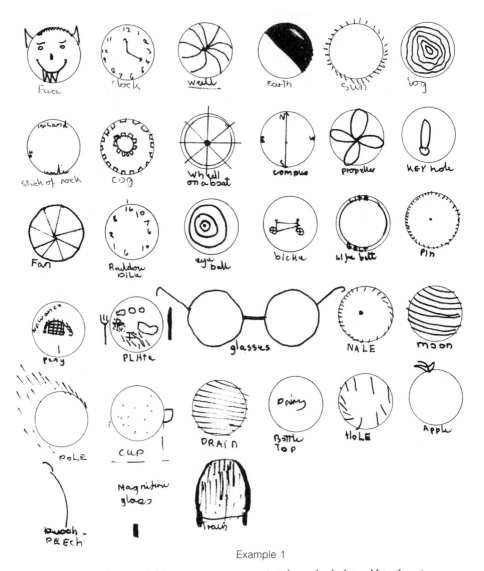

Example 1

FIGURE 13.2 *Circles test: children are given a page of circles and asked to add to them in any way they like. Responses are scored for fluency, flexibility and originality. Some children treat each circle separately (example 1); others combine the circles into larger pictures (example 2h)*

showed that convergent and divergent tests were able to discriminate between science and arts specialists.

A whole battery of tests of divergent thinking were devised (Torrance 1972); one example is 'uses of objects'; a child is asked to think of as many alternative uses of common objects as possible (e.g. uses of a brick, a paper clip, a cardboard box). Responses are scored for fluency and originality. Another example is the 'circles' test, shown in figure 13.2. The tests have, however, been criticized for subjectivity in their scoring and lack of agreement concerning what actually is an original response. The very nature of divergent thinking abilities makes them unsuited to formal timed test situations (Wallach and Kogan, 1965).

There have been other attempts to characterize important ways in which individuals differ in cognitive style. Witkin et al. (1962), for example, differentiated between *field-independence* and *field dependence* in an individual's responses to perceptual patterns. Figure 13.3 shows items from Witkin's Embedded Figure Test, which is designed to differentiate the two types of person.

Some people concentrate on the whole picture and are uninfluenced by the 'field' or surrounding context. These field-independent persons are better at logical, rational tasks and are less likely to be influenced by their social surroundings. Field-dependent persons, by contrast, focus on details of a figure, are less analytical, and more affected by external factors and social influences.

Witkin argues that these characteristic responses to a perceptual field are also reflected in an individual's approach to cognitive tasks. Field-independent people are better at tasks that require a logical solution, at mathematics and science and at

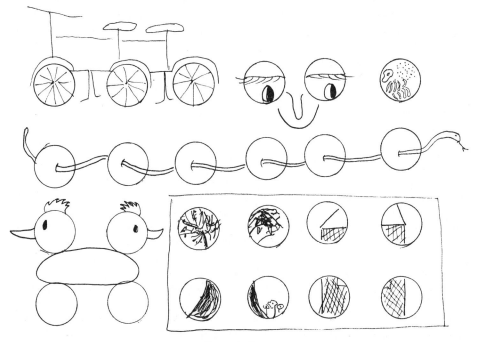

Example 2

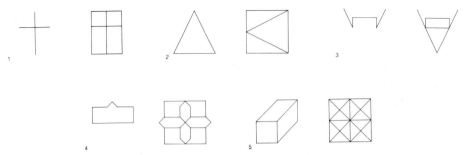

FIGURE 13.3   *Examples of items from Witkin's Embedded Figures Test. The child is asked to outline the simpler left-hand figure in the more complex design on the right. Field-independent persons are quicker and more successful at this task*

spatial tasks; they are also more independent in the social sense and less likely to be swayed in their judgement by other people than are field-dependent subjects. Witkin found high correlations (0.66) between field-independence and certain subtests of the WISC (block design, picture completion and object assembly). He has argued that the Embedded Figures Test can identify spatial abilities which verbal tests overlook. Boys are on average more field-independent than girls. Parallels can also be drawn with work on *brain lateralization theory*, which suggests that each hemisphere of the brain has primary responsibility for certain mental abilities – the left for logical, verbal activities, the right for intuitive, emotional and spatial abilities. The observed differences in cognitive style between males and females may be in part due to differences in hemispheric dominance. Girls talk earlier than boys and tend to score better on language tests (left-hemisphere lateralization); boys tend to perform better than girls on visual-spatial tasks (right-hemisphere lateralization).

The investigation of cognitive style is an exciting field of inquiry which could have considerable implications for education. So far, the difficulty seems to lie in identifying which styles are important and in producing adequate assessment procedures.

### Gardner's multiple intelligences

In what may be considered a variant of the cognitive style approach, Gardner (1983) has proposed a theory of 'multiple intelligences' in a book called *Frames of Mind*. He suggests that there are six distinct kinds of intelligence – linguistic, logical-mathematical, spatial, musical, body-kinesthetic and personal. The first three are already familiar from the psychometric tradition, but the last three constitute more of a radical departure.

Musical intelligence refers to the abilities to comprehend and play or compose music. Bodily-kinesthetic intelligence refers to bodily control and grace of movement as shown, for example, in athletics, dance or skating. Personal intelligence refers to the abilities to understand one's own behaviour and that of others; this is clearly related to social and interpersonal skills and to role-taking ability (see chapters 5 and 11).

Gardner used a number of criteria to select these particular intelligences. These were:

1   Selective impairment of particular kinds of intelligence by brain damage.
2   The existence of individuals with exceptional talent in particular kinds of intelligence.
3   A distinctive developmental history for each kind of intelligence.
4   An evolutionary history demonstrating the adaptive value of each kind of intelligence.
5   A set of core operations or procedures which characterize each kind of intelligence.
6   Experimental evidence that different kinds of intelligence are relatively independent (this is the traditional psychometric method).
7   The connection of each kind of intelligence to some kind of symbolic system (such as words, pictures, musical notation).

Each distinctive intelligence should satisfy most, if not all, of these criteria. Essentially Gardner is criticizing the use of conventional intelligence tests beyond their original purposes which were, as we have seen, to predict academic skills, and which led to an emphasis on verbal and reasoning skills. Gardner focuses instead on the diversity of abilities which human beings can have.

### Intelligence in a social-cultural context

The psychometric approach focuses largely on the internal cognitive processes of individuals but tells us little about the social context within which intelligent behaviour occurs. Wechsler (1975), in fact recognized this aspect of intelligent functioning when he wrote that the assessment of intelligence is inevitably a value judgement. However, despite Wechsler's apparent admission that intelligent behaviour must be meaningful within a particular social setting, this is scarcely reflected in the design of traditional intelligence tests, such as the WISC-R and the Stanford–Binet. These have only been designed and validated in the context of Western educational systems.

   In recent years there has been a growing interest in a broader *contextualist* approach to intelligence. Contextualists take the view that intelligence must be defined within a particular cultural context and that comparisons across cultures can only be made with caution. Berry (1984) argues that it is important to define intelligence in terms of 'cognitive competence' which is needed in a particular culture, and that psychologists should take local or folk conceptions of intelligence into account when they construct tests (figure 13.4). For example, the ability to shoot with a bow and arrow is irrelevant for most people in our society, but skill in the construction and use of the bow and arrow may well be of prime importance among hunter–gatherers. Tests that have been validated in the technologically advanced society would not assess this skill, yet it could not be concluded that the hunter–gatherers were less intelligent.

   Sternberg (1984a), a strong defender of the contextualist approach, defines intelligence as 'consisting of purposive selection and shaping of and adaptation to

"YOU CAN'T BUILD A HUT, YOU DON'T KNOW HOW TO FIND EDIBLE ROOTS AND YOU KNOW NOTHING ABOUT PREDICTING THE WEATHER. IN OTHER WORDS, YOU DO TERRIBLY ON OUR I.Q. TEST."

FIGURE 13.4   *Intelligence needs to be seen in its cultural context (from Current Contents, 1981)*

real-world environments relevant to one's life' (p. 312). From this perspective we can only understand intelligence within the framework of real life situations. He argues that it is far more useful to see intelligence as being embedded in a particular context than as a static quality possessed by an individual; but he does not, however suggest that *everything* is relative and that no comparison is possible across cultures or among groups within the society. More important is the relative emphasis that different cultures place upon certain skills at different historical times. For example, skills needed for reading are present in individuals from pre-literate societies but are not developed and are thus not important until literacy becomes widespread. Within modern Western society, in the past decade or so, children are gaining familiarity with electronic toys and home computers; these depend more on visual, auditory and manual aspects of intelligence – skills that are not so readily measured by traditional intelligence tests. The contextualist view presents a malleable concept of intelligence which can accommodate to such changes over space and time.

Is it possible, then, to measure intelligence from the contextualist stance?

Sternberg suggests that one obvious way of finding out what constitutes intelligence within a particular context is to ask members of the culture. For example, his research in the USA has revealed some overlap between lay-persons' concepts of intelligence and psychologists' views, but the lay-person is more likely to mention *social* competence as an important factor in intelligent functioning. Sternberg identified three broad constellations of behaviour which his American interviewees perceived as being intelligent:

1   *Practical problem-solving ability:* 'Keeps an open mind'; 'responds thoughtfully to others' ideas'.
2   *Verbal ability:* 'speaks clearly and articulately', 'is knowledgeable about a field'.
3   *Social competence:* 'admits mistakes'; 'displays interest in the world at large'; 'thinks before speaking and doing'.

Clearly the constructs of intelligence would vary across cultures, but Sternberg argues that the method could be used to discover what *is* intelligent in different social contexts. There is thus a tension between what Berry (1984) calls 'locally sensitive' or culturally relative concepts of intelligence and the wider aim of arriving at a 'pan-cultural' or universal understanding of cognitive processes. Psychologists are not yet ready to agree that the evidence supports only one position. As Berry writes of the assessment of intelligence within and across cultures:

> If . . . consistent and invariant factors emerge, then a position of general intelligence may be supportable (but it is likely to be a general intelligence construct which differs from our present culture-bound construct). If, however, factors emerge which appear to be culturally relative (that is, patterns exist, but vary according to cultural context), then the cognitive style approach may be supportable (but, again, the styles may be quite different from those identified at the present time). And if no factors emerge, if cognitive abilities are unrelated to each other, then the specific abilities approach will be supported. (1984, p. 355).

*Sternberg's triarchic theory of human intelligence*

Sternberg (1984b) has proposed a 'triarchic' theory of intelligence which embodies the contextualist approach together with an attempt to suggest two universal aspects of human intelligence which can be considered across cultures. These universal aspects cannot be specific *tasks*, since tasks are relative to each culture. Rather, Sternberg considers the *processes* by which tasks are coped with, in line with his definition of intelligence already given (pp. 399–400).

One of these universal aspects is considered to be a 'two-facet subtheory' approach to task demands, which contrasts the novelty or familiarity of the task. At one extreme a task can measure the ability to automatize information processing. Reading skills might provide an example. For the infant school child reading tasks are largely assessing the ability to deal with novel demands; many words, and even the process of reading itself, are fairly new. For most adults, reading has become a rapid automatized process. Differences in reading skill are then a matter of ability to automatize information processing.

The 'two-facet' theory is compatible with the contextualist approach. It makes it clear that what is apparently the same task can put quite different demands on an individual from different contexts or with different prior experiences. Obviously, a verbal test item imposes different demands, depending on the degree of literacy of the person, and the community he or she is from.

The other universal aspect of Sternberg's triarchic theory is what he calls 'componential analysis'. This involves analysing the actual cognitive processes involved in coping with any task. He considers three main kinds of component: *knowledge acquisition* – processes involved in gaining knowledge necessary to deal with a task; *performance components* – encoding symbols and making comparisons, for example; *metacomponents* – executive functions which plan the overall approach to the task, monitor success or failure, and respond to external feedback.

Consider the task of doing a crossword for example. Knowledge acquisition components might include knowing how to use dictionaries or a thesaurus to help solve certain clues. Performance components might include interpreting the clue, and making comparisons of possible solutions with the clue. Metacomponents might include overall strategic decisions such as which clue to tackle first, when to consult a dictionary, or realizing that one word already filled in might be wrong as it does not fit with another one. Again, this kind of analysis of task components could be compatible with the contextualist view.

Sternberg's theory is a relatively new one and has attracted much attention. It is too soon to judge how successful it will be, but this approach and other recent developments (such as the general contextualist approach, and Gardner's theory of multiple intelligences) do seem to herald a major shift in the way psychologists will use the term 'intelligence' in the future.

**Further reading**

A readable view of different approaches to the study of intelligence, including Piagetian theory and information processing approaches as well as the psychometric approach, is R. Kail and J. W. Pellegrino 1985: *Human Intelligence: Perspectives and Prospects*. New York: Freeman. An authoritative sourcebook is A. Anastasi 1982: *Psychological Testing*, 5th ed. New York: Macmillan. Some recent developments are described in H. Gardner 1983: *Frames of Mind*. New York, Basic Books, and R. J. Sternberg, 1985: *Beyond IQ: A Triarchic Theory of Human Intelligence*. Cambridge Cambridge University Press.

A critical review of the social uses of IQ testing is presented in B. Evans and B. Waites 1981: *IQ and Mental Testing: an Unnatural Science and its History*. London, Macmillan. If you want to find out more about the changes which are taking place in the philosophy and practice of educational assessment in Britain, read R. Murphy and H. Torrance 1988: *The Changing Face of Educational Assessment*. Milton Keynes: Open University Press. A comprehensive guide to the theory and practice of integration is the book by S. Hegarty and K. Pocklington 1981: *Educating Pupils with Special Needs in the Primary School*. Windsor: NFER. See also Alan Goddard 1988: 'Processes in special education', in G. Blenkin and A. V. Kelly (eds), *The Primary Curriculum in Action*, London: Paul Chapman.

For an overview of research on gifted children, see J. Freeman (ed.) 1985: *The Psychology of Gifted Children*. Chichester: Wiley.

**Discussion Points**

1   What different abilities or processes underlie intelligent action?

2   Does intelligence mean the same thing in different societies?

3   How valuable are selective procedures in the eduactional system?

4   How do the psychometric methods of assessing intellectual development compare with those of Piaget (chapter 11)?

5   In what ways can the needs of exceptional children be met within the ordinary school system?

**Practical exercises**

1   Ask people from a variety of backgrounds to say what they mean by 'intelligence', or to describe someone they think of as highly intelligent. Sort their answers into categories. Compare with the categories used by Sternberg (p. 401). Which factors, e.g. age, cultural background, level of educational attainment, might contribute towards your interviewee's concept of intelligence?

2   Collaborate with three or four other students to design a test of general information. Each of you contribute five questions that measure knowledge of a particular field (such as music, politics, sport, the peace movement) with which *you* are familiar. Administer the test to other students or to people from different backgrounds and note their reactions. Score the tests and look at the distribution of total scores. How would you assess (a) the reliability of your test and (b) its validity as a test of general information?

3   Design a way in which children's story writing abilities could be assessed. You will need to consider (a) under what conditions the stories should be written; (b) instructions about form and content, if any; (c) what criteria you would use in judging the standard of the stories, and whether qualitative or quantitative methods would be used in assessment. You could try out your method with a small sample of stories obtained from children in say the 8–11 age range at a local school.

# Box 13.1

# Giftedness in a social context

The definition of giftedness varies across cultures and throughout history and thus cannot be viewed apart from its social context. Thus argued Joan Freeman in the introduction to the Gulbenkian Research Project on gifted children which she directed. Her aim was to discover whether the experience of being labelled as 'gifted' had any behavioural effects on children. She was also interested in the part played by parents and teachers in the emotional development of high-ability children. Specifically, she was concerned to test a prevailing view that gifted children may be emotionally disturbed at home or at school because their intellectual maturity makes them out of tune with the others in the environment. Accordingly, she asked three research questions

1 Are children identified by parents as 'gifted' different from other children not so identified?
2 Are the home backgrounds of these children identified as gifted by their parents different from those not so identified?
3 Do gifted children suffer from emotional problems when receiving non-specialist education?

Freeman's sample consisted of three groups with 70 children in each, ranging in age from 5 to 16 years. The Target Group (T) was a sample of children selected from the records of the National Association for Gifted Children (NAGC), i.e. children whose parents had identified them as being of exceptionally high ability. Control Group 1 (C1) was a sample of children who were matched with the above children for ability (as measured by the Raven's Progressive Matrices), age, sex and school. The essential difference was that these children were not in the NAGC. Control Group 2 (C2) was a sample of children of normal ability matched with C1 for age, sex and school class so that they differed only in ability. In this way, each target child was matched with two control children in different ways – one for high ability but not in the NAGC (C1) and one of normal ability (C2).

The children were given a battery of tests covering intelligence (Stanford–Binet), and social adjustment (Bristol Social Adjustment Guides); interviews were carried out with parents (at home) and teachers (at school) about the children's behaviour, their own attitudes to education and views on how educational aims are achieved; in addition, the home background of the children was assessed.

With regard to intelligence, there were significant differences between the target group and control groups C1 and C2. The T and C1 children had been accurately matched for

Based on material in J. Freeman 1980: in R. Povey (ed.). *Educating the Gifted Child*, London: Harper and Row.

BOX TABLE 13.1.1     *Raven's matrices scores and Stanford–Binet IQs of target (T) and control (C) children*

|  | IQ | T | C1 | C2 |
|---|---|---|---|---|
| Raven's | mean | 34.5 | 34.6 | 28.8 |
| matrices | s.d. | 12.9 | 11.5 | 11.6 |
| Stanford– | mean | 147.1 | 134.3 | 119.2 |
| Binet | s.d. | 17.4 | 17.1 | 16.1 |

intelligence on the Raven's Matrices Test but when Stanford–Binet scores were compared, they were found to be significantly different (see box table 13.1.1). Freeman explained these differences as follows. The Raven's Matrices Test is non-verbal and so more 'culture-free' than a verbal test; furthermore, it does not discriminate finely amongst children at upper levels of ability. The Stanford–Binet test, by contrast, does give a more precise assessment at higher levels of intelligence and measures many learned abilities which would put children from privileged, educationally stimulating homes at an advantage. Thus the differences shown in box table 13.1.1 may indicate that the target group had been identified and recognized by their parents as being of exceptional ability.

Interviews with the parents suggested behaviour differences between the T group and groups C1 and C2. The target children were rated as more 'difficult', 'sensitive', 'emotional' and as having 'few friends'. Parents described them as 'very emotional' five times as often as controls and as 'feeling different' 17 times as often as controls. Similarly, teachers' ratings on individual items on the Bristol Social Adjustment Guides indicated that the target children had more problems in making friends and were more likely to be either withdrawn or aggressive in the classroom (see box table 13.1.2).

From home interviews, Freeman observed that the target children were more likely to have unusual backgrounds, e.g. were adopted, came from families where the parents were divorced or separated, or from single-parent families. (One-parent families, for example, were found seven times as often in T as in C groups.) Their mothers were more frequently well-educated but were also discontented about their own achievements. This was surprising since many of these mothers had successful professional or managerial careers

BOX TABLE 13.1.2     *Percentage of children in each group getting high scores from teachers' ratings on items from the Bristol Social Adjustment Guide*

|  | T | C1 | C2 | Significance level |
|---|---|---|---|---|
| Peer maladaptiveness (problems in making friends) | 29 | 14 | 9 | $p < 0.01$ |
| Withdrawal (being socially withdrawn) | 23 | 10 | 10 | $p < 0.01$ |
| Hostility (aggressive and over-reacting) | 39 | 17 | 13 | $p < 0.01$ |

(53 per cent as opposed to 33 per cent in C1 and C2). The homes of the target children were very stimulating, parents encouraged their children's education and attainment. However, this involvement at times took the form of an 'intense pursuit of culture' which in the view of Freeman put some pressure on the children.

What might cause the adjustment problems of the target group of children? In order to find out whether the emotional difficulties were due to intelligence or to other factors, Freeman compared the highest IQ children from the *whole* sample (i.e. children with IQs of 141+ from both target and control groups) with the rest. The features which had distinguished the target groups from the controls were rarely those which distinguished high IQ children from the rest. In fact, Freeman found no evidence to suggest that problems arose simply from being highly intelligent but rather from the way in which giftedness was handled. For example, signs of unhappiness, such as finding it difficult to make friends, did not feature in the list of behaviours that could be identified with high IQ. Although T group parents frequently reported that their children were difficult *because* they were gifted, Freeman's results did not support such a viewpoint.

Freeman suggested that the T group parents had joined the NAGC not only because their children were gifted but because they were difficult. The problems, she suggested, stemmed from parental expectations and handling of these bright children. The parents of the target children were more likely to be dissatisfied with school, but this Freeman saw as being related to the parents' ambitions for their children rather than the children's giftedness by itself. Her overall conclusion was that she could see no good reason for segregating gifted children from normal children. Those gifted children who did have problems were also found to have a number of disturbing environmental factors, such as intense parental pressure, which seemed to be more responsible for the difficulties than giftedness by itself.

This is a challenging study which is unfortunately weakened by the IQ differences between T and C1 children. Freeman's view that the act of labelling a bright child as 'gifted' can have negative effects on the child's behaviour remains controversial.

# Box 13.2

# The assessment of pupils' writing

This report by the Assessment of Performance Unit (APU) was the second in a series aiming to present a national picture of the language performance of 11-year-old pupils in England, Wales and Northern Ireland. Here we consider one part of the survey concerned specifically with writing ability.

The research team was concerned to devise methods of assessment which would reflect the complex nature of the writing process. Thus their aim was to assess not only basic skills, such as spelling and punctuation, but also higher-order skills such as the ability to organize thought, the expression of feeling and sensitivity to the needs of the reader.

In May 1980, 9850 pupils in 691 schools participated in the survey; of these around 3,400 completed tests of writing. A series of ten writing booklets were designed containing four writing tasks to be completed by each pupil:

1  An accurate description of something the pupil had observed. All pupils completed this task.
2  A longer writing task, e.g. an autobiographical anecdote, a letter to a public figure, a personal response to a poem, an explanation of a personal preference. The purpose of this writing was to assess a range of writing skills including narrating, expressing feeling, explaining a point of view, making a request. There were ten of these tasks, distributed among the schools participating in the survey, of which each pupil did one.
3  A text-based exercise such as editing a piece of writing or making notes.
4  Several short questions about pupils' attitudes towards writing in general, their feelings about the tasks in the APU booklet and their preference for writing at home or at school.

The APU team were aware that if the writing tasks were seen as tests the pupils might produce unnatural, stilted writing. To avoid this, the team encouraged teachers to introduce the writing tasks as they would in normal lessons and to allow time for discussion before the children began to write. In this way, they hoped to move away from the model of the pupil writing for the teacher-as-examiner towards the model of the pupil writing in an authentic way for a sensitive and interested reader. However, the writing was still done under test conditions where it could not be assumed that the children would be in the right frame of mind to produce their best writing, and the team admit that the actual contexts in which the children wrote did not provide genuine audiences.

Based on material in Assessment of Performance Unit 1982: Primary Survey Report no.2. London; HMSO.

Two forms of assessment were used, *impression marking* and *analytic marking*. Impression marking involved rapid reading of a script and the allocation of a single mark awarded on a seven-point scale; a score of one indicated that the marker considered the pupil to be a very poor writer for an 11-year-old and a mark of seven corresponded to the marker's judgement that the pupil was a very able writer for this age-group. Each script was double-marked by two members of the team to check on the reliability of this method. Analytic marking was carried out on a random subsample of 10 per cent of the scripts selected from across the whole range of booklets. This involved assessing the pupil writers on a five-point scale with reference to the following set of criteria: relevance of content and coherence of organization in the essays; appropriateness and style, e.g. extent to which vocabulary and form of words were appropriate to the topic; knowledge of grammatical conventions, e.g. punctuation, sentence structure; and knowledge of orthographic conventions, i.e. handwriting and spelling.

Box figure 13.2.1 shows the distribution of marks based on impression marking. In the examiners' opinion, 3.8 per cent of pupils produced work which was extremely poor; 1.8 per cent of pupils produced written work of outstanding quality. Impression marking scores were correlated with each of the analytic criteria and the highest inter-correlation was found between impression marking and the first analytic category of *content and organization* ($r = 0.70$). This result, argue the APU team, indicates that markers of essays written by children are responding to general qualities in the writing rather than specific aspects. The results also indicated that some individual markers 'were inclined to award higher or lower marks than the majority'.

With regard to analytic marking, the results are summarized as follows:

96 per cent of pupils obtained sufficient control of writing to be understood at first reading.

95 per cent had some knowledge of how sentences are separated or related.

15 per cent had numerous errors – i.e. one spelling mistake in each line and one grammatical mistake in each three lines.

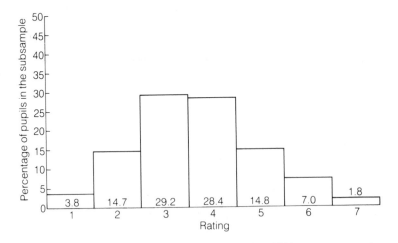

BOX FIGURE 13.2.1 *Distribution of ratings in the APU report: general impression marking*

15 per cent were well in command of spelling and grammar conventions

Pupils' answers to questions on their attitudes towards writing indicated the following factors:

For many 11-year-olds the most enjoyable writing experience is the creation of an exciting story.

Eleven-year-olds do not enjoy writing 'exercises' (e.g. exercises to improve punctuation) or copying from books.

Girls are more likely than boys to become involved in writing long pieces or in writing for their own enjoyment at home.

Many 11-year-olds' perception of writing relates only to one or two uses of the written language, and there is scope for much greater development, e.g. writing for different types of audience.

The APU team expressed the intention of assessing complex cognitive and affective processes involved in writing. However, the general experience of reading the report of the APU is a disappointing one. Many of the results seem rather obvious, including the approximately normal distribution obtained in box figure 13.2.1. Also, little of the children's writing experience comes through. For example, when the team looks at the children's use of dialogue in stories they do not consider the ways in which children use dialogue to express feelings or to show their awareness of psychological states in their characters. Instead, the team limits itself to an analysis of punctuation. This is one example among many of the failures of the team to interpret anything that could not be quantified. In a critique of the study, Rosen (1982) wrote that 'though we may see the team locked in an heroic struggle with the tiger of assessment, we must also see that they should not have ventured on the jungle safari in the first place . . . . There is an alternative; it is the active participation of teachers in assessment, teachers who are close to the children being assessed'. It is such critiques of purely quantitative measures from large-scale surveys which have encouraged the development of teacher-based assessment.

# 14

# Disadvantage and Education

In this final chapter we look at the part played by families, by schools and by society itself in the linguistic development and academic attainment of children, with particular emphasis on those from less advantaged environments. Why are some children at a disadvantage in the educational system? How significant a factor is social class or membership of an ethnic minority? What effects does poverty have on a child's intellectual development? Can schools compensate for deprivation in the home? How does the wider culture shape the direction of a child's aspirations and achievements? None of the answers is simple since these questions concern the complex interaction of many factors, from the parent–child relationship to the social context within which the child develops.

In trying to answer them, it may help to consider Bronfenbrenner's ecological model of human development, summarized in chapter 1 (see figure 1.3). In advocating this model, Bronfenbrenner is warning of the dangers of focusing on the individual without taking into account the context within which he or she exists or the processes of interaction through which the behaviour of individuals in a particular system evolves. He is arguing that when psychologists try to understand the many factors influencing development, they should use methods which are ecologically valid (chapter 1). They should be aware of the effects on the subject of removal from the natural environment to a strange setting (for example, a university laboratory or a psychological testing room). It is useful to bear Bronfenbrenner's ideas in mind as you consider the issues raised in this chapter. But first, let us look at the idea of disadvantage itself.

## The Concept of Disadvantage

We have all had unfavourable experiences which we would say 'put us at a disadvantage' in some way, perhaps socially or intellectually. To the psychologist, however, disadvantage usually means a relatively enduring condition that results in lower academic achievement at school and reduced opportunities in the wider society; this tends to refer to social or cultural characteristics, for example being a member of an ethnic minority group, living in an inner city area, or having a low income. Passow (1970 p.16) defined the disadvantaged child as one who 'because of social or cultural characteristics, for example social class, race, ethnic origin, poverty, sex, geographical location, etc. comes into the school system with knowledge, skills and attitudes which impede learning'. Wedge and Essen (1982 p. 11) defined the disadvantaged as 'that group of children who failed to thrive, who failed to mature as much or as quickly physically, or who have failed to achieve as well in school as other British children'. Important social factors which served to identify such children included family composition (a large number of children in the family, or only one parent figure); low income; and poor housing. Each of these factors was related to poor physical and academic development and less acceptable behaviour.

Historically, this concern coincides with the advent of a universal free education system and the corresponding philosophy of 'equality of opportunity' which arose in most Western societies, including Britain and the USA, in the years following the Second World War. As the Newsom Report (1963) put it, 'all children should have an equal opportunity of acquiring intelligence, and developing their talents and abilities to the full'. It was assumed by many that this would also result in an equality of achievement amongst different social class and racial groups. Yet, surveys over the past 20 years have consistently shown that children from lower social class groups, ethnic minorites and adverse social conditions, such as those described by Wedge and Essen, have on average achieved poorly in the school system.

For example, one nationwide survey of school achievement in the USA, the Coleman Report (Coleman et al., 1966), showed that the best academic performance was obtained by white children from cities in the north-east of the country. As table 14.1 shows, children from other areas, especially the rural south, and of non-white ethnic origin, under-achieved on average by anything up to six grades (six years) by the end of secondary schooling.

TABLE 14.1    *Average under-achievement, in grades (years), of different groups of American children in standardized scores of verbal ability and mathematics, from the Coleman Report of 1966*

|  | Verbal ability | Mathematics |  | Verbal ability | Mathematics |
|---|---|---|---|---|---|
| White children, western cities | 0.5 | 0.8 | Mexican/American children | 3.5 | 4.1 |
| White children, rural south | 1.5 | 1.4 | Puerto Rican children | 3.6 | 4.8 |
| Black children, NE cities | 3.2 | 5.2 | Indian American children | 3.5 | 3.9 |
| Black children, rural south | 5.2 | 6.2 | Oriental-American children | 1.6 | 0.9 |

White children from north-east urban communities are taken as the standard.

The Rampton Report (1981) provides large-scale statistical evidence about the educational attainment from ethnic minority groups in the UK. The report examines CSE, Ordinary and Advanced level results, and destinations, of school leavers from six local education authorities with high concentrations of ethnic minority children – a sample which typified around half the ethnic minority school leavers in the country in 1978/1979. In table 14.2 figures are given for Asian, Afro-Caribbean, and other school leavers. Also given are comparative figures for all maintained school leavers in England during the same period. It is clear from these findings that Afro-Caribbean children are achieving much less well in the educational system than S. Asian or white children.

In the UK the National Child Development Study, a longitudinal study of all children born in one week of March, 1958, found that social class was a strong predictor of school achievement in reading and arithmetic. The children were the subjects of a socio-medical survey soon after birth. At 7, 11 and 16 years, detailed information was obtained about the children's educational progress, psychological development and home circumstances.

The study found a marked relationship between social class, defined by father's occupation, and the children's educational attainment (Davie et al., 1972). Figure 14.1 shows the percentages by social class of those children from the cohort who performed badly on a test of arithmetic at the age of 7. It shows that 41 per cent of children from unskilled families (social class V) had a poor test score as compared to 12 per cent of children from professional families (social class I). Figure 14.2 shows a similar pattern of scores on the Southgate reading test: 48 per cent of children from social class V made low scores compared to 8 per cent of children from social class I. If the criterion of poor reading is made more stringent, the disparity is much larger. The chances of a social class V child being a non-reader are fifteen times greater than those of a social class I child. Teachers were also asked to say whether the children would benefit from special educational treatment. Figure 14.3 shows that around 25 per cent of children from social class V were said to be receiving or in need of specialist teaching; only 3 per cent of children in social class I fell into this category. The gap between children of different social class backgrounds remained at the age of 11, as can be seen from the reading scores presented in table 14.3.

TABLE 14.2   *Evidence of academic under-achievement by young black students*

|  | Asians | Afro-Caribbeans | All other leavers | All school leavers in England |
|---|---|---|---|---|
| Five or more passes at 'O' level or CSE Grade 1 | 18% | 3% | 16% | 21% |
| One or more 'A' level passes | 13% | 2% | 12% | 13% |
| Went to university | 3% | 1% | 3% | 5% |
| $n =$ | 527 | 799 | 4,852 | 693,840 |

*Source*: Rampton Report, 1981

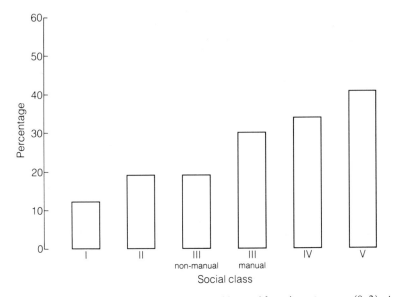

FIGURE 14.1    *Percentage of children with 'poor' problem arithmetic test scores (0–3) at age 7 (adapted from Davie et al., 1972)*

This survey, and others, have therefore identified a strong relationship between social class and educational attainment in reading and arithmetic. There seems to be a clear division in educational attainment between children from non-manual or middle class homes on the one hand and those from manual or working class homes on the other.

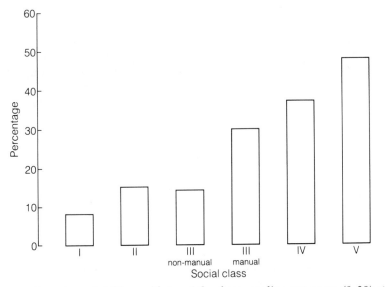

FIGURE 14.2    *Percentage of children with 'poor' Southgate reading test scores (0–20) at age 7 (adapted from Davie et al., 1972)*

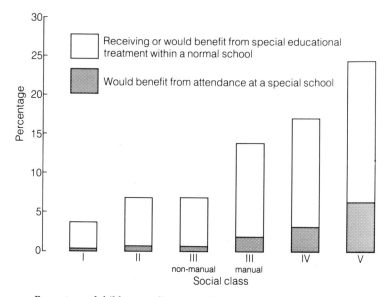

FIGURE 14.3    *Percentage of children needing special educational treatment by social class at age 7 (adapted from Davie et al., 1972)*

## Causes of Educational Disadvantage

In the 1960s and early 1970s many psychologists and educational researchers thought that the reasons for the relative failure in school of children from lower social class groups, and ethnic minorities, must lie in psychological factors such as the quality of parent–child language in the home, or parental attitudes to school. It was felt that parents of these children did not provide the intellectual stimulation which children needed. In the UK the Newsom Report (1963) identified linguistic disadvantage in some home backgrounds; the abilities of boys and girls, it stated, were often unrealized because of their 'inadequate powers of speech'. These ideas came to be known as the 'deficit' model which places blame on the home for failing

TABLE 14.3    *Reading comprehension scores in percentages by social class at 11 years*

| | | Social class | | | | |
|---|---|---|---|---|---|---|
| *Reading score* | *I and II* | *III (non-manual)* | *III (manual)* | *IV* | *V* | *Total* |
| 0–12 | 12.0 | 15.7 | 33.2 | 41.8 | 52.2 | 29.5 |
| 13–19 | 37.5 | 40.8 | 43.7 | 40.4 | 35.6 | 40.9 |
| 20–35 | 50.5 | 43.5 | 23.1 | 17.8 | 12.2 | 29.6 |
| Total | 100 | 100 | 100 | 100 | 100 | 100 |

*n* = 11,961.
*Source*: Davie, 1973

to give an adequate socialization experience for the children; as a result children have poor language skills, and/or inadequate intellectual skills to cope at school.

The term 'cultural deprivation' became popular in this period to describe what was thought of as a lack of 'cultural' stimulation in the homes of 'deprived' children. Such a perspective led naturally to the idea of programmes of 'enrichment' or of 'compensatory education' to remove these children's supposed psychological deficits.

We shall examine the effects of such enriched environments or compensatory education shortly. In certain circumstances, for example institutional rearing, enrichment programmes can have very substantial effects. However, the outcome of compensatory education programmes has seemed more modest, at least at first. The apparent failure of these programmes to remove educational disadvantage led to explanations other than the deficit model being seriously considered.

Advocates of an alternative approach, known as the 'difference' model, argue that schools are essentially white, middle class institutions in terms of their values, the language used by teachers and the content of courses. Hence, children from different backgrounds achieve less well. Difference theorists would wish to see greater tolerance of the values, attitudes and behaviour which the children bring to school from their home background; or even separate kinds of schooling for ethnic minorities. For example, Labov (1969) demonstrated the verbal skills which American ghetto children can display in the right context, but also argued that educators seldom value or encourage the non-standard English of inner city children. Writing about American Indian children, Wax and Wax (1971) argued that educators have been too quick to classify them as 'deprived' or 'lacking in culture' because their homes are without books, radio, newspapers or television. Such an attitude ignores the rich customs, ritual, language, mythology and medical knowledge which is part of the American Indian child's heritage. These authors suggest that the value and meaning of minority groups' culture should be an important part of the educational experience of all children.

Another approach is something of a compromise between the deficit and the difference positions. This emphasizes the 'social disadvantage' of lower social class and ethnic minority groups. Usually, such families have lower income, poor housing and more difficult family circumstances. These factors may be responsible for some real deficits in children's development, which may then show up in psychological or educational tests but which are not primarily psychological in origin. In common with difference theorists, this perspective would not expect too much from compensatory education programmes which did not deal with social and material inequalities. Moreover, such deficits produced by the culture might be exaggerated by actual discrimination against lower class or ethnic minority children in schools, as difference theories suggest.

From a very different and controversial standpoint it has been argued that children from lower social class backgrounds or certain ethnic minorities have, on average, genetically lower potential for intelligence and hence for education. One well-known proponent of this view is Arthur Jensen (1969). This hypothesis naturally raises considerable indignation amongst members of minority groups. Although its supporters argue that it is scientifically valid to present it as a hypothesis, to advance it seems insensitive to the prolonged injustice and discrimination suffered by many ethnic minority groups in Britain and the USA.

Much of the early research on race and intelligence was biased and unsound (see Gould, 1981, and chapter 1), while more recent research is against the hypothesis. For example, Scarr and Weinberg (1976) studied 130 black children adopted by middle class white families in the USA. These children achieved comparable levels of intellectual achievement to adopted white children in similar families. These and other studies (Scarr, 1984) suggest strongly that, while individual differences in intellectual ability may indeed be partly genetic in origin, racial differences in intelligence test scores are overwhelmingly due to environmental factors. Whether these environmental factors are best seen as due to psychological deficits in the home environment, educational prejudice against cultural/subcultural differences, or the consequence of social and material disadvantage, is still actively under debate.

### The Effects of Severe Deprivation and Institutional Rearing

The deficit model of disadvantage supposes that some children experience a deprived or impoverished rearing environment. This is contentious as applied to the homes of lower social class or ethnic minority children. However, it is not contentious in certain extreme circumstances. These include the experience of children reared in orphanages or children's homes in the years before and early after the Second World War. As we also saw in chapter 3, at that time children's institutions provided little stimulation of any kind. The children had few toys or playthings, little conversation with staff, and experienced extreme multiple caregiving. As a result, institutionally reared children scored very poorly on tests of cognitive or linguistic development, as well as showing problems in later social adjustment. It was the work of Bowlby and other psychologists which drew attention to these consequences of institutional rearing, and hence led to great improvements in the quality of the institutional environment. The success of these efforts was one factor contributing to the broad popularity of the deficit model in the 1960s, and the enthusiasm for compensatory education and enrichment programmes.

Two early studies showed dramatically the effects that could be achieved by enriching the environment for institutionally reared children. Skeels and Dye (1939) chanced to notice the effect of environmental change on two apparently retarded children who had been transferred at 18 months from an orphanage to the woman's ward in an institution for the mentally retarded, with an associated school. Their new environment was in fact an enriched one in comparison to the orphanage. Both staff and patients lavished attention and affection on them, played with them and took them on outings, and the children were given a much more stimulating experience than they had had previously. The gains were dramatic and after 15 months of this experience the children were considered to be within the normal range of intelligence. Children who had remained in the unstimulating environment of the orphanage did not make progress in this way.

Skodak and Skeels (1945) then carried out a more systematic longitudinal study in which 13 mentally retarded infants from the orphanage were transferred in the same way as the earlier two. The infants were aged 11-21 months, and had a mean IQ of 64. Again the children made dramatic gains; after an average of 19 months' stay the mean IQ was 92. By the age of 3 or 4 most were adopted by families and went on to attend normal school. A similar, control group of 12 children who stayed in the orphanage, however, actually decreased in IQ from a mean of 87 to 61 over this period. More than 20 years later, a follow-up study (Skeels, 1966) indicated that the gains made by the experimental group of children were lasting. They had obtained significantly more grades at school than the control group, had formed stable partnerships, and had a varied range of occupations (e.g. teacher, beautician, airline stewardess, sales manager). In the control group, all but one were in unskilled occupations, were unemployed or still living in the institution. These dramatic findings suggested that intervention at an early age had crucial effects on later educational and vocational success.

Kirk (1958) advised caution in interpreting Skeels and Skodak's results. Was it the intervention alone which had the effect, or was it the long-term stimulation and care from the adopted families? Kirk followed groups of retarded children during the preschool and first school years. Twenty-eight of his sample were given an enriched preschool experience in the community; 15 remained within the institution but attended an institution nursery school; 12 in a different institution had no preschool education. In terms of intellectual level the community preschool group made an average gain of 12 IQ points, the institution preschool group made an average gain of 10 IQ points, while the institution control group had an average *loss* of 6–7 IQ points. However, some of the differences became smaller after the children had entered school. Much of the intervention effect 'wore off' or 'washed out' after the experimental period was over. The reason for this could have been acceleration on the part of the control children once they experienced the stimulation of school or deceleration on the part of the experimental children once their enriched experience was over. The Kirk experiment suggested that early intervention could have immediate effects, but needed to be reinforced by a continuing experience of enrichment, warmth and stimulation (like that of the adopted children in Skeels and Skodak's study) if the gains were to be permanent.

It was clear from studies such as these that orphanage care for children could be improved. The benefits of better institutional conditions have been shown in a study of London children by Tizard and Rees (1974), discussed in box 3.2. The study started with 65 children who had been placed in the care of institutions by the age of 4 months. Tizard followed up the children at the ages of 2, 4.5 and 8 years. By the age of 4.5 years, 26 remained in the institution, 24 had been adopted and 15 restored to their mothers. There was no evidence of intellectual impairment or language retardation in the institutionalized children; their environment was stimulating with plenty of books and toys, and the staff made efforts to talk with the children. However, the adopted children were more advanced intellectually than those remaining in the institution; they were, in addition, friendlier, more talkative, more cooperative and more relaxed with strangers. The institutionalized children in this study were functioning within the normal range of cognitive and linguistic abilities, but they still showed some problems of social adjustment (see box 3.2). In modern institutions with a more stimulating environment there do not seem to be the adverse effects on cognitive and linguistic development found in earlier studies. The residual effects on social adjustment are probably related to the extreme multiple caregiving which is still an almost inevitable consequence of institutional rearing.

There have also been some case studies of the effects of extreme deprivation and neglect on young children. There have, for example, been anecdotal accounts of 'wild children', that is children discovered in the wild with apparently no form of human contact. When rescued, these children tended to display behaviour more characteristic of animals, such as running on all fours, and this led some to believe that the children had survived through being reared by and among animals. Such cases are generally poorly documented. Whatever the circumstances of their rearing, the prognosis for wild children has been poor. Their linguistic and cognitive attainment has tended to remain low, and their social behaviour strange. However, we cannot be sure that such children were normal when they were abandoned by their parents, and some investigators have suggested that wild children may have been psychotic or retarded in the first instance.

We do have a few more reliable case studies of children who have been reared in conditions of extreme deprivation in their own homes and who have subsequently been rescued. These accounts can help answer the question of how far an enriched environment can compensate for the effects of very severe neglect in the early years.

Koluchova's (1972) case study of Czechoslovakian twins born in 1960 gives evidence to support the argument that these effects need not be irreversible. The twins' mother died when they were born and they spent the next 11 months in an institution where they were said to be making normal progress. The father then took them back into his home but, on his remarriage, they were again put into care until the new household was formed. From around the age of 18 months until 7 years the twins lived with their father and his new wife. However, the stepmother kept them in conditions of extreme deprivation. She forbade her own children to talk to the twins and denied them any affection herself. They spent their time either in a bare, unheated room apart from the rest of the family or, as a punishment, were locked in the cellar. They never went out and lacked proper food, exercise and any kind of intellectual or social stimulation apart from what they could provide for themselves. The neighbours did not know of their existence but from time to time heard strange, animal-like sounds coming from the cellar. By the age of 7, when the authorities became aware of the twins' existence, they had the appearance of 3-year-olds; they could hardly walk because of rickets, they could not play, their speech was very poor and they relied mainly on gestures to communicate. On their discovery, they were removed from the family and placed in a home for preschool children.

They had experienced such severe emotional, intellectual and social deprivation that the prognosis seemed very poor, but once placed in a supportive environment, they began to make remarkable gains. After a year they were ready to be placed in a school for mentally retarded children. There they made such progress that they were transferred the next year to the second class of a normal infant school. At the same time, they were placed in the care of two sisters who gave them the emotional security and intellectual stimulation which had been so lacking in their own family environment. As a result, in the next 15 months, the twins' mental age increased by three years, showing clearly how the environmental change had compensated for early neglect. A follow-up found the twins completely normal in their language development at the age of 14; school performance was good and motivation high. They were now functioning at an average academic level in a class of children who were only 18 months younger than they. They were socially adjusted and had realistic aspirations to go on to take a vocational training. Figure 14.4 indicates the

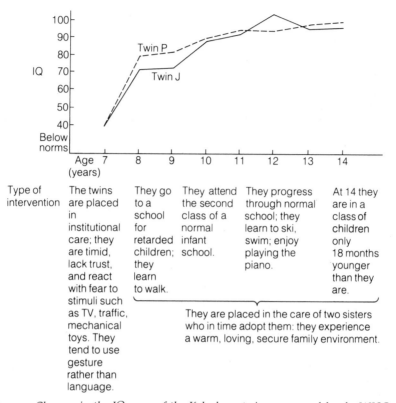

| Type of intervention | The twins are placed in institutional care; they are timid, lack trust, and react with fear to stimuli such as TV, traffic, mechanical toys. They tend to use gesture rather than language. | They go to a school for retarded children; they learn to walk. | They attend the second class of a normal infant school. | They progress through normal school; they learn to ski, swim; enjoy playing the piano. | At 14 they are in a class of children only 18 months younger than they are. |

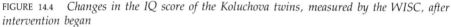

They are placed in the care of two sisters who in time adopt them: they experience a warm, loving, secure family environment.

FIGURE 14.4    *Changes in the IQ score of the Koluchova twins, measured by the WISC, after intervention began*

intellectual progress made by the twins from three months after intervention began. Prior to that, Koluchova had estimated their intelligence to be around an IQ of 40, although no formal assessment was possible because of their unfamiliarity with any of the tasks that appear in intelligence tests.

Koluchova's study indicates how removal from an extremely impoverished environment can reverse the effects of deprivation. It could be argued of course that the success of the intervention was only possible because the twins had experienced some normal nurturing in the first few months of their lives; in addition, they were not totally isolated since they had the support of one another. Finally, the twins were discovered when they were still relatively young. A less favourable outcome was found in another case study, that of a girl called 'Genie', where two of these ameliorative factors were absent (Curtiss, 1977).

Genie's isolation was even more extreme than that of the Czechoslovakian twins and lasted for a longer period of time. From the age of 20 months until she was 13 years old she was imprisoned alone in a darkened room. By day she was tied to an infant potty chair in such a way that she could only move her hands and feet; at night, she was put in a sleeping bag and further restrained by a sort of wire straitjacket. She was beaten by her father if she made any sound and he forbade other members of the family to speak to her. She lived in an almost silent world, deprived of warmth, proper nourishment and normal human contact. She was kept in these conditions until her mother, who was partially blind and dominated by Genie's father, finally escaped with her. At this point, Genie could not walk, she was emaciated, weighing only 59 pounds, she spent much of her time spitting and salivating, and was virtually silent apart from the occasional whimper. When tested soon after admission to hospital, she was functioning at the level of a 1-year-old.

Curtiss (1977), a graduate student of linguistics at the time, has given a moving and detailed account of Genie's development after she was taken into care. Despite the terrible conditions she had endured, Genie did respond to treatment. She soon learned to walk. Her level of intellectual functioning (measured by a non-verbal intelligence test developed for use with deaf children) increased (see figure 14.5) and in some perceptual tasks, such as the Mooney Faces Test which required subjects to distinguish between real and distorted faces, she performed well above average. She also became able to form relationships with other people.

In the area of language, however, Genie's development proved puzzling. During the first seven months in care she learned to recognize a number of words and then began to speak. At first she produced one-word utterances like 'pillow'; later, like any normal toddler, she produced two-word utterances, firstly nouns and adjectives (e.g. 'big teeth') and later verbs ('want milk') (chapter 10). She was even able to use words to describe her experience of isolation and neglect (Curtiss records Genie as saying, 'Father hit arm. Big wood. Genie cry'). However, there were unusual aspects to her language development. She never asked questions, she never learned to use pronouns and the telegraphic speech did not develop into more complex sentences. In fact, she was more inclined to use gestures in order to convey meaning.

Thus, although Genie showed great interest in language and developed some competence, she did not catch up with other children of her own age. Curtiss

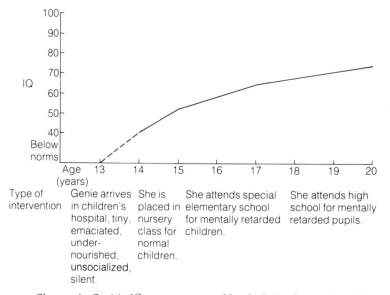

FIGURE 14.5   *Changes in Genie's IQ scores, measured by the Leiter International Performance Scale (a non-verbal test), after intervention began*

speculated that Genie was using the right hemisphere of the brain for language use not the left as is usual. Since the right hemisphere is not predisposed to language, this would explain some of the strange aspects of Genie's speech. Such an interpretation is confirmed by Genie's competence at discriminating faces, which is a right hemisphere task. Curtiss' explanation of Genie's unusual language development is that if language is not acquired at the right time, the cortical tissue 'normally committed for language and related abilities may functionally atrophy'. If Curtiss is right, Genie provides support for the idea that there is indeed a critical period for the development of left hemisphere functioning.

Some of the questions remain unanswered since all research into Genie's development stopped in 1978 when a court allowed her mother to become her legal guardian. At this point Genie's mother filed a lawsuit claiming that Curtiss and others had used Genie for their own personal gain.

Intervention did have a considerable impact on Genie's development, but apparently without such dramatic success as was obtained with the twins in Koluchova's study. A review of these and similar cases has been made by Skuse (1984). In general, it would seem the results of these recent case studies of extreme deprivation, and the improvements made in institutional care of young children, point to the great positive benefits which intervention, based on knowledge of children's psychological needs, can have.

## The Quality of Language in the Home

One of the factors implicated in producing the unstimulating environment of the orphanages of the 1930s was the lack of linguistic stimulation. Infants were largely left to their own devices, with little interaction or conversation with staff or caregivers. Yet, as we saw in chapter 10, there is a large body of evidence to suggest that children's language flourishes in an environment where adults and siblings use rich, varied language themselves, and where they respond with sensitivity to the language which the child produces.

Some deficit theorists have extended this finding to suggest that children in lower social class or ethnic minority groups have also been deprived of an adequate linguistic environment in the home. If so, this might explain their later educational disadvantage. One of the early theorists of this kind was Basil Bernstein, who examined social class differences in the speech of London children

Bernstein (1962) proposed a distinction between two kinds of conversational language, or code: These are a public language, or 'restricted code', and a formal language, or 'elaborated code'. The restricted code is colloquial and context-dependent. Phrases such as 'Do as I tell you', 'Lay off that', 'It's only natural, isn't it?', or 'I wouldn't believe it' are given as examples. These are idiomatic phrases of a fairly simple grammatical type which can be understood in context but not fully out of context (for example, with 'Do as I tell you' we have no idea, out of context, what the child is being asked to do).

By contrast, an elaborated code is more formal and context-independent. The meaning is made explicit for the other person, rather than aspects of meaning being taken for granted. Sentences such as 'I've asked you not to put dirty hands in your mouth since it may make you sick', or 'I know many children are brought up to like sweets, but I believe you can educate them to prefer other more healthy foods', might be examples of elaborated code. You know what the person is meaning, without being present. The sentences also tend to be more complex.

Bernstein proposed that children from middle class backgrounds could use either restricted or elaborated codes, depending on which was most appropriate in the circumstances; but that children from working class backgrounds could only use the restricted code. The restricted code had disadvantages, in that it 'limits the range of behaviour and learning', and leads to 'a low level of conceptualization – an orientation to a low order of causality, a lack of interest in processes'. This could contribute to the educational disadvantage of lower class children in school (see figure 14.6).

Bernstein (1971) also distinguished between 'person-orientated' and 'position-orientated' communications. A person-orientated message uses personal appeal, such as 'I know you don't like kissing grandpa, but he is unwell, and he is very fond of you, and it makes him happy'. A position-orientated message appeals to status roles of a general kind, such as 'I don't want none of your nonsense; children kiss their grandpa'. Bernstein thought the latter to be more characteristic of traditional working class families.

Bernstein and other researchers provided some evidence to support their position. In laboratory or test situations differences in the speech of middle class and working class children seemed to be somewhat along the lines Bernstein's theory suggested. However, this could be either because working-class children lacked the competence to use elaborated code, or because the test environment was more threatening to them and this context did not encourage their use of elaborated code. Lawton (1968) assessed the written and spoken language of 12- and 15-year-olds from different social class groups. In written work the middle class children produced more elaborated essays; but in individual interviews, there were much smaller differences and many examples of abstract thought and generalized content in the conversation of the working class sample.

This and other research suggested that any differences in the language of middle class and working class children in Britain are not so much a matter of competence (the deficit model) as one of the contexts in which particular kinds of language may be used, contexts that are facilitating or threatening to the child (the difference model). In later writings, Bernstein himself went some way to agreeing with this view, thus modifying aspects of his early theories. He also has more recently laid

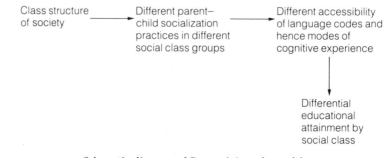

FIGURE 14.6  *Schematic diagram of Bernstein's early model*

greater stress on the direct effects of social disadvantage and inequalities in society. However, his early work was influential in the USA, where it was generalized to racial as well as social class differences.

A much-quoted study by Hess and Shipman (1965) appeared to prove that black children from 'deprived' backgrounds in the USA lacked crucial stimulation from their mothers in the early years so that they failed to acquire the basis for linguistic and cognitive development. This apparently objective study of the effects of deprivation on the intellectual development of children is now seen to have serious flaws in its design and interpretation (see box 14.1). Nevertheless, other language deficit theorists (e.g. Bereiter and Engelmann, 1966) have written about children from ghetto backgrounds as if they had virtually no language which could be of use outside their local environment, and attributed difficulties in reading and writing to the children's deficient, non-standard version of English.

The inadequacy of this sort of conceptualization of lower class black children in the USA was vividly demonstrated by William Labov (1969). He recorded the spontaneous language of black children aged 8–17 years in a ghetto area in Harlem, New York. Many of the boys were gang members, most were failures at school. Labov used black interviewers. Two examples of transcripts follow. In the first, the interviewer, Clarence Robins (C.R.) is talking to an 8-year-old called Leon.

| | |
|---|---|
| C.R. | What if you saw somebody kickin' somebody else on the ground, or was using a stick, what would you do if you saw that? |
| Leon | Mmmmm. |
| C.R. | If it was supposed to be a fair fight – |
| Leon | I don't know. |
| C.R. | You don't know? Would you do anything ... huh? I can't hear you. |
| Leon | No. |
| C.R. | Did you ever see somebody got beat up real bad? |
| Leon | ... Nope??? |
| C.R. | Well – uh – did you ever get into a fight with a guy? |
| Leon | Nope. |
| C.R. | That was bigger than you? |
| Leon | Nope. |
| C.R. | You never been in a fight? |
| Leon | Nope. |
| C.R. | Nobody ever pick on you? |
| Leon | Nope. |
| C.R. | Nobody ever hit you? |
| Leon | Nope. |
| C.R. | How come? |
| Leon | Ah 'on' know. |
| C.R. | Didn't you ever hit somebody? |
| Leon | Nope. |
| C.R. | [incredulous] You never hit nobody? |
| Leon | Mhm. |
| C.R. | Aww, ba-a-a-be, you ain't going to tell me that. |

(Labov, 1969, pp. 200–1)

Although the interviewer is also a black person raised in Harlem, in the formal interview situation he elicits very little from Leon. Is Leon 'deprived of language', or just clamming up in this context? The following extract proves it is the latter.

| | |
|---|---|
| C.R. | Is there anybody who says *your mamma drink pee?* |
| Leon | [rapidly and breathlessly] Yee-ah! |
| Greg | Yup! |
| Leon | And your father eat doo-doo for breakfast'! |
| C.R. | Ohhh!! [laughs] |
| Leon | And they say *your father – your father eat doo-doo for dinner!* |
| Greg | When they sound on me, I say CBM. |
| C.R. | What that mean? |
| Leon | Congo-booger-snatch! [laughs] |
| Greg | Congo-booger-snatch! [laughs] |
| Greg | And sometimes I'll curse with BB. |
| C.R. | What that? |
| Greg | Black boy! [Leon – crunching on potato chips] Oh that's a *MBB*. |
| C.R. | MBB. Whats that? |
| Greg | 'Merican Black Boy! |
| C.R. | Ohh ... |
| Greg | Anyway, 'Mericans is same like white people, right? |
| Leon | And they talk about Allah. |
| C.R. | Oh yeah? |
| Greg | Yeah. |
| C.R. | What they say about Allah? |
| Leon | Allah – Allah is God. |
| Greg | Allah – |
| C.R. | And what else? |
| Leon | I don't know the res'. |
| Greg | Allah i – Allah is God, Allah is the only God, Allah – |
| Leon | Allah is the *son* of God. |
| Greg | But can he make magic? |
| Leon | Nope. |
| Greg | I know who can make magic. |
| C.R. | Who can? |
| Leon | The God, the *real* one. |

(Labov, 1969, p. 201)

Clarence Robins changed the context here by bringing along potato chips, by inviting along Leon's friend Gregory, by sitting down in Leon's room, and introducing taboo words and topics. Leon is transformed from a suspicious non-verbal child into one who is actively competing to speak. From this example it is also apparent that Leon is using a distinct dialect of 'non-standard English' (or NSE) which is different from standard English (SE). NSE used by black American children differs from SE in systematic ways, for example copula deletion (omission of 'is' or 'are'), and the use of double negatives (see table 14.4). These are surface structure differences which reflect a similar deep structure of meaning (see p. 299, chapter 10). There is nothing inferior in these features, and many languages use them. For

TABLE 14.4 *Some differences between non-standard English (NSE) used by black Americans and standard English (SE)*

| | NSE | SE |
|---|---|---|
| Copula deletion | You crazy<br>They mine | You are crazy<br>They are mine |
| Double negative | You ain't going to<br>    no heaven<br>Don't nobody know<br>    it's really a God<br>He don't know<br>    nothing | You are not going to<br>    any heaven<br>Nobody knows that<br>    there really is a God<br>He doesn't know<br>    anything |

example, the double negative is used in French (e.g., 'il ne comprend rien'). Another interview, between interviewer John Lewis (J.L.) and 15-year-old Larry, a gang leader, shows that NSE has just as much potential for formal argument and abstract thought as SE, and Larry is fully capable of it.

J.L.      What happens to you after you die? Do you know?

Larry    Yeah, I know.

J.L.      What?

Larry    After they put you in the ground, your body turns into – ah – bones, an' shit.

J.L.      What happens to your spirit?

Larry    Your spirit – soon as you die, your spirit leaves you.

J.L.      And where does the spirit go?

Larry    Well, it all depends . . .

J.L.      On what?

Larry    You know, like some people say if you're good an'shit, your spirit goin' t' heaven . . . 'n if you bad, your spirit goin' to hell. Well, bullshit! Your spirit goin' to hell anyway, good or bad.

J.L.      Why?

Larry    Why? I'll tell you why. 'Cause you see, doesn' nobody really know that it's a God, y'know, 'cause I mean I have seen black gods, pink gods, white gods, all color gods, and don't nobody know it's really a God. An' when they be sayin' if you good, you goin' t' heaven, tha's bullshit, 'cause you ain't goin' t' no heaven, 'cause it ain't no heaven for you to go to.

(Labov, 1969 p. 203)

Labov thus stressed 'difference' rather than 'deficit' in analysing the language of children from disadvantaged backgrounds. Lower class black children acquire NSE at home and with peers, but are faced with SE at school or in psychological test situations. There is no intrinsic deficit in NSE, but its difference from the SE required in the school, and the biased attitude of educators to NSE, puts lower class black children at a disadvantage.

Criticism of the deficit model also comes from a study by Wells (1983) on social class differences in the UK. He collected a large amount of data in naturalistic settings at home and in school of children's conversations both with adults and with other children. He was especially interested in differences between talk at home and at school, aiming to investigate the claim that 'a major cause of differential success is the difference between children in their ability to meet the linguistic expectations of the classroom as a result of their preschool linguistic experience at home' (p. 127). His Bristol Longitudinal Study followed a representative sample of children through the preschool years into the infant school with recordings of the children's spontaneous talk in the two contexts of home and school. Wells found that there were very few homes which did not provide richer opportunities than are found at school for learning through interaction with adults.

However, Wells pointed out that differences in 'habitual use of language' between home and school could lead to difficulties. Here is an example. One 5-year-old girl, Rosie, from a working class family, already experienced learning difficulties at school because she did not seem to be tuned in to the teacher's expectations of appropriate questions and answers. But Wells did not blame the home. His recordings of interactions between Rosie and her mother indicated that at home she had greater control of language than in class; her difficulty at school stemmed from 'remoteness from direct, personal involvement in a shared or self-initiated activity' (p.137). The formality of the school setting was unfamiliar and threatening to her, so she was put at a disadvantage in her ability to respond to the school environment. Wells argues that teachers should be more flexible in their interactions with children so as to minimize the gaps between home and school. This can happen when the goal of the task is open-ended and where there is an area of negotiation, so that pupils and teachers can share meanings and use language in an exploratory way. Furthermore, Wells argues that it is simply false to suggest that working class children are linguistically 'disadvantaged'; his observations did not identify clear-cut social class differences in the use of language by parents and their children. He stresses the need for teachers to provide opportunities for children to continue the process of learning through the active conversation which has been their experience in the pre-school years.

## Compensatory Education Programmes in the USA

We have seen how, in the later 1960s, a deficit or cultural deprivation model had become the most accepted hypothesis to explain the educational disadvantage and under-achievement of lower social class and ethnic minority children. The early work of Bernstein, and Hess and Shipman (see box 14.1), combined with what psychologists had found out about the successful consequences of early intervention with children reared in orphanages, suggested that the answer to this deficit was early intervention with disadvantaged children, particularly focusing on their language where much of the supposed deficit was thought to be located. This led to a large number of programmes of compensatory education for preschool children in the USA (and also in the UK, see below).

One of the earliest examples, in Illinois, USA was a highly structured language programme for 4-year-old black children devised by Bereiter and Englemann (1966).

This aimed to teach English to non-standard English speakers as if it were a foreign language, by drilling and repetition. Here is a typical interaction between a teacher and a group of children:

| | |
|---|---|
| Teacher | What's this? This is a ... ? |
| Child | Gun. |
| Teacher | Good. This is a gun. Now everybody say, 'This is a gun.' This is a gun. This is a gun. |
| Children | [in unison] This is a gun. |
| Teacher | Good. [trying to hold their interest] Now, what is this? Let's say it one more time. This is an alligator. |
| Child | That ain't no alligator. That a gun. |
| Teacher | That's what I said. This is a bulldog. |
| Child | It ain't neither. It a gun. |
| Teacher | Well, what did I say? |
| Children | You said that a bulldog. |
| Teacher | You're just too smart for me, I can't get away with a thing. I'll start again. This is a gun. Is that correct? |

(Bereiter and Engelmann, 1966, pp. 105–10)

The aim was to change the children's non-standard speech patterns through many repetitions of dialogues and exercises like the one above. Bereiter and Engelmann thought that 'the language of culturally deprived children is not merely an underdeveloped version of Standard English, but is a basically non-logical mode of expressive behavior'. The viewpoint has since been exposed by Labov, and other difference theorists, as biased and completely insensitive to the different features of black American culture or dialect (cf. examples on pp. 423–5 above).

Another early example was the work of Blank and Solomon (1969). They did not require the children in their programmes to speak standard English, nor did they use drilling or repetition. Instead, 'a specialised language program was devised to facilitate abstract thinking in young deprived children through short, individual tutoring sessions on a daily basis'. They involved the children in conversations that arose naturally out of the child's own interests and experiences. Here is an example of a typical conversation;

| | |
|---|---|
| Teacher | Look! I've got some nice toys for you. Do you remember what you wanted to do with them today? |
| Child | [Looks at doll and smiles] Give a bath. |
| Teacher | Yes. That's just what you said yesterday. Now, what do we need to do? |
| Child | Give her a bottle and then she sleep. |
| Teacher | Sleep? We could do that but you said you wanted to give her a bath. What do we need for that? |
| Child | A big bath to put her in. |
| Teacher | Right. Now, where could we give her a bath? |
| Child | There's no bath tub here. |
| Teacher | That's right. There is no bath tub but there is something we could use instead. What is the name of the place where we get water? |
| Child | The sink. |

Teacher   That's a great idea. [Holds up doll] What do we need to do first?
Child     Take off these things.
Teacher   Yes. Take off her clothes. Now you say, 'I have to take her clothes off'.
Child     I have to take her clothes off.

(Blank, M. 1972)

If you read back through the conversation, you will notice that the teacher confirms that the child remembered from the previous day what they had both planned to do with the doll; the sequence which the child suggests is in the wrong order so the teacher corrects her by suggesting 'bath' before 'sleep'. She helps the child focus on the search for an object which will serve for a bath – the sink. When the child gestures the removal of the doll's clothes, the teacher directly asks her to make the statement 'I have to take her clothes off', while at the same time continuing with the game. Blank and Solomon found that children experiencing this programme increased in terms of IQ scores more than did control children, which suggested the programme was having some benefit, and subsequently the Blank language programmes were quite widely used.

Following the apparent success of these kinds of compensatory education programmes, a much more massive policy of intervention occurred in the USA with 'Project Head Start'. This started in the summer of 1965 and built up over the next few years until millions of preschool children across the USA had participated in some form of Head Start programme. The general goal was to give 'deprived' children a head start in schools by some form of early intervention to stimulate cognitive and linguistic development. Up to the 1960s, nursery schools had tended to be more orientated towards the needs of the middle class child. Much of the emphasis was on social and emotional development through free play, and unstructured imaginitive activities. Preschool programmes of compensatory education, by contrast, aimed directly to prepare children for entry into infant school and to give them skills which, it was felt, their homes had failed to provide. Programmes were often based on the assumption that the children's language was deficient, that they lacked cognitive strategies appropriate for school learning, and that their parents used ineffective modes of control. However, no detailed syllabus was laid down and the exact nature and length of programmes varied widely.

## Compensatory Education in the UK

The Plowden Report of 1967 advocated a policy of positive discrimination in favour of children from poor areas throughout Britain which were to be designed 'Educational Priority Areas' (EPAs), through the provision of more resources, more teachers and better school buildings. In response to the recommendations of the Plowden Report, Halsey (1972) mounted a large project, the Educational Priority Area Project, to initiate and evaluate compensatory education programmes in exceptionally deprived communities in London, Birmingham, Liverpool, Yorkshire and Dundee. Each area formulated its own programme within the wider framework of the Project in order to take account of the particular needs of the region. We describe one programme which was mounted in Conisborough and Denaby, a Yorkshire mining community with high levels of unemployment, low wages among the employed and a great deal of ill-health amoung the general population. The research team developed two major programmes in this community: the establishment of preschool education in the area (there had been none before) and intervention with families in their homes.

To establish the first programme, the local education authority set up nursery classes for 3- and 4-year-olds in two schools. Three different curricula were compared: 'normal' nursery provision, i.e. an unstructured approach; the Peabody Language Development kit; and the language programme developed by Blank (see pp. 427–8).

The children were assessed on the English Picture Vocabulary Test at the beginning and end of the first year in nursery school and during the first year of infant school. The groups that had experienced a structured approach – the Peabody and the Blank programmes – showed most improvement. Average scores were above those of groups who had not experienced the programmes; gains were maintained into the infant school.

The second programme involved home visits. Families of children aged 18 months and over were visited with the aim of helping them develop an active learning climate in the home. Thirty-five families were visited each week for 1–2 hours by a researcher who brought toys, books and equipment and who helped mothers to play with their children. Mothers were encouraged to see the educational value of play and helped to extend their children both intellectually and socially. This project was highly successful in the sense that it was appreciated by the families involved, but its effects were not evaluated objectively.

In addition, an educational resource centre called Red House was established. This ran special courses for children at local primary and secondary schools, provided a base for preschool groups and a centre for student teachers. This too was felt to be a success although it was not formally assessed.

The other projects which ran parallel to the programmes based in Conisbrough and Denaby were evaluated in the project report. Halsey's overall conclusion was a positive one. He argued that the concept of Educational Priority Areas was a useful one which enabled positive discrimination to be made in favour of underprivileged children. He advocated the use of structured programmes which are flexible enough to accommodate to local needs and he recommended the development of community schools as one means of bridging the gap between home and school. Although he did not claim that programmes like his could fully compensate for deprived social conditions, he argued that education could play an important role in extending young children's cognitive and linguistic abilities.

## Compensatory Programmes Evaluated

Some of the early evaluation studies showed disappointing results for the compensatory programmes. The first national evaluation of Project Head Start was carried out in 1969 in Ohio University by the Westinghouse Learning Corporation. This research study showed that the intervention programmes had very little, if any, effect on the children who had taken part. Any benefits seemed to be very transient, disappearing after a year or so at school. Some psychologists, such as Arthur Jensen (1969), took this to confirm their view that children from poor families had inherited low academic ability which no amount of compensatory education could make up for. Others thought there should be *more* intervention. This might mean more intensive intervention, involving parent as well as child education; or starting intervention earlier; or following through into the early school years. At an extreme, this might virtually involve removing a young child from a 'deficient' home environment. Yet others – the difference theorists – argued that the whole premise of intervention was biased or racist. As Baratz and Baratz (1970, p. 43) put it, 'Head Start has failed because its goal is to correct a deficit that simply does not exist'. By now the ignorance and insensitivity which many white researchers had shown to black culture and to the thoughts and feelings of black mothers and children had become more obvious. Baratz and Baratz claimed that the 'Head Start programs may inadvertently advocate the annihilation of a cultural system which is barely considered or understood by most social scientists'.

However, the Ohio–Westinghouse study took place only five years after Project Head Start began. By 1976, researchers who were following the long-term effects of intervention programmes began to report encouraging results. One major research project (Lazar and Darlington, 1982) was a collaborative study in which 11 preschool research teams came together to pool their results for a group named the Consortium for Longitudinal Studies. Each researcher had independently designed and carried out preschool programmes in the 1960s; the children who had participated, mainly black children from low-income families, were followed up in 1976 when their ages ranged from 9 to 19.

For example, one project, organized by Weikart et al. (1970) in Ypsilanti, Michigan, involved 123 children from low-waged black families. Half of them, selected at random, experienced an intervention programme; the other half, the control group, had no preschool educational provision. The programme children spent 12.5 hours per week for two years in a special preschool intervention programme which stressed active learning and a great deal of communication between child and adults and between child and child. There were also home visits by the teachers.

The results for IQ scores from the project and later follow-ups are shown in table 14.5. The programme group children showed an initial increase (more than the control group) in the year or so immediately following the intervention, but through the middle school years this showed a familiar falling-off or wash-out effect. However, some long-term effects of the intervention were found in other areas. By the age of 15, the programme group scored on average 8 per cent higher on reading, arithmetic and language tests than the control group. By the end of high school, only 19 per cent of the programme children had been placed in remedial classes compared with 39 per cent in the control group. Socially too there were effects. The programme youngsters were less likely to be delinquent (36 per cent as compared to 42 per cent of the control group). Ten per cent of the programme group went on to college but none of the control group did. These findings were fairly typical of the other ten projects in the survey.

TABLE 14.5 *Changes in IQ with age, for programme and control group children, in Weikart's preschool programme*

|  | Pretest | 3 | 4 | 5 | 6 | 7 | 8 | 9 | 10 | 14 |
|---|---|---|---|---|---|---|---|---|---|---|
| Programme group | 79.6 | 79.9 | 92.7 | 94.1 | 91.3 | 91.7 | 88.1 | 87.7 | 85.0 | 81.0 · |
| Control group | 78.5 | 79.6 | 81.7 | 83.2 | 86.3 | 87.1 | 86.9 | 86.8 | 84.6 | 80.7 |

*Source*: Lazar and Darlington, 1982

As discussed in box 14.2, the Consortium for Longitudinal Studies concluded that early intervention programmes could have significant, long-term effects (Lazar and Darlington, 1982). The interpretation of achievement test scores was difficult because of variability in the tests themselves. However, the authors reported some evidence that children who had experienced early intervention performed better on school attainment tests than controls. But perhaps more important were the non-cognitive differences – the changes in attitudes towards themselves as learners, in aspirations and beliefs in their own competence (box 14.2).

*A continuing debate*

The apparent failure of Project Head Start around 1970 led many workers, such as Baratz and Baratz, to reject the idea of compensatory education and to replace the deficit model with the difference model. The deficit theorists had certainly been naive in their assumptions. Nevertheless, the difference model too may be naive if taken to the extreme of supposing that all kinds of rearing conditions are equally valid. Poor material conditions, inadequate housing and poverty, may well affect the quality of a child's development. Lower social class groups, and many ethnic minorities, tend to suffer from these material and social disadvantages, as well as possible prejudice or bias within and outside the educational system.

Another perspective sees disadvantage as involving both genuine cultural or subcultural differences (as e.g. in standard English and non-standard English dialects) which may be discriminated against in the educational system or wider society; and also more psychological deficits stemming from poor material conditions. As Tulkin (1972) expressed it:

> subcultural influences may represent a legitimate explanation for some of the behaviour observed in particular low-income or minority populations, but these influences should not be regarded as the sole determinant of life styles in these groups. Social scientists must also consider the way in which the majority culture, by its tolerance of social, political and economic inequality, actually contributes to the development, in some subgroups, of the very characteristics which it considers 'depriving'. (p. 331)

From this perspective the evaluation of compensatory education programmes is more difficult than from either a purely deficit or purely difference model. They might have some part to play in the amelioration of genuine deficits, as indeed the long-term successes of Head Start seen to indicate. However, they should be sensitive to the cultural or subcultural differences involved, and to the actual wishes of the parents and the community. In this respect, some of the British projects may have been better designed than many of the early American projects.

In a review of American compensatory education programmes, Bronfenbrenner (1979) argued that the best schemes are those that involve the families, since those that focus on the child alone tend to have only short-term effects. If the parents are involved throughout, they can sustain the effects after the programme is over. He recommends child care education for young people before they become parents, and support for them once the children are born, as well as a network of community support services amongst parents and other members of the community. However, he concluded that programmes of compensatory education are not effective for the most deprived groups if they concentrate only on the parent–child relationship. He calls also for intervention at other levels (cf. figure 1.3) to alleviate the desperate conditions in which some families are forced to live. Removal of educational disadvantage requires that the families themselves have adequate health care, reasonable housing, enough food and a sufficient income. Programmes of compensatory education cannot by themselves undo the inequalities that continue to exist in our society, and should not replace efforts to tackle poverty and racial prejudice.

More recent research shows that material disadvantage, and discrimination in the educational system, remain convincing explanations of much educational under-achievement. There is plenty of evidence to show that poor children perform less well at school than children from better-off families, are less healthy and have a narrower range of opportunities in later life. As we saw earlier, reports from the National Child Development Study (Wedge and Essen, 1982) defined social disadvantage in terms of family composition, poor housing and low income. Children experiencing all three of these were defined as 'disadvantaged' in their analyses. Figure 14.7 shows the populations of children experiencing each of these three kinds of adversities separately, and those defined as disadvantaged, at ages 11 and 16. The number of children included in all three categories amounted to 4.5 per cent at age 11. At 16, the figure was 2.9 per cent. This means that amongst all 16-year-olds in Britain in 1974, there were 46,000 who were socially disadvantaged by these criteria.

These children had more difficulties than ordinary children; besides their poor housing and income, the fathers were more likely to be unemployed, and both parents were more likely to be chronically sick. In school these children were less motivated; at 16 only 41 per cent hoped to continue their education as compared to 71 per cent of their peers. Teachers were asked to say whether the 16-year-olds in the survey were able to do all the calculations normally required of an everyday shopper, and whether they were able to read well enough to cope with everyday needs. Again, the largest proportion of those unable to do these tasks were pupils from disadvantaged homes (figure 14.8).

Was the poor attainment solely attributable to home conditions? Wedge and Essen argue that 'the particularly poor exam records of the disadvantaged could to quite a large extent be attributed to the tendency to enter them for fewer exams, and not necessarily to their performance in those exams'. Figure 14.9 shows that disadvantaged children, even when they scored in the top range on attainment tests

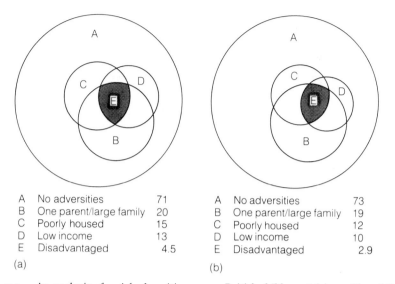

| | | (a) | | | (b) |
|---|---|---|---|---|---|
| A | No adversities | 71 | A | No adversities | 73 |
| B | One parent/large family | 20 | B | One parent/large family | 19 |
| C | Poorly housed | 15 | C | Poorly housed | 12 |
| D | Low income | 13 | D | Low income | 10 |
| E | Disadvantaged | 4.5 | E | Disadvantaged | 2.9 |

FIGURE 14.7   *An analysis of social adversities among British children at (a) age 11 and (b) age 16 in percentages (from Wedge and Essen, 1982)*

in reading and mathematics, were less likely to be entered for examinations in English and mathematics than others in their year group with similar scores. The authors recommended a policy of positive discrimination to encourage the disadvantaged to take examinations which will give them a better opportunity in future life.

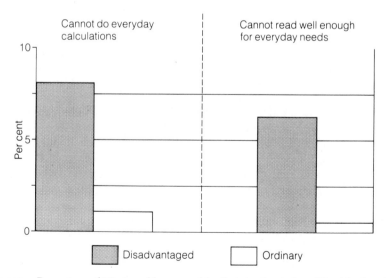

FIGURE 14.8   *Percentage of 16-year-olds assessed by their teacher to be without basic arithmetic and reading skills (from Wedge and Essen, 1982)*

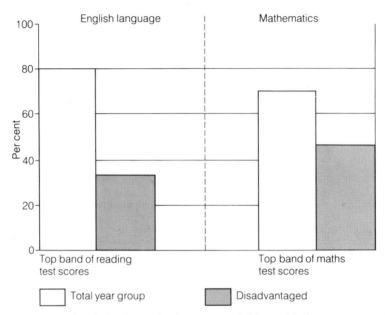

FIGURE 14.9   *Entry for 'O' level examinations among children with the same range of scores in reading and mathematics (from Wedge and Essen, 1982)*

*Ethnic minorities*

Similar results seem to emerge from recent studies of the achievements of young people from ethnic minorities in Britian. Eggleston (1985) carried out an investigation into the educational and vocational experiences of 15- to 18-year-old young people of ethnic minority groups. He studied 593 young people, of whom 157 were South Asian, 110 were of Afro-Caribbean origin and the rest white. In public examinations whites and South Asians did equally well. Afro-Caribbean girls performed as well as white boys, but Afro-Caribbean boys obtained fewest passes in the whole sample. The Eggleston Report suggests that Afro-Caribbean children suffer most from the system of streaming and banding which at present exists in comprehensive schools and that pupils should be assessed more carefully before they are entered for examinations to ensure that they achieve the maximum of which they are capable. As the report states: 'In schools, both at and below sixth-form level, ethnic minority pupils may be placed on courses and entered for examinations at levels below those appropriate for their abilities and ambitions'.

A self-fulfilling prophecy seemed to be operating with teachers expecting less of Afro-Caribbean boys in particular, and the latter then being alienated from conventional schooling. Nevertheless, black students and their parents have academic aspirations and ambitions which, according to the Eggleston Report, are not being met by the present educational system. Cecile Wright (1985), a member of the research team which produced the Eggleston Report, has provided some evidence that bias exists in the allocation of pupils to streams or bands for examination purposes. In table 14.6, for example, Wright presents examination

TABLE 14.6   *Examination marks in English language (Eng.) and science (Sci.) and allocation to upper (U) and lower (L) bands for all Asian, all Afro-Caribbean and a random sample of white pupils in the same year group*

| | Asian | | | Afro-Carribean | | | White | | |
|---|---|---|---|---|---|---|---|---|---|
| | Eng. | Sci. | Band | Eng. | Sci. | Band | Eng. | Sci. | Band |
| Number of pupils with Eng. marks over 43 | 5 | | U | 3 | | U | 6 | | U |
| Individual | 43 | 50 | U | 43 | 35 | L | 42 | 45 | U |
| pupils at upper– | 42 | 27 | U | 42 | 48 | L | 42 | 15 | L |
| lower band | 41 | 36 | U | 37 | 33 | U | 37 | 27 | L |
| boundary (%) | 39 | 27 | U | 36 | 31 | L | 37 | 19 | L |
| | 36 | 34 | U | 36 | 23 | L | 36 | 43 | U |
| | 34 | 41 | U | 35 | 24 | L | 34 | 37 | U |
| | 27 | 33 | U | 27 | 17 | L | 33 | 49 | U |
| | 27 | 21 | L | 24 | 34 | L | 31 | 24 | L |
| | 25 | 26 | L | 21 | 26 | L | 30 | 44 | U |
| | 23 | 16 | L | 21 | 23 | L | 28 | 27 | L |
| | 23 | 43 | U | | | | 27 | 52 | U |
| | 21 | 44 | U | | | | 24 | 35 | U |
| | 21 | 43 | U | | | | | | |
| Below 21% in English, absent or remedial | 6 | | L | 6 | | L | 5 | | L |

*Source*: Wright, 1985

results in English and science for all black pupils and a random sample of white pupils in one year group of a comprehensive school. She points out that the allocation of some Afro-Caribbean pupils to lower bands is puzzling (e.g. the Afro-Caribbean pupil who gains 42 per cent for English and 48 per cent for science); white pupils with comparable marks were placed in the upper band. Wright suggests that teachers may be making their decisions about placement on the basis of behaviour and 'cooperation' as well as ability. For example, one Afro-Caribbean girl with quite high examination performance was allocated to a lower band because, as her teacher explained: 'This pupil is not one of the pleasant Form members. She tends to be arrogant and very insolent. Unless her attitude changes immediately she will not have an enjoyable time in the Upper School'.

The Swann Report (1985), an investigation into the education of children from ethnic minority groups, reached a similar conclusion. Swann also noted that S. Asian children show a pattern of academic achievement which is broadly similar to that of white British children; by contrast, children of Afro-Caribbean origin on average under-achieve at school. He argues that some ethnic minorities are disadvantaged in both social and economic terms and that this is due to racial prejudice and discrimination, especially with regard to housing and employment. Under-achievement at school is also, Swann claims, due to discrimination within the educational system which bears directly on the children.

Under-achievement may have its origins in the very beginnings of school-ing – whether in nursery school or infant school – where preconceived attitudes to children's ability, racist or ethnocentric reading books and the treatment of misdemeanors can give a child a negative picture of himself and his place in the wider society. And these disadvantages become cumulative as the child progresses through the system. (p.109)

As one black child quoted in the report puts it:

In a lot of books you find lovely, pretty pictures, but the pictures are white postmen, white businessmen. You never see a black postman, you never read about black scientists, black whatever. It is always white. If you can't identify yourself with something that you are learning then it is going to kill the incentive in you to learn or go further. (p. 97)

Swann's solution is a long-term policy – a pluralist approach to the curriculum:

We believe it is only through reaching a consensus on the overall task for education both in meeting the needs of ethnic minority pupils and in preparing *all* pupils, both ethnic minority and ethnic majority, through a common educational experience, for life in today's multi-racial Britain, that our aim of a truly pluralist society can be achieved. (Swann Report, 1985, p. 326)

Macdonald (1989), the barrister who chaired the inquiry into the murder of Ahmed Ullah, a pupil at Burnage School, Manchester, argued the case for 'glasnost and power-sharing' to combat racism in schools. His inquiry team recommended principally that schools should create means for pupils' views to be properly heard and opportunities given for pupils to report incidents like racist name-calling and to know that schools have, and operate, an effective anti-racist policy.

Cowie and Rudduck (1991) argue that cooperative learning strategies can make a contribution to the task of creating equal opportunities for *all* pupils and fostering the kind of social climate in the classroom where learning will flourish. American studies (e.g. Johnson et al., 1984; Kagan, 1986) and an Israeli study (Hertz-Lazarowitz et al., 1989) have consistently found that cooperative learning, by reorganizing the social structure of the classroom, can make radical improvements in the interpersonal relationships amongst children from different ethnic backgrounds. As Cowie and Rudduck (1991) point out:

Pupil roles in cooperative classrooms are quite different from those in traditional classrooms. They are more likely to be active, self-directing and communicative. Pupils helps one another and have relationships which are more often characterized by equal status.

A dilemma facing educators is that if the curriculum is changed to accommodate to the knowledge and values which the child brings from home, there is no gaurantee that what is taught will still be valued by society, e.g. by employers or examining boards. However we know that there is a danger that a *laissez-faire* attitude may block the avenues that help children from poor backgrounds gain access to mainstream culture. By failing to take action, educators help to perpetuate injustice in our society. Clearly this is a topic in which the values of society and the political possibilities of the times must be considered together with our psychological knowledge of the processes of children's development.

## Further reading

R. Davie, N. Butler and H. Goldstein 1972: *From Birth to Seven*. London: Longman (National Children's Bureau) is the report of the National Child Development Study at the first follow-up of the 1958 'cohort' at the age of 7. There are many useful analyses of educational attainment, health and environmental conditions in different sectors of British society. A very readable account of the impact of disadvantage is P. Wedge and J. Essen 1982: *Children in Adversity*. London: Pan Books. This looks at the experiences of the same sample of children up to the age of 16, and in particular the consequences of living in disadvantaged circumstances. It is a disturbing book with important implications for educational policy and practice.

A collection of useful articles can be found in A. M. Clarke and A. D. B. Clarke 1976: *Early Experience*. London: Open Books. The authors challenge the belief that the early years have an irreversible effect on later development. The book includes chapters on the effects of parent–child separation, the effects of institutionalization on children's cognitive development, and the case study of severe deprivation in the Czech twins. For a detailed account of the Genie case, see M. Pines 1981: The Civilizing of Genie. *Psychology Today*, 15, (September), 28–34. This describes the effects which an intensive programme of intervention had on the social, intellectual and linguistic development of Genie. A number of important theoretical and practical issues are raised about deprivation and the extent to which its effects can be reversed.

## Discussion points

1   Discuss the meaning of the term 'disadvantage'.

2   How useful are the concepts of 'deficit' and 'difference' in explaining educational disadvantage?

3   Consider the problems involved in evaluating the effects of a programme of compensatory education. How would you attempt to do this?

4   'Black students and their parents have academic aspirations and ambitions which are not being met by the present educational system' (Eggleston, 1985). Discuss how educators might change this state of affairs.

5   What effects do family composition, poor housing and low income have on a child's school performance, and why?

**Practical exercises**

1   Collect examples on tape of individuals speaking in a variety of dialects and accents. Play them to the class and discuss responses to the speakers. How are they perceived? What status do you think they would have in our society? How might they fare in the educational system?

2   Try to teach your classmates a new skill (e.g. understanding some technical language, becoming familiar with computer jargon) using the drilling and repetition techniques advocated by Bereiter and Englemann. Afterwards, compare their subjective impressions of the experience.

3   (a) Look at a selection of textbooks or reading books used in school. To what extent do they acknowledge the existence of ethnic minority groups in our society? Can you find examples of middle class bias or racism in them? (b) Discuss how a teacher might try to develop the pluralist approach to the curriculum which is recommended in the Swann Report.

Box 14.1

# Early experience and the socialization of cognitive modes in children

This study, carried out in the USA, is often quoted in the literature on disadvantage. Hess and Shipman claimed their study showed conclusively that there were striking differences in the ways in which mothers from various social class backgrounds operated as teachers and agents of socialization. They suggested that these differences lay at the very root of the child's social, linguistic and cognitive development and, as a result, were crucial for the child's future educational prospects. Children from 'deprived' backgrounds lack crucial stimulation in the early years and so fail to acquire an adequate basis for language and cognitive development. They demonstrated these differences by analysing the content of interviews carried out in the families' homes, and by observing the mothers as they helped their children solve three tasks in a university laboratory, namely sorting toys by colour and function, sorting blocks by two characteristics simultaneously, and copying designs on an 'Etch-a-sketch' pad.

The participants were 163 black mothers and their 4-year-old children. The social class backgrounds of the mothers were classified as follows:

Group A   college educated: professional and managerial.
Group B   skilled blue-collar workers; had gone no further than high school.
Group C   unskilled or semi-skilled occupational level.
Group D   unskilled or semi-skilled occupational levels with father absent and families supported by public assistance.

The researchers recorded the conversations between mother and child while carrying out the tasks in the laboratory. They analyzed the data on the basis of Bernstein's theories, looking at restricted and elaborated codes, person versus status orientation, mode of classification and maternal teaching style.

The authors reported that the middle class children and their mothers (from group A) performed significantly better on the tasks than the others, and the difference was explained as being due to varying teaching and language styles. The lower class mothers were seen as making more use of restricted and less use of elaborated code than the middle class mothers. For example, mothers in group A were said to use more abstract nouns and verbs than mothers from the other groups. Hess and Shipman give examples of abstract and non-abstract word usage: 'The lion is an animal' shows 'animal' used as an abstract word: 'This animal in the picture is sitting on a throne' does not. The abstraction scores – calculated by taking the proportion of abstract noun and verb types to total number of

Based on material in R. B. Hess and V. C. Shipman 1965: *Child Development*, 36, 869–86

BOX TABLE 14.1.1   *Some social status differences in language usage*

| | Social status group | | | |
|---|---|---|---|---|
| | A | B | C | D |
| Abstraction (use of abstract words) | 5.60 | 4.89 | 3.71 | 1.75 |
| Syntactic structure elaboration | 8.89 | 6.90 | 8.07 | 6.46 |

noun and verb types – are shown in box table 14.1.1. Hess and Shipman give no levels of significance so it is difficult to interpret the importance of these differences among the four groups.

Another measure used by the authors used was syntactic structure elaboration, that is, the use of subordinate clauses ('when I came home … '), participial phrases ('continuing the story, the lion … ') and unusual infinitive phrases ('To drive well you must be alert'). The score was the proportion of these complex structures to the total number of sentences. Results are also shown in box table 14.1.1. The differences among the four groups are small yet Hess and Shipman interpret the results as confirming their hypothesis about the superior quality of middle class communication patterns.

Similarly, they noted differences in the modes of control which the mothers used. The middle class mothers were more likely to be 'person orientated' and to explain actions and ideas to their children. For example, they would use explanations like 'If you are tardy or if you stay away from school, your marks will go down'. Working class mothers were more likely to be 'status orientated' and use an imperative mode of command which demanded unthinking obedience, such as 'Mind the teacher and do what she tells you'. The authors also reported that lower income mothers and children were less mature in their use of concepts for classification tasks, and less successful in maternal teaching style due to an inability to give sufficiently clear and specific instructions.

For a time the Hess and Shipman results were taken to prove the hypothesis that children from working class and low-income families experienced an impoverished intellectual and linguistic socialization in the preschool years. In their words, 'the meaning of deprivation is the deprivation of meaning'. However, criticisms have since been levelled at this study. In their analysis of the data the authors do not give us the levels of statistical significance and for some of the variables (e.g. syntactic structure elaboration) there is no clear trend at all. Working class mothers in the sample did show that they could use abstract nouns and complex syntactical structures. The results did not warrant the conclusion that the working class mothers were 'deprived of meaning'; in fact, the result could equally well have suggested that the mothers had access to meaning but did not always choose to use it.

The linguistic analysis was superficial and did not tap the underlying meaning at all, or the potential complexity of the mother–child dialogues. Labov's work (see pp. 423–5) was to demonstrate that interactions in non-standard English could be articulate and complex when they took place in naturalistic settings.

This leads to a most fundamental criticism. In this study no allowance was made for the context in which the experiment took place – a university laboratory with white, middle class investigators speaking middle class dialect. Even the tests themselves could be described as being culturally biased in favour of the middle class participants. This is a setting in which the middle class, college-educated mothers might well feel more at ease than the others.

Indeed, Hess and Shipman themselves wrote that 'in our testing sessions the most obvious social-class variations were in the total amount of verbal output in response to questions and tasks asking for verbal response.' This would support the idea that the lower class black mothers and children adopted a defensive strategy in an unusual and potentially hostile setting. In retrospect, many psychologists would say that this study reveals more about how the values and expectations of the researchers can lead to lack of awareness and sensitivity on their part, than it does about any deprivation in the development of low-income children.

Box 14.2

# Lasting effects of early education: a report from the Consortium of Longitudinal Studies

Lazar and Darlington attempted an impartial evaluation of the longer-term effectiveness of 11 compensatory education programmes. The individual projects differed; six had used preschool centres, two were home-based and three combined the two methods. The programmes also varied in the content of their curriculum. But what they had in common was that all were concerned with the acquisition of basic cognitive concepts and many stressed language development. All were well-designed studies which had compared the programme children with a control group, and which tested the children before, during and after the intervention began. As many as possible of the children (about three-quarters of the original samples) were traced, assessed on a range of educational and psychological tests, and both they and their families were interviewed. Four main sets of dependent variables were examined:

1  School competence: e.g. whether the child had ever been assigned to a remedial class, or retained in grade (held back to repeat a year in school).

2  Developed abilities: performance in IQ tests and standardized tests of achievement in reading and mathematics.

3  The children's attitudes and values: their self-concept, achievement orientation, and aspirations and attitudes towards education and a career.

4  Impact on family: the effect which participation in an intervention programme had had on the families, how the parents thought about children and what their aspirations were for their children.

Two samples of results are shown in box tables 14.2.1 and 14.2.2. (The number of projects varies, as not all the original projects had data on all the dependent variables.) Box table 14.2.1 shows that in seven out of eight projects fewer programme children were ever held back a year in school, compared to control children. Box table 14.2.2 shows that in six out of six projects more programme children gave achievement-related reasons for being proud of themselves in interview.

Based on material in I. Lazar and R. Darlington 1982: *Monographs of the Society for Research in Child Development*, 47 (nos 2–3).

BOX TABLE 14.2.1   *Percentage of students retained in grade, in programme versus control groups from eight early intervention programmes*

| Location of programme | Programme group | Control group | Significance level |
|---|---|---|---|
| North Central Florida | 27.6 | 28.6 | n.s. |
| Tennessee | 52.9 | 68.8 | n.s. |
| New York | 24.1 | 44.7 | $p<0.01$ |
| Ypsilanti, Michigan | 4.0 | 14.9 | n.s. |
| Philadelphia | 42.9 | 51.6 | n.s. |
| Long Island, NY | 12.9 | 18.8 | n.s. |
| Louisville, Kentucky | 7.8 | 0.0 | n.s. |
| New Haven, Connecticut | 26.6 | 32.3 | n.s. |
| Median all projects | 25.4 | 30.5 | $p<0.05$ |

*Source*: Lazar and Darlington, 1982

These tables show the strength of combining the results of independent studies. Most of the comparisions for individual studies are not statistically significant, but the pooled data are significant and the consistency of individual studies is convincing.

The overall conclusion was that these intervention programmes did have an effect in the long term on the capacity of low-income children to meet school requirements. Other significant findings were that those who had experienced a programme of compensatory education were significantly less likely to be assigned to special education. Scores on intelligence tests did improve among the programme groups but the differences between

BOX TABLE 14.2.2   *Percentage of students giving achievement-related reasons for being proud of themselves, in programme versus control groups from six early intervention programmes*

| Location of programme | Programme group | Control group | Significance level |
|---|---|---|---|
| North Central Florida | 88.2 | 76.5 | n.s. |
| Tennessee | 75.8 | 52.9 | n.s. |
| Ypsilanti, Michigan | 86.2 | 77.1 | n.s. |
| Philadelphia | 65.7 | 60.0 | n.s. |
| Louisville, Kentucky | 78.9 | 71.9 | n.s. |
| Harlem, NY | 77.8 | 52.4 | $p<0.05$ |
| Median all projects | 78.4 | 66.0 | $p<0.01$ |

*Source*: Lazar and Darlington, 1982

the programme and control groups became insignificant over time (cf table 14.5). However, the authors reported some evidence that programme children performed better at mathematics than at reading in relation to controls. More striking were the differences in attitudes towards education. In all groups, children's aspirations far exceeded those of their parents; but the programme children were significantly more likely than controls to give reasons related to school success when asked to describe ways in which they felt proud of themselves. The parents too seemed to have changed as a result of the programmes. Mothers of the programme group children were more likely to report higher educational aspirations for their children than control mothers, and they also reported more satisfaction with their children's performance at school. Interestingly, the authors did not find any significant differences in the long term effects of early intervention programmes among subgroups of their samples. There was no difference reported between boys and girls, between single-parent families and two-parent families, nor did family size appear to be a significant factor.

The long term effects of intervention programmes were found to be not so much on developed abilities (academic test achievement) as on school competence, attitudes and values. The authors conclude that there may be 'mutual reinforcement processes' in that children who take part in early intervention programmes may raise their mothers' expectations of them. The mothers' encouragement may in turn spur them on and furthermore, positive attitudes towards school are rewarded by teachers. Thus, they argue, high quality programmes can be effective for a number of different types of low-income families. The benefits are measurable; some of the qualitative changes are harder to assess objectively but can be inferred from interview material and from self-evaluation reports.

The quality of the Consortium report rests on the quality of data from the individual projects. The main reservation here is that not all the investigators were truly able to assign children randomly to programme or control groups. Thus (to varying degrees) some of the projects are best described as quasi-experiments rather than true experiments (chapter 1). Nevertheless, the findings rank among the most important and substantial in the area of compensatory education and early intervention.

# Appendix A

## Ethical Principles for Conducting Research with Human Participants

### 1  Introduction

1.1  The principles given below are intended to apply to research with human participants. Principles of conduct in professional practice are to be found in the Society's Code of Conduct and in the advisory documents prepared by the Divisions, Sections and Special Groups of the Society.

1.2  Participants in psychological research should have confidence in the investigators. Good psychological research is possible only if there is mutual respect and confidence between investigators and participants. Psychological investigators are potentially interested in all aspects of human behaviour and conscious experience. However, for ethical reasons, some areas of human experience and behaviour may be beyond the reach of experiment, observation or other form of psychological investigation. Ethical guidelines are necessary to clarify the conditions under which psychological research is acceptable.

1.3  The principles given below supplement for researchers with human participants the general ethical principles of members of the Society as stated in the British Psychological Society's Code of Conduct (1985). Members of the British Psychological Society are expected to abide by both the Code of Conduct and the fuller principles expressed here. Members should also draw the principles to the attention of research colleagues who are not members of the Society. Members should encourage colleagues to adopt them and ensure that they are followed by all researchers whom they supervise (e.g. research assistants, postgraduate, undergraduate, A-level and GCSE students).

1.4  In recent years, there has been an increase in legal actions by members of the general public against professionals for alleged misconduct. Researchers must recognise the possibility of such legal action if they infringe the rights and dignity of participants in their research.

This statement was approved by the Council of the British Psychological Society in February 1990. Further copies may be obtained from the British Psychological Society, St Andrews House, 48 Princess Road East, Leicester LE1 7DR

## 2   General

2.1   In all circumstances, investigators must consider the ethical implications and psychological consequences for the participants in their research. The essential principle is that the investigation should be considered from the standpoint of all participants; foreseeable threats to their psychological well-being, health, values or dignity should be eliminated. Investigators should recognise that, in our multi-cultural and multi-ethnic society and where investigations involve individuals of different ages, gender and social background, the investigators may not have sufficient knowledge of the implications of an investigation for the participants. It should be borne in mind that the best judges of whether an investigation will cause offence may be members of the population from which the participants in the research are to be drawn.

## 3   Consent

3.1   Whenever possible, the investigator should inform all participants of the objectives of the investigation. The investigator should inform the participants of all aspects of the research or intervention that might reasonably be expected to influence willingness to participate. The investigator should, normally, explain all other aspects of the research or intervention about which the participants enquire. Failure to make full disclosure prior to obtaining informed consent requires additional safeguards to protect the welfare and dignity of the participants (see section 4).

3.2   Research with children or with participants who have impairments that will limit understanding and/or communication such that they are unable to give their real consent requires special safeguarding procedures.

3.3   Where possible, the real consent of children and of adults with impairments in understanding or communication should be obtained. In addition, where research involves all persons under sixteen years of age, consent should be obtained from parents or from those in *loco parentis*.

3.4   Where real consent cannot be obtained from adults with impairments in understanding or communication, wherever possible the investigator should consult a person well-placed to appreciate the participant's reaction, such as a member of the person's family, and must obtain the disinterested approval of the research from independent advisors.

3.5   When research is being conducted with detained persons, particular care should be taken over informed consent, paying attention to the special circumstances which may affect the person's ability to give free informed consent.

3.6   Investigators should realise that they are often in a position of authority or influence over participants who may be their students, employees or clients. This relationship must not be allowed to pressurize the participants to take part in, or remain in, an investigation.

3.7   The payment of participants must not be used to induce them to risk harm beyond that which they risk without payment in their normal lifestyle.

3.8   If harm, unusual discomfort, or other negative consequences for the individual's future life might occur, the investigator must obtain the disinterested approval of independent advisors, inform the participants, and obtain informed, real consent from each of them.

3.9   In longitudinal research, consent may need to be obtained on more than one occasion.

## 4   Deception

4.1   The withholding of information or the misleading of participants is unacceptable if the participants are typically likely to object or show unease once debriefed. Where this is in any doubt, appropriate consultation must precede the investigation. Consultation is best carried out with individuals who share the social and cultural background of the participants in the research, but the advice of ethics committees or experienced and disinterested colleagues may be sufficient.

4.2   Intentional deception of the participants over the purpose and general nature of the investigation should be avoided whenever possible. Participants should never be deliberately misled without extremely strong scientific or medical justification. Even then there should be strict controls and the disinterested approval of independent advisors.

4.3   It may be impossible to study some psychological processes without withholding information about the true object of the study or deliberately misleading the participants. Before conducting such a study, the investigator has a special responsibility to (a) determine that alternative procedures avoiding concealment or deception are not available; (b) ensure that the participants are provided with sufficient information at the earliest stage; and (c) consult appropriately upon the way that the withholding of information or deliberate deception will be received.

## 5   Debriefing

5.1   In studies where the participants are aware that they have taken part in an investigation, when the data have been collected, the investigator should provide the participants with any necessary information to complete their understanding of the nature of the research. The investigator should discuss with the participants their experience of the research in order to monitor any unforeseen negative effects or misconceptions.

5.2   Debriefing does not provide a justification for unethical aspects of an investigation.

5.3   Some effects which may be produced by an experiment will not be negated by a verbal description following the research. Investigators have a responsibility to ensure that participants recieve any necessary debriefing in the form of active intervention before they leave the research setting.

## 6   Withdrawal from the investigation

6.1   At the onset of the investigation investigators should make plain to participants their right to withdraw from the research at any time, irrespective of whether or not payment or other inducement has been offered. It is recognized that this may be difficult in certain observational or organizational settings, but nevertheless the investigator must attempt to ensure that participants (including children) know of their right to withdraw. When testing children, avoidance of the testing situation may be taken as evidence of failure to consent to the procedure and should be acknowledged.

6.2   In the light of experience of the investigation, or as a result of debriefing, the participant has the right to withdraw retrospectively any consent given, and to require that their own data, including recordings, be destroyed.

## 7   Confidentiality

7.1   Subject to the requirements of legislation, including the Data Protection Act, information obtained about a participant during an investigation is confidential unless otherwise agreed in advance. Investigators who are put under pressure to disclose confidential information should draw this point to the attention of those exerting such pressure. Participants in psychological research have a right to expect that information they provide will be treated confidentially and, if published, will not be identifiable as theirs. In the event that confidentiality and/or anonymity cannot be guaranteed, the participant must be warned of this in advance of agreeing to participate.

## 8   Protection of participants

8.1   Investigators have a primary responsibility to protect participants from physical and mental harm during the investigation. Normally, the risk of harm must be no greater than in ordinary life, i.e. participants should not be exposed to risks greater than or additional to those encountered in their normal lifestyles. Where the risk of harm is greater than in ordinary life the provisions of 3.8 should apply. Participants must be asked about any factors in the procedure that might create a risk, such as pre-existing medical conditions, and must be advised of any special action they should take to avoid risk.

8.2   Participants should be informed of procedures for contacting the investigator within a reasonable time period following participation should stress, potential harm, or related questions or concern arise despite the precautions required by these Principles. Where research procedures might result in undesirable consequences for participants, the investigator has the responsibility to detect and remove or correct these consequences.

8.3.   Where research may involve behaviour or experiences that participants may regard as personal and private the participants must be protected from stress by all appropriate measures, including the assurance that answers to personal questions need not be given. There should be no concealment or deception when seeking information that might encroach on privacy.

8.4    In research involving children, great caution should be exercised when discussing the results with parents, teachers or others *in loco parentis*, since evaluative statements may carry unintended weight.

## 9    Observational research

9.1    Studies based upon observation must respect the privacy and psychological well-being of the individuals studied. Unless those observed give their consent to being observed, observational research is only acceptable in situations where those observed would expect to be observed by strangers. Additionally, particular account should be taken of local cultural values and of the possibility of intruding upon the privacy of individuals who, even while in a normally public space, may believe they are unobserved.

## 10    Giving advice

10.1    During research, an investigator may obtain evidence of psychological or physical problems of which a participant is, apparently, unaware. In such a case, the investigator has a responsibility to inform the participant if the investigator believes that by doing so the participant's future well being may be endangered.

10.2    If, in the normal course of psychological research, or as a result of problems detected as in 10.1, a participant solicits advice concerning educational, personality, behavioural or health issues, caution should be exercised. If the issue is serious and the investigator is not qualified to offer assistance, the appropriate source of professional advice should be recommended. Further details on the giving of advice will be found in the Society's Code of Conduct.

10.3    In some kinds of investigation the giving of advice is appropriate if this forms an intrinsic part of the research and has been agreed in advance.

## 11    Colleagues

11.1    Investigators share responsibility for the ethical treatment of research participants with their collaborators, assistants, students and employees. A psychologist who believes that another psychologist or investigator may be conducting research that is not in accordance with the principles above should encourage that investigator to re-evaluate the research.

# Appendix B

## Resources for Teachers

An especially useful sourcebook for teachers is the volume *Teaching Psychology: A Handbook of Resources*. Leicester: British Psychological Society. This can be obtained direct from The British Psychological Society (address below). The book includes a list of useful films and video tapes on psychological topics, with addresses of distributors; sources of published information such as books, journals and library services; suppliers of psychology laboratory equipment, and suggestions for some do-it-yourself apparatus; the use of microcomputers in psychology teaching; using psychological tests; cinema films and books as sources of psychological material; the teaching of personal and social skills; the literature on the teaching of psychology; ethical issues; careers, and courses.

In addition, some professional societies may provide useful resources for teachers. The British Psychological Society, St Andrews House, 48 Princess Road East, Leicester LE1 7DR (tel.: 0533 549568) represents the professional interests of psychologists in Britain. It publishes a house-journal, *The Psychologist*, a number of specialist journals, and holds regular conferences. Every year it gives a prize to the best A-level candidate in each of the JMB and AEB Psychology examinations. The Association for the Teaching of Psychology can be contacted through the BPS, and a Group of Teachers of Psychology is organized within the society.

The Association for Child Psychology and Psychiatry, Argyle House, 29–31 Euston Road, London NW1 2SD (tel: 071 2784861) is a professional society concerned with the mental health and development of children. It publishes a journal and holds national and regional meetings.

The Association for the Study of Animal Behaviour, c/o Reproduction Research Information Service, 141 Newmarket Road, Cambridge CB5 8HA, aims to promote all aspects of behaviour study. It publishes a journal and holds regular conferences.

The Society for Research in Child Development, 5801 Ellis Avenue, Chicago, Illinois 60637, USA, is the primary professional society in North America designed to further the study of child development. It publishes a newsletter, journal, and monograph series, and holds regular conferences in the USA.

# Appendix C

## Careers in Psychology

Psychology can be studied for intrinsic interest or as part of the general educational process, especially at GSCE or AS and A level. It is also a component of training in many people-orientated professions such as teaching, social work, nursing and occupational therapy, speech therapy and management studies. There are a number of careers, however, for which further training in psychology is required, training at degree level and sometimes beyond. A very helpful booklet entitled 'How about Psychology? A guide to courses and careers' is published by the British Psychological Society, 48 Princess Road East, Leicester LE1 7DR. They also publish several other guides, including A. Gale 1990: *Thinking about Psychology?*, and a booklet, 'Career choices in Psychology: A guide to graduate opportunities'. All these, with other materials, are also provided in the BPS Careers Pack, suitable for schools and careers officers. Another useful book, A. Colman 1988: *What is Psychology? The inside story*. London: Hutchinson, provides a readable introduction to what psychology generally covers, as well as advice on careers.

Educational psychologists work with children of school age and their parents and teachers in cases where there are behavioural or emotional problems manifest at school. A degree in psychology and a postgraduate qualification in educational psychology are needed, as well as teaching qualification and experience.

Clinical psychologists work in hospitals, clinics, or in the community, usually with mentally ill persons, or persons experiencing difficulties of a psychological nature. A good degree in psychology and a postgraduate qualification in clinical psychology are required.

Occupational psychologists work in industry or government, dealing with issues such as personnel selection, job design and the quality of the working environment. A degree in psychology is required, and a postgraduate qualification in occupational psychology is an asset.

Prison psychologists work in prisons and detention centres. They are concerned with aspects of counselling and training of prison staff, and training and rehabilitation of offenders. A degree in psychology is required.

Research psychologists work in universities or polytechnics, government departments, or other organizations, on diverse aspects of psychological inquiry. A degree in psychology is required, and often a postgraduate research qualification such as a PhD.

Teaching in psychology is carried out at universities, polytechnics, institutes of higher education, further education colleges, schools and other educational centres. Would-be teachers require a degree in psychology.

Altogether there are some 5,000 professional psychologists currently employed in the UK. Only a small proportion of psychology graduates become professional psychologists, but many (more than a third) go into careers closely related to psychology, such as social work, teaching, nursing or counselling.

# References

Aboud, F. 1988: *Children and Prejudice.* Oxford: Basil Blackwell.

Ainsworth, M. D. S. 1967: *Infancy in Uganda: Infant Care and the Growth of Love.* Baltimore, Md: Johns Hopkins University Press.

Ainsworth, M. D. S. 1973: The development of mother–infant attachment. In B. M. Caldwell and H. N. Ricciutti (eds), *Review of Child Development Research*, vol. 3, Chicago: University of Chicago Press.

Ainsworth, M. D. S. 1989: Attachments beyond infancy. *American Psychologist*, 44, 709–16.

Ainsworth, M. D. S., Blehar, M. C., Waters, E. and Wall, S. 1978: *Patterns of Attachment: a Psychological Study of the Strange Situation.* Hillsdale, NJ: Lawrence Erlbaum.

Anderson, J. W. 1972: Attachment behaviour out of doors. In N. Blurton Jones (ed.), *Ethological Studies of Child Behaviour.* Cambridge: Cambridge University Press.

Annis, R. C. and Frost, B. 1973: Human visual ecology and orientational anisotropies in acuity. *Science*, 182, 729–31.

Appel, M. H. 1942: Aggressive behavior of nursery school children and adult procedures in dealing with such behavior. *Journal of Experimental Education*, 11, 185–99.

Applebee, A. N. 1978: *The Child's Concept of Story.* Chicago: University of Chicago Press.

Archer, J. 1989: Childhood gender roles: structure and development. *The Psychologist*, 12, 367–70.

Archer, J, and Lloyd, B. 1986: *Sex and Gender* (2nd edn). Harmondsworth: Penguin.

Archer, S. L. 1982: The lower age boundaries of identity development. *Child Development*, 53, 155–6.

Armsden, G. C. and Greenberg, M. T. 1987: The inventory of parent and peer attachment: individual differences and their relationship to psychological well-being in adolescence. *Journal of Youth and Adolescence*, 16, 427–54.

Aronson, E. 1978: *The Jigsaw Classroom.* Beverly Hills: Sage.

Aronson, E. and Rosenbloom, S. 1971: Space perception in early infancy: perception within a common auditory–visual space. *Science*, 172, 116–3.

Astington, J. W., Harris, P. L. and Olson, D. R. (eds) 1988: *Developing Theories of Mind.* Cambridge: Cambridge University Press.

Atkinson, R. L., Atkinson, R. C., and Hilgard, E. R. 1981: *Introduction to Psychology* (8th edition). New York: Harcourt, Brace, Jovanovich.

Avis, J. and Harris, P. 1991: Belief-desire reasoning among Baka children: evidence for a universal conception of mind. *Child Development*, 62.

Baltes, P. B., Reese, H. W. and Lipsitt, L. P. 1980: Life-span developmental psychology. *Annual Review of Psychology*, 31, 65–110.

Bandura, A. 1969: Social learning theory of identificatory processes. In D. A. Goslin (ed.), *Handbook of Socialization Theory and Research.* Chicago: Rand McNally.

Bandura, A. 1971: An analysis of modeling processes. In A. Bandura (ed.), *Psychological Modeling*. New York: Lieber–Atherton.

Banks, M. H. and Ullah, P. 1986: *Youth Unemployment in the 1980s: a Psychological Analysis*. London: Croom Helm.

Banks, M. S., Aslin, R. N. and Leston, R. D. 1975: Sensitive period for the development of human binocular vision. *Science*, 190, 675–7.

Baratz, S. S. and Baratz, J. C. 1970: Early childhood intervention: the social science base of institutional racism. *Harvard Educational Review*, 40, 29–50.

Barker-Lunn, J. C. 1970: *Streaming in the Primary School*. Windsor, Berks: NFER.

Barnes, D. 1976: *From Communication to Curriculum*. Harmondsworth: Penguin.

Baron-Cohen, S. 1987: Autism and symbolic play. *British Journal of Developmental Psychology*, 5, 139–48.

Baron-Cohen, S. 1989: The autistic child's theory of mind: a case of specific developmental delay. *Journal of Child Psychology and Psychiatry*, 30, 285–97.

Baron-Cohen, S., Leslie, A. M. and Frith, U. 1985: Does the autistic child have a 'theory of mind'? *Cognition*, 21, 37–46.

Barrera, M. and Maurer, D. 1981a: The perception of facial expressions by the three-month-old. *Child Developmnet*, 52, 203–6.

Barrera, M. and Maurer, D. 1981b: Discrimination of strangers by three-month-old infants. *Child Development*, 52, 558–63.

Barry, H. III., Bacon, M. K. and Child, I. L. 1957: A cross-cultural survey of some sex differences in socialization. *Journal of Abnormal and Social Psychology*, 55, 327–32.

Bar-Tal, D., Raviv, A. and Goldberg, M. 1982: Helping behavior among preschool children: an observational study. *Child Development*, 53, 396–402.

Bateson, P. P. G. 1982: Preference for cousins in Japanese quail. *Nature*, 295, 236–7.

Becker, H. S. 1952: Social class variations in the teacher–pupil relationship. *Journal of Educational Sociology*, 25, 451–65.

Belsky, J. 1984: The determinants of parenting: a process model. *Child Development*, 55, 83–96.

Belsky, J. 1988: Infant day care and socioemotional development: The United States. *Journal of Child Psychology and Psychiatry*, 29, 397–406.

Belsky, J. and Steinberg, L. D. 1978: The effects of day care: a critical review. *Child Development*, 49, 929–49.

Bem, S. L. 1975: Sex role adaptability: one consequence of psychological androgyny. *Journal of Personality and Social Psychology*, 31, 634–43.

Bem, S. L. 1989: Genital knowledge and gender constancy in preschool children. *Child Development*, 60, 649–62.

Bennett, N. 1979: *Teaching Styles and Pupil Progress*. London: Open Books .

Bennett, N. and Dunne, E. 1989: Implementing cooperative groupwork in classrooms. Paper presented at EARLI conference, Madrid.

Bereiter, C. and Englemann, S. 1966: *Teaching Disadvantaged Children in the Pre-School*. New York: Prentice-Hall.

Bergen, D. 1990: Young children's humour at home and school. Paper given at Eighth International Conference on Humor, Sheffield.

Berndt, T. J. 1979: Developmental changes in conformity to peers and parents. *Developmental Psychology*, 15, 608–16.

Berndt, T. J. 1982: The features and effects of friendship in early adolescence. *Child Development*, 53, 1447–60.

Bernstein, B. 1962: Social class, linguistic codes and grammatical elements. *Language and Speech*, 5, 31–46.

Bernstein, B. 1971: A socio-linguistic approach to socialization: with some reference to educability. In D. Hymes and J. J. Gumperz (eds), *Directions in Sociolinguistics*. New York: Holt, Rinehart and Winston.

Berry, J. W. 1984: Towards a universal psychology of competence. *International Journal of Psychology*, 19, 335–61.

Bertram, B. C. R. 1978: Living in groups: predators and prey. In J. R. Krebs and N. B. Davies (eds), *Behavioural Ecology: an Evoluationary Approach*. Oxford: Basil Blackwell.

Besag, V. 1989: *Bullies and Victims in Schools*. Milton Keynes: Open University Press.

Best, D. L., Williams, J. E., Cloud, L. M., Davis, S. W., Robertson, L. S., Edwards, J. R., Giles, H. and Fowles, J. 1977: Development of sex-trait stereotypes among young children in the United States, England and Ireland. *Child Development*, 48, 1375–84.

Bigelow, B. J. and La Gaipa, J. J. 1980: The development of friendship values and choice. In H. C. Foot, A. J. Chapman and J. R. Smith (eds), *Friendship and Social Relations in Children*. Chichester: Wiley.

Binet, A. and Simon, T. 1905: New methods for diagnosis of the intellectual level of subnormals. *L'Année Psychologique*, 14, 1–90.

Binet, A. and Simon, T. 1916: *The Development of Intelligence in Children*. Baltimore, Md: Williams and Wilkins.

Blakemore, C. and Cooper, C. R. 1970: Development of the brain depends on the visual environment. *Nature*, 228, 477–8.

Blank, M., and Solomon, F. 1969: How shall the disadvantaged child be taught? *Child Development*, 40, 47–61.

Blank, M. (1972) cited in Open University *Language and Learning Activity 5, Block 8*. Bletchley: Open University Press.

Blos, P. 1962: *On Adolescence*. London: Collier–Macmillan.

Blurton Jones, N. 1967: An ethological study of some aspects of social behaviour of children in nursery school. In D. Morris (ed.), *Primate Ethology*. London: Weidenfeld and Nicolson.

Blurton Jones, N. G. and Konner, M. J. 1973: Sex differences in behaviour of London and Bushmen children. In R. P. Michael and J. H. Crook (eds), *Comparative Ecology and Behaviour of Primates*. London and New York: Academic Press.

Blurton Jones, N. G. and Konner, M. J. 1976: Bushmen knowledge of animals behavior. In R. B. Lee and I. De Vore (eds), *Kalahari Hunter-Gatherers*, Cambridge, Mass: Harvard University Press.

Borke, H. 1971: Interpersonal perception of young children: egocentrism or empathy? *Developmental Psychology*, 5, 263–9.

Bornstein, M. H., Kessen, W. and Weiskopf, S. 1976: The categories of hue in infancy. *Science*, 191, 201–2.

Boucher, J. 1989: The theory of mind hypothesis of autism: explanation, evidence and assessment. *British Journal of Disorders of Communication*, 24, 181–98.

Boulton, M. J. and Smith, P. K. 1991: Ethnic and gender partner and activity preferences in mixed-race schools in the UK; playground observations. In C. H. Hart (ed), *Children in Playgrounds*. New York: SUNY Press.

Bower, T. G. R. 1965: Stimulus variables determinating space perception in infants. *Science*, 149, 88–9.

Bower, T. G. R. 1966: The visual world of infants. *Scientific American*, 215, 80–92.

Bower, T. G. R. 1981: Cognitive development. In M. Roberts and J. Tamburrini (eds), *Child Development 0–5*. Edinburgh: Holmes McDougall.

Bower, T. G. R. 1982: *Development in Infancy* (2nd edition). San Francisco: W. H. Freeman.

Bower, T. G. R., Broughton, J. M. and Moore, M. K. 1970: Infant responses to moving objects: an indicator of response to distal variables. *Perception and Psychophysics*, 8, 51–3.

Bowlby, J. 1953: *Child Care and the Growth of Love*. Harmondsworth: Penguin.

Bowlby, J. 1969: Attachment and Loss vol. 1, *Attachment*. London: Hogarth Press.

Bowlby, J. 1988: *A Secure Base: Clinical Applications of Attachment Theory*. London: Routledge.

Bretherton, I. and Waters, E. (eds) 1985: Growing points of attachment theory and research. *Monographs of the Society for Research in Child Development*, 50, nos 1–2.

Bretherton, I., Fritz, J., Zahn-Waxler, C. and Ridgeway, D. 1986: Learning to talk about emotions; a functionalist perspective. *Child Development*, 57, 529–548.

Bridges, S. 1969: *The Gifted Child and the Brentwood Experiment*. London: Pitman's Education.

British Psychological Society. 1990: Psychologists and child sexual abuse. *The Psychologist*, 3, 344–48.

Brittain, C. V. 1963: Adolescent choices and parent–peer cross-pressures. *American Sociological Review*, 28, 385–91.

Bronfenbrenner, U., 1979: *The Ecology of Human Development*. Cambridge, Mass: Harvard University Press.

Brooks-Gunn, J. and Lewis, M. 1981: Infant social perception: responses to pictures of parents and strangers. *Developmental Psychology*, 17, 647–49.

Brophy, J. E. and Good, T. L. 1970: Teachers' communication of differential expectations for children's classroom performance: some behavioral data. *Journal of Educational Psychology*, 61. 365–74.

Brown, A. L. and Palenscar, A. S. 1989: Guided, cooperative learning and individual knowledge acquisition. In L. B. Resnick (ed.), *Knowing, Learning and Instruction*. Hillsdale, NJ: Lawrence Erlbaum.

Brown, G. W. and Harris, T. 1978: *Social Origins of Depression: a Study of Psychiatric Disorders in Women*. London: Tavistock.

Brown, R. 1973: *A First Language*. Cambridge, Mass: Harvard University Press.

Brown, R. and Bellugi, U. 1964: Three processes in the child's acquisition of syntax. In E. H. Lennenberg (ed.), *New Directions in the Study of Language*. Cambridge, Mass: MIT Press.

Brown, R., Cazden, C. and Bellugi, U. 1969: The child's grammar from I–III. In J. P. Hill (ed.), *Minnesota Symposia on Child Psychology*, vol. 2. Minneapolis: University of Minnesota Press.

Brown, R. and Fraser, C. 1963: The acquisition of syntax. In C. N. Cofer and B. Musgrave (eds), *Verbal Behavior and Learning: Problems and Processes*. New York: McGraw-Hill, 158–201.

Browne, K. 1989: The naturalistic context of family violence and child abuse. In J. Archer and K. Browne (eds), *Human Aggression: Naturalistic Approaches*. London: Routledge.

Bruner, J. S. 1963: *The Process of Education*. New York: Vintage Books.

Bruner J. S. 1966: On cognitive growth. In J. S. Bruner, R. R. Olver and P. M. Greenfield (eds), *Studies in Cognitive Growth*. New York: Wiley.

Bruner, J. S. 1971: *The Relevance of Education*. New York: Norton.

Bruner, J. S. 1972: The nature and uses of immaturity. *American Psychologist*, 27, 687–708.

Bruner, J. S. 1983: *Child's Talk*. New York: Norton.

Bruner, J. S. 1986: *Actual Minds: Possible Worlds*. Cambridge, Mass.: Harvard University Press.

Bruner, J. S., and Sherwood, V. 1976: Peekaboo and the learning of rule structures. In J. S. Bruner, A. Jolly and K. Sylva (eds), *Play: its Role in Development and Evolution*. Harmondsworth: Penguin.

Bryant, B., Harris, M. and Newton, D. 1980: *Children and Minders*. London: Grant McIntyre.

Bryant. P. and Bradley, L. 1985: *Children's Reading Problems*. Oxford: Basil Blackwell.

Bryant, P. E. and Trabasso, T. 1971: Transitive inferences and memory in young children. *Nature*, 232, 456–8.

Buis, J. M. and Thompson, D. N. 1989: Imaginary audience and personal fable: a brief review. *Adolescence*, 24, 773-81.

Bullough, V. L. 1981: Age at menarche: A misunderstanding. *Science*, 213, 365–6.

Butterworth, G. 1987: Some benefits of egocentrism. In J. S. Bruner and H. Haste (eds), *Making Sense*. London: Methuen.

Byrne, R. and Whiten, A. 1987: The thinking primate's guide to deception. *New Scientist*, 116, 54–6.

Byrne, R. W. and Whiten, A. (eds) 1988: *Macchiavellian Intelligence: Social Expertise and the Evolution of Intellect in Monkeys, Apes, and Humans*. Oxford: Clarendon Press.

Campos, J. J., Caplovitz, K. B., Lamb, M. E., Goldsmith, H. H. and Stenberg, C. 1983: Socioemotional development. In M. M. Haith and J. J. Campos (eds), *Handbook of Child Psychology: Vol. 2, Infancy and Developmental Psychobiology*. New York: Wiley.

Campos, J. J., Langer, A. and Krowitz, A. 1970: Cardiac responses on the visual cliff in prelocomotor human infants. *Science*, 170, 196–7.

Carlsson-Paige, N. and Levin, D. E. 1987: *The War Play Dilemma: Balancing Needs and Values in the Early Childhood Classroom*. New York: Teachers College, Columbia University.

Cazden, C. B. 1972: *Child Language and Education*. New York: Holt, Rinehart and Winston.

Chomsky, C. 1969: *The Acquisition of Syntax in Children from 5 to 10*. Cambridge, Mass.: MIT Press.

Chomsky, N. 1959: Review of Skinner's *Verbal Behaviour, Language*, 35, 26–58.

Chomsky, N. 1965: *Aspects of a Theory of Syntax*. Cambridge, Mass.: MIT Press.

Christie, J. F. 1986: Training of symbolic play. In P. K. Smith (ed.), *Children's Play: Research Development and Practical Applications*. London: Gordon and Breach.

Chukovsky, K. 1963: *From Two to Five*. Berkeley and Los Angeles: University of California Press.

Claiborn, W. 1969: Expectancy effects in the classroom: A failure to replicate. *Journal of Educational Psychology*, 60, 377– 83.

Clarke, A. M., and Clarke, A. D. B. 1976: *Early Experience: Myth and Evidence*. London: Open Books.

Clarke-Stewart, A. 1973: Interactions between mothers and their young children: Characteristics and consequences. *Monographs of the Society for Research in Child Development*, 38 (serial no. 153).

Clarke-Stewart, A. 1982: *Day Care*. Glasgow: Fontana.

Clarke-Stewart, A. 1989: Infant day care: maligned or malignant? *American Psychologist*, 44, 266–73.

Clutton-Brock, T. H. 1985: Reproductive success in red deer. *Scientific American*, 252 (Feb.), 68–74.

Clutton-Brock, T. H., Guinness, F. E. and Albon, S. D. 1982: *Red Deer: the Behavior and Ecology of Two Sexes*. Chicago: Chicago University Press.

Cohen, L. B., DeLoache, J. S. and Strauss, M. S. 1979: Infant visual perception. In J. Osofsky (ed.), *Handbook of Infant Development*, New York: Wiley.

Cohen, L. J. and Campos, J. J. 1974: Father, mother and stranger as elicitors of attachment behaviour in infancy. *Developmental Psychology*, 10, 146–54.

Coie, J. D. and Dodge, K. A. 1983: Continuities and changes in children's social status: A five-year longitudinal study. *Merrill–Palmer Quarterly*, 29, 261–82.

Coie, J. D. and Krehbiel, G. 1984: Effects of academic tutoring on the social status of low-achieving, socially rejected children. *Child Development*, 55, 1465–78.

Colby, A., Kohlberg, L., Gibbs, J. and Lieberman, M. 1983: A longitudinal study of moral judgement. *Monographs of the Society for Research in Child Development*, 48, nos 1–2.

Cole, P. M. 1986: Children's spontaneous control of facial expression. *Child Development*, 57, 1309–21.

Coleman, J. C. 1980: *The Nature of Adolescence*. London: Methuen.

Coleman, J. S. 1961: *The Adolescent Society*. London: Collier–Macmillan.

Coleman, J. S., Campbell, E. Q., Hobson, C. J., McPortland, J., Wood, A. M. Weinfield, F. D., and York, R. L. 1966: *Equality of Educational Opportunity*. Washington, D. C.: Government Printing Office.

Collins, W. A., Sobol, B. L. and Westby, S. 1981: Effects of adults commentary on children's comprehension and inferences about a televised aggressive portrayal. *Child Development*, 52, 158–63.

Condon, W. D. and Sander, L. W. 1974: Neonate movement is synchronized with adult speech: interactional participation and language acquisition. *Science*, 183. 99–101.

Conger, J. J. 1977: *Adolescence and Youth*, 2nd edn. New York: Harper and Row.

Connolly, J. A. and Doyle, A. B. 1984: Relation of social fantasy play to social competence in preschoolers. *Developmental Psychology*, 20, 797–806.

Cook, T. D. and Cambell, D. T. 1979: *Quasi-experimentation*. Chicago: Rand McNally.

Costanzo, P. R. and Shaw, M. E. 1966: Conformity as a function of age level. *Child Development*, 37, 967–75.

Côté, J. E. and Levine, C. 1988: A critical examination of the ego identity status paradigm. *Developmental Review*, 8, 147–84.

Cowen, E. L., Pederson, A., Babigian, H., Izzo, L. D. and Trost, M. A. 1973: Long-term follow-up of early detected vulnerable children. *Journal of Consulting and Clinical Psychology*, 41, 438–46.

Cowie, H. and Rudduck, J. 1988: *Learning Together, Working Together*. London: BP Publications.

Cowie, H. and Rudduck, J. 1990: Learning from one another: the challenge. In H. C. Foot, M. J. Morgan and R. H. Shute (eds), *Children Helping Children*. Chichester: Wiley.

Cowie, H. and Rudduck, J. 1991: *Cooperative Group Work in the Multi-ethnic Classroom*. London: BP Publications.

Creighton, S. J. and Noyes, P. 1989: *Child Abuse Trends in England and Wales 1983–1987*. London: NSPCC.

Crittenden, P. M. 1988: Distorted patterns of relationship in maltreating families: the role of internal representation models. *Journal of Reproductive and Infant Psychology*, 6, 183–99.

Cromer, R. F. 1974: The development of language and cognition: the cognition hypothesis. In B. Foss (ed.), *New Perspectives in Child Development*. London: Penguin.

Crowell, J. A. and Feldman, S. S. 1988: Mothers' internal models of relationships and children's behavioral and developmental status: a study of mother-child interaction. *Child Development*, 59, 1273—85.

Cullingford, C. 1984: *Children and Television*. Aldershot: Gower.

Cummings, E. M., Iannotti, R. J. and Zahn-Waxler, C. 1985: Influence of conflict between adults on the emotions and aggression of young children. *Developmental Psychology*, 21, 495–507.

Cummings, E. M., Iannotti, R. J . and Zahn-Waxler, C. 1989: Aggression between peers in early childhood: individual continuity and developmental change. *Child Development*, 60, 887–95.

Curtiss, S. 1977: *Genie: a Psycholinguistic Study of a Modern-day 'Wild Child'*. New York: Academic Press.

Damon, W. 1977: *The Social World of the Child*. San Francisco: Jossey-Bass.

Danner, F. W. and Day, M. C. 1977: Eliciting formal operations. *Child Development*, 48, 1600–6.

Dansky, J. L. 1985: Questioning 'A paradigm questioned': a commentary on Simon and Smith. *Merrill–Palmer Quarterly*, 31, 279–84.

Darwin C. 1877: A biographical sketch of an infant. *Mind*, 2, 285–94.

Davey, A. 1983: *Learning to be Prejudiced; Growing Up in Multi-ethnic Britian*. London: Edwards Arnold.

Davie, R. 1973: Eleven years of childhood. *Statistical News*, 22, 14–18.

Davie, R., Butler, N. and Goldstein, H. 1972: *From Birth to Seven*. (Second Report of the National Child Development Study.) London: Longman and National Children's Bureau.

Davies, G. 1988: Use of video in child abuse trials. *The Psychologist*, 10, 20–22.

Davis, L. S. 1984: Alarm calling in Richardson's group squirrels (*Spermophilus Richardsonii*). *Zeitschrift fur Tierpsychology*, 66, 152–64.

Day, R. H. and McKenzie, B. E. 1981: Infant perception of the invariant size of approaching and receding objects. *Developmental Psychology*, 17, 670–7.

DeCasper, A. J. and Fifer, W. P. 1980: Of human bonding: newborns prefer their mother's voices. *Science*, 208, 1174–6.

De Gelder, B. 1987: On not having a theory of mind. *Cognition*, 27, 285–90.

Dehaan, R. F. and Havighurst, R. J. 1960: *Educating Gifted Children*. Chicago: University of Chicago Press.

Department of Education and Science 1985: *General Certificate of Secondary Education: The National Criteria. General Criteria*. London: HMSO.

Departmant of Education and Science 1989: *The Education Reform Act 1988: National Curriculum: Mathematics and Science Orders*, Circular 6/89. London: HMSO.

Department of Education and Science 1990: *Mathematics in the National Curriculum*. London: HMSO.

Department of the Environment, 1973: *Children at Play*. Design Bulletin 27. London: HMSO.

Descartes, R. (1965) La Dioptrique. In R. J. Herrnstein and E. G. Boring (eds) *A Sourcebook in the History of Psychology*. Cambridge, Mass.: Harvard University Press (originally published 1638).

De Villiers, P. A. and De Villiers, J. G. 1979: *Early Language*. Glasgow: Fontana.

Dixon, P. 1986: *The Silver Toilet Roll*. Winchester: Cheriton Books.

Dodge, K. A. and Frame, C. L. 1982: Social cognitive biases and deficits in aggressive boys. *Child Development*, 53, 620–35.

Dodge, K. A., Pettit, G. S., McClaskey, C. L. and Brown, M. M. 1986: Social competence in children. *Monographs of the Society for Research in Child Development*, 51, 2.

Dodge, K. A. and Richard, B. A. 1985: Peer perceptions, aggression, and the development of peer relations. In J. B. Pryor and J. D. Day (eds), *The Development of Social Cognition*, New York: Springer-Verlag.

Dodge, K. A., Schlundt, D. C., Shocken, I. and Delugach, J. D. 1983: Social competence and children's sociometric status: the role of peer group entry strategies. *Merrill–Palmer Quarterly*, 29, 309–36.

Doise, W. and Mugny, G. 1984: *The Social Development of the Intellect*. London: Pergamon Press.

Donaldson, M. 1978: *Childrens' Minds*. London: Fontana.

Douglas, J. W. B. 1975: Early hospital admissions and later disturbances of behaviour and learning. *Developmental Medicine and Child Neurology*, 17, 456–80.

Douglas, J. W. B. and Ross, J. M. 1964: Age of puberty related to educational ability, attainment and school leaving age. *Journal of Child Psychology and Psychiatry*, 5, 185–96.

Douvan, E. 1979: Sex role learning. In J. C. Coleman (ed.) *The School Years*. London: Methuen.

Douvan, E. and Adelson, J. 1966: *The Adolescent Experience*. New York: Wiley.

Drumm, P., Gardner, B. T. and Gardener, R. A. 1986: Vocal and gestural responses to announcements and events by cross- fostered chimpanzees. *American Journal of Psychology*, 99, 1–30.

Dunn, J. 1984: *Sisters and Brothers*. London: Fontana.

Dunn, J. 1988: *The Beginnings of Social Understanding*. Oxford: Basil Blackwell.

Dunn, J. and Kendrick, C. 1982: *Siblings: Love, Envy and Understanding*. Oxford: Basil Blackwell.

Dunphy, D. C. 1963: The social structure of urban adolescent peer groups. *Sociometry*, 26, 230–46.

Durkin, K. 1985: *Television, Sex Roles and Children*. Milton Keynes: Open University Press.

Dyson-Hudson, N. 1963: Karimojong age system. *Ethnology*, 3, 353–401.

Eames, D., Shorrocks, D. and Tomlinson, P. 1990: Naughty animals or naughty experimenters? Conservation accidents revisited with video-stimulated commentary. *British Journal of Developmental Psychology*, 8, 25–37.

Edwards, C. P. and Lewis, M. 1979: Young children's concepts of social relations: social functions and social objects. In M. Lewis and L. A. Rosenblum (eds), *The Child and its Family*. New York: Plenum Press.

Eggleston, J. 1985: *The Educational and Vocational Experiences of 15–18-year-old Young People of Minority Ethnic Groups*. Department of Education, University of Keele.

Eibl-Eibesfeldt, I. 1971: *Love and Hate*. London: Methuen.

Eibl-Eibesfeldt, I. 1972: Similarities and differences between cultures in expressive movements. In R. A. Hinde (ed.), *Non-Verbal Communication*. Cambridge: Cambridge University Press.

Eibl-Eibesfeldt, I. 1989: *Human Ethology*. New York: Aldine de Gruyter.

Eifermann, R. 1970: Level of children's play as expressed in group size. *British Journal of Educational Psychology*, 40, 161–70.

Eimas, P. 1985: The perception of speech in early infancy. *Scientific American*, 252(1).

Eisenberg, N. 1983: Children's differentiations among potential recipients of aid. *Child Development*, 54, 594–602.

Eisenberg-Berg, N. and Hand, M. 1979: The relationship of preschoolers' reasoning about prosocial moral conflict to prosocial behaviour. *Child Development*, 50, 356–63.

Elashoff, J., Dixon, J., and Snow, R. 1971: *Pygmalion Reconsidered: a Case-study in Statistical Inference*. Belmont, Ca: Wadsworth.

Elder, G. H. Jr 1963: Parental power legitimation and its effect on the adolescent. *Sociometry*, 26, 50–65.

Elkind, D. 1967: Egocentrism in adolescence. *Child Development*, 38, 1025–34.

Elliott, C. D., Murray, D. J. and Pearson, L. S. 1979: *British Ability Scales*. Slough: National Foundation for Educational Research.

Ellis, A. W. 1984: *Reading, Writing and Dyslexia: a Cognitive Analysis*. London: Lawrence Erlbaum.

Emmerich W., Goldman, K. S., Kirsh, B. and Sharabany, R. 1976: Development of gender constancy in disadvantaged children. Unpublished report, Educational Testing Service, Princeton, N. J.

Erikson, E. 1968: *Identity: Youth and Crisis*. London: Faber.

Evans, B. and Waites, B. 1981: *IQ and Mental Testing*. London: Macmillan.

Ewer, R. F. 1968: *Ethology of Mammals*. London: Paul Elek.

Fagan, J. F. 1979: The origins of facial pattern recognition. In M. H. Bornstein and W. Kessen (eds), *Psychological Development from Infancy: Image to Intention*. Hillsdale, NJ: Lawrence Erlbaum.

Fagen, R. M. 1974: Selective and evolutionary aspects of animal play. *American Naturalist*, 108, 850–8.

Fagot, B. I. 1978: The influence of sex of child on parental reactions to toddler children. *Child Development*, 49, 459–65.

Fagot, B. I. 1985: Beyond the reinforcement principle: another step toward understanding sex role development. *Developmental Psychology*, 21, 1097–1104.

Falbo, T. and Polit, D. F. 1986: Quantitative review of the only child literature: research evidence and theory development. *Psychological Bulletin*, 100, 176–89.

Fantz, R. L. 1961: The origin of form perception. *Scientific American*, 204 (May), 66–72.

Fantz, R. L. and Fagan, J. F. 1975: Visual attention to size and number of pattern details by term and pre-term infants during the first six months. *Child Development*, 46, 3–18.

Farrell, C. 1978: *My Mother Said*. London: Routledge and Kegan Paul.

Farrington, D. P. 1990: Childhood aggression and adult violence: early precursors and later-life outcomes. In D. J. Pepler and and K. H. Rubin (eds), *The Development of Childhood Aggression*. Hillsdale, NJ: Erlbaum.

Fenson, L. and Schnell, R. E. 1986: The origins of exploratory play. In P. K. Smith (ed.), *Children's Play: Research Developments and Practical Applications*. London: Gordon and Breach.

Fein, G. G. 1975: A transformational analysis of pretending. *Developmental Psychology*, 77, 291–6.

Feinman, S. 1982: Social referencing in infancy. *Merill-Palmer Quarterly*, 28, 445–70.

Feiring C., Lewis, M. and Starr, M. D. 1984: Indirect effects and infants' reaction to strangers. *Developmental Psychology* 20, 485–91.

Ferreiro, E. 1978: *The Relationship between Oral and Written Language: the Children's Viewpoints*. New York: Ford Foundation.

Ferreiro E. 1985: Literacy development: a psychogenic perspective. In D. Olson, N. Torrance and A. Hildyard (eds), *Literacy, Language and Learning*. Cambridge: Cambridge University Press.

Ferri, E. 1972: *Streaming: 2 Years Later*. London: National Foundation for Educational Research.

Ferri, E. 1984: *Stepchildren: a National Study*. London: NFER-Nelson.

Field, T. 1984: Separation stress of young children transferring to new school. *Developmental Psychology*, 20, 786–92.

Finkelstein, N. W. and Haskins, R. 1983: Kindergarten children prefer same-color peers. *Child Development*. 54, 502–8.

Fishbein, H. D. 1976: *Education, Development, and Children's Learning*. Pacific Palisades, California: Goodyear Publishing Company.

Floyd, H. H. Jr and South, D. R. 1972: Dilemma of youth: the choice of parents or peers as a frame of reference for behavior. *Journal of Marriage and the Family*, 34, 627–34.

Fogelman, K. 1976: *Britain's Sixteen-year-olds*. London: National Children's Bureau.

Foot, H. C., Morgan M. J. and Shute, R. H. 1990: *Children Helping Children*. Chichester: John Wiley.

Ford, M. E. 1979: The construct validity of egocentrism. *Psychological Bulletin*, 86, 1169–88.

Fox, N. 1977: Attachment of Kibbutz infants to mother and metapelet. *Child Development*, 48, 1228–39.

Freedman, J. L. 1984: Effect of television violence on aggressiveness. *Psychological Bulletin*, 96, 227–46.

Freeman, D. 1983: *Margaret Mead and Samoa: the Making and Unmaking of an Anthropological Myth*. Cambridge, Mass.: Harvard University Press.

Freeman, N. H., Lewis, C. and Doherty, M. J. 1991: Preschoolers grasp of a desire for knowledge in false-belief prediction: practical intelligence and verbal report. *British Journal of Developmental Psychology*, 9.

Friedrich, L. K. and Stein, A. H. 1973: Aggressive and prosocial television programmes and the natural behavior of preschool children. *Monographs of the Society for Research in Child Development*, 38, no. 4.

Frisch, R. E. 1988: Fatness and fertility. *Scientific American*, March, 71–8.

Frith, U. 1989: *Autism: Explaining the Enigma*. Oxford: Basil Blackwell.

Froebel, F. 1906: *The Education of Man*. New York: Appleton.

Fundudis, T. 1989: Children's memory and the assessment of possible child sex abuse. *Journal of Child Psychology and Psychiatry*, 30, 337–46.

Furman, W., Rahe, D. F. and Hartup, W. W. 1979: Rehabilitation of socially withdrawn preschool children through mixed-age and same-age socialization. *Child Development*, 50, 915–22.

Furrow, D., Nelson, K. and Benedict, H. 1979: Mothers' speech to children and syntactic development: some simple relationships. *Journal of Child Language*, 6, 423–42.

Galloway, D. 1979: *Educating Slow-learning and Maladjusted Children: Integration or Segregation?* London: Longman.

Gallup, G. G. Jr. 1982: Self-awareness and the emergence of mind in primates. *American Journal of Primatology*, 2, 237–48.

Ganchrow, J. R., Steiner, J. E., and Daher, M. 1983: Neonatal facial expressions in response to different qualities and intensities of gustatory stimuli. *Infant Behavior and Development*, 6, 473–84.

Garcia, I. F. and Perez, G. Q. 1989: Violence, bullying and counselling in the Iberian

Peninsula: Spain. In E. Roland and E. Munthe (eds), *Bullying: an International Perspective.* London: David Fulton.

Garcia, J., Ervin, F. R. and Koelling, R. A. 1966: Learning with prolonged delay of reinforcement. *Psychonomic Science,* 5, 121–2.

Gardner, D. E. M. 1942: *Testing Results in the Infant School.* London: Methuen.

Gardner, H. 1980: *Artful Scribbles.* London: Jill Norman.

Gardner, H. 1983: *Frames of Mind: the Theory of Multiple Intelligence.* New York: Basic Books.

Gardner, R. A. and Gardner, B. T. 1969: Teaching sign language to a chimpanzee. *Science,* 165, 664–72.

Garvey, C. 1977: *Play.* London: Fontana/Open Books.

Gelfand, D. M., Hartmann, D. P., Cromer, C. C., Smith, C. L. and Page, B. C. 1975: The effects of instructional prompts and praise on children's donation rates. *Child Development,* 46, 980–3.

Gelman, R. 1969: Conservation acquisition. *Journal of Experimental Child Psychology,* 7, 167–87.

Gelman, R. and Shatz, M. 1977: Appropriate speech adjustments: the operation of conversational constraints on talk to two-year-olds. In M. Lewis and L. A. Rosenblum (eds), *Interaction, Conversation and the Development of Language.* New York: Wiley.

Gibson, E. and Spelke, E. 1983: The development of perception. In P. Mussen (ed.), *Handbook of Child Psychology.* vol III, New York: Wiley.

Gibson, E. J. and Walk R. D. 1960: The 'visual cliff'. *Scientific American,* 202 (April), 64–71.

Gil, D. 1970: *Violence against Children.* Cambridge, Mass. Harvard University Press.

Gillberg, C. 1990: Autism and pervasive developmental disorders. *Journal of Child Psychology and Psychiatry,* 31, 99–119.

Gilligan, C. 1982: *In a Different Voice: Psychological Theory and Women's Development.* Cambridge, Mass.: Harvard University Press.

Gillmartin, B. G. 1987: Peer group antecedents of severe love-shyness in males. *Journal of Personality,* 55, 467–89.

Ginsberg, H. and Opper, S. 1979: *Piaget's Theory of Intellectual Development: An Introduction.* Englewood Cliffs, N.J: Prentice Hall.

Glaser, D. and Collins, C. 1989: The response of young, non-sexually abused children to anatomically correct dolls. *Journal of Child Psychology and Psychiatry,* 30, 547–60.

Gleitman, L., Newport, E. and Gleitman, H. 1984: The current status of the motherese hypothesis. *Journal of Child Language,* 11, 43–79.

Goldberg, S. 1983: Parent–infant bonding: another look. *Child Development,* 54, 1355–82.

Goldfarb, W. 1947: Variations in adolescent adjustment of institutionally reared children. *American Journal of Orthopsychiatry,* 17, 449–57.

Goldman, R. and Goldman, J. 1982: *Children's Sexual Thinking.* London: Routledge and Kegan Paul.

Gordon, F. and Yonas, A. 1976: Sensitivity to binocular depth information. *Journal of Experimental Child Psychology,* 22, 413–22.

Gould, S. J. 1981: *The Mismeasure of Man.* Harmondsworth: Penguin.

Greenberg, B. S. 1976: Viewing and listening: parameters among British youngsters. In R. Brown (ed.), *Children and Television.* London: Collier-Macmillan.

Greenfield, P. M. 1984: *Mind and Media: the Effects of Television, Video Games and Computers.* Aylesbury: Fontana.

Greif, E. B. and Ulman, K. J. 1982: The psychological impact of menarche on early adolescent females: a review of the literature. *Child Development,* 53, 1413–30.

Griffitt, W. and Hatfield, E. 1985: *Human Sexual Behavior.* Glenview, Illinois and London: Scott, Foresman and Co.

Groos, K. 1898: *The Play of Animals.* New York: Appleton.

Groos, K. 1901: *The Play of Man.* London: William Heinemann.

Grossman, K. E., Grossman, K., Huber, F. and Wartner, U. 1981: German children's behavior towards their mothers at 12 months and their fathers at 18 months in Ainsworth's 'strange situation'. *International Journal of Behavioral Development*, 4, 157–81.

Gruber, H. and Vonèche, J. J. 1977: *The Essential Piaget*. London: Routledge and Kegan Paul.

Grusec, J. E. 1982: The socialization of altruism. In N. Eisenberg (ed.), *The Development of Prosocial Behavior*. New York: Academic Press.

Grusec, J. E., Saas-Kortsaak, P. and Simutis, Z. M. 1978: The role of example and moral exhortation in the training of altruism. *Child Development*, 49, 920–3.

Guilford, J. P. 1967: *The Nature of Human Intelligence*. New York: McGraw Hill.

Gurney, R. M. 1980: The effects of unemployment on the psycho-social development of school-leavers. *Journal of Occupational Psychology*, 53, 205–13.

Hadow Report 1926: *The Education of the Adolescent*. London: HMSO.

Hadow Report 1931: *Primary Education*. London: HMSO.

Hainline, L. and Lemerise, E. 1982: Infants' scanning of geometric forms varying in size. *Journal of Experimental Child Psychology*, 33, 235–56.

Hall, G. S. 1908: *Adolescence*. New York: Appleton.

Hallinan, M. T. 1981: Recent advances in sociomentry. In S. R. Asher and J. M. Gottman (eds), *The Development of Children's Friendships*. Cambridge: Cambridge University Press.

Halsey, A. H. 1972: *Educational Priority*, vol. 1 *E.P.A. Problems and Policies*. London: H.M.S.O.

Hamilton, W. D. 1964: The genetical evolution of social behaviour. *Journal of Theoretical Biology*, 7, 1–52.

*Handbook of Suggestions for Teachers* 1937: London: HMSO.

Hargreaves, D. 1967: *Social Relations in a Secondary School*. London: Routledge and Kegan Paul.

Hargreaves, D. 1982: *The Challenge for the Comprehensive School*. London: Routledge and Kegan Paul.

Hargreaves, D. and Colley, A. (eds) 1986: *The Psychology of Sex Roles*. London: Harper and Row.

Harlow, H. F. 1958: The nature of love. *American Psychologist*, 13, 673–85.

Harlow, H. and Harlow, M. 1969: Effects of various mother–infant relationships on rhesus monkey behaviours. In B. M. Foss (ed.), *Determinants of Infant Behaviour*, vol. 4, London: Metheun.

Harris, M. 1968: *The Rise of Anthropological Theory*. London: Routledge and Kegan Paul.

Harris, P. L. 1983: Infant cognition. In P. Mussen (ed.), *Handbook of Child Psychology*, vol II, New York: Wiley.

Harris, P. L. 1989: *Children and Emotion*. Oxford: Basil Blackwell.

Harter, S. 1985: *Manual for the Self-perception Profile for Children*. Denver, Co.: University of Denver.

Hartup, W. W. 1989: Social relationships and their developmental significance. *American Psychologist*, 44, 120–126.

Harvey, O. J. and Consalvi, C. 1960: Status and conformity to pressures in informal groups. *Journal of Abnormal and Social Psychology*, 60, 182–7.

Haste, H. 1987: Growing into rules. In J. S. Bruner and H. Haste (eds), *Making Sense*. London: Methuen.

Haviland, J. M. and Lelwica, M. 1987: The induced affect response: 10-week-old infants' responses to three emotional expressions. *Developmental Psychology*, 23, 97–104.

Hayes, C. 1952: *The Ape in our House*. London: Gollancz.

Hayvren, M. and Hymel, S. 1984: Ethical issues in sociometric testing: impact of sociometric measures on interaction behavior. *Developmental Psychology*, 20, 844–49.

Hearnshaw, L. 1979: *Cyril Burt: Psychologist*. London: Hodder and Stoughton.

Held, R. 1965: Plasticity in sensory-motor systems. *Scientific American*, 213 (Nov.), 84–94.

Held, R. and Hein, A. 1963: Movement-produced stimulation in the development of visually guided behavior. *Journal of Comparative and Physiological Psychology*, 56, 872–6.

Herbert, G. 1989: A whole-curriculum approach to bullying. In D. P. Tattum and D. A. Lane (eds), *Bullying in Schools*. Stoke-on-Trent: Trentham Books.

Hertz-Lazarowitz, R., Feitelson, D., Zahavi, S., and Hartup, W. W. 1981:Social interaction and social organisation of Israeli five-to-seven-year olds. *International Journal of Behavioral Development*, 4, 143–55.

Hertz-Lazarowitz, R., Fuchs, I., Sharabany, R. and Eisenberg, N. 1989: Students interactive and non-interactive behaviours in the classroom: a comparison between two types of classroom in the city and the kibbutz in Israel. *Contemporary Educational Psychology*, 14, 22–32.

Hess, R. D. and Shipman, V. C. 1965: Early experience and the socialization of cognitive modes in children. *Child Development*, 36, 869–86.

Hetherington, E. M. 1988: Family relations six years after divorce. In K. Pasley and M. Ihinger-Tallman (eds), *Remarriage and Stepparenting: Current Research and Theory*. New York: Guilford Press.

Hetherington, E. M. 1989: Coping with family transitions: winners, losers, and survivors. *Child Development*, 60, 1–14.

Hetherington, E. M., Cox, M. and Cox, R. 1982: Effects of divorce on parents and children. In M. Lamb (ed.), *Nontraditional Families*. Hillsdale, NJ: Erlbaum

Hewlett, B. S. 1987: Intimate fathers: patterns of paternal holding among Aka pygmies. In M. Lamb (ed.), *The Father's Role: Cross-cultural Perspectives*. Hillsdale, N.J.: Lawrence Erlbaum.

Heyes, S., Hardy, M., Humphreys, P. and Rookes, P. 1986: *Starting Statistics*. London: Weidenfeld and Nicolson.

Himmelweit, H. T., Oppenheim, A. N. and Vince, P. 1985: *Television and the Child: an Empirical Study of the Effect of Television on the Young*. London: Oxford University Press.

Hinde, R. A. and Stevenson-Hinde, J. (eds) 1973: *Constraints on Learning: Limitations and Predispositions*. London and New York: Academic Press.

Hitchfield, E. 1973: *In Search of Promise*. London: Longman.

Hobson, R. P. 1986: The autistic child's appraisal of expressions of emotion. *Journal of Child Psychology and Psychiatry*, 27, 321–42.

Hobson, R. P. 1990: On acquiring knowledge about people and the capacity to pretend: response to Leslie (1987). *Psychological Review*, 97, 114–21

Hodges, J. and Tizard, B. 1989: IQ and behavioural adjustment of ex-institutional adolescents; and, social and family relationships of ex-institutional adolescents. *Journal of Child Psychology and Psychiatry*, 30, 53–76; 77–98.

Hoffman, M. L. 1970: Moral development. In P. H. Mussen (ed.), *Carmichael's Manual of Child Psychology*, vol. 2, New York: Wiley.

Hold-Cavell, B. C. L. 1985: Showing-off and aggression in young children. *Aggressive Behavior*, 11, 303–14.

Hooff, J. A. R. A. M. van 1972: A comparative approach to the phylogeny of laughter and smiling. In R.A. Hinde (ed.), *Non-Verbal Communication*, Cambridge: Cambridge University Press.

Hopkins, J. R. 1983: *Adolescence: The Transitional Years*. New York and London: Academic Press.

Hudson, L. 1966: *Contrary Imaginations*. London: Methuen.

Humphrey, N. 1984: *Consciousness Regained*. Oxford: Oxford University Press.

Humphreys, A. P. and Smith, P. K. 1984: Rough-and-tumble in pre-school and playground. In P. K. Smith (ed.), *Play in Animals and Humans*. Oxford: Basil Blackwell.

Hunter, F. T. 1984: Socializing procedures in parent–child and friendship relations during adolescence. *Developmental Psychology*, 20, 1092–9.

Huston, A. C. 1983: Sex-typing. In P. H. Mussen and E. M. Hetherington (eds), *Handbook of Child Psychology*, 4th edn, vol. 4, *Socialization, Personality and Social Development*, New York and Chichester: Wiley.

Hutt, C. 1966: Exploration and play in children. *Symposia of the Zoological Society of London*, 18, 61–87.

Hutt, C. 1970: Curiosity in young children. *Science Journal*, 6, 68–72

Hutt, C. and Bhavnani, R. 1972: Predictions from play. *Nature*, 237, 171–2

Huxley, J. S. 1914 (reprinted 1968): *The Courtship Habits of the Great Crested Grebe*, London: Jonathan Cape.

Hwang, P. 1987: The changing role of Swedish fathers. In M. Lamb (ed.), *The Father's Role: Cross-Cultural Perspectives*. Hillsdale, NJ: Lawrence Erlbaum.

Hwang, P., Broberg, A. and Lamb, B. 1990: Swedish childcare research. In E. Melhuish and P. Moss (eds), *Daycare for Young Children: An International Perspective*. London: Routledge.

Hymel, S. 1983: Preschool children's peer relations: issues in sociometric assessment. *Merrill-Palmer Quarterly*, 29, 237–60.

ILEA (Inner London Education Authority) 1982: Secondary education: further developments. *ILEA Contact*, 11, 22.

Inhelder, B. and Piaget, J. 1958 (1955): *The Growth of Logical Thinking from Childhood to Adolescence*. London: Routledge and Kegan Paul.

Isaacs, S. 1929: *The Nursery Years*. London: Routledge and Kegan Paul.

Izard, C. E., Hembree, E. A., and Huebner, R. R. 1987: Infants' emotion expressions to acute pain. *Developmental Psychology*, 23, 105–13.

Jackson, B. and Jackson, S. 1979: *Childminder: a Study in Action Research*. London: Routledge and Kegan Paul.

Jacobson, J. L. 1980: Cognitive determinants of wariness toward unfamiliar peers. *Developmental Psychology*, 16, 347–54.

Jahoda, G. 1983: European 'lag' in the development of an economic concept: a study in Zimbabwe. *British Journal of Developmental Psychology*, 1, 113–20.

James, W. (1890) *Principles of Psychology*. New York: Holt.

Jenni, D. 1979: Female chauvinist birds. *New Scientist*, 82, 896–9.

Jensen, A. R. 1969: How much can we boost IQ and scholastic achievement? *Harvard Educational Review*, 39, 449–83.

Jersild, A. T. and Markey, F. V. 1935: Conflicts between preschool children, *Child Development Monographs*, 21. Teachers College, Columbia University.

Johanson, D. C. and Edey, M. A. 1981: *Lucy: the Beginnings of Humankind*. London: Granada.

Johnson, C. L. 1983: A cultural analysis of the grandmother. *Research on Aging*, 5, 547–67.

Johnson, D. W., Johnson, R. T., Tiffany, M. and Zardman, B. 1984: Cross-ethnic relationships: the impact of intergroup co-operation and intergroup competition. *Journal of Educational Research*, 78, 75–80.

Johnson, J. E., Ershler, J. and Lawton, J. T. 1982: Intellective correlates of preschoolers' spontaneous play. *Journal of Genetic Psychology*, 106, 115–22.

Joravsky, D. 1989: *Russian Psychology*. Oxford: Basil Blackwell.

Kagan, S. 1986: *Beyond Language: Social and Cultural Factors in Schooling Language Minority Students*. Los Angeles: Evaluation, Dissemination and Assessment Center, California State University.

Kail, R. 1979: *The Development of Memory in Children*. San Francisco: W. H. Freeman.

Kant, I. (1958) *Critique of Pure Reason*. New York: Modern Library (first published 1781).

Karniol, R. 1978: Children's use of intention cues in evaluating behavior. *Psychological Bulletin*, 85, 76–85.

Katchadourian, H. 1977: *The Biology of Adolescence*. San Francisco: W. H. Freeman.

Kaye, K. 1984. *The Mental and Social Life of Babies*. London: Methuen.

Kaye, K. and Marcus, J. 1978: Imitation over a series of trials without feedback: age six months. *Infant Behavior and Development*, 1, 141–55.

Kaye, K. and Marcus, J. 1981: Infant imitation: the sensorimotor agenda. *Developmental Psychology*, 17, 258–65.

Keenan, E. O. and Klein, E. 1975: Coherency in children's discourse. *Journal of Psycholinguistic Research*, 4, 365–80.

Kehle, T. 1974: Teachers' expectations: ratings of student performance as biased by student characteristics. *Journal of Experimental Education*, 43, 54–60.

Kempe, C. H. 1980: Incest and other forms of sexual abuse. In C. H. Kempe and R. E. Helfer (eds), *The Battered Child*, 3rd edn. Chicago: Chicago University Press.

Kidscape 1986: *Bullying: a Pilot Study*. Kidscape, 82 Brook St, London.

Kinsey, A. C., Pomeroy, W. B. and Martin, C. E. 1948: *Sexual Behavior in the Human Male*. Philadelphia: W. B. Saunders.

Kinsey, A. C., Pomeroy, W. B., Martin, C. E. and Gebherd, P. H. 1953: *Sexual Behavior in the Human Female*. Philadelphia: W. B. Saunders.

Kirk, S. A. 1958: *Early Education of the Mentally Retarded*. Urbana, Ill.: University of Illinois Press.

Klagsbrun, M. and Bowlby, J. 1976: Responses to separation from parents: a clinical test for young children. *Projective Psychology*, 21, 7–27.

Klaus, M. H. and Kennell, J. H. 1976: *Maternal–Infant Bonding*. St Louis: Mosby.

Klinnert, M. D. 1984: The regulation of infant behavior by maternal facial expression. *Infant Behavior and Development*, 7, 447–65.

Kohlberg, L. 1966: A cognitive developmental analysis of children's sex role concepts and attitudes. In E. E. Maccoby (ed.), *The Development of Sex Differences*, Stanford, Ca: Stanford University Press.

Kohlberg L. 1969: Stages and sequence: the cognitive-developmental approach to socialization. In D. A. Goslin (ed.), *Handbook of Socialization Theory and Research*, Chicago: Rand McNally.

Kohlberg, L. 1976: Moral stages and moralization: The cognitive-developmental approach. In T. Lickona (ed.), *Moral Development and Behavior*. New York: Holt, Rinehart and Winston.

Koluchova, J. 1972: Severe deprivation in twins: a case study. In A. M. Clarke and A. D. B. Clarke (eds), *Early Experience: Myth and Evidence*. London, Open Books.

Kramer, R. 1976: *Maria Montessori: a Biography*. Oxford: Basil Blackwell.

Krasnor, L. R. and Pepler, D. J. 1980: The study of children's play: some suggested future directions. In K. H. Rubin (ed.), *Children's Play*. San Francisco: Jossey-Bass.

Krebs, J. R., Ashcroft, R. and Webber, M. I. 1978: Song repertoires and territory defence in the great tit (*Parus major*). *Nature*, 271, 539–42.

Kucazaj II, S. A. 1986: Language play. In P. K. Smith (ed.), *Children's Play: Research Developments and Practical Applications*. London: Gordon and Breach.

Kuhl, P. (1985) in Eimas, P. The perception of speech in early infancy. *Scientific American*, 252(1).

Kuhn, D., Nash, S. C., and Bruken, L. 1978: Sex role concepts of two-and-three-year-olds. *Child Development*, 49, 445–51.

Kurtines, W. and Greif, E. B. 1974: The development of moral thought: review and evaluation of Kohlberg's approach. *Psychological Bulletin*, 81, 453–70.

Labov, W. 1969: The logic of non-standard English. Reprinted in 1972: *Language in Education: A Source Book*. London and Boston: Routledge and Kegan Paul/Open University Press.

Ladd, G. W. 1981: Effectiveness of a social learning method for enhancing children's social interaction and peer acceptance. *Child Development*, 52, 171–8.

Ladd, G. W. 1983: Social networks of popular, average and rejected children in school settin₀s. *Merrill–Palmer Quarterly*, 29, 283–307.

Lamb, M. E. 1987: Introduction: the emergent American father. In M. E. Lamb (ed.), *The Father's Role: Cross-cultural Perspectives*. Hillsdale, NJ.: Lawrence Erlbaum.

Lamb, M. E., Easterbrooks, M. A. and Holden, G. W. 1980: Reinforcement and punishment among preschoolers: characteristics, effects and correlates. *Child Development*, 51, 1230–6.

Lamb, M. E., Thompson, R. A., Gardner, W. P., Charnov, E. L. and Estes, D. 1984: Security of infantile attachment as assessed in the 'strange situation': its study and biological interpretation. *Behavioural and Brain Sciences*, 7, 127–71.

Langlois, J. H. and Downs, A. C. 1980: Mothers, fathers, and peers as socialization agents of sex-typed play behaviors in young children. *Child Development*, 51, 1217–47.

Lawton, D. 1968: *Social Class, Language and Education*. London: Routledge and Kegan Paul.

Lazar, I. and Darlington, R. 1982: Lasting effects of early education. *Monographs of the Society for Research in Child Development*, 47, nos 2–3.

Leakey, R. E. and Lewin, R. 1977: *Origins*. London: Macdonald and Janes.

Leehey, S. C., Moskowitz-Cook, A., Brill, S., and Held, R. 1975: Orientational anistropy in infant vision. *Science*, 190, 900–2.

Lefkowitz, M. M., Eron L. D., Walder, L. O. and Huesmann, L. R. 1977: *Growing Up to be Violent*. New York and Oxford: Pergamon.

Lenington, S. 1981: Child abuse: the limits of sociobiology. *Ethology and Sociobiology*, 2, 17–29.

Lenneberg, E. H. 1967: *The Biological Foundations of Language*. New York: Wiley.

Leslie, A. M. 1987: Pretence and representation: the origins of 'theory of mind'. *Psychological Review*, 94, 412–26.

Leslie, A. M. and Frith, U. 1987: Metarepresentation and autism: how not to lose one's marbles. *Cognition*, 27, 291–4.

Leslie, A. M. and Frith, U. 1990: Prospects for a cognitive neuropsychology of autism: Hobson's choice. *Psychological Review*, 97, 122–31.

Leventhal, A. G. and Hirsch, H. V. B. 1975: Cortical effect of early selective exposure to diagonal lines. *Science*, 190, 902–4.

Lever, J. 1978: Sex differences in the complexity of children's play and games. *American Sociological Review*, 43, 471–83.

Lewin, K., Lippitt, R. and White, R. K. 1939: Patterns of aggressive behavior in experimentally created 'social climates'. *Journal of Social Psychology*, 10, 271–9.

Lewis, C. 1986: *Becoming a Father*. Milton Keynes: Open University Press.

Lewis, C. and Osborne, A. 1990: Three-year-olds problems with false belief: conceptual deficit or linguistic art: fact? *Child Development*, 61, 1514–9.

Lewis, M. and Brooks-Gunn, J. 1979: *Social Cognition and the Acquisition of Self*. New York: Plenum Press.

Lewis, M., Feiring, C., McGuffoy, C. and Jaskir, J. 1984: Predicting psychopathology in six-year-olds from early social relations. *Child Development*, 55, 123–36.

Lewis, M., Stanger, C., and Sullivan, M. W. 1989: Deception in 3-year-olds. *Developmental Psychology*, 25, 439–43.

Lewis, M., Young, G., Brooks, J. and Michalson, L. 1975: The beginning of friendship. In M. Lewis and L. Rosenblum (eds), *Friendship and Peer Relations*. New York: Wiley.

Lickona, T. 1976: Research on Piaget's theory of moral development. In T. Lickona (ed.), *Moral Development and Behavior*. New York: Holt, Rinehart and Winston.

Liddiard, M. 1928: *The Mothercraft Manual*. London: Churchill.

Linaza, J. 1984: Piaget's marbles: the study of children's games and their knowledge of rules. *Oxford Review of Education*, 10, 271–4.

Locke, J. (1939) An essay concerning human understanding. In E. A. Burtt (ed.), *The English Philosophers from Bacon to Mill*. New York: Modern Library (first published 1690).

Lorenz, K. 1966: *On Aggression*. London: Methuen.

Luepnitz, D. A. 1986. A comparison of maternal, paternal, and joint custody: understanding the varieties of post-divorce family life. *Journal of Divorce*, 9, 1–12.

Maccoby, E. E., and Jacklin, C. N. 1974: *The Psychology of Sex Differences*. Stanford, Ca: Stanford University Press.

MacDonald, I. 1989: *Murder in the Playground*. London: Longsight Press.

McGarrigle, J. and Donaldson, M. 1974: Conservation accidents. *Cognition*, 3, 341–50.

McGhee, P. E. 1979: *Humor: Its Origin and Development*. San Francisco: Freeman.

McGurk, H. and Lewis, M. 1974: Space perception in early infancy: perception within a common auditory-visual space? *Science*, 186, 649–50.

McLoyd, V. C. 1982: Social class differences in sociodramatic play: a critical review. *Developmental Review*, 2, 1–30.

McLoyd, V. C. and Ratner, H. H. 1983: The effects of sex and toy characteristics on exploration in preschool children. *Journal of Genetic Psychology*, 142, 213–24.

McNeill, D, 1966: Developmental psycholinguistics. In F. Smith and G. A. Miller (eds), *The Genesis of Language*. Cambridge, Mass.: MIT Press.

McNeill, D. 1970: *The Acquisition of Language*. New York: Harper and Row.

McNemar, Q. 1972: Lost: our intelligence? Why? In H. J. Butler and D. E. Lomax (eds), *Readings in Human Intelligence*. London: Methuen.

Magnusson, D., Stattin, H. and Allen, V. L. 1985: Biological maturation and social development: A longitudinal study of some adjustment processes from mid-adolescence to adulthood. *Journal of Youth and Adolescence*, 14, 267–83.

Main, M. and Cassidy, J. 1988: Categories of response to reunion with the parent at age 6: predictable from infant attachment classifications and stable over a 1-month period. *Developmental Psychology*, 24, 415–26.

Main, M., Kaplan, N. and Cassidy, J. 1985: Security in infancy, childhood, and adulthood: a move to the level of representation. In I. Bretherton and E. Waters (eds), Growing Points of Attachment Theory and Research. *Monographs of the Society for Research in Child Development*, 50, nos 1–2.

Malina, R. M. 1979: Secular changes in size and maturity: causes and effects. *Monographs of the Society for Research in Child Development*, 44, 59–102.

Mannarino, A. P. 1980: The development of children's friendships. In H. C. Foot, A. J. Chapman and J. R. Smith (eds) *Friendship and Social Relations in Children*. Chichester: Wiley.

Manning, K. and Sharp, A. 1977. *Structuring Play in the Early Years at School*. London: Ward Lock Educational.

Manning, M., Heron, J. and Marshall, T. 1978: Styles of hostility and social interactions at nursery, at school and at home: an extended study of children. In L. A. Hersov, M. Berger and D. Shaffer (eds), *Aggression and Anti-social Behaviour in Childhood and Adolescence*. Oxford: Pergamon, 29–58.

Marcia, J. E. 1966: Development and validation of ego-identity status. *Journal of Personality and Social Psychology*, 3, 551–8.

Marcia, J. 1980: Identity in adolescence. In J. Adelson (ed.), *Handbook of Adolescent Psychology*. New York: Wiley.

Martin, P. and Bateson, P. 1986: *Measuring Behaviour: an Introductory Guide*. Cambridge: Cambridge University Press

Martin, P. and Caro, T. M. 1985: On the functions of play and its role in behavioral development. In J. S. Rosenblatt, C. Beer, M. C. Bunsel and P. J. B. Slater (eds), *Advances in the Study of Behavior*. vol. 15, Orlando, Florida: Academic Press.

Martorano, S. C. 1977: A developmental analysis of performance on Piaget's formal operations tasks. *Developmental Psychology*, 13, 666–72.

Marvin, R., Greenberg, M. and Mossler, D. 1976: The early development of conceptual perspective taking: distinguishing among multiple perspectives. *Child Development*, 47, 511–14.

Matteson, D. R. 1977: Exploration and commitment: sex differences and methodological problems in the case of identity status categories. *Journal of Youth and Adolescence*, 6, 353–74.

Maurer, D. 1983: The scanning of compound figures by young infants. *Journal of Experimental Child Psychology*, 35, 437–48.

Maurer, D. and Barrera, M. 1981: Infants perceptions of natural and distorted arrangements of a schematic face. *Child Development*, 52, 196–202.

Maurer, D. and Salapatek, P. 1976: Developmental changes in the scanning of faces by young infants. *Child Development*, 47, 523–7.

Mayall, B. and Petrie, P. 1977: *Minder, Mother and Child*. Windsor: NFER.

Mayall, B. and Petrie, P. 1983: *Childminding and Day Nurseries: What Kind of Care?* London: Heinemann Educational Books.

Mead, M. 1928: *Coming of Age in Samoa*. New York: Morrow.

Mead, M. 1935: *Sex and Temperament in Three Primitive Societies*. New York: Morrow.

Mead, M. 1949: *Male and Female*. New York: Morrow.

Meilman, P. W. 1979: Cross-sectional age changes in ego identity status during adolescence. *Developmental Psychology*, 15, 230–1.

Melhuish, E. C. 1990: Research on day care for young children in the United Kingdom. In E. C. Melhuish and P. Moss (eds), *Day Care for Young Children: International Perspectives*. London: Routledge.

Meltzoff, A. and Borton, R. 1979: Intermodel matching by human neonates. *Nature*, 282, 403–4.

Meltzoff, A. and Moore, M. 1983: Newborn infants imitate adult facial gestures. *Child Development*, 54, 702–9.

Menyuk, P. and Bernholz, N. 1969: Prosodic features and children's language production. *Quarterly Progress Report*, no. 93, Research Lab of Electronics, Cambridge Mass., 216–19.

Mills, M. and Melhuish, E. 1974: Recognition of mother's voice in early infancy. *Nature*, 252, 123–4.

Milner, D. 1983: *Children and Race: Ten Years on*. London: Ward Lock Educational.

Ministry of Education 1959: *The Handicapped Pupils and Special Schools Regulations*. London: HMSO.

Mischel, W. 1970: Sex-typing and socialization. In P. H. Mussen (ed). *Carmichael's Manual of Child Psychology*, vol. 2 (3rd edn). New York: Wiley.

Mitchell, D. E. 1978: Effects of early visual experience on the development of certain perceptual abilities in animals and man. In R. D. Walk and H. L. Pick, Jr (eds), *Perception and Experience*. New York and London: Plenum Press, 37–75.

Mitchell, R. W. 1986: A framework for discussing deception. In R. W. Mitchell and N. S. Thompson (eds), *Deception: Perspectives on Human and Nonhuman Deceit*. New York: SUNY Press.

Miyake, K., Chen, S. J. and Campos, J. J. 1985: Infant temperament, mother's mode of interaction and attachment in Japan: an interim report. In I. Bretherton and E. Waters (eds), Growing Points of Attachment Theory and Research. *Monographs of the Society for Research in Child Development*, 50, 276–97.

Möller, H. 1985: Voice change in human biological development. *Journal of Interdisciplinary History*, 16, 239–53.

Möller, H. The accelerated development of youth: Beard growth as a biological marker. *Comparative Study of Society and History*, 29, 748–62.

Money, J. and Ehrhardt, A. A. 1972: *Man and Woman, Boy and Girl*. Baltimore, Md: John's Hopkins University Press.

Montemayor, R. and Eisen, M. 1977: The development of self-conceptions from childhood to adolescence. *Developmental Psychology*, 13, 314–19.

Moon, C. 1986: Spot and Pat: living in the best company when you read. In B. Root (ed.), *Resources for Reading*. London: Macmillan.

Moon, C. and Wells, C. G. 1979: The influence of home on learning to read. *Journal of Research in Reading*, 2, 52–62.

Moss, P. 1987: *A Review of Childminding Research*. University of London: Thomas Coram Research Unit.

Mossler, D. G., Marvin, R. S. and Greenberg, M. T. 1976: Conceptual perspective taking in 2- to 6-year-old children. *Developmental Psychology*, 12, 85–6.

Mueller, E. and Brenner, J. 1977: The origins of social skills and interaction among playgroup toddlers. *Child Development*, 48, 854–61.

Munro, G. and Adams, G. R. 1977: Ego-identity formation in college students and working youth. *Developmental Psychology*, 13, 523–4.

Murphy, R. and Torrance, H. 1988: *The Changing Face of Educational Assessment*. Milton Keynes: Open University Press.

Murray, J. P. 1980: *Television and Youth: 25 Years of Research and Controversy*. Boys Town, NE: Boys Town Center for the Study of Youth Development.

Mussen, P. and Eisenberg-Berg, N. 1977: *Roots of Caring, Sharing and Helping*. San Francisco: W. H. Freeman.

Mussen, P. H. and Jones, M. C. 1957: Self-conceptions, motivations and interpersonal attitudes of late- and early-maturing boys. *Child Development*, 28, 243-56.

Myers, B. J. 1984: Mother–infant bonding: the status of this critical-period hypothesis. *Developmental Review*, 4, 240–74.

Nash, R. 1973: *Classrooms Observed*. London: Routledge and Kegan Paul.

Nelson, K. 1981: Individual differences in language development: implications for language and development. *Developmental Psychology*, 17, 170–87.

Nelson, K., Carskaddon, G. and Bonvillian, J. D. 1973: Syntax acquisition: impact of experimental variation in adult verbal interaction with the child. *Child Development*, 44, 497–504.

Newport, E. L., Gleitman, H. and Gleitman, L. R. 1977: Mother, I'd rather do it myself: some effects and non-effects of maternal teaching styles. In C. E. Snow and C. A. Ferguson (eds), *Talking to Children*. Cambridge: Cambridge University Press.

Newsom Report (Central Advisory Council for Education) 1963: *Half Our Future*. London: HSMO.

Newson, J. and Newson, E. 1968: *Four Years Old in an Urban Community*. London: Allen and Unwin.

Nishida, T. 1980: The leaf-clipping display: a newly-discovered expressive gesture in wild chimpanzees. *Journal of Human Evolution*, 9, 117–28.

Novak, M. A. 1979: Social recovery of monkeys isolated for the first year of life: II. Long term assessment. *Developmental Psychology*, 15, 50–61.

Nunnally, J. and Lemond, L. 1973: Exploratory behavior and human development. In H. Reese and L. Lipsitt (eds), *Advances in Child Development and Behavior*, vol. 8. New York: Academic Press.

O'Connell, A. N. 1976: The relationship between life style and identity synthesis and resynthesis in traditional, neo-traditional and non-traditional women. *Journal of Personality*, 4, 675–88.

O'Connor, R. D. 1972: Relative efficacy of modeling, shaping and the combined procedures for modification or social withdrawal. *Journal of Abnormal Psychology*, 79, 327–34.

O'Moore, A. M. 1989: Bullying in Britain and Ireland: an overview. In E. Roland and E. Munthe (eds), *Bullying: an International Perspective*. London: David Fulton.

Oden, S. and Asher, S. R. 1977: Coaching children in social skills for friendship making. *Child Development*, 48, 495–506.

Ogilvie, E. 1973: *Gifted Children in Primary Schools*. London: Macmillan.

Olweus, D. 1978: *Aggression in the Schools: Bullies and Whipping Boys*. Washington D.C: Hemisphere.

Olweus, D. 1989: Bully/victim problems among schoolchildren: basic facts and effects of a school based intervention program. In K. Rubin and D. Pepler (eds), *The Development and Treatment of Childhood Aggression*. Hillsdale, N.J: Erlbaum.

Opie, I. and Opie, P. 1959. *The Lore and Language of School Children*. London: Oxford University Press.

Orloff, H. and Weinstock, A. 1975: A comparison of parent and adolescent attitude factor structures. *Adolescence*, 10, 201–5.

Overton, W. F. and Jackson, J. P. 1973: The representation of imagined objects in action sequences: a developmental study. *Child Development*, 44, 309–14.

Packer, C. 1977: Reciprocal altruism in olive baboons. *Nature*, 265, 441–3.

Parke, R. D. 1977: Some effects of punishment on children's behaviour – revisited. In E. M. Hetherington and R. D. Parke (eds), *Contemporary Readings in Child Psychology*. New York: McGraw-Hill.

Parke, R. D. and Slaby, R. G. 1983: The development of aggression. In P. Mussen (ed.), *Handbook of Child Psychology*. 4th edn vol. IV. New York: Wiley.

Parker, J. G. and Asher, S. R. 1987: Peer relations and later personal adjustment: are low-accepted children at risk? *Psychological Bulletin*, 102, 357–89.

Parker, S. T. and Gibson, K. R. 1979: A developmental model for the evolution of language and intelligence in early hominids. *Behavioral and Brain Sciences*, 2, 367–408.

Parten, M. B. 1932: Social participation among preschool children. *Journal of Abnormal and Social Psychology*, 27, 243–69.

Partington, J. T. and Grant, C. 1984: Imaginary playmates and other useful fantasies. In P. K. Smith (ed.), *Play in Animals and Humans*. Oxford: Basil Blackwell.

Passow, A. H. 1967: *Education of the Disadvantaged*. New York: Holt, Rinehart and Winston.

Passow, A. H. (1970) *Deprivation and Disadvantage: Nature and Manifestations*. Hamburg: UNESCO Institute of Education.

Patterson, F. G. 1978: The gestures of a gorilla: language acquisition in another pongid. *Brain and Language*, 5, 72–97.

Patterson, G. R., DeBaryshe, B. D. and Ramsey, E. 1989: A developmental perspective on antisocial behavior. *American Psychologist*, 44, 329–35.

Peller, L. E. 1954: Libidinal phases, ego development and play. *Psychoanalytic Study of the Child*, 9, 178–98.

Perner, J. 1991: *Understanding the Representational Mind*. Cambridge, Mass.: MIT Press.

Perner, J., Leekam, S. R. and Wimmer, H. 1987: Three-year-olds' difficulty with false belief: the case for a conceptual deficit. *British Journal of Developmental Psychology*, 5, 125–37.

Pfungst, C. 1911: *Clever Hans: a Contribution to Experimental Animal and Human Psychology*. New York: Holt.

Piaget, J. 1929: *The Child's Conception of the World*. New York: Harcourt Brace Jovanovich.

Piaget, J. 1932 (1977): *The Moral Judgement of the Child*. Harmondsworth: Penguin.

Piaget, J. 1936/1952: *The Origin of Intelligence in the Child*. London, Routledge and Kegan Paul.

Piaget, J. 1951: *Play, Dreams and Imitation in Childhood*. London: Routledge and Kegan Paul.

Piaget, J. 1966: Response to Brian Sutton-Smith. *Psychological Review*, 73, 111–12.

Piaget, J. 1972: Intellectual evolution from adolescence to adulthood. *Human Development*, 15, 1–12.

Piaget, J. 1977: Foreward. In H. Gruber and J. J. Voneche (eds), *The Essential Piaget*. London: Routledge and Kegan Paul.

Piaget, J. and Inhelder, B. 1956: *The Child's Conception of Space*. London: Routledge and Kegan Paul.

Plowden Report (Central Advisory Council for Education) 1967: *Children and their Primary Schools*. London: HMSO.

Porter, R. H., Tepper, V. J. and White, D. M. 1980: Experimental influences on the development of huddling preferences and 'sibling' recognition in spiny mice. *Developmental Psychobiology*, 14, 375–82.

Powdermaker, H. 1933: *Life in Lesu*. New York: W. W. Norton.

Premack, D. 1971: Language in chimpanzee? *Science*, 172, 808–22.

Prior, M., Dahlstrom, B. and Squires, T.-L. 1990: Autistic children's knowledge of thinking and feeling states in other people. *Journal of Child Psychology and Psychiatry*, 51, 587–601.

Quinton, D. and Rutter, M. 1976: Early hospital admissions and later disturbances of behaviour: an attempted replication of Douglas's findings. *Developmental Medicine and Child Neurology*, 18, 447–59.

Radin, N., Oyserman, D. and Benn, R. 1991: Grandfathers, teen mothers, and children under two. In P. K. Smith (ed), *The Psychology of Grandparenthood: An International Perspective*. London: Routledge.

Rampton Report 1981. *West Indian Children in our Schools*. London: HMSO, Cmnd 8273.

Raven, J. C. 1958: *Standard Progressive Matrices*. London: H. K. Lewis & Co. Ltd.

Raven, M. 1981: Review: the effects of childminding: How much do we know? *Child: Care, Health and Development*, 7, 103–11.

Reinhold, R. 1979: Census finds unmarried couples have doubled from 1970 to 1978. *The New York Times*, 27 June, p. 1:B5.

Reiss, I. L. 1967: *The Social Context of Premarital Sexual Permissiveness*. New York: Holt, Rinehart and Winston.

Rheingold, H. L. 1982: Little children's participation in the world of adults, a nascent prosocial behavior. *Child Development*, 53, 114–25.

Rheingold, H. L. and Eckerman, C. O. 1973: Fear of the stranger: a critical examination. In H. W. Reese (ed.), *Advances in Child Development and Behavior*, vol. 8, New York: Academic Press.

Rheingold, H. L., Hay, D. F. and West, M. J., 1976: Sharing in the second year of life. *Child Development*, 47, 1148–58.

Rice, B. (1979) The brave new world of intelligence testing. *New Society*, 150 (11 Oct), 63–6.

Richards, M. P. M. 1988: Parental divorce and children. In G. Burrows (ed.), *Handbook of Studies in Child Psychiatry*. Amsterdam: Elsevier.

Riesen, A. H. 1950: Arrested vision. *Scientific American*, 183 (July), 16–19.

Robson, C. 1983; *Experiment, Design and Statistics in Psychology*, 2nd edn. Harmondsworth: Penguin.

Roland, E. 1989: Bullying: the Scandinavian research tradition. In E. Roland and E. Munthe (eds), *Bullying: an International Perspective*. London: David Fulton.

Root, B. 1986: *Resources for Reading*. London: Macmillan.

Rose, S. A., Gottfried, A. W. and Bridger, W. H. 1981: Cross-modal transfer in 6-month-old infants. *Developmental Psychology*, 12, 661–9.

Rose, S. R., Kamin L. J. and Lewontin, R. C. 1984: *Not in our Genes: Biology, Ideology and Human Nature*. Harmondsworth: Penguin.

Rosen, H. (1982) The Language Monitors: a critique of the APU's Primary Survey Report 'Language Performance in Schools'. London: Institute of Education, University of London (Bedford Way Papers: 11).

Rosenthal, R. and Jacobson, L. 1968: *Pygmalion in the Classroom*. New York: Holt.

Rubin, K. H. and Pepler, D. J. 1982: Children's play: Piaget's views reconsidered. *Contemporary Educational Psychology*, 7, 289–99.

Rubin, Z. 1980: *Children's Friendships*. Glasgow: Fontana.

Ruble, D. N., Balaban, T. and Cooper, J. 1981: Gender constancy and the effects of sex-typed televised toy commercials. *Child Development*, 52, 667–73.

Ruble, D. N. and Brooks-Gunn, J. 1982: The experience of menarche. *Child Development*, 53, 1557–66.

Rushton, J. P. 1982: Social learning theory and the development of prosocial behaviour. In N. Eisenberg (ed.), *The Development of Prosocial Behavior*. New York: Academic Press.

Rutter, M. 1981: *Maternal Deprivation Reassessed*, 2nd edn. Harmondsworth: Penguin.

Rutter, M. 1983: Cognitive deficits in the pathogenesis of autism. *Journal of Child Psychology and Psychiatry*, 24, 513–31.

Rutter, M., Graham, P., Chadwick, O., and Yule, W. 1976: Adolescent turmoil: fact or fiction? *Journal of Child Psychology and Psychiatry*, 17, 35–56.

Ryan, J. 1974: Early language development. In M. P. M. Richards (ed.), *The Integration of the Child into a Social World*. Cambridge: Cambridge University Press.

Sahlins, M. 1977: *The Use and Abuse of Biology*. London: Tavistock.

Salapatek, P. 1975: *Infant Perception from Sensation to Cognition*, vol. 1. New York: Academic Press.

Salapatek, P. and Banks, M. 1978: Infant sensory assessment: vision. In F. C. Minifie and L. L. Lloyd (eds), *Communicative and Cognitive Abilities*. Baltimore, Md: University Park Press.

Salmon, P. and Claire, H. 1984; *Classroom Collaboration*. London: Routledge and Kegan Paul.

Samuels, C. A. and Ewy, R. 1985; Aesthetic perception of faces during infancy. *British Journal of Developmental Psychology*, 3, 221–8.

Savage-Rumbaugh, E. S. and Rumbaugh, D. M. 1978: Symbolization, language and chimpanzees: a theoretical reevaluation based on initial language acquisition processes in four young *Pan troglodytes*. *Brain and Language*, 6, 265–300.

Savin-Williams, R. C. 1976: An ethological study of dominance formation and maintenance in a group of human adolescents. *Child Development*, 47, 972–9.

Savin-Williams, R. C. 1980: Social interactions of adolescent females in natural groups. In H. C. Foot, A. J. Chapman and J. R. Smith (eds), *Friendship and Social Relations in Children*. Chichester: Wiley.

Savin-Williams, R. C. and Demo, D. H. 1984: Developmental change and stability in adolescent self-concept. *Developmental Psychology*, 20, 1100–10.

Scaife, M. and Bruner, J. S. 1975: The capacity for joint visual attention in the infant. *Nature*, 253, 265–6.

Scarr, S. 1984: *Race, Social Class, and Individual Differences in I.Q.* London: Lawrence Erlbaum.

Scarr, S. and Weinberg, R. A. 1976: IQ test performance of black children adopted by white families. *American Psychologist*, 31, 726–39.

Scarlett, G. and Wolf, D. 1979: When it's only make-believe: the construction of a boundary between fantasy and reality in story-telling. In E. Winner and H. Gardner (eds) *Fact, Fiction and Fantasy in Childhood*. San Francisco: Jossey-Bass.

Schaffer, H. R. and Emerson, P. E. 1964: The development of social attachments in infancy. *Monographs of the Society for Research in Child Development*, 28.

Schaller, G. B. 1972: *The Serengeti Lion*. Chicago: Chicago University Press.

Schieffelin, B. and Ochs, E. 1983: A cultural perspective on the transition from prelinguistic to linguistic communication. In R. M. Golinkoff (ed.), *The Transition from Prelinguistic to Linguistic Communication*. Hillsdale, NJ: Lawrence Erlbaum, 115-28.

Schaefli, A., Rest, J. R., and Thoma, S. J. 1985: Does moral education improve moral judgement? A meta-analysis of intervention studies using the Defining Issues Test. *Review of Educational Research*, 55, 319–52.

Schofield, J. W. and Francis, W. D. 1982: An observational study of peer interaction in racially mixed 'accelarated' classrooms. *Journal of Educational Psychology*, 74, 722–32.

Schofield, M. 1965: *The Sexual Behaviour of Young People*. London: Longmans.

School Examination and Assessment Council 1990: *A Guide to Teacher Assessment*. London: Heinemann Educational.

Selman, R. L. and Jaquette, D. 1977: Stability and oscillation in interpersonal awareness: a clinical-developmental analysis. In C. B. Keasey (ed.), *The Nebraska Symposium on Motivation*, vol. 25. Lincoln: University of Nebraska Press.

Serbin, L. A., Tonick I. J. and Sternglanz, S. H. 1977: Shaping cooperative cross-sex play. *Child Development*, 48, 924–9.

Seyfarth, R. M. and Cheney, D. L. 1984: The natural vocalisations of non-human primates. *Trends in Neurosciences*, 7, 66–73.

Shaffer, D. R. 1985: *Developmental Psychology: Theory, Research and Applications*. Monterey, Ca: Brooks/Cole.

Shapiro, G. L. 1982: Sign acquisition in a home-reared/free-ranging orang-utan: comparisons with other signing apes. *American Journal of Primatology*, 3, 121–9.

Shatz, M. and Gelman, R. 1973: The development of communication skills: modifications in the speech of young children as a function of listener. *Monographs of the Society for Research in Child Development*, 38, 1–38.

Shayer, M., Kuchemann, D. E. and Wylam, H. 1976: The distribution of Piagetian stages of thinking in British middle and secondary school children. *British Journal of Educational Psychology*, 46, 164–73.

Shayer, M. and Wylam, H. 1978: The distribution of Piagetian stages of thinking in British middle and secondary school children: II. *British Journal of Educational Psychology*, 48, 62–70.

Singer, J. L. 1973: *The Child's World of Make-believe*. New York: Academic Press.

Skeels, H. M. 1966: Adult status of children with contrasting early life experiences: a follow-up study. *Monographs of the Society for Research in Child Development*, 31, no. 3.

Skeels, H. and Dye, H. B. 1939: A study of the effects of differential stimulation on mentally retarded children. *Proceedings of the American Association of Mental Deficiency*, 44, 114–36.

Skinner, B. F. 1957: *Verbal Behavior*. New York: Appleton-Century-Crofts.

Skodak, M. and Skeels, H. M. 1945: A follow-up study of children in adoptive homes. *Journal of Genetic Psychology*, 66, 21–58.

Skuse, D. 1984: Extreme deprivation in early childhood – 11. Theoretical issues and a comparative review. Journal of Child Psychology and Psychiatry, 25, 543–572.

Slavin, R. E. 1987: Developmental and motivational perspectives on cooperative learning: A reconciliation. *Child Development*, 58, 1161–7.

Slobin, D. I. (1973) Cognitive prerequisites for the development of grammar. In C. A. Ferguson and D. I. Slobin (eds). *Studies in Child Language Development*. New York: Holt Rinehart.

Sluckin, A. 1981: *Growing up in the Playground: the Social Development of Children*. London: Routledge and Kegan Paul.

Sluckin, A. M. and Smith, P. K. 1977: Two approaches to the concept of dominance in preschool children. *Child Development*, 48, 917–23.

Smetana, J. G. 1981: Preschool children's conceptions of moral and social rules. *Child Development*, 52, 1333–6.

Smilansky, S. 1968: *The Effects of Sociodramatic Play on Disadvantaged Preschool Children*. New York: Wiley.

Smith, P. K. 1974: Ethological methods. In B. M. Foss (ed.), *New Perspectives in Child Development*. Harmondsworth: Penguin.

Smith, P. K. 1978: A longitudinal study of social participation in preschool children: solitary and parallel play reexamined. *Developmental Psychology*, 14, 517–23.

Smith, P. K. 1980: Shared care of young children: alternative models to monotropism. *Merrill–Palmer Quarterly*, 26, 371–89.

Smith, P. K. 1982: Does play matter? Functional and evolutionary aspects of animal and human play. *The Behavioral and Brain Sciences*, 4, 139–84.

Smith, P. K. 1986: Exploration, play and social development in boys and girls. In D. Hargreaves and A. Colley (eds), *The Psychology of Sex Roles*. London: Harper and Row.

Smith, P. K. and Connolly, K. J. 1980: *The Ecology of Preschool Behaviour*. Cambridge and New York: Cambridge University Press.

Smith, P. K. and Simon, T. 1984: Object play, problem-solving and creativity in children. In P.K. Smith (ed.), *Play in Animals and Humans*. Oxford: Basil Blackwell.

Smith, P. K. and Sloboda, J. 1986: Individual consistency in infant-stranger encounters. *British Journal of Developmental Psychology*, 4, 83–91.

Smith, P. K., Takhvar, M., Gore, N. and Vollstedt, R. 1986: Play in young children: problems of definition, categorization and measurement. In P. K. Smith (ed.), *Children's Play: Research Developments and Practical Applications*. London: Gordon and Breach.

Smith, P. K. and Vollstedt, R. 1985: On defining play: an empirical study of the relationship between play and various play criteria. *Child Development*, 56, 1042–50.

Snarey, J. R. 1985: Cross-cultural universality of social-moral development: a critical review of Kohlbergian research. *Psychological Bulletin*, 97, 202–32.

Snow, C. 1977: The development of conversation between mothers and babies. *Journal of Child Language*, 4, 1–22.

Sorce, J. F., Emde, R. N., Campos, J. J. and Klinnert, M. D. 1985: Maternal emotional signalling: its effects on the visual cliff behavior of 1-year-olds. *Developmental Psychology*, 21, 195–200.

Spearman, C. 1927: *The Abilities of Man: their Nature and Measurement*. London: Macmillan.

Spelke, E. 1981: The infant's acquisition of knowledge of bimodally specified events. *Journal of Experimental Child Psychology*, 31, 279–99.

Spence, J. T. and Helmreich, R. L. 1978: *Masculinity and Femininity: their Psychological Dimensions, Correlates and Antecedents*. Austin: University of Texas Press.

Spencer, H, 1878, 1898: *The Principles of Psychology*. New York: Appleton.

Spens Report 1938: Report of Consultative Committee on Secondary Education. London: HMSO.

Sroufe, L. A. 1977: Wariness of strangers and the study of infant development. *Child Development*, 48, 731–46.

Sroufe, L. A., and Waters, E. 1977: Attachment as an organisational construct. *Child Development* 48, 1184–99.

St. James-Roberts, I. and Wolke, D. 1984: Comparison of mothers' with trained observers' reports of neonatal behavioral style. *Infant Behavior and Development*, 7, 299–310.

Steinberg, L. 1988: Reciprocal relation between parent-child distance and pubertal maturation. *Developmental Psychology*, 24, 122–8.

Sternberg, R. J. 1984a: A contextualist view of the nature of intelligence. *International Journal of Psychology*, 19, 307–34.

Sternberg, R. J. 1984b: Toward a triarchic theory of human intelligence. *Behavioral and Brain Sciences*, 7, 269–87.

Sternglanz, S. H. and Serbin, L. 1974: Sex-role stereotyping in children's television programming. *Developmental Psychology*, 10, 710–15.

Sternglanz, S. H., Gray, J. L. and Murakami, M. 1977: Adult preference for infantile facial features: an ethological approach. *Animal Behaviour*, 25, 108–15.

Stewart, R. B. 1983: Sibling attachment relationships: child-infant interactions in the strange situation. *Developmental Psychology*, 19, 192–9.

Stone, L. H., Miranne, A. C. and Ellis, G. J. 1979: Parent–peer influence as a predictor of marijuana use. *Adolescence*, 14, 115–22.

Stone, M. 1981: *The Education of the Black Child in Britain*. London: Fontana.

Strayer, F. F. and Strayer, J. 1976: An ethological analysis of social agonism and dominance relations among preschool children. *Child Development*, 47, 980–9.

Sullivan, H. S. 1965: *Personal Psychopathology*. New York: Norton.

Suomi, S. J. and Harlow, H. F. 1972: Social rehabilitation of isolate-reared monkeys. *Developmental Psychology*, 6, 487–96.

Sutton-Smith, B. 1966: Piaget on play: a critique. *Psychological Review*, 73, 104–10.

Sutton-Smith, B. 1967: The role of play in cognitive development. *Young Children*, 22, 361–70.

Sutton-Smith, B. and Kelly-Byrne, D. 1984: The idealization of play. In P. K. Smith (ed.), *Play in Animals and Humans*. Oxford: Basil Blackwell.

Swann Report 1985:*Education for All*. London: HMSO, Cmnd 9453.

Sylva, K. and Lunt, I. 1981: *Child Development: an Introductory Text*. Oxford: Basil Blackwell.

Sylva, K., Roy, C. and Painter, M. 1980: *Child Watching at Playgroup and Nursery School*. London: Grant McIntyre.

Symons, D. 1978: *Play and Aggression: a Study of Rhesus Monkeys*. New York: Columbia University Press.

Symons, D. 1979: *The Evolution of Human Sexuality*. New York and Oxford: Oxford University Press.

Takahashi, K. 1990: Are the key assumptions of the 'strange situation' procedure universal? A view from Japanese research. *Human Development*, 33, 23–30.

Tanner, J. M. 1962: *Growth at Adolescence*, 2nd edn. Oxford: Basil Blackwell.

Tanner, J. M. 1973: Growing Up. *Scientific American*, 229 (Sept), 35–43.

Tattum, D. and Herbert, G. 1990: *Bullying: A Positive Response*. Cardiff: South Glamorgan Institute of Higher Education.

Tattum, D. P. and Lane, D. A. 1989: *Bullying in Schools*. Stoke-on-Trent: Trentham Books.

Tempest, N. (1974) *Teaching Clever Children*. London: Routledge and Kegan Paul.

Terman, L. M. 1925–59: *Genetic Studies of Genius*. Stanford, Ca: Stanford University Press.

Terman, L. M. and Merrill, M. A. 1960: Stanford–Binet Intelligence Scale, Third Revision Form L-M. NFER.

Terrace, H. S., Pettito, L. Sanders, R. J., and Bever, T. G. 1979: Can an ape create a sentence? *Science*, 206, 891–902.

Thomas, A. and Chess, S. 1977: *Temperament and Development*. New York: Brunner/ Mazel.

Thompson, R. A., Tinsley, B. R., Scalora, M. J. and Parke, R. D. 1989: Grandparents' visitation rights: legalizing the ties that bind. *American Psychologist*, 44, 1217–22.

Thompson, S. K. 1975: Gender labels and early sex-role development. *Child Development*, 46, 339–47.

Thorpe, W. H. 1972: Vocal communication in birds. In R. A. Hinde (ed.), *Non-verbal Communication*. Cambridge: Cambridge University Press.

Thurstone, L. L. 1938: Primary Mental Abilities. Chicago: University of Chicago Press.

Timney, B. N. and Muir, D. W. 1976: Orientation anisotropy: incidence and magnitude in Caucasian and Chinese subjects. *Science*, 193, 609–11.

Tinbergen, N. 1951: *The Study of Instinct*. Oxford: Clarendon Press.

Tinsley, B. J. and Parke, R. D. 1984: Grandparents as support and socialization agents. In M. Lewis (ed.), *Beyond the Dyad*. New York: Plenum.

Tizard, B., Blatchford, P., Burke, J., Farquhar, C. and Plewis, I. 1988: *Young Children at School in the Inner City*. Hove: Lawrence Erlbaum.

Tizard, B. and Hughes, M. 1984: *Young Children Learning*. London: Fontana.

Tizard, B. and Rees, J. 1974: A comparison of the effects of adoption, restoration to the natural mother, and continued institutionalization on the cognitive development of 4-year-old children. *Child Development*, 45, 92–9.

Tizard, J. and Tizard B. 1971: The social development of two-year-old children in residential nurseries. In H. R. Schaffer (ed.), *The Origins of Human Social Relations*. London: Academic Press.

Tomlinson-Keasey, C. 1978: The structure of concrete operational thought. *Child Development*, 50, 1153–63.

Torrance, E. P. 1970: Causes for concern. In P. E. Vernon (ed.) *Creativity*. Harmondsworth: Penguin.

Torrance, E. P. 1972: Predictive validity of the Torrance Tests of Creative Thinking. *Journal of Creative Behaviour*, 6, 236–52.

Townsend, P. 1957: *The Family Life of Old People*. London: Routledge and Kegan Paul.

Trevarthen, C. 1974: Conversations with a two-month-old. *New Scientist*, 62, 230–5.

Trevarthen, C. 1975: Early attempts at speech. In R. Lewin (ed.), *Child Alive*. London: Temple Smith.

Trivers, R. L. 1971: The evolution of reciprocal altruism. *Quarterly Review of Biology*, 46, 35–57.

Trivers, R. L. 1974: Parent–offspring conflict. *American Zoologist*, 14, 249–64.

Tulkin, S. R. 1972: An analysis of the concept of cultural deprivation. *Developmental Psychology*, 6, 326–39.

Underwood, B. and Moore, B. S. 1982: The generality of altruism in children. In N. Eisenberg (ed.), *The Development of Prosocial Behavior*. New York: Academic Press.

van Cantfort, T. E. and Rimpau, J. B. 1982: Sign language studies with children and chimpanzees. *Sign Language Studies*, 34, 15–72.

Vaughn, B. E. and Langlois, J. H. 1983: Physical attractiveness as a correlate of peer status and social competence in preschool children. *Developmental Psychology*, 19, 561–7.

Vollmer, H. 1937: The grandmother: a problem in child rearing. *American Journal of Orthopsychiatry*, 7, 378–82.

Vygotsky, L. orig. 1934, reprinted 1962; *Thought and Language*. Cambridge, Mass. MIT Press.

Vygotsky, L. 1965 (orig. 1925, published in English 1971): *The Psychology of Art*. Cambridge, Mass.: MIT Press.

Vygotsky, L. S. 1966 (1933): Play and its role in the mental development of the child. *Voprosy Psikhologii*, 12, 62–76.

Vygotsky, L. S. 1978: *Mind in Society*. Edited by M. Cole, V. John-Steiner, S. Scribner and E. Souberman. Cambridge, Mass.: Harvard University Press.

Waddington, C. H. 1957: *The Strategy of the Genes*. London: Allen and Unwin.

Wade, B. 1984: Story at home and school. *Educational Review, Occasional Paper no. 10* University of Birmingham.

Walk, R. D. 1981: *Perceptual Development*. Monterey, Ca: Brooks/ Cole.

Wallach, M. A. and Kogan, N. 1965: *Modes of Thinking in Young Children*. New York: Holt, Rinehart and Winston.

Wallerstein, J. S. 1985: Children of divorce – emerging trends. *Psychiatric Clinics of North America*, 8, 837–55.

Wallerstein, J. S. 1987: Children of divorce: report of a ten-year follow-up of early latency-age children. *American Journal of Orthopsychiatry*, 57, 199–211.

Warnock Report 1978: *Special Educational Needs: Report of the Committee of Enquiry into the Education of Handicapped Children and Young People*. London: HMSO (Cmnd.: 7212).

Waterman, A. W. 1982: Identity development from adolescence to adulthood: an extension of theory and a review of research. *Developmental Psychology*, 18, 341–58.

Waterman, C. K. and Waterman, A. S. 1975: Fathers and sons: a study of ego identity across two generations. *Journal of Youth and Adolescence*, 4, 331–8.

Wax, M. and Wax, R. 1971: Cultural deprivation as an educational ideology. In E. Leacock (ed,), *The Culture of Poverty: a Critique*. New York: Simon and Schuster.

Wechsler, D. 1975: Intelligence defined and undefined. *American Psychologist*, 30, 135–9.

Wedge, P. and Essen, J. 1982: *Children in Adversity*. London: Pan.

Weikart, D., Deloria, D., Lawser, S. and Wiegerink, R. 1970: Longitudinal results of the Ypsilanti Perry preschool project. Monographs of the High-Scope Educational research Foundation, No 1.

Weinraub, M., Clemens, L. P., Sockloff, A., Ethridge, T., Gracely, E. and Myers, B. 1984: The development of sex role stereotypes in the third year: relationships to gender labeling, gender identity, sex-typed toy preference and family characteristics. *Child Development*, 55, 1493–503.

Weinraub, M. and Lewis, M. 1977: The determinants of children's responses to separation. *Monographs of the Society for Research in Child Development*, 42, 1–78.

Weir, R. 1962: *Language in the Crib*. The Hague: Mouton.

Weisel, T. N. and Hubel, D. H. 1963: Single-cell responses in striate cortex of kittens deprived of vision in one eye. *Journal of Neurophysiology*, 26, 1003–17.

Weisler, A. and McCall, R. B. 1976: Exploration and play. *American Psychologist*, 31, 492–508.

Weisner, T. S., and Gallimore, R. 1977: My brother's keeper: child and sibling caretaking. *Current Anthropology*, 18, 169–90.

Wellman, H. 1990: *Children's Theories of Mind*. Cambridge, Mass.: MIT Press.

Wells, C. G. 1980: Adjustments in adult-child conversation: some effects of interaction. In H. Giles, W. P. Robinson and P. M. Smith (eds), *Language*. Oxford: Pergamon.

Wells, C. G. 1983: Talking with children: the complementary roles of parents and teachers. In M. Donaldson (ed.), *Early Childhood Development and Education*. Oxford: Basil Blackwell.

Wells, C. G. 1985: *Language Development in the Preschool Years*. Cambridge: Cambridge University Press.

Werker, J. F. and Tees, R. C. 1985: Cross-language speech perceptions: evidence for perceptual reorganization during the first year of life. *Infant Behavior and Development, 7,* 49–63.

Westcott, H., Davies, G. and Clifford, B. 1989: The use of anatomical dolls in child witness interviews. *Adoption and Fostering, 13,* 6–14.

Westin-Lindgren, G. 1982: Achievement and mental ability of physically late and early maturing school children related to their social background. *Journal of Child Psychology and Psychiatry, 23,* 407–20.

Whitbread, N. 1972: *The Evolution of the Nursery–Infant School*. London: Routledge and Kegan Paul.

Whiten, A. (ed.) 1991: *Natural Theories of Mind: Evolution, Development and Simulation of Everyday Mindreading*. Oxford: Basil Blackwell.

Whiten, A. and Byrne R. W. 1988: Tactical deception in primates. *Behavioral and Brain Sciences, 11,* 233–73.

Whiten, A, and Byrne, R. W. 1991: The emergence of metarepresentation in human ontogeny and primate phylogeny. In A. Whiten (ed.), *Natural Theories of Mind: Evolution, Development and Simulation of Everyday Mindreading*. Oxford: Basil Blackwell.

Whiting, B. and Edwards, C. P. 1973: A cross-cultural analysis of sex differences in the behavior of children aged three through 11. *Journal of Social Psychology, 91,* 171–88.

Whiting, B. B. and Whiting, J. W. M. 1975: *Children of Six Cultures: a Psycho-cultural Analysis*. Cambridge, Mass. and London: Harvard University Press.

Whiting, J. W. M., Kluckhohn, C., and Anthony, A. 1958: The functions of male initiation ceremonies at puberty. In E. Maccoby, T. Newcomb and E. Hartley (eds), *Readings in Social Psychology*. New York: Holt.

Wilcox, J. and Webster, E.: 1980: Early discourse behavior: an analysis of children's responses to listener feedback. *Child Development, 51,* 1120–5.

Wilkins, W. and Glock, M. 1973: *Teacher Expectations and Student Achievement: a Replication*. Ithaca: Cornwall University Press.

Williams, R. L. 1973: Black intelligence test of cultural homogeneity (BITCH). *Newsweek, 19* December, 109.

Willis, P. 1977: *Learning to Labour*. London: Saxon House.

Wilson, E. O. 1978: *On Human Nature*. Cambridge, Mass.: Harvard University Press.

Wimmer, H. and Perner, J. 1983: Beliefs about beliefs: representations and constraining function of wrong beliefs in young children's understanding of deception. *Cognition, 13,* 103–28.

Witkin, H. A., Dyk, R. B. Faterson, H. F. Goodenough, D. R. and Karp, S. A. 1962: *Psychological Differentiation: Studies of Development*. New York: Wiley.

Wohlwill, J. F. 1984: Relationships between exploration and play. In T. D. Yawkey and A. D. Pellegrini (eds), *Child's Play: Developmental and Applied*. Hillsdale, NJ: Lawrence Erlbaum.

Wood, D. J. 1988: *How Children Think and Learn*. Oxford: Basil Blackwell.

Wood, D. J., Bruner, J. S. and Ross, G. 1976: The role of tutoring in problem-solving. *Journal of Child Psychology and Psychiatry, 17,* 89–100.

Wright, C. 1985: The influences of school processes on the educational opportunities of children of West Indian origin. *Multicultural Teaching, 4.1,* Autumn.

Yates, C. and Smith, P. K. 1989: Bullying in two English comprehensive schools. In E. Roland and E. Munthe (eds). *Bullying: An International Perspective*, London: David Fulton.

Yonas, A. 1981: Infants' responses to optical information for collision. In R. N. Aslin, J. R. Alberts and M. R. Peterson (eds), *Development of Perception: Psychobiological Perspectives,* vol 2. New York: Academic Press.

Young, F. W. 1965: *Initiation Ceremonies: a Cross Cultural Study of Status Dramatization.* Indianapolis: Bobbs–Merrill.

Youniss, J. 1980: *Parents and Peers in Social Development.* Chicago: University of Chicago Press.

Zahn-Waxler, C. and Radke-Yarrow, M. 1982: The development of altruism: alternative research strategies. In N. Eisenberg (ed.), *The Development of Prosocial Behaviour.* New York: Academic Press.

Zahn-Waxler, C., Radke-Yarrow, M. and King, R. A. 1979: Child rearing and children's prosocial initiations toward victims of distress. *Child Development,* 50, 319–30.

Zarbatany, L., Hartmann, D. P. and Gelfand, D. M. 1985: Why does children's generosity increase with age: susceptibility to experimenter influence or altruism? *Child Development,* 56, 746–56.

# Index